OFFICERS AND ACCOUNTABILITY IN MEDIEVAL ENGLAND 1170–1300

Officers and Accountability in Medieval England 1170–1300

JOHN SABAPATHY

OXFORD
UNIVERSITY PRESS

Great Clarendon Street, Oxford, OX2 6DP,
United Kingdom

Oxford University Press is a department of the University of Oxford.
It furthers the University's objective of excellence in research, scholarship,
and education by publishing worldwide. Oxford is a registered trade mark of
Oxford University Press in the UK and in certain other countries.

© John Sabapathy 2014

The moral rights of the author have been asserted.

First Edition published in 2014

Impression: 1

All rights reserved. No part of this publication may be reproduced, stored in
a retrieval system, or transmitted, in any form or by any means, without the
prior permission in writing of Oxford University Press, or as expressly permitted
by law, by licence or under terms agreed with the appropriate reprographics
rights organization. Enquiries concerning reproduction outside the scope of the
above should be sent to the Rights Department, Oxford University Press, at the
address above.

You must not circulate this work in any other form
and you must impose this same condition on any acquirer.

Published in the United States of America by Oxford University Press
198 Madison Avenue, New York, NY 10016, United States of America

British Library Cataloguing in Publication Data
Data available

Library of Congress Control Number: 2014934195

ISBN 978–0–19–964590–9

Printed and bound by
CPI Group (UK) Ltd, Croydon, CR0 4YY

Links to third party websites are provided by Oxford in good faith and
for information only. Oxford disclaims any responsibility for the materials
contained in any third party website referenced in this work.

For my parents
with love and gratitude

Acknowledgements

A first book gathers many debts. This study exists thanks to numerous institutions and individuals. The Arts and Humanities Research Council funded the doctoral research that underlies it. St John's College, Oxford elected me to a Junior Research Fellowship, allowing me to complete the thesis and begin thinking beyond it. Before and after that UCL History Department has given it a very happy home, both as thesis and as book. It was finished during a period of research leave provided under my Department's model leave policy. The work is dependent on the collections and librarians of the Bodleian, British Library (whose Board provide my cover image), Institute of Historical Research, National Archives, Senate House Library, St John's College Oxford, UCL (especially the Royal Historical Society Collection which it houses), Warburg Institute, and Institute of Advanced Legal Study. I thank them all. At OUP I am indebted to Christopher Wheeler, Stephanie Ireland, Cathryn Steele and Emma Lonie for welcoming and chaperoning the book through the Press. Sylvie Jaffrey was the most comradely of editors and patiently re-taught me my *trivium*. It was my great loss that pneumonia interrupted our editing and I am grateful to staff at OUP and Newgen, and Francis Eaves for picking up our threads.

Audiences at seminars and conferences in Leeds, London, Manchester, Metz, and Oxford have given valuable comments. I am indebted to colleagues who generously provided suggestive and corrective readings at various points: Paul Brand, David Carpenter (thrice), Michael Clanchy, Roger Highfield, Matthew Kempshall, Sandy Murray, Nigel Ramsay, Susan Reynolds, Magnus Ryan, and Julia Walworth. John Gillingham and Robert Bartlett examined the doctoral thesis from which the book stems and gave sane, generous, and constructive counsel. Several complementary projects became happily apparent at different stages and I thank Richard Cassidy, Moritz Isenmann, and Julien Théry for sharing important unpublished work at helpful points. Discussion at different points and in different forms with Bob Berkhofer, Tom Bisson, Richard Cassidy, Andrew Hershey, Nick Karn, Frédérique Lachaud, Yossi Rapoport, Nick Vincent, Sethina Watson, and Chris Wickham has been equally valuable. In addition to commenting on portions Michael Clanchy and Susan Reynolds have let me crawl all over them since I was a masters student—as Sir Richard Southern said the best teachers would. OUP's anonymous reader provided attentive, insightful, and helpful suggestions and questions. None are responsible, accountable, or otherwise liable for errors, deficiencies, or idiosyncrasies that persist.

My colleagues at UCL have been as supportive as I could wish—I am particularly grateful to Nikki Miller, Stephen Conway, Jason Peacey, Sophie Page, and Antonio Sennis. At or through Wadham College, Oxford I have longstanding and deep debts of support and encouragement owed to Cliff Davies, Jane Garnett, Gervase Rosser, Matthew Kempshall (especially), and, more recently in London, David Carpenter, Jinty Nelson, and Magnus Ryan.

My most unredeemable debts cannot be well-expressed in such a note. David d'Avray's generosity, thoughtfulness, and enthusiasm as *Doktorvater* and now colleague has been, and is, greater than one could ever rightfully hope for. He has acutely commented on this work more times than I can recall, and saved me from innumerable errors along the way. My parents have supported me in countless selfless ways for a lifetime. To them I owe my appreciation of learning and much more, and to them this book is dedicated. Finally my wife, enthusiastically, unstintingly, and with great patience, has made the process of researching and writing it not only possible, but also enormously happy. My daughter has shown me how proper teachers teach, and my son has laughed. *Sine quibus nihil.*

J.W.W.S.

24 Gordon Square
London, June 2014

Office will reveal the man.
Aristotle, quoting Bias, *Nicomachean Ethics* (1130a1)

Let us torture the stewards.
'Quintilian', *Lesser Declamations* (353)

Contents

Abbreviations   xiii

1. Introduction   1
   A Francophone Florentine in London   1
   Themes and Argument   5
       Roles and Rules: Character and Office   5
       Political Thinking, Political Thought, Institutions, and
          Administrative History   10
       Concepts, Accountability, and Comparisons   19
       Arguments   23

2. Bailiffs and Stewards   25
   Two Cases   26
       Robert of Chilton   26
       John de Valle   29
   'A Reasonable Account of His Time as a Bailiff'   38
       The Twelfth and Early Thirteenth Centuries   38
       c.1225–1258   44
       The Period of Legislation, 1259–1285   47
   The 'Political Economy' of the Action of Account   52
       Bailiffs' Accountability and Demesne Farming   52
       Early Prescriptive Texts on Estate Management and *la moralisation de
          l'administration*   55
       Tenure, Law, Accounts: The Political Economy of Bailiffs   60

3. Sheriffs   83
   'Exchequer Rules': Accountability and the *Dialogue of the Exchequer*   91
       The Culture of Accountability at the Exchequer in the Late
          Twelfth Century   92
       The *Dialogue of the Exchequer*: 'That edifies, *this* enables'   95
       The Purpose of Shrieval Accountability: Utility, the Fisc, and the
          Kingdom's Good   101
       A Game of Chess: The Sheriff's *conflictus* at the Exchequer   103
   Sheriffs' Accountability Beyond Exchequer Accounting   110
       Exchequer of Pleas, Eyres, and ad hoc Inquiries   110
       Tensions and Contradictions within Shrieval Accountability   113
   Comparisons: Preferences, Structures, Royal Self-image   121
   Conclusions   132

4. Bishops   135
   The Accountability of Inquisition   140
   Law in Motion: The Complaints against Archbishop Geoffrey of York,
       1194–1202   142

Geoffrey of York's Inquisitions in Context	148
Legal Learning	148
The Politics of Inquisitorial Accountability	154
Sociological Aspects of Canonical Inquisitions	165
The Inquisition into Walter Langton, Bishop of Coventry and Lichfield	173
Conclusions	183
5. Wardens and Fellows	185
Wardens and Colleges	185
The View from Merton College, Oxford	187
Pecham at Merton	187
Lessons from Merton	191
'College Peculiars'	209
Intellectuals, Poverty, Self-administration	210
Sources and Reasons	214
Conclusions: *Omnibus et singulis*	220
6. Conclusions	222
Parallels, Differences, Similarities	226
'Who, Whom?'	226
Delegation and Access	229
Control of Officers: Insiders and Outsiders	231
Local Political Structures, Values, and Officers' Accountability	232
Causes, Conditions, Correlations	236
Institutional Development, Intellectual Capability, and the *rector*'s Conscience	236
Étatisation and Official Accountability?	239
Elective Affinities	241
Effects	246
Unintended Consequences	246
Effects and Their Problems	248
Accountability and Justice?	253
Bibliography	261
List of Manuscripts and Rolls Consulted	261
Editions of Sources	262
Secondary Sources	273
Online Resources	302
Indices	303

Abbreviations

AHR	*American Historical Review*
BL	British Library
Bod.	Bodleian Library, Oxford
BRUO	*A Biographical Register of the University of Oxford to A.D. 1500*, A. B. Emden, 3 vols. (Oxford, 1957–9)
Calendar Documents Ireland	*Calendar of Documents relating to Ireland*, ed. H.S. Sweetman (vol. v with G. F. Hancock), 5 vols. (London, 1875–86).
Calendar Justiciary Rolls Ireland	*Calendar of the Justiciary Rolls, or, Proceedings in the Court of the Justiciar of Ireland, preserved in the Public Record Office of Ireland*, ed. James Mills [vols. 1–2]; Herbert Wood, Albert E. Langman, and rev. Margaret C. Griffith, 3 vols. (1905–56, Dublin).
C&S	*Councils and Synods with Other Documents Relating to the English Church*, i. *A.D. 871–1204*, ed. Dorothy Whitelock, Martin Brett, and C. N. L. Brooke, 2 vols. (Oxford, 1981); ii. *A.D. 1205–1313*, ed. F. M. Powicke and C. R. Cheney, 2 vols. (Oxford, 1964)
C&Y	Canterbury and York Society
CCR	*Calendar of Charter Rolls*
CIC	*Corpus iuris canonici*, ed. E. Richter, rev. E. Friedberg, 2 vols. (Leipzig, 1879; repr. Graz, 1959)
Comp.	*Quinque Compilationes Antiquae, nec non collectio canonum Lipsiensis*, ed. E. Friedberg (Leipzig, 1882; repr. Graz, 1882)
CPR	*Calendar of Patent Rolls*
CR	*Calendar of Close Rolls*
CRR	*Curia Regis Rolls*
CS	Camden Society
CUL	Cambridge University Library
CUP	*Chartularium Universitatis Parisiensis*, ed. H. Denifle and E. Chatelain, 4 vols. (Paris, 1891–99)
Decretum	'Gratian', *Decretum* (giving references to the *CIC* edition)
DBF	*Dictionnaire de biographie française*, ed. J. Balteau et al., 19 vols. (Paris, 1933–)
DBI	*Dizionario biografico degli Italiani*, 71 vols. (Rome, 1960–)
DBM	*Documents of the Baronial Movement of Reform and Rebellion, 1258–1267*, ed. R. E. Treharne and I. J. Sanders, OMT (Oxford, 1973)
DS	*Dialogus de scaccario: The Course of the Exchequer by Richard Fitz Nigel and Constitutio domus regis: The Establishment of the Royal Household*, ed. Charles Johnson, rev. F. E. L. Carter and D. E. Greenway, OMT (Oxford, 1983)

EEA	English Episcopal Acta, gen. eds. David M. Smith and Philippa M. Hoskin, 43 vols. (Oxford, 1980–2012)
EHD i, ii, iii	*English Historical Documents*, i. *c.500–1042*, ed. D. Whitelock, rev. edn. (London, 1979); ii. *1042–1189*, ed. D. C. Douglas and G. W. Greenaway (London, 1953); iii. *1189–1327*, ed. H. Rothwell (London, 1975)
EHR	*English Historical Review*
Foedera	*Foedera, conventiones, litteræ et cujuscunque generis acta publica inter reges Angliæ, et alios quosvis imperatores, reges, pontifices, principes vel communitates: ab ingressu Gulielmi I. in Angliam, A.D. 1066, ad nostra usque tempora habita aut tractata*, ed. Thomas Rymer and Robert Sanderson, rev. Adam Clarke, Frederic Holbrooke, and John Caley, 4 vols. in 7 (London, 1816–69)
FSI	Fonti per la storia d'Italia pubblicate dall'Istituto storico italiano (Rome, 1887–)
Innocent III English Calendar	*The Letters of Pope Innocent III (1198–1216) Concerning England and Wales: A Calendar with an Appendix of Texts*, ed. C. R. Cheney and Mary G. Cheney (Oxford, 1967)
Innocent III English Letters	*Selected Letters of Pope Innocent III Concerning England (1198–1216)*, ed. C. R. Cheney and W. H. Semple, NMT (Edinburgh, 1953)
Jaffé	*Regesta pontificum romanorum: ab condita ecclesia ad annum post Christum natum MCXCVIII*, ed. P. Jaffé, rev. S. Loewenfeld, F. Kaltenbrunner, and P. Ewald, 2 vols. (Leipzig, 1885–8) [citing Jaffé 'number']
JEH	*Journal of Ecclesiastical History*
Layettes	*Layettes de trésor des chartes*, ed. A. Teulet, J. de Laborde, E. Berger, and H.-F. Delaborde, Inventaires et documents, 5 vols. (Paris, 1863–1909; repr. Nendeln, 1977)
LHP	*Leges Henrici Primi*, ed. L. J. Downer (Oxford, 1972)
MGH	Monumenta Germaniae Historica
	BdK: Briefe der deutschen Kaiserzeit
	Const.: Constitutiones et acta publica imperatorem et regum
	LdL: Libelli de lite imperatorem et pontificum saeculis XI et XII
	SRG: Scriptores rerum Germanicarum in usum scholarum separatim editi
	SS: Scriptores
MS/MSS	Manuscript/s
NMT	Nelson's Medieval Texts
ODNB	*Oxford Dictionary of National Biography* (Oxford, 2004–) [cited from the online edn. and omitting web references]
OHS	Oxford Historical Society
OMT	Oxford Medieval Texts
Paris, *Chronica majora*	*Matthaei Pariensis, monachi Sancti Albani, Chronica majora*, ed. H. R. Luard, RS, 7 vols. (London, 1872–83)
P&P	*Past and Present*

PL	Jacques-Paul Migne (ed.), *Patrologiae cursus completus [. . .] omnium SS. patrum: doctorum scriptorumque ecclesiasticorum... ad aetatem Innocentii III [. . .] series latina*, 221 vols. (Paris, 1844–55, 1862–5)
Potthast	*Regesta pontificum romanorum inde ab a. post Christum natum MCXCVIII ad a. MCCCIV*, ed. Augustus Potthast, 2 vols. (Berlin, 1874–5; repr. Graz, 1957) [citing Potthast 'number']
PR	*Pipe Rolls*
PROME	*Parliament Rolls of Medieval England 1275–1504*, gen. ed. Chris Given-Wilson, 16 vols. (Woodbridge, 2005)
RCA	*I Registri della Cancelleria angioina*, ed. Riccardo Filangieri et al., Testi e documenti di storia napoletana, 49 vols. (Naples, 1950–)
Reg. Bon. VIII	*Les Registres de Boniface VIII: Recueil des bulles de ce pape publiées ou analysées d'après les manuscrits originaux des archives du Vatican*, ed. Georges Digard, Maurice Faucon, Antoine Thomas, and Robert Fawtier, 4 vols. (Paris, 1882), iii
Reg. Clem. V	*Regestum Clementis papae V*, 10 vols. in 8 (Rome, 1885–92)
Reg. Greg. IX	*Les Régistres de Grégoire IX*, ed. Lucien Auvray, Bibliothèque des Écoles françaises d'Athènes et de Rome. 2nd ser., Registres des papes du 13. Siècle 9, 4 vols. (Paris, 1896–1955)
Reg. Hon. III	*Regesta Honorii Papae III*, ed. Petrus Pressutti, 2 vols. (Rome, 1888–95; repr. Hildesheim, 1978)
Reg. Inn. III	*Die Register Innocenz' III*, ed. Othmar Hageneder et al., Historischen Instituts beim Österreichischen Kulturinstitut in Rom. II. Abt.: Quellen. 1, 10 vols. in 13 (Graz, 1964–) [up to January 1210 to date; for later dates see *PL* 216–17]
Reg. Peckham	*Registrum epistolarum fratris Johannis Peckham Archiepiscopi Cantuariensis*, ed. C. T. Martin. RS, 3 vols. (London, 1882–6)
Reg. vat.	Archivio Segreto Vaticano, Registra vaticana
RHF	*Recueil des historiens des Gaules et de la France*, gen. ed. L. Delisle, 24 vols. in 25 (Paris, 1869–1904; repub. Farnborough 1967)
RIS²	*Rerum Italicarum Scriptores*, new edn., 34 vols. in multiple parts (various publishers, 1900–)
RS	Rerum Britannicarum Medii Aevi Scriptores ('Rolls Series'), 99 vols. in multiple parts (London, 1858–96)
RSI	*Rivista Storica Italiana*
SCH	Studies in Church History
SR	*The Statutes of the Realm: From Original Records, etc. (1101–1713)*, ed. A. Luders, T. Edlyn Tomlins, J. France, W. E. Tauton, and J. Raithby, 11 vols. (London, 1810–28)

SS	Selden Society
Statutes of the Colleges of Oxford	*Statutes of the Colleges of Oxford: With Royal Patents of Foundation, Injunctions of Visitors*, ed. E. A. Bond, 3 vols. (London, 1853) [documents paginated separately by college]
TCE	*Thirteenth Century England*
TNA	The National Archives (formerly PRO, the Public Record Office)
	C 150: Abbey of St Peter, Gloucester: Cartulary and Deeds
	E 13: Exchequer of Pleas: Plea Rolls
	E 101: King's Remembrancer: Accounts Various
	E 159: Exchequer: King's Remembrancer: Memoranda Rolls and Enrolment Books
	SC 1: Special Collections: Ancient Correspondence of the Chancery and the Exchequer
TRHS	*Transactions of the Royal Historical Society*
TSMAO	*Typologie des sources du Moyen Age occidental*, 86 vols. (Turnhout, 1972–)
Walter of Henley	*Walter of Henley and Other Treatises on Estate Management and Accounting*, ed. Dorothea Oschinsky (Oxford, 1971)
X	*Liber extra* (giving references to the *CIC* edition)
ZRG Kan. Abt.	*Zeitschrift der Savigny-Stiftung für Rechtsgeschichte, Kanonistische Abteilung*

I give full references on first citation and abbreviated titles subsequently. The bibliography lists medieval sources by author, if known, or title. For long series of record editions (e.g. pipe rolls) I cite only the volume's relevant chronological coverage (e.g. *CPR 1292–1301*). In large dictionary series I cite only the entry, and a page reference if appropriate. If citing the document number in a text ('#') is as accurate as giving page references I do so, e.g. in the *CUP*. Column/page numbers are additionally cited if appropriate. Page references using 'p./pp.' are generally avoided except when providing cross-references within the book. References to Aristotle are taken from the revised Oxford translation. Canon law references follow the 'modern form' as set out by James A. Brundage in *Medieval Canon Law* (London, 1995), Appendix 1. Translations are mine unless noted.

1

Introduction

A FRANCOPHONE FLORENTINE IN LONDON

Item. I leave to London Guildhall's chamber a great book [*magnum librum*] of English acts, in which are contained many useful things [*utilia*], and another book concerning old English matters, together with a book called *Britton* and a book called the *Mirror of Justices* and a further book composed by Henry of Huntingdon. Item. One other book of English statutes with many liberties and other things touching the city.[1]

These were the books that Andrew Horn, London's chamberlain, bequeathed to London between 1320 and 1328, the year he died. A number (*Britton*, the *Mirror of Justices*) figure below in relation to the accountability of various English officers. As chamberlain Horn was the city's chief financial and judicial officer, with a longstanding interest in its law and custom.[2] In thinking about official conduct, however, Horn did not restrict himself to English models only.

It seems clear that his 'great book' contained an expanded version of the early thirteenth-century *Leges Anglorum*, numerous charters from Henry III's reign, statutes and tracts of Henry and Edward I, lists of London officers, and a set of more recent documents relating to London.[3] This compilation of customs, precedents, rules, laws, and lists is extant but now divided.[4] In the 'great book' Horn inserted a quire. It comprised Henry of Huntingdon's description of Britain (*c.*1130–57),

---

[1] Corporation of London Records Office (CLRO), Hustings Roll 57, #16, cited from Jeremy I. Catto, 'Andrew Horn: Law and History in Fourteenth Century England', in R. H. C. Davis and J. M. Wallace-Hadrill (eds.), with R. J. A. I. Catto and M. H. Keen, *The Writing of History in the Middle Ages: Essays Presented to Richard William Southern* (Oxford, 1981), 367–91 at 370–1. I have elided a gap in the MS. See also Catto, 'Horn, Andrew (*c.*1275–1328)', *ODNB*.

[2] Catto, 'Andrew Horn', 369, 372; Caroline M. Barron, *London in the Later Middle Ages: Government and People 1200–1500* (Oxford, 2004), 176–85.

[3] Catto, 'Andrew Horn', 376–8, on the basis of Ker's work (see n. 4).

[4] Between BL Cotton MS Claudius D II, Corporation of London *Liber custumarum*, and Oriel College MS 46. The manuscript history of the two original custumals which Horn was responsible for is messy (the *Magnum librum* is the earlier). N. R. Ker reconstructed Sir Robert Cotton's division and recombination of them in '*Liber Custumarum*, and other manuscripts formerly at the Guildhall', *The Guildhall Miscellany* 3 (1954), 37–45, and *Medieval Manuscripts in British Libraries*, i. *London* (Oxford, 1969), 20–2. The modern arrangement of the Corporation's *Liber custumarum* is different from the medieval MS's contents. I use *Magnum librum* to denote the original, complete medieval MS.

William fitz Stephen's description of London (*c*.1173–4), and excerpts addressing the election, conduct, and accountability of elected, fixed-term, Italian 'mayors' (*podestà*) taken from Brunetto Latini's *Livres dou Tresor* (*c*.1260–*c*.1265).[5] Horn, then, was also interested in the office, character, and accountability of Italian communal officers.

Latini had been a notary, scribe, and secretary for the Florentine *primo popolo* regime (1250–60), and Florence's ambassador to Alfonso X of Castile in 1260 when it pressed the King to act on his claims for the imperial crown against Manfred, allied with the rival Sienese. During the embassy, the Guelphs were badly defeated at Montaperti on 4 September and Latini's return home became instead a French exile.[6] It was during this that he wrote the *Livres dou Tresor*, a book of instruction for *podestà*.[7]

According to Latini the *Livres* were a treasure for 'that lord who wishes to find in a small place things of the greatest value not only for his delight but also to augment his power and to guarantee his estate in war and peace'.[8] A sequential encyclopedia, the book first discussed the 'beginning of the created world and the ancient time of the old histories, the establishment of the world and in sum the nature of all things'.[9] It then 'treats of vice and virtues [. . .] that is to say what one should do and what not, and shows the reason why'.[10] The third book was 'of fine gold. That is to say, it instructs man to speak according to the doctrine of rhetoric, and how a lord should govern the people who are his, likewise according to the Italians' customs.'[11] Only having led his readers up this ascent could Latini finally fulfil his promise to 'define politics, that is the government of cities which is the most noble and high science and the most noble office that there is on earth, in so far as politics covers generally all the arts which pertain to the community of men'.[12] This goal terminates the book. It was from these last thirty odd chapters of the *Tresor* that Horn took what Latini had to say about *podestà*, and actively and selectively adapted it for another annually elected municipal officer, the London mayor.[13]

The final chapters of the *Livres dou Tresor* discuss the transition from one *podestà* to the next. This transition included the procedure of *sindacatio*: the formal accounting

---

[5] For the *Magnum librum* see *Munimenta Gildhallæ Londoniensis: Liber albus, Liber custumarum, et Liber Horn*, ed. Henry Thomas Riley, RS, 3 vols. in 4 (London, 1859–62), ii.1. 15–25 (French excerpts from *Tresor*). Brief comment in Susan Reynolds, *Kingdoms and Communities in Western Europe, 900–1300*, 2nd edn. (Oxford, 1997), 197–8.

[6] G. Inglese, 'Latini, Brunetto', *DBI*.

[7] See now *Tresor*, ed. Pietro G. Beltrami, Paolo Squillaciotti, Plinio Torri, and Sergio Vatteroni (Turin, 2007); earlier editions are: P. Chabaille's *Li livres dou Tresor* (Paris, 1863) and Francis J. Carmody, *Li livres dou tresor* (Berkeley, Calif., 1948). Escorial MS L-II-3 is the basis of *Li livres dou tresor*, ed. Spurgeon Baldwin and Paul Barrette, Medieval and Renaissance Texts and Studies 257 (Tempe, 2003). For Latini on *sindacatio*, the thirteenth-century British Library manuscript of the *Tresor* used below, and further comments about accountability, see my 'A Medieval Officer and a Modern Mentality? *Podestà* and the Quality of Accountability', *The Mediæval Journal* 1.2 (2011), 43–79.

[8] BL Add. MS 30024, fo. 8ᵛ (§1.1). [9] BL Add. MS 30024, fo. 8ᵛ (§1.1).

[10] BL Add. MS 30024, fos. 8ᵛ–9ʳ (§1.1). [11] BL Add. MS 30024, fo. 9ʳ (§1.1.)

[12] BL Add. MS 30024, fos. 226ᵛ–227ʳ (§3.73). On this practical 'lay' privileging of politics as the greatest science, Ruedi Imbach, *Dante, la philosophie et les laïcs: initiations à la philosophie médiévale*, Vestigia 21 (Fribourg, 1996), 37–41.

[13] Horn's *Magnum librum* excerpts have 8 caps. (*Munimenta Gildhallæ*, ii.1. 15–25). They correspond to *Tresor* as follows: Horn cap. 1 to Latini §3.74–5; Horn 2–3 to Latini 3.75; Horn 4 to Latini 3.102; Horn 5 to Latini 3.104; Horn 6 to Latini 3.97 and, partly, 98; Horn 7–8 to Latini 3.96. Latini's preferred term for the *podestà* is *poeste* when he refers specifically to the Italian officer

of *podestà* after their term of office.[14] *Podestà* would remain in town, in their residence. Public announcements would be made in advance of their *sindacatio*. They would account for their own actions and those of their officers. In the hiatus anyone could complain about the *podestà* or his officers' conduct when in office, to which the *podestà* would respond.[15] Then, the *Tresor* ends, 'when it should please God you may be honourably discharged [*asolt*]. You will take your leave of the council, of the commune, and of the town, and you will go on your way home in glory and with honour amen.'[16] It is clear that before and during Latini's life, *sindacatio* could be a serious, sometimes hazardous moment for a *podestà*.[17] It is an interesting aspect of Latini's account of *sindacatio* that he presents it not as account exacted from an unwilling *podestà*, but as a bounty given by an eloquent and courteous one. In fact this makes great sense. Latini's *Tresor* is a book dedicated to the skilful cultivation of a *podestà*'s character. Since there is no skill in being simply held to account, it is logical that Latini should stress how his readership could express through *sindacatio* their responsible official character as *podestà*. Latini places his stress on character not coercion, responsibility not accountability.[18]

Given this, and the absence of a London equivalent of *sindacatio* for mayors at the end of their term of office, it was easy for Horn to develop the theme. Horn excerpts in and around these passages, but his version of a city magistrate's accountability at the end of his tenure is rather different.[19] Completing his term of office, Horn's mayor is a model of official courtesy, offering, outside any coercive legalism, redress for wrongs done.

> But in no way should [the mayor] forget to describe anything he has done which has profited the commune, and which seems good to him; and as for that which he mistook

---

(e.g. 3.73) and *seignor/chief* when speaking more generally (e.g. 3.75). *Governeor* is also used (3.96). Horn keeps this term (*Munimenta Gildhallæ*, ii.1. 23, cap. 7 using *Tresor* §3.96). *Governour* can also be synonymous with *meire* for Horn (*Munimenta*, ii.1. 16) who also uses *meire/meyre* to replace Latini's *chief* and *seignor* (*Munimenta*, ii.1. 16, 19, caps. 1, 3 using *Tresor* §3.74, 75). Horn sometimes replaces *sire* with *soverain* (*Munimenta* ii.1. 16 cap. 1 using *Tresor* §3.74).

[14] The procedure has antecedents in Roman Law: see Cod. Just. 1. 49 requiring provincial governors to remain at hand for fifty days after completing their term of office.

[15] BL Add. MS 30024, fos. 244ʳ–5ʳ (§3.103–5). Cf. the *compotum* of the English sheriff, including the public notices of accounting, the obligation to attend and reside, and the ritual of the audit as described in Richard of Ely's *Dialogus scaccarii* (1170s), *DS*, I.v, II.iii, II.iv, II.xx–xi esp. at 21, 79, 84–5, 116–18). See Ch. 3.

[16] BL Add. MS 30024, fo. 245ʳ (§3.105). In some copies (not MS 30024) a closing rhymed prayer follows.

[17] Philip Jones, *The Italian City-State: From Commune to Signoria* (Oxford, 1997), 532, 642–3; on later changes to *sindacatio* see Trevor Dean and Kate Lowe, 'Writing the History of Crime in the Italian Renaissance', in eid. (eds.), *Crime, Society and the Law in Renaissance Italy* (Cambridge, 1994), 1–15 at 8–9.

[18] See further Sabapathy, 'A Medieval Officer and a Modern Mentality', 53–66, 76–9, and 'Accountable *rectores* in comparative perspective: the theory and practice of holding *podestà* and bishops to account (late twelfth to thirteenth centuries)', in Agnès Bérenger and Frédérique Lachaud (eds.), *Hiérarchie des pouvoirs, délégation de pouvoir et responsabilité des administrateurs dans l'Antiquité et au Moyen Âge*, Centre de Recherche Universitaire Lorrain d'Histoire, Université de Lorraine—Site de Metz 46 (Metz, 2012), 201–30. For a different interpretation of Latini, Lauro Martines, *Power and Imagination: City-States in Renaissance Italy* (Harmondsworth, 1980), 155–67.

[19] *Munimenta Gildhallæ*, ii.1. 20, cap. 5.

against reason or against the law of the town, he is greatly sorry, and he shall be ready to make amends to both the greatest and the least, at any time, according to his power. And so he should pray to God that He should give them a governor which will know better, and who can guide them such as he could not during his time [in office]. And then he should commend them to God, great and small, and give to them his good will and thanks.[20]

Horn seems to have excerpted from Latini with a view to applicability. He does not transpose the constitutional accountability of Italian *sindacatio* to London, but builds on Latini's stress on courteous responsibility. Horn shows a greater interest in what Latini has to say about the election of mayors and of the characteristics and qualities they should have. Horn is also preoccupied with differing styles of government: whether governors do better to be feared or loved and how this in turn reflects differences between tyrants and kings. His interests clearly correlate with London's wider political context around the early 1320s, the generally agreed date for the 'great book's' composition.[21] The renewed 'popular' London charter of 8 June 1319 undoubtedly increased educated Londoners' appetite for food for thought about city governance.[22] Latini provided this. Horn's own interests in such matters predated his responsibilities as the city's principal financial and judicial officer (from 13 January 1320). The following year saw the 'intrusive' six-month-long London eyre that precipitated complaints about the oligarchical basis of the mayor's election, his deposition, and the appointment of a temporary royal warden.[23] For much of the following decade Horn's fellow fishmonger, the divisive Hamo Chigwell, was mayor, supported by the King and, until 1326, only nominally elected.[24] Chigwell would hold the mayoralty four times. It is in this charged context of un-free communal government, dubious municipal elections, politically compromised magistrates, and multiple, successive incumbencies that Horn's reading and rewriting of Latini should be placed.[25] As in communal Italy, questions about whether officers could be relied on to be responsible or should be more strictly required to be accountable were real issues. Horn was more interested in responsible officers; less in *sindacatio* as the means of predictably securing good mayoral rule.[26] His ostensible preference—like

---

[20] *Munimenta Gildhallæ*, ii.1. 20, cap. 5.
[21] Catto, 'Andrew Horn', 378, on the basis that the *Librum*'s list of London officers for 1276–1321 makes a date much later than 1321 unlikely.
[22] *The Historical Charters and Constitutional Documents of the City of London*, ed. W. de Gray Birch, rev. edn. (London, 1887), #22, 45–50, esp. caps. 1–2, 4–5, 13, 19, and the final remarks on self-assessed tallages.
[23] *The Eyre of London, 14 Edward II, AD 1321*, ed. H. M. Cam, 2 vols., SS 85–6 (1968–9), i. 42–4; Barron, *London in the Later Middle Ages*, 33, 149.
[24] Mayor 1321–3, 1324–6; for a full breakdown, see Anne Lancashire's lists in Barron, *London in the Later Middle Ages*, 326–8. Chigwell was freely elected in 1327 and then barred in 1328. See Elspeth Veale, 'Chigwell, Hamo (d. 1332)', *ODNB*.
[25] Cf. Catto, 'Andrew Horn', 370.
[26] It is striking that, given his own title and function, Horn does *not* excerpt Latini's passages relating to the 'chamberlain', his 'conte', and his accountability (Add. MS 30024, fos. 239ᵛ–240ʳ, *Tresor*, §3.93). Horn uses Latini to get at some very specific aspects of *mayoral* government which were clearly preoccupying him.

Latini's—was to provide for good government through norms of responsibility, rather than enforce it through rules of accountability.

THEMES AND ARGUMENT

The relationship between these two men, their offices and writings and administrative preferences provides a miniature synecdoche of this study's broader themes: first the relationship between norms, rules, practices, and official conduct; secondly, a distinction I wish to draw between 'political thinking' and 'political thought', applied especially to an institutional context; and thirdly a desire to place English developments within a broader European context. These themes are sketched below in a historiographical context. The example can also illustrate the broader substantive argument, and this chapter closes with a summary of it. I outline first the three themes.

Roles and Rules: Character and Office

A central theme of this study is the question of how it was hoped given officials would behave, how they were required to behave, and the relationship between the two. Texts expressing some ideal of official conduct may have articulated those hopes quite differently from those implied by institutions which practically sought to secure medieval officers' accountability. The contrast proposed above between Latini's comments on the ideal character of *podestà* and the institution of *sindacatio* is one example. The issue of official accountability is of great importance given the rapid expansion of officers of all sorts in this period.[27] That expansion was consequent on the proliferation of all kinds of institution in the period. At the heart of any interpretation of the twelfth and thirteenth centuries must lie some account of Europeans' appetite and aptitude for institutionalization.[28] One of the most significant recent contributions to this theme, Thomas Bisson's *Crisis of the Twelfth Century*, might partly be characterized as a study of the problem and possibility of distinguishing *at all* between two ideal types of official in the twelfth century: between, 'private' lordly agents, and 'public' regnal officials with some meaningful sense of a public interest. For Bisson, lordship is generally associated with the first and cuts against the second, which is associated with a normative idea of office, the prerequisite for a politics aspiring beyond the interests of merely

---

[27] See e.g. the complex *familia* of Roger of Pont l'Evêque, Archbishop of York, at the beginning of the period studied here, *York, 1154–1181*, ed. Marie Lovatt, EEA 20 (Oxford, 2000), xliii–liv.

[28] It is an interesting question whether 'institutionalization' should be seen as a self-justifying dynamic. Cf. Thomas Bisson's comments on creating fiscal institutions in Catalonia: 'Building efficient institutions was not yet an end in itself in the early thirteenth century. It was only a means, one among other still more favored means [e.g. violence] in support of the militant designs of a baronial monarchy', *Fiscal Accounts of Catalonia under the Early Count-Kings (1151–1213)*, 2 vols. (Berkeley, Calif., 1984), i. 150.

selfish lordship.²⁹ The accountability of agents thus becomes a proxy for the existence of that idea of office.³⁰

The reference to 'ideal types' in this context speaks to a Weberian practice of thinking about both officials and ideal types. 'Ideal types' have been much misunderstood. To use them is not to adjudicate on how far given officers diverged or conformed to some supposed blueprint. Rather 'the ideal type is a mental picture, which should neither be construed as historical reality, nor still the "real" truth, still less so as a schema which reality is orientated to like an exemplar; rather its meaning is to demarcate a completely ideal boundary, by which reality is measured or compared, so as to clarify particular, significant components of its empirical content.'³¹ Medieval categories of person and the importance of thinking through types has produced an important historiography addressing how actual individuals inhabited and moulded their variously stiff robes of office.³² A good deal of this historiographical thought has been interested in representation in and through types, influenced by the post-1967 *Annales équipe*.³³ The most influential French historiography of this sort has often been less interested in political, administrative, or legal structures and practices, which have tended to figure as a background, not foreground, element. This is in contrast to the longer constitutionalist tradition of historiography on officers of one sort or another. That historiography was principally interested in officers for the structure they provided to government. Some rapprochement, or at least rebalancing, seems evident more recently. More is said about these changes later in the chapter, but it is worth first explaining the approach to selecting officers taken here.

In its own literature, the period understandably left an enormous range of reflections on status and roles (*ad status* sermons, encyclopedias, etc.). The most famous typology is that of the three orders (those of fighting, praying, and cultivating), but far more finely grained gradations were developed—such as the social meanings seen

---

[29] Thomas N. Bisson, *The Crisis of the Twelfth Century: Power, Lordship, and the Origins of European Government* (Princeton, NJ, 2009), *passim*. Yet even lordship could be construed as an office for which one was capable or worthy (*idoneus*): see Edmund King, *King Stephen* (New Haven, Conn., 2010), 8–9, on William of Blois and Robert Curthose. On *idoneitas* from the Carolingians to Adolf of Nassau see Edward Peters, *The Shadow King: Rex Inutilis in Medieval Law and Literature, 751–1327* (New Haven, Conn., 1970), 42, 44, 61–2, 65–7, 70, 233–4.

[30] Though cf. pp. 45–6, 252 how the thirteenth-century action of account could produce a means of holding to account that (sometimes) legally fabricated the officer—bailiff—needed to express it.

[31] 'Die »Objectivität« sozialwissenschaftlicher und sozialpolitischer Erkenntnis', in Max Weber, *Schriften zur Wissenschaftslehre*, ed. Michael Sukale (Stuttgart, 1991), 21–101 at 77.

[32] Exceptional studies significantly structured by consideration of their subjects' roles are M. T. Clanchy, *Abelard: A Medieval Life* (Oxford, 1997) and Jacques Le Goff, *Saint Louis* (Paris, 1996). See also Le Goff's work on *exempla* and on medieval 'types': id., *Héros du Moyen Âge, le saint et le roi* (Paris, 2004); Claude Bremond, Jacques Le Goff, and Jean-Claude Schmitt, *L'"Exemplum"*, *TSMAO* 40 (1982); *The Medieval World*, ed. Jacques Le Goff, trans. Lydia G. Cochrane (London, 1990); Aaron Gurevich, *The Origins of European Individualism*, trans. Katharine Judelson (Oxford, 1995).

[33] Le Goff's own 'inside-out' study, *Saint Louis*, focused less on politics and administration and more on the effects of the linguistic turn, medieval exemplary types, the constraints of genres of regal representation, and applying Louis Dumézil's Indo-European tri-functional regal ideal of sacred, military, and productive functions to Louis IX. Cf. in a different idiom the equally authoritative studies of Louis's brother-in-law and contemporary Henry III executed by David Carpenter in *The Minority of Henry III* (London, 1990) and *The Reign of Henry III* (London, 1996). The contrast is only partly explained by differences in the English/French archival base.

reflected in the game of chess and its pieces.[34] Such reflections on social and functional roles provided the exemplary content for how officers should conduct themselves.[35] At least two of the greatest works of medieval literature (Dante's *Commedia* and Chaucer's *Canterbury Tales*) are rule-bending demonstrations of how these roles and characters can vibrate with life when put under immense poetic pressure.

This can be explored further in relation to twelfth-century *dictatores*—those trained in the formal writing of letters. They thought hard about the correct forms of address to, and between, different addressees, and therefore between different social groups. Consequently they thought about how to divide those groups up: popes and emperors at the top, peasants at the bottom. The group in between was harder and it is upon them—neither the apex nor absolute bottom of medieval societies—that this study draws. This great middling group (the *mediocres*) contained, according to the mid-twelfth-century *dictator* Bernard of Bologna, everyone from archbishops to laymen holding offices of one sort or another.[36] Other *dictatores*, such as Peter of Blois (1125 x 1130–1212), offered further subdivisions, into a middling (*mediocris*) and a more exalted (*sublimis*) group. The latter included archbishops and bishops; the former, *prepositi, prefecti*, and *consules*. What was important in such segregations was 'not profession in the technical sense of the word, but dignity, power, and office, and to a lesser extent [. . .] birth and nobility'.[37]

Medieval office denoted function,[38] honour, and responsibility.[39] This study takes up those topics of dignity, power, responsibility, and accountability. Its purpose is to examine how some of the members of these groups were deemed, and made, accountable—whatever 'accountable' may turn out to mean. Since *dictatores*' hierarchical filing systems varied, their groupings do not structure this analysis. But they

---

[34] On medieval orders see George Duby, *Les Trois Ordres ou l'imaginaire du féodalisme* (Paris, 1978); Alexander Murray, *Reason and Society in the Middle Ages* (Oxford, 1978); Giles Constable, 'The Interpretation of Mary and Martha' and 'The Orders of Society', two of his *Three Studies in Medieval Religious and Social Thought* (Cambridge, 1995). On chess see the comments below at pp. 103–10 on the *Dialogue of the Exchequer* and S. I. Luchitskaya, 'Chess as a Metaphor for Medieval Society', in *Saluting Aron Gurevich: Essays in History, Literature and Other Related Subjects*, ed. Yelena Mazour-Matusevich and Alexandra S. Korros (Leiden, 2010), 277–99; Jenny Adams, *Power Play: The Literature and Politics of Chess in the Later Middle Ages* (Philadelphia, 2006); Olle Ferm and Volker Honemann (eds.), *Chess and Allegory in the Middle Ages* (Stockholm, 2005); Michel Pastoureau, *L'Échiquier de Charlemagne: Un jeu pour ne pas jouer* (Paris, 1990) and *Une histoire symbolique du Moyen Âge occidental* (Paris, 2004), 303–29.

[35] On the importance for societies of their emblematic characters and traditions see Alasdair MacIntyre's, *After Virtue: A Study in Moral Theory*, 2nd edn. (London, 1985), 27–31, 73, and on traditions and institutions 221–5; *Whose Justice? Which Rationality?* (London, 1988), 164–82; and *Three Rival Versions of Moral Enquiry: Encyclopaedia, Genealogy, and Tradition* (London, 1990), 149–69.

[36] Giles Constable, 'The Structure of Medieval Society According to the Dictatores of the Twelfth Century', in Kenneth Pennington and Robert Somerville (eds.), *Law, Church and Society: Essays in Honour of Stephan Kuttner* (Philadelphia, 1977), 253–67 at 256, 264 n. 20. See also Constable, *Three Studies*, 342–60.

[37] Constable, 'Structure of Medieval Society', 253–67 (261 for Constable's quote and 260, 267 for Peter of Blois).

[38] Richard Kieckhefer, 'The Office of Inquisition and Medieval Heresy: The Transition from Personal to Institutional Jurisdiction', *JEH 46* (1995), 36–61 at 47–9.

[39] *Innocent III English Letters*, #25 (1205), 'Cum sit honori adnexum, exequi debet officium qui beneficium est sortitus.'

are useful as a point of departure about medieval hierarchies—where hierarchies of responsibility followed from positions of responsibility.[40] One presumption of taking this sample of *mediocres* is that there are things just as interesting to say about medieval political thinking respecting *mediocres* as there are respecting *sublimes*—kings and emperors. After all, the highest officers (and the most highly-strung in terms of the tension surrounding their accountability to others) may not offer the most representative perspective on accountability in the Middle Ages. Even if they have, logically, dominated the historiography of medieval political thought, the dominance of kings, emperors, and popes has arguably limited it, and likewise limited the history of political accountability, an issue developed below.[41]

In one important respect the study disregards an important axiom of many *dictatores*' social filing systems, and some modern historiography. That axiom is that secular officers and religious officers are magnetically repellant to each other, such that each field should be considered separately. There are practical reasons why complex fields tend to be treated discretely; but a consequence is a diminished understanding of the connections between them. (Legal historiography often exemplifies both features.) There was an interplay between different ideas of officers and techniques for regulating them, whether this was causally direct or just observable in fact (e.g. the relationship between secular inquests and canonical inquisitions). Individuals moved between secular office and ecclesiastical office. A bishop could be thought a *rector* no less than a secular ruler such as a *podestà*.[42] Hubert Walter, Justiciar, Chancellor, and Archbishop of Canterbury was involved (as we shall see) in a number of both secular and ecclesiastical *inquisitiones* as well as the canonization inquiries into Gilbert of Sempringham. Robert Grosseteste (also discussed below), was both Bishop of Lincoln and a translator of Aristotle's *Politics* and writer on estate management. John of Crakehall was both Grosseteste's steward and between 1258 and 1260 Exchequer Treasurer to the Baronial Council.[43] The conjunction of functions is relevant to an understanding of these men's conduct in office.[44] There is a value in comparing different sorts of officer. Biblical norms

---

[40] Cf. Gregory the Great on this theme: Carole Straw, *Gregory the Great: Perfection in Imperfection* (Berkeley, Calif., 1988), 86–9.

[41] Ernst H. Kantorowicz infamously and classically addressed emperor and king in *Kaiser Friedrich der Zweite* (Berlin, 1927; Eng. trans. 1931) and *The King's Two Bodies: A Study in Mediaeval Political Theology* (Princeton, NJ, 1957). Parallel rationales to mine for examining middling royal officials are offered by Romain Telliez, «*Per potentiam officii*»: *Les Officiers devant la justice dans le royaume de France au XIVe siècle* (Paris, 2005), 8; Cristina Jular Pérez-Alfaro, 'The King's Face on the Territory: Royal Officers, Discourse and Legitimating Practices in Thirteenth and Fourteenth Century Castile', in Isabel Alfonso, Hugh Kennedy, and Julia Escalona (eds.), *Building Legitimacy: Political Discourses and Forms of Legitimacy in Medieval Societies*, The Medieval Mediterranean 53 (Leiden, 2004), 107–37 at 108–9. Arguing that there are other, less charged officers worth examining obviously does not deny the central importance of issues of office, delegation, and answerability in relation to these highest offices.

[42] For bishop as *rector* see e.g. *Innocent III English Letters*, #23, 27 October 1205 (*Reg. Inn. III*, viii. #143 (142)).

[43] Adrian Jobson, 'John of Crakehall: The "Forgotten" Baronial Treasurer, 1258-1260', *TCE* 13 (2011), pp. 83–99.

[44] Cf. Telliez, «*Per potentiam officii*» pp. 7–8.

seeped through thinking about religious and lay officers (the Gospel parable of the unjust steward could be cited regarding both secular and religious officers' accountability). Legal learning could interpenetrate theology.[45] The relationship between learned argument and administrative practices could be one of informed reciprocity.[46] (Latini's introduction to the *Tresor* explicitly indicates what pertains to *théorique* and what *pratique*.)[47] But more holistic pictures of medieval political thinking have been hampered by a tendency to segregate secular government, administration, and law from its ecclesiastical partners. Bringing administration, law, theology, and political thinking under the same analytical consideration here with respect to secular and religious officials of different qualities is intended to address this.

The group discussed here, then, enables a sampling of differences and similarities within important medieval institutions: churches (bishops), seigneurial and 'private' administration (bailiffs and stewards), royal government (sheriffs), and charitable foundations (wardens), and to a much lesser extent, towns (mayors and *podestà*). There is a rich historiography on almost all of them.[48] Other individual officers have received sustained treatment: ambassador,[49] Flemish general receiver (*général recheveur*),[50] notary,[51] coroner.[52] Some seemed too particular to provide a focus here. Others seemed too large to accommodate on this scale (judges, lawyers, abbots).[53] Princes (*principes*) with *dominium*, to put it legalistically, are, as noted, largely

---

[45] William Marx, 'The Conflictus inter Deum et Diabolum and the Emergence of the Literature of Law in Thirteenth Century England', *TCE* 13 (2011), 57–66.

[46] e.g. Jean Dunbabin, *The French in the Kingdom of Sicily, 1266–1305* (Cambridge, 2011), 222–3 (on the Neapolitan nature of Aquinas's political thinking), 224–5 (likewise James of Viterbo).

[47] BL Add. MS 30024, fos. 8ᵛ–11ᵛ (§§1.1, 1.3–4).

[48] Indicatively: on bailiffs, T. F. T. Plucknett, *The Mediaeval Bailiff* (London, 1954), repr. as *Studies in English Legal History* (London, 1983), essay V; Paul Brand, 'Stewards, Bailiffs and the Emerging Legal Profession', in Ralph Evans (ed.), *Lordship and Learning: Studies in Memory of Trevor Aston* (Woodbridge, 2004), 139–53. On sheriffs: W. A. Morris, *The Medieval English Sheriff to 1300* (Manchester, 1927); Judith A. Green, *English Sheriffs to 1154*, Public Record Office Handbooks 24 (London, 1990); D. A. Carpenter, 'The Decline of the Curial Sheriff in England 1194–1258', *EHR* 91 (1976), 1–32, repr. in his *Reign of Henry III*, 151–82. For *podestà* see the bibliography in Sabapathy, 'A Medieval Officer and a Modern Mentality', nn. 21, 23, 29. For bishops: Robert L. Benson, *The Bishop-Elect: A Study in Medieval Ecclesiastical Office* (Princeton, NJ, 1968); Robert Brentano, *Two Churches: England and Italy in the Thirteenth Century*, new edn. (Berkeley, Calif., 1988); Kenneth Pennington, *Pope and Bishops: The Papal Monarchy in the Twelfth and Thirteenth Centuries* (Philadelphia, 1984). I have not found a study of college wardens. For hospital wardens see Sethina C. Watson's '*Fundatio, Ordinatio* and *Statuta*: The Statutes and Constitutional Documents of English Hospitals to 1300' (D.Phil. thesis, Oxford, 2004), and ead., 'The Origins of the English Hospital', *TRHS*, 6th ser. 16 (2006), 75–94.

[49] Donald E. Queller, *The Office of the Ambassador in the Middle Ages* (Princeton, NJ, 1967).

[50] Ellen E. Kittell, *From Ad Hoc to Routine: A Case Study in Medieval Bureaucracy* (Philadelphia, 1991).

[51] R. Aubenas, *Étude sur le notariat provençal au Moyen Âge et sous l'Ancien Régime* (Aix-en-Provence, 1931); C. R. Cheney, *Notaries Public in England in the Thirteenth and Fourteenth Centuries* (Oxford, 1972).

[52] R. F. Hunnisett, *The Medieval Coroner* (Cambridge, 1961).

[53] On legal professionals, James A. Brundage, *The Medieval Origins of the Legal Profession: Canonists, Civilians, and Courts* (Chicago, 2008) and Paul Brand, *The Origins of the English Legal Profession* (Oxford, 1992). Accountability in religious orders is touched on at pp. 202–4.

excluded.[54] The focus here, however, is on the norms, rules, and practices of accountability relating to officials at intermediate points in their hierarchies.

In evaluating these relationships between norms, rules, and practices I have tried not to presume any causal current naturally flowing in a given direction. Ideas may be instrumental in producing social change. Equally norms may be invoked *ex post facto* to justify emerging practices that fulfil some functional need. The polarity of a current running between intellectual ideas and social practices cannot be presumed. The potential intricacy of such issues is illustrated by Robert Bartlett's discussion of the medieval ordeal. The ordeal, Bartlett argues, did not die a natural 'functional' death but was assiduously strangled *c*.1050–1215 by reforming clerical intellectuals.[55] Generally law has provided the most familiar field in which older ideas (e.g. Roman) are presumed to power or inspire new or reinterpreted practices. Sometimes this seems too easy an answer, but sometimes it may well just be right.[56] The tendency herein is to presume that a demonstrable genealogical precedent for a given form of accountability is *not* necessarily a sufficient explanation for its medieval versions. 'The important thing is not the putative descent of some practice or institution, but its function and significance in the living society in which it has a place' is quoted several times.[57] Likewise Maitland's view that 'legal ideas never reach very far beyond practical needs'.[58] This is probably too optimistic, but it is a better starting point than many. That Justinian's Code 1.49 requires end-of-term auditing for military and civil provincial governors seems to me insufficient alone to explain the existence and form of Italian *sindacatio*—we obviously must look too at the practical needs that gave the rule life.

Political Thinking, Political Thought, Institutions, and Administrative History

This implies a further general theme of the study: the relationship between theories and practices of accountability (a formulation deliberately avoiding that of 'ideal versus reality'). Given the focus on practices and institutions, it follows that many

---

[54] See Kenneth Pennington, *The Prince and the Law, 1200–1600: Sovereignty and Rights in the Western Legal Tradition* (Berkeley, Calif., 1993); Peters, *Shadow King*; Marguerite Boulet-Sautel, 'Le Princeps de Guillaume Durand', in *Études d'histoire du droit canonique, dédiées à Gabriel Le Bras*, 2 vols. (Paris, 1965), ii. 803–13.

[55] Robert Bartlett, *Trial by Fire and Water: The Medieval Judicial Ordeal* (Oxford, 1986), esp. pp. 42–43, 62, 69, 70–102, 139, 153, 164–5.

[56] See Andrew Lewis's sensitive consideration of whether either Henry II's possessory assizes or the institutional idea of an Islamic charitable foundation (*waqf*) owe their existence to Roman legal ideas, 'On Not Expecting the Spanish Inquisition: The Uses of Comparative Legal History', *Current Legal Problems* 57 (2004), 53–84 at 57–62.

[57] Bartlett, *Trial by Fire and Water*, 154. He is criticizing the question that asks whether the ordeal should be seen as 'really' Christian or 'really' pagan. My quotation should not imply that Bartlett is arguing for a purely functionalist approach to legal change. Cf. a more basically sceptical view of the instrumentality of (Roman, legal) ideas in Michael Prestwich (ed.), *Documents Illustrating the Crisis of 1297–1298 in England*, CS 4th ser. 24 (1980), 28–30, and Michael Prestwich, *Plantagenet England, 1225–1360* (Oxford, 2005), 171.

[58] Frederic William Maitland, *Township and Borough* (Cambridge, 1898), 27.

of the texts analysed are 'lower' rather than 'higher' in terms of their apparent intellectual standing: anonymous texts on estate management and Aquinas's advice to the Duchess of Brabant both figure, but the former receive more attention than the latter. All points on that spectrum merit the same quality of attention. This approach is in line with three distinct historiographical trends, relating respectively to the history of philosophy, the history of political thinking, and what could be called 'new' administrative history.

In his *Introduction to Medieval Philosophy*, Kurt Flasch writes 'in praise of mediocre authors', specifically Macrobius, who provided the central prosecution evidence in Manegold of Lautenbach's *c.*1080 letter to Wolfhelm of Cologne attacking Philosophy's challenge to Christianity, and the Emperor's challenge to the Pope.[59] It is through Manegold's use of this mediocre author (middling like the *mediocres* selected here) that, Flasch says, we can see the articulate tensions of this late eleventh-century world.[60] The perspective taken here is broadly similar. What light do these 'middling' texts and individuals offer about ideas of accountability in this period?

The study also addresses these ideas working in action through social institutions and practices. The second trend then derives from a distinction implicitly drawn by Janet Nelson between the history of 'political thinking' and that of 'political thought'. Such a distinction seems useful because it indicates a difference in the sources focused on, the questions therefore asked, and the histories consequently written.[61] So, political thinking would denote the applied reasoning which can be inferred from institutional practices whether legal, administrative, or other. Judicial practice (as distinct from only formal law) is especially important here, given the 'medieval tendency to assimilate politics to law' such that medieval justice 'structurally occupied a far more pivotal position within the total political system [than modern justice]' and 'was the ordinary name of power'.[62] Since so much medieval legal business was also administrative business one might

---

[59] Using the translation by Janine de Bourgknecht, *Introduction à la philosophie médiévale* (Paris, 1998), 71–4, 82–8; also John Marenbon's lecture, 'Ce que les historiens de la philosophie anglophones pourraient apprendre en lisant Kurt Flasch' (2005), 10–11, and downloaded from <http://www.trin.cam.ac.uk/show.php?dowid=200>, accessed January 2014. Imbach, *Dante*, is a parallel move.

[60] Flasch's distinction is compatible with David d'Avray's tripartite distinction about what may be included under the rubric of 'the history of ideas and attitudes', namely 'original ideas, ideology and social development, and "ordinary" beliefs'. D. L. d'Avray, *The Preaching of the Friars: Sermons Diffused from Paris Before 1300* (Oxford, 1985), 258–9. The present study focuses mainly on the latter two.

[61] This is my version of a distinction I infer from Nelson. Nelson's sadly unpublished 1999 Oxford Carlyle Lectures in the history of political thought, 'Political Thinking in the Early Middle Ages', would offer further substantive and methodological insights (her titles were: 'Trends', 'Peers', 'Patriarchs', 'Councils', 'Rites', 'End-times'). Her 2001–4 Royal Historical Society Presidential Addresses on 'England and the Continent in the Ninth Century' touch on some similar themes. For debate about what 'count as "sources"' in this context see Nelson's and Joe Canning's 1997 exchange concerning the latter's *A History of Medieval Political Thought, 300–1450*, 1st edn. (London, 1995) at <http://www.history.ac.uk/reviews/review/33>, accessed January 2014. For an integrating view of intellectuals (writ large) as rooted figures in their landscapes see Nelson's 'Organic Intellectuals in the Dark Ages?', *History Workshop Journal* 66 (2008), 1–17.

[62] The first quote is Susan Reynolds's, *Kingdoms and Communities*, 189 (talking about *podestà*), the latter Perry Anderson's in *Passages from Antiquity to Feudalism* (London, 1974), 153.

go on to say that administration (writ large) should occupy a far more significant place in accounts of medieval political thinking. It is for instance unhelpful that the Provisions of Westminster of October 1259, a vital record of the principled conflict between Henry III and the barons, should be given modern rubrics apparently distinguishing between 'legal resolutions' and 'administrative and political resolutions'.[63] Administration is politics by routine means, often legal ones.

Political thought, by contrast, generally denotes the reasoning expressed in more, rather than less, self-conscious texts synthesizing political issues—be these treatises such as Dante's *Monarchia* or legal commentaries such as that of Johannes Teutonicus. (Both figure later in the book: there is equally no presumption that intellectual ideas remain 'just' ideas.)[64] Still, an important consequence of looking outside formal or 'high' 'political' writing for evidence of political thinking in action is that the resulting history is, it is hoped, different. There is much law in what follows and judicial practice ought to be a good bridge between political thought and political thinking, given its natural engagement with both theory and practice.[65] An exemplification comes from Alain Boureau's account of monasteries' impact on English legal practice. Boureau argues for a connection between liturgical thinking and Benedictine legal thinking in the late eleventh through to thirteenth centuries, focusing on an English version of what he calls *l'abstraction judiciaire*—the ability to resolve complex disputes into formal elements and standard procedures, itself produced by the *practice* of litigation, and relatively autonomous with respect to the Continental *ius commune*. By so doing Boureau wanted to offer

> not a fragment of a history of juridical doctrines, nor a history of justice [but rather between these two] a sort of historical morphology of norms, attentive to the forms of the action and interaction, which would show in a context with a suberabundance of normative references (Roman law, canon law, common law, feudal laws, monastic

---

[63] *DBM* ##11, 12. The rubric originated with Sir Maurice Powicke, according to Treharne and Sanders.

[64] For an argument that publicly expressed ideas constrain behaviour irrespective of whether they are an agent's actual motivation see Quentin Skinner, 'The Principles and Practice of Opposition: The Case of Bolingbroke versus Walpole', in Neil McKendrick (ed.), *Historical Perspectives: Studies in English Thought and Society in Honour of J. H. Plumb*, (London, 1974), 93–128 at 128: 'The agent's principles will also make a difference [not just if those principles can be shown to have provided a motive for action] whenever he needs to be able to provide an explicit justification for them. This will make it necessary for the agent to limit and direct his behaviour in such a way as to make his actions compatible with the claim that they were motivated by an acceptable principle and that they can thus be justified. This in turn means that such an agent's professed principles invariably need to be treated as causal conditions of his actions, even if the agent professes those principles in a wholly disingenuous way.' There are important unstated terms in this formulation: (*a*) that some public exists with some sufficient sanction to make a lack of compatibility undesirable for the agent, so, (*b*), leading to self-constraint. Separately, (*c*), it is presumed that there is singular way to establish this compatibility. On the problem of detecting incompatibilities between verbal statements and non-verbal actions see Raymond Geuss, 'Moralism and Realpolitik', in his *Politics and the Imagination* (Princeton, NJ, 2010), 31–42 at 35–7.

[65] Cf. Charles Donahue Jr., *Why the History of Canon Law Is Not Written*, SS Lecture (London, 1986), on case law as a window into political thinking (15), law and political thinking (14), the constant if implicit relationship between practice and 'theory' (21–2), and the challenge of comparative work (9, 19).

discipline, customs, natural law, law of nations), how monastic actors constructed their own forms of intervention or defence by playing with institutional and ideological constraints.[66]

That approach tallies with the 'legal realist' approach that Michael Clanchy perceived in Barnwell Priory's legal historian of the 1290s who compiled a register composed 'by interweaving the texts of official records from the royal plea rolls with a commentary allegedly explaining what really happened'.[67] No analysis claims any more to explain *wie es eigentlich gewesen ist*. What this study does share with the Barnwell realist is a desire to look 'at the system from the middle'. For the Barnwell realist, 'above him is the mysterious and hazardous territory of the king's justices and learned counsel and beneath him are the prior's tenants and dependants'. Clanchy thought this view from the middle useful since 'the vast records of the king's courts have caused historians of medieval England to view the legal system too often from above: from the unique standpoint of the sovereign king, his justices and their clerks'.[68]

This last point relates to both the earlier one about *mediocres* and the 'history of accountability' itself. After all, the latter appears to be a largely unwritten chapter in the history of political thought. Or, rather, discussion of it has generally occurred from those 'unique standpoints' of sovereigns and pontiffs. The possibility of opposing, deposing, replacing, and holding to trial popes, kings, and emperors was obviously real—as, in different ways, Pope Gregory VII, Henry IV of Germany, John and Henry III in England, Frederick II in Germany, and Boniface VIII well knew. Histories have been written about them. To describe thus the history of accountability as unwritten then is partly to argue about the subjects and terms from which that history has been written. Yet the focus on the political accountability of those at the top of medieval hierarchies has largely not trickled down historiographically to a consideration of the *mediocres* beneath. The contrast sketched above between Latini's framing of *sindacatio* and its hazardous reality is offered as a case in point of the value of reading together medieval 'theory' and 'practice' in relation to officials' accountability.[69] The conjunction

---

[66] Alain Boureau, *La Loi du royaume: Les Moines, le droit et la construction de la nation anglaise (XIe–XIIIe siècles)* (Paris, 2001), 14; method sketched at 12–20, partly appearing in English as 'How Law Came to the Monks: The Use of Law in English Society at the Beginning of the Thirteenth Century', *P&P* 167 (2000), 29–74. Legal historians and anthropologists elsewhere have been giving attention to 'legalism' as a mode of thought: see the papers in Paul Dresch and Hannah Skoda (eds.), *Legalism: Anthropology and History* (Oxford, 2012) and Fernanda Pirie and Judith Scheele (eds.), *Legalism: Community and Justice* (Oxford, forthcoming). A compatible and similarly independent line of thought is D. L. d'Avray, *Rationalities in History: A Weberian Essay in Comparison* (Cambridge, 2010).

[67] M. T. Clanchy, 'A Medieval Realist: Interpreting the Rules at Barnwell Priory, Cambridge', in Elspeth Attwooll (ed.), *Perspectives in Jurisprudence* (Glasgow, 1977), 176–94 discussing BL Harley MS 3601 (*c.*1295–6) and ed. John Willis Clark, intr. F. W. Maitland, *Liber memorandum ecclesie de Bernewelle* (Cambridge, 1907), trans. as John Willis *The Observances in Use at the Augustinian Priory of S. Giles and S. Andrew at Barnwell, Cambridgeshire*, ed. John Willis Clark (Cambridge, 1897).

[68] Clanchy, 'Medieval Realist', 186.

[69] Explored further in Sabapathy, 'A Medieval Officer and a Modern Mentality'. More recent historiography has focused on *podestà, sindacatio*, and political thought often in terms of rhetoric—again

14 *Introduction*

has precedents.[70] Especially amongst early medievalists it has become the focus of more self-conscious study during the last twenty-five years or so, as the work of the 'Bucknell Group' demonstrates.[71]

Much of what such historians have focused on are social practices and social institutions, and this historiographical trend leads into, but is often surprisingly distinct from, the third historiographical trend: administrative history.[72] The constitutional interests of nineteenth-century historiography entailed administrative histories that thrived well into the twentieth, and, in places, continue to do so.[73] But in general more fashionable twentieth-century historiography (at least in Europe and North America) can crudely be characterized as a reaction against the implicit empiricist values and narrowly political perspectives of such legal/constitutional/administrative historiographies. A large reason for the fame and success of the *Annales* 'School' was that when Bloch and Febvre pollarded the dry trunk of their French tradition they were hacking away in time with other historians' equivalent assaults.[74] Many focused on constitutional/institutional history. One hatchet-job was that of Jaime Vicens Vives. He argued that legal history (and the connected 'myth of the document') had produced

---

moving away from the constititional/administrative focus of earlier generations' work. See e.g. Paolo Cammarosano, 'L'Éloquence laïque dans l'Italie communale (fin du XIIe–XIVe siècle)', *Bibliothèque de l'École des Chartes* 158 (2000), 431–42; Enrico Artifoni, 'Retorica e organizzazione del linguaggio politico nel Duecento italiano', in Paolo Cammarasono (ed.), *Le forme della propaganda politica nel Due e nel Trecento*, Collection de l'École française de Rome 201 (Rome, 1994), 157–82; Artifoni, 'Sull'eloquenza politica nel Duecento italiano', *Quaderni medievali storici* 35 (1993), 57–78; Artifoni, 'I podestà professionali e la fondazione retorica della politica comunale', *Quaderni storici* 63 (1986), 687–719.

[70] Of Anglophone scholarship the work of Jolliffe, Bisson, Clanchy, Dunbabin, Holt, and Reynolds is of lasting value: J. E. A. Jolliffe, *Angevin Kingship*, 2nd edn. (London, 1963); T. N. Bisson, *Fiscal Accounts of Catalonia*; Bisson, *Tormented Voices: Power, Crisis and Humanity in Rural Catalonia, 1140–1200* (Cambridge, Mass., 1998); and Bisson, *Crisis of the Twelfth Century*; M. T. Clanchy, 'Remembering the Past and the Good Old Law', *History* 55 (1970), 165–76; Clanchy, 'Law, Government, and Society in Medieval England', *History* 59 (1974), 73–8; Clanchy, '*Moderni* in Education and Government in England', *Speculum* 50 (1975), 671–88; Clanchy, 'Medieval Realist'; Clanchy, 'Law and Love in the Middle Ages', in John Bossy (ed.), *Disputes and Settlements: Law and Human Relations in the West* (Cambridge 1983), 47–67; Jean Dunbabin, 'Aristotle in the Schools', in Beryl Smalley (ed.), *Trends in Medieval Political Thought* (Oxford, 1965), 65–85; Dunbabin, 'Government', in J. H. Burns (ed.), *The Cambridge History of Medieval Political Thought, c.350–c.1450* (Cambridge, 1988), 477–519; Dunbabin, 'Guido Vernani of Rimini's Commentary on Aristotle's Politics', *Traditio* 44 (1988), 373–88; Dunbabin, *Charles I of Anjou: Power, Kingship and State-Making in Thirteenth-Century Europe* (London, 1998); Dunbabin, 'Charles I of Anjou and the Development of Medieval Political Ideas', *Nottingham Medieval Studies* 45 (2001), 110–26; J. C. Holt, *The Northerners: A Study in the Reign of King John*, rev. edn. (Oxford, 1992); and Holt, *Magna Carta*, 2nd edn. (Cambridge, 1992); and Reynolds, *Kingdoms and Communities*.

[71] Wendy Davies and Paul Fouracre (eds.), *The Settlement of Disputes in Early Medieval Europe*, *Property and Power in the Early Middle Ages*, and *The Languages of Gift in the Early Middle Ages* (Cambridge, 1986, 1995, 2010). For a critique of the effect that concentrating on dispute settlement has had on recognizing modes of legal thought see Paul Dresch, 'Legalism, Anthropology and History: A View from Part of Anthropology', in Dresch and Skoda (eds.), *Legalism*, 1–37, esp. 3–15.

[72] I give a complementary analysis of 'institutional' history in relation to the Sorbonne in Sabapathy, 'Regulating Community and Society at the Sorbonne in the Late Thirteenth Century', in Fernanda Pirie and Judith Scheele (eds.), *Legalism: Community and Justice* (Oxford, 2014).

[73] Two excellent, recent, relevant, British examples are J. R. Maddicott, *The Origins of the English Parliament, 924–1327* (Oxford, 2010), and Sandra Raban, *A Second Domesday? The Hundred Rolls of 1279–80* (Oxford, 2004).

[74] 'A nos lecteurs', *Annales d'histoire économique et sociale*, 1 (1929), 1–2.

a cold and sterile history of institutions [...] Importance was bestowed upon the framework instead of the contents, upon the conduit of energy instead of the charge which the conduit [that is the institution] merely transfers passively. [...] [Medievalists have] forgotten that any institution, by the simple act of encasing a vital tension or of achieving a new equilibrium of forces, is stillborn or at least inert [...] Neither regulations, nor privileges, nor laws, nor constitutions bring us close to human reality. These are formulas that establish limits, but nothing more than limits. The expression of life is to be found in the application of the law, statute, decree, or regulation; in the way in which individuals distort the desire of a state, of a corporation, or of an oligarchy to impose a certain order. An institution should be considered not in and of itself, but in terms of the human fervor that stirs in its innermost recesses.[75]

Similar comments have been made of other European historiographies. Chris Wickham commented of Italian history about the twelfth century that it has seemed 'curiously dead, curiously institutional', each perhaps amounting to much the same thing.[76] Even a sympathetic critic such as John Gillingham can reasonably complain that 'historians of administration tend to be impressed only by the evidence of administrative documents'.[77] Just so—up to a point—and a general effect has been to render such history relatively unfashionable, at least for medievalists, and at least, so to speak, beyond the large map and documents room of the National Archives or the seminar rooms of the École des Chartes.[78] Le Goff's 'annaliste' *Saint Louis* is a deeply 'institutional' history—but principally regarding social practices constitutive of Louis's kingship and character, not in the organizational-constitutional sense. Without criticism Chiffoleau has asked whether the richness of *exempla*, narratives, and hagiographies around Louis IX has not been to the detriment of his 'practical acta'.[79] Such a split has problematic consequences. With a reduced focus on institutions *qua* organizations and their reflexive relationship with institutions *qua* practices, an important perspective for explaining political domination becomes blinkered. Yet the importance of institutions in both senses is clear: 'It is because there are institutions everywhere that there is domination everywhere'.[80] That formula may exaggerate, depending on one's theory of human nature. Less arguable would be the claim

---

[75] Jaime Vicens Vives, *Approaches to the History of Spain*, trans. Joan Connelly Ullman, 2nd edn. (Berkeley, Calif., 1970), xvi–xvii (orig. pub. 1952).

[76] Chris Wickham, *Courts and Conflict in Twelfth-Century Tuscany* (Oxford, 2003), 312. Cf. Timothy Reuter's critique of institutionalized history in 'Modern Mentalities and Medieval Polities', *Medieval Polities and Modern Mentalities*, ed. Janet L. Nelson (Cambridge, 2006), 3–18 at 13–14.

[77] John Gillingham, *Richard I* (New Haven, Conn., 1999), 276 n. 29, also 275.

[78] The fine collection by Werner Paravicini and Karl Ferdinand Werner (eds.), *Histoire comparée de l'administration (IVᵉ–XVIIIᵉ siècles): Actes du XIVᵉ Colloque historique franco-allemand, Tours, 27 mars–1ᵉʳ avril 1977*, Beihefte der Francia 9 (Munich, 1980), could be taken as a watershed of the older European tradition. For American historians' commitment to 'institutions', one could take the three volumes on *The English Government at Work, 1327–1336* comprising, i. *Central and Prerogative Administration*, ed. James F. Willard and William A. Morris, ii. *Fiscal Administration*, ed. William A. Morris and Joseph R. Strayer, iii. *Local Administration and Justice*, ed. James F. Willard, William A. Morris, and William H. Dunham (Cambridge, Mass., 1940, 1947, 1950).

[79] Jacques Chiffoleau, 'Saint Louis, Frédéric II et les constructions institutionelles du XIIIᵉ siècle', *Médiévales* 34 (1998), 13–23 at 19.

[80] Luc Boltanski's characterization of 'critical sociology's' approach to the subject: *De la critique: Précis de sociologie de l'émancipation* (Paris, 2009), 86. He is alive to the various valencies of 'institutional'.

that 'there are no institutional facts without brute facts'.[81] Ceasing to attend to the one implies an increasing inability to explain the other. There is an irony that it was just as the social sciences engaged with institutions and administration that historians' interest in them declined, but 'institutions' have also waned as an object of social scientific interest.[82]

The obvious drawbacks of such blinkering may be a sufficient explanation of more recent approaches to institutional history in the broadest sense and with the broadest sympathies. That begs a question about my deliberately imprecise use of the word 'institutional' so far.[83] Is one talking about 'institutions' as political-juridical phenomena (e.g. fiefs and homage *à la* Ganshof);[84] as rule-based organizations (e.g. a monastery); or as flexible social practices *tout court* (e.g. oaths in general)?[85] The intention here is to show how institutions (*qua* social practices) gave life to institutions (*qua* organizational forms), and also how the latter gave shape and form to the former (e.g. at the Curia, Merton College, the Exchequer). I use 'institution' throughout in either sense, clarifying particular senses as seems useful. I have avoided any sharp lexical differentiation simply because it seems to me that institutions are the sum of both their practices and their organizational forms.

This integrated view of institutional history is no novelty of the present study and can be illustrated specifically in the field of administrative accountability, responsibility, and office by numerous recent, important European collections.[86] A permissible generalization might be that these papers (many not by French historians) are interested in asserting the vitality and importance of administrative activity, and interested

---

[81] John R. Searle, *The Construction of Social Reality* (London, 1995), 34, also 55–6, 104–12, 113–19; Searle, 'What Is an Institution?', *Journal of Institutional Economics* 1 (2005), 1–22; Searle, *Making the Social World: The Structure of Human Civilization* (Oxford, 2010), 141–4, 145–73.

[82] For a sketch of sociological engagement with institutions, Boltanski, *De la critique*, 83–93.

[83] On historians' failure to distinguish these two: Hannah Skoda, 'A Historian's Perspective on the Present Volume', in *Legalism: Anthropology and History*, ed. Dresch and Skoda, 39–54 at 44.

[84] François-Louis Ganshof's characterization of feudalism in terms of fiefs and homage is commonly referred to as 'institutional' and commonly contrasted with a more 'social' approach. See e.g. Sverre Bagge, Michael H. Gelting, and Thomas Lindkvist (eds.), *Feudalism: New Landscapes of Debate*, The Medieval Countryside 5 (Turnhout, 2011), *passim*. The institutional/social distinction seems to have been especially important in Spanish historiography: see in this volume Adam J. Kosto, 'What about Spain? Iberia in the Historiography of Medieval European Feudalism', 135–58; also Jular Pérez-Alfaro, 'King's Face on the Territory', 109.

[85] See Jacques Revel, 'L'institution et le social', *Un parcours critique: Douze exercices d'histoire sociale* (Paris, 2006), 85–110. Patrick Fridenson argued for a renewed history of institutions as organizations in 'Les organisations, un nouvel objet', *Annales: Histoire, Sciences Sociales* 44 (1989), 1461–77.

[86] Claude Gauvard (ed.), *L'Enquête au Moyen Âge*, Collection École française de Rome 399 (Rome, 2008); Thierry Pécout (ed.), *Quand gouverner c'est enquêter: Les Pratiques politiques de l'enquête princière (Occident, XIII*ᵉ*–XIV*ᵉ *siècles): Actes du colloque international d'Aix-en-Provence et Marseille 19–21 mars 2009* (Paris, 2010); Armand Jamme and Olivier Poncet (eds.), *Offices, écrit et papauté (XIII*ᵉ*–XVII*ᵉ *siècle)*, Collection École française de Rome 386 (Rome, 2007), and *Offices et papauté (XIV*ᵉ*-XVII*ᵉ *siècle): charges, hommes, destins*, Collection de l'École française de Rome 334 (Rome, 2005); Laurent Feller (ed.), *Contrôler les agents du pouvoir. Actes du colloque organisé par l'Équipe d'acceuil «Histoire Comparée des Pouvoirs» (EA 3350) à l'Université de Marne-la-Vallée, 30, 31 mai et 1*ᵉʳ *juin 2002* (Limoges, 2004), incl. Xavier Hélary, 'Délégation du pouvoir et contrôle des officiers: Les Lieutenants du roi sous Philippe III et sous Philippe IV (1270–1314)', 169–90; Romain Telliez, 'Le Contrôle des officiers en France à la fin du Moyen Âge: Une priorité pour le pouvoir', 191–209; Bérenger and Lachaud (eds.), *Hiérarchie des pouvoirs*. On the first two see Élisabeth Lalou, 'L'Enquête

Themes and Argument 17

also in the often political ideas inherent in administrative practices and organizational forms. Important monographs might equally illustrate this.[87] Lachaud's *L'Éthique du pouvoir* is a fine example of a history of political thinking focusing on both normative treatises and governmental *ordonnances*, statutes, and records of counsel.[88] A simple way to describe the distinctiveness of what might be called such 'new' administrative history is that it produces a history of political thinking using administrative records of various sorts. But it returns to the subject of institutional practices, organizations, and administration informed by *'Annales'* work on *mentalités*, discourses, political anthropology, ritual, and communities, to describe 'how institutions think', work, and do not work.[89] While these idioms have enabled historians to see administrative/institutional history afresh, energy remains in older idioms. J. R. Maddicott's *Origins of the English Parliament* comes from a different direction to (e.g.) Lachaud, but is a history of important political ideas deduced from the records and accounts of parliamentary assemblies. Maddicott is working in a long-established idiom of constitutional history, but his is a comparative one, and one well aware of, if unevangelical about, recent historiographical trends.[90] One cannot step in the same stream twice however; it could not be mistaken for older work.

Work on fiscal accountability specifically has proved a fertile field, and accounting itself has now its own historiography and journals.[91] Thomas Bisson's important large-scale interpretation placing political accountability at the centre

---

au Moyen Âge', *Revue historique* 313 (2011), 145–53. Jean-Philippe Genet, Christopher Fletcher, and John Watts (eds.), *Governing in Later Medieval France and England: Office, Network, Idea. A Study in Comparative Political History* (Cambridge, forthcoming) should add much of interest.

[87] Cristina Jular Pérez-Alfaro, *Los Adelantados y Merinos Mayores de León (siglos XIII–XV)* (León, 1990); Romain Telliez, *«Per potentiam officii»: Les Officiers devant la justice dans le royaume de France au XIVe siècle* (Paris, 2005); Moritz Isenmann, *Legalität und Herrschaftskontrolle (1200–1600): Eine vergleichende Studie zum Syndikatsprozess: Florenz, Kastilien und Valencia* (Frankfurt, 2010); Julien Théry, 'Justice et gouvernement dans la Chrétienté latine: Recherches autour du modèle ecclésial (v. 1150–v. 1330). «Excès» et «affaires d'enquête»: Les Procès criminels de la papauté contre les prélats, XIIIe–mi-XIVe siècle', 2 vols. (Université Paul-Valéry—Montpellier III, Dossier pour l'habilitation à diriger des recherches en histoire médiévale, 2010); Frédérique Lachaud, *L'Éthique du pouvoir au Moyen Âge: L'Office dans la culture politique (Angleterre, vers 1150–vers 1330)*, Bibliothèque d'histoire médiévale 3 (Paris, 2010); Serena Morelli, *Per conservare la pace: I Giustizieri del regno di Sicilia da Carlo I a Carlo II d'Angiò* (Naples, 2012); Sarah Rubin Blanshei, *Politics and Justice in Late Medieval Bologna* (Leiden, 2010); Caroline Burt, *Edward I and the Governance of England, 1272–1307* (Cambridge, 2013).

[88] Lachaud, *Éthique du pouvoir*, 27–9, 630, and esp. 319–456, 539–88.

[89] To quote the title of Mary Douglas's 1986 book. Various interesting perspectives are illustrated in the issue 'Que faire des institutions?', *Tracés. Revue de Sciences humaines* 17 (2009).

[90] Maddicott quotes Bishop Stubbs, *Constitutional History*, with justifiable approval: 'The History of Institutions cannot be mastered—can scarcely be approached—without an effort.' Maddicott, *Origins of the English Parliament*, ix. For Maddicott's awareness of other idioms (e.g. medieval political anthropology) and his comparative lens see 93, 376–453.

[91] e.g. *Accounting History Review* (formerly *Accounting, Business and Financial History*); *Financial History Review*; *Accounting History*; *Comptabilité(S)* (http://comptabilites.revues.org/, accessed January 2014); *De Computis: Revista Española de Historia de la Contabilidad* (<http://www.decomputis.org/>, accessed January 2014). See also Jean Durliat, 'De conlaboratu': faux rendements et vraie comptabilité à l'époque carolingienne', *Revue historique de droit français et étranger*, 4th ser. 56 (1978), 445–57; Geoffrey de Ste. Croix, 'Greek and Roman Accounting' in A. C. Littleton and B. S. Yamey (eds.), *Studies in the History of Accounting* (London, 1956), 14–74; Glautier, 'A Study in the Development of Accounting in Roman Times', *Revue internationale des droits de l'antiquité*, 3rd ser. 19 (1972), 311–43.

of 'the origins of European government' has its origins in his invaluable work on Catalonian fiscal accounts.[92] A number of his students have also addressed the theme[93] and there is lively work convened from Lille on accounting per se, using diplomatic approaches and Aix (the work coordinated by Pécout already cited also has its roots in work on Provençal fiscal records).[94] This (rightly) has not prevented accountability being firmly placed in political contexts, as in the ancient historiography on *euthyna* and associated practices,[95] early medieval[96] and Byzantine

I have been unable to consult a number of items by Jean Durliat: 'La Comptabilité publique protomédiévale (notes de cours de l'année 1978–1979, deposés à la bibliothèque de l'U.E.R. d'Histoire de l'Université de Toulouse-le-Mirail)'; 'Les Comptes multiples dans la comptabilité protomediévales', *Histoire, gestion et management* (Toulouse, 1993), 25–46; and 'Notes brèves sur le comptabilité pré-capitaliste', *Comptabilité et nouvelles technologies* (Toulouse, 1993).

[92] See *Fiscal Accounts of Catalonia; Tormented Voices: Crisis of the Twelfth Century*; 'Les Comptes des domaines au temps du Philippe Auguste: essai comparatif', *Medieval France and her Pyrenean Neighbours: Studies in Early Institutional History* (London, 1989), 265–83; and 'Medieval Lordship', *Speculum*, 70 (1995), 743–59. A collection edited by Bisson as *Cultures of Power: Lordship, Status and Process in Twelfth-century Europe* (Philadelphia, 1995) includes wider reflections as does one edited for him: Robert F. Berkhofer III, Alan Cooper, and Adam J. Kosto (eds.), *The Experience of Power in Medieval Europe, 950–1350* (Aldershot, 2005). Questions of accountability were also themes in Bisson's contributions to the *P&P* 'Feudal Revolution' debate: T. N. Bisson, 'The "Feudal Revolution"', *P&P* 142 (1994), 6–42, and 'The "Feudal Revolution": Reply', *P&P* 155 (1997), 208–25. The other *P&P* contributions: Dominique Barthélemy, 152 (1996) 196–205; Stephen D. White, 152 (1996), 205–23; Timothy Reuter, 155 (1997), 177–95; and Chris Wickham, 155 (1997), 196–208. Bisson's *Crisis of the Twelfth Century* offers a forceful interpretation of accountability *c*.875–*c*.1225.

[93] Most explicitly Robert F. Berkhofer III, *Day of Reckoning: Power and Accountability in Medieval France* (Philadelphia, 2004).

[94] The Lille project is *Enquêtes historiques sur les comptabilités, XIVᵉ–XIXᵉ siècles* (<http://irhis. recherche.univ-lille3.fr/00-Comptabilites/Index.html>, accessed January 2014). Pécout is also part of the *équipe* led by Armand Jamme working on *Genèse médiévale d'une méthode administrative: Formes et pratiques des comptabilités princières (Savoie Dauphiné, Provence, Venaissin) entre XIIIᵉ et XVIᵉ siècle*, which will edit various records and registers from French departmental holdings.

[95] The term means literally 'straightening', see s.v. *Euthyna, euthynai* in *The Oxford Classical Dictionary*, ed. Simon Hornblower and Anthony Spawforth, 3rd edn. (Oxford, 1996). Edward M. Harris reviewing Fröhlich (end of this note) in the *Bryn Mawr Classical Review* 18/7/2005 notes that in fifth-century BC Greek the term means 'to punish' or 'to inflict a fine', later acquiring the meaning 'to exercise control over officials' (<http://ccat.sas.upenn.edu/bmcr/2005/2005-07-18.html>, accessed January 2014). There are also references to *euthyna* in Herodotus' *Histories* (§3.80, where Otanes praises Persian self-rule following the 'Conspiracy of the Seven'); the *Constitution of Athens* at §§4.2, 27.1, 31.1, 39.6, 48.3–5, 54.2, 59.1–6; and Plato's *Protagoras* (325d), and *Laws*, 12 (945b–948b). For discussion of Greek and Athenian practice see Jennifer Tolbert Roberts, *Accountability in Athenian Government* (Madison, 1982), John Davies, 'Accounts and Accountability in Classical Athens' in Robin Osborne and Simon Hornblower (eds.), *Ritual, Finance, Politics: Athenian Democratic Accounts Presented to David Lewis* (Oxford, 1994), 201–12; Edwin M. Carawan, '"Eisangelia" and "Euthyna": The trials of Miltiades, Themistocles and Cimon', *Greek, Roman and Byzantine Studies* 28 (1987), 167–208; Marcel Piérart, 'Les Euthenoi athéniens', *L'Antiquité classique* 40 (1971), 526–73 and; P. J. Rhodes, *Euthynai (Accounting): A Valedictory Lecture Delivered before the University of Durham* (Durham, 2005). For accountability in archaic poetic texts, Deirdre Dionysia von Dornum, 'The Straight and the Crooked: Legal Accountability in Ancient Greece', *Columbia Law Review* 97 (1997), 1483–518. For accountability beyond Athens, Pierre Fröhlich, *Les Cités grecques et le contrôle des magistrats (IVᵉ–Iᵉʳ siècle avant J.-C.)* (Geneva, 2004).

[96] For the Carolingian Empire see Mayke de Jong, *The Penitential State: Authority and Atonement in the Age of Louis the Pious, 814–840* (Cambridge, 2009), esp. ch. 3; Abigail Firey, *A Contrite Heart: Prosecution and Redemption in the Carolingian Empire* (Leiden, 2009) Paul Fouracre, 'Carolingian Justice: The Rhetoric of Improvement and Contexts of Abuse', in *La giustizia nell'alto medioevo (secoli v–viii)*, Settimane di studio del Centro italiano di studi sull'alto medioevo 42 (Spoleto, 1995), 771–803; Rosamund McKitterick, *Charlemagne: The Formation of a European Identity*

historiography,[97] or early modern historiography on officers and accounting.[98] Since I am principally interested in accountability in its wider political aspects, however, this study does not view fiscal accounting as coterminous with accountability, and focuses on accountability often in non-fiscal terms.

One could designate these historiographies overall as a kind of new administrative history, in so far as they recognize the importance of the subject yet approach it from a variety of perspectives informed by changes in post-war European, British, and American historiography. This alone makes them quite distinct from their predecessors. A good example would be Olivier Mattéoni's 2007 article on French *chambres des comptes*—as sensitive to the ritual or dramatic as the fiscal aspects of accounting.[99] Such work is quite distinct from the somewhat misleadingly named 'new institutional history', really a species of new economic history that seeks to apply a sort of rational choice theory to explain history, seemingly taking 'institutions' as synonymous with 'economic practices and market frameworks'.[100] The study contributes much less to that institutional history, but rather hopes to contribute to this new administrative history.

Concepts, Accountability, and Comparisons

A criticism of the old-style legal/constitutional/administrative history was that its default object of interest was, at least implicitly, the emergence or anticipation of

---

(Cambridge, 2008), esp. 142–55, and chs. 4–5; Janet L. Nelson, 'Kingship and Royal Government', in Rosamund McKitterick (ed.), *The New Cambridge Medieval History*, ii. *c.700–c.900* (Cambridge, 1995), 383–430 at 410–27: Jennifer R. Davis, 'A Pattern for Power: Charlemagne's Delegation of Judicial Responsibilities', in Davis and Michael M. McCormick (eds.), *The Long Morning of Medieval Europe: New Directions in Medieval Studies* (Aldershot, 2008), 235–46. For a slightly later period, Wendy Davies's article, 'Judges and Judging: Truth and Justice in Northern Iberia on the Eve of the Millennium', *Journal of Medieval History* 36 (2010), 193–203, esp. 194–5, 202–3, takes an interesting if sceptically functional view of the meaning of the rhetoric of 'truth' and 'justice' in dispute resolution.

[97] Byzantine political thinking about responsible household management (*oikonomia*) seems to have played a similar, transferable role as ideas of stewardship and *villicatio* did in European thinking. See Leonara Neville, *Authority in Provincial Byzantine Society, 950–1100* (Cambridge, 2004), 99–105, and Gilbert Dagron, *Emperor and Priest: The Imperial Office in Byzantium*, trans. Jean Birrell (Cambridge, 2003), indexed under 'economy'. Dimiter Angelov, *Imperial Ideology and Political Thought in Byzantium, 1204–1330* (Cambridge, 2007) is also relevant, esp. chs. 7–10.

[98] e.g. D. R. Hainsworth, *Stewards, Lords and People: The Estate Steward and his World in Later Stuart England* (Cambridge, 1992); Conal Condren, *Argument and Authority in Early Modern England: The Presupposition of Oaths and Offices* (Cambridge, 2006); Mark Goldie, 'The Unacknowledged Republic: Officeholding in Early Modern England', in *The Politics of the Excluded, c.1500–1800* (Basingstoke, 2001), 153–94; Gary W. Cox, 'War, Moral Hazard, and Ministerial Responsibility: England after the Glorious Revolution', *Journal of Economic History* 71 (2011), 133–61; Jacob Soll, 'Accounting for Government: Holland and the Rise of Political Economy in Seventeenth-Century Europe', *The Journal of Interdisciplinary History* 40 (2009), 215–38; and more widely and recently, Soll, *The Reckoning: Financial Accountability and the Making and Breaking of Nations* (New York, 2014).

[99] Olivier Mattéoni, 'Vérifier, corriger, juger: Les Chambres des comptes et le contrôle des officiers en France à la fin du Moyen Âge', *Revue historique* 641 (2007), 31–69.

[100] See e.g. Thomas A. Koelble, 'The New Institutionalism in Political Science and Sociology', *Comparative Politics* 27 (1995), 231–43. An excellent critical example is Sheila Ogilvie, 'Whatever Is, Is Right? Economic Institutions in Pre-Industrial Europe', *Economic History Review* NS 60 (2007),

secular, parliamentary, sovereign states. That is, it expected to apply a relatively uniform set of institutional measures and concepts, imposing uniformity and enabling comparability. To be fair, a focus on states, or 'princely' regimes, still dominates the historiography. It is not the dominant optic here. If one is trying to set English medieval officers' accountability in a comparative perspective, the question is can a more comparative approach be developed—one that is less monomaniacally focused on states?

In the specific field of medieval officers' accountability there are two issues: conceptual comparability (Are ideas of accountability anachronistic or appropriate?); and institutionalized comparability (Are social practices used to exact that accountability from officers responsive to both similarity and difference across geography and types of officer?). I have argued elsewhere that if accountability can be taken at a high level of generality as an 'empty shell' concept it can only be filled with meaning when analysed with respect to specific, historical, social values and practices.[101] Max Weber famously proposed a set of characteristics relating to contemporary bureaucratic officials which could be successfully used to analyse non-modern forms of bureaucracy: the specification of jurisdictional areas (duties, rules, and ability); super- and subordination within some hierarchy; management based on files and documents; training and specialization of officers; the full-time use of the officer; management following general, acquirable rules.[102] A more recent *longue durée* analysis focusing on the Middle Ages applies a Weberian framework to the 'essential characteristics of the concept of office': the connection between actions and specific tasks; the provision of resources for them that do not belong to the official; the officials' ordering in a hierarchy; the separation of roles intended to eliminate conflicts of interest between the personal and the official; the establishment of general rules for management; and the interchangeableness of officeholders in order to ensure continuity of office.[103] This definition occurs within the *Geschichtliche Grundbegriffe*, a multi-author *dictionnaire raisonnée* of political-social language from antiquity onwards. The orientation of the *Geschichtliche Grundbegriffe* is towards a projected turning-point (*Sattelzeit*, lit. 'saddle-time') of c.1750–1850 in which Germanic Europe experienced a series of significant conceptual/social changes bound up with the precipitation of an idea of Modernity. There is a temptation to use the *Grundbegriffe* as the basis for a general European account, but it is a specifically German one, even though its treatment of some concepts (e.g. medieval ecclesiastical ones) may be more widely applicable.[104] Weber seems more elastic here because

---

649–84. A different approach is set out in d'Avray, *Rationalities in History*, including, at pp. 29–58, a critique of the rational choice approach so influential in political science.

[101] Sabapathy, 'A Medieval Officer and a Modern Mentality', esp. 62–79.

[102] Max Weber, *Wirtschaft und Gesellschaft: Grundriss der Verstehenden Soziologie*, ed. Johannes Winckelmann, 5th edn. (Tübingen, 1972), 551–2 and generally to 579.

[103] Udo Wolter, 'Verwaltung, Amt, Beamter, V–VI', in Otto Brunner, Werner Conze, and Reinhart Koselleck (eds.), *Geschichtliche Grundbegriffe: Historisches Lexikon zur politisch-sozialen Sprache in Deutschland*, 8 vols. in 9 (Stuttgart, 1972–97), vii. 26–47 at 27–8 (this is the medieval portion of the article; each chronological section was written by a different specialist with Koselleck providing the introduction).

[104] Wolter, in 'Verwaltung, Amt, Beamter, V–VI', in Otto Brunner, Werner Conze, and Reinhart Koselleck (eds.), *Geschichtliche Grundbegriffe: Historisches Lexikon zur politisch-sozialen Sprache in*

of his ideal type approach (i.e. here his definition of officials), and its flexibility (as already described).[105] Weber's approach is concrete and functional, granting a role for ideas and values. A basically similar approach is taken here. Wolter's definition above is also relatively functional, but I am not convinced that changes in conceptual use are an infallible guide to changes in practices, so the broader *Grundbegriffe* approach is not itself foregrounded here. Both Weber's and Wolter's definitions are avowedly focused on a modern idea of office, although Weber's is arguably the more flexible. They imply but do not per se say very much concrete about accountability. Elsewhere, through reflection on Thomas Bisson's and Jean Glénisson's work, I have suggested a framework for thinking about officers' accountability comparatively, and I develop this here.[106] Again, 'accountability' is not used here in a narrow fiscal sense, but in relation to individuals' conduct more widely.[107] Partly because accountability is relational, partly because there is a risk of imposing expectations, I have not elaborated a set of ideal characteristics of officials' accountability. One can imagine what a set might be, perhaps: (1) the official is accountable to his superiors; (2) the official's accountability is specified in relation to his functions; (3) the official is accountable as a matter of course; (4) the official is dismissible. Other criteria could be added. I have, however, preferred to keep a loose questionnaire as a grid to guide (but not slavishly structure) my analysis of medieval officers' accountability. Those questions are:

1. '*Kto kogo?*', 'Who, whom?', in the phrase attributed to Lenin.[108] Who exacts what of whom? This is the question I refer back to most frequently, and the subsequent questions are to a degree simply extrapolations from it.

2. What is the texture, or dynamic, of the conflict encouraged by the given institutionalization of accountability?

3. Are the justifications for a given officer's accountability specific to that officer, or do they relate to some wider, common pattern of justifying official accountability applicable to many sorts of officer? If some pattern is apparent, how is it to be explained?

Deutschland, 8 vols. in 9 (Stuttgart, 1972–97), frames his discussion in terms of a 'begriffsgeschichtlichen Analyse die Herausbildung und Entwicklung der Elemente des modernen Amtsbegriffs im Mittelalter' (28). Mostly Wolter stressses that the roots (*Wurzeln*) of modern administration are to be sought in the later Middle Ages (46), but at others (e.g. also 46) Wolter is explicit that there is no direct line of development (*Entwicklungslinie*) from a medieval concept of administration and office to a modern one.

[105] See n. 31 and associated text.
[106] Sabapathy, 'Accountable *rectores* in comparative perspective', 219–30.
[107] David d'Avray kindly provided me with Leo Cullum's *New Yorker* cartoon (8 November 2010) of two businessmen seated at a paper-strewn table in an office wallpapered with graphs. 'Remember', says the senior to his bright-eyed junior, '"accounting" and "accountability". Nothing in common'. It is worth noting that the French *comptabilité* and the Italian *contabilità* relate more narrowly to just the 'accounting' semantic field.
[108] Given its later fame, Lenin's recorded uses of 'Kto kogo?' are notably late and few. See Lars T. Lih, 'The Soviet Union and the Road to Communism', in Ronald Grigor Suny (ed.), *The Cambridge History of Russia*, iii. *The Twentieth Century* (Cambridge, 2006), 706–31 at 718–22. On the question, Jonathan Wolff, *An Introduction to Political Philosophy*, rev. edn. (Oxford, 2006), 1–3; Raymond Geuss, *Philosophy and Real Politics* (Princeton, NJ, 2008), 23–30.

4. What is the relationship between the practice of holding officers to account and any related organizational form?
5. Do processes of holding officers accountable invariably deliver judgements of justice on those being held to account—or is that a separate process?

The questions are intended to enable an analysis focused on borrowings, parallels, divergences, and similarities between different sorts of officer and different regional jurisdictions. The study is neither comparative in the sustained dialectical manner of, say, Brentano's diptych of the English and Italian churches in the thirteenth century, nor following the multiple paired mosaics of Wickham's socioeconomic analyses.[109] Less ambitiously, it introduces comparisons and contrasts to its core English material where this promises insights of either convergence or divergence. These points of comparison are sometimes from England's neighbour France, but also from further afield.

The study is more systematically comparative along a different axis. Its central chapters provide analytical case studies of a sequence of officers from distinct fields not often addressed together (seigneurial, princely, ecclesiastical, clerical/educational, and, to a much lesser extent, urban). Each also focuses on these officials' accountability through particular mechanisms of holding them to account: *sindacatio* (*podestà*, earlier), action of account (bailiff), Exchequer audit and judicial enquiry (sheriff), canonical *inquisitio* (bishop), audit and *scrutinium* (warden).

It is a basic thesis of this study that in these forms such practices are novelties of the twelfth and thirteenth centuries. The claim to novelty for this period is qualitative and quantitative, but not absolute in relation to the earlier medieval period. The officers and the methods for holding them to account which comprise this series are compared together in the final chapter, with an interpretation of their significance. Since I do not presume the primacy of kingdoms or polities in the development of officers' accountability, the officers analysed here quite deliberately do not all pertain to 'state' institutions. The question of state innovation is addressed again in the final chapter. Behind this lie several arguments that the analysis seeks to test, and whose significance should be obvious given the historiographical agenda and analysis offered earlier. No doubt increasing the range and numbers of officers analysed would have improved the study. The officers I have analysed here have been selected because their experiences illustrate the practices of accountability developed in this period to regulate them. My approach is to take this relatively small number of detailed cases and interpret them widely through other relevant, comparable material. In the chapters on bailiffs, stewards, and bishops I have paired an earlier case with a later one. In Chapter 3, on sheriffs, the *Dialogue of the Exchequer* acts as my earlier focus. The chronology of collegial foundations means that it is hard to find sufficiently detailed earlier thirteenth-century sources for Chapter 5 and so the focus on Oxford from the 1260s is paired with some contemporary French, and later English and European,

---

[109] Robert Brentano, *Two Churches: England and Italy in the Thirteenth Century* (Princeton, NJ., 1968); Chris Wickham, *Framing the Early Middle Ages: Europe and the Mediterranean 400–800* (Oxford, 2005).

material. The comparisons, though, are intended to be suggestive, not exhaustive or definitive. That would have required a quite different book.

Arguments

This study develops the following arguments. Firstly, that the relationship between norms of office and rules of accountability is central to an understanding of how, and how far, institutions of all sorts encouraged officers towards a narrower conception of accountability or more broadly characterized ideas of responsibility. The period examined here is interestingly schizophrenic since it tended to *say* that the characters of officers could be cultivated so as to guarantee their conduct.[110] This seems especially so with higher 'officers', where status made accountability to inferiors especially problematic (hence again the value of looking at *mediocres*). 'Ruler, rule yourself' was often the expressed solution.[111] What people in the period tended to *do* implied that there was a real anxiety that strict statutes and biting curbs were necessary to enforce right conduct for want of responsibility.[112] Avowed belief in responsible conduct was belied by repeated reliance on a thinner accountability in practice. We have Guibert of Tournai's treatise for Louis IX, the *Eruditio regum et principum* (*c*.1259) offering to the problem of official insolence its solution of appointing those who love God and hate sin.[113] We have also the massive documentation of Louis' *enquêtes* into officials' misconduct (ongoing 1247–69).[114] Secondly, ironically, that this hope wagered on more formal regulation of officials' accountability did not always produce more responsible officers. Often its consequence seems to have been greater complexity of law and administration. Still, in all the areas discussed here, that this tendency did minimally mean that reasonably clear, reasonably rational ground rules were established. Thirdly, that in this legal-administrative sphere one should recognize the role of a 'vernacular' pragmatism in responding to officers' (un)accountability. By 'vernacular' I mean that local practice and solutions mattered. Accountability did not invariably boil down only to learned precepts, but was often the product of local experimentation.[115] The

---

[110] Dunbabin, 'Aristotle in the Schools', 68–9 (on kings). Relevant remarks in Philippe Buc, *L'Ambiguïté du livre: Prince, pouvoir et peuple dans les commentaires de la Bible au Moyen Âge* (Paris, 1994), 400–1; Reynolds, *Kingdoms and Communities*, 189.

[111] See e.g. Gerald of Wales, *Liber de principis instructione* in *Giraldi Cambrensis Opera*, RS, 8 vols. (London, 1861–91), viii. ed. George F. Warner, esp. Dist. 1, Dist. 3, cap. 31.

[112] In H. L. A. Hart's terms, internal rule-following did not produce evident external rule-application, though a shared sense of the internal rule existed: *The Concept of Law*, 2nd edn. (Oxford, 1994), esp. 56–7, 84–91, 102–13 where 'internal' pertains to self-regulation through following a rule/norm; 'external' pertains to our ability to see a rule in fact exists out in the world by its being visibly followed. Of the internal aspect Hart said, 'What is necessary is that there should be a critical reflective attitude [within a community] to certain patterns of behaviour as a common standard, and that this should display itself in criticism (including self-criticism), demands for conformity, and in acknowledgements that such criticism and demands are justified, all of which find their characteristic expression in the normative terminology of 'ought', 'must', and 'should', 'right' and 'wrong'' (57). See further Nicola Lacey, *A Life of H. L. A. Hart: The Nightmare and the Noble Dream* (Oxford, 2004), 225–9.

[113] *Le Traité Eruditio regum et principum de Guibert de Tournai*, O.F.M, ed. A. de Poorter, Les Philosophes belges 9 (Louvain, 1914), 78–9, section beginning, 'Ergo tales in. . .'

[114] *RHF*, xxiv.

[115] Cf. Jason Peacey's study of 'common politics' in seventeenth-century Britain, *Print and Public Politics in the English Revolution* (Cambridge, 2013), esp. the introduction and conclusion.

more learned logic that may frame these responses need not always be quite the engine driving them. Fourthly, that different types of office were sometimes permeable to ideas from other types of office. Finally, fifthly, and above all: that although a number of ways of holding officers accountable developed in relation to regnal ('state') institutions, by no means all of them did. To see accounts, inquests, inquisitions, and accountability more generally as principally and necessarily expressions of The State's emergence is to mistake a part for a broader whole. An increased attention to officers' responsibility and accountability is part of a far more generally widespread way of thinking in this period. This study explores it.

2
Bailiffs and Stewards

Alongside the 'great book' containing the excerpts from Brunetto Latini, Andrew Horn had a large collection of English statutes and other materials copied out, the Liber Horn, which was likewise left to the Guildhall in his will. It contains two French texts that include discussion of a manorial bailiff's duties: the father–son dialogue, *Walter of Henley*, and the *Seneschauncy*.[1] Horn, we have seen, had an interest in Italian communal as well as manorial accountability. The Liber Horn itself is part of a striking and distinct English tradition of didactic estate management texts, and invites reflection on the relationship between changing twelfth- and thirteenth-century practices and rules for manorial officials' accountability, and texts such as *Walter of Henley* and *Seneschauncy*. That is this chapter's focus. In particular the chapter examines the development of a legal action ('writ') for securing bailiffs' accountability—the 'action of account'.

Changes in manorial official's accountability in England during the twelfth and thirteenth centuries are reflected in these treatises and reinforced by those legal changes—themselves reflecting broader social and economic developments over the period. What follows addresses this first by describing two lawsuits, one from the early twelfth, the other from the late thirteenth century. Robert of Chilton's lawsuit (the first case), shows the early existence of some basic expectation of bailiffs' liability to account, one where scriptural precept gives the key warrant and whose legal life is relatively simple. John de Valle's (the second), shows how far this had evolved by 1291. It is a case bristling with writs that qualify, respond, and extend the initial legal action—the product of significant legislative work between 1259 and 1285 on the 'action of account'. Fully worthy of *Bleak House*'s Chancery, the writ's legal potential grants the case an improvised life of its own, ultimately quite abandoning the original intent of holding John de Valle himself accountable. Both cases also beg questions about what a 'bailiff' was. Robert of Chilton refused to be treated like a manorial official. John de Valle's responsibilities look more like a steward's, yet he was held to account legally as a 'bailiff'. Both indicate how broad and contested a bailiff's responsibilities, and liabilities, might be. These legal developments—and the political economy that produced them—are examined after discussing the cases, together with an examination of non-legal texts such as *Seneschauncy* which are their satellites.

---

[1] London Guildhall, MS Liber Horn, fos. 158r–168r (*Walter*), 168r–176r (*Seneschauncy*). See *Walter of Henley and Other Treatises on Estate Management and Accounting*, ed. Dorothea Oschinsky (Oxford, 1971), 22, 53. I am indebted to Paul Brand and David Carpenter for discussion of the material that follows.

TWO CASES

Robert of Chilton

During a vacancy at Battle Abbey early in Henry I's reign, probably *c.*1102, the King appointed as *procurator* the monk Geoffrey of St Calais—'a man who, though unlearned, was full of pragmatism and prudence with the greatest worldly foresight'.[2] Geoffrey immediately 'showed the prudence in which he was so skilled'.[3] Under his custodianship (*procurationum*), Battle's cupboards are promptly restocked, the church's rights and brothers' honour both breathe again, and the estates' wealth is restored.

> But when he [Geoffrey] had gone to the church's chief manor at Wye [in Kent], which a certain servant of the dead abbot [Henry], Robert, surnamed 'of Chilton', had been looking after, and [Geoffrey] had found it completely broken up, he sought the reasons from that manager [*preposito*] and demanded an account of his stewardship [*rationemque requirere uillicationis*].[4]

Robert rejects the need to give any such account. Since 'he had satisfied his now dead lord' he would not summon witnesses, presumably proving how satisfied—or not—Henry had been. Geoffrey finally charged Robert in the Wye manorial court as manifestly guilty (*convictum*). 'But with the force of the county [i.e. Kentish] nobility whom he had associated himself with, [Robert] completely refused to stand to justice. So the procurator of the church [i.e. Geoffrey] summoned him, and his supporters who were there [by writ] in the king's name to appear at Battle court on a set day.'[5]

Four named Kentish men and 'other barons' duly appear at Battle, given 'the force and terror of the king's name'. 'My dearest lords,' asks Geoffrey, 'since you have presented yourselves to the court following a summons, I ask have you come here for the seeking and receiving of justice [*rectitudinis*]?'[6] They 'retorted that they should be liable to all justice in their own county [court], not here'.[7] After much wrangling (*controuersiam*) Geoffrey realizes he has an ace to play.

> 'If therefore, as you say, you are not subject to legal pleas except in your own county [court], surely you would not obstruct settling the complaint were you admitted to the king's court?'
>
> 'In no way', they said.
>
> 'So on that basis,' he said, 'you will be unable to oppose this present court which stands for the king.'[8]

---

[2] *The Chronicle of Battle Abbey*, ed. Eleanor Searle, OMT (Oxford, 1980), 108. Partly excerpted in *English Lawsuits from William I to Richard I*, ed. R. C. van Caenegem, SS, 106–7, 2 vols. (London, 1990–1), i. #174; cf. Patrick Wormald, *Lawyers and the State: The Varieties of Legal History*, SS Lecture (London, 2006), 14.

[3] *Chronicle of Battle*, 108.   [4] *Chronicle of Battle*, 108.   [5] *Chronicle of Battle*, 110.

[6] *Chronicle of Battle*, 110.

[7] *Chronicle of Battle*, 110. Nigel Ramsay helpfully suggests this is as much a Sussex (Battle) vs. Kent (Wye) dispute as anything else.

[8] *Chronicle of Battle*, 110–12.

Left with no recourse except to reason with violence (*ui ratiocinatione freti*), the defendants try to break out of the court, but Geoffrey, ever skilled in prudence, locks the door. Lured up a legal dead end, the bailiff and his barons have found themselves in a physical one. With such a captive audience Geoffrey loses no time in detailing the ruin of the manor at Wye and the incapacity of a manager to give an account of his stewardship [*uillicationis reddere rationem*] until at last, after the spinning of many words, Robert stands guilty before the common judgement.[9]

Robert, cornered, accepts the judgement and is forgiven—at the cost of ten pounds of silver and ten measures of corn. Careful to ask (with the doors still locked) if anyone objects to the court's judgement, Geoffrey then dissolves the court. The chronicler closes the episode by recounting that Geoffrey

> committed that manor and the rest of the church's possessions to men faithful to himself and to the church entrusted to him, to be thoroughly restored, while he himself, though closely supervising the prosperity of the servants of God in every aspect, concentrated his attention on the building and buttressing of the house and on putting up a wall around the precincts.[10]

What does the story show?[11] Robert is an early twelfth-century *prepositus* (in a mid-twelfth-century chronicle) entrusted with the manor of Wye. He manages Wye as a farmer of its revenues, not its direct cultivator. Geoffrey after all seems only to realize there is a problem at Wye once he visits it, after sorting out—in the Chronicle's telling—the immediately visible problems at Battle. If the manor was failing to produce its dues and renders this would presumably have been visible earlier. If, however, it had been farmed out for cash then the abbey might not be able to see the dilapidation. It would only be when the lease was due for renewal and if its damage meant the lessee had to renegotiate its price that any alienation or dissipation might be apparent. This would make sense of how, when Geoffrey arrives at Wye (around twenty-six miles north-east of Battle), he finds the manor all *distractum*, presumably sub-let and split from Robert's direct control.[12] This is also what Geoffrey remedies at the end of the episode when he removes Robert. It is *not* clear that Geoffrey changed the structure of how Wye was run (e.g. from lease management to direct management)—we are told only that he 'committed it to those faithful to him'.[13] This could be contrasted with the famously hands-on management of both Samson of Bury St Edmunds and Suger of St Denis.[14]

---

[9] *Chronicle of Battle*, 112.   [10] *Chronicle of Battle*, 112, Searle's trans.

[11] On chronicles, norms, and cases, see John Hudson, 'Court Cases and Legal Arguments in England, *c*.1066-1166', *TRHS* 6th ser. 10 (2000), 91–115, esp. 107–11.

[12] Searle comments that Wye's tenements were prone to this because they were discrete and 'probably enclosed', *Chronicle of Battle*, 108 n. 2. A map is in Eleanor Searle, *Lordship and Community: Battle Abbey and its Banlieu, 1066–1538*, Pontifical Institute of Mediaeval Studies, Studies and Texts 26 (Toronto, 1974).

[13] *Chronicle of Battle*, 112.

[14] *The Chronicle of Jocelin of Brakelond Concerning the Acts of Samson, Abbot of the Monastery of St Edmund*, ed. H. E. Butler, NMT (London, 1949), 32 (Michaelmas 1182), following an Easter visitation; Suger, *Œuvres*, ed. Françoise Gasparri, Classiques de l'histoire de France au Moyen Âge 37, 41, 2 vols. (Paris, 1996–2008), i. 54–155, for the *Gesta Suggerii abbatis* (*De administratione*).

The *Battle Chronicle* describes Robert as a *prepositus*, a reeve, literally 'one set above'; he is also described as a 'servant of the dead abbot' (not necessarily denoting servile status).[15] The Gospel precept from Luke 16 that a *villicus* (steward) is obliged to give an account of his stewardship is explicit in the Chronicle's Latin (see pp. 41–4). The norm appears twice in the story and in ways signalling its contribution to the episode's structure, not simply as a biblical piety projected onto a story that could work just as well without it.[16] On the contrary. Geoffrey does not challenge Robert's right to the manor. The legal ground on which Geoffrey chooses to fight is the question of whether Robert is prepared to give the proverbial account for his stewardship. That question is the immediate and formal prelude to Geoffrey's attempted legal proceedings in the Wye manor court. Geoffrey's gloating discourse on the biblical precept—once he has Robert and his baronial pleaders captive—serves to strop both its legal and its ideological edge in front of barons and brothers alike: this is what happens if stewards do not cultivate the abbey's assets.

The following are notable. First, Robert as a *prepositus*-farmer is a man of some local status. He is able to draw on the support of the 'county nobles' and his four named pleaders or 'barons' included Fulbert I of Dover, one of Bishop Odo's Domesday tenants.[17] Secondly, high on the list of desirable skills for *prepositus*-farmers was some subtlety in the law.[18] This is worth noting. Robert accepts an accountability for Wye, but he tries at least to claim this is only personally due to the dead Abbot Henry of Battle, and says he has satisfactorily discharged it. That accountability, both Robert and Geoffrey implicitly agree, relates to the care of the Wye manor, and the conservation of its value. Their disagreement is whether Robert has satisfactorily carried out his liability to account. Robert's assertion that he has is surely partly an attempt to try lines of defence that he thinks will, at least, delay Geoffrey. Robert's defence that he is accountable to the individual abbot he contracted with and not some temporary *procurator* must have had some basic contemporary legal integrity.[19] It may also be noteworthy that Geoffrey does not challenge Robert's assertion that Abbot Henry had been satisfied with Robert's administration of Wye. It is possible there was some proof of that which Geoffrey knew of. The third aspect of the case worth stressing is Geoffrey's difficulty in finding a satisfactory (to him) court in which to confront Robert. Wye's manorial court proves ineffective, if not procedurally then politically, thick as it was with the county nobles' latent violence (*ui nobilium provincie*). Robert

---

[15] *Chronicle of Battle*, 108. On terminology, P. D. A. Harvey, *Manorial Records*, Archives and the User 5, rev. edn. (London, 1999), 6.

[16] See Searle's comments on the value and reliability of the 'Main Chronicler' for twelfth-century law in *Chronicle of Battle*, 8–15.

[17] References for the named pleaders at *Chronicle of Battle*, 110–11 nn. 1–4. Searle hypothesizes they were the tenants to whom Robert had sub-let the manor's lands.

[18] Cf. Jocelin of Brakelond's praise in the 1180s on the legal subtlety of another monastic administrator, Abbot Samson of Bury St Edmunds: 'tam subtilis ingenii erat quod omnes mirabantur, et ab Osberto filio Heruei subuicecomite dicebatur: "Iste abbas disputator est: si procedit sicut incipit, nos omnes execabit quotquot sumus." ', *Chronicle of Jocelin*, 34.

[19] Robert's specific legal arguments are not wholly clear. The chronicler however does not present Robert's formal argument as hingeing per se on his status; it hangs on his personal affinity with Abbot Henry.

on the other hand is angling to get the case heard in the county court, where, again, he and the barons will hold sway. Ultimately it is at Battle's own court that Geoffrey triumphs, through his adroit elision of the abbey court and the king's court, given the royal writ that had drawn the barons there.[20]

Lastly, it is not only unclear from this episode precisely what Robert was accountable for; it is also unclear precisely how he was to account. *Prepositus* and *procurator* thought about the former's accountability quite differently. Robert thought of himself as a man free to dispose of Wye as he saw fit. Geoffrey thought of Robert—or wanted Robert to be thought of—as a delegated official on a limited leash with some duty of care for the manor's integrity. That is the intended effect of citing the Gospel precept from Luke. The principle was shared with what would become the later legal action of account in the thirteenth century. The following features are notable here: a *prepositus* of some independence and legal skill; a contest between him and the landlord over appropriate jurisdiction for the holding to account; a debate about the liability to account and whether this had been satisfactorily discharged; a wrestling match between *prepositus* and *procurator* over the former's latitude and status as an agent; the role of the writ.

John de Valle

Robert of Chilton's relatively simple case can be contrasted with a later, longer case concerning a bailiff's accountability. But what comprised the core of the Chilton case here formed only the preliminaries. In fact the story to be narrated deals solely with what happens *after* an initial alleged failure of a bailiff to account for himself, the bailiff's subsequent forced accounting and charging with debt, and his consequent appeal against that verdict.

It is at this third point that John de Valle's story appears in the records. This case's interest is to show the system of holding bailiffs to account in a mature phase late in the thirteenth century. The record of the case begins as an *ex parte* writ from Edward I to the Treasurer and Barons of the Exchequer dated 11 November 1291.[21] *Ex parte* was a way of disputing an allegedly overdue account—so the case emerges in the records a long way in. From the writ we learn that John de Valle, a former bailiff in Ireland of Agnes de Valence, had been imprisoned in London's Fleet prison for arrears in the account due to her. Her auditors had allocated to John receipts that he said 'he has not received'. They, he alleged, likewise refused to allow him 'expenses and reasonable payments' for this office. The King, says the writ, since he did not want John to be injured [*iniurietur*] because of this, ordered the barons of

---

[20] This seems to be as much a rhetorical as a legal move. It was certainly a political one, since Geoffrey was an appointee of the king 'among the remaining leaders of the kingdom then at court' and 'not customarily excluded from the secrets of the king's court' (*Chronicle of Battle*, 114).

[21] *Ex parte* is a writ available to 'bailiffs' who allege they have been unjustly seized for wrongly failing to account for themselves in office. See *Registrum omnium brevium, tam originalium quam judicalium* (London, 1634), 137ᵛ–138ʳ, and on various writs of account, 135–8. I put 'bailiffs' in quotes given the legalistic, not functional way in which they are principally defined in relation to actions of account. See the Florentine merchants discussed on pp. 45–6.

the Exchequer to agree sureties for John and a date when he would return before them to stand to right 'according to the form of the statute provided by the common counsel of our realm' (*iuxta formam statuti de communi consilio regni nostri provisi*). Agnes, for her part, was to come 'with the rolls and tallies' John had offered originally on his side.[22] This order from Edward I prefaces the subsequent proceedings in the Exchequer of Pleas where the case then continued.

This summary makes clear both implicitly and explicitly that we are dealing with a much more sophisticated world than Robert of Chilton's in terms of seigneurial officers' accountability. Here are standardized legal actions for bailiffs' accounting (writs); statutes agreed by counsel; a mass of accounts, receipts, rolls, and tallies; concepts of equity ('reasonable' payments); and the involvement of one of the Crown's oldest and most powerful courts (the Exchequer). In many ways the techniques of holding officers to account appear to have progressed.

Agnes de Valence (d. 1310) was the daughter of William de Valence, Earl of Pembroke, and granddaughter of Hugues X of Lusignan and Isabella of Angoulême, King John's widow. Henry III was thus her uncle and her family stood at the heart of England's enormous political dispute about 'alien' influences over the King in the mid-thirteenth century.[23] Her own marriages display a judicious taste for well-placed British and Continental husbands, and included John de Balliol's eldest son Hugh (d. 1271) and Jean d'Avesnes, lord of Beaumont and the second son of the Countess of Hainault (d. 1283).[24] Her first husband was the Irish Fitzgerald heir, and that connection provides the basis for this case.

The Valences' Irish connections began, however, with Agnes's father's marriage to the Marshall heir Joan of Munchensi in 1247, through whom William obtained the lordship of Wexford.[25] Agnes obtained lands in her own right in 1266 at Kenilworth (during the siege) when her marriage to Maurice Fitzgerald (grandson and namesake of the former Justiciar of Ireland, d. 1257), was formalized. The charter accompanying the marriage gave Agnes a life interest in the Fitzgerald's Limerick lands.[26] Maurice was dead by 1268 and the apparently childless marriage meant the Fitzgerald lands passed to a son from a previous marriage, the palindromic Gerald

---

[22] TNA E 13/17 m. 6. Calendar summary in *Calendar Documents Ireland*, ii. *1285–1292*, ed. H. S. Sweetman (London, 1886), #993. Henry III's and Edward I's extant Exchequer plea records are listed in *Select Cases in the Exchequer of Pleas*, ed. Hilary Jenkinson and Beryl E. R. Formoy, SS 48 (London, 1932), xxi–xxv, here at xxiii. There is brief commentary in Noël Denholm-Young, *Seignorial Administration in England* (London, 1937), 158 and n. 3. The story is thoroughly analysed from the wider perspective of Agnes and John fitz Thomas's relationship in Cormac Ó Cléirigh, 'The Absentee Landlady and the Sturdy Robbers: Agnes de Valence'. in Christine Meek and Katharine Simms (eds.), *'The Fragility of her Sex'? Medieval Irishwomen in their European Context* (Blackrock, 1996), 101–18.

[23] *The Complete Peerage of England, Scotland, Ireland, Great Britain and the United Kingdom, extant, extinct or dormant*, ed. G. E. C. Cokayne et al., 14 vols., new edn. (London, 1910–59), x. 377–81; H. W. Ridgway, 'Valence, [Lusignan], William de, earl of Pembroke (d. 1296)', *ODNB*.

[24] *Complete Peerage*, x. 16–17.

[25] Married on 13 August 1247, noted in Paris, *Chronica majora*, iv. 628–9. For royal grants and allowances to William, see e.g. *CPR 1232–1247*, 505–6, 508–9; *CPR 1247–1258*, 10.

[26] 1 November 1299 reconfirmation of the charter: *CPR 1292–1301*, 450–1 = *Calendar Documents Ireland*, iv. *1293–1301*, #672. See also *Complete Peerage*, x. 16. There is a helpful family tree in Beth

fitz Maurice Fitzgerald. In spring 1269 Agnes and William de Valence bought his wardship from Thomas of Clare for 3,500 marks.[27] The following spring William de Valence visited Ireland to help in Agnes's court case with Thomas over this deal.[28] Her stepson Gerald died seventeen years later, granting before his death Lea Castle, Kildare, and the Offaly lands to his cousin, the future Earl of Kildare, John fitz Thomas Fitzgerald.[29] The subsequent dispute between this Fitzgerald and Agnes de Valance lasted for the rest of her life. The dispute over de Valle's debts lasted at least until 1306.

The Exchequer of Pleas' record (TNA E 13/17 m. 6-6d) has the following stages: Edward I's writ of 19 November 1291 and a late Michaelmas 1291 session at the Exchequer; sessions in the Hilary and Easter terms of 1292; and the Hilary and Trinity 1293 sessions.[30] At the start the spotlight was entirely on de Valle, yet some fifteen years later as the case dragged on, de Valle had evaporated from citations and the focus, by the end, was entirely on his pledges.[31]

It is hard to be sure who John de Valle was, and when records for this name are for 'our' John de Valle.[32] The de Valles ('Dale') came from Pembrokeshire and held land in Carlow, Wexford, and Kilkenny.[33] If Agnes's John de Valle is one of the Ardbristan and Inchyolaghan line then he must be the knight John de Valle the younger, succeeding his father sometime between c.1279 and c.1293.[34] In 1285 a man by that name was paid 10s. by Bishop Stephen of Waterford for carrying harness to Connaught on the Justiciar's orders.[35] On 10 July 1292 the patent rolls record letters of attorney granted at Berwick-upon-Tweed for two years to Adam of St Edmund and David fitz Roger for a John de Valle (this does sound like Agnes's John) who remained 'by licence' in England.[36] A John

---

Hartland, 'English Lords in Late Thirteenth and Early Fourteenth Century Ireland: Roger Bigod and the de Clare Lords of Thomond', *EHR* 122 (2007), 318–48 at 341.

[27] 30 March–2 April 1270, *Calendar Documents Ireland*, ii. *1252–84*, ##866–8 = *CR 1268–1272*, 258–60. See also #1039 (Michaelmas 1274).

[28] On Agnes's fight with Thomas de Clare over the Offaly custody see *Royal and Other Historical Letters Illustrative of the Reign of Henry III*, ed. W. W. Shirley, RS, 2 vols. (1862–6), ii. #683 (1272); Robin Frame, 'Fitzgerald, Maurice [called Muiris Ruadh] (d. 1268)', *ODNB*.

[29] Cormac Ó Cléirigh, 'Fitzgerald, John fitz Thomas, First Earl of Kildare (d. 1316)', *ODNB*.

[30] For Exchequer of Pleas sessions see Paul Brand's comments in *A Handbook of Dates for Students of British History*, ed. C. R. Cheney, rev. Michael Jones, Royal Historical Society Guides and Handbooks 4 (Cambridge, 2000), 105–6.

[31] The trail seems finally to run cold with the long 27 January 1306 entry from the Dublin Court of Pleas, *Calendar of Justiciary Rolls Ireland*, ii. *1305–1307*, 204–13. These records were almost entirely destroyed by civil war in 1922.

[32] For the difficulties arising from the name's proliferation see e.g. *Calendar of Ormond Deeds*, ed. Edmund Curtis, 6 vols. (Dublin, 1932–43), i. #816. For the region in general, Beth Hartland, 'The Liberties of Ireland in the Reign of Edward I', in Michael Prestwich (ed.), *Liberties and Identities in the Medieval British Isles* (Woodbridge, 2008), 200–16.

[33] Eric St. John Brooks, *Knights' Fees in Counties Wexford, Carlow, and Kilkenny (13th–15th Century)* (Dublin, 1950), 66–8.

[34] 1293 is the latest, from *Register of the Hospital of S. John the Baptist*, ed. Eric St. John Brooks (Dublin, 1936), #413; c.1279 the earliest (St. John Brooks, *Knights' Fees*, 67). See also *Calendar of Ormond Deeds*, i. ##159, 226, 257, 361, 559.

[35] *Calendar Documents Ireland*, iii. *1285–1292*, #169 at 74.

[36] *Calendar Documents Ireland*, iii. *1285–1292*, #1134.

de Valle (along with numerous others, including some of our John's pledges) received letters enjoining him to obey the newly appointed Justiciar of Ireland John Wogan and then to bring his men to Whitehaven in March 1296 to aid in the Scottish war.[37] It is harder to be sure of Agnes's ex-bailiff being the free tenant John de Valle who held two carucates of land at Kilsethith for service of 6*s.* 8*d.* and rendered 2*s.* yearly in 1298/9.[38] Around 1279 a John de Valle received with relatives a grant of land and pasture in Ballyverneen; around 1300 he and his heirs gained fourteen arable acres in Cnockaslam.[39] In June 1307 Roger Bigod's wife Alice gained his rights over numerous knight's fees, including one held by 'John de Val' in Ardbristan.[40] It was presumably this same John de Valle who elsewhere is noted as holding a knight's fee of 40*s.* at Ardbristan and doing suit at the court of Forth again in 1306/7.[41] Irrespectively, Agnes's John seemingly held land, making the question of *monstravit*'s use striking given its predication on a bailiff's landlessness. Agnes's John is explicitly cited in a case of 1300 as the co-holder with John of Hothum of a tenement at Poynston at Rathmore and Hothum's disseisin of it by Agnes's bailiff is justified on the grounds of John de Valle's debts to her.[42]

Internal evidence from the case at least clarifies de Valle as a bailiff.[43] He had access to up-to-date legal brains (his own?), as well as the right people. The case begins after all with de Valle using the recent *ex parte* writ to get out of the Fleet and procure the King's order to the Exchequer to investigate the problem. De Valle's pledges would include the King's co-crusader and former Irish justiciar Geoffrey de Geneville, Lord of Trim, whose daughter enjoyed a short-lived marriage (1284 x 1297) to Agnes's stepson;[44] the soon-to-be justiciar William Dodingseles;[45] John fitz Thomas Fitzgerald, the Geraldine heir apparent to Agnes's stepson Gerald fitz Maurice Fitzgerald;[46] and the knights Walter l'Enfaunt (a future royal justice) and

---

[37] *Calendar Documents Ireland*, iv. *1293–1301*, ##270, 276. Wogan was a tenant of William de Valence and married to a Margaret de Valle (see *ODNB* entry for Sir John). For further references for the Irish contingent in the war, see Michael Prestwich, *Edward I* (London, 1988), 470 n. 4.

[38] *Calendar Documents Ireland*, iv. *1293–1301*, #551 at 257.

[39] *Calendar of Ormond Deeds*, i. #226 at 361.

[40] *Calendar Documents Ireland*, v. *1302–7*, #673.

[41] *Calendar Documents Ireland*, v. *1302–7*, #617 at 173, 179; *Calendar of Ormond Deeds*, #559.

[42] *Calendar Justiciary Rolls Ireland*, ii. *1295–1303*, 322. The calendaring of this now destroyed roll implies that the seisin was justified since Valle 'had bound himself to pay her said money (or that) all his lands should be forfeited to her, and she might enter them'.

[43] For local administrators of English lords in Ireland generally see Beth Hartland, '"To serve Well and Faithfully": The Agents of Aristocratic English Lordship in Leinster *c.*1272–*c.*1315', *Medieval Prosopography* 24 (2003), 195–246.

[44] Justiciar from 1273 to 1276. See James Lydon, 'The Years of Crisis, 1254–1315' and 'A Land of War', in Art Cosgrove (ed.), *A New History of Ireland*, ii. *Medieval Ireland 1169–1534* (Oxford, 1987), 179–204 and 240–74 at 189–91, 257–9.

[45] Justiciar, from 18 October 1294 to pre-19 October 1295. See A. J. Otway-Ruthven, *A History of Medieval Ireland* (London, 1968), 211 n. 58.

[46] 'Apparent' because Gerald fitz Maurice Fitzgerald had not completed the transfer before his death, exacerbating the conflict between Agnes and John fitz Thomas Fitzgerald. On this complicated story see Ó Cléirigh, 'Absentee Landlady', 105, 107–9.

James Keating.[47] When this bailiff took his lady to law he did so well prepared politically and legally.

What had happened to de Valle was this. He had been the bailiff of Agnes and her husband, Jean d'Avesnes, in Ireland, 'guarding' unspecified 'lands and tenements' there.[48] When the relationship had broken down is unclear, but it may predate 1283 when Avesnes died, since de Valle is specified as his bailiff as well as Agnes's. There had then been a dispute about de Valle's accounting and debts on behalf of the couple. We know this because *ex parte* was an appeal against such accountings which the 1285 legislation known as Statute of Westminster II (cap. 11) provided for.[49] So in 1291 de Valle had *already* been forced to account and his answers found wanting by his plaintiff-lord. Avesnes's auditors had taken up their legal right to then commit the defendant-bailiff to the king's prison. Obliged by *ex parte*, the law then unrolled, requiring a second audit to be undertaken at the Exchequer, by its appointed auditors, William of Carleton, Exchequer baron, and Walter of Castello.[50]

They found that the total of John's original receipts and issues (*receptus et exitus*) was £5,313. 2s. 12d: John had been originally allowed £3,840. 8s. 11¼d. of this. Aside from this, three further debts were attributed to John. A further £1,023. 6s. 11d. was disputed, which, John said, 'he had delivered to various merchants on the order of the aforesaid John [d'Avesnes] and Agnes for the same John and Agnes's debts' [*quos dixit se liberasse diversis mercatoribus ex precepto predictorum Iohannis et Agn' pro debitis eorundem Iohannis et Agn'*]. The ex-bailiff lacked, however, 'letters of quittance proving the said payment' [*litteras acquietancie predictam solutionem testificantes*]. Secondly, John remained liable for £23. 6s. 8d. for the cost of 36 crannock[51] of wheat and 43 crannock of oats which he said he had delivered to William of Loges, Agnes's clerk at Rathmore, on leaving Ireland. But, again, John 'did not have a letter from the said William proving the same delivery' [*non habuit litteram predicti Willelmi predictam liberacionem testificantem*], so Agnes's auditors had not conceded this either. Thirdly, even allowing for this, John was still £426 short [*debuit de claro*] of his total liabilities, 'for which he had been committed to the King's prison of the Fleet by the auditors of the said Agnes' [*pro quibus commisus fuit prisone Regis de Fflete per auditores predicte Agn'*]. Now John de Valle newly produced, in front of William of Carleton and Walter of Castello, new accounts of these debts and much more about 'the different outlays and expenses which he says he had to make in the service of the said John [d'Avesnes] and Agnes in parts of Ireland, regarding which he seeks justice for himself.' [*de diversis misis et expensis quas dicit se necessarie fecisse in servicio predictorum Iohannis et Agn' in partibus Hibernie', de quibus petit iustitiam sibi fieri*].[52]

The following are noteworthy. De Valle had discretion over very large amounts of money. He appears to be liaising directly with merchant-bankers (from England,

---

[47] These last two are from de Valle's second batch of pledges. [48] TNA E 13/17 m. 6.
[49] *SR*, i. 80–1. [50] Paul Brand, 'Carleton, William (*c*.1250–1311)', *ODNB*.
[51] A 'dry measure formerly in use in Wales, the West of England, and Ireland. It varied greatly in different places, and according to the commodity. For corn, the crannock of 2 or 4 bushels is mentioned; for salt it appears to have been much larger' (*OED*).
[52] Quotes in this paragraph are from TNA E 13/17 m. 6.

Hainault, Brabant, and Lombardy as it turns out), again for large amounts of money. Since Valence does not dispute his right to do so (it is his quittances she hangs him on), de Valle was presumably empowered to do so. Significantly, de Valle appears at the mercy of those from or to whom he had taken or given assets, either through his own incompetence in obtaining, or their refusal to give him, receipts. Yet he does not seem to have been so incompetent that he lacked 'some detailed accounts from the said arrears' which he could bring before the court to prove his good faith (presumably either notes, accounts, or tallies of his own).[53] It is possible therefore that de Valle's were legitimate debts. Nor is it hard to imagine the power a lord (or lady) might gain over a servant-employee by withholding such receipts or quittances—a powerful incentive for future 'good behaviour'.[54] The Valences had a reputation for hard estate management, on both the male and female side. The exploits of one steward, William de Bussey, have been well-analysed.[55] But Agnes's mother Joan, Lady of Wexford also had form as a hard financial taskmistress. Her steward Adam de le Roche submitted a detailed petition in 1300/1 to the King's Council complaining at how over £250 of allowances allowed and documented were being refused.[56] The Valence reputation would be a good explanation of John de Valle's own facility at law.

Written records could prove a poor defence anyway. In 1295, the King received numerous petitions from London citizens concerning crimes alleged against William March, Bishop of Bath (1293–1302), Treasurer at the Exchequer (dismissed later that year). These included Nicholas of Clere's complaint that while he was accounting at the Exchequer, 'the bishop himself took his [Clere's] royal letters patent and another guarantee showing that he had loyally delivered the treasure of the king following his command and these letters and guarantees [March] wrongfully disallowed and withheld and, although he owes nothing, for arrears in his account and for other illicit judgements, he imprisoned him and held him in prison for three years since the morrow of Epiphany'.[57] A more graphic case is the earlier one of John le Waleys, who, when trying to serve a citation on the serial pluralist Bogo of Clare, was forced by Clare's *familia* to 'eat those letters, and even the seals attached to them, by force and against his will', before being beaten and imprisoned.[58]

[53] Looking, presumably, not dissimilar from TNA E 101/505/34, John of Tarrant's 1296–9 bundle of tallies, notes, and lists for Ufford church.
[54] Agnes was instructed to come with 'the rolls and tallies and with all other instruments through which she can burden [*onerare*] the said John with the aforesaid account and further accounts and certain demands [*certas occasiones*] for which the said John, because of the said account was arrested and his imprisonment explained', TNA E 13/17 m. 6.
[55] Andrew H. Hershey, 'The Rise and Fall of William de Bussey: A Mid-Thirteenth Century Steward', *Nottingham Medieval Studies* 44 (2000), 104–21.
[56] *Documents on the Affairs of Ireland Before the King's Council*, ed. G. O. Sayles (Dublin, 1979), #64. Cf. Robert Immer's plea to Joan to be released from prison to account and discussed in Hartland, '"To Serve Well and Faithfully"', 203, 226.
[57] *Select Cases before the King's Council, 1243–1482*, ed. I. S. Leadam and J. F. Baldwin, SS 35 (1918), 10–18 at 12.
[58] *Querela* at the Easter 1290 parliament, *PROME*, i. *Edward I, 1275–1294* (ed. Paul Brand), 193 (his trans.). Since Clare argued that his ignorance of who did this was a sufficient defence, the case illustrates a later point (pp. 65–7) about the accountable line between servants' actions and masters' liabilities. On Bogo see n. 231.

Agnes de Valence's own rough justice was less imaginative but not unpractised. In Wodeholm her bailiffs' trespasses and amercements led to a petition in the Michaelmas 1290 parliament.[59] There also John Francis, another former Valence bailiff, petitioned to be freed from the Fleet where he too had been for 'a year and a half for a certain account which Agnes de Valence demands from him'.[60] Was Francis sinner or sinned against? Agnes de Valence was also accused of champerty (participating in a suit to profit from it)—enticing the justiciar and Lord of Kildare William de Vescy to support her case against John fitz Thomas Fitzgerald.[61] It is not clear therefore that Valence had been made soft by life in the 'home counties of England', nor that de Valle's case was a fraudulent one.[62]

The difficulty of establishing whether servants had accounted to masters is illustrated by a case connected to de Valle's. In 1300, a freeholder of Poynston by Rathmor, John of Hothum, brought a successful action of novel disseisin against Valence and another bailiff of hers who had thrown Hothum off his tenement—which he had held for many years of Reyner de Valle and John de Valle. In unsuccessful defence, Valence's bailiff argued all of de Valle's property was forfeit to his lady, and so this tenement was forfeit.[63] Now none of this prevented Hothum himself becoming a Valence bailiff (for Rathmor!). He then experienced exactly the same problem as de Valle, and John Francis: that is, he became indebted to Valence for £171. 11s.—and admitted as much. *Afterwards*, Hothum realized that his only way out was to cover over this admission. So Hothum,

> suggesting to the court that the auditors of the account unduly aggrieved him on the account, charging him with receipts which he did not receive, and not allowing expenses and reasonable payments, sued a writ by which he was delivered by mainprise to be before the Treasurer and barons of the Exchequer, Dublin, at a certain day [. . .] In suing which writ, he did not mention the fact of the acknowledgement of said arrears which he made before said justices, which fact if he had stated he would not have obtained the writ.[64]

Hothum's case is a useful pendent to de Valle's. It shows the difficulty in these cases of really knowing who is defrauding whom, and shows that bailiffs and lords could act against each other with equal cynicism. It also implies a court was likely to credit lord and bailiff as equally unaccountable, equally capable of manipulating the very

---

[59] *PROME*, i. *Edward I: 1275–1294*, 292.   [60] *PROME*, i. *Edward I: 1275–1294*, 296.
[61] *PROME*, i. *Edward I: 1275–1294*, 662 (Michaelmas 1293).
[62] Pace Ó Cléirigh, 'Absentee Landlady', 116 and 117, 'absentee landladies were an unaffordable luxury'. It is certainly true that slippery tricks were used against Agnes—notably the disseisin of her lands by John fitz Thomas Fitzgerald on the back of his false claim that she was dead! See *PROME*, ii. *Edward I: 1294-1307* (ed. Paul Brand), 172–3, 267–8, 339 (for 28 February 1305). I am not convinced that systematic comparison with other female landlords would prove their greater general inferiority. Cf. on Margaret de Lacy, Countess of Lincoln, Louise J. Wilkinson, 'Pawn and Political Player: Observations on the Life of a Thirteenth Century Countess', *Historical Research* 73 (2000), 105–23 (and text and nn. 155, 156 on Grosseteste's *Rules*); cf. on Isabella de Fortibus, Denholm-Young, *Seignorial Administration*, passim.
[63] *Calendar Justiciary Rolls Ireland*, i. *1295–1303*, 322 (7 May 1300).
[64] *Calendar Justiciary Rolls Ireland*, ii. *1305–7*, 19–20 at 20 (27 January 1305). Although Hothum is discharged because Agnes sends no one to court, he remains a marked man.

machinery that was designed to produce accountability, in order to obscure their own negligence, corruption, or debt.[65]

In de Valle's case, the barons of the Exchequer agreed that any analysis of who had done what was impossible 'regarding the discharges and expenses given in the regions of Ireland', and that 'they could not have a just and sufficient knowledge (*iustam et sufficientem cognitionem*) except through men from Irish lands'.[66] John and Agnes could not agree, however, on who could help in the investigation (*discussio*) of these accusations and altercations (*calumpniis et altercationibus*). The case therefore defaulted to sessions in Hilary and Easter 1292 when the Treasurer and Justice of Pleas, Robert Bagot, were agreed as auditors. The remainder of the story can be briefly summarized. De Valle asks for more time to be given to get hold of acquittances from the numerous merchants. The barons grant him nine months (to 14 January 1293) on condition that he secures more pledges[67] and that if he does not then appear he will pay the whole of the £1,023 figure. Come January 1293, de Valle defaults and absconds (*omnino se subtraxit* as a later summary says). Through 1293 the case pivots, tipping from its tight hold on de Valle to a broad and ultimately unfocused grasp on a mass of first and second pledges and their proxies. The sheriffs of Devon, Warwickshire, and Somerset are drawn into the search for them, many of whom then also disappear.[68] In fact only one, Dodingseles, appeared in January 1293, 'for the reason that he could in no way fly off (*devolitare*) or excuse [himself]'. Given de Valle's absence, Dodingseles, together with the first set of pledges, becomes liable for the original 'undisputable debt' of £426 for which de Valle was in the Fleet.[69] The final judgement with which this plea record ends, however, is this. Since neither de Valle, nor his second batch of pledges came,

> It is adjudged that the aforesaid Agnes should recover her property against the aforesaid John [fitz Thomas Fitzgerald], Walter [son of Walter Lenfaunt], James [Keating], John [of Ffulburn], Walter [of Bodynton] and John [Punchardun] for the aforesaid £1,023 6s. and 11d.[70]

From this point Agnes and the courts turn to pursue the pledges, a long and involved set of claim and counter-claim of progressively diminishing returns, only wearing itself out in 1306.[71]

These two cases provide two illustrations of two bailiffs at the start of the twelfth and at the end of the thirteenth century. They suggest questions and offer answers regarding what bailiffs were and did, how this changed, and why.

---

[65] So J. H. Baker: 'Practising lawyers know that success in litigation is not always, or even often, dependent upon a pure matter of law. It is more a matter of how a tribunal can be persuaded of the facts as the party sees them, and how it can be persuaded to see those facts in a warm light which does not relegate the party's best point of law to the shadows', *Why the History of English Law Has Not Been Finished* (Cambridge, 1999), 10–11.

[66] TNA E 13/17 m. 6.

[67] TNA E 13/17 m. 6, 'John FitzThomas Fitzgerald [again], Walter, son of Walter Lenfaunt, James Ketyng, John of Fulburne knight, Walter of Bodynton, and John Punchardun'.

[68] TNA E 13/17 m. 6d.   [69] TNA E 13/17 m. 6d.   [70] TNA E 13/17 m. 6d.

[71] The coda is *Calendar Justiciary Rolls Ireland*, ii. *1305–7*, 204–13 (27 January 1306). For the wider political-territorial context see Ó Cléirigh, 'Absentee Landlady'.

'Who, whom?' is a good question to ask here. What did Robert of Chilton do as a *prepositus*? He fought with his superior—intensely. He contested the terms of his 'contract' with some—but not enough—legal skill. He sub-let his *villicatio* presumably to increase his gain from the manor, but in a way that its owner was unhappy with. And when it came to a fight, he jostled—as did his land-lord—to place the case in a jurisdiction that was likely to favour him. Finally, he lost.[72] What did John de Valle do as a bailiff? Asking 'Who, whom?' produces more interesting answers here. The scale of his responsibilities and management of large sums of money estates imply he was more steward than bailiff functionally if not legally. Like Robert of Chilton, he too fought with his employer/lord, Agnes, and for it suffered imprisonment. To free himself he enlisted an impressive clutch of pledges with strong local knowledge as well as political clout. He was, again, legally well informed.

We do not know the detail about any informal means Agnes de Valence used to resolve the dispute with John de Valle before going to law, or whether he evaded customary accountings. We can assume an enforced accounting preceding the *ex parte* writ (its premise). One contrast with the Wye case is the total displacement of accountability from John de Valle to his pledges, notwithstanding the limited success of this shift. Although well-rooted enough in his locale to procure these pledges, de Valle seems to cut his losses. If this John de Valle is one of those we can see—perplexingly—holding land thereabouts then he disappeared sufficiently to leave the courts and Valence with no choice but to turn to his pledges. Another contrast is that the Irish dispute was less over the terms of any quasi-contract and more a procedural game of cat and mouse, where questions of receipts and quittances were critical. It can be hard indeed to tell cat from mouse. Each case therefore, almost two centuries apart, produces its puff of confusion in different places.[73] This seems a function of where each bailiff could best stand his ground: on a question of status (Chilton), or on a question of records (de Valle). This difference could be exaggerated, but it is a real contrast. The final contrast, between these two cases, is obvious. Robert of Chilton lost. After a fashion John de Valle won. At least, if he did indeed owe Agnes the 'clear' £426, *plus* the £1,023. 6*s*. 11*d*., *plus* the £23. 6*s*. 8*d*. worth of grain, he seems never to have paid it back. If his arguments were genuine his victory was more sour, since it was only through 'completely absconding' that he obtained his own rough justice and evaded the attempt to hold him to account, whether that was sought of him in good faith or bad.

---

[72] Had that 'legal realist' at Barnwell offered his assessment of bailiffs' accountability, it might have sounded something like that. See BL Harley MS 3601 (*c*.1295–6), ed. as *Liber memorandum ecclesie de Bernewelle*, analysed in M. T. Clanchy, 'A Medieval Realist: Interpreting the Rules at Barnwell Priory, Cambridge', in Elspeth Attwooll (ed.), *Perspectives in Jurisprudence* (Glasgow, 1977), 176–94. Unfortunately the chronicler does not discuss such actions.

[73] Cf. Susan Reynolds's ironic comment on common law actions becoming 'more enchantingly complex' over the thirteenth century, 'How Different was England?', *TCE* 7 (1999), 1–16 at 2.

'A REASONABLE ACCOUNT OF HIS TIME AS A BAILIFF'

How did the liability of bailiffs to account for their office 'get' from Robert of Chilton to John de Valle? An answer is given here as a case study in the institutionalizing of a practice as a legal norm. The answer is split into three: developments up until the early thirteenth century; developments 1225–58; and the great period of legislation 1259–85 which would produce what Edward I referred to in John de Valle's case as the rule 'according to the form of the statute provided by the common counsel of our realm', i.e. Statute of Westminster II (1285) cap. 11.[74]

The Twelfth and Early Thirteenth Centuries

Both the Chilton and the de Valle cases are predicated on the existence of some sort of enforceable custom or law that a bailiff was obliged to account for his bailiffship to the person from whom he held it. The Wye case mentions a writ summons of Robert of Chilton to Battle *ex regis nomine*.[75] The de Valle case talks about the 'statute provided for by the common counsel of our kingdom'.[76] The 1291 *ex parte* writ of Edward I was a response to what had become a sequence of legislative interventions. What was the quality of these norms and how did they develop?

A handful of twelfth-century cases points towards the existence of some legal means of obliging an accounting between a bailiff and his lord-principal, which have been classed as 'actions of account'.[77]

One should be disqualified. Raoul van Caenegem argued that an 1163 x 1172/3 writ from the King and witnessed by Richard of Ilchester, doyen of Exchequer auditing, was an action of account.[78] It orders Emelina de Ros to 'respond reasonably' (*juste respondeas*) to the Abbot of St Augustine's Canterbury for 'works and expenses

---

[74] *SR*, i. 80–1.   [75] *Chronicle of Battle*, 110.   [76] TNA E 13/17 m. 6.
[77] A first gathering was *Royal Writs in England from the Conquest to Glanvill*, ed. R. C. van Caenegem, SS 77 (London, 1959), 188, 345–6. Searle makes the connection between the Wye case and the action in *Chronicle of Battle*, 108 n. 2. Paul Brand noticed an 1198 case, *Kings, Barons and Justices: The Making and Enforcement of Legislation in Thirteenth-Century England* (Cambridge, 2003), 65 n. 96. Brand's work here and elsewhere on TNA records massively advances the thirteenth-century history of this action. Other important authors for the action of account are: T. F. T. Plucknett, esp. *Mediaeval Bailiff* (London, 1954), and *Legislation of Edward I* (Oxford, 1949), and Denholm-Young's *Seignorial Administration*. Maitland was fairly dismissive of the action: Frederick Pollock and Frederic William Maitland, *The History of English Law before the Time of Edward I*, reissued edn. by S. F. C. Milsom, 2 vols. (Cambridge, 1968), ii. 221–2, 347. Maitland gave the 1232 case as the first instance of an action of account. See also his posthumous *The Forms of Action at Common Law* (Cambridge, 1954), 48. For the period from *c*.1300 see S. J. Stoljar, 'The Transformations of Account', *Law Quarterly Review* 80 (1964), 203–24. More generally on the action: J. H. Baker, *An Introduction to English Legal History*, 3rd edn. (London, 1990), 410–13; S. F. C. Milsom, *Historical Foundations of the Common Law*, 2nd edn. (London, 1981), 275–82; T. F. T. Plucknett, *A Concise History of the Common Law*, 5th edn. (London, 1956), 28, 30–1, 365, 448–9; Michael Prestwich, *Plantagenet England, 1225–1360* (Oxford, 2005), 431–2; Frédérique Lachaud, *L'Éthique du pouvoir au Moyen Âge: L'Office dans la culture politique (Angleterre, vers 1150–vers 1330)*, Bibliothèque d'histoire médiévale 3 (Paris, 2010), 551–3.
[78] On Richard of Ilchester see pp. 92 n. 61, 251.

from your part of land at Plumstead, as you and your ancestors were accustomed to do at the time of King Henry my grandfather. And unless you do so, the sheriff of Kent will make it so, such that on this I will hear no further complaint for want of right.'[79]

At Domesday Plumstead was held by the Abbot from Odo of Bayeux, and a Ros family is visible in Kent during this period.[80] No bailiff or manorial official is mentioned in this writ though, nor is an accounting clearly specified. Rather a custom is at issue. It seems more reasonable to see this writ not as a proto-action of account, but simply as an issue of the upkeep of defence works on the Thames at Plumstead.[81] It seems a weak case for the institutionalized accountability of twelfth-century bailiffs.

The Chilton case itself comes second given the *Battle Chronicle*'s *terminus* of *c*.1184.[82] A royal writ figured (the summons *ex regis nomine*), but its contents are unclear. Eleanor Searle suggested that Geoffrey of St Calais' writ could have simply recapitulated the terms of an 1101 grant whereby Abbot Henry was empowered to hear any tenants' cases in his court or to transfer it to the King's court if he wished.[83] She plausibly suggests this general writ might be the source of the 'terror' that resulted in Robert of Chilton attending the Battle court. Thus the case presupposes no specific rule about *bailiffs*' accountability. The way Luke 16 is cited implies, however, that it was a unexceptional norm (see later in this section). The discrepancy may be explained by suggesting that the norm became established after the date of the incident (*c*.1102) and during the chronicle's composition (1125 x 1138–*c*.1184).

Two further cases indeed date from 1185 and come from the pipe rolls. For Essex and Hertfordshire's 1185 'new pleas and agreements from Roger fitz Renfrid and William de Ver and William Ruffus and his companions', it was noted that:

> Michael clerk of Hadfield renders account for 20*m*. for having a legal account against Richard of Brunesho for the pledge of Michael fitzGodfrey. In the treasury 10*m*. And he owes 10*m*.
> Thomas of La Mailanda renders account for 3 marks for having a legal account against Brien de Purley. In the treasury, 6*s*. And he owes 34*s*.[84]

---

[79] *Royal Writs in England*, #125, at 345 n. 8; Thomas of Elmham, *Historia monasterii S. Augustini Cantuariensis*, ed. Charles Hardwick, RS (London, 1858), #38 at 409.

[80] *Domesday Book*, trans. Ann Williams and G. H. Martin, repr. (London, 2002), 15, 29.

[81] I am grateful for discussion to Paul Brand, to whom I owe the explanation of Plumstead's significance here. I do not find a reference to an Emelina de Ros of Plumstead appearing in the pipe rolls 1163–73. Barons of Ros are identifiable in Kent for this period, but I cannot connect Emelina. See K. S. B. Keats-Rohan, *Domesday Descendants: A Prosopography of Persons Occurring in English Documents 1066-1166*, ii. *Pipe Rolls to Cartae Baronum* (Woodbridge, 2002), 671–2. Van Caenegem (*Royal Writs in England*, 346) argues that the case was 'an executive measure, outside the courts and to the benefit of individuals, [it] is at the origin of what was later to become a distinct plea in the royal courts'.

[82] *Chronicle of Battle*, 9.

[83] *Chronicle of Battle*, 111 n. 5. The 1101 notification is summarized in *Regesta Regum Anglo-Normannorum 1066–1154*, ed. C. Johnson, H. A. Cronne, and H. W. C. Davis, 4 vols. (Oxford, 1913–69), ii. #529.

[84] *PR 1184–1185*, 17. Caenegem (*Royal Writs in England*, 345 n. 7) cites *PR 1185–1186*, 14, where the debt is this 10 marks.

Further payments were made: Michael was quit in 1187, Thomas of his final seven shillings only in 1192.[85] Both cases indicate payments for royal writs. In neither is the relationship between suer and sued clear. The shorthand phrase *pro habendo legali compoto* does point towards some established legal practice of requiring an accounting by this time though.

A last brief twelfth-century case comes from the *curia regis* roll for 1198. Under pleas for York, 'A day is given to Richard Malebiss[86] and Andrew of ?Magnebus for a plea of account to be rendered when the justices come [i.e. in eyre], by the parties' prayer [*prece partium*].'[87] Here the parties (one of whom presumably owes an account to the other) appear to have agreed on the county justices in eyre as their way out of disagreement. The justices held this eyre in York during January and February 1199, but the pipe rolls and final concords give no further information on this plea of account.[88]

These few cases imply that a semi-regular mechanism for obliging one private individual to account for the discharge of some duty of care to a further private individual had been established by the end of the twelfth century. By 1198 it was coherent enough to be described as a plea. It is not clear that this mechanism presumed a defendant must be responsible for a fixed function (e.g. a bailiffship) in relation to the purchaser of the writ. That though is possible in just some slightly later cases. The first clear reference to a *bailiff's* having to account is only two year's after the Malebiss entry (see p. 43). It is not clear there was a fixed price for obtaining the writ for such a 'legal account' (the variance in the 1185 prices perhaps implies not). It is not precisely clear how far the writ was *de cursu* or *de gracia*—i.e. how standardized it was.[89] However, the legal principle does seem long established that a person with some duty of care owed towards another could be obliged to give an account of it.

A potential problem with this narrative is that no writ of account is mentioned in *Glanvill*—the important treatise on procedure and writs in royal courts compiled for Henry II in the 1180s. But since *Glanvill* was 'concerned primarily with civil litigation by writ before the king's justices', and county and seigneurial courts are excluded from its consideration, this may not be problematic.[90] An 'early'

---

[85] *PR 1185–1186*, 14–15 for 'pleas of Roger fitzRenfrid and his companions', *PR 1186–1187*, 124, for Michael's quittance, *PR 1191–1192*, 169, for Thomas's.

[86] The culpable ringleader responsible for the murder of the few Jews of York left in 1190 after the majority had committed suicide for fear of being murdered: *The Chronicle of Walter of Guisborough*, ed. Harry Rothwell, CS 3rd ser. 89 (1957), 95; *Cartularium prioratus de Gyseburne, Ebor. dioceseos, ordinis Sancti Augustini, fundati A.D. MCXIX*, ed. William Brown, 2 vols., Surtees Society, 86, 89 (1889–94), ii. 60 n. 3.

[87] *Memoranda Roll 1207–1208*, 105.

[88] *PR 1200*, 111–17. For the eyre and its records: David Crook, *Records of the General Eyre*, Public Record Office Handbooks 20 (London, 1982), 59. Malebiss appears variously in the rolls, but I have not found further signs of this plea.

[89] On writs *de cursu* and *de gracia*, see *Brevia Placitata*, ed. G. J. Turner and T. F. T. Plucknett, SS 66 (1951), xlviii–lix. It would be a much longer legal and historical question why this vehicle contributed so little to the history of trusts in English law.

[90] *The Treatise on the Laws and Customs of the Realm of England Commonly Called Glanvill*, ed. G. D. G. Hall, NMT (London, 1965), xi; Michael Clanchy on Glanvill's modesty in his 'Guide to Further Reading' in the 1993 OMT reissue, lxxiii, lxxviii–lxxix.

action of account may not have interested *Glanvill*. Furthermore, the elements this action addressed *are* discussed in the early twelfth-century *Leges Henrici Primi* (rootless manorial officials, audits and accounts, jurisdictional problems, unaccountable reeves). It has also been suggested that much-maligned *Leges* may have been written by a hundred court bailiff especially concerned with hundredal courts.[91] If so he would have been operating at just the relevant level to express an interest in these issues, which *Glanvill* was not (see further pp. 61–2, 70 on the *Leges*).

Like the later, formal, action of account (and like *Leges Henrici Primi*), the Wye case expresses a similar concern for the state of lands at farm, the accountability of a lease-farmer who was a *prepositus*, and the problem (for Battle) of pinning him in one of a number of potential courts. (And discussed further on pp. 47–52, 60–82.) In articulating a rule that a manorial official-cum-farmer is liable to account for his management, the Battle case gives expression to an idea with legal power. But rather than appealing to a legal rule, Geoffrey of St Calais licenses his actions through a scriptural precept that obligates his *villicus* to be accountable to him: 'he demanded an account of his stewardship'. The norm was structural, not decorative (at least in the *Battle Chronicle*). One hypothesis would be that Scripture provided a way of naturalizing the institutionalization of the norm as a legal rule, a justification that obviously became legally superfluous once the rule was established.[92]

The etymological origins and scriptural usage of *villicus* are needed to make sense of this. Luke 16: 1–14 comprises the disturbing parable of the unjust *villicus* who has been embezzling his lord's goods. He is discovered and summoned to give an account of his stewardship. Faced with the prospect of penury and expulsion from office, the *villicus* seeks to ingratiate himself with his lord's debtors by forging receipts and accounts. His lord, on discovering this, disconcertingly endorses the manager's misconduct by extrapolating from his conduct that, in its light, he will be so much the keener for eternal life. (This text will furnish Pope Innocent III with one proof for his decretal establishing inquisitions as a method of investigating negligent prelates; see pp. 159–62.) Other bailiff-like terms emphasize accountability in the Bible. *Prepositus*, which can mean simply 'one set above', or, in an English manorial context, 'reeve', is used in the same way biblically.[93] The connection between being a *prepositus*

---

[91] Nicholas Karn, 'Rethinking the *Leges Henrici Primi*', in Stefan Jurasinski, Andrew Rabin, and Lisi Oliver (eds.), *English Law before Magna Carta: Felix Liebermann and Die Gesetze der Angelsachsen* (Leiden, 2010), 199–220 at 214–18. He is producing a new edition of the *Leges Henrici Primi* for the Early English Laws project (<http://www.earlyenglishlaws.ac.uk/>, accessed January 2014).

[92] Cf. Mary Douglas's idea that social rules are founded on analogies that reflect 'natural' or cosmic norms, in *Natural Symbols: Explorations in Cosmology*, 2nd edn. (London, 2003 edn.) and *How Institutions Think* (Syracuse, 1986). See the 'how to' manorial treatises edited in *The Court Baron*, ed. Frederic William Maitland and William Paley Baildon, SS 4 (London, 1891), citing biblical precepts: the Lord's allusion to the parable of the wicked servants regarding a serial non-attender of court (50, *La Court de baron*, #27); the duty of manorial officers holding court to do so honourably given the need to render what is God's to God and what is Caesar's to Caesar (70, *De placitis et curiis tenendis*); a reference to the Judgement Day, invoked at the re-swearing of frankpledges (93, *Modus tenendi curias*).

[93] e.g. Hebrews 13: 17. 'Oboedite praepositis vestris et subiacete eis ipsi enim pervigilant quasi rationem pro animabus vestris reddituri'. On the importance of this citation in the development of

or *villicus* and some sort of accountability was consequently a common one, from the high to the later Middle Ages.[94]

The other relevant element regarding manorial officials is that classically *villicus* meant 'rural administrator'. Isidore of Seville defines it: 'A *villicus* is properly the manager of a "country estate" (*villa*), whence the *villicus* takes his name from *villa*. Yet sometimes *villicus* does not signify the management of a country estate, but, according to Cicero, the oversight of all the household business, that is, he is overseer of all the property and estates.'[95]

Scripture and etymology can be seen in two earlier, different contexts. The first relates to two letters of Charles the Bald to Pope Hadrian II in which Charles complained about the Pope's interference in the suppression of his son Carloman's 870 revolt and appointments to the Bishop of Laon's lay estates.[96] The letters asserted that although bishops lived under their own laws this in no way implied that Frankish kings were 'bishops' bailiffs' (*episcoporum villici*). Augustine says, recounts Charles, that 'Property is possessed by the laws of kings, but not by episcopal *fiat* [*per episcopale imperium*] do kings become estate-managers [*villarum actores*].'[97] A second letter some six months letter again rejected the idea that Frankish kings were bishops' bailiffs.[98] Charles's objection can be expressed as a pragmatic rejection of the idea that he needed to account to anyone else when disposing of ecclesiastical lands whose bishop was deposed (here Hincmar of Laon).[99] A dismissable *villicus* was the opposite of how powerful men regarded themselves.[100] A second illustration makes the same point. This time, in 1075, an ecclesiastical *potens* attacks the idea that he and *his* fellow bishops are the pope's mere *villici*: so Bishop Liemar of Bremen, when

---

Pope Gelasius I's ideas of papal accountability and authority in 494 see Janet L. Nelson, 'Gelasius I's Doctrine of Responsibility, a Note', in *Journal of Theological Studies* 18 (1967), 154–62 at 156–8.

[94] e.g. for the earlier period in *The Ecclesiastical History of Orderic Vitalis*, ed. Marjorie Chibnall, OMT, 6 vols. (Oxford, 1969–80), iii. 14 (V.3, Bishop Hugh of Lisieux's deathbed confession); iv. 42 (VII.8, William's arrest of Odo of Bayeux), and for the later period, Thomas Wimbledon's 1386/8 St Paul's Cross sermon, ed. Ione Kemp Knight, as *Wimbledon's Sermon: redde racionem villicationis tue, a Middle English Sermon of the Fourteenth Century* (Pittsburgh, 1967). For useful references in this later period, Christopher Fletcher, 'Morality and Office in Late Medieval England and France', in *Fourteenth Century England* 5 (2008), 178–90. It should be said conversely that scriptural passages that are not literally about bailiffs can be used by preachers to illustrate stories about bailiffs, e.g. D. L. d'Avray, *The Preaching of the Friars* (Oxford, 1985), 218–19, citing Matthew 6: 33 ('Seek first the kingdom of God') and 1 Samuel 7: 3 ('Prepare your heart for the lord'). *Baillivus* is again used broadly.

[95] *The Etymologies of Isidore of Seville*, trans. Stephen A. Barney, W. J. Lewis, J. A. Beach, and Oliver Berghof (Cambridge, 2006), 205 (IX. iv. 33).

[96] Following Janet L. Nelson, ' "Not Bishops' Bailiffs but Lords of the Earth": Charles the Bald and the Problem of Sovereignty', in Diana Wood (ed.), *The Church and Sovereignty, c.590–1918*, SCH Subsidia 9 (Oxford, 1991), 23–34.

[97] *PL* 124, Ep. 7, col. 878, letter of *c*.6 September 871. Comment in Nelson, 'Not Bishops' Bailiffs', 28. Nelson argues that the authorial voice here is genuinely Charles's (33).

[98] *PL* 124, Ep. 8, cols. 886–7, February/March 871; Nelson, 'Not Bishops' Bailiffs', 30–1.

[99] In August 871 at Douzy in Lotharingia: Janet L. Nelson *Charles the Bald* (London, 1992), 229.

[100] On the status of *villici* see the discussion in Heinrich Fichtenau, *Living in the Tenth Century: Mentalities and Social Orders*, trans. P. J. Geary (Chicago, 1991), ch. 16, esp. 360–7. For the different *ministeriales* see Gerd Althoff, *Family, Friends and Followers: Political and Social Bonds in Early Medieval Europe*, trans. C. Carroll (Cambridge, 2004), 133–5. On *villicatio/villicus* see J. R. Niermeyer and C. van de Kieft, rev. J. W. J. Burgers, *Mediae Latinitatis Lexicon Minus*, 2 vols. (Leiden, 2002), ii. 1439–41.

Pope Gregory VII's cardinal legates suspend him following his opposition to the Pope's reforms.[101]

These cases show first, unsurprisingly, how the scriptural precept to 'give an account of your stewardship' was transposed across many sorts of officer. Secondly they highlight how central the liability to justify one's actions was to the idea of being a manager of any sort and to an association of accountability with servility, or at least subordination. To these men being a *villicus* implied very clear answers to 'Who, whom?'. It was the political subordination consequent on accepting such accountability that both Charles the Bald, Liemar of Bremen—and Robert of Chilton—resisted. Status mattered when determining which way the current of accountability flowed. On this line of thinking, men of status are not accountable to those beneath them.

Further terse actions of account can be seen in the early thirteenth century, and it is then that the first extant reference to a bailiff per se having to account occurs in 1200, very soon after the Malebiss case. The plea is for Norfolk, mid-June 1200.

> Ranulph clerk of the Archbishop of Canterbury, offers himself on the fourth day against Ralph son of Anketill for a plea of chattels which he had in custody while he was his bailiff and for which he has not rendered an account as he claims. And he himself did not come or excuse himself, and he was pledged, namely by Richard Sorrell and Ranulph Fabrum.[102]

In July,

> a day was given from the quindene of St Michael's [i.e. 13–19 October] to Ranulph clerk and Ralph son of Anketill for a plea of chattels and account at the parties' agreement; and they have leave to come to an agreement.[103]

Here, the court appears as much as a means of arbitration and dispute resolution as of more formally legal proceedings. A 1206 plea shows the same arbitration going on between Samson of Pomeroy and William of Upton for a Buckinghamshire plea. Samson seeks an account from William (William is not specified as a bailiff).[104] That Easter

> William put himself upon Richer of Belle Field and Bartholemew, dean of Duniton, or upon two others, if he is unable to have them; and Samson put himself upon Peter of

---

[101] Liemar of of Bremen to Hezilo of Hildesheim, January 1075: 'Periculosus homo vult iubere, que vult, episcopis ut villicis suis', in *Briefsammlungen der Zeit Heinrichs IV.*, ed. Carl Erdmann and Norbert Fickermann, MGH, BdK (Weimar, 1950), v. Hildesheimer Briefe #15 at 34. See also Wenrich of Trier, *Epistola* in MGH, *LdL*, 3 vols. (Hannover, 1891–7), i. 289, ll. 32–6. Commentary in I. S. Robinson, '*Periculosus homo*: Pope Gregory VII and Episcopal Authority', *Viator* 9 (1978), 103–31; id., *Authority and Resistance in the Investiture Contest* (Manchester, 1978), 124–7, 169–70, and *Imperial Lives and Letters of the Eleventh Century*, ed. and trans. T. E. Mommsen and K. F. Morrison, rev. edn. (New York, 2000), 29.

[102] *CRR, 1196–1201*, 191; *Royal Writs in England*, 345 n. 4; C. T. Flower, *Introduction to the Curia Regis Rolls, 1199–1230*, SS 62 (London, 1944), 292, and, on local officers, 419–33; Brand, *Kings, Barons and Justices*, 65 n. 97.

[103] *CRR, 1196–1201*, 249.   [104] *CRR, 1205–1206*, 64 (Hilary 1206).

Wod [. . .] and Ralph of Wakering, or upon two others, if they cannot be present. And each of them commits himself to the decision of the said four and William of Neketon, and with the truth heard from each party, they shall abide by their decision.[105]

Here the court acts as a forum for agreeing acceptable arbitrators for the accounting, much as parties in a papal judge-delegate case would.[106] This is striking, a notable difference from later post-1260 developments where the choice of auditors became a major site of disagreement (as with John de Valle). The tone, such as can be deduced from such stark material, appears more consensual—or at least more flexible than in later cases.

Some accepted, customary basis for forcing people to account for goods or duties they held in care seems apparent then from the late twelfth century. The legal cases, such as they are, do not always make clear that those liable to account are bailiffs, but some do. Some—scant—material implies, that the rule, at least as a norm, was being applied to the actual liability of manorial agents or lease-holders *c.*1184, possibly earlier in the century. The core of what was later formalized as the action of account was evolving in the second half of the twelfth century.

*c.*1225–1258

These slim pickings though do not imply that the *need* for a legal power forcing manorial officers to account was clear, great, or frequent by the early thirteenth century. From the early thirteenth century the quantity and quality of such actions appears to change. There are problems in normalizing the earlier material with this later material given the latter's increasing volume and fullness. From 1200 to 1230 there are some eight recognizable cases and another eight from 1230 up to 1260, contrasting with the five *c.*1100–1200. From 1260 the number seems to increase. From 1260 until 1270 I note seven; twenty during the 1270s; fifteen until the end of the century; and another fifteen during the rest of Edward I's reign—a total of seventy-eight.[107] These totals are only indicative and impressionistic.[108] Nevertheless, the increase is there, and would presumably be greater on analysis of unedited material in the National Archives. The increase from the 1260s seems unlikely to be pure coincidence since, as we will see, in 1259/60 a variant form was

---

[105] *CRR, 1205–1206*, 145 (Easter 1206).

[106] Cf. Jane E. Sayers, *Papal Judges Delegate in the Province of Canterbury 1198–1254* (Oxford, 1971), 104–7, 109–14.

[107] There are also (at least) fourteenth- and fifteenth-century borough custumal rules regarding the action of account, but they are not factored in here. See Mary Bateson, ed., *Borough Customs*, 2 vols., SS 18, 21 (1904–6), i. 219–21, for Kilkenny, Lydd, and Lincoln.

[108] They could not be exhaustive without much further work on unedited rolls. Still, they are drawn from 1173–1307 printed *PR, CPR*, Year Books, *CRR*, Memoranda Rolls, Flower's *Introduction to the Curia Regis Rolls*, Stenton's *Pleas before the King or His Justices* and *Rolls of the Justices in Eyre*, Harding's *Roll of the Shropshire Eyre of 1256*, Leadam and Baldwin's *Select Cases before the King's Council*, Hall's *Select Cases concerning the Law Merchant, 1239–1633*, and, especially for the 1270s, Brand, *Kings, Barons and Justices* (esp. 314 nn. 58–73). My total's reliance on printed material means pre-1250 material is not fully reflected and only very broad inferences are worth drawing. Brand (65) notes that writs ordering accountings at county courts may have been more frequent than records allow us to see in this period.

introduced, the *monstravit de compoto*, and the action of account was fitted with a new set of teeth.

Qualitatively, the texture of the legal material also seems more defined even by the 1220s, in (e.g.) a Norfolk case from Trinity Term 1225:

> John of Stowe seeks against Hubert, fitzWilliam, son of Gery that he gives to him his reasonable account of the time when he was his bailiff in Helmstead. Whence the same John says that [Hubert] was his bailiff for four years and in no year did [Hubert] account to [John] except for 4 marks, so [Hubert] is in arrears to him by a year for 13 marks; and [John] seeks that [Hubert] renders to him his arrears etc. And Hubert comes and acknowledges that he was his bailiff; and freely he will reply to him as his lord [*respondebit ut domino suo*]. And so he is handed over to the same John as his servant [*ut serviens suus*].[109] And John gives to him respite up to the 8th day after Michaelmas, that meanwhile he satisfies the same John.[110]

A lord has an official that he deems has discharged his duty inadequately. He obtains a writ to secure this bailiff's adequate accounting. The bailiff is charged, concedes, replies. A concept too has been given—newly?—legalized form here: 'a reasonable account of his time as a bailiff'. The formulation may have passed from shrieval accounting, and imply the need for written proofs.[111] It implies that kings, barons, and justices had digested and responded to a perceived need for a clearer but elastic legal criterion to determine what an accountant was liable *for*. Before this point actions of account apparently conflated two things: (1) getting someone to account for a duty of care, where there was a dispute about their carefulness; and (2) getting someone to account when there was a dispute about whether he had accounted or not.

Another striking case is that of 6 October 1234, a plea by certain Florentine merchants in London. The merchants used the legal rule against their own *procurator*, Bonacursus, for debts owed to them.[112] Significantly, at this early point the action is used not only for those with estate management responsibilities but also those involved in entirely non-agricultural commercial activity. The boundaries between rules, practices, and applications could be fluid, as Andrew Horn's wide-ranging *Magnum librum* collations implied. From the 1230s the expectation to account for your time as a bailiff could apparently apply to men who were not bailiffs functionally but were considered bailiffs legally.[113] In this case accountability existed

---

[109] Remembering that *serviens* can connote a bailiff or reeve in a manorial context.
[110] *CRR 1225–1226*, 120–1 #605. For the start of the case, 82 #428.
[111] John required the indebted Robert of Vieuxpont, sheriff of Nottinghamshire and Derbyshire, to give a 'racionabilem conpotum' for the counties as part of the deal cut to handle his debts in December 1208 (*Rotuli chartarum in Turri londinensi asservati*, ed. T. D. Hardy (London, 1837), i.1. 184a). The phrase does not seem recurrent in John's charters, though one finds royal bailiffs are to pay their debts to the crown as *racionabiliter* as possible (60a) and common references to 'reasonable' donations, charters, concessions (e.g. 6b, 116b). On Vieuxpont in 1208 see *PR 1208*, 45, and Holt, *Northerners*, 226–7. 'Reasonable expenses' (*conuenables despens*) occurs in an accounting context in the 1258 'ordinance of sheriffs' (*DBM* #8 at 122). For *racionabilis*, implying written, see Robert C. Palmer, *The County Courts of Medieval England 1150–1350* (Princeton, NJ, 1982), 198–215.
[112] *CRR 1233–1237*, #1181 at 291.
[113] Five mercantile cases of the later sort are in Cam, *Eyre of London 1321*, i. cv–cvi. A separate line against 'receivers/agents' developed later. For these writ forms see Elsa de Haas and G. D. G. Hall

semi-independently of any particular office or role—the only relevant role here being the liability to account.

Another notable case comes from Shropshire in mid-1254. It concerned Thomas Corbet, sheriff of Shropshire. He had arrested and imprisoned from 11 June to 19 August 1254 William Cadigan, a bailiff of the King (*ballivus domini regis*). William Cadigan complains at the eyre, but the case is rejected on a technicality. Thomas Corbet then clarifies what happened. Corbet says:

> William was a bailiff of the lord king when he himself was sheriff, and that he [William] ought to have answered to him for his bailiwick, so that the same William should have rendered his account for the said bailiwick before R[obert] of Grendon then sheriff and the other faithful men there present, when he [William] was 40 shillings or more in arrears with his account. So Robert said to him [Thomas] that he should deal with him according to the law of England [*legem Anglie*], and for that reason he [Thomas] arrested him [William] as one convicted of [a deficient] account. Afterwards it was testified that the said William Cadigan is a pauper and has nothing, so he is quit.[114]

The case is interesting for the following reasons. First, a bailiff's liability to account to his superior is taken as a rule. Plucknett thought cases at this date must be extra-judicial.[115] Harding's judgement seems right though: 'the confidence and success of Corbet's defence suggests that the imprisonment of defaulting bailiffs was generally condoned' at this date.[116] That this was a recognized legal recourse seems warranted by Robert of Grendon's encouragement to Thomas Corbet to deal with Cadigan 'according to the law of England'. Secondly, the case involves not a seigneurial bailiff, but one of the king's. Given earlier and later seigneurial examples of 'actions of account', this implies that what was fit for a lord was fit for a king. Liabilities to account were shared—and perhaps developed—between private and regnal 'bailiffs', whatever the 'publicness' of their duties. Thirdly, a routine accounting for a bailiwick is expected at the start of the superior's term of office, and this duty seems owed both to a bailiff's immediate superior (Grendon) and—perhaps because there was a problem—to Grendon's predecessor, Corbet. There is nothing especially sophisticated in this, but there is a parallel with a *podestà*'s liability to account at the end of his term of office. This accounting is to the communal franchise though, rather than the *podestà*'s incoming replacement. Grendon's reference to *legem Anglie* implies that there was some explicit recognized rule for a bailiff's accountability by 1254. Since he and Grendon had poor reputations their action may have been narrowly legal rather than fair though. Still, the 1225 Norfolk case's tag 'a reasonable account of his time as a bailiff' implies that there may have been some established common law by then. Given on the one hand the modest but clear number of cases

---

(eds.), *Early Registers of Writs*, SS 87 (London, 1970), 376; Hubert Hall (ed.), *Select Cases concerning the Law Merchant, 1239–1633*, ii. *Central Courts*, SS 46 (London, 1930), *s.v.* 'accounts', 'writs of account'. See also Plucknett, *Mediaeval Bailiff*, 14–24, 26–7; Brand, 'Stewards, Bailiffs and the Emerging Legal Profession', 146, 150.

[114] Alan Harding (ed.), *The Roll of the Shropshire Eyre of 1256*, SS 96 (1981), #738 at 257–8, his trans., modified.

[115] Plucknett, *Legislation of Edward I*, 152.   [116] *Roll of the Shropshire Eyre of 1256*, xxii.

before both 1225 and 1254, and on the other the absence of any early extant formal justification for this action before these dates, we can suggest the actual *development* of this legal accountability was dependent on a legal warrant that came out of emerging 'vernacular' procedures.[117]

The edges of these thirteenth-century cases feel sharper than before. The law seems to be milling its grist more easily. Turning to formal warrant and registers of writs we can find some correlation. The earliest extant writ forms given in a register for an action of account is for the *justicies* form of the Norfolk 1225 case. It was a viscontiel *justicies* writ (i.e. addressed to a sheriff or other locally responsible officer) and would have enabled him to take action at the county courts if the writ itself proved ineffective.[118] An action of account does not figure in an early register (christened 'CA' by Maitland), datable to the 1220s.[119] But an unedited Cambridge register CUL MS Kk.v.33 ('CB') does include the action at no. 83: 'You [the local official] are to oblige so-and-so [i.e. the accused bailiff] to render to such-and-such [i.e. the lord-plaintiff] his reasonable account of the time when he was his bailiff.'[120] This sequence of writs is pre-1236 in *form* and the MS itself was dated by Maitland to 1236–59.[121] Inclusion implies that the action was *de cursu*: that is, a generally accessible action available centrally to plaintiffs as a *pro forma* for a set fee.[122] This and other variants of the action appear in registers thereafter. The evidence of the registers therefore tallies with that of the case records themselves. From the second quarter of the thirteenth century the action of account appears increasingly stable and increasingly recognized as a standard legal action in these fora.

The Period of Legislation, 1259–1285

The post-1259 increase in the numbers of known actions of account was probably a function of new legislation. The action is thus caught up in that extended period of

---

[117] Cf. Searle's comments to this effect on the legal developments that the Battle chronicler charts, *Chronicle of Battle*, 10.

[118] On the classification of writs see Palmer, *County Courts*, ch. 7, esp. 212–15; Milsom, *Historical Foundations*, 243–6; *Brevia Placitata*, xliii–lix; Baker, *Introduction to English Legal History*, 83. For the action in *Brevia Placitata*, cxxxviii–cxxxix, 23–4, 68–9, 176–7. The core of this treatise is probably 1260 (xviii–xix). Hall thought that is was not impossible that a *praecipe* form of this action existed by the 1180s (i.e. one returnable to a royal court). See *Glanvill*, 189.

[119] CUL MS Ii. vi. 13. See *Early Registers of Writs*, xl, xl–xliv. The Irish register known as 'Hib.' (BL Cotton MS Julius D. II) I do not discuss, because although it is arguably *c*.1227, its complexity makes it too slippery a guide. Discussion: *Early Registers of Writs*, xxxiii–xl.

[120] 'The History of the Register of Original Writs', in *The Collected Papers of Frederic William Maitland*, ed. H. A. L. Fisher, 3 vols. (Cambridge, 1911), ii. 110–73 at 146, #83; Brand, *Kings, Barons and Justices*, 65 n. 98.

[121] Their precise wording cannot therefore be taken as a reliable reflection for the earlier date: *Early Registers of Writs*, xxxiv n. 4. Hall notes that the MS was copied after 1259, but that the early actions may follow the form of the 1250s. Also Maitland, 'History of the Register of Original Writs', 141–2.

[122] *Early Registers of Writs*, xviii–xxi. Actions of account are explicitly included as *de cursu* in the Inner Temple Library Edwardian MS 511.9. The listing is printed in *Early Registers of Writs* as App. B (xxvii–xxviii) where writs of 'racionabili compoto' are listed amongst those available 'pro precio ad bancum concedenda'. The later harsher *monstravit* (see next section) is listed under 'breuia que dicuntur esse de precepto et gratia' (xxviii).

legal and administrative change arising from the conciliar government of 1258–61. The action was given a new writ form in the 1259 'new provisions of the Barons' (cap. 19), extant from 1260. The legislation was reissued in 1263–4 (cap. 17); re-endorsed in the Statute of Marlborough in 1267 (cap. 23); and lent a further twist through additional sanctions against bailiffs granted by the Statute of Westminster II in 1285 (cap. 11).[123]

The provisions read out in Westminster Hall on 24 October 1259 followed some eight months of debate, negotiation, drafting, and redrafting between reformist and royalist barons, 'bachelors', and the King. They had increasingly stressed the need for baronial as much as regal reform.[124] Cap. 19 strengthened the legal recourses available to those saddled with unaccountable bailiffs:

> It has also been provided that, if bailiffs who are obliged to render account to their lords flee from them and do not have lands and tenements by which they may be distrained, then they are to be attached by their bodies, so that the sheriffs in whose bailiwicks they are found are to make them come to render their account.[125]

Within the wider drafting process the issue of bailiffs' accountability to their lords first appeared in the draft immediately preceding the final provisions, that is the French draft produced for the Michaelmas 1259 parliament.[126] It did not, significantly, figure in the reform-focused 'Petition of the Barons', drafted for the June 1258 parliament.[127]

The Close Rolls for 1260 duly provide the corresponding text for a 'new writ of account', its name (*monstravit de compoto*) taken as usual from the opening words.

> The king to the better men and sheriffs of London, greetings. Master Michael rector of Ockendon has shown to us [*monstravit nobis*] that since Godfrey of Fornham who recently stood [*extiterit*] as his bailiff in Ockendon, having care and administration for all of his things and goods, the same Godfrey with his account not discharged, seeks through subterfuge [*subterfugia*] to hide in your bailiwick so that he cannot be found, or distrained to render the said account. And because the provision is, by the common counsel of the whole of our kingdom, that if bailiffs who are liable to render account to their masters abscond [*se subtraxerint*] and they lack lands or tenements through which they can be distrained, they are to be attached by their bodies, so that the sheriffs in whose bailiwicks they are found can make them come to render their account— so we order you that if the said master Michael gives you security that the complaint should be taken forward [*fecerit te securum de clamore suo prosequendo*], then you are to ensure the said Godfrey is attached, so that you have his body before you in your court of our City of London for the rendering to the said Michael his aforesaid account, as

---

[123] Brand, *Kings, Barons and Justices*, discussion at 65–6, 312–33, 402–3, texts in appendices I–III for Provisions of Westminster, and the Statute of Marlborough; *SR*, i. 80–1 (cap. 11) for Westminster II.

[124] Brand, *Kings, Barons and Justices*, 15–41; Prestwich, *Plantagenet England*, 104–9.

[125] Text and translation from Brand, *Kings, Barons and Justices*, 424–5; also *DBM* #11 at 146. *Brevia Placitata* includes a note on a post-1267 version of the older writ noting that landless bailiffs may be physically held by the sheriff to force an account (*Brevia Placitata*, cxxxviii–cxxxix, 23 n. 4).

[126] Brand, *Kings, Barons and Justices*, 34–7.   [127] *DBM* #3.

the same Michael can reasonably [*racionabiliter*] show that [Godfrey] ought to render [it] to him, so that we will not hear this plaint a second time. Witness.[128]

The addition of summary imprisonment is a significant legal tightening. The *Mirror of Justices* (1285–9) thought the initial imprisonment sanction should be restricted to a mere summons.[129] Imprisonment as an initial step in the case seems only to have been commonly used for homicide.[130] Another striking aspect is the requirement of *monstravit* that bailiffs be landless. The second Statute of Westminster would take this further in 1285 and in cap. 11 add instant outlawry to the sanctions available against landless, absconding bailiffs.[131] The *Mirror* complained this should be reserved for 'mortal sins' only.[132] This was the law that Edward I alluded to in 1291 when he wrote of 'the complete form of the statute provided for by the common counsel of our kingdom' in the *ex parte* writ regarding John de Valle quoted earlier.

Monstravit de compoto was actively pro-landlord. It presumed in the first place that an account is really due.[133] It summarily empowered a lord's auditors, putting answerable bailiffs at a proportionate disadvantage ('so the evil of auditors goes unpunished').[134] The legislation's revealed preferences were clear to the *Mirror of Justices*, which inveighed against landlords' auditors in its section *De Abusions* (again, the *Mirror of Justices* was one of Andrew Horn's books):

---

[128] *CR 1259-61*, 162. Discussion: Brand, *Kings, Barons and Justices*, 117–18.

[129] *Mirror of Justices*, ed. William Joseph Whittaker, intr. Frederic William Maitland, SS 7 (London, 1895), 184, apropos of the provision in cap. 23 of the Statute of Marlborough. On dating, xxiv. This was Maitland's dating; however a passage relating directly to the action of account (76), states that an absconding bailiff cannot be outlawed. This portion of the treatise therefore seems to predate the 1285 Statute of Westminster II cap. 11. The view is now that Andrew Horn did not write the *Mirror* (Jeremy I. Catto, 'Andrew Horn: Law and History in Fourteenth Century England', in R. H. C. Davis and J. M. Wallace-Hadrill (eds.), with R. J. A. I. Catto and M. H. Keen, *The Writing of History in the Middle Ages: Essays Presented to Richard William Southern* (Oxford, 1981), 373–4). See now on the *Mirror*, Lachaud, *Éthique du pouvoir*, 635–62.

[130] Brand, *Kings, Barons and Justices*, 66. [131] *SR*, i. 80–1.

[132] *Mirror of Justices*, 192–3, apropos of Westminster II cap. 11.

[133] Brand, *Kings, Barons and Justices*, 35. Provision was later made for cases where the action was obtained under false pretences. This seems to be the problem behind the 1230-2 action of account noted in *Bracton's Note Book*. Here Theobald Hautein alleges John of Preston owes him an account for his bailiffship of Mereflet (Yorks). Preston retorts that he owes no such thing since he did not hold land of Hautein but of Adam of Mereflet to whom he accounted and was quit. It was *Adam*, says Preston, who was Hautein's bailiff and liable to him. Case: *CRR 1230-1232*, 189 (#930), 306 (#1442), 430 (#2004); also *Bracton's Note Book*, ed. F. W. Maitland, 3 vols. (London, 1887), ii. 668 #859. Comment: Caenegem, *Royal Writs in England*, 345 n. 4 ('a much noticed action of account'); Pollock and Maitland, *History of English Law*, ii. 221, giving the case as the first extant example of the action of account. The issue concerns who is accountable to whom where there are intermediate and delegated liabilities.

[134] *Mirror of Justices*, 193 on Statute of Westminster II cap. 11. The latter may be an attempt to fine-tune the legislation and regularize auditors' behaviour (as well as increasing the penalties on absconding bailiffs), since it offers bailiffs a recourse for auditors who have unjustly 'oppressed [the bailiff] with goods received which he did not receive, or by refusing him expenses or reasonable costs', *SR*, i. 80, 'conqueratur quod auditores compoti ipsum injuste gravaverunt, onerando de receptis que non recepit, vel non allocando expensas aut liberaciones racionabiles. . .'. Paul Brand argues that *monstravit* did provide some security for bailiffs (personal communication). See also Plucknett, *Mediaeval Bailiff*, 26–7.

86. Abuse it is that auditors are given by the lords to hear accounts, without the assent of bailiffs.
87. Abuse it is that bailiffs cannot recover a thing in damages from criminous auditors.
88. Abuse it is that regard is given to status, since by such law [i.e. actions of account] bailiffs are not allowed to recover debts against their lords, as contrariwise lords can do of them.[135]

Later along the same lines,

123. Abuse it is of the writ of account of *monstravit* whereby someone can imprison another [i.e. a bailiff] wrongly.[136]

The answer to 'Who, whom?' is clear: 'Lords, bailiffs'.

It is striking indeed in these complaints that the auditor himself has become an actor in the action. The *Mirror of Justices* at points leaves it ambiguous whether the lord or auditor unfairly imprisons the bailiff (another example of the head not knowing what the right hand does?). The author clearly has more sympathy for bailiffs than landlords, and so is a useful guide to the aspects of the law that some saw as inequitable.[137] Such complaints of course return us to John de Valle's own case: his complaints against the auditors who have disallowed his reasonable expenses, imprisoned him unfairly, and left him liable for transactions undertaken for his master and mistress (or so he said).

Cap. 19 of the 1259 Provisions sits rather oddly amidst some of the other provisions of Westminster addressing *lords*' accountabilities to *communities*. In particular the Provisions' so-called 'administrative and political resolutions' include the important commitment that the justices in eyre 'should also inquire into the bailiffs of the rich men of the land, and into the rich men themselves'.[138]

There had been much agitation about unaccountable, seigneurial bailiffs—but from communities', not lords' perspectives. The 'administrative' provision tallies directly with the February–March 1259 'Ordinance of the Magnates', which records the barons' explicitly reciprocal commitment to restrain and correct their bailiffs, in so far as Henry III would do so for his officers.[139] The principle of seigneurial bailiffs' accountability had indeed been floated the previous summer at Oxford.[140]

---

[135] *Mirror of Justices*, 164–5.   [136] *Mirror of Justices*, 172.

[137] Maitland detected some 'reactionary' as well as 'curious leanings towards liberty and equality' in the author as well as a persistent critique of royal agents and justices (*Mirror of Justices*, respectively xliii, xxxix, xlvi–xlix).

[138] *DBM* #12 cap. 6 at 150, 'Ausi enquergent des baillifs as riches homes de la terre, e des riches homes memes'. The provisions were not proclaimed at the county courts. For a reconstruction of the drafting process see Brand, *Kings, Barons and Justices*, chs. 1–3, and on this point 38–41; R. F. Treharne, *The Baronial Plan of Reform, 1258–1263*, rev. edn. (Manchester, 1971), 164–9, on this point, 187 n. 1.

[139] *DBM* #10 at 132. For the November 1259 implementation, again making clear that seigneurial *and* regnal agents are under review #13 at 160–2 (caps. 6–8). Henry cancelled the eyre on 5 June 1260 (#27).

[140] *DBM* #5 ('Provisions of Oxford'), 98, providing for four 'discreti et legales' knights who would 'conueniant ad audiendum omnes querelas de quibuscumque transgressionibus et inuiriis quibuscumque personis illatis per uicecomites, balliuos, *seu quoscumque alios*, et ad faciendum tachiamenta que ad dictas querelas pertinent', my stress.

(Valence's steward, William de Bussey experienced it in practice at the end of 1258.)[141] Matthew Paris gives the text of the 1258 inquisition ordered into a whole range of bailiffs and sheriffs—both regal and seigneurial.[142] But the pre-1259 context of actions of account—like cap. 19 in 1259—is one of deficient service or breach of private trust, not one of wider equity or justice. Still one can imagine it being presented otherwise: 'If you want me to stop my bailiffs biting, give me stronger legal leashes to call them to heel.' It is not hard to see cap. 19 of the Provisions being presented by its baronial supporters as a contribution to this general reform of local government—whatever the self-interested ends it happily also provided its baronial advocates. Indeed it looks exactly like the sort of thing Agnes's father William de Valence would have endorsed (although he had fled England in July 1258).

Did barons—or 'land-lords' more generally—need *monstravit de compoto*? Brand argues the clause could have been a proportionate response to an actual problem. He is equally open to the possibility that cap. 19 was not a response to 'a widespread problem but was prompted by just one or two recent instances of landless bailiffs absconding without rendering an account and that it was those instances alone which prompted this general legislation'.[143] The cases Brand himself has unearthed for the 1270s might argue in favour of some 'need' in that period.[144] At least they argue in favour of the enhanced legislation's usefulness to greater land-lords.[145] It is possible too that the subset of extant cases at higher courts covers a greater number of cases at county courts than *curia regis* roll references enable us to see.[146] The latter are conceivably the subset of the most problematic cases that plaintiffs brought to the king's court. Cap. 11 of the Statute of Westminster II itself may offer further proof that *monstravit de compoto* was no accident: why, after all, compound a gratuitous legal penalty by extending it still further?

Bracton, the mid-thirteenth-century legal treatise, states 'there ought to be a remedy for every wrong; if some new wrong be perpetrated, then a new writ may be invented to meet it'.[147] Maitland's version of the same principle has been quoted—'legal ideas never reach very far beyond practical needs'.[148] These axioms, it is true, imply that legal innovation is usually a proportionate response

---

[141] Hershey, 'Rise and Fall of William de Bussey', 113–18.
[142] *Chronica majora* vi. 397–400, e.g. opening clause and 399, 'de vicecomitibus [. . .] et de omnibus ballivis quicunque fuerint'.
[143] Brand, *Kings, Barons and Justices*, 66. Legislation did develop like this, cf. Prestwich, *Edward I*, 270.
[144] A problem in deciding this will always be that land-lords, like bankers, routinely feel that the regulatory regime under which they operate is insufficiently supportive.
[145] Examples: Brand, *Kings, Barons and Justices*, 314. It should be remembered that lesser landlords continued to have recourse to the old action of account.
[146] Brand, *Kings, Barons and Justices*, 65; *Early Registers of Writs*, xlii; Plucknett, *Mediaeval Bailiff*, 23; *Brevia Placitata*, lvii–lix, lxiv–lxv.
[147] Cited in *Early Registers of Writs*, xii, but I cannot find the quote in *Bracton* at fo. 413^b as cited. The closest match I do find on this folio is: 'quia tot erunt formulae brevium quot sunt genera actionum, quia non potest quis sine brevi agere'. *Bracton on the Laws and Customs of England*, ed. George E. Woodbine, rev. S. E. Thorne, 4 vols. (Cambridge, Mass., 1977), iv. 286. See also fo. 111^b.
[148] Frederic William Maitland, *Township and Borough* (Cambridge, 1898), 27.

to objectively demonstrable needs. That argument is wrong absolutely speaking (extraordinary rendition and *Bleak House*'s Chancery would be inconceivable). The analysis above has argued for the existence of practices, norms, and rules for holding bailiffs to account some time before the 1259 legislation was passed. Perhaps this implies 'needs must'—at least up to a point. Perhaps *monstravit de compoto* was the timely and reasonable response to an acute or worsened problem. But if the 1259 legislation is not accidental (nor, by extension, that of 1285), what could such legislation be a function of, and what might it signify?

THE 'POLITICAL ECONOMY' OF THE ACTION OF ACCOUNT

'Cases have two histories: the first is the story of the decision itself, as a single event, and the other is the story of its legal effect, of its transmission and reception.'[149] 'Why it exists' could be added when asking whether changes in legal ideas follow social change. What then were any practical needs—social, economic, and/or political—that produced the political thinking that the action of account expressed when it sought to address manorial officers', or at least 'bailiffs' accountability? In many ways the dimensions of the question can be read off the contours of the action itself. The action of account is concerned with the quality of the lord–bailiff bond (a bailiff will not account/has absconded); with legal jurisdictions (where is the bailiff to be held to account, especially if he is no longer in the county?); and bailiffs' mobility and remuneration (by definition actions of account that deal with landless bailiffs are dealing with bailiffs whose link to their lord is contractual not tenurial). What role, if any, do those distinctive features of English agriculture play—demesne farming, sophisticated records of manorial accounting, and an unusual English literature on estate management—and is politics as coincidental as the hypothesis in the previous section about cap. 19 of the Provisions of Westminster implies? In the final section of this chapter I argue that we have enough evidence to argue for a line of connection threading them all.

Bailiffs' Accountability and Demesne Farming

Over forty years ago Dorothea Oschinsky suggested there was a direct causal connection between: (*a*) the Statute of Westminster II, cap. 11; (*b*) the English intensification of demesne farming (i.e. direct cultivation of land by its lord and his immediate agents); (*c*) a marked sophistication of English manorial accounting technique from the second half of the thirteenth century; and (*d*) the production of a sophisticated if short-lived practical English literature addressing in French or Latin the management of both officials and land, most of whose earliest

---

[149] Baker, *Why the History of English Law has not been Finished*, 23.

manuscripts date from c.1300.[150] Paul Harvey argued that there were chronological problems with Oschinsky's argument.[151] Westminster II cap. 11 (1285) happened later than some of the phenomena it was supposed to cause. A shift to demesne farming can be first documented from 1184, moving most quickly on lay estates, but still slow and concentrated in the Midlands and southern and eastern England.[152] Harvey has been sceptical of any in-principle link between demesne farming, more sophisticated accounting, and then the literature of estate management.[153] Furthermore the later type of manorial accounts that Harvey has christened 'phase 2' (see pp. 70–6) are a phenomenon of the 1250s on.[154] Oschinsky's analysis of the estate management literature can also be modified— but so as to push it earlier and therefore closer to the other phenomena she wished to connect it with.

These English mid-thirteenth- to mid-fourteenth-century texts are well known.[155] The earliest are the 1245 x 1253 French *Rules* of Robert Grosseteste, a private work for Margaret de Lacy, the widowed Countess of Lincoln.[156] The shorter Latin version,

---

[150] *Walter of Henley*, 72–4, 144–5, and her preparatory articles 'Notes on the Editing and Interpretation of Estate Accounts', pts. 1 and 2 in *Archives* 9 (1969–70), 84–9 and 142–52 at 149.

[151] P. D. A. Harvey, 'Agricultural Treatises and Manorial Accounting in Medieval England', *Agricultural History Review* 20 (1972), 170–82 at 179–80. Agriculture and law are both discussed in C. Noke, 'Agency and the Excessus balance in Manorial Accounts', in R. H. Parke and B. S. Yamey (eds.), *Accounting History: Some British Contributions* (Oxford, 1994), 139–59 at 152–5 and Plucknett, *Mediaeval Bailiff*. Noke though is interested in the applicability of modern management theory about principals and agents to medieval accounting. Plucknett discusses both the action of account and the manorial manuals but does not really ask about their relationship.

[152] P. D. A. Harvey, 'The Pipe Rolls and the Adoption of Desmesne Farming in England', *Economic History Review* NS 27 (1974), 345–59 at 353–4; for distribution, Christopher Dyer, *Making a Living in the Middle Ages: The People of Britain 850–1520* (London, 2003), 137; for comments on the institutional/social features of seigneurial agriculture see B. M. S. Campbell, *English Seignorial Agriculture, 1250–1450*, Cambridge Studies in Historical Geography 31 (Cambridge, 2000), 419–24. More work on the relationship between politics, agriculture, and law would be valuable.

[153] Harvey, 'Agricultural Treatises and Manorial Accounting', 179–80.

[154] *Manorial Records of Cuxham, Oxfordshire, circa 1200–1359*, ed. P. D. A. Harvey, Oxfordshire Record Society 50/Historical Manuscripts Commission Joint Publications 23 (London, 1976), 17–18, noting all such pre-1250 accounts are from large secular and religious estates.

[155] Oschinsky's *Walter of Henley* replaced *Walter of Henley's Husbandry together with an anonymous Husbandry, Seneschaucie and Robert Grosseteste's Rules*, ed. Elizabeth Lamond (London, 1890). Oschinsky argued for the early fourteenth century as the highpoint of the treatises' use and therefore for the immediately prior period as the significant one in causing that literature (*Walter of Henley*, 72–3). Harvey discussed the risks with Oschinksy's dating very clearly in 'Agricultural Treatises and Manorial Accounting', 172–5. Oschinksy's own datings range from 1235 to 1276 with *Walter of Henley* the latest, dated to c.1286. But if Westminster II is a cause of change many key texts are being written significantly sooner than they should be. Oschinsky's sequence for the 'non-accounting' treatises is: 'private' Latin *Statuta* of Robert Grosseteste 1235–42; French *Rules* version for the Countess of Lincoln 1240–2 and *its* Latin version 1240–53 (but see following note); *Seneschauncy* c.1260–76; *Walter of Henley*, a commentary on *Seneschauncy*, c.1276 x c.1290 possibly 1286. See respectively *Walter of Henley*, 196–7, 88–9, 76–82, and 144–5.

[156] Dating of Grosseteste's (French) *Rules* has recently been resolved by Louise Wilkinson. Wilkinson and Michael Burger, while endorsing Grosseteste's authorship, challenged Oschinsky's 1240–2 dating. Burger argues that if the *Rules* need to be allocated to an unmarried (or even widowed) Countess of Lincoln during Grosseteste's episcopate, Margaret de Quincy/Lacy is not the only possible option (his 'The Date and Authorship of Robert Grosseteste's *Rules*', *Historical Research* 74 (2001), 106–16, esp. at 108–11). If accepted, the *Rules* date to 1235–53. Wilkinson ingeniously adds that Grosseteste's reference to shopping in Caversham (obtained through the Marshal marriage) specifically

Statuta, is a roughly contemporary summary. The *Rules* instruct the Countess in the good management of her estates. *Seneschauncy* is a French manual on the 'management and improvement of manors which are entrusted to stewards and bailiffs' and describes a series of subordinate manorial offices, probably dating to *c*.1260. *Walter of Henley* is a French treatise, in a sermon form, 'spoken' by a father to his son, advising him on the good management of his farms, stock, and servants. *Walter* is dependent on *Seneschauncy*'s pattern and datable perhaps to *c*.1262–*c*.1272. Most recensions have adapted it to emphasize its textbook elements.[157] In the cartulary of St Peter's Gloucester are the Latin rules of conduct to be read out monthly by the reeve, recorded during John of Gamages's abbacy, 1284–1301.[158] The underlying text is a more general manual but this version is possibly a response to the critical visitation by Archbishop Winchelsey on 27 July 1301.[159] There are also the *c*.1350 French notes on the supervision of the grange in the Mohun Cartulary.[160] More informal sets of instructions survive in letters.[161]

In addition a large number of accounting manuals are extant, giving guidance on how to account, specimen forms, and instructions on procedure and problems.[162] *Husbandry* is arguably better associated with these texts than the estate management ones since it is for manorial auditors, outlining, in French,

---

pins the treatise to de Lacy's second widowhood following Walter Marshal's 1245 death and before Grosseteste's in 1253. See Louise J. Wilkinson, 'The *Rules* of Robert Grosseteste Reconsidered: The Lady as Estate and Household Manager in Thirteenth Century England', in Cordelia Beattie et al. (eds.), *The Medieval Household in Christian Europe, c.850–c.1550* (Turnhout, 2003), 294–306, esp. 299–300, also Wilkinson, *Women in Thirteenth-Century Lincolnshire*, Royal Historical Society Studies in History NS (Woodbridge, 2007), 58–64, and 51 for de Lacy's contacts with the court in the 1250s.

[157] The earliest version closest to the projected original of *Walter*, according to Oschinsky, is CUL MS Dd.VII.14 (= 'Oschinsky' MS 42), *Walter of Henley*, 121–2; Harvey's dating, 'Agricultural Treatises and Manorial Accounting', 173–4.

[158] TNA C 150/1, fos. 326ᵛ–330ᵛ (modern foliation); *Historia et cartularium monasterii Sancti Petri Gloucestriae*, ed. William Henry Hart, RS, 3 vols. (London, 1863–7), iii. 213–21; discussion at xciii–c. The manual occupies the end of a gathering and follows a description of manors, the last being of Cubberley. It is followed on the same gathering by another text on accountability; a description of how to take the view of frankpledge. Various items of a later hand follow in this gathering. The cartulary also contains an extension of Winchelsey's injunctions at fos. 285ᵛ–287ʳ: rubric, 'Constitutio quedam necessaria super peccunia commune, et aliis rebus' beg. 'Nulla pecunia de cetero spectans', ends 'assisa ad panem veniat certis diebus ad pistrinum' (Hart's edn., iii. 105–8).

[159] *Registrum Roberti Winchelsey, Cantuariensis Archiepiscopi, A.D. 1294–1313*, ed. Rose Graham, C&Y 51–2, 2 vols. (1952–6), ii. 856–64 (Winchelsey's injunctions 28 July 1301); *The Victoria History, of the County of Gloucester* 2, ed. William Page (London, 1907), 55–6. Oschinsky's references, *Walter of Henley*, 241, 254–7; Harvey, 'Agricultural Treatises and Manorial Accounting', 177.

[160] BL Egerton MS 3724, fos. 19–20ʳ and 39ʳ–40ᵛ, 'En sa veillesce set li prudhom', a poem of instruction drawing on caps. 1–5, 12–16 of *Walter of Henley*. The grange treatise is edited in *Walter of Henley*, 475–8.

[161] e.g. *Registrum Thome de Cantilupo, Episcopi Herefordensis, A.D. 1275–1282*, ed. R. G. Griffiths and W. W. Capes, C&Y 2 (London, 1907), 108–11 with numerous concrete recommendations for minimizing corruption (18 November ?1276).

[162] Oschinsky lists thirty-six such manuscripts (*Walter of Henley*, 235–57). Harvey listed seven additional accounting treatises in 'Agricultural Treatises and Manorial Accounting', 178–9. All these are in English collections. A French variant of the St Peter's treatise is in BNF MS Fr. 400 (Harvey, 'Agricultural Treatises and Manorial Accounting', 177 n. 4). See also *Legal and Manorial Formularies, Edited from Originals at the British Museum and the Public Record Office in Memory of Julius Parnell Gilson* (Oxford, 1933).

'headings regarding the rendering of accounts and likewise headings of things upon which an account should be charged'.[163] Possibly of Kentish origin, its dating is less certain; Oschinsky put it at *c*.1300.[164]

As to the relations between these phenomena Harvey is sceptical of estate officers' legal interest or competence—at least officials who are not stewards with responsibility for a great lord's aggregated estates. Harvey instead focuses on why *landlords* would need to have legally competent manorial officials, rather than on what the benefits of legal competence would be for *bailiffs* themselves.[165] (It is of course a complicating feature of the law that a 'bailiff' might only be so legally, not in terms of manorial duties.) Harvey has also argued for a shift over the second half of the thirteenth century *from* more centralized supervision of estates *to* a more decentralied supervision—a tendency seemingly opposed to the simultaneous trend charted here of an tighter legal grip by land-lords over bailiffs.[166] Notwithstanding the problems, it is a very great merit of Oschinsky's approach that she considered the connections between these phenomena.

Early Prescriptive Texts on Estate Management and *la moralisation de l'administration*

The issue is where to go from there. It should be said immediately that the thirteenth century is not needed to initiate a tradition in England of reflective, practical, and—sometimes—moralistic thinking about estate management and the conduct and control of manorial officers. The so-called *Institutes of Polity*, a text composed from 1008 by Archbishop Wulfstan of York (d. 1023) comprises prescriptive reflections addressed to different social groups (*ad status*, as later medievalists would say) to offer a 'programme for a Christian society'.[167] One group is

---

[163] 'Articuli de compoto reddendo et similiter de articulis super quibus compotus debet carcari', title to the best copy of *Husbandry*—in Bod. Ashmole MS 1524 (SC 8232), fos. 127ᵛ–132ʳ (cf. *Walter of Henley*, 44–5, 247, for 'Oschinsky MS 69'). This copy is preceded by a *Modus ordinandi compotum alicuius prepositi* (fos. 126ʳ–127ʳ) and followed by an *Extenta manerii* (fos. 132ʳ–133ʳ), instructions *De homagio et fidelitate* (fo. 133), and *Walter* fragment (fos. 133ᵛ–134ᵛ).

[164] *Walter of Henley*, 200–1; Harvey, 'Agricultural Treatises and Manorial Accounting', 172.

[165] Harvey, 'Agricultural Treatises and Manorial Accounting', 175–6. Cf. Oschinsky on the content of manorial officials' professional instruction, *Walter of Henley*, 61–72, 233–4, and Plucknett, *Mediaeval Bailiff*, 8–15. For recent work underscoring the legal competence of *stewards* see Brand, 'Stewards, Bailiffs and the Emerging Legal Profession' with notices on the manorial treatises at 148–50, and David Crook, 'Freedom, Villeinage and Legal Process: The Dispute between the Abbot of Burton and his Tenants of Mickleover, 1280', *Nottingham Medieval Studies* 44 (2000), 123–40.

[166] Harvey's view that 'phase 2' accounts implies more decentralised lordly control and greater latitude on the part of the local agent has critics. See reviews of Harvey's *Manorial Records* and *Manorial Records of Cuxham*, by Christoper Dyer (*Economic History Review* NS 38 (1985), 448), and Ian Kershaw (*EHR* 93 (1978), 862–4 at 863–4). Edmund King ('Estate Management and the Reform Movement', in W. M. Ormrod (ed.), *England in the Thirteenth Century: Proceedings of the 1989 Harlaxton Symposium*, Harlaxton Medieval Studies 1 (Stamford, 1991), 1–14 at 9–10) is important. See pp. 76–82.

[167] Patrick Wormald, *The Making of English Law: King Alfred to the Twelfth Century*, i.*Legislation and its Limits* (Oxford, 1999), 197, see also 394, 458–65, and dating the first version of the *Institutes* 1008–14, 458 n. 153). It is an important part of Wormald's wider argument that law and theology are

reeves (*gerefan*).[168] Initially considered along with earls (*eorlum*) Wulfstan asserts that all must 'love what is right in front of God and the world and nowhere neglect their wisdom through injustice, either for gain or friendship'.[169] The section on reeves themselves begins with the basic precept: 'Right it is that reeves work vigorously and constantly profit their lords with right.'[170] What this means in practice is not expanded—the remainder of the chapter is a lament that since Edgar's death (975) reeves have been 'robbers who should be herdsmen of Christian folk'.[171] They have done worst who should know best, but, beyond the important recognition of reeves' place within England's political-eschatological future, there is nothing specific to reeves per se. Two pre-Conquest tracts are more specific on manorial duties: *Rectitudines singularum personarum* ('Duties of individuals', possibly mid-tenth century, connected possibly with Bath Abbey, possibly the crown), and *Bege sceadwisan gerefan* ('On the canny reeve') known as *Gerefa* and late tenth/ early eleventh century.[172] What is most interesting about *Rectitudines*, the more functionally detailed treatise, is that it is in the 'voice' of an over-reeve (*ealdorman*), advising others about estate expectations and impositions.[173] It seems quite distinct from Carolingian capitularies, 'concerned with higher levels of oversight'.[174] More striking still is the sensitivity these over-reeves are encouraged to display. *Rectitudines* runs through functional categories and establishes norms ('the taxable swineherd ought to pay...') while also stressing that these norms must flex with the estate's customs:

> All estate customs are not alike. On some estates a tenant must pay tax in honey, on some tax in food, on some tax in ale. He who looks after the administration is to take

---

deeply connected in such texts—see 333 for a comment on the 'reluctance—or inability—to distinguish the status of law-code and homily', apropos the running together in Corpus Christi Cambridge MS 201 of the law-code Æthelred 'V' and the *Institutes of Polity*.

[168] *Die «Institutes of polity, civil and ecclesiastical»: ein Werk Erzbischof Wulfstans von York*, ed. and trans. (into German) Karl Jost, Schweizer Anglistische Arbeiten 47 (Berne, 1959). An English trans. of the second version is in *Anglo-Saxon Prose*, trans. Michael Swanton, rev. edn. (London, 1993), 187–201. The versions have a complex manuscript history. In Jost's edition 'I. Polity' refers to the earlier version; 'II. Polity' the later.

[169] «*Institutes of polity*», ed. Jost (II) cap. IX, §85 at 78.
[170] «*Institutes of polity*», ed. Jost (II) cap. X, §94 at 81.
[171] «*Institutes of polity*», ed. Jost (II) cap. X, §95 at 81.
[172] On dating and explication see P. D. A. Harvey, '*Rectitudines Singularum Personarum* and *Gerefa*', *EHR* 426 (1993), 1–22, and for dating 7, 11, 17–19; Wormald, *Making of English Law*, 232–3, 387–9; *Charters of Bath and Wells*, ed. S. E. Kelly, Anglo-Saxon Charters, 13 (Oxford, 2007), #24 ('Sawyer', §1555) at 150. Both treatises are translated as 'two estate memoranda' in *Anglo-Saxon Prose*, trans. Swanton, 26–33. Kelly argues that a royal official is as likely an author as a Bath reeve given the estate's royal connections, but the references to royal obligations in the text imply to me that the king is a different person from the estate's lord (*Anglo-Saxon Prose*, trans. Swanton, 26, 27).

[173] *Anglo-Saxon Prose*, trans. Swanton, 28, 29 (*Rectitudines*). Harvey argues this usage of *ealdorman* suggests an earlier dating given that it only occurs elsewhere in this context in Alfred's translation of Bede, Harvey, '*Rectitudines Singularum Personarum* and *Gerefa*', 18–19. Harvey and others see the first person singular as the sign of a reviser, 17 n. 1).

[174] Harvey, '*Rectitudines Singularum Personarum* and *Gerefa*', 20. Aside from capitularies, cf. Hincmar of Reims, *De ordine palatii*, ed. Thomas Gross and Rudolf Schieffer, MGH Leges, Fontes iuris germanici antiqui 3 (Hannover, 1980); Rosamund McKitterick, *Charlemagne: The Formation of a European Identity* (Cambridge, 2008), 142–8.

care that he always knows what is the ancient arrangement on the estate, and what the custom of the people.[175]

Having run through the different tasks/people, the text closes by reiterating this need for discrimination:

> As I said before, estate laws are various. Nor do we apply these regulations, which we have previously spoken about, in all districts. But we tell what the custom is where it is known to us. If we learn better, we will readily delight in and maintain it, according to the custom of the people among whom we then live. Wherefore one must learn the laws in the district lovingly, if one does not wish to lose good opinion on the estate.[176]

A concern with one's professional standing ('profession' seems justified); an awareness that simple autocracy is managerially inadequate; the need for local knowledge—such an approach is readily comprehensible, yet we may still be struck by the sophistication of management, instruction, and knowledge-sharing implied. The sophistication is comparable to that of Robert Grosseteste's *Rules*, addressed to the landlady's perspective, some 240–300 years later:

> When your bailiffs and the servants of your lands and manors come before you address them well and speak pleasantly to them, ask them discreetly and gently how your men are doing, how the corn stands, about the progress of your ploughs and your stock. Make these enquiries openly and your knowledge shall be much respected.[177]

The tone may be more courteous, but a comparable balance between rigour and responsiveness is sought.

Gerefa by contrast (perhaps written by a colleague of Wulfstan's) has generally been seen as less 'practical' because more 'literary'.[178] It is true that beyond its itemized shopping list of desirable tools and equipment it sticks to general principles of managing people. But what it says on this count seems no less practical than what the *Rules* or *Walter of Henley* or *Rectitudines* have to offer. If *Gerefa* is influenced by a reading of Cato or Columella, as Harvey has argued, that seems in itself no reason to discount some perfectly sensible insights into effective estate management. So the reeve

> should never allow his servants to over-rule him, but he is to command each one with the authority of the lord according to the rights of the people; it is better for him to be forever out of office than in, if those whom he should govern can govern him; it is not prudent for a lord to allow that.[179]

An analysis of these early prescriptive texts perhaps offers ways to soften two important interpretations. One is the tendency—implicit at least—to presume that administration only becomes 'moralized' in the later twelfth and certainly in the thirteenth century (after a supposed Carolingian false start). Certainly there are later

---

[175] *Anglo-Saxon Prose*, trans. Swanton, 28 (*Rectitudines*).
[176] *Anglo-Saxon Prose*, trans. Swanton, 30 (*Rectitudines*).
[177] *Rules*, cap. 27, *Walter of Henley*, 406 (Oschinsky's trans.). Cf. also the lady's speech to her 'haut seneschal devaunt aucun de ses bons amis' in cap. 3.
[178] Harvey, '*Rectitudines Singularum Personarum* and *Gerefa*', 12; Wormald, *Making of English Law*, 389.
[179] *Anglo-Saxon Prose*, trans. Swanton, 31 (*Gerefa*).

highly significant royal actions expressing the 'moralisation de l'administration'—as with Louis IX's 1254 *ordonnances* on local administrators.[180] But in terms of the quality of their moral concern it is hard to perceive much difference between a Wulfstan and a Louis IX. The difference must lie elsewhere—perhaps quantitative, perhaps administratively technical. Secondly, *Rectitudines*' emphasis on exercising discrimination and respecting local custom and dues may imply that we should not overemphasize the static, descriptive, imposed nature of early surveys.[181] This is *not* to presume such sensitivity to local customs is by any means normal. It *is* to argue that the practice behind the parchment may be more pliable than we can perceive, as Harvey has argued about much later manorial accounts. They are 'virtually a dialogue, a debate between local officials and auditors'; 'the purpose of a manorial account was to establish the state of reckoning between lord and local official: we should never take for granted that it records what really happened on the manor'.[182] Accounts were negotiated. Can the same principle hold earlier? If dues have been specified, there may yet be some flexibility in negotiating or exacting them.[183]

It is possible that this can be seen in an arguably contemporaneous Anglo-Saxon survey of Tidenham, which may be an 'application' of *Rectitudines* (whose vocabulary implies Somerset).[184] There is a hint that labour dues there are notable ('From Tidenham much labour is due'), implying a sense of wider norms to measure them against—which *Rectitudines* would provide.[185] In both texts the *geneat* tenant is obligated to ride, provide horse-service (*auerian* is attested only in these two texts), and give carrying service.[186] *Rectitudines* says that a *gebur*'s services vary, and indeed those specified at Tidenham do not precisely match *Rectitudines*. At Tidenham he gives 6*d*. and half a jar of honey at Easter; six jars of malt at Lammas; a ball of 'good net yarn' at Martinmas. In *Rectitudines* at Easter a young sheep or 2*d*. is due; at Martinmas twenty-three jars of barley and two hens; no Martinmas levy is specified but 10*d*. is due at Michaelmas about which Tidenham says nothing. It is hard to prove, and any argument for *Rectitudines*'s 'flexible' approach being applied at Tidenham may simply reflect that the Tidenham survey has less, not more, connection with *Rectitudines*. No clinching argument is available—but it is possible that precepts similar to *Rectitudines*'s were applied at Tidenham.

---

[180] The phrase is Jacques Le Goff's, *Saint Louis* (Paris, 1996), 218, with usage by Laure Verdon, 'Le Roi, la loi, l'enquête et l'officier: procédure et enquêteurs en Provence sous le règne de Charles II (1285–1309)', in Claude Gauvard (ed.), *L'Enquête au Moyen Âge*, École française de Rome (Rome, 2008), 319–29 at 328–9; Lachaud, *Éthique du pouvoir*, 412–13.

[181] Cf. Thomas N. Bisson, *Crisis of the Twelfth Century: Power, Lordship, and the Origins of European Government* (Princeton, NJ, 2009), 325–9.

[182] Harvey, *Manorial Records*, 33, 34.

[183] This would also soften Bisson's contrast between earlier prescriptive accounts and later twelfth/thirteenth-century ones in *Crisis*.

[184] *Charters of Bath and Wells*, ed. Kelly, #24. Kelly is sceptical of a Bath Abbey and *Rectitudines*' connection. I cannot judge Wormald's claims for the Somerset dialect (*Making of English Law*, 233). See also Wormald's Appendix to 'Archbishop Wulfstan and the Holiness of Society', in Wormald, *Legal Culture in the Early Medieval West. Law as Text, Image and Experience* (London, 1999), 225–51.

[185] *Charters of Bath and Wells*, ed. Kelly, #24 at 148, her translation.

[186] *Charters of Bath and Wells*, ed. Kelly, #24 at 147; *Anglo-Saxon Prose*, trans. Swanton, 27.

Looking at these mid-tenth/eleventh-century texts the development of a sophisticated 'functional' and 'normative' literature for manorial agents seems neither an intrinsically royal nor necessarily twelfth- or thirteenth-century story. It suggests some general tradition of thinking about effective estate management. That may imply this tradition can be at most a precondition, not cause, of later developments around accounting and bailiffs' legal accountability. Perhaps it could soften sharp lines in a story about a post-Carolingian 'evolution from patrimonial exploitation to public administration', at least as a general rule.[187] Wulfstan did not see a contradiction between the two—just as Grosseteste would be as sharp on good management as fair management. Stephen Baxter has suggested that Wulfstan saw it as his religious duty to 'exploit' God's property, to make it as productive as it should be—and that he did.[188] It is true that a prelate has different values to call on when justifying productive ecclesiastical estate management ('*Deus lo vult!*') than a seigneurial lord may ('I want it!'). But even in a post-Carolingian, pre-twelfth-century renaissance England we can see practical 'managerial' concerns arising from a moral obligation to give a lord—divine or human—his economically expressed due.

The point is that thinking in England about estate management and officers' conduct was sophisticated—both practically and morally—from an early date. There is also a case that estate surveys may be more flexible than they seem at even that early date. What the sources just analysed do *not* clearly express is a particular idea of how any estate officers should be held to account. These texts seem concerned with responsibilities before accountability. *Rectitudines* is focused on the estate agents whom reeves supervise, so it is unsurprising it says nothing of the reeve's own liabilities. The implicit means of controlling estate officers in *Rectitudines* is simply direct supervision. Wulfstan's *Institutes of Polity* explicitly decries reeves' abuses. Its solution, however, is simply the character-improving one of more prayer and repentance. In Michael Clanchy's terms, love (affective self-regulation) not law (imposed direction) is the preferable order.[189] But conscience, love, is what has already failed on the *Institutes*' own account. Likewise the Wulfstan-influenced *Gerefa* says the reeve 'is to take care that he protect and promote everything according to what is best' for the estate. But it does not say what to do if the reeve is not just canny but crafty and corrupt. If agents' responsibility is lacking these texts do not offer a solution beyond 'more responsibility'.[190] My suggestion in the final part of this chapter is that a difference between these earlier and later texts—a difference between a Wulfstan, a Louis IX, or a Grosseteste so to speak—is that later texts *are* more preoccupied with the

---

[187] The evolution that Thomas Bisson has argued for in Catalonia 1151–1213: Bisson, *Fiscal Accounts of Catalonia under the Early Count-Kings (1151–1213)*, 2 vols. (Berkeley, Calif., 1984), i. 151–8.
[188] Stephen Baxter, 'Archbishop Wulfstan and the Administration of God's Property', in *Wulfstan, Archbishop of York: The Proceedings of the Second Alcuin Conference*, ed. Matthew Townend, Studies in the Early Middle Ages 10 (Turnhout, 2004), 161–205, esp. 162–5, 176, 186–90.
[189] Clanchy, 'Law and Love'.
[190] On the reluctance to acknowledge structural conflicts of interest and the preference for solutions based on hopes wagered on 'good character' see Dunbabin, 'Aristotle in the Schools', 69; Susan Reynolds, *Kingdoms and Communities in Western Europe, 900–1300*, 2nd edn. (Oxford, 1997), 189.

accountability, as distinct from the responsibility, of a lord's men, and that this preoccupation is a function of a partially changed political economy.

Tenure, Law, Accounts: The Political Economy of Bailiffs

The question then is what produces changes in a bailiff's accountability—as expressed in the action of account. The argument has numerous threads so it is useful to summarize. The first two parts of this chapter argued that fragmentary elements of the later action of account are visible in the twelfth century. They also suggested that the later thirteenth century's high formalization of a procedure was arguably meaningful, not just a coincidental function of well-placed barons whom the legislation served. The first part of this third section accepted the argument that demesne farming did not drive the legal changes, even when the elements of the action of account can be dated considerably earlier than Oschinsky argued (and so closer to the start of demesne farming). It then argued for an extension of English estate management literature to well before the twelfth century, but noted that while this literature is, in some ways, as sophisticated as its more famous thirteenth-century analogues, the earlier literature was principally interested in estate officers' responsibilities, not their accountability. That interest continued into the period focused on here, but it was modified by new sorts of focus on officials' accountability (as seen in the action of account). Oschinsky was right to put demesne farming and a 'practical' or 'moral' estate management literature into the same sequence with bailiffs' accounts and accountability, but demesne farming may have been a necessary not sufficient condition for changes in bailiffs' and stewards' accountability.

Connections in the Minds of Contemporaries

A late legal text connected some of these phenomena, as Oschinsky noted.[191] Around 1290–1300, a sometime resident of the Fleet prison in London compiled a large legal handbook that both revised and enhanced *Bracton's* earlier treatise and included much other material, including from the manorial manuals *Seneschaucy* (for stewards) and *Husbandry* (for the lord's manorial auditors). This intentionally practical handbook dealt with charters and statutes; personal, criminal, real, and mixed actions; and other administrative material. It could be called *Fleta*, its author suggested, after its place of composition.[192]

Book 2 of *Fleta* deals with civil personal actions and runs through (amongst other things) descriptions of different types of court (caps. 1–3), household officers of the king's court, the Exchequer and its officers (caps. 4–33), aspects of the Common

---

[191] *Walter of Henley*, 73.
[192] *Fleta*, ed. H. G. Richardson and G. O. Sayles, 3 vols. SS 72, 89, 99 (1955–84), ii. 3. This edition remains incomplete since vol. i, an introduction, notes, and indices, was never published. Volume ii contains the prologue and books 1–2 of the treatise, vol. iii books 3–4, vol. iv books 5–6. The medieval author's hope that readers would augment the text by correcting their own copies went apparently unfulfilled. It survives in only BL Cotton MS Julius B.viii. Some passages are also to be found in Cotton MS Nero D.vi. See David J. Seipp, 'Fleta (*fl.* 1290–1300)', *ODNB*.

Bench (caps. 34–9), forest law (caps. 39–40), and *mesne* processes (cap. 50). The discussion circles around various legal questions arising from contractual and quasi-contractual problems such as debt (caps. 56–64), then focuses for several chapters on how to deal with sheriffs' wrongdoings (caps. 67–9). From here it associatively moves on to the wrongdoings of bailiffs and the idea of debt caught up in their transgressions and works through the various writs of account associated with bailiffs (cap. 70). Book 2 then makes one final pivot and turns to address questions of manorial and agricultural management in general, profit, and how to get the most out of various manorial servants, ranging from dairymaids to auditors (caps. 71–88).

Fleta thus associates the action of account and the agricultural developments of the second half of the thirteenth century. But *Fleta* comes long after the action of account has tried to bolt the door behind the absconding bailiff. *Fleta* is too late to prove any early causal relationship between these things.

One very early text, however, suggesting a causal connection between these phenomena in contemporaries' minds, is the so-called *Leges Henrici Primi* (before *c*.1108). As noted (p. 41), it has been convincingly argued that the *Leges Henrici Primi* is not a hopeless jumble, but a text produced by a hundred bailiff relating to hundred and other local courts. It remained a 'live' text consulted and used in the twelfth century (hence the cross-purpose interpolations and rubrics that have encouraged readers to reckon it an amateurish mess). So understood the *Leges Henrici Primi*'s coherence is apparent.[193]

If the *Leges Henrici Primi* is a 'live' early twelfth-century text related to hundred and seigneurial courts (therefore addressing courts that *Glanvill* does not), its considered comments in cap. 56. 1–7 on lord–lease-farmer–*prepositus* relationships are especially interesting.[194] This section discusses what to do when a dispute arises (*controuersia oriatur*) 'between someone and his lease-farmer who is not also his man' (*inter aliquem et firmarium suum quo non etiam sit homo suus*). 'Not his man' seems to mean that he does not 'have the lease-farm as a fee *and* that he has not done homage for it, whether he resides there or not' (emphasis added).[195] At least, this is the sort of the person the *Leges* immediately discuss in contradistinction to the *homo* just discussed. In case of a dispute a person with a fee and in homage will simply satisfy (*satisfaciat*) his lord on any dispute in the lord's court (*curia domini*).[196] For the lease-farmer *without* homage any dispute 'will be dealt with on that manor'— presumably the manor court (*sit in ipso manerio*). These are passages concerned with clarifying where and how disputes are settled, and what lease-farmers' liabilities are to their lord or landlord. It is notable that immediately after this discussion the *Leges* offers an itemized audit list of what should be evaluated when the manor is 'returned' (*in redditione*). Attention then shifts to complaints about the reeve. The reeve may

---

[193] Karn, 'Rethinking the *Leges Henrici Primi*'.
[194] Even disposing of the rubric 'De firma tenenda', 'cap. 56' retains its coherence. See Karn, 'Rethinking the *Leges Henrici Primi*', 200–4, 211–14.
[195] *LHP*, cap. 56.2. On homage by free men for property see Susan Reynolds, *Fiefs and Vassals: The Medieval Evidence Reinterpreted* (Oxford, 1994), 370–3.
[196] For terms, Reynolds, *Fiefs and Vassals*, 323–4, 353–8.

have damaged the tenancy and the lessee wish to accuse him at this end-of-lease inquiry (remember Robert of Chilton):

> If someone should complain that the reeve has taken something from him injuriously, he should be heard in that same manor or in his lord's court, just as a reeve should reply to his subjects [*subditis suis*]. If he has resigned his reeveship and is with another lord, whoever will speak in this way about the reeve [i.e. accuse him] will come to the reeve's [current] hundred court.[197]

The logic of the sequence is: lord–tenant relationships → disputes and liabilities between lords and tenants and the relevant courts → accounts and inquiries into leased farms at the end of lease → complaints about reeves → what to do with retrospective complaints when the reeve has moved on and is no longer liable to the lord under whom he committed the offences. There is a lively interest in the problems of getting tenants (including those who have not done homage) to account for their management of lease-land and its state on return. Associated with this is a concern with the accountability of a *prepositus* and the problems of pinning him in a court when his office may have expired and he is serving under another lord.[198] In the early twelfth century the *Leges Henrici Primi* are worried about how to get tenants to account for the state of land at lease. They even offer a sketch of the inquiry that should follow at the end of a lease (see p. 70). With this they connect the question of the *prepositus*'s accountability and the problem his mobility poses for his legal liability. There is no action of account here. But there is an active intelligence bringing together those manorial dynamics that the action of account would later coalesce and address.

The *Mirror of Justices* should be recalled here, since it brings law, maths, and love between lords and bailiffs together. The relevant passage is at the end of the chapter *De Contract*. If the legalistically contractual way of thinking was not applicable throughout our period, the seigneurial problem sounds very similar to that envisaged in the *Leges Henrici Primi*.

> As for a contract for a baillia [*baille*] and the administration of another's goods and money, it is perfectly permissible for anyone [i.e. a land-lord] to dispose of his goods wisely or foolishly waste them as he sees fit, and so everyone should have such bailiffs and administrators as it seems will well preserve each fee. And if he is damaged by some stupid or bad servant, he [the land-lord] can put this rightly down to his own stupid contract, in so far as he did not take sufficient surety for complete loyalty and discretion, and so the contrary: since against him who has nothing the law gives nothing for recovery, nor any remedy beyond vengeance. If however there should be some such bailiff who will not render any loyal account to his lord, he can be chased down by a writ of account—which is a mixed action—if he has anything by which he can be made justiciable. And if he should not be distrainable nor hold a fee, and flees his lord, and will

---

[197] *LHP*, cap. 56. 4–5.
[198] *Britton* perhaps implies that one reason behind the later action of account was the desire to solve the question of where a former bailiff should be liable to account. *Britton*, ed. Francis Morgan Nichols, 2 vols. (Oxford, 1865), i. 176.

not render an account, for such disobedience the action stands mixed for the personal trespass.[199]

Tenure and Contract

In an important article Scott Waugh cited a series of common law actions where the effects of a shift from tenure to contract may be observed—annuity, covenant, debt.[200] *Monstravit de compoto* should probably be included. It responded to the mobility that bailiffs had acquired. Its use implies that that bailiff is unlikely to be re-employed. It implies a fixed-term office. Such mobility was unrooted in land tenure (since the question of bailiffs' landlessness was central). It was rooted in salaried payment. The action of account then looks like a further instance of lordly clients turning 'to the royal courts for the protection of their contractual claims'.[201] The problem—if not the solution of royal courts—was visible from the twelfth-century *Leges Henrici Primi*.

Bailiffs' mobility is a predicate of *monstravit* itself. 'The sheriffs in whose bailiwicks they are found are to make them come to render their account', stated the 1259 Provisions of Westminster (cap. 19). The bailiffs could be anywhere. The manorial manual *Husbandry*, addressed to manorial auditors, makes clear the problem:

> And be sure to know, as for manors which are entrusted to bailiffs, where there is no reeve [*provost*] beyond the bailiff, that whatever damage comes to pass under the bailiff, the bailiff will answer for every thing, just as if he were the reeve. And the lord should look out carefully that [the bailiff] should have pledges, so whatever damage comes to pass under the bailiff, who has nothing of his own [in terms of property], that these pledges shall answer for him.[202]

John de Valle's evasiveness is one example of this. He has no trouble evading the distraint to which he is liable. Indeed it is his success at doing precisely this that forces Agnes de Valence down the channel through which her action flows chasing de Valle's pledges.

Was such mobility a consequence of being salaried? Historians have noted the general decline in land grants by lords to tenants and followers *c*.1200–*c*.1275 in England, seeing a partial shift in the way lords rewarded followers and household servants.[203] This is the hinge between a bailiff being literally a bailee for his lord of some manor, to a position where he is a salaried official.[204] Plucknett gave the

---

[199] *Mirror of Justices* 76. The question of what the bailiff *owns* is, again, central.
[200] Scott L. Waugh, 'Tenure to Contract: Lordship and Clientage in Thirteenth Century England', *EHR* 101 (1986), 811–39 at 828–32.
[201] Waugh, 'Tenure to Contract', 828.
[202] *Walter of Henley*, 442 (*Husbandry*, cap. 57).
[203] Waugh, 'Tenure to Contract', esp. 816–24; D. A. Carpenter, 'The Second Century of English Feudalism', *P&P* 168 (2000), 30–71, esp. 34–6, 50–5 on (e.g.) the Ferrers' use of both tenured and untenured officials, and 57–8 for tenured stewards.
[204] See *Fleta's* presumption, discussed by Plucknett, *Mediaeval Bailiff*, 2; Harvey, 'Pipe Rolls and the Adoption of Desmesne Farming', 351; Prestwich, *Plantagenet England*, 427, associates salaried manorial officials with direct management of desmesnes and periods of inflation (as in the early thirteenth century).

question no explicit consideration at all in his Creighton Lecture and bailiffs per se perhaps lose out historiographically to stewards or even reeves.[205] At least during the heyday of demesne farming in the second half of the thirteenth century bailiffs seem to have inhabited something of an intermediary position between the unfree, firmly rooted reeve and the free and sometimes familial, sometimes official steward.[206] It is not necessary for the argument here that any shift from tenure to contract should be absolute; simply that it was sufficient and prevalent enough to cause a real problem in bailiffs' accountability. *Seneschauncy* (*c.*1260–76) takes it for granted that bailiffs were salaried.[207] The bailiffs at the Priory of Ely were salaried in this period at 2*d.* a day.[208] A letter of Bishop Thomas Cantilupe of Hereford clearly presumes a market of mobile bailiffs and a licence to go where they would. In a very detailed letter to his steward about numerous matters of estate management, Cantilupe ordered John of Bradeham to 'appoint Robert of Furches to the bailiwick [of Whitbourne], and this quickly lest he be lured into putting himself in service to someone else'.[209] The timing of the letter may be significant—18 November—precisely the period following on from the Michaelmas audit when landlords would review bailiffs' past conduct with a view to future redeployment (much of Cantilupe's letter is taken up with this), and therefore when bailiffs themselves might be hawking their services. A late fourteenth-century Durham manuscript assumes that a manorial reeve or bailiff will newly enter into office at the start of the (presumably financial) year and 'secure for himself a clerk who can competently order his roll and estate'.[210]

---

[205] For stewards see Carpenter, 'Second Century'; Hershey, 'Rise and Fall of William de Bussey'. For reeves see P. D. A. Harvey, 'The Manorial Reeve in Twelfth Century England', in Ralph Evans (ed.), *Lordship and Learning: Studies in Memory of Trevor Aston* (Woodbridge, 2004), 125–38. The question is particularly problematic since, as was noted at the outset, two men could both be called bailiffs yet be doing very different jobs. Paul Brand, 'Stewards, Bailiffs and the Emerging Legal Profession', in Ralph Evans (ed.), *Lordship and Learning: Studies in Memory of Trevor Aston* (Woodbridge, 2004), shows a sequence of lordly officials acting legally as 'bailiffs' but who then turn out to be stewards functionally. The bailiff here evaporates into a completely fictional legal person. For service remittances given to *reeves* in lieu of payment see Noke, 'Agency and the *Excessus* Balance' at 149–50. For an example *c.*1230, see *Select Documents of the English Lands of the Abbey of Bec*, ed. Marjorie Chibnall, CS 3rd ser. 73 (1951), 65.

[206] Harvey, 'Manorial Reeve in Twelfth Century England'. Although bailiffs could themselves be villeins: see the 28 October 1282 note by the Abbot of Ramsey that he has appointed Robert of Vandry and Roger Smith 'villeins of ours at Gravenhurst, as our bailiff and attorney for the custody of . . . [the] manor of Gravenhurst'. They were to account for it too. Translated in J. Ambrose Raftis, *The Estates of Ramsey Abbey: A Study in Economic Growth and Organziation*, Studies and Texts 3 (Toronto, 1957), App. D, 315 [=CUL MS Hh.vi.11, fo. 66ʳ].

[207] *Seneschauncy*, cap. 80 (*Walter of Henley*, 293, comment 94–6).

[208] Edward Miller, *The Abbey and Bishopric of Ely: The Social History of an Ecclesiastical Estate from the Tenth to the Early Fourteenth Century* (Cambridge, 1951), 255; similarly, Raftis, *Estates of Ramsey Abbey*, 263–4 (post-1348). Ramsey also used wage labour, see 199–201.

[209] *Registrum Thome de Cantilupo*, 108 (18 November 1276). Borough custumals' prohibitions against luring another's servants from service correlate this at a far more general level. See e.g. for Northampton *c.*1260 and Waterford *c.*1300, *Borough Customs*, i. 215–16.

[210] Durham Dean and Chapter Library MS Loc. 2, 15 (v) cited from *Walter of Henley*, 464–7 at 464. For dating, *Walter*, 249 (='Oschinsky' MS 83). Compare the late thirteenth-/early fourteenth-century rule that 'All bailiffs after accounting are to be inquired into in place without delay by good and lawworthy men [*bonos et legales homines*] who are sworn and assigned for this in every vill', from CUL MS Dd. VII. 6, cited from *Walter of Henley*, 463-4 (='Oschinsky' MS 41).

In this context the prevalence of 'merely prominent royal servants'[211] amongst those bringing actions of *monstravit* in the 1270s may be *not* that it shows *monstravit* was just a matter of laws for the boys. Its significance may rather be that *even* powerful servants of the crown apparently lacked satisfactory means to discipline or hold accountable their own senior officials.

This is striking in the common law context which often took bailiffs as equivalents for, or extensions of, their lords. *Glanvill* talks about bailiffs or stewards being appointed to 'dispose of someone's lands or goods' with the qualification that this did not entitle them per se to act as the person's representative in court (implying that they were doing precisely that).[212] Famously, in the writ of novel disseisin, the bailiff of the lord who had unjustly seised a plaintiff's land could be summoned if his lord could not be found.[213] The Court of the Fair of St Ives speaks in 1275 about the 'peace of the abbot and the bailiffs', the one an extension of the other.[214] The conflation of agency and hence liability could be problematic. Conscientious rulers worried about it. A Duchess of Brabant included questions about her liability for the exactions of her officers in a questionnaire she put to Aquinas in the 1260s or early 1270s.[215] In 1219 William Marshal II's bailiffs ejected the Countess of Huntingdon (she said) from the manors of Baddow, Tottenham, and Kempston.[216] Responding that autumn to Henry III's written reproach and censure, Marshal expressed how

> my spirit was astonished—more than is scarcely possible—that you could have believed that I should have so offended against your dignity and excellence, since I have never done anything, or ordered anything to be done, against your excellence or dignity which could provide grounds for such an evil, suspicious surmise. As for your claim in your letters to me that when Earl David had died, my bailiffs, armed and with main force, injured his men and violently took off with the cattle which had been his, on my orders, dearest lord, I reply thus to your Excellency, that if this should have been done by my bailiffs, I know nothing about it, nor do I consent to any such acts, and that I will undertake to correct any excesses [*excessus*] of my bailiffs, should they have committed them, according to your will, and according to the laws and customs of the kingdom.[217]

The faultline between servants doing what they saw their master wanted but had not asked for and masters indicating what they wanted without ordering it

---

[211] Brand, *Kings, Barons and Justices*, 314.
[212] *Glanvill*, 133. He goes on to provide the writ to effect this. Also *Britton*, i. 305–6. See S. F. C. Milsom's comments in *The Legal Framework of English Feudalism* (Cambridge, 1976), 18–21 esp. 20, on 'vicarious liability' and Plucknett, *Mediaeval Bailiff*, 14–15.
[213] *Glanvill*, 167–8.
[214] *Select Pleas in Manorial Courts and Other Seignorial Courts*, ed. F. W. Maitland, SS 1 (London, 1889), 138.
[215] 'De regimine judaeorum' (*c.*1261–1271), in *Aquinas: Selected Political Writings*, ed. A. P. d'Entrèves, trans. J. G. Dawson (Oxford, 1974), 92–4. It is unclear which Duchess of Brabant Aquinas addressed: Aquinas, *Political Writings*, trans. R. W. Dyson (Cambridge, 2002), xx.
[216] *Royal and Other Historical Letters [...] Henry III*, ed. W. W. Shirley, RS, 2 vols. (London, 1862–6), i. #40. For William Marshal I's bailiffs encroachments on Earl David of Huntingdon's land in 1217 see i. #5.
[217] *Royal and Other Historical Letters [...] Henry III*, i. #41.

was a persistent problem. Thomas Becket's murder is merely the most emblematic twelfth-century instance.[218]

Simon of Senlis's letters show the upside of such a close identification by bailiff-agents with their lords' interests. Senlis worries about his lord's interests when buying London herring and St Ives cloth (a concern Grosseteste would repeat in his *Rules* for the Countess of Lincoln).[219] The 'damage et hontage' (to use the *Court de Baron*'s refrain)[220] done to a lord by bailiffs who did *not* identify with their lords' interests is made clear in Henry III's *gravamina* against his council in March 1261, a highly politicized instance. Henry described how his council went against this natural order to 'appoint new bailiffs for conserving the king's rights, but do so at their own pleasure without respect to the king, such that these bailiffs [*balliui*] do not think of themselves as the king's men, and ignore his rights in order to please others rather than him'.[221]

Given the strong impetus to conflate agents' and masters' interests, the action of account is striking in that it indicates that such a happy conjunction had, too often, passed. Instead of being agents serving their lords' interests and carrying out their orders, actions of account imply the bond between lord and bailiff worked differently towards the later thirteenth century. Robert of Chilton had been a man rooted in local Kentish politics. His bond with Battle was longstanding and it was a newcomer—Geoffrey of St Calais—who ruptured it. Chilton thought of himself as someone merely holding land of his lord. John de Valle was in status lesser, but in responsibilities greater. Despite his friends in high places de Valle was clearly an official of Agnes de Valence but curiously 'unpropertied' from *monstravit*'s perspective given the related case admitting his involvement in a tenement.[222] Yet records from (e.g.) the 1240s show powerful men and women seemingly at a loss to control such officials: Ralph de Neville, Chancellor and Bishop of Chichester;[223] Drogo, a member of the Turberville family;[224] Isabella de Fortibus, daughter of Gilbert de Clare;[225] later Gilbert himself;

---

[218] As a wider problem see *Petri Cantoris Parisiensis Verbum adbreviatum*, ed. Monique Boutry, Corpus Christianorum Continuatio Mediaevalis 196 (Turnhout, 2004), 171 (§1.18).

[219] TNA SC 1/6/141 (1226–32). See further Jeanne Stones and Lionel Stones, 'Bishop Ralph Neville, Chancellor to King Henry III, and His Correspondence: A Reappraisal', *Archives* 16 (1984), 227–57. Grosseteste's *Rules* (cap. xii[28]): 'buy your wine, and your wax and your wardrobe at the fair of St Botolph [. . .] your robes purchase at St Ives' (*Walter of Henley*, 398).

[220] *Court Baron* at e.g. 22, 23.

[221] *DBM* #30 cap. 10 [6] at 214. See also cap. 5 [3] at 212. The 'new bailiffs' are in practice sheriffs, but Henry, I think, uses the wider term to stress the unnaturalness of the outcome. For the Council's retort, *DBM* #31 (March–April 1261), caps. 3 [5] at 220–2; 6 [10] at 224. Here they certainly *avow* the principle that baronial agents were accountable. Cf. Edward's retort to criticisms of Walter Langton as Treasurer in 1301, Prestwich, *Edward I*, 526.

[222] *Calendar Justiciary Rolls Ireland*, ii. *1295–1303*, 322.

[223] *CRR 1237–1242*, 430 #2121 (May 1242); *CRR 1242–1243*, 336 #1708 (February 1243), against John Blund for Sussex lands.

[224] *CRR 1242–1243*, 298 #1530 (January/February1243) against William of Bretevill for lands in Devon).

[225] For 1256–60 (for Roger of Donescumbe, her chaplain, for land at Lambeth and Kennington): TNA E 13/1e mm. 2d and 9 (Exchequer plea rolls); E 159/43 m. 8 (King's Remembrancer Memoranda Rolls) against Richard of Halstede for Holderness, 1269, and notwithstanding Denholm-Young's remark, *Seignorial Administration*, 159.

Geoffrey de Lusignan; etc.[226] Given that the Clares and Lusignans had significant reputations themselves for having aggressive bailiffs, their inclusion may be notable. Licensing hard bailiffs to do hard business did not immunize barons from being ultimately unable to hold their own men to account.[227] A significant minority of baronial bailiffs seem distinct liabilities by the mid-thirteenth century.

What is striking is not that bailiffs should themselves want to profit in the course of service to their lord. It is that lords could get neither local compromise nor constrain bailiffs when they disagreed. Legal jurisdictions are important here. Robert of Chilton's case showed that the question of jurisdiction was key to securing bailiffs' accountability even in the early twelfth century. Chilton initially refused Battle's jurisdiction but was 'tricked' into conceding it. His argument against a liability to account hinged (to recap) first on his own self-regard as an agent and secondly on his claim for the personal nature of that liability to the dead Abbot Henry For him, accepting Battle's jurisdiction does seem to have been a matter of personal fidelity, not of official responsibility—and on something like those terms.[228]

The 'old', traditional form of the emerging action of account was directed towards a sheriff to secure an accounting at the county courts. Given the rough subsidiarity principle of English lawcourts, this implies several things jurisdictionally. It implies that any private rapprochement between bailiff and lord had failed. It then implies (predictably) that any attempt to resolve matters at the seigneurial court had failed.[229] The county court was the next step up. Even that though was a significant concession, given the unavoidable, public recognition that a lord's 'disciplinary jurisdiction' had failed—and in his relations with his own officer.[230] Reputationally, none of these cases

---

[226] Further examples and references from 1267, Brand, *Kings, Barons and Justices*, 314–18.

[227] Clare's bailiffs' reputation: *CPR 1258–1266*, 53 (July 1259 inquiry and public invitation for plaints against into Richard de Clare's bailiffs); generally, David Carpenter, *The Struggle for Mastery: Britain 1066–1284* (London, 2003), 371, 461. Geoffrey's bailiffs' reputation: Matthew Paris, *Chronica majora* v. 737–9 (on William de Bussey, actually a steward); TNA JUST 1/82 m. 24d (use of his Trumpington mill as a fatal prison) (1261 eyre, Cambs.); *The 1258–9 Special Eyre of Surrey and Kent*, ed. Andrew H. Hershey, Surrey Record Society 38 (Woking, 2004), ##114–5, 124, 146, 182. Commentary: Hershey, 'Rise and Fall of William de Bussey'; Carpenter, *Reign of Henry III*, 102, 327–8; J. R. Maddicott, 'Magna Carta and the Local Community', *P&P* 102 (1984), 25–65 at 57.

[228] See the contrast Bisson draws between an accountability of fidelity and an accountability of office (*Crisis of the Twelfth Century*, esp. 316–49). I take this distinction as a contrast, and avoid the presumption of an absolute opposition or chronological progression from an 'accountability of fidelity' to an 'accountability of office': e.g. 'was an accountability of fidelity ultimately self-contradictory?' (350); 'realization that fidelity might not always entail competence' (336). See e.g. *Chronicle of Jocelin*, 42, noting Abbot Samson's appointment to offices on merit not affection (*nisi essent idonei*). See also Bisson's slightly different distinction about the compatibility of 'lordship' and 'office', 351. Bisson's negative definition of the old (fidelitarian) accountability whose deficiencies he sees the new (official) accountability remedying are best summarized at *Crisis of the Twelfth Century*, 324. Udo Wolter, 'Verwaltung, Amt, Beamter, V–VI', in Otto Brunner, Werner Conze, and Reinhart Koselleck (eds.), *Geschichtliche Grundbegriffe: Historisches Lexikon zur politisch-sozialen Sprache in Deutschland*, 8 vols. in 9 (Stuttgart, 1972–97), vii. 38, on German officials, takes a similar approach in detecting a move from personalized service to functional objectification of tasks, implicitly in the later thirteenth and fourteenth centuries.

[229] For analogous comments on the difficulties of tenants getting real due process from a seigneurial court when they contested dues and services, Milsom, *Legal Framework*, 26–7, 33–4.

[230] The phrase is Milsom's, *Legal Framework*, ch. 1, but esp. 25–35. He is using it in the context of enforcing tenurial dues and services.

can have enhanced lordly status in tenants' or neighbours' eyes. It is possible that the 1259/1285 statutes were so strict because of the embarrassment that unaccountable bailiffs caused lords. Actions of account may have been not so much expressions of landlordly strength so much as expressions of landlordly loss of control.

What may it imply for dispute resolution at a county level when actions of account pass through the Exchequer of Pleas, Common Bench, or the eyre sessions?[231] We cannot tell how many cases occurred, and were resolved, at the county level or lower. A number of factors are at work, though: the seniority (political or official) of those bringing such cases; the argument that any action of account is some admission of failure; and the pre-1259 cases that we can see involving less powerful people. This implies that such cases are unlikely to constitute only a modest molehill. Yet evidence is lacking to claim they are all that is left of a mountain. The truth is probably somewhere in between, but, I suspect, more mountain than molehill. It may also imply something about 'jurisdiction shopping'. It is hard to be certain that any tendency for cases to ascend jurisdictionally speaking implies an increased inability of lower jurisdictions to deal with unaccountable bailiffs. It may be simply that greater lords found these higher fora preferable. If so they most probably preferred them because they found them most congenial to winning. Either way the preferences of the powerful played a role.[232] A clear implication is that these visible cases must always be a subset of a bigger universe of cases that got resolved at lower jurisdictions.

S. F. C. Milsom, analysing lordly 'disciplinary jurisdiction', has seen a shift during the thirteenth century from tenurial relationships that had an 'organic life in which tenement and dues are interdependent and kept in balance by the lord's court' to one where dues and services are 'independent properties fixed in an external system of law'.[233] Actions of account, mostly brought after periods of service, offer some correlation. This contrast between organic, affectual relations and more formally legalized obligations seems similar to Michael Clanchy's pithy contrast between 'love and law', or Thomas Bisson's between the accountability of fidelity and the accountability of office. It is important though that any shift in disciplinary jurisdiction, 'tenure

---

[231] For a famous case at the Exchequer see *Select Cases in the Exchequer of Pleas*, cix–cx, on Bogo de Clare's 1286 case against his wardrober (*sic*, not his bailiff), Walter of Reygni. Jenkinson and Formoy refer here to *two* actions involving Bogo, but I have neither found this on the rolls nor found further references. They edit it as #170 (=TNA E 13/12 m. 32d). See also TNA SC 1/12/147 (Edward I to Edmund of Cornwall, 15 February 1288, re the case). For commentary: M. S. Giuseppi, 'The Wardrobe and Household Accounts of Bogo de Clare, A.D. 1284-6', *Archaeologia* 70 (1920), 1–56 (including an edition of the accounts cited as evidence during the case, 19–56); Denholm-Young, *Seignorial Administration*, 156–8; Plucknett, *Legislation of Edward I*, 153 n. 2, and *The Mediaeval Bailiff*, 28 n. 2; and Alan Harding, *England in the Thirteenth Century* (Cambridge, 1993), 150–1. On Bogo: F. M. Powicke, *The Thirteenth Century, 1216–1307*, 2nd edn. (Oxford, 1962), 475; John R. H. Moorman, *Church Life in England in the Thirteenth Century* (Cambridge, 1945), 26–30; Henry Sumerson, 'Clare, Bogo de (1248–1294)', in *ODNB*.

[232] I am grateful to David Carpenter for discussion. On cases floating to higher jurisdictions in France see Fredric L. Cheyette, '"Suum cuique tribuere"', *French Historical Studies* 6 (1970), 287–99, esp. 289–90, 297–8.

[233] Milsom, *Legal Framework*, 34–5.

to contract', 'law and love', from 'fidelity' to 'office' is not interpreted absolutely.[234] The development of actions of account corresponds with Milsom's shift from the personal to the impersonal (from Chilton's personal ideal of accountability to de Valle's broken contracts)—but it clearly coexisted with modes of fidelity.[235] Bailiffs and stewards swore oaths. In the transition from one bailiff (John of Crakehall, who will reappear) to another, Adam Marsh lamented in 1251 that Robert Grosseteste was suffering 'considerable damage at the hands of some persons [servants of various sorts] who have no compunction in violating their fealty [*aliquos qui uiolate fidei culpam non uerentur*]'.[236]

In Bisson's terms, Marsh was talking about competent, official estate agents,[237] but he happily frames the issue in terms of broken faith rather than breach of contract, even at this 'late' date.[238] After all, bailiffs' oaths obligate them to uphold their lords' interests writ large, as well as their wider communal duty, as is well expressed in John of Oxford's 'Luffield Book'. It gives a bailiffs' oath:

> Any bailiff receiving a bailiwick will swear so: Hear this Lord N., that I N. will faithfully conduct myself in my bailiwick and bear myself honestly towards the country, towards rich and poor and that I will reclaim as far as I can anything that was lost from my lord's rights, or from your rights by my predecessors as bailiffs, and make known to my lord or to your council etc.[239]

There may have been progression from one to the other, but it is not clear from a case such as John de Valle's that it was progress; nor is it clear that law triumphed ineluctably over love, however intricately it tangled relations between servants and masters. A drift from tenure to contract interacted with a change in conceptualizing and exacting accountability from bailiffs.[240] What our actions

---

[234] Clanchy, 'Law and Love' suggests a distinction, not a progression. In the common law Milsom also saw no master plan. See Clanchy's helpful review to Milsom's revised *Historical Foundations of the Common Law* in *Modern Law Review* 44 (1981), 597–600. On the distinction between accountability of fidelity and of office, again Bisson, *Crisis of the Twelfth Century*, esp. 316–49.

[235] David Carpenter has made this point in arguing for the waxing *and* waning of 'fiscal feudalism' in thirteenth-century England e.g. with reference to the 1207 tax writ that 'precisely contrasted the two ways [royal, official if you like, and honorial, fidelitarian à la Bisson] of thinking about power', Carpenter, 'Second Century', 63, also 71. By 'fiscal feudalism' Carpenter means relations that produce money for lords, formally grounded in tenurial bonds but where the question at issue is whether that bond carries any meaning beyond the fiscal (44). He argues it does (58–71).

[236] *The Letters of Adam Marsh*, ed. C. H. Lawrence, OMT, 2 vols. (Oxford, 2006–10), i. #22 at 52–3, Lawrence's translation.

[237] Bisson, *Crisis of the Twelfth Century*, e.g. 324, 329.

[238] Cf. Marc Bloch, *La Société féodale* (Paris, 1994 edn.), 617–19.

[239] '(De jure jurandi ballivorum). Aliquis ballivus recipiens ballivam jurabit sic. Hoc auditis domine N. quod ego N. fideliter me geram in balliva mea et honeste me portabo erga patriam scilicet erga divitem et pauperem, et quod alienatum fuit de jure domini mei vel de jure vestro per ballivos antecessores meos revocabo pro posse meo, et scire faciam domino meo vel vobis et consilio vestro etc.', *Court Baron*, 77. The *Modus tenendi curias* gives a somewhat circular oath for reeves: 'You will be loyal to your lord and loyally do what pertains to a reeve and loyally will you take on all receipts and loyally will you discharge yourself of loyal [*sic*, 'lealx'] costs, by your ability and your knowledge, so help you God and his saints,' 103.

[240] This is what Mary Douglas would call changes in thought styles: Douglas, *Thought Styles* (London, 1996), xii, 'a distinctive thought style develops as the communicative genre for a social unit speaking to itself about itself, and so constituting itself'. Also Douglas, *How Institutions Think*.

70 Bailiffs and Stewards

of account do seem to show are the limitations of *both* love and law. In this respect they are not dissimilar to twelfth- and thirteenth-century *podestà*. There too there are grounds for thinking that the 'law' expressed by *sindacatio* and the 'love' expressed by the character-building literature of the *podestà* manuals did not provide an infallible guarantee of professional, official conduct.[241]

Accounts, Audits, Inquiries

If law was one 'hard' means of control that the *Leges Henrici Primi* connected with the problem of manorial officials' tenure, conduct, and accountability so too were accounts, audits, and inquiries. The *Leges*, it was noted, give a checklist for when an estate is returned, following immediately from the discussion of jurisdictional problems in judging reeves who are not their lords' men. The *Leges* are asking about how the *prepositus* has done his job:

> And in returning the manor the shepherds should be questioned about the beasts, their number and state. From the other servants each about his office, whether all things are held fully and at their value; about the availability of men and of livestock; if there has been any deterioration of the manor in demesne or men, in pastures, woods; if anyone has increased his rent, if anyone has wrongly withheld them; what is in the granaries, what sown.[242]

This implies a regular re-evaluation of an estate/manor's value. The approach seems comparable to, if less detailed, that taken by later manuals. The following comes from a late thirteenth-/early fourteenth-century manuscript and sets out the annual headings for the manorial audit. The layout retains the format of the manuscript (including the lines drawn in to connect different items, but not the alternating red–blue colouring of the gallow marks).

> The beginning of what to inquire into—first headings regarding bailiffs, sub-bailiffs, reeves, haywards, shepherds, and other ministers of the court—how they have conducted themselves [*qualiter se habent*] in their office, and whether they are people the lord should keep in his service.
> **CONCERNING** lands, how well-cultivated they are [*lucrantur*], how they are sown, and how they are composted by both sheepdung [*falda*] and cart [*carecta*]. ¶ About the sheep, whether those that ought to lie in the lord's sheepfold, lie as they ought to or not, and if they do not so lie, then on whose account and to what loss.[243]

---

[241] See John Sabapathy, 'A Medieval Officer and a Modern Mentality: *Podestà* and the Quality of Accountability', *Mediaeval Journal* 1.2 (2011), 43–79.

[242] *LHP*, cap. 56.3.

[243] I try to give a sense of how the MS works by reproducing deliberate breaks and marks, putting in bold illuminated words, interlinear notes with pointing lines, etc. In the MS gallows marks alternate in red and blue. Such lists were really intended to be of practical application in the field. Oschinsky's edition masks this by running edited text as a continuous block. The same considerations would apply to, say, Bod. Barlow MS 49 (SC 6414) (the Faringdon accounts of Beaulieu Abbey, 1269–70) whose elaborate coloured hierarchy of lines provides a visual flowchart for following the *Regule compoti*'s rules (fos. 59r–65r and the 90r–v 'tabula quantitatis mercennis mercennariorum'). It would be instructive to apply Malcolm Parkes's ideas of *ordinatio et compilatio* or Mary Carruthers's

- ⁋ Of pasture sales, etc ⎱ if they are well sold or not
- ⁋ Of fishpond sales etc ⎰
- ⁋ Of the safekeeping of hay in autumn, done well or not
- ⁋ Of hay threshing, done well or not
- ⁋ Of the measurement made by the reeve outside the grange
- ⁋ Of sales of the same, if it is badly sold or not and on whose account and to what loss etc
- ⁋ Of seed how it is guarded in the fields
- ⁋ Of hay sold, etc as above
- ⁋ Of ploughs and carts, in whose interests it is kept and on whose say-so and to what loss etc
- ⁋ Of straw and chaff sold ⎱ as above
- ⁋ Of pasture sold etc ⎰
- ⁋ Of wood sold and how many acres in the great wood and the underwood etc
- ⁋ Of turf sales etc as above
- ⁋ Of custody by whomever of stock and of murrain to the same and by whose stupidity etc
- ⁋ Of rose sales etc
- ⁋ Of sales of bracken etc
- ⁋ Of stock sales etc — as above
- ⁋ Of straw sold etc
- ⁋ Of [rabbit] warrens, how they are guarded etc
- ⁋ Of furze sold etc
- ⁋ Of guarding of the liberty, how it is guarded etc, and if homages are taken as they ought to be taken, and if badly by whom etc
- ⁋ Of sheep from ewes having two lambs and from cows having two calves, whether they are [both] in the account etc
- ⁋ Of all other things and profits [*proficuis*] of the lord, pertaining to sales; if they are sold in the lord's interest [*ad commodum domini*] or not and if they are in the account etc.

The end regarding the actions of servants.[244]

It is worth noticing that while sales, profits, and growth are the refrain of such lists, they are not the only concern. Competence and conduct are also audited even at this modest level.[245] In the same way, the *Leges* after setting out its audit headings move on associatively to complaints about the reeve's conduct in office.

Concern about manorial officers' accountability reached a peak in the 'new writ of account' of 1259/60 and its later elaborations. At some level, as we have seen, these legal developments were a product of the *c*.1259–*c*.1261 'reform movement'. Concurrently, a 'management revolution'[246] occurred in the mid-thirteenth century,

---

work on manuscript layout and memory to this very interesting class of 'miscellaneous' manuscripts. Cf. Mattéoni, 'Vérifier, corriger, juger', 55 n. 113.

[244] BL Royal MS 9 A. VII fos. 227ʳ⁻ᵛ = 'Oschinsky' MS 25, App. VI 467–8. I am grateful to Paul Brand for help with some terms.

[245] Cf. Bernard Williams on the question 'what should the lawyer do?' vs. 'how should the lawyer be?' in relation to 'Professional Morality and its Dispositions', in his *Making Sense of Humanity and Other Philosophical Papers 1982–1993* (Cambridge, 1995), 192–202 at 200.

[246] Prestwich, *Plantagenet England*, 429.

manifested by both a highly distinctive genre of English manorial manuals and a change in demesne accounting which Harvey, doyen of English manorial specialists, has characterized as 'phase 2'.[247] The transition from 'phase 1' to 'phase 2' is relevant.[248] The typology can be summarized as follows. Phase 1 characterizes the records from the first half of the thirteenth century and consists of *agreed, final accounts* centrally produced by the lord's men.[249] They correlate with the early phase of concentrated demesne farming (in the Midlands and southern and eastern England) and show the hierarchy of demesne workers at its most elaborate. The accounts themselves tend to have a greater variety of forms at the start than at the end of the period. 'Phase 2' characterizes records from the mid-thirteenth century through to the mid-fourteenth, the height of English demesne farming. The tendency for the reeve and bailiff to account together (with the reeve holding sole financial liability) disappears as the levels of manorial officials decrease. The audit itself provides the main supervisory function.[250] Phase 2 are uniform, *unagreed* accounts, produced *locally* by manorial officials. That is, they represent the accounts manorial officers have compiled before audit, and often include notations showing the negotiated changes made during the course of the audit. Phase 2 accounts have notably similar structures, with the accountants' cash incomes, dues, and debits on the front and the corn and stock account on the dorse. Harvey's stress on the negotiated nature of the account is important.[251] Just as we will see at the Exchequer, the accounts and their content furnished the weapons for a *conflictus* between accountant and auditor.[252]

There are two broad groups of manorial treatises, one focusing on management, the other on financial controls. Harvey criticized Oschinsky's association of the two because she connected the accounting manuals with demesne cultivation, which in turn produced the need for the estate manuals.[253] Harvey has argued that there is no 'essential link between the treatises on husbandry, written for estate owners and their stewards, and the treatises on accounting, written for the clerks who drew up the manorial accounts'.[254] But the difference rather implies the complementarity of the two types. Treatises on the conduct of officials and those on accounting and auditing are functionally the two halves of the same tally. Each approaches the same problem of bailiffs' accountability with a different stick. One seeks to guide land-lords and agents to the problems of managing people and the likely temptations arising

---

[247] For a recent summary, Harvey, *Manorial Records*.
[248] The typology was first set out in *Manorial Records of Cuxham*, 16–34. I draw on Harvey's more recent *Manorial Records*, 29–37.
[249] See e.g. *The Pipe Roll of the Bishopric of Winchester for the Fourth Year of the Pontificate of Peter des Roches, 1208–1209*, ed. Hubert Hall (London, 1903); *The Pipe Roll of the Bishopric of Winchester 1210–1211*, ed. N. R. Holt (Manchester, 1964), and *The Winchester Pipe Rolls and Medieval English Society*, ed. Richard Britnell (Woodbridge, 2003), *passim*.
[250] The fact that the action of account concentrates on *bailiffs'* liabilities while phase 2 manorial accounts themselves do not require a 'bailiff' per se to account reinforces the earlier argument that a bailiff is better defined as an agent with a particular liability rather than an agent with a particular job.
[251] Harvey, *Manorial Records*, 33, 34.   [252] See Ch. 3.
[253] *Walter of Henley*, 3–4, 213–15, 233–4.
[254] 'Agricultural Treatises and Manorial Accounting', 179–80.

from doing particular jobs. The other seeks to overcome the question of individuals through accounting and auditing.

The latter broadly correlates with phase 2 accounting, which sought to reduce hierarchy by placing greater weight on the audit. An interesting, if late, Durham text of *c*.1380–1 illustrates this simply in relation to tallies themselves. The text is a set of instructions on how to manage the clerk used by the manorial officer. After the bailiff/reeve had secured his clerk at the start of the year,

> Then the clerk should give to the reeve or the bailiff a stick [*baculum*][255] on which he may put receipts in one side and disbursements on the other [*recepta. . . deliberaciones*]; he ought either to teach himself to make the tally or other sign for the court regarding granary calculations or [do so] by some other means so that he can securely enroll receipts and disbursements. And thus that reeve will always be in a good state and not in arrears.[256]

The same text makes clear that the manorial professionals were perfectly capable of ranking qualitatively the effectiveness of different techniques for ensuring reeves'/bailiffs' accountability.

> There are three ways in which the reeve or bailiff is liable [*onerari*] for the quality [*genere*] of corn, namely via reckoning [*estimacionem*] of the sheaves, and this is poor reckoning [*mala oneracio*] for the lord and by the bailiff[257] because therein can lie great deception, but should he be liable for a reckoning [*estimacionem*] of this sort particular sheaves should be threshed and winnowed under the bailiff's eyes so that he knows what he has. The second form of reckoning is to answer for the grain to a quarter, fifth, or sixth and a half, according to the custom of the manor or place, and this is a better form of reckoning for the lord and by the bailiff[258] and orders everything so that he answers for a fixed amount [*certum*]. If it is really answered to the grain [*vero oneretur ad granum*], there is not a good surplus of seed to put [aside] because they will reply for the seed in the second year according to the custom of the land or place. The third form of reckoning is that someone should answer for the tallies of the counter-tally holder [*contratalliatoris*] and as with one thief there will be sometimes two thieves notwithstanding that they may have sworn [to be faithful] since everyone will prove [*prestabit*] his oath with a counter-tally; the reeve or bailiff should always have tallies against whoever has an office [*officium*] on the manor, because if a reeve says that he handed over money or corn or whatever, unless he has a letter or tally for himself he may well be bound by his hands and feet on the say-so of the auditor [*per preceptum auditoris*] until he has completely satisfied his lord for his arrears.[259]

---

[255] Cf. on the *verges* of royal county officials *Britton*, i. 21; the steward's rod for admission into tenancies, Harvey *Manorial Records*, 50; use of rods of office for conveyancing, Bisson, *Crisis of the Twelfth Century*, 122. The encyclopedia Omne bonum illustrates its bailiff entry with a trio holding rods that could as well be spears (BL Royal MS 6 E. VI (i), fo. 208ʳ).

[256] Durham Dean and Chapter Library MS Loc. 2. 15, cited from the edn. in *Walter of Henley*, 464–7 at 464–5 (=Oschinsky MS 83).

[257] *baillivo*, could be 'for the bailiff'.   [258] *baillivo*, could be 'for the bailiff'.

[259] Durham Dean and Chapter Library MS Loc. 2. 15, cited from the edn. in *Walter of Henley*, 465.

The author of this text is no fool. Sampling is hit and miss.[260] Setting a fixed threshold guarantees a return, but will allow officers to benefit from any surplus accruing (since they don't have to answer for it). Tallies work, but only if the foils are held centrally by the bailiff, otherwise they are a licence to gull the reeves/bailiffs.

The longest item in the *c.*1301 St Peter's Gloucester text aggressively sets out this style of securing officers' accountability. Here is the text that reeves were supposed individually to swear before each other, at least monthly. It concerned their own propensity for fraud and the cooking of books.[261]

> Item. Because of those who subvert and cook [*correatores*] accounts the truth is suppressed many times and falsehood set down in the reeves' accounts; [so] it is ordained and ordered that any reeve should receive in his official capacity two or more rolls of parchment [*rotulos percameni*] from the steward's hand, in which rolls will be set down the heading [*titulus*], written in the steward's clerk's hand, or the hand of another, namely, 'This heading is the roll of such a reeve for his account of that manor etc'. And in this roll clearly and openly should be set down in itemised detail [*per particulas*] what he receives, spends, or to whomsoever he hands [anything] over, and this by tallies and testimony, and in the same rolls [is to be set down] once a month or more according to his need his expenses, but not on wax, nor some scrap [*in cedula*], nor in any other such place, except for those rolls, should it be written before that person who is deputed to tally against him [*coram illo qui ad talliandum contra illum deputatur*], and before whom [i.e. those two] it is to be recited at least once monthly [*quolibet mense recitetur ad minus semel*] whatever they have set down in those rolls. And by no other covering order [*ordine dealbato*] are the accounts of the reeves to be heard except by those rolls, nor is anything beyond those rolls to be allowed in the accounting of any reeve, and the same form is to be observed for the checking and reconciling of tallies at least once every fortnight [*de talliis ad minus infra quindenam semel visitandis et concordandis*], and the reeve should know that nothing will be allowed him in his account unless he can produce the aforementioned rolls and tallies in testimony.[262]

This lengthy and complex passage well illustrates the policy of relying principally on routinized procedure to ensure accountability. The original accounting system has not produced the responsible conduct it ought. A further more complicated intervention is therefore introduced to overcome the earlier manipulations. The mutual swearing is intended presumably to have the sort of 360-degree effect Bentham later aimed for in his *Panopticon*.

Accounting is expensive, and dealing with the fallout of poor accounting, poor systems, or bad accountants even more so. It is expensive both for the landlords who have to police a system and the officials who have to comply with it, so good reasons

---

[260] Cf. *Walter of Henley*'s caps. 55–8 (*Walter of Henley*, 324).
[261] The oath is clearly closed by the instruction: 'Ista sunt injugenda prepositis non tamen iuranda', i.e. what follows (TNA C 150/1 fo. 328ʳ). The opening passage (fo. 326ᵛ) had stipulated that 'Prepositus quolibet mense semel ad minus articulos istius | scripti distincte coram eo et socio suo messore aperte fa|ciat recitare et formam preceptorum in eo contentam cum summa | diligentia et sollicitudine sub pena restitutionis omnium obmitten|dorum pro posse suo ad plenum observabit. . .' Cf. on seigneurial officers' oaths, Lachaud, *Éthique du pouvoir*, 491–5.
[262] TNA C 150/1 fo. 328ʳ (=*Historia Sancti Petri Gloucestriae*, iii. 216).

are needed for it.[263] *Monstravit de compoto* shows that barons considered these costs acceptable. How might a *bailiff* respond to the legal changes of 1259/60 and 1285?

He would certainly wish to avoid the application of these severe sanctions to him. As we have seen, the new writs were pro-landlord, especially with respect to the use of lordly auditors and the sanctions of imprisonment and (from 1285), outlawry. That is irrespective of the legal cost of contesting an action or of the disruption and displacement it could entail (John de Valle's case moves from Ireland to London). Bailiffs will not have been complacent about such risks.

What could they do to protect themselves against them? 'Cultivate good relationships with their masters and mistresses' is one answer (see pp. 76–82). But with masters like Geoffrey of Lusignan or Gilbert de Clare this would not always be easy. A second approach would be more bureaucratic: furnish themselves with the documentary proof that as bailiffs they had accounted, did have receipts, and had been acquitted of their charges. At least by so doing bailiffs could arm themselves against malicious or 'bad faith' attempts by their masters to offload costs that were not rightly theirs. A John de Valle would thereby have his receipts from the English, Hainault, Brabantine, and Lombard merchants he had contracted with. The problem of what constituted 'reasonable expenses' might also be rendered more soluble. For bailiffs then, better accountancy on their part might protect them against the action of account (although not against masters who sought to destroy these records or make their officials eat them). Such records might also seem attractive from a landlord's perspective, in so far as they offered greater discouragement to bailiffs who might well try to inflate 'reasonable' expenses into private profits.[264]

There is a chronological correlation between a change in manorial accounting and the growing profile of actions of account. The change to phase 2 accounts occurs mid-century, the same decade in which landlords' concern about bailiffs produced the action of account.[265] But such accounts may indicate a different strategy of landlordly control, rather than decentralization.[266] It is credible to suggest that as the sanctions increased against bailiffs who lacked written proofs of account it should be of interest both to bailiffs and lords to address this. It makes particular sense in this context that accounts should be produced locally and include some acknowledgement of the debate between lordly auditors and local accountants of what the latter sought by way of expenses and what the former allowed. The stress on 'reasonable

---

[263] Comments from twentieth-century and early medieval accounting perspectives in respectively Michael Power, *The Audit Society: Rituals of Verification* (Oxford, 1997), *passim*, and Chris Wickham, *Framing the Early Middle Ages: Europe and the Mediterranean 400–800* (Oxford, 2005), 264–72.

[264] The value from lords' perspective: Harvey, *Manorial Records of Cuxham, EHR* 93 (1978), 15–16.

[265] For various instances as well as an 'archaic' set of obedientiary accounts in BL Harley MS 645 fos. 193–9, 252–3, 260–5 (for 1247–50 and 1256–7) see P. D. A. Harvey, 'Mid-Thirteenth Century Accounts from Bury St Edmunds Abbey', in Antonia Gransden (ed.), *Bury St. Edmunds: Medieval Art, Architecture, Archaeology, and Economy* (Leeds, 1998), 128–38; Gransden, *A History of the Abbey of Bury St Edmunds 1182–1256: Samson of Tottingham to Edmund of Walpole*, Studies in the History of Medieval Religion 31 (Woodbridge, 2007), App. III. Some manors/lords produce both actions of account and accounting experiments, such as Isabella de Forz and Gilbert de Clare. Denholm-Young, *Seignorial Administration*, 159–60, Brand, *Kings, Barons and Justices*, 314; *Manorial Records of Cuxham*, 20, 22–3, 26.

[266] A point made by Kershaw reviewing Harvey, *Manorial Records of Cuxham* in *EHR* 93 (1978), 863–4.

expenses' should be recalled. Audit 'workings' might later be needed in court, as they are in de Valle's case or the action between Bogo de Clare and Walter de Reygni (see p. 68 n. 231). Further, the sanction of the new writs of account firmly placed the burden of proof on accountant-bailiffs. It was they who undertook business for their lord, they who contracted with third parties, and they who needed to claim their expenses, deliveries, and profits. A shift from central accounting to local accounting and from final to pre-audited accounts makes sense in the context of the legislation. Whichever side this impetus to experiment with accounting models came from, it fitted very well into the manorial legal and political economy, both from bailiffs' and lords' perspectives. It need imply no decentralized slackening of lordly interest. The action of account, accounting traditions, and estate management treatises need taking together to understand the way in which law, administration, and agriculture were likely to have interacted.

Politics and Political Economy

What was the relationship between politics and the changing political economy of bailiffs? In specific ways they seem mutually permeable. Edmund King argued for a connection, given the tendency in the thirteenth century to think quite literally about how 'political reform turned, in large part, on how that [great estate of England] was best managed'. Should we define 'reform a little more broadly, and speak of administrative and legal changes in which the landlord class played a prominent role, there is scope to look again at the records of the great estates'.[267] The 1259 action of account qualifies as one in which baronial interests figure prominently. Its self-interest was discussed earlier, but a question remains as to whether bailiffs' accountability intersected with the public good of the common realm.

The old English tradition of Wulfstan's early eleventh-century *moralisation de l'administration* should be recalled.[268] That was also a feature of the thirteenth-century estate literature. But Louis IX had no monopoly on this *mentalité*, neither in the eleventh nor thirteenth centuries. Walter of Henley directs his son, 'If you need to choose a bailiff or servant, do not choose them because of their parentage or appearance, nor lest they are of good reputation [*bon renum*], and if they will be loyal and perceptive, and know how about fields and stock.'[269] Issues of renown will resurface, especially in Chapter 4. The question of whose interests the bailiff or other officer

---

[267] King, 'Estate Management and the Reform Movement', 1, 12. The relationship between *communities'* concern about seigneurial bailiffs' accountability (as opposed to seigneurial concern) and the 'reform movement' is a very longstanding part of the historiography. See esp. E. F. Jacob, *Studies in the Period of Baronial Reform and Rebellion, 1258–1267*, Oxford Studies in Social and Legal History 8 (Oxford, 1925), esp. 25–6, 28–34, 90–2, 96–8, 106–17, 337–49, 354–65; Treharne, *Baronial Plan of Reform*, esp. 109–14, 137–9, 149–56, 175–6, 186–8, 199–202, 246–7, 356–76; Maddicott, 'Magna Carta and the Local Community', esp. 25, 54–61, and 'Edward I and the Lessons of Baronial Reform: Local Government, 1258-80', *TCE* 1 (1986), 1–30; Andrew H. Hershey, 'Success or Failure? Hugh Bigod and Judicial Reform during the Baronial Movement, June 1258–February 1259', *TCE* 5 (1995), 65–87, esp. 70, 77–8, 80–2; Maddicott, *Simon de Montfort* (Cambridge, 1994), esp. 164–72, incl. comparison with Louis IX's *enquêtes* at 168–9.

[268] Le Goff, *Saint Louis*, 218 (of Louis's *ordonnances* of 1254).

[269] *Walter of Henley*, cap. 33 (*Walter of Henley*, 316).

'Political Economy' of the Action of Account 77

served is a key theme in the manuals, just as it was an important practical problem. Walter of Henley closes his sermon thus: 'Those that take care of another man's things should accordingly avow four things by right: to love their lord, and fear him, and as for getting profit [*pru*] should think of his things as theirs, and as to making spend [think of them] as another's.'[270]

That is, they should seek to maximize gain and minimize costs. Yet, as Walter goes on to remark, 'many servants only aver the last, seeking to minimize their costs while making the most out of their masters'.[271] The problem of whose interests a bailiff serves and how close is the identification of his own and his lord's interests has resurfaced. Counting and character cannot be separated, economics and politics melt to the same currency.

A later fourteenth-century encyclopedia well expresses the same problem. The English Exchequer clerk James le Palmer's Omne bonum (1360–75)[272] includes an entry on *baiuli*.[273] Le Palmer's rubric covers 'the testing of bailiffs and the signs by which they may be known as good or bad in their counsel'.[274] Le Palmer is thinking about bailiffs, drawing on the Pseudo-Aristotelian *Secretum secretorum*'s advice to rulers.[275] A marginal note recommends a reader to 'note here the virtues and behaviour of a good bailiff and, here, how they can be recognized' and points to the *Secretum*'s fifteen characteristics of a good bailiff.[276] (Another sign of the permeable boundaries between texts and officers.) Both are clearly thinking of bailiffs with real responsibilities for their lords' goods (and good). The first test of a bailiff is given thus:

¶ The first way [to test him] is to show him you lack money. ¶ If therefore he encourages you to waste that which is in your treasury and argues that this is expedient, you know that he places you in no esteem. ¶ And if he encourages you to seize your subjects' [*subditorum*] money, he will be the corruption of your rule [*regiminis*] and they will hate you beyond measure. ¶ But if rather he sets out before you what he has and says, 'This is what I bought by your grace and gift', offering himself to you; then this [bailiff] is deservedly to be trusted and worthy of all possible praise [since] he chooses and wants difficulties for himself for your glory.[277]

---

[270] *Walter of Henley*, cap. 111 (*Walter of Henley*, 340). Texts on *podestà* also discuss the roles of love and fear.

[271] Compare Adam Marsh's less worldly advice to Grosseteste, 'You know that a divine precept instructs lords to study much more to be loved by their people than to be feared, and prelates should understand that they are fathers of the poor rather than princes of the people', *Letters of Adam Marsh*, i. #42, Lawrence's trans. Grosseteste was particularly sensible of a bishop's duty of care and divine accountability.

[272] Lucy Sandler Freeman, *Omne Bonum: A Fourteenth Century Encyclopedia of Universal Knowledge*, British Library MSS Royal 6 E. VI—6 E. VII, 2 vols. (London, 1996), i. 22, 25.

[273] BL Royal MSS 6 E. VI and VII (each MS is then in two vols.). This entry is at VI (i) fo. 208ʳ⁻ᵛ. A related, earlier MS is Bod. MS Bodley 784, a copy of the *notabilia* le Palmer used for Omne bonum.

[274] 'De baiulis experiendis et de signis quibus cognoscintur an boni an mali sint consiliari', BL Royal MS 6 E. VI (i) fo. 208ʳ.

[275] *Opera hactenus inedita Rogeri Baconi*, ed. Robert Steele, 16 vols. (Oxford, 1905–40), v. *Secretum secretorum cum glossis et notulis*, 140–1, 'De temptacione bajulorum' (§3.12).

[276] 'Notatur hic virtutes et mores boni baiuli et per que potest cognosci ut hic', BL Royal MS 6 E. VI (i) fo. 208ᵛ (*Secretum secretorum*, 141–3 (§3.13)).

[277] BL Royal MS 6 E. VI (i) fo. 208ʳ, '¶ Primo | modo quod ostendas ei te indigere pecunia. ¶ Si ergo inducat te ad distractionem eorum que sunt in thesauro tuo et ostendat hoc esse expediens, scias

This is late, and one might argue negligibly relevant to any reform movement, Montfortian or otherwise. The currency of thought was, however, a broader one.[278] Furthermore, specific connections can be drawn in relation to the one known author of an estate management manual, Grosseteste's *Rules* on estate management (1245 x 1253).

Grosseteste's direct influence on Montfort himself is well established.[279] His influence had other paths. The baronial council's choice of John of Crakehall as Treasurer in November 1258 was practical and symbolic. Crakehall was Grosseteste's former steward, as intimate and familiar with Grosseteste's views on royal self-sufficiency as equitable estate management. The council's commitment to Exchequer equity could not be better embodied.[280] Indeed, while there are Exchequer precedents for the detailed county auditing by vill and individual that Crakehall tested in 1258, it also conforms to Grosseteste's manorial level recommendations in the *Rules* to assess all parcels of land, rents, customs, franchises, etc. with a view to being able to audit bailiffs' efficiency.[281] Still more striking is the correlation between the *Rules*' stress on *bailiffs*' just and equitable conduct and the norms for *sheriffs*' just and equitable conduct as prescribed in numerous schemes developed 1258/9.[282] Chapter 3 will argue that there was a striking lack of articulate reflection about the positive content of the office of sheriff. In 1258/9 it looks as if part of what plugged the gap was articulate reflection about *bailiffs*. So it may be that ironically bailiffs' accountability contributed to the 'common good' less through the action of account's baronial self-interest, and more through that tradition of thought about stewardly conduct that seems to have influenced ideas about shrieval conduct.[283]

---

quod nullum caput precii ponit in te. ¶ Et si inducat te ad rapiendum peccuniam subditorum, erit corrupcio regiminis et odient te ultra modum. ¶ Si vero exponat tibi quod habet et dicat: hoc est quod ex gracia et dono vestro adquisivi offerens ipsum tibi: iste est merito commendandus et omni laude dignus ut pote, eligens et volens sui ipsius confusionem pro tua gloria.' The text in BL Royal MS 12 C. VI fol. 37ʳ is slightly closer than that edited in *Secretum secretorum*, 140–1. See also 148–9 (§3.17).

[278] More widely cf. Philippe de Beaumanoir, *Coutumes de Beauvaisis*, ed. André Salmon, 2 vols. (Paris, repr. 1970), i. cap. 1 on *baillis*, ii. cap. 50 §1516–32 on governance and accountability in towns.

[279] Maddicott, *Simon de Montfort*, 77–105, 167–9.

[280] *DBM* #37b at 260, cap. 8; Adrian Jobson, 'John of Crakehall: The "Forgotten" Baronial Treasurer, 1258-1260', *TCE* 13 (2011), 89–96; Sophie Ambler, 'On Kingship and Tyranny: Grosseteste's Memorandum and its Place in the Baronial Reform Movement', *TCE* 14 (2013), 115–28 at 124–7.

[281] Jobson, 'John of Crakehall', 93–4 on the Exchequer reforms; *Walter of Henley*, 388, 395.

[282] See the stress on manorial officers' conduct and trustworthiness in *Rules*, caps. 1, 3 (esp.), 4, 5, 6, 7, 27, in *Walter of Henley*, 388–406. There is a similar stress for household officials. Cf. the Provisions of Oxford (*DBM*, #5 esp. caps. 16, 17), order for inquiries (#6), Provisions of Westminster (#11, cap. 4, #12, caps. 5, 7, 9, 20), provisions for inquiries (#13), 1264 justifications to Louis IX (#37b, caps. 7–8, 10–12); Paris, *Chronica majora*, v. 719–20, vi. 397–400.

[283] Especially ironic given earlier Angevins' habit of treating the state as their estate. See further pp. 102–3, 240–1, also 52–60, 66. The parallelism of the state as an estate runs right through the period: see Edward I's 1301 comparison in *The Chronicle of Pierre de Langtoft*, ed. Thomas Wright, RS, 2 vols. (1866–8), ii. 330, with interesting comment in J. R. Maddicott, '"1258" and "1297": Some Comparisons and Contrasts', *TCE* 9 (2003), 1–14 at 12. Cf. *Willelmi Rishanger, Chronica et annales*, ed. Henry Thomas Riley, RS (1865), 460.

There were also possible routes from royal accounting experiments back into seigneurial administration. In 1236/7 the membership of Henry III's council changed.[284] One of the consequences of that change was a far-reaching but short-lived experiment between 1236 and 1240 in managing the crown estate. It was divided into chunks and large sections of it taken into direct demesne management.[285] There was a strong interest in the accountability of estate officers. In 1240 the experiment was abandoned because, it seems, of its expense.[286] Similar experiments were tried between 1275 and 1282, and perhaps discussed in parliament.[287] One of the 1236 councillors closely involved in this programme was John de Lacy, Constable of Chester, and from 1232, Earl of Lincoln. In 1221 de Lacy married Margaret de Quincy, daughter of Robert of Quincy and granddaughter of the Earl of Winchester, a diocese that was an experimental furnace of English government and accounting. It was to this Margaret de Quincy, a woman who had connections at court in the 1250s and with the Montforts into the 1260s, that Robert Grosseteste gave his *Rules*.[288] The connections between private and public were multiple and could flow in numerous directions.

Grosseteste's *Rules* are interesting. There is a courtesy in Grosseteste's *Rules* and the *Statuta*, one that seeks to show and instruct by example, as when the lord or lady calls the steward 'before some of their good friends'.[289] Having inspected there the rolls and inquests pertaining to the manors, the Countess is given a long speech, both an exhortation and an oath for the steward:

> Good sir, you see well that to clarify my rights and to know more certainly [*esclarzir e pur saver plus certeynement*] the state of my people and lands [. . .] I have had made these inquests and enrolments. Now I beg of you as he to whom I have entrusted [*baylle*, lit. bailled] everything beneath me to protect and rule [*a garder e governer*], I strictly command you [. . .] to keep [everything of mine] whole and unblemished and what

---

[284] N. Denholm-Young, 'The "Paper Constitution" Attributed to 1244', *EHR* 232 (1943), 401–23 at 412.
[285] Robert C. Stacey, *Politics, Policy, and Finance under Henry III 1216–1245* (Oxford, 1987), 52–66 and 'Agricultural Investment and the Management of the Royal Desmesne Manors, 1236–1240', *Journal of Economic History* 46 (1986), 919–34.
[286] Cf. the partial abandonment in 1259 of the experiment with custodial sheriffs during the 'reform' government, H. W. Ridgeway, 'Mid Thirteenth-Century Reformers and the Localities: The Sheriffs of the Baronial Regime, 1258–1261', in P. F. Fleming, A. Gross, and J. R. Lander (eds.), *Regionalism and Revision: The Crown and its Provinces in England, 1200–1650* (London, 1998), 59–86 at 71–2. It seems reasonable to associate this shift with the fact that the 'custodian system enabled a closer control over the sheriff and his revenue, but for that reason was more troublesome to run', D. A. Carpenter, 'The Decline of the Curial Sheriff in England 1194–1258', *EHR* 91 (1976), 1–32 at 3 n. 2.
[287] Maddicott, 'Edward I and the Lessons of Baronial Reform', 21–3; Prestwich, *Plantagenet England*, 127; Prestwich, *Edward I*, 102–3. Perhaps the sixteenth-century tradition of a 'parliamentary' discussion 4 Edward I (20 November 1275–19 November 1276) about efficient land management should be connected with the November 1275 'Statutes of the Exchequer' experiment (*SR*, i. 197–8). Oschinsky tried to connect the parliamentary references with the treatise on making a manorial extent, *Extenta manerii, Walter of Henley*, 70–2.
[288] Louise J. Wilkinson, *Women in Thirteenth-Century Lincolnshire* (Woodbridge, 2007), 51, 57–8.
[289] One might object that the courtesy here is a function of the *Rules* having been written for an aristocratic lady. But Grosseteste thought them good enough to stand for his own household in the Latin translation of the *Statuta*. As Agnes de Valence shows, there is no reason to presume any softness in female administrators in the thirteenth century.

is diminished or damaged by the neglect or wrong of others to repel it with all your power.[290]

The steward is endorsed to attend as much to the growth of her property as to its equitable increase. No bailiffs are to achieve such growth at the expense of her tenants and they are to 'neither oppress, nor hurt, nor abuse the people who hold land of me, rich or poor'.[291] This topic forms the longest entry of the Latin version and equally emphasizes the balance between profit and equity which the lord/lady should seek.

> [Item] That all trust [*diligencia*] is to be placed completely in the head steward [*senescallo superiori*] that rights, liberties, and fixed assets [*possessiones imobiles*] of his lord will be preserved intact and undiminished, and should any of them through negligence or unjustly be unprotected by his care [*immunitum per suam diligenciam*], on this account he may be justly recalled [*revocetur*]. And similarly, that moveable goods [*possessiones mobiles*] are to be multiplied in a just and honest way, and faithfully guarded and should come to the hands of the lord without fraudulent reductions, so that he may spend them to the honour of the Lord and the good of the dead.[292]

Conferring trust itself produces accountability or rather responsibility. There may be more theory here than meets the eye. The emphasis on establishing a mean in one's actions as a lord is very marked in Grosseteste's household and manorial advice: 'household service in food and drink should be courteous [*curiale*] expressing graceful service in voice, face and gesture, and with moderate [*moderamine*] generosity, neither notably stingy nor excessive'.[293] Likewise, while increase of assets should be sought, it should not come at the expense of unjust exactions or extortions. Since this is Grosseteste, translator of the *Nicomachean Ethics*, it is not fanciful to associate his emphasis on striking a balance between extremes with Aristotle's discussion of the mean in the *Ethics*. Likewise the brisk practical emphasis on *lordly* economic self-sufficiency in the *Rules* should be tallied with Grosseteste's stress on it as an Aristotelian principle of self-control and justice for *kings* in his commentary on the *Ethics* and his attack on papal placemen at Lyons in 1250.[294] Such connections certainly put the *Rules* and *Statuta* at the rarefied end of the manorial manual genre, but no less practical for that.[295] The permeability of offices to others is also illustrated. Ideals for kings flowed back and forth from ideas for bailiffs.

---

[290] *Rules*, cap. 3 (*Walter of Henley*, 390).   [291] *Rules*, cap. 3 (*Walter of Henley*, 390).
[292] *Statuta*, cap. 3 (*Walter of Henley*, 409).   [293] *Statuta*, cap. 3 (*Walter of Henley*, 409).
[294] The *Rules* stresses this from the outset: 'Ki le reules vout tenir ben e bel del son demeyne porra vivre e soy meymes e les son sustenir' (*Rules*, edn. in *Walter of Henley*, 388).). For sufficiency and kingship see Ambler, 'On Kingship and Tyranny', 122–4. Servus Gieben edited the documents, 'Robert Grosseteste at the Papal Curia, Lyons 1250. Edition of the documents', *Collectanea Franciscana* 41 (1971), 340–93.
[295] *Nicomachean Ethics* II.6–9 (1105a20–1109b25). A fully integrated reading of the *Rules* within the context of Grosseteste's other writings is needed. See the stress on the mean in Grosseteste's *Templum Dei, edited from MS 27 of Emmanuel College, Cambridge*, ed. Joseph Goering and F. A. C. Mantello (Toronto, 1984), 51 (1220–30). R. W. Southern's *Robert Grosseteste: The Growth of an English Mind in Medieval Europe*, rev. edn. (Oxford, 1992), focused principally on Grosseteste's ecclesiastical and 'intellectual' activities. The dating of Grosseteste's Aristotelian corpus to the 1240s, even

In terms of bailiffs' conduct the *Rules*' point is that it is the lady's good example that provides the pattern for the responsible conduct of her officers. Her character produces their character produces their responsible stewardship. The 27th rule 'teaches how you ought to bear yourself before your bailiffs of your lands and manors when they come before you':

> When your bailiffs and the servants of your lands and of your manors come before you, address them most kindly, and speak warmly with them privately and gently and inquire of them how your people do, and your corn in the fields, how your ploughs and your stock thrive, and make such inquiries openly and your good sense shall be greatly respected.[296]

Clanchy's useful distinction between love and law bears repeating, where 'love [...] is a bond of affection, established by public undertakings before witnesses and upheld by social pressure [...] and [Law is] imposed by authorities from above through codes of rules.' Grosseteste's 'loving' approach directed lords in the selection, cultivation, and character of their officers; he was as interested in responsibility as in accountability.[297] There is a comparable intermixing of responsibility and accountability in Philippe de Beaumanoir's *c*.1283 account of a *bailli*'s office, indeed here the former comes firmly first.[298] This was not a merely a theoretical matter. Simon of Senlis's letters show how important was the sheer temperament of individual officers. But it was theorized (with or without Aristotle), and what that theory stressed in the manorial manuals offers a final insight into those aspects of responsibility and accountability which sanctions such as the action of account could not so well engage.

In phase 2 accounts, sophisticated accounting is intended to compensate for officials' defects of character or competence. However while *Seneschauncy* does stress stewards' personal oversight of bailiffs, it also clearly emphasizes the need for men whose autonomy can be simply relied on because of their character. A bailiff

> should be loyal and profit-making, able to bring good gain and wise, such that he need send neither to their lord, nor to the steward to get counsel or advice on any matter touching their bailiwick, unless it is some strange problem or some great peril. For a bailiff is little use in business who knows little, and is incapable without others' advice.[299]

This is not a credulous theory of 'love'. The hayward should be 'vigorous and sharp'; the bailiff 'fair in all his actions', but the latter is still to be accompanied by the steward when collecting fines, reliefs, or dowers.[300] As in other cases examined in this study, the remedy of accountability (whether manifest in the action of account or accounts themselves) could not really address these aspects of officers' conduct. The

---

c.1246–7, closely correlates with the date range for the *Rules* (i.e. 1245–53) for which Wilkinson argues (this chapter, n. 156). Dating Grosseteste's Aristotle: Jean Dunbabin, 'Robert Grosseteste as Translator, Transmitter, and Commentator: the "Nicomachean Ethics"', *Traditio* 28 (1972), 460–72 at 461 and n. 3. I am grateful to Frédérique Lachaud for pointing out the complementarity of Paul Binski, *Becket's Crown: Art and Imagination in Gothic England, 1170–1300* (New Haven, Conn., 2004), 43, 181–6, esp. 186.

[296] *Rules*, cap. 27 (*Walter of Henley*, 406).   [297] Clanchy, 'Law and Love', 47, 50.
[298] *Coutumes de Beauvaisis*, i. cap. 1, esp. §11–22, 29–30, 40, 53.
[299] *Seneschauncy*, cap. 17 (*Walter of Henley*, 268).
[300] *Seneschauncy*, caps. 47, 21 (*Walter of Henley*, 280, 270).

addressing of character in this way seeks to cultivate *responsibility* to proportionately reduce the reliance on accountability. Internal rules create a framework that ideally makes external ones less essential.[301] Both love and law were elaborated in relation to bailiffs' and stewards' conduct in office. This was a contrast with sheriffs and ideas about bailiffs were arguably transposed to fill out a positive ideal of sheriffs' characters in 1258/9.

The argument of this chapter can be summarized as follows. There were limits to what institutionalized accountability could produce in terms of official conduct. English bailiffs' accountability to their lords becomes particularly problematic in the mid-thirteenth century. This arose from changes in bailiffs' relationships with lords, land, and communities. It was in part a function of professionalization. This though relocated rather than solved problems in lord–officer relationships. What is interesting for these manorial officers—most *mediocres* of those officers considered here—was the range of experiments for regulating their conduct in quite distinct ways. How much legalistic approaches such as the action of account left to say about stewardly conduct is indicated by the Chilton and Valle cases already reviewed. The issue was how practices of accountability interacted with norms of responsibility (how 'law' interacted with 'love' so to speak).[302] That problem provided the centre of gravity for several different types of attempted solution that circled around it: the action of account; accounting in its various 'phases'; the genre of manorial manuals. These solutions—law, maths, love—articulated different approaches to the same problem of manorial officers' accountability. It is interesting that in the case of bailiffs solutions premised both on accountability ('law') and on responsibility ('love') were articulated. That comparable ideas were diffuse and diffused in different institutions is part of this study's overall argument. Mentalities of accountability, and responsibility, got into everything. The phenomena they gravitated towards were parts of the same universe and inflected each other's particular orbits, even when those lines are hard to trace and their dynamics quite distinct. These spheres are so large and their historiographies so separate that it is as difficult as it is important to try to reconnect them as they were connected for medieval bailiffs and lords.

---

[301] See further Chs. 1 and 6. Cristina Jular Pérez-Alfaro has argued for essentially the same distinction for Castilian *adelantados* and *merinos*, but in terms of a 'positive' model of ideal official norms and a 'negative' regulatory, corrective one: '"King's Face on the Territory"': Royal Officers, Discourse and Legitimating Practices in Thirteenth and Fourteenth Century Castile', in Isabel Alfonso, Hugh Kennedy, and Julia Escalona (eds.), *Building Legitimacy: Political Discourses and Forms of Legitimacy in Medieval Societies*, The Medieval Mediterranean 53 (Leiden, 2004), 111, 119–20.

[302] Cf. Bisson, *Crisis of the Twelfth Century*, 4, 'Power attached to persons', also e.g. 94, 'confusion between official and affective action'.

3
Sheriffs

The English shrievalty was not a static office and consideration of it alone could constitute a monograph.[1] The sheriff can be defined crisply: 'a royal official who held his position at the king's pleasure and fulfilled a range of duties, primarily judicial and administrative. He presided over the county court and was responsible for the annual payment that each shire made to the king' at the Exchequer, as well as other debts owed to the king.[2] The sheriff was the most senior local officer in England's thirty-nine-odd counties,[3] could hold more than

---

[1] I am very grateful to David Carpenter for discussion of this subject. For lists, *List of Sheriffs for England and Wales: From the Earliest Times to A.D. 1831*, Public Record Office, Lists and Indexes 9, repr. (New York, 1963). W. A. Morris, *The Medieval English Sheriff to 1300* (Manchester, 1927) remains valuable. For the earlier period see Judith A. Green, *The Government of England under Henry I* (Cambridge, 1986), 194–214, and *English Sheriffs to 1154*, Public Record Office Handbooks 24 (London, 1990), 9–19. For the later period see Richard Gorski, *The Fourteenth-Century Sheriff: English Local Administration in the Late Middle Ages* (Woodbridge, 2003), esp. ch. 4. There are valuable comments throughout Frédérique Lachaud, *Éthique du pouvoir au Moyen Âge: L'Office dans la culture politique (Angleterre, vers 1150–vers 1330)*, Bibliothèque d'histoire médiévale 3 (Paris, 2010): her focus is complementary to mine. See also Robert Bartlett, *England under the Norman and Angevin Kings, 1075–1225* (Oxford, 2000), 149–51, 159–77; Flower, *Introduction to the Curia Regis Rolls, 1199–1230*, SS 62 (London, 1944), esp. 419–33. *The New Oxford Dictionary of Biography* now includes many studies of individual sheriffs. For two recent studies elsewhere see Hugh Doherty, 'Robert de Vaux and Roger de Stuteville, Sheriffs of Cumberland and Northumberland 1170–1185', *Anglo-Norman Studies* 28 (2006), 65–102; Nicholas Karn, 'Secular Power and its Rewards in Dorset in the Late Eleventh and Early Twelfth Centuries', *Historical Research* 82 (2009), 2–16. Studies with wider implications include Emilie Amt, 'The Reputation of the Sheriff, 1100–1216', *Haskins Society Journal* 8 (1996), 91–8, and for Henry II, Julia Boorman, 'The Sheriffs of Henry II and the Significance of 1170', in George Garnett and John Hudson (eds.), *Law and Government in Medieval England and Normandy: Essays in Honour of Sir James Holt* (Cambridge, 1994), 255–75. For Richard I: Richard Heiser, 'The Sheriffs of Richard I: Trends of Management as Seen in the Shrieval Appointments from 1189 to 1194', *Haskins Society Journal* 4 (1993), 109–22; Heiser, 'Richard I and His Appointments to English Shrievalties', *EHR* 112 (1997), 1–19. For John and Henry III: J. C. Holt, 'Philip Mark and the Shrievalty of Nottinghamshire and Derbyshire in the Early Thirteenth Century', *Transactions of the Thoroton Society of Nottinghamshire* 56 (1952), 8–24; D. A. Carpenter, 'The Decline of the Curial Sheriff in England 1194–1258', *EHR* 91 (1976). For the Barons' War: H. W. Ridgeway, 'Mid Thirteenth-Century Reformers and the Localities: The Sheriffs of the Baronial Regime, 1258–1261', in P. F. Fleming, A. Gross, and J. R. Lander (eds.), *Regionalism and Revision: The Crown and its Provinces in England, 1200–1650* (London, 1998); Richard Cassidy, '*Adventus Vicecomitum* and the Financial Crisis of Henry III's Reign, 1250–1272', *EHR* 126 (2011), 614–27, and 'Bad Sheriffs, Custodial Sheriffs, and Control of the Counties', *TCE* 15 (forthcoming 2015). For Edward see J. R. Maddicott, 'Edward I and the Lessons of Baronial Reform: Local Government, 1258–80', *TCE* 1 (1986).

[2] Bartlett, *England under the Norman and Angevin Kings*, 149; also John Hudson, *The Oxford History of the Laws of England*, ii. *871–1216* (Oxford, 2012), 265–6, 506–7 with 37–40.

[3] The number of counties fluctuated in the twelfth century (Bartlett, *England under the Norman and Angevin Kings*, 147–9). The model of sheriff/Exchequer/county was also used in colonial government in Ireland and Wales.

one shrievalty[4] and could hold it in tandem with another.[5] He could be a cleric.[6] He could hold the job over successive block terms.[7] He had deputies.[8] 'He' was occasionally 'she'.[9] The post could be held by successive members of the same family, although—excepting Stephen's reign—it did not ossify into a hereditary sinecure.[10] By 1130, the date of the first extant annual Exchequer audit, the sheriffs answered for 'county farms'—the bundle of money due from the royal estates, individual debts due to the king, payments due from towns, proceeds from cases in the county and hundred courts, and other land payments, such as wardpenny.[11] The sheriff also collected the geld, the Anglo-Saxon de facto annual land tax liable on freely owned ('demesne') land.[12] The shrievalty allowed for a rentier system—aspirant sheriffs could offer money to the crown in exchange for holding a county farm over a given period of time. Equally it allowed sheriffs to buy themselves out of the burden of office.[13]

Shrieval judicial and administrative activities were broad. The sheriff generally carried out the King's orders, with an armed county posse if necessary.[14] Equally he could be the object of violence.[15] The sheriff attended the county court with other local worthies and was probably often the greatest figure actually present.[16] He could

---

[4] In 1110 Hugh of Buckland was sheriff of eight counties, including Berkshire, Hertfordshire, Bedfordshire, Buckinghamshire, Essex, and London and Middlesex. See Henry Bradley, 'Buckland, Hugh of (d. 1116 x 19)', rev. John Hudson, *ODNB*.

[5] So Richard Basset and Aubrey de Vere jointly held Bedfordshire, Buckinghamshire, Cambridgeshire, Essex, Hertfordshire, Huntingdonshire, Leicestershire, Norfolk, Northamptonshire, Suffolk, Surrey, and Lincolnshire between 1129 and 1130. See *List of Sheriffs for England and Wales*; Green, *Government of England*, 65–6 and their entries in her biographical appendix.

[6] e.g. Hilary, Bishop of Chichester, sheriff of Sussex in 1154–5, *The Red Book of the Exchequer*, ed. Hubert Hall, RS, 3 vols. (London, 1896), ii. 654.

[7] e.g. Osbert the Sheriff held Yorkshire from 1100 to *c.*1115, Green, *English Sheriffs*, 89.

[8] For the earlier period see e.g. *Cartularium monasterii de Rameseia*, ed. William Henry Hart and Ponsonby A. Lyons, 3 vols., RS (London, 1884–93), i. ##61, 81. In general, Robert C. Palmer, *The County Courts of Medieval England 1150–1350* (Princeton, NJ, 1982), 40–55; M. L. Holford, 'Under-sheriffs, the State, and Local Society, *c.*1300–1340: A Preliminary Survey', in Chris Given-Wilson, Ann Kettle, and Len Scales (eds.), *War, Government, and Aristocracy in the British Isles, c.1150–1500: Essays in Honour of Michael Prestwich* (Woodbridge, 2008), 55–68.

[9] Louise J. Wilkinson, 'Women as Sheriffs in Early Thirteenth Century England', in Adrian Jobson (ed.), *English Government in the Thirteenth Century* (Woodbridge, 2004), 111–24.

[10] e.g. Sweyn succeeded his father Robert FitzWymarc at Essex at some point after the Conquest and is addressed as sheriff at points between 1066 and 1085 (Green, *English Sheriffs*, 39). One should not necessarily presume that the reissuing of the office to a member of the same family implied royal indifference to competence. For (e.g.) John's 1205 grant of Rutland to Radulf of Normanvilla see *Rotuli chartarum in Turri londinensi asservati*, ed. T. D. Hardy (London, 1837), i.1. 149a.

[11] Green, *English Sheriffs*, 10–11, and *Government of England*, 63–6.

[12] The geld's origin as an anti-Viking military levy is claimed by the Peterborough Anglo-Saxon Chronicle ('E') for 1012: *The Anglo-Saxon Chronicles*, trans. Michael Swanton, rev. edn. (London, 2000), 142–3. The tax lapsed 1162–94, re-emerged as 'carucage', and came under attack again in 1220. See Bartlett, *England under the Norman and Angevin Kings*, 165–6; J. C. Holt, *Magna Carta*, 2nd edn. (Cambridge, 1992), 399–400; J. R. Maddicott, *The Origins of the English Parliament, 924–1327* (Oxford, 2010), 150.

[13] Early and later examples: *PR 1130*, 117 (new edn. Judith Green); eight instances in May 1253 in *CPR 1247–1258*, a decade when it was a particular problem (J. R. Maddicott, 'Magna Carta and the Local Community', *P&P* 102 (1984), 45).

[14] e.g. *CPR 1247–1258*, 223–4, a 1253 order for Dorset and Somerset.

[15] e.g. *CPR 1247–1258*, 225, about the beating of those shires' sheriff, Walter de Burges (1253).

[16] *LHP*, cap. 7.2; Green, *English Sheriffs*, 10; Morris, *Medieval English Sheriff*, 88–94.

be ordered to carry out particular investigations.[17] His precise judicial competence early on is not wholly clear. He presided over the county courts, but was not per se judge.[18] The *Leges Henrici Primi* implies that the sheriff was a justice of the King, but this role was dwindling, the general eyre partly supplanting it.[19] His jurisdiction was cut back in 1274, following a series of inquiries (the 'hundred rolls' inquiries) into royal rights and local wrongs on Edward I's return to England.[20] There were already formal limits. The *Leges* specifies the crown pleas in which the sheriff needs an explicit dispensation to act with sufficient stress for us to infer sheriffs' intrusion into them.[21] It was the sheriff too who summoned the monthly hundred courts, the administrative tier below many counties.[22] Here he took his 'tourn', the biannual 'view of frankpledge' at which he checked that all adult free men were in 'tithings', the ten-strong groups that bound members as liable sureties for one another should they break the law.[23] He was also instrumental in disseminating important political statements locally, such as reissues of Magna Carta.[24]

The English sheriff has his equivalents elsewhere in Western Christendom. Appointed regional officials of a central delegating authority who combined administrative and judicial functions existed elsewhere: *bailli* and *prévôt* in France, *vicarius* or *baiulus* in Catalonia, *dapifer*, *senescalus*, and *prepositus* in Flanders, names that may be found more generally and generically.[25] As with bailiffs, these are not exact matches but they broadly embrace the same type of agent. It is as 'public' officials that this chapter examines shrieval officers (the adjective is therefore used generically). *Ministerialis* may be used more generally, but German *ministeriales* are less comparable, remaining a clear *Dienstadel* or aristocracy of service.[26] Comparators can also be found earlier, as with Carolingian *missi dominici*[27] or *fiscalini*,[28] while the sheriff himself grew clearly out of an Anglo-Saxon stem.[29]

---

[17] e.g. *CPR 1247–1258*, 197, sheriff of York's inquisition into a homicide.

[18] e.g. Hugh of Buckland presided over the Berkshire county court, see Morris, *Medieval English Sheriff*, 89; Palmer, *County Courts*, 28, 35–7.

[19] *LHP*, cap. 53.1 refers to the summoner of the county court—a shrieval function—as *iusticia regis*.

[20] Palmer, *County Courts*, 228–9; Maddicott, 'Edward I and the Lessons of Baronial Reform'.

[21] *LHP*, caps. 10.1, 10.4, 19.1.   [22] *LHP*, cap. 51.

[23] *LHP*, caps. 8.1, 8.2. In general W. A. Morris, *The Frankpledge System* (Cambridge, Mass., 1910); Hudson, *Oxford History of the Laws of England*, 555–6. Not all counties had a tourn.

[24] *CPR 1247–1258*, 281 (24 March 1254, regarding the 1253 reissue).

[25] On regional terms, W. C. Jordan, *Louis IX and the Challenge of the Crusade: A Study in Rulership* (Princeton, NJ, 1979), 46; Pascale Bourgain and Marie-Clotilde Hubert, *Le Latin médiéval*, L'Atelier du médiéviste 10 (Turnhout, 2005), 100 and examples at 254–5, 315–18.

[26] For introductions to specialized literature, Benjamin Arnold, 'Instruments of Power: The Profile and Profession of *Ministeriales* within German Aristocratic Society (1050–1225)', in Thomas Bisson (ed.), *Cultures of Power: Lordship, Status and Process in Twelfth-Century Europe* (Philadelphia, 1995), 36–55; Arnold, *German Knighthood, 1050–1300* (Oxford, 1985), and Karl Leyser, 'The German Aristocracy from the Ninth to the Early Twelfth Century: A Historical and Cultural Sketch', *P&P* 41 (1968), 25–53.

[27] Nelson, 'Kingship and Royal Government', esp. 411–14; McKitterick, *Charlemagne, passim*; de Jong, *Penitential State, passim*.

[28] Stuart Airlie, 'Bonds of Power and Bonds of Association in the Court Circle of Louis the Pious', in Peter Godman and Roger Collins (eds.), *Charlemagne's Heir: New Perspectives on the Reign of Louis the Pious (814–840)* (Oxford, 1990), 191–204, arguing that *fiscalini* did not uphold an ideal of dispassionate service for some sort of public good (193–4). They were answerable for their conduct, though (198–200).

[29] *Scir-gerefa*, or shire-reeve in Old English, *vicecomes*, in Latin; the *comes* was a military rank introduced by Constantine. *Vicarius* was also a Roman title of the provincial governors, technically the deputies of praetorian prefects.

It is uncontroversial that English sheriffs were accountable. In the context of Henry II's ad hoc 1170 investigation into shrieval behaviour which left 26 per cent of sheriffs in post, Robert Bartlett argues the sheriffs 'remained dismissable and accountable'.[30] Describing the Exchequer, Judith Green argues cogently that it functioned more as an 'aid to accountability, than as a help for the illiterate'.[31] Michael Clanchy concludes that the Chancery (the King's writing office) and the Exchequer 'contributed to the theory of kingship and the philosophy of government by making royal orders accountable, repeatable and widespread'.[32]

What was the quality of this accountability? Sheriffs were, in principle, highly accountable, in two broad ways. The first was through the Easter and Michaelmas audit of sheriffs' expenses and income at the Exchequer at Westminster—an institution that attracted both attention and some opprobrium in the later twelfth century. The records of these audits (which summoned other debtors beyond the sheriff) survive in the Pipe Rolls unbroken from 1156, one of the earliest continuous sets of administrative sources in European history.[33]

The second way was through a wide range of irregular, but not infrequent, central governmental inquiries. One of these, the itinerant late twelfth- to late thirteenth-century 'general eyre' of royal justices heard civil and criminal county pleas, including complaints against sheriffs.[34] In addition the crown commissioned specific inquiries into the conduct in office of sheriffs and other officials during the twelfth and thirteenth centuries. The sheriff was in this period therefore the

---

[30] Bartlett, *England under the Norman and Angevin Kings*, 150. For example, the 21 July 1253 power given to Eleanor and Richard of Cornwall to remove sheriffs who 'fall short in their offices' while Henry III is on the Continent, *CPR 1247–1258*, 214.

[31] Green, *Government of England*, 40.

[32] M. T. Clanchy, *England and its Rulers, 1066–1307*, 3rd edn. (Oxford, 2006), 58.

[33] A fragment of an earlier roll has been found by Mark Hagger in a St Albans cartulary, see 'A Pipe Roll for 25 Henry I', *EHR* 122 (2007), 133–40. Judith Green argues that the 1130 roll reflects 'fundamentally the same department of government as that described in the *Dialogus*, but at a slightly earlier stage of development', '*Praeclarum et Magnificum Antiquitatis Monumentum*: The Earliest Surviving Pipe Roll' [*Bulletin of the Institute of*] *Historical Research* 55 (1982), 1–17 at 2. See now her new edn. *The Great Roll of the Pipe for the Thirty First Year of the Reign of Henry I, Michaelmas 1130 (Pipe Roll 1)*, ed. Judith A. Green, Pipe Roll Society ns 57 (95) (Loughborough, 2012). For a thirteenth-century overview, Richard Cassidy, '*Recorda splendidissima*: The Use of Pipe Rolls in the Thirteenth Century', *Historical Research* 85 (2012), 1–12.

[34] David Crook, *Records of the General Eyre*, Public Record Office Handbooks 20 (London, 1982), 47–52; Hudson, *Oxford History of the Laws of England*, 544–8. In general see C. A. F. Meekings' introductions to his *Crown Pleas of the Wiltshire Eyre, 1249*, Wiltshire Archaeological and Natural History Society 16 (Devizes, 1961) and *The 1235 Surrey Eyre*, ed. C. A. F. Meekings, completed by David Crook, 3 vols., Surrey Record Society 31, 32, 37 (Guildford, 1979–2002), i. A general synthesis, building on the many individual analyses, is now needed. Eyre records edited since 1982 include Adrian Jobson, 'The Oxfordshire Eyre Roll of 1261', 3 vols. (University of London Ph.D. thesis, 2006), *The Civil Pleas of the Suffolk Eyre of 1240*, ed. Eric James Gallagher, Suffolk Record Society 52 (Woodbridge, 2009); *The Earliest English Law Reports*, vols. iii–iv, ed. Paul A. Brand, SS 122–3 (London, 2005–7); *The Worcester Eyre of 1275*, ed. Jens Röhrkasten, Worcestershire Historical Society NS, 22 (Trowbridge, 2008); *The Northumberland Eyre Roll for 1293*, ed. Constance M. Fraser, Surtees Society 211 (Woodbridge, 2009); *The 1263 Surrey Eyre*, ed. Susan Stewart, Surrey Record Society 40 (Woking, 2006); *The Buckinghamshire Eyre of 1286*, ed. Lesley Boatwright, Buckinghamshire Record Society 34 (Aylesbury, 2006); *The 1258–9 Special Eyre of Surrey and Kent*, ed. Andrew H. Hershey, Surrey Record Society 38 (Woking, 2004); *1235 Surrey Eyre*, ed. Meekings with Crook; *The Rolls of the 1281 Derbyshire Eyre*, ed. Aileen M. Hopkinson, intr. Crook, Derbyshire Record Society 27

target of both ad hoc and routine modes of accountability. The question here is what was the quality of accountability in either of these two broad fora; what was their relationship, and how did ideas of accountability change and differ from one to the other—especially in relation to comparable Continental practices?

The question is usefully approached by noting the broad separation of enquiries into shrieval fiscality on the one hand and wider conduct on the other, and its parallel with two interesting European frameworks developed separately by Thomas Bisson and Jean Glénisson.[35]

Glénisson's schema was developed on the basis of his work on Louis IX's France-wide enquiries into *baillis'* and *prévôts'* behaviour before and after the 1248–54 Crusade.[36] Glénisson described his interest as 'administrative inquiries', although wary of its potentially anachronistic formulation. He defined that type of inquiry as 'all information summarily required by a power in a matter and focusing on an object which concerns either the rights and duties of the sovereign and the state, or the manner in which delegated authorities exercise their functions'.[37] Hence, Glénisson sees two families with different goals but both nevertheless arising from the state's 'permanent need for control'. 'The first has as its goal the investigation of information useful to the good administration of the state's domanial and fiscal business. The second aspires to correcting and reforming abuses.'[38]

(Chesterfield, 2000); *The Oxfordshire Eyre, 1241*, ed. Janet Cooper, Oxfordshire Record Society 56 (Oxford, 1989); *Crown Pleas of the Devon Eyre of 1238*, ed. Henry Summerson, Devon and Cornwall Record Society NS 28 (Torquay, 1985); *The Eyre of Northamptonshire: 3–4 Edward III, A.D. 1329–1330*, ed. Donald W. Sutherland, SS 97–8, (1983). For the forest eyre, Jane Frances Winters, 'The Forest Eyre, 1154–1368' (University of London Ph.D. thesis, 1999).

[35] I expand here on Sabapathy, 'Accountable *rectores* in comparative perspective: the theory and practice of holding *podestà* and bishops to account (late twelfth to thirteenth centuries)', in Agnès Bérenger and Frédérique Lachaud (eds.), *Hiérarchie des pouvoirs, délégation de pouvoir et responsabilité des administrateurs dans l'Antiquité et au Moyen Âge*, Centre de Recherche Universitaire Lorrain d'Histoire, Université de Lorraine—Site de Metz 46 (Metz, 2012), 220–4.

[36] Jean Glénisson, 'Les Enquêtes administratives en Europe occidentale aux XIIIe et XIVe siècles', in Werner Paravicini and Karl Ferdinand Werner (eds.), *Histoire comparée de l'administration (IVe–XVIIe siècles)*, Beihefte der Francia 9 (Munich, 1980), 17–25. Glénisson's plan to extend and apply this framework more generally never materialized. The earlier work is summarized in Jean Glénisson, 'Les Enquêteurs-réformateurs de 1270 à 1328', in *Positions des thèses soutenues par les élèves de la promotion de 1946 pour obtenir le diplôme d'archiviste paléographe*, École nationale des chartes (1946), 81–8. For discussion and/or application see e.g. Anne Mailloux, 'Pratiques administratives, définition des droits et fixation territoriale d'après l'enquête ordonnée par Robert sur les droits de l'évêque de Gap entre 1305 et 1309', in Jean-Paul Boyer, Anne Mailloux and Laure Verdon (eds.), *La Justice temporelle dans les territoires angevins aux XIIIe et XIVe siècles: Théories et pratiques*, Collection de l'École française de Rome 354 (Rome, 2005), 249–62; Marie Dejoux, 'Mener une enquête générale, pratiques et méthodes: l'exemple de la tournée ordonnée par Louis IX en Languedoc à l'hiver 1247–48', in Thierry Pécout (ed.), *Quand gouverner c'est enquêter: Les Pratiques politiques de l'enquête princière (Occident, XIIIe–XIVe siècles)* (Paris, 2010), 133–55. I have been unable to consult Jean-Paul Boyer, 'Construire l'état en Provence. Les "Enquêtes administratives" (mi-XIIIe–mi-XIVe siècle)', in Bernard Demotz (ed.), *Des principautés aux régions dans l'espace européen* (Lyons, 1994), 1–26.

[37] Glénisson, 'Enquêtes administratives', 18–19.

[38] Glénisson, 'Enquêtes administratives', 19. Different original dynamics for ecclesiastical and secular inquisitions are suggested in Theodor Bühler-Reimann, '*Enquête—Inquesta—Inquisitio*', *ZRG Kan. Abt.* 61 (1975), 53–62. More useful is R. I. Moore's stress on transference between secular and ecclesiastical practices. See his *The War on Heresy: Faith and Power in Medieval Europe* (London,

Glénisson worried about the risk of anachronism in his schema. Can Louis's *enquêtes* really be thought of as 'administrative'?[39] An unanachronistic distinction between 'useful administration' and 'correction and reform' is available through the actual classical and medieval distinction between acting advantageously (*utile*) and acting with integrity (*honeste*).[40] Glénisson's two categories of *inquisitiones* stress the supposedly different social function of each. In practice though, his understandable stress on *inquisitiones*' juridical form and etymological roots would underplay this aspect.[41] A preoccupation with etymological parallels risks paying insufficient attention to functional similarities when such parallels are lacking. One reason for the lack of sustained comparisons between eyres (English judges itinerating on their *ex officio* judicial tours with wide-ranging and variable mandates) and Continental *inquisitiones* such as that specified in the Constitutions of Melfi (judges and administrators *ex officio* investigating behaviour of various types)[42] is perhaps the lack of a shared etymological link.[43] Lastly, Glénisson's two-family model risks an unhelpful

2012), 171–2 (Philip of Alsace's 1163 code for Arras), 193 (cap. 21 of the 1166 Assize of Clarendon), 205–6 (*Ad abolendam*, 1184), 299–302 (1236 Montauban inquisitions) and his *The First European Revolution, c.970–1215* (Oxford, 2000), 171–3.

[39] Glénisson, 'Enquêtes administratives', 19–20. Cf. the October 1259 Provisions of Westminster in England, also described by their editors as 'administrative and political resolutions', which stipulated that there should be investigations into sheriffs and baronial and royal bailiffs (*DBM* #12, caps. 5–6).

[40] The Pseudo-Ciceronian *Rhetorica ad Herrenium* placed *utilitas* as the criterion of action, of which security (*tuta*) and integrity (*honestas*) were the two subtypes. Cicero himself sought to integrate the *utile* with the *honestum*, arguing that the action expressing both should be chosen, and in *De officiis* arguing that any contradiction between the two was apparent rather than real. On this see Matthew Kempshall, *Rhetoric and the Writing of History, 400–1500* (Manchester, 2011), 229–34, and 234–42 for later usages.

[41] The juridical form he emphasizes is that of testimony and witnessing, Glénisson, 'Enquêtes administratives', 17–18. Sandra Raban, 'Edward I's Other Inquiries', *TCE* 9 (2003), 43–57 at 44, commented that this was too generic a form to be a useful distinguishing characteristic. Cf. Bühler-Reimann, '*Enquête—Inquesta—Inquisitio*' and see the many interesting papers in Claude Gauvard (ed.), *L'Enquête au Moyen Âge*, Collection École française de Rome 399 (Rome, 2008).

[42] e.g. *Die Konstitutionen Friedrichs II. für das Königreich sizilien*, ed. Wolfgang Stürner, MGH Leges, Const. Suppl. 2 (Hannover, 1996), caps. 1.17, 1.28, and (in 1246) 1.62.2.

[43] The question of Continental influences on English *inquisitiones* has been, at times, obstructed by a tedious possessive chauvinism about wishing to demonstrate that it is 'really' English or 'really' Frankish. Helpful contributions are: R. Besnier, '«*Inquisitiones*» et «*Recognitiones*». Le Nouveau Système des preuves à l'époque des Coutumiers normands', *Revue historique de droit français et étranger* 28 (1950), 183–212; R. C. van Caenegem, 'Public Prosecution of Crime in Twelfth-Century England', *Legal History: A European Perspective* (London, 1991), 1–36; Sandra Raban, *A Second Domesday? The Hundred Rolls of 1279–80* (Oxford, 2004), 26–36. Alan Harding, *Medieval Law and the Foundations of the State* (Oxford, 2002), esp. 33–7, 118–23, 134–5, 147–60; Lachaud, *Éthique du pouvoir*, 404–16. A recent discussion rejecting Continental sworn inquests as parallels for the Domesday *descriptio* is David Roffe, *Domesday: The Inquest and the Book* (Oxford, 2000), ch. 3, esp. 54–5. There are differences of scale and intent but the approach and mentality are comparable. On this see R. H. C. Davis, 'Domesday Book: Continental Parallels', in *Domesday Studies: Papers Read at the Novocentenary Conference of the Royal Historical Society and the Institute of British Geographers, Winchester 1986*, ed. J. C. Holt (Woodbridge, 1987), 15–39. For Carolingian practices see e.g. the c.809–12 Lyons church survey in Alexandre Coville, *Recherches sur l'histoire de Lyon du Vme siècle au IXme siècle, 450–800* (Paris, 1928), 283–8; *Capitulare de villis* in MGH Leges, *Capitularia regum Francorum*, ed. Alfred Boretius and Victor Krause, 2 vols. (Hannover, 1883–7), i. #32; the possibly 807 *Capitula de causis diversis* 4 (*Capitularia regum Francorum*, i. #49); the 811–13 capitulary on justice (*Capitularia regum Francorum*, i. #80); the possible template for inventories *Brevium exempla* (*Capitularia regum Francorum*, i. #128); and the commissioned survey into Holy Land churches

either/or approach to different modes of accountability.[44] If the apparently principled purge of English sheriffs in 1170 is reformist it cannot be fiscal or *utile*. It is unhelpful to be obliged to make such choices, and there is no reason why '1170' cannot pertain to both.

Thomas Bisson's key distinction is determined by the quality of the relationship between servant and superior. In a series of important publications Bisson has argued for a 'revival of office' across many parts of Europe over the twelfth century. During this period, a 'failing system of fidelitarian management' was replaced by a 'concept of accountable functional competence', the 'most nearly revolutionary change of the twelfth century'.[45] Techniques (such as dynamic accounting and auditing)[46] are both a cause and effect of the generally fiscal, functional competence that ties officer and superior by a quite different knot from that of a tie of fidelity. That latter accountability of fidelity dominates European polities before the later twelfth century and Bisson argues that in the eleventh and twelfth centuries

> Sheriffs, viscounts (notably in Normandy) and (lay) vicars were entrusted with public powers of command and demand [. . .] If the form of such service remained administrative or official, its essence had become proprietary or personal. The men sent out to collect and command were not so much agents as companions in lordship [. . .] Of official appointment or election there is very little evidence before the later twelfth century; and of stipulated accountability on the part of bailiffs and provosts, none at all [. . .]

---

c.801–10 in Michael McCormick, *Charlemagne's Survey of the Holy Land: Wealth, Personnel, and Buildings of a Mediterranean Church between Antiquity and the Middle Ages* (Washington DC, 2011), esp. 148–9, 155–159, 200–217. For older comparisons of different aspects of accountability/bureaucracy see e.g. Charles Petit-Dutaillis, *La Monarchie féodale en France et Angleterre, X^e–XIIIe siècle* (Paris, 1933); and Heinrich Mitteis, *The State in the Middle Ages: A Comparative Constitutional History of Feudal Europe*, trans. H. F. Orton (Amsterdam, 1975). Adriaan Verhulst and Bryce Lyon, *Medieval Finance*, is valuable but can be unclear. See also the works cited by W. C. Jordan, T. N. Bisson, and R. I. Moore. Stubbs's stress on admixture remains strikingly sane: William Stubbs, *The Constitutional History of England in its Origin and Development*, 3rd edn. 3 vols. (Oxford, 1880), i. 275–6, 434–9.

[44] For criticism within the French *enquêtes* context see Dejoux, 'Mener une enquête générale', and Olivier Canteaut, 'Le Juge et le financier: Les Enquêteurs-réformateurs des derniers Capétiens (1314–1328)', in Gauvard (ed.) *L'Enquête au Moyen Âge*, 269–318. For editions of post-Louis IX *enquêtes* see the *Enquêtes menées sous les derniers Capétiens*, ed. Xavier Hélary and Élisabeth Lalou, Ædilis, Publications scientifiques 4 (Orléans, 2006–9), online only at http://www.cn-telma.fr/enquetes/, accessed February 2014. From an English perspective, Sally Harvey's forthcoming *Domesday: Book of Judgement* (Oxford, 2014) would argue Domesday entailed an 'inquest of sheriffs' that was interested in both shrieval conduct and royal fiscality.

[45] Bisson reviewing Moore, *First European Revolution*, *c.970–1215* (Oxford, 2000), in *Speculum* 77 (2002), 1366–8 at 1367. More widely, see T. N. Bisson, *Fiscal Accounts of Catalonia under the Early Count-Kings (1151–1213)*, 2 vols. (Berkeley, Calif., 1984), i. Introduction; 'Les Comptes des domaines au temps du Philippe Auguste: essai comparatif', in his *Medieval France and her Pyrenean Neighbours: Studies in Early Institutional History* (London, 1989); the *P&P* ' "Feudal Revolution" debate' (references at p. 18 n.92); 'Medieval Lordship', *Speculum* 70 (1995); *Tormented Voices: Power, Crisis and Humanity in Rural Catalonia, 1140–1200* (Cambridge Mass., 1998); *The Crisis of the Twelfth Century: Power, Lordship, and the Origins of European Government* (Princeton, NJ, 2009).

[46] Bisson, *Crisis of the Twelfth Century*, 326–49. By 'dynamic' Bisson means that the demands made and so the accounts offered are not fixed and ideal ('prescriptive') but based on fresh assessments of value that are regularly reviewed. Cf. my comments about Tidenham and the *Rectitudines*, pp. 56–8.

accountancy was a matter of lordly or courtly sociability: [. . .] it was informal, remedial, and occasional.[47]

These two currents (fidelity/office) flow in contrary directions because they are premised on different relationships between officer and superior. Bisson's general argument is that the 'accountability of fidelity' runs out and is gradually displaced by 'the accountability of office' from the late twelfth century. The two types have been taken as mutually exclusive, although Bisson argues that they are rather sliding scales—and this is a more useful way of understanding the contrast he draws.[48] On Bisson's interpretation holding officers to account for their managerial competence is a sign of office; office is sign of government; and government is the premise for real politics. Shrieval accountability at the Exchequer would therefore be a sign of functional, fiscal, official competence. Shrieval liability at eyres and shrieval-specific ad hoc inquiries by contrast might be a sign of what Bisson elsewhere calls moral or remedial accountability. How these elements actually combine in the figure of the sheriff is problematic as will become clear, but Bisson is surely right overall about the increasing stress given to office-holding and accountability (it is, after all, the subject of this study).

Bisson's and Glénisson's schemas appear to complement and correlate with forms of shrieval accountability. Sheriffs are subject to one sort of fiscal audit focusing on competence and money-management. Sheriffs are also subject to inquiries attentive to more equitable aspects of their conduct.[49] Money and fiscal competence in one arena; ethics, conduct, lawbreaking in another is the apparent division of labour.

One way to assess the quality of shrieval accountability—and to see how far these models work—is to see how people thought Exchequer accountability worked. Rather than looking at a particular sheriff in the first instance, since there are numerous individual studies, and since it provides important insights and merits a rereading, I will focus on an important Exchequer insider's view: that of Richard of Ely,

---

[47] Bisson, 'Medieval Lordship', 752–3, and developed in *Fiscal Accounts of Catalonia*, i, *Tormented Voices*, and *Crisis*.

[48] I am grateful to Professor Bisson for discussion and comment. I take his types in a Weberian rather than a Platonic spirit—i.e. rather than proving them by demonstrating their absolute manifestation in history one uses such ideal types as guides for 'things to look for' à la Wickham (see pp. 6, 20–1, and John Sabapathy, 'A Medieval Officer and a Modern Mentality: *Podestà* and the Quality of Accountability', *Mediaeval Journal* 1.2 (2011), 76–9). The point is first whether ideal types are helpful rather than whether they are right, although with any ideal type its basic premises may turn out to be sufficiently wrong as to be no longer helpful (as many would argue is the case with Weber on towns). For interesting reviews of Bisson's *Crisis* see that by Theo Riches, *Reviews in History* (2009), together with Bisson's response (http://www.history.ac.uk/reviews/review/754 and http://www.history.ac.uk/reviews/review/754/response, both accessed February 2014); Robert Bartlett, 'Lords of "Pride and Plunder"', *New York Review of Books* 57/11 (24 June 2010), 47–50, with Bisson's response by letter on 11 November 2010; Judith Green, *English Historical Review*, 125 (2010), 680–2; and R. I. Moore, *American Historical Review* 115 (2010), 172–4.

[49] Cf. Bernard Williams, 'Professional Morality and its Dispositions', in his *Making Sense of Humanity and Other Philosophical Papers 1982–1993* (Cambridge, 1995), 200. For the existence of substantive rather than formal standards in thirteenth-century England, see Paul Brand, 'Ethical Standards for Royal Justices in England, c.1175–1307', *University of Chicago Law School Roundtable* 8 (2001), 239–79.

Treasurer at the Exchequer (1158 x 1160–c.1196) and author of a treatise about it. To gauge his perspective I need to look first at some critics of the Exchequer.

'EXCHEQUER RULES': ACCOUNTABILITY AND THE *DIALOGUE OF THE EXCHEQUER*

The late twelfth-century English Exchequer had a formidable reputation. Both a court and the counting house,[50] historians have described it as 'the most relentless financial system in Europe', the 'gyroscope that kept the whole structure of [English] government and administration on an even keel', the 'eye of the storm'.[51] The bare mechanics of shrieval accountability at the late twelfth-century Exchequer worked as follows.[52] Written summonses to account specifying the amount due were issued in advance of the two sessions at Easter and Michaelmas. These went out to sheriffs, other royal agents, and those with significant royal debts or agreements.[53] Half the sheriffs' 'farm' was due at the Easter 'view', the sheriff then receiving notched wooden tallies indicating the amount actually paid in to the Treasury. He would bring these, his summons, royal writs authorizing expenditure, his receipts, and cash at Michaelmas for the final account which was taken at the Upper or Greater Exchequer at Westminster.[54] It was from this complex mix of wood, parchment, and coin that the final reckoning was made. If it all tallied with the Exchequer's record of what the sheriff owed, the accountant was deemed quit. Debts frequently rolled on into successive accounting years, however.

The English king therefore had a complex set of moneys to spend. He might have feudal dues (wardships, proffers for marriages), or moneys arising from the

---

[50] The first reference to the (barons of the) Exchequer exemplifies this mix; a writ exempting St Mary of Lincoln from the 3s. hide tax of 1110, *Regesta Regum Anglo-Normannorum 1066–1154*, ii. at #963. *Select Cases in the Exchequer of Pleas* provides a valuable introduction to the court side of the Exchequer, esp. xxxix, xliv, liii–liv.

[51] First quote, R. W. Southern, *The Making of the Middle Ages* (London, 1953), 180; following quotes, Warren, *Henry II*, new edn. (London, 1991), 315, 316. The historiography of the twelfth-century Exchequer is large. Editions of *DS* provide bibliographies, as do many newer Pipe Rolls editions (e.g. *PR 1221*). The last monograph was Reginald L. Poole's *The Exchequer in the Twelfth Century* (Oxford, 1912); see also F. Liebermann *Einleitung in den Dialogus de Scaccario* (Göttingen, 1875). More recent studies include H. G. Richardson, 'Richard fitz Neal and the *Dialogus de Scaccario*', *EHR* 43 (1928), 161–71, 321–40; H. G. Richardson and G. O. Sayles, *The Governance of Mediaeval England from the Conquest to Magna Carta* (Edinburgh, 1963), *passim*; and Green, *Government of England*, esp. 38–50. For sharp commentary see Clanchy, *England and its Rulers*, 54–9, and *From Memory to Written Record: England 1066–1307*, 3rd edn. (Chichester, 2013), *passim*; John Hudson, 'Administration, Family and Perceptions of the Past in Late Twelfth-Century England: Richard FitzNigel and the Dialogue of the Exchequer', in Paul Magdalino (ed.), *The Perception of the Past in Twelfth Century Europe* (London, 1992), 75–98, and *The Formation of the English Common Law: Law and Society in England from the Norman Conquest to Magna Carta* (London, 1996), 151–5.

[52] For the 1170s, *DS*, II.ii, at 72–5. I have preferred to use the 1983 edn.; for discussion of the 2007 edn. see Nicholas Karn's review in *EHR* 126 (2011), 408–10. For clear summaries of procedure see David Carpenter, *Struggle for Mastery: Britain 1066–1284* (London, 2003), 152–4, and Green's introduction to *PR 1130*, new edn., ix–xv, xxiv–xxxi; Stacey, *Politics, Policy and Finance*, 201–5.

[53] *DS*, II.ii at 69.

[54] For partial Exchequer mobility in the early thirteenth century, see Holt, 'Philip Mark', 10–12.

county plumbing that underlay England and through which law and administration flowed (as with the diocesan grid in the religious sphere). The English combination is unusual in Western Christendom in the twelfth century.[55] Administratively England was bigger than France, in that the directly administered French royal domain was much smaller than the area where the English king had legislative, judicial, and fiscal rights.[56] The French royal domain (before John's loss of Normandy in 1204) ran only from Evreux, north of Paris, south down to Orléans, with Sens in the west, and the bubble around Bourges furthest south.[57] Size-wise England contrasts also with the county of Flanders, the core of the Aragonese crown, and Sicily: that is, the other major Western European principalities with advancing administrative machinery in the late twelfth century.[58] In England, by contrast too with Flanders or France, payments were made solely in cash by the late twelfth century.[59] In Flanders, sheep were still being brought into localized collection points for comital assessment.[60] It was the particular balance struck between tallies, writs, and receipts held by shrieval-accountants and records held centrally at the Exchequer that allowed the system to reconcile shrieval action and royal order while avoiding hideous over-sophistication. England was complicated.[61]

The Culture of Accountability at the Exchequer in the Late Twelfth Century

Accountability at the Exchequer could, however, be dismissed as mere, mean, bean counting—and sometimes was. In his *Invectives* (*c*.1200–16), Gerald of Wales inveighed in just such terms against Hubert Walter (d. 1205), Chancellor (from 1199) and, as Archbishop of Canterbury (from 1193), a guilty party in foiling

---

[55] The practical question of the English monarchs' management of proportionately greater non-feudal revenues can also be usefully compared to other monarchs *vis-à-vis* theoretical ideas of 'public vs. private' management of regnal assets.

[56] A wonderful extended consideration making this amongst other points is ch. 7 of Maddicott's *Origins of the English Parliament*, here 381–2, 389. On the reach of French royal *authority*, as distinct from *legislative* reach see André Gouron's remarks in 'Royal *Ordonnances* in Medieval France', in Antonio Padoa-Schioppa (ed.), *Legislation and Justice* (*The Origins of the Modern State in Europe, 13th to 18th Centuries*) (Oxford, 1997), 57–71 at 59–61. Gouron argues that the former is visible by the mid-twelfth century, the latter by the early thirteenth.

[57] Map 12, *New Cambridge Medieval History*, iv. c.*1024–c.1198, part II*, ed. J. Riley-Smith and D. Luscombe (Cambridge, 2004), 550–1. Comment on the smallness of the domain and hence the ease of supervising regional administration in John W. Baldwin, *The Government of Philip Augustus: Foundations of French Royal Power in the Middle Ages* (Berkeley, Calif., 1986), 44.

[58] T. N. Bisson, *The Medieval Crown of Aragon: A Short History* (Oxford, 1986), 91; the combination of Catalonia and Aragon from 1134 under Ramon Berenguer IV and Petronilla of Aragon, 31–48.

[59] *DS*, I.vii at 40–1.

[60] A. Verhulst and M. Gysseling (eds.), *Le Compte Général de 1187, connu sous le nom de «Gros Brief», et les institutions financières du comté de Flandre au XIIe siècle* (Brussels, 1962), *passim*. Verhulst and Gysseling argue that payments were made both in kind and in coin (54–8). See Bryce Lyon and Adriaan Verhulst, *Medieval Finance: A Comparison of Financial Institutions in Northwestern Europe* (Bruges, 1967), 20–2 for the centres, 29, 36–8 for renders in kind.

[61] Over-sophistication could occur, as under the Exchequer baron Richard of Ilchester (d. 1188): he introduced the copying of summonses, a practice abandoned because of the proliferating records it led to. *DS*, II.ii at 74–5.

Gerald's attempts to become (Arch)bishop of St David's.[62] Walter's Exchequer training, said Gerald, being learnt 'where fiscal returns are tallied and totted', provided no basis for properly responsible forms of office—such as the episcopacy.

> That good man, namely the bishop-elect of Bangor, had been called from the cloister, I from the schools, and whence the archbishop? From the Exchequer, and what is the Exchequer? It is the place in England where the public treasure is, that is, a four-square table in London, where fiscal assessments are tallied and totted. From this 'school', from this 'gymnasium', through all the grades of his rank was he called, like nearly all the English bishops, and there he grew old. From here he can reckon well, dispute well, since—for sure—he who can reckon well can philosophize well.[63]

Such sarcasm could not apply to Walter's successor at Canterbury. Stephen Langton taught, like Gerald, at Paris as a master. But Langton too complained about bishops who were elected, not according to the Holy Spirit, but rather according to the 'spirit of the Exchequer in London'.[64]

More slippery are Walter Map's scurrilous comments on the Exchequer in his Angevin satire, *De nugis curialium* (c.1181–2 with later revisions). Map, a royal clerk and sometime royal justice (as was Richard of Ely), is writing of the Exchequer after it settled in London and received the institutional form Richard describes in the *Dialogue*. Talking ironically of the wider court, Map says it 'is milder than hell only in that those whom the court tortures can die'.[65] He describes at length the curial equivalents of Charon, Sisyphus, Ixion, Tityus, Belus's daughters, Cerberus, and the perverted court judgements of its King Dis (Hades), and the judges Minos and Rhadamanthus (the latter two brothers who gave laws to humans and ended as infernal judges).[66] Map names the Exchequer as the one chink of light in this darkness: the only place where 'mother purse with her wrinkled mouth' does not work miracles. The contrast Map draws between the rest of the court and the Exchequer is so extreme that irony seems at work. It is unclear, true, whether Map is distinguishing between the Exchequer as court or counting house, but the crown's discretion to decide and vary the rate of debtors' repayment at the Exchequer was one of its greatest political powers (as we shall see). It seems likeliest too then that Map was thinking of the Exchequer barons when he wrote:

---

[62] On Gerald and St David's, see Michael Richter, *Giraldus Cambrensis: The Growth of the Welsh Nation*, rev. edn. (Aberystwyth, 1976); Robert Bartlett, *Gerald of Wales: A Voice of the Middle Ages*, repr. edn. (Stroud, 2006), 44–53.

[63] Gerald of Wales, '*De Invectionibus*', ed. W. S. Davies, *Y Cymmrodor* 30 (1920), 97. Cf. 114–15. See also C. R. Cheney, *Hubert Walter* (London, 1967), 97–9.

[64] In a commentary on Numbers 27: 17–19 concerning the selection of priests in BNF Lat. 14415 fo. 242ᵛᵇ, cited by Buc, *Ambiguïté du livre*, 62. Cf. Peter of Blois, *Tractatus de institutione episcopi* in *PL*, 207, cols. 1097–12 at 1107.

[65] *De nugis curialium*, ed. M. R. James, rev. C. N. L. Brooke and R. A. B. Mynors, OMT (Oxford, 1983), 500 (§5.7). Map's original incomplete version was drafted c.1181–2. See now Björn K. Weiler, 'Royal Justice and Royal Virtue in William of Malmesbury's *Historia Novella* and Walter Map's *De Nugis Curialium*', in István P. Bejczy and Richard G. Newhauser (eds.), *Virtue and Ethics in the Twelfth Century* (Leiden, 2005), 317–39; and Weiler, 'The King as Judge: Henry II and Frederick Barbarossa as Seen by Their Contemporaries', in Patricia Skinner (ed.), *Challenging the Boundaries of Medieval History: The Legacy of Timothy Reuter*, (Turnhout, 2009), 115–40.

[66] Fittingly, Rhadamanthus figures in one of Plato's extended discussions of *euthyna* when discussing how perjury is common and oaths no longer effective (*Laws* XII, 945b–949c at 948b–e).

I do not call them accountants [*bursarios*] whom the king has chosen to be the greatest of all, but [I do so call] those whom cupidity and office-holding [*procuracio*] has led to their own bench [of judgement]. Nor is it surprising if those whom Simon [Magus, seller of offices] promoted to rule, count for Simon. It is the custom of businessmen that what they buy, they sell.[67]

Mother Purse seems to have re-entered through the back door. It also seems odd for Map to claim that the reason for the Exchequer's justice is that 'the eye of the just king seems to be ever fresh there', that Henry II's proximity leads to prompt Exchequer judgement.[68] As Map would have known, and as Richard's *Dialogue* describes, Henry II is the Exchequer's absent centre. Everything is keyed to his interest but he is not there. Henry is no Alphonse II of Aragon (1162–96) where the king is so close he himself accounts.[69] Part of the point of the Exchequer was that, by the late twelfth century, it generally stayed put while the king itinerated. Map himself, just after this passage, notes how judges at (unspecified) courts encourage the king to be *absent* so as to profit the better from them. When it comes to the king's fresh eye, Map implies the opposite of what he says about Exchequer justice.

Map's criticism of the king's judges and officers is that what should not be bought and sold, is. Gerald and Langton are critical of the norms characterizing one set of officers (Exchequer men) infecting another (bishops). Gerald does not esteem the skills cultivated at the Exchequer. Langton does not like how its spirit ('culture' we might say) seeps out to other institutions. The fairness of these subjective, select complaints is not the issue. What matters is that their bite came from the easy presumption that others would recognize the verdict. If the *Dialogus* says that 'Clearly the exchequer stands by its own laws (*suis legibus*), not rashly, but on the advice of the great', it is clear how some perceived the spirit of those laws, as well as the motivations of the great.[70] The culture—specifically the culture of accountability—at the Exchequer had a very particular reputation amongst Richard of Ely's late twelfth-century contemporaries.

The Exchequer structured the accountability of sheriffs to a very great degree. The *Dialogue of the Exchequer* offers a view of why the Exchequer mattered, and what it was interested in. It is an exceptional, some would say distorting, text speaking specifically to late twelfth-century Exchequer practices. A dialogue between an experienced Exchequer *magister* (i.e. 'Richard') and his neophyte *discipulus*, prefaced with a dedication to Henry II, it describes first the approach of the Exchequer, then the tasks and officers of the lower Exchequer of receipt (book 1), and then the tasks and officers of the upper Exchequer (book 2).

---

[67] *De nugis curialium*, 508 (§5.7).
[68] *De nugis curialium*, 508 (§5.7). David Carpenter suggests Map may be suggesting the vigilance of the Exchequer on behalf ot the king, though Map has some satirical goal here.
[69] First person singular accounting by King Alphonse II of Aragon: *Fiscal Accounts of Catalonia*, ii. ##27, 33, 35, 46 (examples from 1174–83). See also ##41, 42. For accounting by Peter II (1196–1213) see ##115, 120, 122, 128 (examples from 1205–9). See also *Fiscal Accounts of Catalonia*, i. 84–5, 142. One could also compare Wace's image of Richard II of Normandy—see p. 100.
[70] *DS*, Dedication, 3.

Richard's views on Exchequer practice were doubtless one of many (he acknowledges that by framing his *tractatus* as a dialogue with an over-assertive Exchequer *discipulus*). But given his office and its forty-odd-year duration, Richard's opinions must express an influential view of what the Exchequer thought worth privileging, and what it did not, when it held sheriffs to account.[71]

The *Dialogue of the Exchequer*: 'That edifies, *this* enables'

Richard of Ely was keen to make powerfully clear the direct, practical value of the Exchequer to Henry II. The 'observances necessary at your Exchequer' enabled the King to be, in practice, king, 'since a glut or lack of portable wealth exalts or humbles princes' powers'.[72] This is what made the Exchequer such a remarkable system and why its Treasurer was keen to explain and extol its—and concurrently his—virtues. Richard's encomium to his own institution was so great he could compare his father, restoring the lost laws of the Exchequer following the civil war, to Ezra, the great restorer of Jewish law.[73] The *Dialogue* itself, as a practical manual, is taken widely and rightly as exceptional.[74] It is not at all clear what its next or nearest equivalents are.[75] Such is its value that historians have devoutly wished equivalents existed for other Angevin institutions.[76] That is why dedicating such an exceptional treatise to it, and

---

[71] On the problems of reading texts such as this see J. C. Holt, *The Northerners: A Study in the Reign of King John*, rev. edn. (Oxford, 1992), 189–90. On the distinct matter of technical Exchequer practice the *Dialogus* should not be taken as necessarily accurate beyond the late twelfth century. See Cassidy, 'Recorda splendidissima', 3, 6.

[72] *DS*, Dedication, 1.   [73] *DS*, I.viii at 50.

[74] R. W. Southern grouped the *Dialogus* with John of Salisbury's *Policraticus* and the legal treatise and collection of legal writ forms called *Glanvill* and argued that 'they were not simply manuals or text-books for office use [. . .]: they aspired [. . .] to invest the routine of government with an intellectual generality', 'The Place of England in the Twelfth Century Renaissance', in Southern, *Medieval Humanism and Other Studies* (Oxford, 1970), 158–80 at 176. Similar comments: Frederick Pollock and Frederic William Maitland, *The History of English Law before the Time of Edward I*, reissued edn. by S. F. C. Milsom, 2 vols. (Cambridge, 1968), i. 161–2; C. H. Haskins 'Henry II as a Patron of Literature', in A. G. Little and F. M. Powicke (eds.), *Essays in Medieval History Presented to Thomas Frederick Tout* (Manchester, 1925), 71–7 at 77 (paired again with *Glanvill*); Richardson and Sayles, *Governance of Mediaeval England*, 242–3 (expressed negatively); M. T. Clanchy, *From Memory to Written Record: England 1066–1307*, 3rd edn. (Chichester, 2013), 69 (twinned with *Glanvill*); Bisson, 'Medieval Lordship', 757; Moore, *First European Revolution*, 144.

[75] On Byzantium see Pierre Toubert, 'Byzantium and the Mediterranean Agrarian Civilization', in *The Economic History of Byzantium from the Seventh through the Fifteenth Century*, gen. ed. Angeliki E. Laiou, 3 vols. (Washington DC, 2002), i. 377–91, with brief discussion (389–91) of the parallel between the *villicus* of the *Capitulare de villis* and the *epitropos* of the *Geoponika*. Nicolas Oikonomides, 'The Role of the Byzantine State in the Economy (*Economic History of Byzantium*, iii. 973–1058), suggests many lines of enquiry, including (994–5) the appearance of the central and provincial accountants (*logariastai*) in 1012 and Alexios Komnenos's two new auditing institutions from 1094. Hugh Kennedy suggests the Būyid administrator/historian Miskawayh (*c.*932–?1030) as a potential Islamic comparator given his *Tajārib al-umam* (*Experiences of the Nations*) and *Tahdhīb al-akhlāq* (*Health of the Soul*) (personal communication). Parts trans. in *The Eclipse of the 'Abbasid Caliphate: Original Chronicles of the Fourth Islamic Century*, ed. H. F. Amedroz and D. S. Margoliouth, 7 vols. (Oxford, 1920–1), and *The Refinement of Character: A Translation from the Arabic of Aḥmad ibn-Muḥammad Miskawayh's Tahdhīb al-Akhlāq*, trans. Constantine K. Zurayk (Beirut, 1968). See M. Arkoun's entry on Miskawayh in *The Encyclopaedia of Islam* ed. H. A. R. Gibb et al., 12 vols. (Leiden, 1960–2009).

[76] Nicholas Vincent, 'Why 1199? Bureaucracy and Enrolment under John and his Contemporaries', Adrian Jobson (ed.), *English Government in the Thirteenth Century* (Woodbridge, 2004), 17–48 at 17 (on chancery).

Henry II, would have marked out the forty-something Exchequer clerk from any run-of-the-mill accountant.[77] It must have seemed a good career move to a man who was then running the Ely diocese in the shadow of his sick father, still yet to attain any significant senior ecclesiastical post.[78] It seems unlikely that Richard of Ely did not have hopes for the effect the *Dialogus* might have on his prospects.[79]

Given the critiques of Exchequer culture, it is striking that the *Dialogue of the Exchequer* offers a explicitly pragmatic, fiscal justification of 'Exchequer rules'. It does not assert its own integrity by appealing to the sorts of conventional ethical justifications that would please a Walter Map or a Gerald of Wales. The political thinking it offers is unusual and its own.[80] Clanchy has argued that the *Dialogue*, 'with its emphasis on the efficacy of money rather than virtue, looks like the first work by a British empiricist'.[81] It is not a flippant comparison.

The heart of Richard's pragmatic, instrumental picture of government is set out in the *Dialogus*'s dedication to Henry II. The dedication is short, but worth analysing in detail since the sheriff's accountability flows from the Exchequer's approach here.

The opening of Richard's dedication is conventional enough, echoing St Paul's de facto justification of political power from Romans 13: 'To the powers ordained by God it is necessary to be both subject and subservient in all fear. For every power is from the Lord God.'[82] Henry's virtues as a king follow as a demonstration of that scriptural proof. But the core of Richard's praise of Henry is of a notably material cast. When Richard calls Henry 'greatest of worldly princes' the stress falls on 'worldly'.[83] The King had much money to spend. What he spent it on varied: castles and wages in war, churches, the poor, and charity in peace.[84] And the more money he spent the more of a king he was.[85] Richard's point is that the Exchequer enabled this. More interestingly, Henry's gloriousness is visible because he spends money well, 'in places, at times, on persons on the basis of legitimate

---

[77] On Richard's abilities and achievements, see Richardson's comments, 'Richard fitz Neal and the *Dialogus de Scaccario*', 166.

[78] In terms of his secular office as Treasurer at the Exchequer, Richard is keen to emphasize both the importance of this office and the fact that it is not one of the most senior: 'Officium thesaurarii uel cura uel sollicitudo ipsius uix explicari posset uerbis etiam si esset mihi "calamus scribe uelociter scribentis"' and 'Numquid a thesaurio compotus suscipitur cum illic multi sint qui ratione potestatis maiores uideantur?', respectively *DS* I.v and I.i at 28, 7.

[79] If the treatise was finished by the end of the 1170s (notwithstanding later amendments) something shifted soon afterwards in Richard's fortunes: he was made Dean of Lincoln in 1183 and (eventually) Bishop of London in 1189—under Richard—and the Archbishop of Canterbury's stand-in during his crusading absence in 1190. Wace and Gerald of Wales are good comparators of Angevin literacy, ambition, and disappointment entangled.

[80] The *Dialogue*, because of its great importance as a source for the functioning of the Exchequer, has been underestimated and not infrequently despised as a text in its own right. This is most manifest in historians' willingness to take literally the obviously contradictory statement by the *discipulus* that the *magister* will write 'not subtly but usefully'. I hope to discuss the *Dialogue*'s subtlety more generally elsewhere, focusing here only on its account of Exchequer political thinking and accountability.

[81] Clanchy, *England and its Rulers*, 59.

[82] *DS*, Dedication, 1.   [83] *DS*, Dedication, 2.   [84] *DS*, Dedication, 2.

[85] Cf. John Gillingham and Robert Bartlett's comments that it was a sign of regal success *not* to be in England, but (spending money) abroad fighting: respectively, *The Angevin Empire*, 2nd edn. (London, 2001), 1, 73, 115, and *England under the Norman and Angevin Kings*, 13.

reasons'.[86] Regal largesse had obviously mattered before Henry II and before even *Beowulf*, but Richard's praise of right spending tastes distinctive. It is as a guide to getting and managing money so that the King can spend it that the *Dialogue* is dedicated to Henry. So concerned was Henry about Exchequer procedure, says Richard, that, 'having sent discreet men from your side you [Henry] summoned the then Lord of Ely', Nigel, the *magister*'s/Richard's own father.[87] 'Nor', adds Richard, 'was it ridiculous for [you], a man of such enormous insight, a prince of such singular power, to attend to this amongst other, greater things.'[88]

Richard's implication is that there was little of greater importance. Yet denying its ridiculousness also signals Richard's concern that others might think just that. One can see why by looking at more conventional measures of praise for Henry in, say, Jordan Fantosme's romance *Chronicle* (*c*.1174–5) about the 1173 rebellion of Henry's sons.[89] Here Henry vows to attack the rebels no matter how much gold he should be offered (l. 143).[90] Henry's views about the just seisin of estates (ll. 217–18) are equally some distance from Richard's pragmatic defence of Henry's properties, irrespective of how they were obtained. The style of regality is quite different from Richard's. Given Fantosme's genre this is no surprise, but the point is that Fantosme's criteria of regality were more common, Richard's more unusual.

A more comparably 'practical' treatise, also dedicated to Henry II, is the very nearly contemporaneous English legal treatise *Glanvill* (completed 1187–9) and with which the *Dialogue* is often paired.[91] *Glanvill*'s dedication is far more conventional. Where Richard stresses what money can resolve, *Glanvill* stresses how fitting and decorative is the law to kingship, a more usual theme, and one expressed in a less hard-nosed or assertive manner.[92] But for Richard, 'In either [war or peace] the glory of princes lies in vigorous action, but it *excels* in those where, for a worldly outlay, they obtain a happy bargain which lasts.'[93]

When Richard does acknowledge the place of the cardinal virtues in ruling, his concession sounds rather perfunctory. We know 'indeed how kingdoms are ruled and laws upheld, principally through prudence, fortitude, temperance or

---

[86] *DS*, Dedication, 2.   [87] *DS*, Dedication, 2–3.   [88] *DS*, Dedication, 3.

[89] Both texts are written about actual events but expressed through very different discourses (a master–pupil dialogue; the *chanson de geste*). The use of 'real' events appears something of a feature of texts connected with Henry II—compare also Peter of Blois the younger's *Dialogus inter regem Henricum II et abbatem Bonaevallensem*, based on an actual meeting.

[90] *Jordan Fantosme's Chronicle*, ed. R. C. Johnston (Oxford, 1981), e.g. ll. 109–18. Contrast also the offer of money and gold by William I of Scotland to Robert de Vaux in exchange for abandoning the defence of Carlisle castle (ll. 1397–1412).

[91] See n. 74 in this chapter.

[92] *The Treatise on the Laws and Customs of the Realm of England Commonly Called Glanvill*, ed. G. D. G. Hall, NMT (London, 1965), 1–2. Outside the dedication there is more conventional praise of Henry, e.g. *DS*, II.ii at 75–7. Richardson suggested this was a interpolation ('Richard fitz Neal and the *Dialogus de Scaccario*', 339–40). Amt thinks it a revision, *Dialogus de Scaccario: The Dialogue of the Exchequer and Constitutio Domus Regis: Disposition of the King's Household*, ed. Emilie Amt and S. D. Church, OMT (Oxford, 2007), xxxiii. Certainly the prologue's emphases correlate better with the values expressed through the *Dialogue* as a whole.

[93] *DS*, Dedication, 2. The stress is mine. 'Felici mercimonio mansura' gestures towards an eternal (heavenly), reward, but seems to fall short of specifiying it.

justice and other virtues'.[94] But, he goes on, 'it sometimes turns out that what is proposed by admirable counsel or excellent insight takes root more quickly through the intercession of money, and that what seemed difficult then turns out to be easy, as in any type of business'.[95] Ruling a kingdom is just like any other sort of business.[96] By their own admission, Walter Map's 'businessmen' are at work in the Exchequer for the king. 'It is proper to serve them [kings and other powers] not only by protecting the dignities through which the glory of the king's power shines out, but [by protecting] the wealth of worldly means which pertains to them by reason of their status. For that edifies, but *this* enables.'[97] Richard is interested in what works, and money works. In book 2 the *magister* discusses offerings (*de oblatis*) made to the king, including those made *in spem*, 'in hope' of some future conduct by the king. The *magister* is very quick however to say that this is not offered '*so that* justice may be done—lest you flare up and say he puts justice up for sale—but rather so it may be done without delay' (my stress).[98] The *magister's*—Richard's—sensitivity belies just how credible such suspicions must have seemed (it also shows a mastery of subtlety, Exchequer style). It was neither very far nor long from this suspicion to cap. 40 of Magna Carta proscribing the selling, denying, and delaying of justice.[99] In less sensitive areas Richard's hard-nosed pragmatism was more assertive, willing to countenance support for possibly unlawful, and certainly questionable, royal actions.

> Those who lack [wealth] become the spoils of their enemies, while those who have it take their enemies as spoils. Clearly much of this wealth comes to kings, not according to the strict letter of the law, but sometimes because of the laws of countries, sometimes because of the hidden counsels of [kings'] hearts, and sometimes even because of the licence of their will [*sue uoluntatis arbitrio*]. However their deeds cannot be either discussed or condemned by their inferiors.[100]

---

[94] DS, Dedication, 2. On virtues see István P. Bejczy, *The Cardinal Virtues in the Middle Ages: A Study in Moral Thought from the Fourth to the Fourteenth Century* (Leiden, 2011).

[95] DS, Dedication, 2.

[96] Richard must have known how provocative this would be. Cf. the far more conventional rejection of justice as *negotiationis species* in *The Letters of John of Salisbury*, i. *The Early Letters*, ed. W. J. Millor and H. E. Butler, rev. C. N. L. Brooke, NMT (London, 1955), #100 at 160. By the late thirteenth century this view was less shocking, but still indicative of a particular political pragmatism. Cf. the *c*.1297 *Dispute between the Priest and the Knight*, ed. Norma N. Erickson, Proceedings of the American Philosophical Society 111 (1967), 288–309 at 299–300. The knight argues in favour of the view that money (and therefore taxes) contribute to the public good: 'Clara enim ratione conceditur ut respublica reipublice sumptibus defendatur. . .' (299).

[97] DS, Dedication, 1.

[98] DS, II.xxiii at 120. Comment on the wider political manipulability of writs in Andrew H. Hershey, 'Justice and Bureaucracy: The English Royal Writ and "1258"', *EHR* 113 (1998), 829–51, esp. 834–5, 840 n. 2.

[99] Holt, *Magna Carta*, App. 6, cap. 40.

[100] DS, Dedication, 1. David Carpenter argues that the *Dialogue* seems embarrassed about the king's arbitrary will (*Struggle for Mastery*, 295). I think that Richard would not have mentioned it if he did feel embarrased, especially not in the Dedication. I take it rather as a further sign of Richard's desire to describe how he understands power actually working. I do think he wishes to show that the Exchequer has a powerful degree of discretion (see here pp. 103–10). I am grateful to him for discussion. *Arbitrium* in the later thirteenth century *ius commune* tradition could be a complex nuanced term: Massimo Vallerani, *Medieval Public Justice*, trans. Sarah Rubin Blanshei, Studies in Medieval and Early Modern Canon Law 9 (Washington, 2012), 60–5, 72.

Richard seems reasonably content to accept a king's arbitrary will. If we presume these views reflect a wider Exchequer 'culture' they are important because they set both the tone and limits for officials' conduct, a culture whose influence should not be underestimated.[101]

This justification of royal *arbitrium* seems distinct from the Roman law tag, 'what pleases the prince has the force of law', a mechanism for legitimating the prince's desires.[102] For Richard the answer to '*Kto kogo?*' is clear and clearly different between this world and the next. All officers are accountable here to the king, and no subject or subordinate has the power (given Romans 13: 1) to hold the king to account.

> Therefore, whatever may appear to be the basis or nature of such [regal] acquisitions, for those who are appointed their official guards there should be no let-up in care, but a solicitous love in collecting, conserving and distributing these things—as if an account of the kingdom's status will be required—[and] by which its integrity endures [cf. Hebrews 13: 17].[103]

In Hebrews 13: 17 obedience follows from leaders' liability to account for the souls in their keeping.[104] In Richard's version officials' accountability pertains not to souls but to the liquidity of the *status regni*.[105] This view is to be internalized by Exchequer officials the better to uphold it. The preservation and the perpetuation of king and kingdom is Richard's goal, obtained by that worldly wealth that sticks to the king because of his status, and to whose protection his officials are bound.[106] That is the purpose of acceding to any apparent royal impropriety. Any royal accountability is deferred to God.

> For their [kings'] hearts and the movements of their hearts are in the hands of God; and those who have been entrusted with the care of their subjects by God Himself will on that account stand or fall by divine not human judgement. For no one, however so rich he is should deceive himself that he will flout expectations unpunished, since it is written thus, 'the powerful will suffer powerful torments'.[107]

---

[101] Cf. Thomas Nagel's observation that 'the degree to which ruthlessness is acceptable in public life—the ways in which public actors may have to get their hands dirty—depends on moral features of the institutions through which public action is carried out', 'Ruthlessness in Public Life', in his *Mortal Questions* (Cambridge, 1979), 74–90 at 82–3.

[102] Institutes 1.2.6; Digest 1.4.1. This tag is used in *Glanvill*, 2. For Roman law in *Glanvill*, see van Caenegem, *Royal Writs in England*, 379–86. For discussion of the principle see Pennington, *Prince and the Law*, 28, and the index of Roman law citations for Digest 1.4.1. On tags see Paul Hyams in 'Due Process versus the Maintenance of Order in European Law: The Contribution of the ius *commune*', in Peter Coss (ed.), *The Moral World of the Law* (Cambridge, 2000), 62–90 at 86–90.

[103] *DS*, Dedication, 1–2.

[104] 'Oboedite praepositis vestris et subiacete eis, ipsi enim pervigilant quasi rationem pro animabus vestris reddituri ut cum gaudio hoc faciant et non gementes, hoc enim non expedit vobis.'

[105] *DS*, Dedication, 1.

[106] Gaines Post's argument that the *Dialogus* provides important evidence of Romanizing *ratio status* seems somewhat over-egged to me. See *Studies in Medieval Legal Thought: Public Law and the State, 1100–1322* (Princeton, NJ, 1964), *passim* and esp. '*Ratio publicae utilitatis, ratio status*, and "reason of state"', 1100–1300', 241–309. Post also overlooks the relevant context for Richard: his family's erstwhile tormentor, Stephen, had banned Roman law, thereby sweetening whatever romanesque allusions Richard cared to make. See R. W. Southern, *Scholastic Humanism and the Unification of Europe*, ii. *The Heroic Age* (Oxford, 2001), 156–8.

[107] *DS*, Dedication, 1, drawing on Proverbs 21: 1, Romans 14: 4, and Wisdom of Solomon 6: 7.

The political thinking Richard endorses is not completely idiosyncratic. Other Norman and Anglo-Norman texts express a confident association between measurement, judgement, and ruling which complement Richard's picture of shrieval accountability at the Exchequer.

Hugo Falcandus presented the Norman Roger II of Sicily (1130–1154), as preoccupied with saving rather than spending, as did Romuald of Salerno (in contrast to the English stress on spending).[108] Wace's portrait of Henry's Norman ancestor, Richard II Duke of Normandy (d. 1026) is of direct interest since Wace was another member of Henry's court, and the *Roman de Rou* (*c*.1170–82) was commissioned by the King. Wace has this Richard auditing in a counting house of his own.[109] A learned Lombard, Master Bernard, travels all the way to Rouen having heard of Richard's excellence and goodness. Upon arrival though Richard is too busy and his host tells Bernard:

> You will not be able to speak to him at all for a week. He remains in that high tower and does not leave it night or day; no one can enter the tower unless he is summoned by name. He has brought together all the provosts, bailiffs, tax-collectors and vicomtes in this land; he is doing his reckoning and accounts. After dinner, when he is tired he leans out of a window which overlooks the Seine and sits there for a good long time, gazing at the woods and the people crossing the bridge.[110]

The monastic historian Orderic Vitalis described William Rufus's ministerial *exactor* Ranulf Flambard who measured the country with a rope to revise its tax burden.[111] Such practice was arguably all of a piece with the overall set of inquiries and evaluations that produced the Domesday records.[112] In Naples, Roger II was described pacing the city walls by night, working out they were 2,363 paces long, duly amazing its inhabitants with this datum and his wisdom.[113] Roger indeed looks

---

[108] 'Ingentes etiam thesauros ad regni tuitionem posteritati consulens preparavit ac Panormi reposuit', *La historia o liber de regno Sicilie e la epistola ad Petrum Panormitane urbis thesaurium di Ugo Falcando*, ed. G. B. Siragusa, FSI 22 (Rome, 1897), 6; also *Romualdi Salernitani Chronicon*, ed. C. A. Garufi, *RIS*² 7.1 (1914–35), 237: 'In acquirenda pecunia multum sollicitus, in expendenda non plurimum largus.'

[109] Given the connection with Henry II, the relative chronology, and the image of a 'Richard' who is counting or associated with counting in a high tower that looks out over a river it seems to me likely that Wace's image of Richard II is the principal source for the famous opening image of the *Dialogue* proper: 'In the twenty-third year of King Henry II when I was sitting at a tower window next to the flowing Thames a man called urgently to me' (*DS*, Prologue, 5). I hope to address these textual aspects of the *Dialogue* elsewhere. Richard II was Henry II's great-great-great-grandfather.

[110] *The History of the Norman People: Wace's Roman de Rou*, trans. Glyn S. Burgess, notes with Elisabeth van Houts (Woodbridge, 2004), 113–14.

[111] *Ecclesiastical History of Orderic Vitalis*, iv. 172 (VIII.8), discussion in R. W. Southern, 'Ranulf Flambard', *Medieval Humanism*, 183–205 at 190, 194. *Exactor* was a technical term for the king's shire reeve responsible for revenue collection. See Sally Harvey, 'Domesday Book and Anglo-Norman Governance', *TRHS* 5th ser. 25 (1975), 175–93 at 180.

[112] Harvey, 'Domesday Book and Anglo-Norman Governance, 188–93, arguing for Domesday as an synthesis of both more recent and longer-established administrative practices, and building on her 'Domesday Book and its Predecessors', *EHR* 86 (1971), 753–73.

[113] Falcone di Benevento, *Chronicon Beneventanum: città e feudi nell'Italia dei Normanni*, ed. Edoardo D'Angelo (Florence, 1998), 236 (for 1140 at 5.9–11); discussion, Hubert Houben, *Roger II of Sicily: A Ruler between East and West*, trans. Graham A. Loud and Diane Milburn (Cambridge, 2002), 105.

like the Norman *calculator* par excellence. The Sicilian or North African scholar al-Idrisi explicitly correlates his political and arithmetical skill,[114] and describes how Roger wanted to know the 'condition of his state', commissioning new maps and measurements of his territories, seas, and harbours which he then personally checked with an iron compass.[115] If it was 'always school' under Henry II that may have been a kindergarten compared with Alexander of Telese's workaholic Roger.[116]

> [Roger] hardly ever gave way to idleness or relaxation, so much so that if and when it should happen that he was not involved with some more profitable [*utilioribus*] occupation, then either he supervised the public exactions or checked what had been, or ought to have been given, or ought to be received, with the result that through studying the accounts he always understood better the revenues which had to be paid to his treasury, and from where they ought to be drawn.[117]

One is reminded of the connection suggested between estate management, accountability, accounting, and rulership discussed earlier (pp. 76–82 and 78 n. 283).

These parallels illustrate the stream of twelfth-century thinking, some specifically Angevin, which praised royal fiscal and administrative skill, and with which the *Dialogue* flows. But the tenor of Richard's description of Exchequer political thinking is subtler. It is not just that Richard takes money seriously. The criticisms of Walter Map, Gerald of Wales, and Stephen Langton show the unoriginality of doing that. Like Wace or Alexander, but far more systematically, Richard's originality is his willingness to offer fiscality as an explicit, considered programme for government—without embarrassment, adornment, or hypocrisy. Government is like any other business. Regality is filtered unapologetically through the lens of fiscality. The perspective is a notable one for a twelfth-century clerical administrator to articulate.[118] It was doubtless more novel in expression than fact, but it is a reflection of the Exchequer's standing—and Richard's gimlet-eye—that it could find expression at all.

The Purpose of Shrieval Accountability: Utility, the Fisc, and the Kingdom's Good

Richard's political pragmatism does not, however, lack scruples, ethics, or a sense of equity. The question (Who, whom?) is rather who defines the purpose of Ezra-like

---

[114] *Biblioteca Arabo-Sicula*, ed. and trans. Michele Amari, 2 vols. (Turin, 1880), i. 35. The encomium starts at 33.
[115] *Biblioteca Arabo-Sicula*, 36–40. See the discussion in Houben, *Roger II*, 103–4, and further in *Roger II and the Creation of the Kingdom of Sicily*, trans. Graham A. Loud (Manchester, 2012), 355–63.
[116] The boast made by Peter of Blois to the Archbishop of Palermo, *c*.1177, *PL* 207, Ep. 66 at col. 198. It is frustratingly impossible to reconstruct the Sicilian–English administrative connection.
[117] *Alexandri Telesini abbatis Ystoria Rogerii regis Sicilie Calabrie atque Apulie*, ed. Ludovica De Nava and Dione Clementi, FSI 112 (Rome, 1991), IV.3–4 at 82–3, trans. drawing on Houben, *Roger II*, 157. Alexander is also keen to point out that Roger 'was not headlong, but before he did anything he was careful always to study it with the eye of prudence [*providentie oculo*]' and when on military expeditions 'wherever possible he overcame without bloodshed and thus always tried to avoid risk [*discrimen*] to his army' (IV. 4). Further, Loud, *Roger II and the Creation of the Kingdom of Sicily*, 121–2.
[118] Further comparison with Hugo Falcandus's unillusioned, moral pragmatism would be interesting (e.g. *Historia o liber de regno Sicilie*, 6).

reformed Exchequer accountability—a central issue in the great crises of 1213–15 and 1258–66. For Richard the re-establishment of a solvent, stable kingdom justifies the administrative and fiscal means to get to it. Fiscality enables regality. Mammon produces mercy.[119] For Richard the end justifies the means, and the end is equity and utility of king and kingdom. Michael Clanchy suggested that the *Dialogue* can be seen as the first work of British empiricism. It can also be seen, literally but not trivially, as the first work of British political utilitarianism.

While, says Richard, the offices of those who sit at the upper Exchequer 'seem to have distinct properties, all the offices have the one intention, to attend to the utility of the king—reserving equity of course—according to the ordained rules of the Exchequer'.[120] Elsewhere we are told that the head of the Exchequer, the Chief Justiciar, manages the Exchequer so that everything 'rightly promotes the utility of the lord King'.[121] This utility has its summary definition at the very end of the *Dialogue*'s dedication.

> Clearly the Exchequer operates following its own laws, not blindly but following the deliberations of great men, and if this logic is served in all things, individuals will get their rights [*poterunt singulis sua iura servari*][122] and what is owed to your fisc will flow fully to you, which your administering hand can disburse as your most noble mind sees fit.[123]

The King's interest is the primary point of reference for justifying officers' accountability (Exchequer or shrieval), presented within a context of the *regni statum*.[124] Richard explicitly justified the business of accountability (shrieval and otherwise) at the Exchequer as a matter of public concern, not purely regal concern.[125]

---

[119] 'Et ceteris operibus misericordie insistendo mammona distribuitur', *DS*, Dedication, 2. The allusion is probably to Matthew 6: 24 (non potestis Deo servire et mamonae); Richard will also allude to Matthew 6: 21: *DS*, I.v at 16; I.xiv, at 61–2. Editions of the *Dialogue* have identified this as an allusion to the parable of the unjust steward. At the end of the parable the finagling, embezzling, fraudulent steward has falsified his masters' debtors' receipts and bills, attempting to ingratiate himself with them before being fired, and is actually re-employed by his master, in full awareness of what he has done. 'And the lord praised the unjust steward because he had acted prudently, because the sons of this age are the more prudent' (Et laudavit dominus vilicum iniquitatis quia prudenter fecisset, quia filii huius saeculi prudentiores filiis lucis in generatione sua sunt, Luke 16: 8). Cryptically Christ endorses this behaviour: 'Make for yourselves friends of the mammon of iniquity, that when you fail they will receive you the eternal tabernacles' (Facite vobis amicos de mamona iniquitatis ut cum defeceritis recipiant vos in aeterna tabernacula, Luke 16: 9). Both readings of this passage in the *Dialogue* are possible, but taking this as an allusion to Matthew 6: 24 seems simpler.

[120] *DS*, I.iv at 13.

[121] *DS*, I.v at 16. I find thirteen discussions of *utilitas/utilis* etc. in total: Prologue, 5 (the contrast with *subtilis* is made several times); I.iv, at 13; I.v, at 16, 27; I.vi, at 34; I.vi, at 38; I.vii, at 43; I.xviii, at 65; II.vii, at 88; II.xiii, at 109 (the word is *commodis* but the sense is the same); II.xiv, 111 (the word is *necessitate* but the sense is the same); II.xvi, at 113; II.xxiii, at 119.

[122] Cf. the Roman legal idea of justice as rendering to each his due: 'suum cuique tribuere'. See Institutes 1.1.3; Digest 1.1.10. See also *DS*, I.xvi at 63.

[123] *DS*, Dedication, 3. The Dedication overall is Richard's definition of utility. The word is not used in the Dedication but then appears immediately and throughout the treatise proper.

[124] The 'state of the kingdom' is cited in the Dedication, 2, and II.ii, at 77. For reform in the context of *status regni* see Harding, *Medieval Law and the Foundations of the State*, 158–60.

[125] Part of the impetus behind this 'public' stress may have been the Angevin tendency to treat their *imperium* precisely as dynastic estate, not state. See Gillingham, *Angevin Empire*, 32, 116, and Richard

'Exchequer Rules' 103

That Richard could distinguish the two is clear in his discussion of the assay (the spot-checking of the quality of a sheriff's coin by melting a portion). Richard tells us his great-uncle, Roger, Bishop of Salisbury 'ordered that there should be a burning or testing of the farm [. . .], having consulted with the king himself, so as to provide simultaneously for the utility of the king and the public'. This specifically regal/public distinction is then stressed by the *discipulus* who asks, 'How so "for the public"?' The *magister*/'Richard' explains this is because a sheriff who has lost out by having light money discounted will then ensure that moneyers coin at the right percentage of silver to copper and bronze.[126] Shrieval accountability was justifiable on both royal and public grounds. How did the *Dialogue* analyse that accountability?

A Game of Chess: The Sheriff's *conflictus* at the Exchequer

The first of the *Dialogue*'s two books focuses on the officials who admit, run, and judge the sheriff's account of himself at the Exchequer. Book 1[127] of the *Dialogue* addresses the mechanics of Exchequer rules. It has very little to say directly about the sheriff himself, a topic purposely reserved for the second book. There the *magister* says he and the *discipulus* will discuss the Exchequer's 'greater and more indispensable practices'. This is where the 'more excellent, more useful [*utilior*] and more elevated science of the Exchequer' lies.[128] Stressing always the intellectual integrity of Exchequer knowledge (*scientia*), Richard points his readers towards book 2's main contribution to regal and regnal utility: managing sheriffs.

Famously, the emblematic image offered by Richard of the sheriff accounting for himself at the Exchequer is that of a player in a game of chess. The whole set-up of the Exchequer audit is that of a serious game.[129] The overt reason why the Exchequer (*scaccarium*) is so called arises from the chequered abacus board used to mark the sheriffs' workings at the account (different columns represented different denominations).[130] But the 'more hidden' (*occultior*) reason, explains the *magister*, is that

> As in a game of chess there are certain orders of fighters, who stop or start according to given rules [*legibus*] or limits, some outranking, others in the vanguard, so in this

---

Heiser, 'Richard I and his Appointments', 10. Henry II was perfectly capable of drawing a public/private distinction when it was in his interests. See William of Newburgh's obituary for Henry citing his defence of regalian rights from vacant bishoprics on the grounds that 'Nonne melius est ut pecuniae istae impendantur necessariis regni negotiis, quam in episcoporum absumantur deliciis?' Newburgh dismissed this 'defence as a stupid sophism' (*defensionem inanem ratiunculam*): William of Newburgh's *Historia rerum Anglicarum* in *Chronicles of the Reigns of Stephen, Henry II and Richard I*, ed. Richard Howlett, RS, 4 vols. (London 1884–9), i. 280–1 (§3.26).

[126] e.g. the assay of the quality of coin paid in at the Exchequer is discussed in terms of 'regie simul et publice prouideretur utilitati', *DS*, I.vii at 43.

[127] Irrespective of successive, inconclusive editorial disagreement over whether the text is really divided into two books, there is a clear break/transition between 'book 1' and 'book 2'.

[128] *DS*, I.xviii at 65.

[129] On serious games for managing conflict see also Johan Huizinga, *Homo Ludens: A Study of the Play-Element in Culture* (London, 1949). The Exchequer itself is, of course, also conceived in the *Dialogus* as both event and institution, *DS*, I.i at 6–7.

[130] *DS*, I.i at 7.

[the Exchequer account and audit], some preside and others assist *ex officio*, and there is no one who is free to infringe the constituted rules [*leges*] [. . .] And as also in the game, a battle is waged between kings, so in this, the conflict [*conflictus*] where battle is waged is principally between two people, namely the treasurer and the sheriff who sits to account, while others sit like judges so that they can watch and judge.[131]

In the same way there is a more hidden way of translating the *magister*'s statement that 'the summonses are sent out so that there can be an Exchequer'—'The summonses are sent out that there may be a game of chess'.[132] The treatise could even be titled 'How to play the game of chess'.[133] The ritual of the setting, the stage of the account, and the loving, hierarchical progression through officers' tasks, are all emphasized in the *magister*'s description of his spectator sport.[134] The drama of Exchequer theatre was still thought worth reasserting in the 1320s when the then treasurer Walter Stapeldon complained of the need for 'grant diligence et bone quiete' lest the sheriffs' accounts be neither 'suffisaument renduz, oyz, ne espleites [finished]'.[135] It does not seem excessive to think of the *conflictus* metaphorically as a chess game. During the earlier discussion of chess and fortune, the *magister* endorsed as 'praiseworthy' his *discipulus*'s attempts 'to dig for the flowers of symbolic understanding amidst worldly thorns'.[136] Applying Richard's injunction yields interesting points about how the accountability of sheriffs at the Exchequer was understood.

Accurate measurement of money and its quality was, as book 1 describes, a fundamentally important part of Exchequer business. Counting a debtor's money in at the Exchequer was a straightforward, empirical matter. Alongside counting went exaction. One of the first things book 2 describes is the question of what the sheriff's rate of repayment would be. This was a matter of political judgement. Summonses were issued for each term. The barons, at the end of one term and before the next, then sat privately together, the clerks having compiled lists of everyone's outstanding debts and, going through each county, 'from its individual debtors they determine [*decernent*] how much ought to be demanded, taking into account the quality of the person, the nature of their business, and the basis on which it is owed to the King'.[137]

---

[131] *DS*, I.i at 7. It fits Richard's purposes, of course, that it is the Treasurer who is the sheriff's key antagonist in this presentation.

[132] 'Fiunt autem summonitiones ut scaccarium fiat', *DS*, II.i at 69.

[133] 'De scaccarii tui necessariis obseruanciis', *DS*, Dedication, 2.

[134] The subject of much of book 1. See esp. *DS*, I.i at 6–7 for the setting, I.v at 15–17 for the progression according to status, II.iv at 84–5 for attention to the isolation of the sheriff immediately before giving his account. Diagrams of the described layout of the Exchequer room are given in *DS*, xlii. Given his symbolic-functional analyses of Kabyle domestic space, Pierre Bourdieu would have enjoyed reading the *Dialogue of the Exchequer*. For an analysis of the later medieval French *Chambre des comptes* stressing ritual aspects see Olivier Mattéoni, 'Vérifier, corriger, juger: Les Chambres des comptes et le contrôle des officiers en France à la fin du Moyen Âge', *Revue historique* 641 (2007), esp. 41–7, 51–2.

[135] *Red Book of the Exchequer*, iii. 850. Stapeldon seems as self-conscious as Richard of Ely of the Exchequer's momentous need for 'grant occupation de temps et diligence graunde, et conoissance a le faire' (*Red Book of the Exchequer*, iii. 856, and generally 848–909).

[136] *DS*, I.v at 26.   [137] *DS*, II.i at 70.

This due consideration of what to exact is the complement of the King's consideration about what to spend that received such stress in Richard's Dedication.[138] The overall process of holding sheriffs to account could be as much a question of political arithmetic as pure maths. The discretion of the barons was vital. As, Richard said, if '10' was called in for the Easter term (the start of the Exchequer year) then a debtor might presume a total of '20' would be required for the whole year at the Michaelmas account. But 'to that said "10" might be added a further "10"—*or more—as is the view of those presiding and evaluating*' (my stress). Debtors are liable *ad arbitrium* of those presiding at the Exchequer.[139] It is specifically in the handling of these summonses containing this decision that Richard identifies the more 'elevated science of the Exchequer'.[140] This then was a potentially highly political accountability.[141] The judgement of how to vary exactions and to pin down evasive sheriffs was the more useful and elevated science of the Exchequer. Exacting and counting were the two sides of the coin, the former more loaded than the level latter.[142] Richard's openness about this process is, again, striking. The stakes could be large. It was, after all, Thomas Becket's alleged £30,000 Exchequer debt that in 1164 was called in as a weapon against him during his dispute with Henry.[143] The Briouze family, with almost equal infamy, found itself pursued by King John 'secundum consuetudinem regni nostri, et per legem scaccarii nostri', for William III's alleged financial delicts, for which William's wife and eldest son would be starved to death in 1210.[144]

There was then a 'discretionary' side to this, and it is one that Richard describes as, again, *occultior*.[145] The *Dialogue* places a curious stress on the more arbitrary aspects of accountants' fortune at the chessboard. In describing the mechanics of the abacus system—again at just the point when he might emphasize the rationalizing *scientia* of the procedure—Richard instead foregrounds the wilfulness of it. The *magister* describes how counters may be reassigned numerical significations on the counting board, either up or down, 'so that if it pleases the person calculating, what signifies 1,000, descending by degrees, may instead signify 1'.[146] This would

---

[138] *DS*, Dedication, 2 and text cited at n. 123. For discussion of the situation under John see Holt, *Northerners*, 232–3, 237. David Carpenter's forthcoming study and edition of Magna Carta will address 'standards of judgement' under John.

[139] *DS*, I.ii at 73. This presumes that the '10' originally summonsed was less than half of the actual amount owed. It is not that more than was *due* was illegitimately summonsed.

[140] *DS*, II.ii at 78.

[141] It seems useful to characterize the barons' decisions on amounts due, then specifying, verifying, and auditing them, as comprising accountability at the Exchequer.

[142] See David Carpenter's sharp remark that the Exchequer 'was central to the exaction of revenue, the control of local officials, and the web of political control which the king could spin over the country, for nearly everyone of importance owed money to the crown and could be punished or rewarded by varying the rates of repayment', *Struggle for Mastery*, 154. See e.g. Philip Marmyn's repayment plan for debts from his time as sheriff of Warwick and Leicester, *CPR 1247–1258*, 268 (12 February 1254).

[143] Frank Barlow, *Thomas Becket* (London, 1986), 111.

[144] *Foedera*, i.1. 107–8 at 107, John's sworn and witnessed justification.

[145] The arbitrariness of regal court culture is not an original theme. See e.g. Map's *De nugis curialium*, 2–10 (§1.1–9), 498–512 (§5.7). Much earlier Boethius's *Consolation of Philosophy* discusses the same issue—and is, of course, also a dialogue.

[146] *DS*, I.v at 25–6.

be an innocuous enough demonstration of the versatility of the counters, were it not that the *discipulus* replies,

> Thus it may be that any ordinary person, should he be a man and no more, can have his temporalities added to at the will [*uoluntate*] of the president [of the Exchequer], and ascend from the depths to the heights and then, once fortune's law's been served, be flung down to the bottom, remaining as he was, although he seems changed by his dignity and state.[147]

This is a very striking allusion to the potentially arbitrary nature of Exchequer exactions (and subtler than anything Walter Map had to say). The maths at the Exchequer was one thing. But rates of exaction were quite another and could easily become a political judgement. Olivier Mattéoni has made similar arguments about why the later French *Chambre des comptes* in Paris did not always apply the penalty sanctions its auditing process permitted.[148] Debts cannot be paid unless they are owed.[149] The value of the Exchequer's *scientia* was that whatever was accounted there was objective by definition. But what was summonsed for payment was not. Exchequer judgements always looked fair and sometimes might even have been fair (much as in the manorial accounts discussed in Chapter 2). That was a good part of their usefulness. Snakes and ladders begins to seem a better image than chess.

The *Dialogue*'s images of chess and dice are not innocent images to conjure with here either.[150] The *magister* and the *discipulus* themselves refer to their dialogue as a game of dice in which they take turns to speak.[151] Lightheartedness about dicing was not so uncontroversial, however. Nor is it clear that Richard assumed such allusions were uncomplicated. Around 1060–1, having watched the Bishop of Florence play chess all evening, the hardline church reformer Peter Damian wrote to the pope-elect Alexander II. Identifying chess with gambling he lamented 'how shameful, how senseless, how disgusting this sport is in a priest'. Chess was banned in the Knights Templars' rule of 1129 at the Council of Troyes. Alexander Nequam condemned it in his *De naturis rerum* (*c.*1200–4).[152] Louis VII (1120–80) was berated by Count William II of Nevers for playing chess, the Count contrasting its frivolity unfavourably with the 'heavy stewardship' (*strenuum prouisorem*) needed from kings to attend to God's people.[153] For Frederick II at Melfi in 1232, dicing was infamous enough to

---

[147] *DS*, I.v at 25–6. Cf. *Walter of Henley*, cap. 3, in *Walter of Henley*, 308; Charles M. Radding, 'Fortune and her Wheel: The Meaning of a Medieval Symbol', *Mediaevistik. Internationale Zeitschrift für interdisziplinäre Mittelalterforschung* 5 (1992), 127–38.

[148] Mattéoni, 'Vérifier, corriger, juger', 61–5 on the extra-accountancy considerations that could affect the Chambre's failure to impose the fines it might.

[149] For John's advantage in using the Exchequer court to establish, exact, and vary debts see Holt's account of the debts of Peter de Brus, Thomas of Moulton, Nicholas de Stuteville, Robert de Vaux, John de Lacy, in *Northerners*, 171–4 and 164, 183.

[150] See generally Michel, Pastoureau, *L'Échiquier de Charlemagne: Un jeu pour ne pas jouer* (Paris, 1990), and *Une histoire symbolique du Moyen Âge occidental* (Paris, 2004), 303–29.

[151] *DS*, I.v at 25.

[152] James Robinson, *The Lewis Chessmen* (London, 2004), 46–55. For emphasis of the rational aspects, Alexander Murray, *Reason and Society in the Middle Ages* (Oxford, 1978), 204–5.

[153] Adam of Eynsham, *Magna Vita Sancti Hugonis*, ed. Decima L. Douie and Hugh Farmer, OMT, 2 vols. corr. ed. (London, 1985), ii. 56 (§4.12).

bar one from public office for life, or invalidate the testimony of knights who should know better.[154] Henry II himself had legislated against dice.[155] One interpretation of the chess game represented in S. Savino, Piacenza's mosaic, is that it is an extension of the central roundel's depiction of the wheel of fortune on which figures rise and fall.[156] The offensiveness of chess to churchmen was that they associated it with luck, chance, and gambling. Thirteenth-century *Bibles moralisées* often used *scaccarium* images as shorthand for lustful, worldly, or intemperate behaviour.[157] Choosing chess as the key motif of the ostensibly rational, equitable struggle between sheriff and Treasurer is wilfully dicey. As the central image characterizing the quality of the trial by battle between Treasurer and sheriff, it indicates a far from innocuous presumption about the 'justice of accountability'.[158]

Richard sails closest to the wind though when he discusses the president of the Exchequer, the Chief Justiciar, 'who is entrusted with the king's heart'. It is only right, the Treasurer says, that he should be so entrusted, since, as Christ said, 'where your treasure is, there will your heart be also'.[159] This is, of course, the precise *opposite* of Christ's actual meaning to put aside worldly wealth. It was completely consonant, however, with a vision of accountability dedicated to the utility of king and kingdom and which both *Dialogue* and Exchequer promoted. The *magister*'s endorsement of his *discipulus*' 'praiseworthy' digging for symbolic understanding amidst worldly thorns during the discussion of chess and fortune has already been noted.[160] Digging in the *Dialogus* reveals much more than Europe's first audit manual.

In making these points I am not at all suggesting that Exchequer accounting is 'merely' symbolic or irrelevant to the eventual exactions imposed on debtors. The counting is real yet the rate of repayment could be highly political. Richard is well aware of the political nature of Exchequer accountability and the gamesmanship of the process is admitted, even welcomed. The rules are there to be played and the barons are there to outplay sheriffs and other debtors.[161] But the formal process validates the political outcome, and the ritual lends the proceedings an objectivity that is fundamental in ensuring the institution generates belief in itself.[162] This explains Richard's

---

[154] *Konstitutionen Friedrichs II. für das Königreich sizilien*, cap. 3.90.
[155] *Chronica magistri Rogeri de Houedene*, ed. William Stubbs, RS, 4 vols. (London, 1868–71), ii. 336–7.
[156] William L. Tronzo, 'Moral Hieroglyphs: Chess and Dice at San Savino in Piacenza', *Gesta* 16/2 (1977), 15–26, but preferring a positive association of chess with virtue (esp. 19–21). The debate exemplifies the imagery's ambiguousness.
[157] e.g. BL Add. MS 18719 (London, late 1280s–early 1290s) at fos.7ᵛ, 22ʳ, 24ʳ, 44ʳ, 53ʳ, 118ᵛ, 150ᵛ, 203ᵛ, 208ᵛ, 211ʳ, 270ʳ. On this MS, see further pp. 253–5.
[158] The subtitle of Bisson, *Crisis of the Twelfth Century*, 316–49. See here pp. 253–60.
[159] *DS*, I.v at 16, quoting Matt. 6: 21. The point is repeated at I.xiv at 61–2.
[160] *DS*, I.v at 26.
[161] Cf. the *magister*'s account of how debtors tried to move taxable capital out of their county during the sheriff's predictable visits so that a sheriff with a county mandate would not be able to evaluate nor collect it, *DS*, II.i at 71–2. This is not catching *sheriffs* out but stopping sheriffs from being bamboozled by over-subtle legalistic approaches by other debtors.
[162] Genet has provocatively asked whether the men of the *Chambre des comptes* even counted. He wished to make a similar point, that political arithmetic influenced the question of what was summed (Jean-Philippe Genet, 'Chambres des comptes des principautés et genèse de l'état moderne',

loving care in iterating the members, responsibilities, peculiarities, rules, layout, procedure, and history of his institution. The Exchequer clears an ostensibly rational, but not necessarily level, space for rule-based conflict between sheriff and Treasurer.

As a text concerned with both fiscality and a particular idea of *utile* equity, and one that describes how these ends are secured by the professionalism of its central court and counting house's officers, and which specifies the management of sheriffs at the Exchequer as its highest science, it is nevertheless surprising what aspects of sheriffs' conduct are absent from the *Dialogue of the Exchequer*. The greatest European 'manual' of the twelfth century on office-holding and a governmental institution has barely anything to say about the character of the sheriff, the key officer who faces the Treasurer at the audit. It may be argued this is to be expected. Richard is principally describing his side of the *conflictus*, thus the professional, managerial competence that is so dominant a feature of what Richard says relates strictly to the Exchequer officials, not at all to the sheriffs. Yet book 2 gives a great deal of time and discussion to the sheriff. Richard's handling of the sheriff is interesting. It is not clear that Richard deigns to consider sheriffs as officers.[163] Book 1 lovingly rotates through the lower Exchequer offices of treasurer's clerk, deputy chamberlains, pesour, melter, usher, watchman, and then the upper Exchequer's justicier, chancellor, constable, chamberlains, marshal, and the many others.[164] Even the lowly watchmen and ushers' jobs are described as *officia*.[165] Richard, however, generally avoids describing the sheriff's activities as an elevated *officium*.[166] His preference is for the plainer *agenda* or sometimes *negotium*.[167] One would not want to exaggerate the significance of this, but given the liberal allocation of formal offices to everyone else in the *Dialogue*, the sheriff's virtual exclusion from this category is notable.[168] The sheriff's oath as discussed in the *Dialogue* is relatively 'thin' too. It seems only to have concerned his thorough investigation of debts due to the king and his own claim that he had accounted correctly. (It will contrast with the 1258 oath.) There is no mention at all of *how* the sheriff was expected to discharge this responsibility.[169]

---

in Philippe Contamine and Olivier Mattéoni (eds.), *La France des principautés: Les Chambres des comptes XIVe et XVe siècles. Colloque tenu aux Archives départementales de l'Allier, à Moulins-Yzeure, 6, 7, 8 avril 1995* (Paris, 1996), 267–79 at 271–2. Less dramatic but still subtle are Mattéoni's comments on the *Chambres des comptes*, 'Vérifier, juger', esp. 61–7. A useful theorization of the norms and limits of institutional self-objectification is Pierre Bourdieu's idea of *officialisation* in *Le Sens pratique* (Paris, 1980), 183–8 (referenced by Bisson, *Crisis of the Twelfth Century*, 350, and cf. his discussion of the Exchequer, 462–9). Even Jeremy Bentham understood that his panopticon's accountability was significant as a 'new mode of *obtaining power*, power of mind over mind, in a quantity hitherto without example: and that, to a degree equally without example, secured by whoever chooses to have it so, against abuse. Such is the engine: such the work that may be done with it' [my emphasis], *Panopticon; or The Inspection House*, 2 vols. (Dublin and London, 1791) i. i–ii.

[163] See also e.g. *DS*, II.iv at 81, where he implies he is a servant (*seruiens*). This is a quite distinct register from Richard's in speaking about 'his' men.
[164] See the listing in *DS*, at lv–lvii.   [165] *DS*, I.iii, I.vii at 8, 12–13, 44–5.
[166] An exception is *DS*, II.xii at 105.
[167] *DS*, I.v, II.i, II.ii, II.iii, II.iv at 25, 29, 30, 69, 78, 79, 82, 84, 85.
[168] For an example of Richard's use of *officium* for *his* men see e.g. *DS*, I.v at 26.
[169] *DS*, I.v, II.xii–xiii, II.xiii, II.xvii, xxviii at 21, 106–7, 109, 113–14, 124, 126. Also II.iv (81) on the oaths of his representatives. For officers' oaths more widely, see now Lachaud, *Éthique du pouvoir*, 473–507.

There is also little discussion of shrieval misconduct in the *Dialogue of the Exchequer*, but it is instructive about the sheer possibility of independent shrieval action. The question of fraud surfaces when the *discipulus* asks whether a sheriff could tamper with his summons. The *discipulus* reflects that the summons remains

> in his and his mens' hands for a long time, the summons' integrity reliant on his faith alone. So [a sheriff] could, if he wished, delete, distort or diminish it with impunity, since there is no copy in the barons' hands.[170]

The *magister* replies:

> He could perhaps if he wished, but this would be proof of total insanity, to open himself willingly to so great a risk, particularly when he could not thereby strike off his debts to the king, scarcely indeed put them off. For every single debt which summons are made out for, has already been carefully noted down, so that it is not possible for anyone to free themselves by such devices, even were the sheriff to help them.[171]

Shrieval conduct is determined by Exchequer controls, rather than by any internal professionalism. (One could contrast *podestà* treatises such as Latini's *Tresor* and to some extent the manorial ones of Chapter 2.) Utility—mostly royal, sometimes specifically regnal—is its operative watchword. On Richard's account, the simple sheriff is the revolving object at the centre of the Exchequer's panopticon. At the epicentre of the institution for managing sheriffs there is little attention to their professional character. There could have been. Sheriffs' broader conduct in office had been the focus of a major and controversial inquest in 1170. In John of Salisbury's *Policraticus* we can find extensive discussions of the sheriff's character and office.[172] Interestingly this seems to have been little read in thirteenth-century England—by contrast with France.[173] Certainly from Richard's perspective there were limits to the Exchequer's interest in sheriffs' accountable, functional, professional competence.

This, to repeat, is not to say that the *Dialogue* is indifferent to right or justice.[174] It is rather that those are defined principally from the king's perspective ('Who, whom?'). Sometimes this is differentiated from the interests of the kingdom; sometimes the two are deemed identical. But such attention as Richard gives to issues of right and justice beyond the king's interest is strictly limited. In turn the sheriff as a professional official receives a quite different and unflattering treatment compared to his chessboard opponents. The Treasurer's description of how his institution works is little concerned with how the sheriff conducts himself in office so long as the king is not at a loss. Of course the Exchequer as a court remained an important venue for disputes about debts exacted by sheriffs, but the overwhelming stress of Europe's first audit manual was on the accountability of debtors understood in a very particular, political, fiscal way. It is not surprising that this was the case. It is more surprising that

---

[170] *DS*, II.ii at 74. [171] *DS*, II.ii at 74.
[172] See now Lachaud, *Éthique du pouvoir*, 177–216.
[173] Frédérique Lachaud, 'La Notion d'office dans la littérature politique en France et en Angleterre, XIIe–XIIIe siècles', *Comptes rendus de l'Académie des Inscriptions et Belles-Lettres* (November–December 2009), 1543–70. I am grateful to Professeur Lachaud for a copy.
[174] Cf. Amt, 'Reputation of the Sheriff', for another perspective.

the Treasurer of the Exchequer makes this the bare ground on which to demonstrate his institution's governmental mastery.

The Exchequer audit was not the only way in which sheriffs were accountable at the Exchequer, since the Exchequer was also a court. Issues of shrieval conduct were also raised at eyres and at 'bespoke' inquiries into sheriffs. Nor, as conceded, was Richard's the only relevant perspective on shrieval accountability. Did these approaches ameliorate or exacerbate the tensions between *utile* fiscality and *honestum* conduct within the sheriff's office?

SHERIFFS' ACCOUNTABILITY BEYOND EXCHEQUER ACCOUNTING

Exchequer of Pleas, Eyres, and ad hoc Inquiries

The *Dialogue of the Exchequer* gives only a partial picture of Exchequer practice since it stresses the audit and accounting side of the Exchequer's work, at the expense of its court side as the Exchequer of Pleas. Some of its records (though not regarding a sheriff) have already been discussed since the Valle case was heard there.[175] Walter Langton, who will be discussed as a bishop in the next chapter, fell foul of the Exchequer court as Treasurer.[176] Exchequer pleas certainly included complaints about shrieval abuses. One such, from the end of the period, was Eda of Bolton's 1299 complaint against the sheriff of Cumberland, William of Molecastre, and his men for trespass and novel disseisin 'under the pretext of office'.[177] Eda's complaint was successful, if only for a quarter of the 20 marks damages she claimed. The Exchequer as a court was an important potential means of redress even if its interests were especially concerned with fiscal abuses.

A second way to put sheriffs on the spot, this time *in situ*, was through the periodic itineration of justices 'on eyre', a practice flourishing from the 1170s to 1294.[178] The eyre was a real means of constraining sheriffs. Its jurisdiction included all civil pleas and crown pleas since the last eyre. If the Exchequer was centripetal, the eyre was centrifugal. Local juries responded to set articles of the eyre (*capitula itineris*), by mid-century 'a somewhat shapeless code of enquiry into the assumption of franchises and the misdeeds of local officials'.[179] One gains a sense however of the central administration's awareness of shrieval conduct as an issue from changes made to the *capitula itineris*. So, additions (caps. 39–54) made under Justice William of York's

---

[175] The first extant plea record is 1236–7 (TNA E 13/1a). For a sampling see *Select Cases in the Exchequer of Pleas*.
[176] *Records of the Trial of Walter Langeton, Bishop of Coventry and Lichfield, 1307–1312*, ed. Alice Beardwood, CS 4th ser. 6 (1969).
[177] *Select Cases in the Exchequer of Pleas*, #213. See e.g. also ##84, 167, 188, 205, 208.
[178] See Crook, *Records of the General Eyre*; Meekings, *Crown Pleas of the Wiltshire Eyre*, 1–16; Pollock and Maitland, *History of English Law*, ii. 520–1, 644–56. For the case that the eyre was obsolete not overburdened by 1294, see Caroline Burt, 'The Demise of the General Eyre in the Reign of Edward I', *EHR* 120 (2005), 1–14.
[179] Meekings, *Crown Pleas of the Wiltshire Eyre*, 6–7.

influence *c*.1245–6 included a significant number addressing shrieval and other officials' misconduct (caps. 40, 42, 43, 44, 45, 46, possibly 52–4).[180] Explicit concern with royal officials' conduct was added to the 1254 eyre articles, perhaps connected with the difficult Hilary parliament that year.[181] Hugh Bigod's Surrey and Kent eyre of 1258–9 produced numerous accusations of sheriffs' 'raising' new, more profitable 'customs', especially relating to the tourn, but also abuse of power through extortion and double-counting.[182] From Edward's reign, concern with shrieval conduct became more emphatic. It is evident in numerous *capitula* of the 1274 Hundred Roll inquiries[183] as well as the Statute of Westminster I (1275).[184] The 1275 Statutes of the Exchequer confirmed three surveyors for reviewing crown wards and escheats to whom sheriffs were answerable. It also made explicit provision for dealing with abusive sheriffs and false accounting, and gave, in 1276, the surveyors licence to hear complaints against sheriffs.[185] The Statute of Rhuddlan (1284) provided for local inquiries into the state of debts, bypassing sole reliance on the sheriffs' affadavit.[186]

In Glénisson's terms such a complex of provisions were *both* administrative *and* reformist. General eyres were as interested in the raising of judicial fines for the king as in the wrongs against counties. It was the capacity of pleas to produce royal fines that made them legitimate eyre pleas. Eyres could therefore contribute to the governmental oppressiveness that petitioners wished to use them to resolve. Again, Walter Map's testimony is easy to discount since it is clear satire. But as a sometime itinerant judge himself, Map cast a trained eye on late-twelfth-century justices in eyre—his 'creatures of the night':

> These are commissioned to go round about, to seek out diligently and to report accurately what of good happens that may concern Jupiter [i.e. the King] [. . .] their first concern is to follow up the odour of carrion. This they devour in secrecy, or conceal, and upon their return lay any accusations they please, besides what they gain for themselves in private by robbery.[187]

---

[180] Helen M. Cam, *Studies in the Hundred Rolls: Some Aspects of Thirteenth-Century Administration*, Oxford Studies in Social and Legal History 6 (Oxford, 1921), 22–5, corr. by Meekings, *Crown Pleas of the Wiltshire Eyre*, 27–33; *Roll of the Shropshire Eyre of 1256*, xxii–xxiv. On William of York, see C. A. F. Meekings and David Crook, *King's Bench and Common Bench in the Reign of Henry III*, SS Suppl. Ser. 17 (London, 2010), 75–6.

[181] Articles for 1254 eyres in Staffordshire (*Annales monastici*, ed. H. R. Luard, RS, 5 vols. (London, 1864–9), i. 329–33 from Burton) and Gloucestershire (*Historia et cartularium monasterii Sancti Petri Gloucestriae*, ii. 276–80. The parliament: Cam, *Studies in the Hundred Rolls*, 25; Maddicott, *Origins of the English Parliament*, 210–18.

[182] *1258–9 Special Eyre*, ed. Hershey, e.g. ##54–6, 80, 152, 295, 322, 385 (tourn abuses); ##363, 364 (extortion and double-counting).

[183] Helen, M. Cam, *The Hundred and the Hundred Rolls: An Outline of Local Government in Medieval England* (London, 1930), App. 1 where the following caps. make explicit reference or imply concern with shrieval or royal officers' conduct: 12–13, 15–38, 42; also *Foedera*, i.2. 517–18; *Yorkshire Hundred and Quo Warranto Rolls*, ed. Barbara English, Yorkshire Archaeological Society, Record Series, 151 (Leeds, 1996), 23–6.

[184] *SR*, i. 27–33, e.g. sheriffs' retinues in cap. 1, and caps. 2 (shrieval judgement), 4 (handling of wrecks), 9 (handling of felonies), 15 (replevin), 18–19 (amercements, quittances, complaints), 25–6 (champerty, extortion). Further: Maddicott, 'Edward I and the Lessons', 14–15.

[185] *SR*, i. 197b–198, caps. 13, 17, 18. Discussion in Maddicott, 'Edward I and the Lessons', 21–3; Michael Prestwich, *Edward I* (London, 1988), 102–3.

[186] *SR*, i. 70. On Rhuddlan's wider fiscal purpose see Prestwich, *Edward I*, 242–3.

[187] *De nugis curialium*, 12–13 (§1.10), eds.' trans.

In 1198 Roger Howden argued that Richard's general and forest eyres 'had reduced the whole of England from sea to sea to poverty'.[188] Paris said of the 1240 eyre that its correction of the *excessus* of many was a pretext for gathering endless amounts of money for the king.[189] In 1242 the barons' own record of their complaints at the January parliament stressed the impoverishment produced by the eyre.[190] Indeed during the 1240s revenue from the eyre did nearly double.[191] If gathering royal judicial profits could coincide with disciplining errant officials so much the better. But it was the former which seems particularly to have impressed contemporaries.

Some sense of the wider accountabilities that sheriffs were subject to can be seen by a brief example. In 1255, Robert le Vavasur, sheriff of Nottinghamshire and Derbyshire since 1246, sometime custodian of Bolsover, Nottingham, and Harstan castles, the honour of Peverel, the manor of Melleburne, a man free from onerous judicial obligations, 'lost his bailiwick, and, being accused by many, finished by owing the King 200 marks'.[192] In May 1254 the Barons of the Exchequer had been ordered to investigate how much Robert and others had siphoned off in relation to the Tickhill honour.[193] On 29 March 1255 the Abbot of Pershore was instructed to investigate Maud of Stratleg's complaints that Robert had run her off her land unjustly, a particular offence since Robert as sheriff is 'specially bound to keep the peace', meaning his 'trespasses shall not go unpunished'.[194] The contradictory state whereby the sheriff of Nottingham summoned himself to appear for this was over by 11 May when Roger de Lovetot was made sheriff. From 22 May the abbot and rising justice William de Wilton were commissioned to investigate further 'various rumours' (presumably made by plaint) that Robert, his son, and others of his household had misappropriated assets due to Nottingham's castle, as well as royal mill, fish, and hay rights; further commissions followed.[195] On 24 January 1256 they were pardoned the 200 marks fine resulting from the trespasses against the King, but held liable for judgement in court by others who wished to complain against them.[196] In January 1257, having confessed his debts, Henry III ordered the new sheriff of Nottingham to take Robert's goods into royal protection until he should make satisfaction.[197] By June 1258 Robert was dead and his son William struggling to negotiate his debts at the Exchequer and in court cases there.[198] Only on 18 October 1270 were Robert's grandchildren and great-grandchildren pardoned 'all accounts, arrears and

---

[188] Howden, *Chronica* iv. 62–3, 84, for unflattering epitaphs of Richard.

[189] Paris, *Chronica majora*, iv. 34. For justice as royal profit see Cam, *Studies in the Hundred Rolls*, 190–2, and Paul A. Brand, 'Edward I and the Judges: The "State Trials" of 1289–93', *TCE* 1 (1986), 31–40 at 34.

[190] Paris, *Chronica majora*, iv. 185–7 at 186–7; further, Maddicott, *Origins of the English Parliament*, 229.

[191] Cassidy, 'Bad Sheriffs'.

[192] *List of Sheriffs for England and Wales*, 102; *CPR 1247–1258*, 22, 39, 121, 240, 410; *CPR 1266–1272*, 465; *Annales monastici*, iii. 199 (Dunstable).

[193] *CR 1253–1254*, 60–1.   [194] *CPR 1247–1258*, 430–1.

[195] *CPR 1247–1258*, 432; *Calendar of Inquisitions Miscellaneous*, i. *1219–1307*, 74. For plaints and *querelae* see Alan Harding, 'Plaints and Bills in the History of English Law, Mainly in the Period 1250–1350', in Dafydd Jenkins (ed.), *Legal History Studies 1972* (Cardiff, 1975), 65–86.

[196] *CPR 1247–1258*, 459. Vavasur had accepted the royal case in November 1255 (507).

[197] *CR 1256–1259*, 115–16.

[198] *CR 1256–1259*, 313–14, 487; *Select Cases in the Exchequer of Pleas*, #100 (Michaelmas 1260).

reckonings' Robert owed, for having paid 60*l.* and 'in consideration of [his] service' (his accomplices were pardoned too).[199] This must have been insufficient to prevent further claims since Robert's granddaughters Elizabeth and Annora sought repetition of the pardon as late as 1285—thirty years after Robert's dismissal as Sheriff of Nottingham and Derbyshire.[200] It is a minor story of petty abuses—less extravagant than others—but it illustrates the complex web of courts, plaints, ad hoc inquiries and pursuits that augmented the routine accountability of sheriffs at the Exchequer.[201] Equity undoubtedly had a voice in these proceedings but not the only one.

Nevertheless, as this makes clear, alongside shrieval accountability to the king and Exchequer barons went some sort of shrieval accountability to sheriffs' county communities. The persistent pulse of grievances against sheriffs makes clear the long-term nature of the problem. The ongoing tinkering with the eyre's *capitula itineris* indicates some governmental sensitivity to the problem. Rather than a solution to a problem, though, this pattern implies a structural tension between sheriffs' accountability to crown fiscality and their accountability to their local communities.

Tensions and Contradictions within Shrieval Accountability

The political thinking Richard of Ely described at the Exchequer finds its practical expression in the intensity and manner in which the English crown focused on sheriffs' fiscal accountability increasingly from the late twelfth century through at least to the second baronial rebellion of 1258–66. This focus seems to have prevented the crown from fully conceptualizing or addressing other aspects of shrieval conduct. That double bind in no small way contributed to the complaints about sheriffs' extortions and misconduct that were so major a feature of the baronial and knightly rebellions of 1214–16 and 1258–66.[202] Even when the crown was supposed to be championing the *honestum* against the fiscally *utile* one can see an important ambivalence. Something of these tensions is visible right from the beginning of the period addressed here in the 1170 inquest of sheriffs.

---

[199] *CPR 1266–1272*, 465.   [200] *CR 1279–1288*, 315.

[201] For some more extravagant examples see Holt, 'Philip Mark', 18–22; for Girard d'Athée and Engelard de Cigogné see *Pleas of the Crown for the County of Gloucester, A.D. 1221*, ed. F. W. Maitland (London, 1884), ##92, 93, 100, 108, 126, 130, 144, 154, 156, 217, 227, 245, 246, 250, 325, 327, 362, 364, 374, 378, 380, 402, 407, 439, 441, 444, 482, 505, and pp. 118, 119, 121, 129, 131, and *Rolls of the Justices in Eyre: Being the Rolls of Pleas and Assizes for Gloucestershire, Warwickshire and Staffordshire, 1221, 1222*, ed. Doris Mary Stenton, SS 59 (London, 1940), #232; Holt, *Northerners*, 229; Richard Cassidy, 'William Heron, "Hammer of the Poor, Persecutor of the Religious", Sheriff of Northumberland, 1246–1258', *Northern History* 50 (2013), 9–19; for William de l'Isle see Paris, *Chronica majora*, v. 577–81, 715–16, *CR 1256–1259*, 174–5, 293–4, Andrew H. Hershey, 'An Introduction to and Edition of the Hugh Bigod Eyre Rolls June 1258–February 1259: P.R.O. Just 1/1187 & Just 1/873', 2 vols. (Ph.D. thesis, University of London, 1991), i. 413–14; and with Hugh de Manneby see Jacob, *Studies in the Period of Baronial Reform and Rebellion*, 10–12, and Hershey, 'Introduction to and Edition of the Hugh Bigod Eyre', i. 49; for Thomas Corbet see *Roll of the Shropshire Eyre*, xxi–xxv and references.

[202] Holt, *Northerners*, 152–6, 228–33; Holt, *Magna Carta*, 61–7, 212–15; Maddicott, 'Magna Carta and the Local Community'; Cassidy, 'William Heron'; Hershey, 'Success or Failure'.

In March 1170, after four years' absence and a dreadful sea crossing from Normandy, Henry II held an Easter council celebrating the coronation of his son and the 'statutes of his kingdom'. He then 'dismissed almost all the sheriffs of England and their bailiffs because they had badly treated the men of his kingdom'. The sheriffs and bailiffs, says Roger of Howden, then swore to 'offer redress to the King and to the men of the kingdom as they ought to offer redress for their exactions'. Gervase of Canterbury describes how Henry 'gathered all of his best men and fixed the abbots and clerks, the earls and knights who would tour the land [*circuierent terram*] giving them the written form which they were to observe'. Meanwhile those in the regions swore to tell the truth about what these men had done. They were particularly to recount, said Howden, 'what and how much the sheriffs and their bailiffs had taken from them, and what with due judgement, and what without, and for what sorts of infringement'. Unexpectedly we are then told, 'But from this the people of England suffered a great injury, because after the inquisition, the King replaced a number of those sheriffs in their places, and these same people showed themselves to be much crueller than they had been previously'.[203] This holding to account does not seem to have produced an equitable effect.

The mechanics of who went in and out of the sheriffs in 1170 have been well analysed.[204] Only three shires seem to have experienced a long-term change in their administrators (Hampshire, Nottinghamshire and Derbyshire, Northumberland).[205] The years 1159/60 and 1163/4, furthermore, saw a greater number of sheriffs removed for those years as a whole, without any of 1170's fanfare.[206] The *Gesta regis Henrici secundi* presents the *inquisitio* as taking a broader view of sheriffs' conduct in its account. There is a reference in the articles of inquiry to how 'the land and the men have been oppressed'. But the principle concern of the *modus inquisitionis* is to rectify this with respect to losses suffered by the King, not to reduce the overall burden on the kingdom.[207] Damage and loss from the King's perspective is the main focus. A comparable pattern is visible in Richard's 1194 eyre following his return from captivity at Dürnstein. Originally this was conceived as a broader *inquisitio* into prises and payments 'of all the bailiffs of the lord king, both justices and sheriffs and constables and foresters, and their servants' since Richard's coronation. The *inquisitio* in these terms though was postponed on Hubert Walter's order. What was left focused on the interests and dues of the crown.[208] The *utile* created more pressing

---

[203] Roger of Howden, *Gesta regis Henrici secundi Benedicti abbatis*, ed. William Stubbs, RS, 2 vols. (London, 1867), i. 4–5; Gervase of Canterbury, *The Historical Works of Gervase of Canterbury*, ed. W. Stubbs, RS, 2 vols. (1879–80), i. 216–19, quote at 216.

[204] Boorman, 'The Sheriffs of Henry II'. Complementary comment in Amt, 'Reputation of the Sheriff'.

[205] Boorman, 'The Sheriffs of Henry II', 274.

[206] Boorman, 'The Sheriffs of Henry II', 258–67.

[207] Text of the headings for investigation in *Select Charters and Other Illustrations of English Constitutional History from the Earliest Times to the Reign of Edward I*, ed. W. Stubbs, rev. H. W. C. Davis, 9th edn. (Oxford, 1913), 175–8. An extant set of instructions for those witnessing at the inquests is in *The Letters and Charters of Gilbert Foliot: Abbot of Gloucester (1139–48), Bishop of Hereford (1148–63), and London (1163–87)*, ed. Z. N. Brooke, Adrian Morey, and C. N. L. Brooke (Cambridge, 1967), App. VII #5 at 523–4.

[208] Roger of Howden, *Chronica*, iii. 262–7, and repr. *Select Charters*, 252–7 at cap. 25, also Roger of Howden, *Chronica*, iii. 241. John Gillingham, *Richard I* (New Haven, Conn., 1999), 276, argues

demands than the *honestum* for Richard. Naturally this cannot but have ethical overtones, but those are not what dominate the articles of the inquiry.

There is no mention at all of what will happen to sheriffs found wanting in relation to the terms of the 1170 inquest. Having specified in detail the fourteen headings (a modern invention) that the itinerant barons are to investigate, the fifteenth simply says, 'And after they have been inquired into, my sheriffs are to be set to my other business and swear that they will legally look into the inquisitions to be made into the lands of the barons.'[209] Inspectors may inspect inspectors, but it is implied that notwithstanding any shrieval failings identified by the barons, the sheriffs may well carry on regardless.

The extant (financial) returns to the inquiry unsurprisingly read mainly as a set of taxable liabilities, not as a broader evaluation.[210] Grievances are audible. In Worcester the sheriff was alleged to exact an unaccustomed castle-guard service and avoid taxes due on his burgage land.[211] In Ely, during the illness of the Bishop (and therefore during its de facto administration by Richard of Ely) the farm of the hundred of Milford and the half hundred of Dereham was increased to '£8 by reason of which the men were so heavily burdened that, unless it be amended they will all be paupers'.[212] On the Earl of Arundel's land, Matthew of Candos had had 405 sheep driven off by the Earl's servants for debts they alleged. Matthew blamed the Earl, who accepted the debts were unfair and blamed his steward.[213] At Docking, unfair dues had been extorted when, 'in the time of King Henry [I] they paid nothing except a just rent'.[214]

The inquest of sheriffs is explicable if its objective was to give sheriffs a bit of a fright, to let them know that other parts of the Angevin machine could well mobilize to keep an eye on them and discourage them from pulling a fast one on the crown. That aim was not trivial, nor was the publicity of the venture coincidental. But there may have been limits to how far such an inquest could put a general stop to shrieval insolence of office.[215] Rather few sheriffs seem to have been seriously disciplined. It seems reasonable to interpret the inquest of sheriffs as an exercise in a fiscal accountability of a familiar sort, and which echoed some wider ideal of rectification. But that rectification was essentially expedient and appears to have been mostly in the fisc's interest. Other senses of accountability can be heard only dimly, expressing fairness financially as they must.

---

it was an initiative of Richard's. See also 270 and Heiser, 'Richard I and his Appointments'. The Norman Exchequer official, Abbot Robert of Caen, was commissioned in 1196 to review the English Exchequer's practice, but died before he could carry this out. Hubert Walter, said Newburgh, was opposed to this review too. See Newburgh, *Historia*, in *Chronicles*, ii. 464–5 (§5.19). On the investigation, John Gillingham, 'The Historian as Judge: William of Newburgh and Hubert Walter', *EHR* 119 (2004), 1275–87 at 1283–4.

[209] *Select Charters*, 178.

[210] *Red Book of the Exchequer*, ii. App. A to Preface, cclxvii–cclxxxi, trans. *EHD* ii. #49; James Tait, 'A New Fragment of the Inquest of Sheriffs (1170)', *EHR* 39 (1924), 80–3.

[211] Tait, 'New Fragment', 83.   [212] *EHD* ii. #49, 447.   [213] *EHD* ii. #49, 442.

[214] *EHD* ii. #49, 448.

[215] Bisson's view that the inquest 'surely stirred the English masses while jolting their masters as never before' (*Crisis of the Twelfth Century*, 383) seems exaggerated. Marc Bloch, *La Société féodale* (Paris, 1994 edn.) took the same view.

Contemporaries' impressions of royal attitudes are important here, and some thought comparatively. Newburgh's obituary of Henry contains a relatively benign picture of regal supervision of officials. 'In extracting money [Henry] was a little excessive—but the growth of this evil beyond measure in the times which followed excused [*justificavit*] him in this respect, and showed that it had been within decent limits under him.'[216] Henry 'imposed no serious burden on the kingdom of the English or his overseas lands until that most recent Tenth because of the expedition to Jerusalem [i.e. the 'Saladin Tithe' of 1188]'.[217] These were observations about sheriffs and their officers, since it was they who extracted the money. Newburgh had identified that officials extracting improper dues was a problem at the start of Henry II's reign.[218] But if Henry was bad, Richard was worse.[219] The Cistercian Ralph of Coggeshall—happy to praise Richard elsewhere—said 'no age can remember nor history tell of any past kings, however long they reigned, who demanded and took so much money from his kingdom as this king extorted and amassed within the five years after his return from his captivity' (i.e. 1194–9).[220] Newburgh's comparison was sharper still. 'The present experience of evils [i.e. under Richard] created a memory of [Henry II's] goodness, and the man who had been hateful to almost everyone in his own time [i.e. Henry], was declared an extraordinary and useful prince.'[221] Faced with such political amnesia, Newburgh's judgement on the English is that 'this stupid people is thrashed now by scorpions with less complaint than in those years past when it was thrashed with whips' by Henry II.[222] The stings Newburgh and Coggeshall must have had in mind doubtlessly included the English contribution to Richard's ransom (150,000 marks), and that of the Norman campaign—but also of the shrieval expedients Richard initiated.

From Richard's return in 1194, the crown became increasingly preoccupied with sheriffs' fiscal accountability, pressurizing them as never before, and necessarily pressurizing other aspects of shrieval conduct.[223] Lands that had escheated to the crown were now accounted for by crown-appointed escheators, not sheriffs, in an attempt to increase the value drawn from these assets. New increments were added to nine county farms, increasing the amount sheriffs had to account for, or forcing them to fine in order to pay the lower, lesser rates. Up-front gifts for appointments to shrievalties declined in value, but incremental increases more than compensated the

---

[216] Newburgh, *Historia*, in *Chronicles*, i. 280 (§3.26).
[217] Newburgh, *Historia*, in *Chronicles*, i. 282 (§3.26). See Gillingham, 'Historian as Judge', 1275–87.
[218] Newburgh, *Historia*, in *Chronicles*, i. 102 (§2.1).
[219] Note, however, the remarks of Ralph Diceto stressing Henry's attempts to find good judges to look into shrieval actions in 1179, *Radulfi de Diceto Decani Londoniensis, Opera historica*, ed. William Stubbs, RS, 2 vols. (London, 1876), i. 434–5.
[220] *Radulphi de Coggeshall Chronicon Anglicanum*, ed. Joseph Stevenson, RS (London 1875), 93. Further, Gillingham, *Richard I*, 332, 342–4. David Carpenter argues convincingly that Coggeshall's account of 1195–1200 was written in 1201: D. A. Carpenter, 'Abbot Ralph of Coggeshall's Account of the Last Years of King Richard and the First Years of King John', *EHR* 113 (1998), 1210–30.
[221] Newburgh, *Historia*, in *Chronicles*, i. 283 (§3.26).
[222] Newburgh, *Historia*, in *Chronicles*, i. 283 (§3.26), echoing 2 Chron. 10: 11.
[223] For the following changes see Heiser, 'Richard I and his Appointments'; Carpenter, 'Decline of the Curial Sheriff'; Holt, *Northerners*, 152–7; Brian E. Harris, 'King John and the Sheriffs' Farms', *EHR* 79 (1964), 532–42; Robert C. Stacey, *Politics, Policy, and Finance under Henry III 1216–1245*

Exchequer. The emphasis was shifted from candidates' ability to pay on entry to sheriffs' ability to get more money out of shrieval farms.[224] Sheriffs, however, could not cope with the new increments, and Barratt's analysis shows the declining yield to the crown.[225] As with Richard, so with John, and the attempt to muster resources for Continental reconquest after 1204 focused John's attention back on England, prompting him to increase exploitation there.[226] From 1204 a system of 'custodian' sheriffs was introduced, tax-gatherers who simply accounted for all revenues that passed through their hands, not the simple total of the farm they previously held responsibility for.[227] Increased shrieval accountability went in uneven tandem with the complex decline of the curial sheriff—reducing the attractiveness of the office and the status of incumbents.[228] Thirteen shrievalties changed hands in 1204, nine being handed on to lesser men more pliable to Exchequer pressure.[229] From 1207 individual debtors' debts were aggregated at the Exchequer so a global total could be seen, and managed, more clearly.[230] Sheriffs' fiscal accountability at the Exchequer was under pressure as never before. From 1194 to 1215 the income from the county account drops below £20,000 only in 1196–7; between 1208 and 1212 it averages £39,354, more than three times as much as the 1189 county total of £11,363.[231] The pressure on other debtors is staggering. In 1204 £523 of debt was called in. In 1205, £1,398, and a similar figure in 1206; between 1207 and 1210 an annual average of £4,685 was taken; and between 1210 and 1212, £10,513, 16 per cent of the annual average revenue for 1210–12 of £63,939 (in 1200 it was 6 per cent of annual revenue).[232] As Barrett argues, 'John's attempts to maintain his financial position in this period represent the greatest level of exploitation seen in England since the Conquest.'[233] Such a single-minded focus on fiscal accountability could only hamstring any efforts to take a broader-minded conception of shrieval office. In part Magna Carta was the effect.[234]

(Oxford, 1987), ch. 2, esp. 66–92 and Stacey, 'Agricultural Investment and the Management of the Royal Desmesne Manors, 1236–1240', *Journal of Economic History* 46 (1986); Cassidy, '*Adventus Vicecomitum*'.

[224] Heiser, 'Richard I and his Appointments', 14–16.

[225] For data and analysis Nick Barratt, 'The English Revenues of Richard I', *EHR* 116 (2001), 635–56, Table 8 and 650.

[226] Holt, *Northerners*, 148, 152–3.

[227] Carpenter, 'Decline of the Curial Sheriff', 3 n. 2, 21 n. 3.

[228] Carpenter, 'Decline of the Curial Sheriff', 9–10.

[229] See *Lists of Sheriffs for England and Wales*.

[230] *PR 1207*, e.g. 81, 82 on Roger de Montbegon; discussion: Holt, *Northerners*, 170–1.

[231] Using financial year (29 September–29 September) figures from table 2 of Barratt, 'English Revenues of Richard I' and table 2 of Nick Barratt, 'The Revenue of King John', *EHR* 111 (1996), 835–55. While these tables are not completely comparable (e.g. for escheats), on this axis they appear to be. Inflation needs to be factored in, but doing so makes clear that John's revenues were powerfully expanding whichever way the data are looked at (Barratt, 'Revenue of King John', table 6.2 and discussion). See also Barratt, 'English Revenues of Richard I', 653–4.

[232] Figures are calculated from tables 2, 4 of Barratt, 'Revenue of King John'. Using table 5.1, which has only debts associated with the country pipe roll totals, would reduce these figures. Some of these calculated totals differ from Barratt's since he (legitimately) seems to exclude credit revenue from some of his calculations. Barratt's comment on these figures, 851.

[233] Barratt, 'Revenue of King John', 855.

[234] *Magna Carta*, caps. 4 (shrieval answerability for handling of wardships), 9 (non-seisin of capital while a debtor is solvent nor of his sureties if he is solvent), 25 (return to the old farm rates), 28, 30–1

Henry III did not radically diverge from the pattern and well-known changes in 1236 to shrieval tenure pushed this further.[235] 'Cleverly packaged and proclaimed as reforms to meet the aspirations and grievances of county society', twenty-two of twenty-seven counties were made custodial shrievalties: instead of answering for a fixed farm, sheriffs were to answer for all their profits.[236]

The effect was to exacerbate the manipulability of sheriffs. Further, the changes glossed over the fundamentally extractive nature of the shrieval office by appealing to good behaviour. But the longer-term problem was structural: on weaker men heavier demands were being placed. The best recent evaluation is that by 1250/1 counties were expected to produce 16.4 per cent more than in 1241/2 and a further 5.3 per cent by 1256/7 (to £4,689). The increase lay overwhelmingly in the incremental profit demanded of the sheriff outside the county farm's income. Here the increase was 75 per cent between 1241/2 and 1256/7.[237]

Such a commitment to royal fiscality did not preclude good intentions. On 7 October 1250 Henry III famously spoke at the Exchequer to 'all the sheriffs of England then in post'. The sheriffs were to maintain the liberties of Holy Church, those of wards, orphans, and widows and 'bring them swift justice'. They were to deal with blasphemers and not distrain peasants for their solvent masters' debts. They should 'diligently and rightly inquire into how the magnates conduct themselves towards their men [. . .] and correct their transgressions in so far as they can'. If they 'cannot fully correct them, then they should bring these same transgressions before the lord king'. They were to shop short-weighting merchants to the King. They were 'not to sell on the right to hear complaints in hundreds, wapentakes or other bailiwicks unless it is to someone who will treat the people with justice'.[238] Other requirements stipulated the terms on which they hold pleas. There was no explicit mention of the fiscal aspects of their job. The attention given to other matters is very different from the priorities attended to at the Exchequer, making the choice of location symbolic as well as practical. Six years later the picture was a very different one when Henry again spoke at the Exchequer. This time it was in reaction to sheriffs and accountants failing to appear at the Michaelmas 1256 account.[239] The object of this second royal intervention was simple fiscal accountability. Those who do not appear are to be fined £5 daily up to five days when the fine will be 'ad voluntatem domini regis'. All elevated talk has evaporated.

(restrictions on sheriffs' exactions), 45 (demand for local men as sheriffs), 48 (order for investigation into evil customs of sheriffs and other officials), ed. in Holt, *Magna Carta*, App. 6.

[235] Stacey, *Politics, Policy, and Finance*, 52–66; Carpenter, 'Decline of the Curial Sheriff', *passim*.

[236] Carpenter, 'Decline of the Curial Sheriff', 17. See Mabel H. Mills, 'Experiments in Exchequer Procedure, 1200–1232', *TRHS* 4th ser. 8 (1925), 151–70; Mills, 'Reforms at the Exchequer, 1232–1242', *TRHS* 4th ser. 10 (1927), 111–33; Cassidy, *Adventus Vicecomitum*; Cassidy, 'Bad Sheriffs'.

[237] Using figures in Richard Cassidy, 'The 1259 Pipe Roll', 2 vols. (Ph.D. thesis, University of London, 2012), i. 104–6. I am very grateful to him for discussion and a copy of this very important thesis. He is preparing an edition for the Pipe Roll Society.

[238] Edn. in Michael Clanchy, 'Did Henry III Have a Policy?', *History* 53 (1968), 203–16 at 216.

[239] D. A. Carpenter, 'Matthew Paris and Henry III's Speech at the Exchequer in October 1256', in his *Reign of Henry III*, 137–50, printing the text and Paris's account at 149–50.

It would be easy to be censorious about the crown's failure to balance the need for equitable and fiscally successful officers. The crown *did* express a concern with sheriffs' behaviour, but that expression was intermittent, hampered by John and Henry's underlying, ongoing inability to modify their financial needs. Like his father, Henry was forced to do so in 1258–66 by a baronial and knightly uprising.

The baronial council's sheriff's oath of October 1258 demonstrates the centrality of shrieval equity to thirteenth-century politics.[240] The 1258 oath contrasts sharply with the Exchequer sheriff's oath as can be reconstructed for the twelfth century. This seems only to have concerned his thorough investigation of debts due to the king and his own claim that he had accounted correctly.[241] It was suggested in Chapter 2 that the 1258 change may have owed something to the manorial treatises' expectations of those officers' conduct (pp. 76–80). Extant in French, but issued in Latin and English too, the oath is very long. Limitations and restrictions on the hospitality he could expect, ceilings on the size of his entourage, stipulations on the quality of these men, bans on the sub-farming of jurisdictions, warnings of punishment to those making illegal exactions, bans on bribes, instructions that only reasonable expenses will be met, and a strict one-year limit on terms of office: all these are set out in the letter that was to be sent out to all counties and read out by their sheriffs (presumably at the county court). The 1258 oath is the serious assertion of the concerns articulated in 1236 when the great curial sheriffs were removed and more manipulable sheriffs installed.[242] It went alongside widespread dismissals of sheriffs and Exchequer officials and a principled and applied attempt to marry solvency with equity.[243] As custodians the 1258/9 sheriffs had no profit target but had to account for all their 'workings' in submitted *particule*.[244] When 'farmer' sheriffs were reintroduced in 1259/60 their targets were (somewhat) reduced to 80 per cent of those of 1256/7.[245]

The dynasty's longstanding problem in taking both money and conduct seriously with respect to sheriffs is clearly brought out in the 1264 dossier presented to Louis IX. (On Edward I's attitude see pp. 122, 126, 128, 133.) In January Louis was trying to settle the dispute between the barons and his brother-in-law. The barons were absolutely clear about the structure of the problem with respect to sheriffs. The pre-1258 shift from 'a fixed and moderate farm' to 'recently imposed permanent increments' 'with ongoing increases' was a major complaint.[246] The

---

[240] Printed, *DBM* #8. Copies: BL Cotton MS Vespasian E. III, fos. 85ᵛ–86 (= *Annales monastici*, i. 453–55 from Burton; *CPR 1247–1258*, 655–6); BL Add. MS 15668 fo. 32ʳ; variant TNA E 159/32 m. 2. See Brand, *Kings, Barons and Justices*, 25–6; Lachaud, *Éthique du pouvoir*, 486–9. Cf. *Konstitutionen Friedrichs II. für das Königreich sizilien*, caps. 1.62.1, 1.62.2.

[241] See p. 108 and *DS*, I.v, II.xii–xiii, xiii, xvii, xxviii, at 21, 106–7, 109, 113–14, 124, 126.

[242] Paris, *Chronica majora*, iii. 363.

[243] See Provisions of Oxford (*DBM* #5, esp. caps. 16, 17), order for inquiries (#6), Provisions of Westminster (#11, cap. 4, #12, caps. 5, 7, 9, 20), provisions for inquiries (#13), 1264 justifications to Louis IX (#37b, caps. 7–8, 10–12); Paris, *Chronica majora*, v. 719–20, vi. 397–400. Cassidy, *1259 Pipe Roll*, i. 127–8 is more reserved.

[244] Jobson, 'John of Crakehall', 93–4; Cassidy, '1259 Pipe Roll', i. 92–103; Cassidy, 'Bad Sheriffs'.

[245] Using Cassidy, '1259 Pipe Roll', i. 110–12. See also his 'Bad Sheriffs'.

[246] *DBM* #37c at 274, cap. 6. For a convincing argument about the correct ordering of *DBM* #37a–b see Robert C. Stacey, 'Crusades, Crusaders, and the Baronial *Gravamina* of 1263–1264', *TCE* 3 (1991),

attempt to make sheriffs bureaucratic publicans was also alleged to have failed since 'the sheriffs and bailiffs, seeking their profit at the expense of others, each schemed to outbid the other, and thus, not being able to pay otherwise the payments thus imposed and so frequently increased, of necessity had recourse to illicit extortions and rapine, thus reducing the whole land to an incredible state of poverty'.[247] The problem was precisely that which Aquinas advised the Duchess of Brabant would probably result from the sale of offices when 'those are offered for sale at so great a price that the holders cannot recoup the cost without damage to your subjects'.[248] In England, there was no means of redressing such abuses 'on account of the protectors whom the oppressors had at court as partners in their ill-gotten gains'. Furthermore, the sheriffs were not 'prudent and knowledgeable knights of the counties, as was of old custom, but men coming from far away and utter strangers in the counties'.[249] The complaints parallel many from Magna Carta.[250] As a whole, the heading of the 1264 dossier effectively summarizes a century's worth of resentment about sheriffs. It was precisely responsiveness to these aspects of shrieval behaviour that had been fudged in 1170 and abandoned in the county *inquisitio* of 1194. The *utile* created more pressing demands than the *honestum* for Richard on his return from the Crusade. John had started to take them seriously in 1213, but too late.[251] Any reformist dabbling of Henry's was overwhelmed by his need for money, latterly connected with his Sicilian crusading ambitions for his son Edmund.

Two thirteenth-century rebellions forced the Angevins to express a less faltering interest in shrieval conduct writ large. They had failed to do so themselves almost by definition since the fiscal stress of shrieval accountability at least between 1194 and 1258 precluded it. Further, it was attempts to tweak the sheriff's office so that it was more of a professional and less or a curial position that ended up making it more offensive between 1236 and 1274 (when Edward returned to England).[252] As a less powerful local figure he was less responsive to local concerns and more wholly accountable to those of the Exchequer. Increased fiscal liability, reduced social standing, plus possibly worsened financial wherewithal sustained or exacerbated sheriffs' interest in extracting money from the counties.[253] The problem with sheriffs' accountability was that its stress on the fiscally *utile* undercut county concern about the *honestum*. Some comparisons with Continental European 'shrieval' officers sheds further light on England and enables reflection on wider interpretative frameworks.

137–50, arguing that C precedes B, where C is the baronial summary of events and royal wrongs that B continues, going on to C to rebut the king's grievances as stated in A.

[247] *DBM* #37c at 275, cap. 6, eds.' trans.

[248] 'De regimine judaeorum' in *Aquinas: Selected Political Writings*, ed. A. P. d'Entrèves, trans. J. G. Dawson (Oxford, 1974), 88.

[249] *DBM* #37c cap. 6 at 275–7, eds.' trans.   [250] See n. 234.

[251] See the Barnwell Chronicler's account, *Memoriale fratris Walteri de Coventria*, ed. William Stubbs, RS, 2 vols. (London, 1872–3), ii. 214–15; Holt, *Magna Carta*, 212–16.

[252] For Edward's 1274–8 reforms, Maddicott, 'Edward I and the Lessons of Baronial Reform', 19–28.

[253] e.g. the May 1258 *Petitio Baronum, DBM* #3 at 82, cap. 16; Ridgeway, 'Mid-Thirteenth Century Reformers', 61.

COMPARISONS: PREFERENCES, STRUCTURES, ROYAL SELF-IMAGE

Various schemas suggest themselves. Sir Richard Southern suggested a contrast between France and England in which sophistication of governmental machinery was inversely proportionate with regnal solidarity and regal security. The great machinery of the Exchequer was contrasted with more rudimentary French mechanisms. In France the fiscal system was 'very simple. When men are very rich and are getting richer they have no need for elaborate organization or for novelties of procedure.'[254] Different administrative infrastructures precipitated different political weather.

> England came to possess the most highly developed secular administrative machine in Europe. But this was never enough. This was the English tragedy. The French kings grew rich without strain; the English kings strained every nerve but could never be rich enough. There is a direct connection between the over-great financial and military burden of [the English] Continental policy and the failure of the English kings to create any warmth of sentiment operating in their favour among the most powerful classes of society.[255]

The effect was that 'in England we have a tradition of service without affection; in France a tradition of domesticity without, at this time, much professional service'.[256] This could be transposed into Thomas Bisson's terms: in late twelfth-century England, accountability of office; in France, accountability of fidelity.[257] Jean Glénisson's typology of inquiries might suggest a related answer. It would lie in the difference between Exchequer accountability—relating to his inquiries dedicated to 'administration of the state's domanial and fiscal business'—versus eyres and other inquiries incorporating 'correcting and reforming abuses'.[258] How did thirteenth-century England experience such deep political problems, so tightly associated with shrieval officers, in comparison with France and also with the Regno?

First, quite distinct strategies for managing sheriffs/*baillis* were in operation in France and England. Magna Carta cap. 45 had stipulated that sheriffs and other officials should know customary practice and law.[259] Sometimes counties could bid collectively to get the sheriff of their choice appointed. In England the ideal in the

---

[254] R. W. Southern, 'England's First Entry into Europe', in his *Medieval Humanism*, 135–57 at 153.
[255] Southern, 'England's First Entry into Europe', 152. There is a sophisticated debate about whether French revenues were indeed significantly higher than English ones by the late twelfth/early thirteenth century. Even if previous estimations of French financial superiority need to be reduced significantly, the point about the relative effort of exacting these revenues remains. See Nick Barratt, 'Revenue of King John', esp. 835–56, 844–5; Barratt, 'English Revenue of Richard I', 651–2, 656; Barratt, 'The Revenues of John and Philip Augustus Revisited', in S. D. Church (ed.), *King John: New Interpretations* (Woodbridge, 1999), 75–99; Gillingham, *Angevin Empire*, 95–102; Baldwin, *Government of Philip Augustus*, 152–75.
[256] Southern, 'England's First Entry into Europe', 151.
[257] Bisson, *Crisis of the Twelfth Century*, 316–49.
[258] Glénisson, 'Enquêtes administratives', 19.
[259] Holt, *Magna Carta*, App. 6, discussion 61–6; Maddicott, *Origins of the English Parliament*, 135–6, 256, 315–17.

localities was that a locally credible man would be selected.[260] In Philip Augustus's and Louis IX's France the preference was different. Limiting links between *baillis* and their billeted regions was the aim. In 1254 Louis ruled that a *bailli* could not buy land in his bailiwick, he could not marry into it, he could not sell his offices on. He would stay in the vicinity after leaving office for forty days in order to be answerable to his successor or any complainants.[261] At the March 1283 San Martino parliament, Louis's nephew, Charles of Salerno, responded to the disastrous Vespers rebellion by regulating for a very 'Italian' *sindacatio* for his officers, as well as attempting to legislate against officers exercising undue influence on the communities in which they worked.[262] Like '1258' in England, the Vespers had been caused in large part by (officials') excessive fiscal pressure. But the same cause produced a different effect. The political psychology of Louis's and Charles's policies here was as with Italian *podestà*: guarantee independence from partisan politics by minimizing 'shrieval' ties with the locality. The traditional English model was more, perhaps too, sophisticated: political answerability to the county; fiscal answerability to the Exchequer. The basis for ongoing political dispute about whom the sheriff really was responsible to was thus established. It did not matter that shrieval 'localism' was fallible.[263] The bad taste left by sheriffs perceived as the King's more than the counties' friends under John was long-lasting.[264] His grandson's 1278 acceptance of the shrieval localism principle was simply acceptance of a worn plea.[265] This dynamic finds suggestive support in patterns of Edwardian sheriffs. If Edward was indeed central to shrieval policy in the late 1260s, as Caroline Burt has argued, the partial shift in 1270 from knightly sheriffs to that of curial or 'professional' sheriffs implies a concern about lesser men's openness to local magnate influence. Irrespective of the principle, adoption of local sheriffs in 1278 was acceptable because the return of the King enabled sharper supervision.[266] Regnal preferences about 'shrieval' officers were a part product of institutional structures. They inflected the development and fortunes of royal political thinking about 'shrieval' officers' accountability in different ways.

The novelty of French administrative self-assertion may have rendered structures there more flexible making liability to the centre easier to stress.[267] But even if France had 'caught up' by the 1220s, the relative age of the institutions was significant. The English shrieval system's age made attempts to modify the office both inevitable and inevitably explosive. The *baillis* by contrast were barely fifty years old when

---

[260] Maddicott, *Origins of the English Parliament*, 135–6; Ridgeway, 'Mid-Thirteenth Century Reformers', 61–2.
[261] Joinville, *Histoire de Saint Louis*, ed. M. Natalis de Wailly, 9th edn. (Paris, 1921), ch. 140 (§§703, 704, 709–10, 714).
[262] Romualdo Trifone, *La Legislazione Angioina*, Documenti per la storia dell'Italia meridionale 1 (Naples, 1921), #59 at 104, 102, 103. Earlier practices, Dunbabin, *Charles I of Anjou*, 74.
[263] Cassidy, 'William Heron', analyses a local boy gone bad.
[264] Holt, 'Philip Mark', 12–13 and on the 'King's friends', Holt, *Northerners*, 217–36. Complaints about 'alien' officers' impunity as a function of their proximity to Henry III, 1258–64 was a variation of the 'King's friends' complaint. See *DBM* #37c, cap. 3.
[265] See Maddicott, 'Edward I and the Lessons of Baronial Reform', 26.
[266] See the discussion of possible interpretations in Burt, *Edward I and the Governance of England*, 109–14.
[267] Cf. Bloch, *Société féodale*, 585–8.

Louis initiated his 1247 investigations. But age and function were long connected. Extracting money nationwide through the county 'plumbing' using a royal officer who was also a county officer over time led to sheriffs' accountability becoming enormously pressurized. Thanks to a long conciliar tradition, it contributed to his and the county unit's politicization, resulting in an ultimately parliamentary forum.[268] The dynamic was very different from France's, as Maddicott has sharply shown. *Baillis* were less politicized than sheriffs. Greater French royal demesne wealth, greater royal itineration, greater provincial fragmentation partly because of towns' roles, and greater mutability of administrative units simultaneously reduced the centrality of French 'shrieval' officers while forestalling a similar space for the politicization of complaint.[269] It was easier for Capetians than for Plantagenets to take the *honestum* aspect of their 'shrieval' officers seriously because the stakes were lower. A wider Capetian emphasis on the integrity of office-holding threatened a cadre and its customs proportionately less.

How far the relative youth of the French system actually produced more equitable *baillis* is far from certain. Before leaving for crusade in 1190 Philip Augustus offered regular appeal sessions against the abuse of office. How far it was taken up is unclear.[270] So is its continuation on Philip's return.[271] The implication of the complaints made in response to his grandson's inquiries may well be that as the responsibilities of these officials expanded over Philip II's reign, controls over them did not.

Cadoc of Pont Audemer can provide a partial indication of both French practice and developments, and a counterpoint to the English material. Cadoc, an important leader of *routier*s (mercenary bands), or better a 'captain of irregulars' (Powicke) for Philip Augustus, was also the only one of the new *baillis* there to be removed. Delisle described him as un 'étrange personnage, un véritable aventurier, dont l'audace et le talent aidèrent puissamment Philippe Auguste à conquérir la Normandie, et à affermir la domination française dans une partie de cette province'.[272] Cadoc figures relatively frequently in French chronicles: fighting for Philip with Richard and John, wounding Richard in the siege of Gaillon Castle in 1196, taking the town of Angers, and, *c.*1213, sailing with the fleet destroyed by the Flemish.[273] The *Roman*

---

[268] Cf. Maddicott, *Origins of the English Parliament*, 415, 393–4, 405, 432–3.

[269] Key points of Maddicott, *Origins of the English Parliament*, ch. 7, but see esp. 386 (wealth), 389–90 (itineration), 382, 406, 408, 415 (fragmentation, towns), 409–410 (mutable administration).

[270] *Actes du Parlement de Paris. 1. série, de l'an 1254 à l'an 1328*, ed. E. Boutaric, 2 vols. (Paris, 1863–7), i. ccxcvii–ccxcviii (*Arrêts et enquêtes*, #2).

[271] Baldwin, *Government of Philip Augustus*, 138–9 citing *RHF*, xxiv.1. *277 as a slim demonstration that it did.

[272] For Cadoc, see *RHF*, xxiv.1. *130–3; index entries in *Cartulaire Normand, de Philippe-Auguste, Louis VIII, Saint Louis, et Philippe-le-Hardi*, ed. Léopold Delisle (Caen, 1882, repr. Geneva, 1978); M. Prevost's entry 'Cadoc', in *DBF*; Baldwin, *Government of Philip Augustus*, 223, 135 n. 289 and in C. Warren Hollister and John W. Baldwin, 'The Rise of Administrative Kingship: Henry I and Philip Augustus', *AHR* 83 (1978), 867–905 at 903; F. M. Powicke, *The Loss of Normandy, 1189–1204: Studies in the History of the Angevin Empire*, 2nd edn. (Manchester, 1961), 231, 271 n. 119, 272–3, 172; Powicke, review of Audoin's *Essai sur l'armée royale au temps de Philippe Auguste*, *EHR* 30 (1915), 114.

[273] *Œuvres de Rigord et de Guillaume le Breton: historiens de Philippe-Auguste*, ed. H.-François Delaborde, Société de l'histoire de France, 2 vols. (Paris, 1882–5), ii. *Philippidos*, 5 l. 262; 7 ll. 158, 396; 9 ll. 296, 394, 461.

d'Eustaches le Moine questionably attributes to him the seneschalcy of Normandy.[274] Before that, Cadoc had already benefited from France's conquest of Normandy in 1204 when the temporary, second-tier Norman *bailliage* of Pont-Audemer was created.[275] Cadoc administered 'dans son intérêt personnel les populations du territoire confié à sa garde'.[276] Before that he had already figured in the one extant set of Capetian accounts for Philip, including a payment offered for 4,400*l. Angevin*.[277] He is found assisting in the French equivalent of the Easter 'view of account' in 1209.[278] Following the conquest he took over Gaillon whose usufruct he gained in 1216. This seems to have been the centre of his operation: he founded the chapel of Notre Dame there in 1218 and perhaps in *c.*1215 conducted an inquiry into its resources and those of Evreux.[279]

In March 1207 the King ordered him not to vex the monks of Valasse by the levy of the Norman hearth tax, the 'fouage'.[280] Exactions from La Pommeraie forest were cited in complaints against him (*c.*1230).[281] Importantly, further complaints about Cadoc's behaviour surfaced only following Louis IX's 1247 campaign to investigate the conduct of regional agents.[282] Cadoc rehabilitated himself by 1227, then died, probably *c.*1232.[283] But it was *c.*1219–20 that Cadoc was removed for failing to account in Paris for some 14,200*l. Parisis*.[284] The formal grounds for Cadoc's removal and the social memory of his abusive conduct appear totally

---

[274] *RHF*, xxiv.1. *132; *Le Roman d'Eustache le moine*, ed. A. J. Holden and J. Monfrin (Louvain, 2005), ll. 1955–2126.

[275] Cf. Powicke, *Loss of Normandy*, 71; J. R. Strayer, *The Administration of Normandy under Saint Louis* (Cambridge, Mass., 1932), 7–9.

[276] *RHF*, xxiv.1. *130.

[277] Ferdinand Lot and Robert Fawtier (eds.), *Le Premier Budget de la monarchie française: le compte général de 1202–1203*, Bibliothèque de l'École des Hautes Études, Sciences historiques et philologiques, Fasc. 259 (Paris, 1932), 203, CCV; *RHF*, xxiv.1. *130. See the note on coinage in Baldwin, *Government of Philip Augustus*, xv.

[278] *RHF*, xxiv.1. *131; *Recueil de jugements de l'échiquier de Normandie au XIIIe siècle (1207–1270) suivi d'un mémoire sur les anciennes collections de ces jugements*, ed. Léopold Delisle (Paris, 1864), 14 n. 3.

[279] *RHF*, xxiv.1. *131; Léopold Delisle, *Catalogue des actes de Philippe-Auguste: avec une introduction sur les sources, les caractères et l'importance historique de ces documents* (Paris, 1856), #1677, 1790 = respectively *Recueil des Actes de Philippe Auguste, roi de France*, gen. ed. Élie Berger, Chartes et diplômes relatifs à l'histoire de France, 6 vols. (Paris, 1916–), iv. #1441, 1509. See also *Mémoires et notes de M. Auguste Le Prévost pour servir à l'histoire du département de l'Eure*, ed. Léopold Delisle and Loius Passy, 3 vols. (Evreux, 1862–9), ii. 148–9 (chapel). Le Prévost gives 24 February 1205 as the date of the foundation of the chapel. For the inquiry, see *Les Registres de Philippe Auguste*, ed. John W. Baldwin with Françoise Gasparri, Michel Nortier, and Élisabeth Lalou, *Recueil des historiens de la France*, Documents financiers et administratifs 7 (Paris, 1992), 95–6 (*inquisitiones*, #47) = *Layettes*, i. 300–1 (#797).

[280] *Cartulaire Normand*, #1084 = *Catalogue des actes de Philippe-Auguste*, #1018 = *Recueil des Actes de Philippe Auguste*, iii. #966. On *fouage* see Baldwin, *Government of Philip Augustus*, 159–60.

[281] *RHF*, xxiv.1. *132 and for the inquest into rights in the wood, *Cartulaire Normand*, #1143.

[282] See *RHF*, xxiv.1. *132. For these 1247 investigations, *Querimoniae Normannorum*, *RHF*, xxiv.1. 6 (§32), 10 (§62), 11 (§70), 14 (§84), 16 (§102), 36 (§278), 38 (§§284, 287), 42 (§316), 65 (§491), 66 (§§494, 496), 67 (§501).

[283] For his rehabilitation by 1227, when he took an oath to Louis IX, *Layettes*, ii. #1937–8 = *Cartulaire Normand*, #364, 363 also 365; *Registres de Philippe Auguste*, 437 (*securitates*, #83); *RHF*, xxiv.1. *132-3.

[284] *RHF*, xxiv.1. 132*, 40–1 (§305), 66 (§496), 67 (§503), and 68 (§512); *Layettes* ii. #1937–8.

separate (as they might well at the English Exchequer). Furthermore, the substantive grounds for his removal are some thirty to forty years prior to the investigations that provide us with most of our knowledge into Cadoc's bearing while a *bailli*. (The timespan is pointed out by some 1247 complainants.) Many also claimed that the crown had simply continued Cadoc's unfair exactions. It had seized his assets and applied his 'customs'. They were complaining—doubtless with due care—about the crown as much as they were appealing to the king. Ethics came after exploitation, and the crown found itself investigating its own (unwitting?) complicity in its officers' abuses.

In France the early storage of and responsibility for royal revenue with the Templars meant Paris's *Chambre des comptes* emerged into focus relatively late, in the period between Louis IX's 1254 reforms and the 1320 Vivier-en-Brie *ordonnance* of Philip V (r.1316–22) regulating the Chambre.[285] This chronological inversion meant that, by contrast with England, 'in France royal justice was not born of the institution which had control of the administration of the [royal] demesne, it preceded it'.[286] Certainly Louis IX has his officials swear their heavily moralized oaths of office at the full assizes; Philip V has them swear it at the *Chambre des comptes*.[287] English institutional fiscal practice was uninfluential except where dynastic contacts prompted influence, such as Savoy.[288] It has been further argued that accountability at the French *Chambre des comptes*—growing as it did from the same conscientious Crusade-related reformist urge that produced the massive *enquêtes* into officials' broader conduct—was likewise informed by that same reformist spirit.[289] If true, this would provide an obvious, immediate contrast with the picture in the *Dialogue*. But, as was shown earlier, Exchequer accountability was also conceived (on Richard of Ely's account) within a context of 'reform', and broadly within the context of giving to each his due. Its stress was on a particular idea of *utilitas* which, it was argued above, can be seen in financial practice. It was from these premises that the Exchequer was 'the cradle of the professionalization of justice' in England.[290] Both English and French 'exchequers' were premised on 'reformist' ideas; but those ideas and their stresses were distinct.

The issue is not simply that England has an advanced administrative machinery by 1200. What Bisson describes as the accountability of office is present and correct amongst the officials of the late twelfth-century Exchequer. There is nothing

---

[285] Élisabeth Lalou, 'La Chambre des comptes de Paris: sa mise en place et son fonctionnement (fin XIIIᵉ–XIVᵉ siècle)', in Contamine and Mattéoni (eds.), *La France des principautés*, 3–15, esp. 4–9. She re-edits the Vivier-en-Brie *ordonnance* in 'La Chambre des comptes du roi de France', in Philippe Contamine and Olivier Mattéoni (eds.), *Les Chambres des comptes en France aux XIVᵉ et XVᵉ siècles: Textes et documents* (Paris, 1998), 1–18 at 3–8.

[286] Genet, 'Chambres des comptes des principautés et genèse de l'état moderne', 270; cf. Maddicott, *Origins of the English Parliament*, 402–7, 421.

[287] Joinville, *Histoire de Saint Louis*, ch. 140, §701; Lalou, 'La Chambre des comptes du roi de France', 7 (cap. 22 of the Vivier-en-Brie *ordonnance*).

[288] Genet, 'Chambres des comptes des principautés et genèse de l'état moderne', 269–70.

[289] Mattéoni, 'Vérifier, corriger, juger', 57–8; Jacques Le Goff, *Saint Louis* (Paris, 1996), 323–5; cf. Lalou, 'La Chambre des comptes de Paris', 4.

[290] The phrase is Genet's, 'Chambres des comptes des principautés et genèse de l'état moderne', 269.

informal or occasional about Exchequer accountability, an institution and process predating both the writing of the *Dialogue* and the first extant 1130 pipe roll.[291] Nor does the Exchequer immediately appear a likely place of courtly sociability, such as would characterize Bisson's fidelitarian accountability.[292] The ongoing problem in England was that fiscal accountability implied relatively little for some positive sense of shrieval responsibility. Richard of Ely's seeming inability to think of sheriffs as responsible officers, rather than as chancers who needed to be put in their place on the chessboard, is instructive. But it is unhelpful to characterize Exchequer agents' accountability as 'official' if that means, by contradistinction, that they necessarily lacked any felt fidelity to the King. With an acquisitive Exchequer and an aggressive King sheriffs such as John's Philip Mark combined an accountability of office and one of fidelity to produce the worst of both worlds. (That John was John detracts not a jot).

Some broader sense of official conduct does not seem to have branched naturally from the Exchequer's highly developed fiscal stem. In the shadow of one sort of accountability another one withered. Bursts of hectic watering altered little. The interest of Bisson's types here is how awkwardly sheriffs fitted them; how little one sort of accountability (fiscal) led on to other sorts of official responsibility.

In France the relatively late emergence of a royal fiscal cadre at the *Chambre des comptes* offers a similarly problematic proof for the argument that real politics emerges principally *out of* a dispassionate fiscal competency.[293] Louis IX's particular concern with accountability provides an interesting application. Louis stressed official fiscal competence *pari passu* with an ostensibly archaic 'moral, remedial, judicial' accountability of fidelity.[294] Louis's *enquêtes* absolutely fit this bill, yet they also conform to an ideal of fiscal competence. If one wishes to take these as two separate types, in Louis' *enquêtes* they are vigorously intermixed.[295] Before Edward I, at least, sophisticated English fiscal accountability did not lead to a broader regal concern for shrieval conduct in office except under heavy duress. This was partly because of the crown's financial needs, needs that were linked to the very strong fiscal mentality that found expression not only in royal policies, but also pre-eminently in the *Dialogue of the Exchequer*. In France such official fiscal competence arose at least equally out of

---

[291] The same is true of the regular accounting in France and Flanders; see Lyon and Verhulst, *Medieval Finance*, *passim*. For England see *PR 1130*.

[292] Earlier incarnations might have been more 'courteous' and it was part of Richard's goal to show how 'officializing' it was.

[293] Cf. Bisson, *Crisis of the Twelfth Century*, 5, 94, 325–8, 490, 577, 579–81. See also my discussions on pp. 5–6, 67 n. 228, 82 n. 302, 89–90, 132, 170 n. 97, 249–50.

[294] The quotation is from an important passage where Bisson (*Crisis of the Twelfth Century*, 324), contrasts the two types in discussing the still-fidelitarian accountability of Guimann of Saint Vaast, c.1170.

[295] See the general ordinance for crown officials as given in Joinville, *Histoire de Saint Louis*, ch. 140, §§693–714. Louis stresses the personal nature of the service ('tant comme il seront en nostre service', 'soit en nostre service', *passim*) at the same time as he articulates their duties in official, functional terms. These terms (e.g. §§694, 696) are both ethical ('il feront droit à chascun sanz excepcion de persones, aussi aus povres comme aus riches', etc.) and self-interested ('jureront que il garderont loialment nos rentes et nos droiz', etc.). See further pp. 157, 256–7.

the moral concerns that drove Louis IX before and after his failure in Outremer. If fiscal policy lacked the institutional base it had in England, that also made it easier to develop a system of *enquêteurs* who were directed towards both money and conduct. It seems likely that in England it was harder to countermand the incentives that sheriffs facing their *conflictus* at the Exchequer were conditioned to respond to.

So it is possible to distinguish impulses for inquiring into officers (Glénisson), and different 'modes' of accountability (Bisson), as well as variable emphases within kingdoms (Southern) but unhelpful to polarize these contrasts as a matter of course.

Nor should one presume that the 'administrative' and 'reformist' auditing of sheriff-like officers was inherently separate. It may look as if England's interest in inquiring into sheriffs' activities is limited to what Glénisson would call 'enquêtes administratives ou domaniales': inquiries and audits principally undertaken for the economic good of the crown. In France, it may seem such enquiries are reforming, undertaken in the spirit of equity and justice or—better—as a means of making royal power acceptable.[296] On 27 November 1236 Henry III commissioned an interesting *inquisitio* prompted by complaints against royal officers in the Bordelais area of Gascony. The mandates and inquiries show that Henry III was interested in both the claimed customs and liberties of Entre-deux-Mers and the wrongs committed by royal officials.[297] In France Philip II's sworn inquests (*inquisitiones*) expressed a perfectly sharp interest in investigating and specifying royal rights, as distinct from the 'equitable' use his grandson Louis IX made of them.[298] Besides, Louis IX's interest in urban governance was as 'administrative' as it was 'reformist'. This is nicely embodied in the 1262 mayoral requirement to account.[299] In Normandy, on 29 October the outgoing mayor should present his preliminary annual accounts to three annually elected 'good men' selected by all of such men; on 18 November the outgoing mayor should appear before the King's men in Paris to account for the city's expenditure, when the next mayor would also be chosen from the three men co-presenting the accounts.[300]

---

[296] Gérard Sivéry, 'Le Mécontentement dans le royaume de France et les enquêtes de saint Louis', *Revue historique* 269 (1983), 3–24 at 9, 23–4.

[297] *Archives historiques du département de la Gironde*, 58 vols. (Paris/Bordeaux, 1859–1932), iii. ##35–8; *CR 1234–1237*, 351–2, 371; *CPR 1232–1247*, 169, 201. The *inquisitio* is analysed by Frédéric Boutoulle, 'L'Enquête de 1236–1237 en Bordelais', in Pécout (ed.), *Quand gouverner c'est enquêter*, 117–31, also Raban, *A Second Domesday?*, 27. Boutoulle categorizes this as an 'enquête administrative ou domaniale' (118, 126). If the replacement of Henry de Trubleville as Seneschal Gascony by one of the *enquêteurs*, Hubert Hosat, in 1237 was connected with the complaints, it did Trubleville no damage; he led the English contingent against the Lombard cities for Frederick II in 1238 and took the cross with Richard of Cornwall in 1239 (Boutoulle, 'L'enquête de 1236–1237', 131; C. J. Tyerman, 'Trubleville, Sir Henry de (d. 1239)', *ODNB*).

[298] '*Registres de Philippe Auguste*, 35–180. These are mostly focused on establishing royal rights but include cases touching on officials' tenure and conduct, e.g. ##89–90 (inquiry 1220 or later into crimes at Roye and Montdidier, with Philip himself issuing punishments, 'Rex fecit inde justiticiam et cepit...'); 67, 63, 98, 112, 113, 100, 103, 81. For statistics and discussion of Philip II's *inquisitiones* see Baldwin, *Government of Philip Augustus*, 41, table 2, 141–4, 248–57.

[299] The context was Louis's ostensible disquiet at the state of communal governance following his attempt to raise a levy on them 1257/9 to compensate Henry III for his expected renunciation of French lands.

[300] Le Goff, *Saint Louis*, 229–32; William Chester Jordan, 'Communal Administration in France, 1257–1270: Problems Discovered and Solutions Imposed', *Ideology and Royal Power in Medieval*

And while there are 'structural' differences one should discount neither the importance of political mismanagement nor the character of individual kings in explaining why shrieval accountability proved so stubborn an English problem. 'There were few things more calculated to endear a prince to his subjects than a display of stern retribution on unjust officials', writes Jean Dunbabin of twelfth-century France.[301] That lesson was learnt variously and with various effects in France, the Regno, and England. Henry II made capital out of it 1170, whatever the chroniclers said. By 1274 Edward I had learnt the lesson better than his father and grandfather.[302] When *Britton* ventriloquized the King *c*.1291 and had him speak a *summa* on the common law, his chapter providing solutions for abusive *ministres*, notably sheriffs, rang better than it would have done in his father's mouth.[303] The complaints about sheriffs would recur, but less explosively. Still, Edward would protect his treasurer Walter Langton in 1301–2 when Langton's exploitative control of shrieval appointments contributed to the crisis that produced the *Articuli super cartas* and Langton's denunciation at the 1301 Lincoln parliament.[304] (This secular political context was probably connected to the canonical inquisition into Langton as bishop analysed in Chapter 4.) John and Henry III were both forced to see the sense of a broader interest in sheriffs' conduct. Under them there tended to be either interest in sheriffs' accountability understood fiscally, or a concern with the fairness of their conduct within their communities, but seldom the two together, and when the latter appeared it was often under baronial and knightly coercion.

By contrast, in France inquiries into the conduct of officials were not imposed on the crown, but assumed on its initiative. This is an important difference.[305] In France the campaign against shrieval misconduct was instigated, led, and carried through voluntarily by the king. Philip II ostensibly regulated his *prévôts* by *baillis* with respect to the *utile* and the *honestum*, at least in principle, before leaving on a Crusade in 1190.[306] But it was his grandson Louis IX who really took the question seriously.[307]

France: Kingship, Crusades and the Jews (Aldershot, 2001), iii. 292–313, with an appendix of the 1262 Normandy and Francia *ordonnances*.

[301] Jean Dunbabin, *France in the Making, 843–1180*, 2nd rev. edn. (Oxford, 2000), 286; also Michael Prestwich, *Plantagenet England 1225–1360* (Oxford, 2005), 132. For a prince's lengthy denunciation of his own officials see Charles I of Anjou's 10 June 1282 judgement following the Easter Vespers, *RCA*, xxv. Documenti tratti da altre fonti, #5 at 194–208.

[302] Maddicott, 'Edward I and the Lessons of Baronial Reform'; Raban, 'Edward I's Other Inquiries'. The contrast between Edward's dismissals on returning to England in 1289 and the continuity of personnel in 1274 is interesting. For 1289: T. F. Tout and Hilda Johnston (eds.), *State Trials of the Reign of Edward the First, 1289–1293*, Camden Society, 3rd ser. 9 (1906); Brand, 'Edward I and the Judges' (tempering Tout and Johnston); Richard Huscroft, 'Robert Burnell and the Government of England, 1270–1274', *TCE* 8 (2001), 59–70.

[303] *Britton*, ed. Francis Morgan Nichols, 2 vols. (Oxford, 1865), i. 85–97 (§1.22, *De ministres*).

[304] *SR*, i. 136–41, caps. 8–9, 11–15, 19; Maddicott, ' "1258" and "1297" ', 7–12; Prestwich, *Edward I*, 525–7.

[305] Sivéry, 'Mécontentement dans le royaume', 3, 5. William Chester Jordan, 'Anti-corruption Campaigns in Thirteenth-century Europe', *Journal of Medieval History* 35 (2009), 204–19 at 214–15, is inclined to see the English and French moves on the same continuum.

[306] *Recueil des Actes de Philippe Auguste*, i. #345. See also Rigord, *Histoire de Philippe Auguste*, ed. Élisabeth Carpentier, Georges Pon, and Yves Chauvin (Paris, 2006), 277–85. On Rigord: Baldwin, *Government of Philip Augustus*, 396–9.

[307] See the 1254–6 *ordonnances* in *Ordonnances des roys de France de la troisième race: recueillies par ordre chronologique*, 21 vols. (Paris, 1723–1849), i. (ed. Eusèbe Jacob de Laurière), 65–81. For the earlier

Louis famously inquired into his officials' conduct both before and after of his disastrous Egyptian crusade, in 1247 and 1254.[308] In 1247 Louis licensed his mendicant inquisitors[309] to

> hear and summarise in writing and to inquire into complaints—according to the form given to them by us—if anyone have any against us on whatever reasonable grounds, or on account of us or our ancestors, and further to hear and write and to inquire simply and plainly about injuries and exactions, undue services, receipts and other damages; whether they were done by others, or whether they were done by our *baillis*, *prévôts*, foresters, servants or their associates, during our reign, and to require them or their heirs that they themselves should restore those things to their compensation, either by their own confessions or by other proofs (*probationes*).[310]

It was Louis's piety before the Crusade and his attempt to atone for its failure afterwards that impelled him to investigate 'shrieval' behaviour.[311] At the end of his life he included similar injunctions in his *envoi* to his son:

> Dear son, carefully ensure that there should be good *baillis* and *prévôts* through your land, and act frequently in order to ensure that they themselves do justice well, and that they do not do injury to others, nor anything which they ought not, since while you should hate all evil, you should hate more than others the evil in another which comes from those who have power of you, and you should do more to guard and forestall against this should it happen.[312]

By contrast, the extensive sheriff's oath of 1258 was imposed on the crown, not offered. Its extensiveness is here a sign that it was intended to constrain and limit, and a sign that the norms it specified were not being taken as read. When a further sheriff's oath is documented at the start of Edward's reign in 1274–5 its significance was that it was novel, substantive, and not coerced from the crown.[313] Charles I of Anjou (r. 1266–85)—another king with extensive dynastic plans and therefore a gimlet eye for money—also took a hard, and principled line on his officers' conduct. The parallel tendencies may have been genuinely polarized there. One can hear the gears screeching as the King's need for money ground against his desire for equitable officers.[314]

January 1247 letters of commission, Teluet, *Layettes*, v. #490, *RHF*, xxiv.1. 4*. See further Jordan, *Louis IX and the Challenge of the Crusade*, 45–63, 158–71; Louis Carolus-Barré, 'La Grande Ordonnance de 1254 sur la réforme de l'administration et la police du royaume', in *Septième centenaire de la mort de Saint Louis: actes des colloques de Royaumont et de Paris, 21–27 mai 1970* (Paris, 1976), 85–96.

[308] See generally Jordan, *Louis IX and the Challenge of the Crusade*, ch. 3 and 6; Ch.-V. Langlois, 'Doléances recueillis par les enquêteurs de Saint Louis et des derniers Capètiens directs', *Revue historique* 92 (1906), 1–41; Gérard Sivéry, *Saint Louis et son siècle*, (Paris, 1983), 158–224; Sivéry, 'Mécontentement dans le royaume'; Le Goff, *Saint Louis*, 179–81, 225–8; Jean Richard, *Saint Louis: Roi d'une France féodale, soutien de la Terre sainte* (Paris, 1983), 278–303.

[309] On mendicants' unease about conducting secular comital inquisitions for Alphonse of Poitiers 1262–70, see Yves Dossat, 'Inquisiteurs ou enquêteurs? Á propos d'un texte d'Humbert de Romans', *Bulletin philologique et historique* (1958), 105–13; Jordan, *Louis IX and the Challenge of the Crusade*, 53–4.

[310] *Layettes*, v. #490 at 165–6.

[311] Jordan, *Louis IX and the Challenge of the Crusade*, 51, 55–64, 141–2, 148, 152–4, 158.

[312] Anonymous of St Denis, *Gesta sancti Ludovici noni*, in *RHF*, xx. 49.

[313] TNA, E 159/49, m. 1d, applied e.g. at 2d. Discussed in Prestwich, *Edward I*, 93; Maddicott, 'Edward I and the Lessons of Baronial Reform', 20.

[314] See Jean Dunbabin, 'Charles I of Anjou and the Development of Medieval Political Ideas', *Nottingham Medieval Studies*, 45 (2001) at 122.

The difficulty of extracting money was critical, as Southern and Maddicott have argued. Richard of Ely asserted that 'Exchequer rules' were only the projection of the king's fiscal *utilitas* onto the wider world. John and Henry III's need for money encouraged the over-dominance of those rules; they could not afford to have an 'ethical shrieval policy', so to speak. 'No policy is better than the capacity of the government of the day and its agents to deliver it.'[315] One can see something similar in the Regno. The oscillating fortunes of the office-holding Della Marra, Rufolo, and De Braida under Charles I in the Regno suggest an ambiguous picture of officials variously blamed, fined, freed, and reappointed to bolster the reputation of the King, his need for money, and his desire to assert himself as the source of all patronage.[316] Even after the great Vespers rebellion (30 March 1282), Charles's expressed ideal of greater and lesser officials' conduct makes plain that circumscribing their freedom of manoeuvre remained problematic no matter how much one stressed some descending theory of delegation and answerability.[317] Administrative structures and fiscal 'need' were key in shaping royal approaches to 'shrieval' officers.

Traditions of kingship seem to have mattered too in so far as they encouraged kings to see officers' conduct as mirrors for their own image. It is interesting to find in both France and the Regno around the time of Henry II's 1170 inquest royal *acta* which stress this.

The Assizes of Roger II (1140s) are not principally concerned with the regulation of shrieval agents' behaviour but still include pertinent headings. The stress on reform writ large is notable. They open with a pious preamble. God

> has reformed [*reformavit*] the integrity of our kingdom, both spiritually and physically, by his most gracious tranquility, so we are forced likewise to reform [*reformare*] the pathways of justice and piety, where we see them miserably distorted [. . .] So rightly we who, through his grace, have authority by right and law [*iuris et legum*], ought partly to set them in a better state, partly to reform [*reformare*] them [. . .][318]

Specific headings show how good conduct and public offices were entertwined. *De officialibus publicis* rules that

> The quality of a person increases or reduces the penalty for fraud. State officials [*officiales reipublice*] or judges who have stolen public money while administering, those who are guilty of the crime of fraud are to be punished capitally, unless regal piety shows leniency.[319]

Under *De bonis publicis* Roger ruled that

> Whoever by his negligence will damage or diminish public goods [*bona publica*] is to be declared guilty in his own person and goods, at the discretion of royal piety.

---

[315] *Mutatis mutandis*, Anthony King and Ivor Crewe, *The Blunders of our Governments* (London, 2013), 413.

[316] The argument of Serena Morelli, '«*Ad extirpenda vitia»:* normativa regia e sistemi di controllo sul funzionariato nella prima età angioina', *Mélanges de l'École française de Rome: Moyen-Âge, temps modernes* 109.2 (1997), 463–75, esp. 469–73. Also Dunbabin, *Charles I of Anjou*, 74–6, 107–8.

[317] See the ruling 'Post corruptionis amara discrimina' (10 June 1282), *RCA*, xxv. Documenti tratti da altre fonti, #5 at 194–208

[318] Gennaro M. Monti, *Lo stato normanno svevo, lineamenti e ricerche* (Trani, 1945), 114–15 (Vatican lat. MS 8782).

[319] Monti, *Stato normanno*, 135–6 (cap. 25).

Whoever knowingly connives with such thieves will be held to the same rule.[320]

De iudice depravato rules that

> If a judge, having received money, finds a defendant guilty and [worthy of] death, he exposes himself to the death penalty.
>
> If a judge fraudulently and deceitfully hands down a sentence against the law he loses his judicial authority irrevocably, is branded with infamy and all his goods are forfeit to the public [*publicatis*]. However, if his legal judgement is an aberration arising from ignorance, he will be subject to royal mercy and providence, blameworthy because of his clear mental stupidity.[321]

The driving logic behind the inclusion of these headings is an emphasis on the status of the king, and the consequent damage done to it by wayward agents. Again, both a regal/regnal self-interest and a concern with the manner of its execution on the ground is apparent.

Philip Augustus's 1190 *ordonnance* providing for his crusading absence defines

> The royal office of the king is to provide in all appropriate ways for the interests of [his] subjects, and to place the public interest before his own private interest [*Officium regium est subjectorum commodis modis omnibus providere et sue utilitati private publicam anteferre.*][322]

It is in that context that Philip legislates for the royal dues and non-financial accountability of his 'shrieval' *baillis*.

> [...] And in our lands we have placed, clearly by name, our *baillis* who in their bailiwicks are to set aside one day every month which will be called assize, in which all those who make appeals [*clamorem facient*] will receive through them their rights [*jus suum*] and justice without delay, and we our rights and our justice; wherefore what is rightly ours will be there written.
>
> [...] But if any of our *baillis* falls short [*deliquerit*], excepting murder, theft, homicide, breach of trust [*proditione*], and this is accepted by Archbishop [Guillaume de Reims] and the Queen and others present to hear of our aforesaid *baillis*' deeds, we order them to advise us [of this] on the set days by their letters every year, three times a year, which *bailli* has fallen short, and what he has done, and what he has received [*acceperit*], and from whom, with respect to money or duty or service because of which our men lack their legal rights or we ours.
>
> Similarly our *baillis* will notify us regarding our *prévôts*.
>
> But the queen and the archbishop cannot remove our *baillis* from their bailiwicks, unless for murder, theft, homicide, breach of trust [*proditione*]; nor the *baillis* the *prévôts*, unless it is for the same. But we, with the counsel of God will make judgement of them, when the aforesaid men will have reported to us the truth of the matter, so that others cannot be intimidated [*deterreri*] without reason.[323]

This is an important form of redress in principle, if cumbersome in practice. By contrast, the tendency of English kings to see (or claim to see) shrieval misconduct as

---

[320] Monti, *Stato normanno*, 136–7 (cap. 26).
[321] Monti, *Stato normanno*, 157 (cap. 44, the title is from the Cassinense MS).
[322] *Recueil des Actes de Philippe*, i. #345 at 416.
[323] *Recueil des Actes de Philippe*, i. #345 at 417–18.

an offence to their own integrity seems distinctly erratic until Edward's reign. Philip II's proprietorial concern about 'shrieval' accountability had famous descendants.[324] Roger II's had both Staufer and (French) Angevin ones.[325] In Capetian and Staufer spheres 'shrieval' conduct seems to have been resolved more commonly as a corollary of regal service. Louis IX, Frederick II, and Charles I took this view readily. Henry III and John by contrast seem to have arrived at this conclusion far more reluctantly, at least in so far as their willingness to respond to generalized complaints of shrieval conduct went. As '1215' and '1258' showed this was not for want of the conceptual or administrative wherewithal, but rather of interest, will, and money.

CONCLUSIONS

This analysis cuts across the applicability of the models proposed by Glénisson and Bisson. There seem no inherent or diplomatic grounds for separating Glénisson's 'administrative' from 'reformist' inquisitions. Inquisitions into shrieval officers more or less focus on both as a function of their commissioners' interests.[326] With respect to Bisson's argument the position is interesting. Any analysis of the English sheriff between 1194 and 1274 cannot claim him as a model of the justice of accountability, notwithstanding the sophistication of the administrative system. Politics (in Bisson's strong sense of principled disputing) and official integrity do not appear to be the consequential effect of accountability—at least not straightforwardly so. Politics *was* the product of disputing *about* the content *of* the sheriff's office as the reform agendas of '1215' and '1258' show. Nor need accountability be a sign of 'proper' office when that office is limited to a narrow fiscality. In the case of sheriffs, there were conceptions of a wider office, but the crown was reluctant to institutionalize them, as Richard of Ely seemed in the *Dialogue of the Exchequer*. There were no manuals on shrieval office as there were for *podestà, baillis*, bishop, or even the lesser (English) bailiff or reeve. Even 'only' German knightly *ministeriales* had their custumals setting out their liable duties.[327] Philippe de Beaumanoir may not have been representative but his *c*.1283 *coutumier* showed how far a French *bailli* could internalize norms encouraged by the crown.[328] It is a contrast that the *Policraticus*, one

---

[324] For the idea in France from *c*.1254–*c*.1380, Telliez, «*Per potentiam officii*», 62–70, 681–3, 411–14.

[325] See *Konstitutionen Friedrichs II. für das Königreich sizilien*, caps. 1.36.1, 1.36.2, 1.37 (all drawn from earlier legislation). Also caps. 1.30, 3.41 on officials as representative extensions of the King's person; severe punishment for officials guilty of crimes against the *res publica*.

[326] Strayer argued one could even see Louis IX's preferences played out in *enquêteurs*' relative handling of different appeals (good for women, less so for bishops): Joseph R. Strayer, 'La Conscience du roi: Les Enquêtes de 1258–1262 dans la sénéchaussée de Carcassonne-Béziers' in *Mélanges Roger Aubenas*, Recueil de mémoires et travaux publié par la Société d'histoire du droit et des institutions des anciens pays de droit écrit 9 (Montpellier, 1974), 725–36. I am grateful to Antonia Fitzpatrick for obtaining a copy of this for me.

[327] Arnold, *German Knighthood*, 76–99.

[328] Cf. Joinville, *Histoire de Saint Louis*, ch. 140, with *Coutumes du Beauvaisis*, ed. André Salmon, 2 vols. (Paris, repr. 1970), *passim*; esp. i. cap. 1 §11–22, 29–30, 40.

of the most relevant English texts, received scant attention at home. More focused attention seems to have been paid in England to manorial officers than to sheriffs, and ideas about the former may well have been poured onto the latter in 1258 (see pp. 78–80). Given the governmental centrality of sheriff this is striking. Reflective thought about responsible shrieval office did not connect well with sheriffs' accountability in England between 1194 and 1274 except under the duress of 'reform'. It had to be cultivated, forced, to sprout.

What this implies for the actual quality or conduct of governmental officials is problematic (see further pp. 246–60). Well-meant does not mean well-governed, as Louis IX's inquiries showed. Conversely extractive government per se *may* not necessitate abusive government. Charles I of Anjou saw 'red tape as the best insurance of governmental effectiveness' in the Regno and certainly the 'Vespers' rebellion of 1282 was provoked by his attempt to tie that tape tight for tax reasons.[329] It is interesting at least that by 'comparison with the English reform movement of 1258, the San Martino [1283 parliamentary reform] canons expressed little discontent with the operation of the legal system, no outrage at the arbitrariness of government, no build-up of anger among the barons'.[330]

The crown was late to embrace practices of responsible shrieval office in England. Sheriffs were too important fiscally. But because they were important politically as well as fiscally, perceptions of official irresponsibility produced real problems in the crises of '1215' and '1258'. An explanation is based partly on the peculiarity of English administrative structures; partly on the English crown's financial need; and partly on kings' personalities. The English crown's predominant interest in shrieval accountability as seen through an Exchequer optic prevented it properly gauging the seriousness of other aspects of sheriffs' conduct. A basic conflict of interest jammed the two against each another. Before Edward I, one mentality of accountability occluded the fuller development of its counterbalancing pair, except when the crown was under duress from barons and knights. In an important respect this was simply a necessary cost of doing (royal) business. But the basic liability of sheriffs to both county and Exchequer guaranteed that it would be problematic. The ways in which the crown did and did not stress sheriffs' accountability during the late twelfth and thirteenth centuries contributed in basic ways to the civil wars of the thirteenth. This was not for want of the right intellectual equiment. The *acta* analysed above of Henry II, Philip II, and Roger II show that *c.*1140–90 all had the capability to stress the *utile* and the *honestum* when it came to their agents' accountability, as well as, sometimes, the inclination. But English dynastic ambitions and their costs were crucial in

---

[329] Dunbabin, *Charles I of Anjou*, 23 and ch. 8 on the Vespers. See her incisive comments on Charles's 'competent if not particularly amiable government' in Provence (54); that the *regnicoli* 'felt the pinch of [Charles's] fiscalism more [. . .] because his civil service was more efficient' (66) and that 'Angevin justice was well-meaning, thorough, ferocious (though not more so than that of other effective monarchies of the period), and usually principled' (67) while Charles's bureaucratic passion 'made even the contemporary English kings look negligent in recording' (70). David Abulafia stresses Staufer administrative continuity: *The Western Mediterranean Kingdoms, 1200–1500: The Struggle for Dominion* (Harlow, 1997), 72–5, 79.
[330] Dunbabin, *Charles I of Anjou*, 111, cf. 113.

restricting how far more generous ideas of shrieval conduct could be taken seriously. And what one king had affirmed another could disavow. If Edward I accommodated himself somewhat to reforming ideals once king, Exchequer practice under his son's sometime treasurer Walter Stapeldon was so offensively extractive that in October 1326 Stapeldon died beneath a London mob who sawed his head off with a bread-knife. It is disconcerting to recall this as one reads the smooth, obsessive, oppressive detail of the Exchequer rules that Stapeldon was responsible for drafting between 1323 and 1326.[331] Rulers' characters (and Exchequer officials') could matter. A fuller assertion of royal officers' accountability and responsibility was a stronger assertion of the contours of kingship itself. That was no guarantee of regal success, as Charles I discovered in Sicily. As John and Henry III knew equally well, however, narrower conceptions of shrieval accountability were no guarantee of regal success either.

---

[331] *Red Book of the Exchequer*, iii. 848–97. Stapeldon's peculiar blend of acquisitiveness, piety, and 'nineteenth-century' educational fervour is well captured by John Maddicott in *Founders and Fellowship: The Early History of Exeter College, Oxford, 1314–1592* (Oxford, 2014), ch. 1, esp. 34–6, 39, 50–62. Stapeldon's skill as a canny administrator and founder of Stapeldon Hall/Exeter College recurs in Ch. 5.

4

Bishops

As his comments on Hubert Walter showed, Gerald of Wales did not think much of the competencies required of Exchequer officials—at least as qualifications for episcopal office.[1] 'A bishop should be deemed most vile if he who has the greatest honour does not excel in knowledge and sanctity since, praiseworthy by neither conduct nor learning, such a person has presumed to lord it over others (*preesse*), ignorant of how to serve them (*prodesse*).'[2] The sentiment was widespread and venerable: *pastores* should strive to *prodesse*, not *preesse*.[3] Yet in England, Gerald complained, 'whoever is good at being a tax collector immediately deserves to be deemed a great prelate in the English Church'. It was from the Exchequer's 'gymnasium' that 'almost all the English bishops are raised to honours'.[4] Gerald's insinuation is that one's numeracy says nothing for one's literacy, yet it is through the latter spiritual learning that men merit high religious office.[5] For Gerald it was not appropriate to transfer norms from one office to another. Accountancy and the prelacy should not mix. In Gerald's eyes, Walter was further compromised because of the royal offices he held, first Justiciar,

---

[1] See pp. 92–3.
[2] Gerald of Wales, '*De Invectionibus*', ed. W. S. Davies, *Y Cymmrodor* 30 (1920), 97. Gerald used the same contrast to distinguish princes from tyrants: *Liber de principis instructione* in *Giraldi Cambrensis Opera*, RS, 8 vols. (London, 1861–91) viii. ed. George F. Warner, 54, 56 (Dist. 1, cap. 16), their comparability, 142 (Dist. 1, cap. 20).
[3] For the Augustinian and Gregorian origins of the reference see R. A. Markus, *Gregory the Great and His World* (Cambridge, 1997), 30 and n. 54 (esp. Augustine, *City of God*, §19.19 and *Enarrationes in Psalmos*, §126.3). Bernard of Clairvaux, *De consideratione*, §III.i.2, was an important formulation, ed. in *Sancti Bernardi opera*, ed. J. Leclercq, C. H. Talbot, and H. M. Rochais, 8 vols. in 9 (Rome, 1957–77), iii. 381–493. The pairing was a favourite of Innocent III: e.g. *Innocent III English Letters*, #62, Innocent to Nicholas Bishop of Tusculum (13 October 1213) at 166, and generally John C. Moore, *Pope Innocent III: To Root Up and to Plant* (Leiden, 2003), 255–60. In Angevin and Capetian circles cf. e.g. Peter of Blois, *Tractatus de institutione episcopi* in *PL*, 207, cols. 1097–12 at 1102–1108; Philip Augustus's debate with Peter the Chanter in Léopold Delisle, 'Etienne de Gallardon, clerc de la chancellerie de Philippe Auguste, chanoine de Bruges', *Bibliothèque de l'École des chartes* 60 (1899), 5–44 at 24; or in the section on the disciplining of officials in *Le Traité Eruditio regum et principum de Guibert de Tournai, O.F.M.*, ed. A. de Poorter, Les Philosophes belges, 9 (Louvain, 1914), 44 (§2.1.1). For the thirteenth-century scholastic handling of a related Augustinian-derived distinction between rule as *dominandi cupiditate* (will to dominate) or *officio consulendi* (duty to counsel) see Markus, *Saeculum: History and Society in the Theology of St Augustine*, rev. edn. (Cambridge, 1988), App. C. On *preesse* see further Thomas Bisson, *Crisis of the Twelfth Century: Power, Lordship, and the Origins of European Government* (Princeton, NJ, 2009), 455 n. 92.
[4] Gerald of Wales, *De invectionibus*, 114, also 97. Cf. a similar critique in *Nigellus de Longchamp dit Wireker, i. Introduction, Tractatus contra curiales et officiales clericos*, ed. A. Boutemy (Paris, 1959), 190.
[5] Cf. Alexander Murray, *Reason and Society in the Middle Ages* (Oxford, 1978), 217, and his following section on the 'lucrative sciences'. Gerald's complaint about Walter's education correlates with Murray's subsequent argument that clerical complaints about properly literate ecclesiastics were a product of competition for finite benefices (*Reason and Society*, 292–314, esp. 308–9).

then Chancellor, the former of which he was forced to abandon, following the Canterbury monks' complaints before Innocent III.[6] He was, scorned Gerald, like 'a fish out of water, when he cannot live without worldly cares or the court, ignorant—or feigning ignorance—of having read the Apostle, that no-one fighting for God involves himself in the world's work'.[7] Bishops were different from the other officers analysed here. Those others lacked sacramental powers. Sacramentally all bishops were equivalent, even the bishop of Rome who claimed his power complete because it was from St Peter, and his responsibility [*sollicitudo*] greater, if shared.[8] Nor were episcopal appointments temporary. Gerald would be right in those respects about the qualitatively different nature of the bishop's office. But as Gerald's protests show, there was anxiety about the episcopate being reduced to 'just another office'. Almost at the end of his *Gemma ecclesiastica* he bemoans how close have become the institutions and interests of prelate and prince. That inappropriate convergence means that prelates' eminence and the standing of their office has become extremely hazardous. 'I do not say that bishops cannot be saved; but I do say that in these days it is harder for bishops than for other men to be saved'.[9] In the period under discussion, for better or worse, an important strand in the church's solution to this was the tendency to make bishops increasingly accountable and dismissible largely at the Bishop of Rome's discretion, in relation to the contours of their office, and in relation to the inquisitorial methods analysed below.

Gerald's attitude to Hubert Walter oscillated, partly in line with his hopes for Walter's patronage.[10] Around 1194 Gerald had even dedicated the *Description of Wales* to Walter, having already given him a copy of the *Journey through Wales*. The second version of the *Journey* (c.1197) Gerald dedicated to the Bishop of Lincoln, Hugh of Avalon, of whom he would also write a *Life* (c.1213–19), completed shortly before Hugh's rapid ten-month canonization process (16 February 1220).[11] Adam of Eynsham's *Life* of Hugh (c.1212) also offered criticism of Hubert, describing Hugh's frequent reproofs of the Archbishop for his excessive attention to the 'administration

---

[6] Roger of Howden, *Chronica*, iv. 47–8. If Howden is reliable here the complaint was specifically about the conflict between the spiritual values Walter was supposed to uphold as archbishop and those secular political values he was upholding when making 'judgements of blood' and smoking the London demagogue William fitz Osbert out of his St Mary le Bow sanctuary to his death. See John Gillingham, 'The Historian as Judge: William of Newburgh and Hubert Walter', *EHR* 119 (2004)', 1280–1.

[7] Gerald of Wales, *De invectionibus*, 97 (2 Timothy 2:4).

[8] J. A. Watt, 'The Theory of Papal Monarchy in the Thirteenth Century: The Contribution of the Canonists', *Traditio* 20 (1964), 179–317 at 250–60 and Kenneth Pennington, *Pope and Bishops: The Papal Monarchy in the Twelfth and Thirteenth Centuries* (Philadelphia, 1984), ch. 2, on the thirteenth-century crystallization of the idea that the Pope summons bishops to a share of responsibility, but not to the fullness of power he had.

[9] Gerald of Wales, *Gemma ecclesiastica* (c.1197–8) in *Giraldi Cambrensis Opera*, ii. ed. J. S. Brewer, 359, and more widely 358–62 (Dist. 2, cap. 38).

[10] Cf. the *Retractationes* (c.1217) in *Giraldi Cambrensis Opera*, i. ed. Brewer, 426–7; C. R. Cheney, *From Becket to Langton: English Church Government 1170–1213* (Manchester, 1956), 36.

[11] Robert Bartlett, *Gerald of Wales: A Voice of the Middle Ages*, repr. edn. (Stroud, 2006), 208 n. 10 and App. 1; David H. Farmer, 'The Cult and Canonization of St Hugh', in Henry Mayr-Harting (ed.), *St Hugh of Lincoln: Lectures Delivered at Oxford and Lincoln to Celebrate the Eighth Centenary of St Hugh's Consecration as Bishop of Lincoln*, (Oxford, 1987), 75–87 at 82.

of the *res publica*' at the expense of his 'pontifical office'. Adam pointedly related how Hugh then recalled his diocesan subordinates, both clerks and priests, to the 'path of straighter living and the integrity of clerical discipline'.[12]

Gerald of Wales, Hubert Walter, Hugh of Avalon: scholar and bishop-aspirant, royal minister and archbishop, bishop and saint. Each exemplifies a different set of later twelfth- and thirteenth-century values and abilities, and entry points for reflection on episcopal character. All of those entry points pertain to conceptions of episcopal responsibility. That relationship between projections of a bishop's character, his responsibilities—and, if need be, his accountability—therefore requires explanation. Two *exempla* from Adam of Eynsham's *Life* of Hugh can open out many of these themes. The first concerns Hubert Walter.

On his deathbed in 1200 Hugh was visited by Hubert Walter. Hugh's primate and superior began solicitously enough, inviting Hugh to ask forgiveness of any he had hurt. The Archbishop went on to make clear that he was thinking of *himself*—to whom Hugh should apologize for all his provocations, offences given despite the obedience the Bishop of Lincoln owed. Hugh replied,

> It is true that after making a thorough examination of conscience I know well that I have often angered you. Yet I do not consider that I should repent of this, but I rather grieve that I did not do so more frequently and earnestly. I am, however, firmly resolved under God's all-seeing eyes to do so more often if I am spared [death]. I remember how often I weakly kept silent about matters where I should have spoken out but did not do so in order to appease you, because I knew that you would not take it patiently if I did. My sin was that I declined to offend you rather than my heavenly Father. For this reason, I ask pardon for my serious offence against God and against you, my father and my primate.[13]

Adam does not relate Hubert Walter's response.

The anecdote raises important themes in relation to episcopal responsibility and accountability. First, conscience played a central role in bishops' own expression of their episcopal responsibilities.[14] Secondly, conscience was extended to the responsibility for the direct denunciation of colleagues with ostensibly defective consciences, even and including one's superiors.[15] Fraternal correction, first in private, following the apostolic tradition, was a basic model.[16] Thirdly, reproofs by an inferior were

---

[12] Adam of Eynsham, *Magna Vita Sancti Hugonis*, ed. Decima L. Douie and Hugh Farmer, OMT, 2 vols. (London, 1985), ii. 96 (§5.5).

[13] Adam of Eynsham, *Magna Vita Sancti Hugonis*, ii. 188–9 (§5.16), adapting Douie and Farmer's trans. See also Farmer, 'Cult and Canonization of St Hugh', 76–7.

[14] e.g. the *De consideratione* (1148/9–1152/3) of Bernard of Clairvaux, addressed to Pope Eugenius III, stressed Eugenius's standing as a bishop (§IV.vi.22 and see also §II.ix.17), and the importance of conscience to right rule (§§II.i.4; II.iii.6). The fifth book, the solution to the curial litigiousness and spiritual enervation Bernard has criticized, is best seen as a highly structured means of ordering the Pope's conscience.

[15] Bernard again might be cited in relation to *De consideratione* §§II.i.4 and III.iii.13, a spiritual, though not a formal reproof to Eugenius.

[16] Matthew 18: 15–17. e.g. in the famous 'Novit ille qui' letter of April 1204 from Innocent III to the French prelates (*Innocent III English Letters*, #21 at 64; *Reg. Inn. III*, vii. #43 (42) at 73). See further on conscience and correction pp. 158, 237–9, 256–7.

problematic in fact—in that the inferior would probably feel constrained from correcting his superior and the superior conceivably disinclined to accept any criticism.

A second *exemplum* from the *Life* of Hugh is interesting for its method of correcting faults. The case concerns an adulterous parishioner of Hugh's, when as a young deacon he administered the 'rule [*regimen*] of a parish'. When Hugh 'learned of the evil rumour [*famam mali*] I took it badly; I looked into the matter with the utmost care', and it was indeed 'discovered and confirmed'. He brought the man before him, privately, and confronted him with the allegation. Both this and a second confrontation before two or three other witnesses (following the Gospel precept) failed to shift the parishioner's obdurate impenitence. So, again following the Gospel precept, since the matter was 'plain to everyone' [*omnibus manifestum*] Hugh 'one solemn day put it to him openly in church' [*media in ecclesia quadam die sollempni palam coargui*].[17] He denounced the 'hideousness of his shame, his handover to Satan for the destruction of his flesh' at which, finally, the man, 'completely terrified and desperate, dashed into the middle of the church' [*territus uehementer et confusus, in medium prosiliuit*] to renounce his sins, 'not without sobbing and showers of tears'.

Adam's primary concern is to demonstrate how Hugh fulfilled the Gospel precept of correction, by following the correct sequence of reproof. The procedure (its *ordo*) which Hugh followed in practice also requires attention, however. First, Hugh is made aware of a public belief about a person's guilt of a crime—in this case a 'parishioner defamed [*infamatam*] of adultery' (part of Adam of Eynsham's chapter heading). He then acts on his own authority, *ex officio* as it were. There is no accusation made against the parishioner. Hugh acts because of the *infamia* and because the parish's governance (*regimen*) is entrusted to him. Addressing the former is a responsibility of the latter. Thirdly, Hugh investigates (*inquisiui*) the matter. Adam's framing of Hugh's account is important. It was prompted by a question Adam says he asked Hugh once about fraternal correction, when Hugh was 'sitting down with many learned men', including men specifically 'skilled in both canon and civil law'.[18] It is striking and of immediate interest to this chapter that the procedural components of the case follow canonical inquisitorial procedure, that emerging means of inquiring *ex officio*, on the basis of *infamia*, into crimes (*excessus*), particularly those attributed to prelates and clerics.[19]

A Burgundian aristocrat by birth, Hugh was a deacon at St Maximus there between *c*.1160 and *c*.1163. Hugh died in 1200. Adam finished writing the *Life* *c*.1212. The timespan is precisely that during which inquisitorial procedure was being developed, before its emergence into the mainstream of canonical law at the Fourth Lateran Council of 1215, where inquisitorial procedure figured as canon eight, *Qualiter et quando* (its opening words).

---

[17] Cf. Ecclesiasticus 15: 5.
[18] Adam of Eynsham, *Magna Vita Sancti Hugonis*, i. 20–1 (§1.6).
[19] Cf. another *en passant* illustration of inquisitorial procedure in Herman of Tournai's description of an *ex officio* inquisition on the basis of rumour in his *De Miracula S. Mariae Laudunensis, PL* 156, cols. 961–1020 at 1009 (2nd version 1146/7).

The suggestion is not that Hugh of Avalon invented 'inquisitorial procedure'. (Adam may, in 1212, easily have wished to present Hugh as having been intuitively prescient in his own approach to pastoral correction during the 1160s.) The point of this second *exemplum* from Adam of Eynsham is rather to illustrate that one can identify relatively 'untheorized', 'vernacular' illustrations of inquisitorial procedure in non-legal records. By this I mean simply that important aspects of the relevant formal action can be indicated that may not be the designed product of legal theory. Such instances encourage an analysis that places a greater stress on the reciprocal relations between the 'high' formal theory of romano-canonical procedure and more intuitive ad hoc responses within a given society.[20] The corollary is that a lesser emphasis is put on the idea that lawyers' autonomous reflection is a sufficient explanation of socio-legal change or the notion that the inherent aesthetic attraction of legal systems per se is sufficient to explain their success.[21] This is a slightly different furrow to the productive one ploughed by Susan Reynolds in relation to legal change.[22] Reynolds's general thesis has been that there is a fundamental qualitative difference between customary pre-1200 law and professional post-1200 law: that the former was characterized by more communal judgements rooted in society, the latter by a more professional law that became 'more esoteric, rigid and expert', and whose canons have been mistakenly presumed to connote a greater normative rationality.[23] My stress is on the stitching from materials diffused through Christendom (*infamia*, *scandalum*, official investigation, 'inquisition'), into a respectable uniform for responding to officers' *excessus*, one of which was the ultimately formalized canonical inquisitorial procedure. Where Reynolds has stressed distinctions between *un*learned law and learned law, I wish to make suggestions about communication between the two.

This chapter explores the development of inquisitorial procedure to hold bishops to account, using case law and formal law, and making some comparative observations about inquisitions. A working axiom is Maitland's suggestion that 'legal ideas never reach very far beyond practical needs'.[24] The challenge ultimately is to explain the similarities and differences between multiple sorts of inquisition and why the particular nature of canonical inquisitorial procedure was produced

---

[20] See also R. I. Moore's stress on connections between heretical and secular inquisitions in *The War on Heresy: Faith and Power in Medieval Europe* (London, 2012), 171–2 (Philip of Alsace's 1163 code for Arras), 193 (cap. 21 of the 1166 Assize of Clarendon) and his *First European Revolution, c.970–1215* (Oxford, 2000), 171–3.

[21] Cf. e.g. Raoul van Caenegem, 'L'Histoire du droit et la chronologie. Réflexions sur la formation du «Common Law» et la procédure romano-canonique', in *Études d'histoire du droit canonique dédiées à Gabriel Le Bras*, 2 vols. (Paris, 1965), ii. 1459–65; Caenegem, 'History of European Civil Procedure', *International Encyclopedia of International Law*, XVI.2 (Tübingen, 1973), 16–23. In the former van Caenegem argues for a pragmatic make-do-and-mend attitude on the part of Henry II's counsellors; in the latter for the normatively more coherent and greater rationality of the *ius commune* and its aesthetic ability to compel assent.

[22] See Susan Reynolds, *Fiefs and Vassals: The Medieval Evidence Reinterpreted* (Oxford, 1994), and *Kingdoms and Communities in Western Europe, 900–1300*, 2nd edn. (Oxford, 1997).

[23] The pre-/post-1200 characterization, *Fiefs and Vassals*, 73–4; 'esoteric, rigid, and expert', 478; on 'rationality' and law, *Kingdoms and Communities*, 64–6.

[24] Frederic William Maitland, *Township and Borough* (Cambridge, 1898), 27.

by its sociological matrix. This chapter will suggest that it was the comparable ambitions, and pretensions, on the part of different élites that led them to assemble, from learned laws and improvised practices, legal systems for regulating societal—and official—conduct.

THE ACCOUNTABILITY OF INQUISITION

In November 1215 at the Lateran Palace, Pope Innocent III opened a general council of the Western Church, the fourth and at that time the largest ever held.[25] It famously legislated on many (arguably all) of the institutions later emblematic of the medieval church: private confession (cap. 21), the regulation of heresy (cap. 3), excommunication (caps. 47–9), crusading (cap. 71), the regulation of Jewish–Christian relations (caps. 67–70), the regulation of new religious orders, including mendicants (cap. 13),[26] preaching (cap. 10), and inquisition (cap. 8).[27] Inquisition here constituted neither an organization nor an interest in heresy. Canonical inquisition was simply a legal mechanism for identifying, investigating, and correcting the delicts of clerics, including prelates.[28] Since *inquisitio* was also used generically without implying the use of a canonical procedure, one needs to be careful when determining whether references to *inquisitio* do or do not imply that specific procedure. *Canonical* inquisitions integrated distinct Roman legal concepts[29] and had the following features:[30]

---

[25] Colin Morris, *The Papal Monarchy: The Western Church from 1050 to 1250* (Oxford, 1989), 447–51; Stephen Kuttner and Antonio García y García, 'A New Eyewitness Account of the Fourth Lateran Council', *Traditio* 20 (1964), 115–78; Jakob Werner, 'Die Teilnehmerliste des Laterankonzils vom Jahre 1215', *Neues Archiv der Gesellschaft für ältere deutsche Geschichtskunde* 31 (1906), 575–93, with attendees at 584–92.

[26] Dominic was told at the Council to base his order's rule on an existing one; no Franciscan 'rule' was formally ratified at Lateran IV, but Innocent III had verbally endorsed the group in 1209–10.

[27] For the Council see the introduction to *Constitutiones Concilii quarti Lateranensis una cum Commentariis glossatorum*, ed. Antonio García y García, Monumenta iuris canonici, Ser. A: Corpus glossatorum 2 (Vatican City, 1981), 6–11 arguing that the council's *acta* were decided between its summoning on 19 April 1213, and its November 1215 opening (excluding caps. 1–3 and 71 on religious belief and the crusade). See also J. A. Watt, 'The Papacy' in David Abulafia (ed.), *New Cambridge Medieval History*, v. c.*1198*–c.*1300* (Cambridge, 1999), 107–63 at 119–26; John W. Baldwin, 'Paris et Rome en 1215: Les Réformes du IVᵉ Concile de Latran', *Journal des Savants* 1 (1997), 99–124.

[28] On this distinction and the gradual institutionalization of heretical inquisitions, Richard Kieckhefer, 'The Office of Inquisition and Medieval Heresy: The Transition from Personal to Institutional Jurisdiction', *JEH* 46 (1995); Kenneth Pennington, 'Law, Criminal Procedure', *Dictionary of the Middle Ages: Supplement* 1 (New York, 2004), 309–20; and Edward Peters, *Inquisition* (New York, 1988).

[29] See p. 153, n. 96.

[30] On non-heretical inquisitorial procedure see esp. Lotte Kéry, '*Inquisitio—denunciatio—exceptio*: Möglichkeiten der Verfahrenseinleitung im Dekretalenrecht', *ZRG Kan. Abt.* 87 (2001), 226–68, and Winfried Trusen, 'Der Inquisitionsprozeß, seine historischen Grundlagen und frühen Formen', *ZRG Kan. Abt.* 74 (1988), 168–230; Henry Ansgar Kelly, 'Inquisitorial Due Process and the Status of Secret Crimes', in *Proceedings of the Eighth International Congress of Medieval Canon Law, Proceedings of the Eighth International Congress of Medieval Canon Law*, ed. Stanley Chodorow, Monumenta iuris canonici, Ser. C: Subsidia 9 (Vatican City, 1992), 407–27, repr. in his *Inquisitions and Other Trial*

1. The basis on which an *inquisitio* was ordered was the *clamor* and *infamia* attributing misconduct to an individual. No accuser was needed, and initiation was consequently much easier procedurally and politically. As God at Sodom, he judge would 'descend and see' the *clamor* for himself (Genesis 18: 21).
2. Inquisitions were accordingly *ex officio* of the investigating magistrate. In the formal law of Roman accusation, an accuser was liable to a retaliatory punishment, a *poena talionis*, if the accusation failed; such considerations did not apply to inquisitions since the *clamor* acted as accuser.
3. An inquisition investigated the truth of the allegation, depending on which charges then followed.
4. Any punishment liable from an inquisition was caritative and medicinal not punitive, again in contrast to accusations.

What is novel is the combination of the *ex officio* investigation with the role of *infamia*. Inquisitorial procedure was explicitly intended to address clerical accountability. The innovation begins to emerge during Alexander III's pontificate (1159–81).[31] The legal form was taken further under Innocent III (1198–1216).[32] Under Innocent the mechanism was worked out through responses to cases (decretals), one of which was adapted as canon 8 of Lateran IV, and therefore injected throughout all Christendom's bloodstream.[33] Keeping these three components in mind (inquiring *ex officio* on the basis of *infamia*), the core of this

---

Procedures in the Medieval West (Aldershot, 2001) no. II; Linda Fowler-Magerl, *Ordines iudiciarii and Libelli de ordine iudiciorum (from the middle of the twelfth to the end of the fifteenth century)*, TSMAO 63 (Turnhout, 1994), 49–55; James A. Brundage, *Medieval Canon Law* (Harlow, 1995), 91–6, 139–53. Older works include: A. Esmein, *A History of Continental Criminal Procedure, with Special Reference to France*, trans. J. Simpson (London, 1914); Paul Fournier, *Les Officialités au Moyen Âge: Étude sur l'organisation, la compétence et la procédure des tribunaux ecclésiastiques ordinaires en France, de 1180 à 1328* (Paris, 1880), 270-8; and H. C. Lea, *A History of the Inquisition of the Middle Ages*, 3 vols. (London, 1888), i. 14–16, on non-heretical inquisitions; Augustin Fliche's comments in Augustin Fliche, Christine Thouzellier, and Yvonne Azais, *Histoire de l'Église depuis les origines jusqu'à nos jours: 10. La Chrétienté romaine (1198–1274)* (Paris, 1950), 161–3, 209.

[31] 'Cum in ecclesia' (*PL* 200, #811, cols. 743–4; Jaffé, #11930) (October 1170–October 1172) regarding the Bishop of Amiens' *ex officio* investigations into simoniacal presentations in Tournai on the basis of *fama*. Also e.g. 'Nos inter alios' (X 5.34.6; 1 Comp. 5.29.7; Jaffé, #13970) on the reliance of *publica fama* for forcing a parishioner to purge himself.

[32] On Innocent and inquisitions, see Markus Hirte, *Papst Innozenz III., das IV. Lateranum und die Strafverfahren gegen Kleriker: Eine registergestützte Untersuchung zur Entwicklung der Verfahrensarten zwischen 1198 und 1216*, Rothenburger Gespräche zur Strafrechtsgeschichte 5 (Tübingen, 2005). For the period 1198–1342 Julien Théry's *habilitation*, based on 243 inquisitorial cases, is of great importance: 'Justice et gouvernement dans la Chrétienté latine: recherches autour du modèle ecclésial (v. 1150–v. 1330). «Excès» et «affaires d'enquête»: Les Procès criminels de la papauté contre les prélats, XIIIe–mi-XIVe siècle', 2 vols. (Université Paul-Valéry—Montpellier III, Dossier pour l'habilitation à diriger des recherches en histoire médiévale, 2010). I am extremely grateful to Professor Théry for a copy which I was able to access in this study's late stages.

[33] Helene Tillmann, *Innocent III*, trans. Walter Sax (Amsterdam, 1980), 201–11; Trusen, 'Inquisitionsprozeß' (esp. 187–215); Kéry, '*Inquisitio—denunciatio—exceptio*'; and Hirte, *Papst Innozenz III*, are now the starting points for consideration of the Innocentine legislation, notably: *Inter sollicitudines nostras*, 7 May 1199 (X 5.34.10; 3 Comp. 5.17.1; *Reg. Inn. III*, ii. #60 (63); Potthast #693); *Licet Heli summus*, 2 December 1199 (X 5.3.31; 3 Comp. 5.2.3; *Reg. Inn. III*, ii. #250 (260); Potthast #888); *Per tuas nobis*, 29 January 1204 (X 5.3.32; 3 Comp. 5.2.4; *Reg. Inn. III*, vi. #243 (244), Potthast #2134); *Super his de*, February 11 1203 (X 5.1.16; 3 Comp. 5.1.3; *Reg. Inn. III*, v. #152 (153), Potthast #1824); and the 'original' 29 January 1206 version of *Qualiter et*

chapter examines two bishops and the investigations of episcopal misconduct into them. The first, early, case allows an exploration of proto-inquisitorial procedure before the Fourth Lateran Council, in a country where the influence of canon law has been disputed, a country moreover, where some, at least, of the untheorized elements of inquisitorial procedure concurrently existed in vernacular forms. The second very late thirteenth-century case allows us to explore how inquisitions developed, in their wider context, during the intervening period.

LAW IN MOTION: THE COMPLAINTS AGAINST ARCHBISHOP GEOFFREY OF YORK, 1194–1202

Some of the protagonists described above also played roles in the first case, involving Henry II's 'formidable bastard', Geoffrey of York, Archbishop of York 1189–1212.[34] Gerald of Wales would write a biography of Geoffrey. Hubert Walter would be Geoffrey's sometime opponent, and metropolitan rival. Hugh of Avalon would be called on by Celestine III to judge Geoffrey. The story of Geoffrey's struggle with the canons of York Minster has been told before, but, as elsewhere, my focus is on the political thinking in the legal-administrative process.[35] In order to draw out their interest it is worth describing the inquiries in some detail.

Geoffrey provoked strong feelings.[36] Gervase of Canterbury described him as an 'illiterate youth, stammering and stuttering [. . .] known to all as someone who plotted about everything proudly and impiously'.[37] It seems quite likely that Geoffrey's reluctance to be ordained a priest was a function of his hope that he might yet be king.[38] His father had memorably said he was the only one of his sons who was not a bastard.[39] Not all of Geoffrey's chapter felt like that and it would be Geoffrey's relationship with his chapter that lay at the heart of the inquisitions. In 1193 canon Henry Marshal, younger brother of William Marshal, was promoted to Bishop of Exeter. He had had a very poor relationship with Geoffrey, but replacing him fostered still worse bad blood between archbishop and chapter.[40] Geoffrey's rejection of the chapter's candidate for dean—the Italian canonist Simon of Apulia—prompted

---

quando addressed to the Bishop of Vercelli and the Abbot of Tiglieto (X 5.1.17; 3 Comp. 5.1.4; *Reg. Inn. III*, viii. #201 (200); Potthast #2672). See also *Ut famae tuae*, 10 December 1203 (X 5.39.35; 3 Comp. 5.21.8; *Reg. Inn. III*, vi. #181 (183); Potthast #2038).

[34] Decima L. Douie's phrase: *Archbishop Geoffrey Plantagenet and the Chapter of York*, Borthwick Institute of Historical Research 18 (York, 1960), 3.

[35] Marie Lovatt's work is essential for a study of Geoffrey: *York, 1189–1212*, EEA 27 (Oxford, 2004), introduction, esp. xlii–l; Lovatt, 'Geoffrey (1151?–1212), Archbishop of York', *ODNB*.

[36] Gerald of Wales, *De vita Galfridi archiepiscopi Eboracensis*, in *Giraldi Cambrensis Opera*, iv., ed. Brewer, e.g. 374–83, 387–96; *Gesta regis Henrici secundi Benedicti abbatis* [Roger of Howden], ed. William Stubbs, RS, 2 vols. (London, 1867), ii. 91, 100.

[37] *The Historical Works of Gervase of Canterbury*, ed. William Stubbs, RS, 2 vols. (1879–80), i. 520.

[38] John Gillingham, *Richard I* (New Haven, Conn., 1999), 109–10.

[39] Gerald of Wales, *Vita Galfridi* in *Giraldi Cambrensis Opera*, iv. 368; Douie, *Archbishop Geoffrey Plantagenet*, 4–8.

[40] *York, 1189–1212*, EEA 27, xxxvii–xviii, xliv.

them to appeal to King Richard and Celestine III.⁴¹ The disruption of services by some canons led in January 1194 to Geoffrey removing the offending officers. A group of York canons, with Robert, Abbot of St Mary's York, Roger of Selby, and eleven Premonstratensian canons 'at once proceeded to the diffamation [*ad diffamationem*] and accusation [*accusationem*]' of Geoffrey arguing that he was a

> violent despoiler of his own and other clerics' goods, a wicked extortioner, that he broke down church doors with force, distributed and kept ecclesiastical benefices simoniacally, would not concede appeals, despised the privileges of the Roman Church [. . .] they claimed he was a man who despised the office [*officium*] of every bishop, a man given up to hawking and hunting and other military concerns. And for these, and other reasons, they sought to depose [*deponere*] him.⁴²

The consequence of the complaint was a papal letter of 8 June 1194 ('Mediator Dei et') ordering the Bishop of Lincoln, Hugh of Avalon, the Archdeacon of Northampton, and the Prior of Pontefract to conduct an inquisition.⁴³ The chronicler Roger of Howden, our source and well-appraised because of his Yorkshire prebend, describes another simultaneous, secular inquiry. At the same time as they complained to the Pope, the York canons also complained to the Archbishop of Canterbury, Hubert Walter, and then Richard's Justiciar. Walter, 'with the King's authority, on which he acted', sent seven senior barons, including Roger Bigod, William of Warenne, and William of Stuteville to

> hear the dispute between the Archbishop of York and his canons, and resolve it as the law would determine. When the [barons] came and heard the canons' appeal and the responses of the Archbishop and his men, they ordered the Archbishop's men who had been accused of robbery to be seized and imprisoned. And although the Archbishop guaranteed their actions, the Archbishop could not however pledge them.⁴⁴

---

⁴¹ Howden, *Chronica*, ii. 229–30. On Simon as a canonist, S. Kuttner and E. Rathbone, 'Anglo-Norman Canonists of the Twelfth Century', *Traditio* 7 (1949–51), 279–358 at 305–8; repr. with corrections in Kuttner's *Gratian and the Schools of Law 1140–1234* (London, 1983), #VIII.

⁴² Howden, *Chronica*, iii. 230. Howden gives two accounts of these proceedings. The first (230–1) is under 1194, the second fuller account is given at the point when the commissioners arrived in York (15 January 1195) and includes Celestine's 8 June 1194 letter of commission (Jaffé # 27882). On the complex chronology see Lovatt, *York, 1189–1212*, EEA 27, xlv–xlviii.

⁴³ 'Mediator Dei et', in Howden, *Chronica*, iii. 279–81. Texts and chronology here are inconsistent. There is a *second* letter of 8 June 1194 ('Quanto venerabilis frater') also to Bishop of Lincoln and Hugh of Avalon together with the Archdeacon of Northampton and Prior of Pontefract, also instructing them to discipline Geoffrey at York, but distinct, and lacking the inquisitorial stress of 'Mediator Dei et'. See James Raine (ed.), *The Historians of the Church of York and its Archbishops*, RS, 3 vols. (London, 1879–94), iii. #76 at 99–101. 'Quanto venerabilis frater' is given by these judges-delegate in their undated account of their investigation, which began, according to Howden, on 15 January 1195 (*Chronica*, iii. 278). Perhaps the concurrent letters of 8 June reflect the Curia's indecision about how to proceed. On the chronology see further *York, 1189–1212*, EEA 27, xlvii n. 100. On 31 May 1194 Celestine had ordered a different trio of judges (but ones also from Lincoln and Northampton) to evaluate damages alleged by Geoffrey, eventually assessed at 1,000 marks (Howden in *Chronica*, iii. 285–6). This is less than, but of a comparable order with, the damages assessed by Hugh of Lincoln in 1195.

⁴⁴ Howden, *Chronica*, iii. 261–2.

Finding, as Celestine would, that Geoffrey was reluctant to appear before the judges, they disseized him of all but one manor at Ripon.[45] By the end of summer 1194 then, there were two enquiries into Geoffrey of York. One was ecclesiastical. The other, although initiated by a justiciar who was also the Archbishop of Canterbury, was secular, and shortly behind it followed a general judicial tour (eyre) of England by the justices.

On 15 January 1195 the papal judges arrived in York, attempting to cite Geoffrey, found he was en route to Rome, heard the complaints anyway, and totalled over 1,000 marks worth of damages against him.[46] Discussing the canonical inquiry, Howden talked about 'accusation'; the canons' desire for punishment speaks to this too. 'Mediator Dei et' itself is somewhat more equivocal, since it appears to blend parts of an accusatorial procedure with aspects stressing inquiry on the basis of public rumour and the need to avoid damage to the body ecclesiastic. It begins with language Innocent III would have been proud of, stressing Christ's particular reservation to Rome of disciplinary and corrective powers in relation to *excessus* through plenitude of power.[47] (The problematic parallel letter of 8 June, 'Quanto venerabilis frater' speaks of the need for bishops to minister to, not lord it over, subjects.) Celestine seems careful not to describe what has happened as an *accusatio*. Committing the case to Hugh of Avalon and the others, Celestine spoke of the 'report' (*insinuatio*) he had received from the chapter, which 'appears to show by manifest testimony' the charges laid against Geoffrey.[48] Further, having recapitulated in great detail the charges against Geoffrey, Celestine laid out his commission to the two Hughs:

> so, if [Geoffrey] lives like this, and his conduct has been like this for a long time, it should be feared that he is a stone of horror and a rock of scandal [*scandali petra*] to the flock entrusted to him, rather than an example of enlightenment, or a comfort or guardian against spiritual worthlessness. Therefore, because what has been set out demands the attention [*sollicitudinem*] of an enquiry, we have been led to commit the inquisition of these things to your discretion, in which we have complete confidence.[49]

The prelate-judges were to go to York and call the Church together and 'inquire more carefully whether he treated the Church and Province of York so damagingly

---

[45] *Historical Works of Gervase of Canterbury*, i. 528, says Geoffrey's estates were confiscated in August at Richard's command for a debt of over 1,000 marks.

[46] *Historians of the Church of York and its Archbishops*, iii. 101–4.

[47] On *excessus* see Bruno Lemesle, 'Corriger les excès. L'extension des infractions, des délits et des crimes, et les transformations de la procédure inquisitoire dans les lettres pontificales (milieu du XIIe siècle-fin du pontificat d'Innocent III)', *Revue historique* 313 (2011), 747–79.

[48] Howden, *Chronica*, iii. 279–81, 8 June 1194. Under 'simony', X 5.3.28 (2 Comp. 5.2.10); Jaffé #17634), a letter of Celestine's, 'Dilectus filius noster', is likewise addressed and concerns the *prepositus* R who, in one manuscript tradition, offered 'our venerable brother G. Archbishop of York' money if he would cease from troubling him, but who, having received the money did not cease from troubling R. Friedberg preferred an alternative reading of 'archdeacon' for 'archbishop'. Stubbs had earlier connected this letter with the case analysed here (Howden, *Chronica*, iii. 279 n. 1) but gives an incorrect reference to it. A reading of 'archbishop' seems consonant with the material described here. For Avalon's *acta, Lincoln, 1186–1206*, ed. David M. Smith, EEA 4 (Oxford, 1986), #214A–C.

[49] Howden, *Chronica*, iii. 280–1; for the rock see 1 Peter 2: 8, an interesting citation given that chapter's wider stress on self-subjugation to instituted authorities.

and perniciously [*tam inutiliter et perniciose*]'.[50] However Celestine does seem to allow for the procedure to indeed become accusatorial, since he envisages two alternatives. In one, *legitimi accusatores* will appear. In the other,

> if there are inadequate accusers [*accusatores defecerint*],[51] *and the public outcry* [*fama publica*] *is against him*, you will proclaim, on our authority, with the obstacle of appeal removed, his purgation by three bishops, and the same number of abbots. In the event that he fails in this, you will have him present himself in person to the Pope, suspended from archiepiscopal office and administration, so that he may be here instructed more fully through the Lord Founder how he and his peers should minister in the house of God.[52]

That is, Celestine sketches how the investigation could become accusatorial (always formally clear), but should that fail he also allows how it can proceed further on the basis of *fama publica*.[53] Even if the York canons intended an accusatorial process from the outset (and Howden might not be technically right about that), Celestine seems to have reframed the process. At the same time Celestine set limits, since Geoffrey could purge himself. The purgative penalty at this point might be compared to that within the different proceedings *per notorium* (where open notoriety was the trigger for proceedings).[54] Here purgation was required if unprovable allegations against clerics risked popular scandal.

It is tricky to be sure of what is going on here partly because one wishes to make sense of it through later guidelines which were not yet stable, and partly because what is going on procedurally (the *modus*) appears to evolve en route. Still, the initiation of proceedings into Geoffrey's conduct illustrates the pooling of several deep streams in canonical practice: the question of accusation, delegated inquisitions, canonical purgation, clerical delict as *excessus*, action by *fama publica*, and a very 'inquisitorial'-looking result. At different points the case seems capable of developing in different ways but the central elements of *Qualiter et quando* are visible: inquiring *ex officio* at the demand of reliable *infamia* in order to avoid *scandalum* to the church—a more serious technical term than *fama publica*.[55] Celestine's later recapitulation (23 December 1195) of his initial reasons for ordering the inquisition gives a clearer picture. In this letter Celestine stresses that the 1194 inquisition was into whether there was a *fama* about Geoffrey, not whether he had actually done these things. Those rumours had circulated not once but often. They came not only from those at the

---

[50] Howden, *Chronica*, iii. 281.
[51] The Latin seems to allow they might be inadequate both in numbers and in quality.
[52] Howden, *Chronica*, iii. 281, my stress. On canonical purgation see R. H. Helmholz, *The Ius Commune in England: Four Studies* (Oxford, 2001), ch. 2.
[53] Cf. X 5.3.31 (*Licet Heli summus*) where Innocent III in 1199 allowed for a process initiated by denunciation to proceed even if the denunciation was formally quashed.
[54] *Tua nos duxit*, 11 May 1199 (X 3.2.8). Friedberg's attribution of this decretal *Exonensi episcopo* (who would have been Richard Marshal, Geoffrey's former dean), is incorrect. See *Reg. Inn. III*, ii. #62 (65). See also Brundage, *Medieval Canon Law*, 144–7; Kéry, '*Inquisitio—denunciatio—exceptio*', 261–6.
[55] See Richard Helmholz, '*Scandalum* in the Medieval Canon Law and in the English Ecclesiastical Courts', *ZRG Kan. Abt.* 127 (2010), 258–74, at 260, and 266 n. 33 noting how *scandalum* and *fama publica* came together in inquisitorial practice.

church of York, but 'from other prelates in the kingdom of England, and also those placed in the province of York'. That is, implicitly, they came from those lacking York Minster's active interest in the case.

This retelling seems at variance with what we ostensibly know about the case's origins. Howden says that it originated with those who had a definite 'interest'. In contrast to Howden's suggestion that York Minster's aim was deposition, Celestine says in 1195 that the canons' motive was 'to deter [*deterrere*] [Geoffrey] from his excesses [*excessibus*] and to recall him to the due pursuit of his pastoral office'.[56] It was corrective and implicitly therefore not malicious. (Deposition by contrast was the aim of accusation.)[57] In 1194 Celestine is not clear that the inquisition is only into whether there are nasty stories in circulation, implying actually that it was also into their substantive truth.[58] In 1195 he is clearer that it was just an *inquisitionem famae*.[59] The ambiguity between these two letters shows us the papacy and perhaps the canons at York trying to get their *modus* straight.

Geoffrey anyway prevaricated and missed the 1 June 1195 deadline for appearing at Rome, and the revised one of 18 November.[60] Probably petitioned to suspend Geoffrey in relation to the papal letters' original delegated powers, Hugh declined to suspend Geoffrey 'preferring to be suspended myself than suspend him'.[61] (One compares Hugh's later self-criticism to Hubert Walter.) On 23 December 1195, Celestine enforced the suspension himself. In 1196 Geoffrey did eventually appear before the Curia in Rome and 'repeatedly claimed all the charges were false'. His opponents, 'having been asked whether they could prove their claims, after a pause had been asked for and granted, [...] replied that they did not want to bear the burden of proof [*onus probationis*]'. So the Archbishop showed himself to be sufficiently immune to the allegations.[62] Celestine restored Geoffrey, declaring that 'everything that his adversaries had rumoured about him was false and fictitious' [*falsa et fictitia*].[63] There was, however, another inquisition into Geoffrey yet to come.

At the end of May or start of June 1202, a weary Innocent III wrote to Bishop Eustace of Ely, Roger Dean of Lincoln, and the Archdeacon of Bedford that 'the variety of quarrels and the frequency of the complaints regularly put forward before us

---

[56] Howden, *Chronica*, iii. 314 (to the judges), cf. the similar phrase to Geoffrey in the letter the same day (310).

[57] See the slightly later 1203 *Super his de* (X 5.1.16) and the 1211 *Inquisitionis negotium quam* (X 5.1.21; PL 216, cols. 715–17, ep. #191 for Innocent's 15th year). The idea that inquisitions could not entail punishment was now modified, especially in relation to serious crimes (e.g. simony, homicide). See further, Kéry, 'Inquisitio—denunciatio—exceptio', 255.

[58] Howden, *Chronica*, iii. 281, 'diligentius inquiratis, utrum Eboracensem ecclesiam et provinciam tam inutiliter et perniciose tractaverit'.

[59] See the two 23 December 1195 letters in Howden, *Chronica*, iii. 310 (non statim formavimus judicium contra eum, sed inquisitionem famae [. . .] duximus committendam), 312–13 (auditis excessibus [. . .] destitimus laborare), 314 (inquisitio famae; 'inquireretis veritatem' is also used, but of the truth of the *fama*). Cf. Lemesle, 'Corriger les excès', 772; Massimo Vallerani, *Medieval Public Justice*, trans. Sarah Rubin Blanshei, Studies in Medieval and Early Modern Canon Law 9 (Washington, 2012), 101–3.

[60] Howden, *Chronica*, iii.. 231, 282.

[61] Howden, *Chronica*, iii. 306; *York, 1189–1212*, EEA 27, xlviii n. 107.

[62] Howden, *Chronica*, iv. 7.   [63] Howden, *Chronica*, iv. 7.

against our venerable brother Geoffrey of York are exceptionally tiring to hear'.[64] This time the chapter seems to have tried a slightly different legal tack, one that they could do because they had (evidently) rebuked Geoffrey so often in the interim. So the three judges-delegate were to carry out another investigation, formally *per denunciationem*. Geoffrey, although 'he has often been reprimanded and corrected, so that he could improve his behaviour for the better, neither accepts the warnings, as he ought, nor the corrections'. This was even though he had been 'carefully admonished', 'like a father by sons', by the Dean and Chapter of York, neighbouring bishops, and other religious men, 'so that he should have ceased from unduly harassing them, and borne himself towards them and his other subjects like a kind shepherd'. Geoffrey 'should have corrected his own excesses'. Precisely 'because of this his effect on those people is so much worse, like someone who constantly glories in molesting such people'. The Pope did not wish that 'these and other things which have often been denounced [*denuntiata*] before us should go on out of neglect any more' and so ordered Eustace and his companions to go and investigate. They were

> to go to the church of York, having summoned abbots, priors, and other, proper persons of whatever order, and, with the Archbishop present, if he wishes, and—if he can—defending himself, under penalty of excommunication, and without appeal, you may charge these people as necessary that they should bring forward the testimony of the truth—on which the same Archbishop has already received an admonition from the said dean and chapter— and you will receive the witnesses which they shall produce to prove those things in which they say the Archbishop himself has committed excesses in [*excessise*]; inquiring [*inquirentes*] through them and also the common report [*famam communem*] whether the Archbishop himself is competent [*utilis*] and able [*sufficiens*] to the exalted role of episcopal governance [*regimen*]. . .[65]

The judges were also to investigate any allegations of Geoffrey against the chapter, and then to send a report of everything to Innocent, setting a time for them all to appear at the Curia before him. The trail runs cold here, however. Innocent's letters include a string of further complaints about Geoffrey (often about his evasiveness in instituting postulated clerics to benefices), but how this investigation died, or was abandoned, is not known.[66] By April 1204, Archbishop and chapter were back at it, with Innocent audibly weary, once more, at their disputes, and Eustace, once

---

[64] 'Querelarum diversitas et', *Reg. Inn. III*, v. #57 (59), (= Potthast #1686; *Innocent III English Calendar*, #414). Geoffrey had most recently been rebuked in 1201 regarding Master Honorius and his archdeaconry at Richmond (*Innocent III English Calendar*, ##283, 303–5) and a 1202 investigation into Guisborough Priory had been ordered (#392). Cf. Hirte's analysis of 'Querelarum diversitas et' as denunciatory procedure, *Papst Innozenz III*, 91–3, 96, 98–9, 103–4, 182.
[65] This and previous quotes *Reg. Inn. III*, v. #57 (59) ('Querelarum diversitas et').
[66] This is quite common. See Théry, '«Excès» et «affaires d'enquête»', i. 520. There are letters involving Geoffrey from Innocent regarding institutions at Durham on 13 December 1202 and 5 January 1203 (*Innocent III English Calendar*, ##499 and see 591, 759). Geoffrey's movements from late 1201 to February 1204 are difficult to pin down. See *York, 1189–1212*, EEA 27, App. II. The complaint to Innocent about the former legate John of Salerno, written for Geoffrey by Peter of Blois (*York, 1189–1212*, EEA 27 #29), is datable to early 1203–March 1204, and implies Geoffrey was at Ripon at Christmas in either of those years. It betrays no presumption of an ongoing investigation. In May 1203 Geoffrey was asked to guarantee Bernard, former Archbishop of Ragusa as the titular

148   *Bishops*

more, in charge of their resolution.[67] Geoffrey lived to continue wrangling with his half-brother the King, until his death in Norman exile in 1212.[68]

GEOFFREY OF YORK'S INQUISITIONS IN CONTEXT

There are several themes to be drawn from this material. First it is worth summarizing the legal learning revolving around Geoffrey's case, in order to interpret the attempts to hold Geoffrey to account within their legal matrix. Secondly, since this episcopal accountability was not uncontroversial, some account is needed of the a priori political ideas that allowed canonical inquisitorial procedure to exist.

Legal Learning

Those involved in Geoffrey Plantagenet's case included clerics highly skilled and informed in current and emerging canon law.[69] They would have been up to date with legal thinking as it was emerging around the Curia, often in response to problems posed by prelates across Christendom, some of whom were in England.

According to Gerald of Wales, Geoffrey 'once studied liberal arts for some time' at Northampton, which had an important legal *studium* at the time.[70] From *c*.1200 on Geoffrey's *familia* included clerks endorsed by Innocent III himself.[71] Geoffrey had skilled canonists before then too. William Longchamp was Geoffrey's clerk until 1189 during which time he wrote a *Practica legum* on romano-canonical procedure (1181–9).[72] Other sometime members of Geoffrey's *familia* included Simon of Apulia (perhaps a former clerk) and the important canonist and Oxford teacher,

---

bishop of Carlisle (*Innocent III English Calendar*, #474). In June Eustace again was appointed to lead a party of judges mandated to resolve Geoffrey's failure to grant institutions at Kirkham (*Innocent III English Calendar*, #499 and see ##591, 759).

[67] *Reg. Inn. III*, vii. #35, 1 April 1204 ('Quia omne regnum' = *Innocent III English Calendar*, #552); *Reg. Inn. III*, viii. #6, 26 February 1205 ('Venerabilis frater noster' = *Innocent III English Calendar*, #605).

[68] EEA 27, lvii and n. 163. Innocent's defence of Geoffrey against John's attacks: *Innocent III English Calendar*, ##775–7, 792, 867 (respectively December 1207, May 1208, May 1210).

[69] On late twelfth-century Angevin learning in canon law see Kuttner and Rathbone, 'Anglo-Norman Canonists of the Twelfth Century'; Charles Duggan, 'The Reception of Canon Law in England in the Later-Twelfth Century', *Proceedings of the Second International Congress of Medieval Canon Law: Boston College, 12–16 August 1963*, ed. Stephan Kuttner, J. Joseph Ryan (Vatican City, 1965), 359–90, repr. as #XI of Duggan's *Canon Law in Medieval England: the Becket Dispute and Decretal Collections* (London, 1982). See also Alain Boureau, *La Loi du royaume: Les Moines, le droit et la construction de la nation anglaise (XI*ᵉ*–XIII*ᵉ *siècles)* (Paris 2001), chs. 3–5, on Benedictine legal aptitudes; R. H. Helmholz, *The Oxford History of the Laws of England*, i. *The Canon Law and Ecclesiastical Jurisdiction from 597 to the 1640s* (Oxford, 2004), 120–34; Sam Worby, *Law and Kinship in Thirteenth Century England* (Woodbridge, 2010).

[70] Gerald of Wales, *De Vita Galfridi Archiepiscopi Eboracensis* in *Giraldi Cambrensis Opera*, iv. 410; H. G. Richardson, 'The Schools of Northampton in the Twelfth Century', *EHR* 56 (1941), 595–605; Kuttner and Rathbone, 'Anglo-Norman Canonists of the Twelfth Century'.

[71] *York, 1189–1212*, EEA 27, xcviii and xcvi–c on the *familia* and Geoffrey's relative failure as a patron.

[72] Ed. Exupère Caillemer, 'Le Droit civil dans les provinces anglo-normandes au XIIᵉ siècle', *Mémoires de l'Académie nationale des Sciences, Arts et Belles-Lettres de Caen* (Caen, 1883) and internally

Honorius (briefly Geoffrey's Official).[73] It was a falling-out with Honorius and a consequent dispute about his Archdeaconry at Richmond that in fact resulted in Geoffrey's inadvertant contribution to canon law, since two of Innocent III's rulings on this would be included in Gregory IX's *Liber extra*.[74] Further, if X 5.3.28 is to be connected with Geoffrey's misconduct, then he provided the grounds for three decretals in the *Corpus iuris canonici*.[75] Geoffrey's peer at Canterbury was just as well equipped. When Honorius left Geoffrey's service he moved to Hubert Walter's. Walter's roster of canonists included the ostensible leader of the Oxford canonist group, John of Tynemouth, as well as Simon of Sywell.[76] It was also Walter who received early in the summer of 1201 the important letter *Dilectus filius magister*, which drew distinctions between accusatorial and inquisitorial penalties, and the variable consequences permitted through either procedure.[77] An earlier Archbishop of Canterbury, Richard of Dover (r.1173–84), was also the recipient of an important letter (26 June 1174 x 1176) ordering him to restrain the *ex officio* investigations of Coventry's archdeacons into lay and clerical misdeeds.[78] This was not the only letter addressed to an English prelate regarding overenthusiastic clerics acting *ex officio*. Alexander III also ordered the same abuse by an Archdeacon 'R' of Chester to cease, an order that also made its way into *Compilatio prima* and the *Liber extra*.[79] Finally, Bishop Eustace of Ely—also Hubert Walter's predecessor as Chancellor—figured prominently in the later investigations into Geoffrey. Eustace himself was the recipient of some thirty-five papal letters, often mandates to act as judge-delegate. For a Paris-trained scholar that judicial experience prompted numerous practical questions

---

datable (48–9); 'Rectifications et additions' by Gérard Fransen and Pierre Legendre, *Revue historique de droit français et étrange* 44 (1966), 115–18; comment in Fowler-Magerl, *Ordines iudiciarii*, 64.

[73] Charles Duggan, 'Honorius (d. *c.*1213)', *ODNB*; Frank Barlow, 'Apulia, Simon of (d. 1223)', *ODNB*; James A. Brundage, *The Medieval Origins of the Legal Profession: Canonists, Civilians, and Courts* (Chicago, 2008), 112–14.

[74] X 3.7.6; X 3.8.7; Douie, *Archbishop Geoffrey Plantagenet*, 13–14.   [75] See p. 144 n. 48.

[76] *Canterbury, 1162–1190*, ed. C. R. Cheney and Bridgitt E. A. Jones, EEA 2 (Oxford, 1986), xxviii–xxix; C. R. Cheney, *Hubert Walter* (London, 1967), 164–6; Thomas of Marlborough, *History of the Abbey of Evesham*, ed. Jane Sayers and Leslie Watkiss, OMT (Oxford, 2003), 232–4 and notes.

[77] X 5.3.30, *Dilectus filius magister* (May–June 1201) (*Innocent III English Calendar*, #331; Potthast #1403). Since it might otherwise be presumed relevant it is worth noting (as others have) that the important decretal *Ut famae tuae* (10 December 1203, X 5.39.35), which addresses this theme, is addressed not to the Bishop of London, but the Archbishop of Lund, and so does not have an English matrix. Richard M. Fraher's important article on this subject is unaffected by this misattribution: see 'The Theoretical Justification for the New Criminal Law of the High Middle Ages: "rei publicae interest, ne crimina remaneant impunita"', *University of Illinois Law Review* (1984), 577–95. On Fraher see p. 163 note 151.

[78] X 5.37.3 (1 Comp. 5.32.3; Jaffé 14315), reiterated in Richard's mandate to the Archdeacons, *Canterbury, 1162–1190*, EEA, 2 #115. Comment in Caenegem, 'Public Prosecution of Crime', 27.

[79] 'Mandamus, quatenus prohibeatis' (X 1.23.6). This 'R' would fit with Archdeacon Robert of Chester appearing in Coventry *acta* from the second half of the century, but is it not clear whether 'Robert' is the same Robert throughout the period, let alone this 'R'. See *Coventry and Lichfield, 1160–1182*, ed. M. J. Franklin, EEA 16 (Oxford, 1998), 113. Charles Duggan's *Decretals and the Creation of 'New Law' in the Twelfth Century: Judges, Judgements, Equity and Law* (Aldershot, 1998) and Walther Holtzmann's *Decretales ineditae saeculi XII*, ed. and rev. Stanley Chodorow and Charles Duggan, Monumenta iuris canonici, Ser. B: Corpus collectionum 4 (Vatican City, 1982) do not appear to discuss this decretal. It appears elsewhere with a variant *incipit* ('Mandamus ut ex nostra parte—durius'), see 1 Comp. 5.32.4, Jaffé #13857, and *Collectio Rotomagensis prima* in Walther Holtzmann, *Studies in the*

for the Pope. One 21-point set of queries from Eustace ('this lengthy examination paper', Maitland called it) elicited the extensive reply, *Pastoralis officii diligentia*, all of whose rulings passed into canon law.[80]

It is clear then that many of the prelates involved in the investigations into Geoffrey had a high level of knowledge about current procedure. This is important because it provides a basis for interpreting the significance of the investigations into Geoffrey.

In 1202 there was an investigation formally *per denunciationem*. In 1194 there had been one that seemed to oscillate between accusation and inquisition. Such experimentation—perhaps the consequence of discussion at the Curia—shows both the selecting of legal mechanisms and their limits.[81] Notwithstanding the formal differences between procedures their functional content here was very similar—*ex officio* investigation on the basis of reliable report into publicly alleged conduct.[82] A significant difference between accusatory and inquisitorial procedure was that it lacked, formally, an accuser. That was a *raison d'être*. But commentators on Lateran IV cap. 8 who wrote very soon after its promulgation were quite clear that inquisitions can be *ex officio* or *cum aliquo promovente*.[83] Indeed, the tone of some of their comments implies that they presumed that it would be *normal* for there to be an *impetrator inquisitionis*—and the rule whereby an inquisition can be pursued on *fama alone* needed to be reiterated in the case of inquisitions where the *impetrator* is removed *a prosecutione eius inquisitionis*.[84] That is, from early on the very rule that was ostensibly the point of procedure *per inquisitionem* and which made it easier than accusatorial cases needed reiterating in case it was overlooked. In practice, then, and notwithstanding that inquisitions were easier to procure than accusations, inquisitions often needed someone—beyond the investigating prelate—to get the ball rolling. Geoffrey of York's cases show that, in his case, a strong cathedral chapter was more than willing to oblige. The same would continue to be true after Lateran IV.[85] York Minster had a good sense of what it had to play with procedurally, especially if Howden was not

---

Collections of Twelfth-Century Decretals, ed. C. R. Cheney and Mary G. Cheney, Monumenta iuris canonici, Ser. B: Corpus collectionum 3 (Vatican City, 1979), 188 #13.

[80] *Reg. Inn. III*, vii. #169, trans. *Innocent III English Letters*, #22, 19 December 1204. Others count the number of legal issues raised in this text differently. On Eustace, see Dorothy M. Owen, 'Eustace (d. 1215)', *ODNB*. Maitland's remark is in *Roman Canon Law in the Church of England: Six Essays* (London, 1898), 126. Maitland views these questions as an underemployed jurist's 'what if's (124), but given Eustace's extensive experience as a judge-delegate it seems more likely that he had simply deduced from experience a large set of questions whose answers he thought it least troublesome to request in one go.

[81] Susan Reynolds might describe the mechanisms as inchoate: *Fiefs and Vassals*, 389.

[82] See also Jacques Chiffoleau, '«*Ecclesia de occultis non iudicat*»? L'Église, le secret, l'occulte du XII\ⁿ au XIV\ⁿ siècle', in *Il Segreto, The Secret*, Micrologus 14 (Florence, 2006), 359–481 at 419–20.

[83] Johannes Teutonicus, *Apparatus in concilium quartum Lateranense*, in *Constitutiones Concilii quarti Lateranensis*, 197.

[84] Vincentius Hispanus, *Apparatus in concilium quartum Lateranense*, in *Constitutiones Concilii quarti Lateranensis*, 300. On these commentators, see Antonio García y García, 'The Fourth Lateran Council and the Canonists', in Wilfried Hartmann and Kenneth Pennington (eds.), *The History of Medieval Canon Law in the Classical Period, 1140–1234: From Gratian to the Decretals of Pope Gregory IX* (Washington DC, 2008), 367–78.

[85] e.g. Richard Marsh at Durham in the 1220s or Anselm de Mauny at Laon in the 1230s. The most complete set of cases is available in Théry, '«Excès» et «affaires d'enquête»'.

using the language of 'accusation' technically, but in terms of the chapter's political intentions. The legal *savoir faire* of those involved allows some presumption in their favour. Nor does Geoffrey's seemingly successful evasion denote the chapter's failure. Such inquisitions played roles in local political conflicts whose importance is hard to evaluate counterfactually. A contemporary cabinet minister who has survived a tabloid scandal is not the same person politically as the pre-scandal minister. The papal letters in turn imply the clarification and even the *ex post facto* re-rationalization of procedure going on in midstream. The different approaches would anyway continue to be procedurally fluid.[86] The investigations into Geoffrey show how the interaction of lawyers, popes, and prelates was beginning to produce political 'facts on the ground' through legal means very similar to those that Innocent III would continue developing. The argument, anyway, is not that here we see inquisitorial procedure 'invented' (just as it was not the case that Adam of Eynsham's *exemplum* about Hugh of Lincoln shows him inventing it). Rather, Geoffrey's case demonstrates that in late twelfth- and early thirteenth-century England there were local, ongoing experiments to find satisfactory ways of holding prelates to account, using the legal material and methods to hand and which were ostensibly the result of the back-and-forth of particular cases.[87]

England seems indeed an apposite place for such experiments, given its familiarity with summary procedure in the secular sphere. We have early English examples of archdeacons being reprimanded for overenthusiastic *ex officio* conduct at Coventry and Chester—rulings that made their way into canon law. These may imply a wider ease with *ex officio* action in England. *Ex officio* inquiries were certainly familiar in the field of secular executive action. We have seen Hubert Walter change hats to order just such a secular '*ex officio*' enquiry, in the context of York Minster's *ecclesiastical* complaints against Geoffrey. Further, there is the well-known habit of senior prelates holding simultaneously or concurrently *both* high ecclesiastical and high secular office in this period: Thomas Becket, Hubert Walter, Geoffrey himself, William

---

[86] On the organic growth and intermixing of relevant procedural elements even after their formalization, cf. Kéry, '*Inquisitio—denunciatio—exceptio*', 267–8; Théry, '«Excès» et «affaires d'enquête»', i. 60, 530–1; Chiffoleau, '«*Ecclesia de occultis non iudicat*»?', *passim*. For a late thirteenth century Franciscan critique of the modes as a single complex, see Richard de Mediavilla, *Questions disputées*, ed. Alain Boureau, 6 vols. (Paris, 2012–14), vi. q. 45 esp. art. 3–4, comment, xxx–xxxiv; Alain Boureau, 'Une parole destructrice: La Diffamation. Richard de Mediavilla et le droit individuel au péché', in Julie Claustre, Olivier Mattéoni, and Nicolas Offenstadt (eds.),*Un Moyen Âge pour aujourd'hui: Mélanges offerts à Claude Gauvard* (Paris, 2010), 306–14.

[87] This is consonant with others' recent arguments that Innocent III did not invent inquisitorial procedure *ex nihilo*. Cf. the argument by Hirte that Innocent's activities in this field impress as 'mehr evolutionär denn revolutionär', although they still have a 'gewisse neue Qualität' (*Papst Innozenz III*, 294). See also Kéry's argument that the key Innocentine developments build on work done from Alexander III's pontificate on ('*Inquisitio—denunciatio—exceptio*', 227–8). But there is no reason why the Curia should have a monopoly on relevant legal experimentation. A strong argument for what would be parallel (if more influential) developments in France has been made by Jessalynn Bird in 'The Wheat and the Tares: Peter the Chanter's Circle and the *Fama*-based Inquest Against Heresy and Criminal Sins, c.1198–c.1235', in *Proceedings of the Twelfth International Congress of Medieval Canon Law: Washington, D.C. 1–7 August 2004*, ed. Uta-Renate Blumenthal, Kenneth Pennington, and Atria A. Larson, Monumenta iuris canonici, Ser. C: Subsidia 13 (Vatican City, 2008). Bird argues that Parisian Masters played a key experimental role in developing *fama*-based inquests.

Longchamp, Eustace of Ely, Peter des Roches—the list could be extended.[88] Such individuals would consequently have been familiar with forms both of secular *ex officio* action and of ecclesiastical *ex officio* and summary action—such as they existed. Again, as a simple example, one can point to the letter *Dilectus filius magister* from Innocent III to Hubert Walter about inquisitorial and accusatorial procedure. It would be entirely natural for an administrator such as Walter to have an interest in both the lay and the ecclesiastical sides of the coin used to initiate summary procedure. Again, the suggestion is not that England invented inquisitorial procedure. Rather the suggestion is that, given the existence of cases early on involving prelates and inquisitions; and the presence of informed Anglo-Norman canonists dealing with such cases during the period of the romano-canonical procedure's development; and the frequency with which senior prelates held senior secular offices in this period; and the existence of concurrent secular English summary procedures of inquisition; and the canon law's working out of such theoretical problems through case questions, that it *then* seems entirely likely that English thought and practice more than played their role in the development of the 'theory in practice' that ultimately produced Lateran IV cap. 8. This is the opposite of making an argument for English 'exceptionalism'.[89] It is rather to make an argument for a useful consonance between English 'vernacular' practice and romano-canonical practice.[90] It suggests a meaningful coincidence between the two.[91] It is in the nature of the material that it should be difficult to point to proof texts connecting one legal forum to another. What is clear is the concurrent elaboration of comparable procedures involving those on both sides of the lay and ecclesiastical 'fence'.

---

[88] Cf. comment in Murray, *Reason and Society*, ch. 13.

[89] See Raoul van Caenegem's comments on chauvinism in interpreting the 'English' jury, *The Birth of the English Common Law*, 2nd edn. (Cambridge, 1988) 76; Vallerani, *Medieval Public Justice*, 58–9; Maddicott, *Origins of the English Parliament*, ch. 7 for illuminating relevant analysis of English exceptionalism as a variation on a European pattern. Karl Blaine Shoemaker, 'Criminal Procedure in Medieval European Law', *ZRG Kan. Abt.* 85 (1999), 174–202 argues that post-1215 England and the Continent diverge legally, the former's jury system continuing a communal 'ordeal'-type mentality; the latter increasingly committed to written records and objective fact-finding. The contrast seems exaggerated. Cf. (e.g.) the parallelisms noted by Laura Ikins Stern, 'Public Fame: A Useful Canon Law Borrowing', in *Proceedings of the Eleventh International Congress of Medieval Canon Law: Catania, 30 July–6 August, 2000*, ed. Manlio Bellomo and Orazio Condorelli, Monumenta iuris canonici, Ser. C: Subsidia 12 (Vatican City, 2006), 661–72 at 670.

[90] For a parallel argument, R. H. Helmholz, 'The Early History of the Grand Jury and the Canon Law', *University of Chicago Law Review* 50 (1983), 613–27. John Hudson, *Oxford History of the Laws of England*, ii. 871–1216 (Oxford, 2012), 532–3, 735–8, is sceptical. But *pace* Hudson's reservation (736 n. 166) that secular and canonical inquiries differed importantly in relation to the indisputable *infamia* triggering them, they seem comparable to me in that canonical inquiries are initiated where there is 'enough' concern about *infamia* to justify further investigation. Similarly, English juries could still require further investigation of allegations after presenting suspicions, indicating their *infamia* was also to be proven (*Glanvill*, 171). *Britton* too worried about the reliability of jurors' opinions (*Britton*, ed. Francis Morgan Nichols, 2 vols. (Oxford, 1865), i. 32). A helpful questionnaire for such problems is John Hudson, 'Magna Carta, the Ius Commune, and English Common Law', in J. S. Loengard (ed.), *Magna Carta and the England of King John* (Woodbridge, 2010), 99–119 at 101.

[91] Underlying this is the idea of elective affinities as adapted by Max Weber: that two distinct social phenomena can have complementary features which, if they were brought together, can strengthen the parts and the whole. See pp. 241–6.

If these parallels are suggestive, what *does* this coincidence mean, and what were the factors that may lie behind it? Suggestions can be offered by considering the nature of the interests served by the development of both canonical and secular English inquisitions. It is easier to demonstrate the nexus of individuals in England who would have both awareness of English and canonical inquisitions than it is to demonstrate a direct causality from one to the other. But to do so might anyway risk missing the important question of why such comparable inquisitorial techniques should be useful to both papal and secular English institutions. Robert Bartlett has made this point in relation to the medieval ordeal's origins: 'The important thing is not the putative descent of some practice or institution, but its function and significance in the living society in which it has a place'.[92] This is to restate Marc Bloch's critique of the 'quest for origins'.[93] It is one thing, Bloch argued, to describe the historical antecedents of a practice or institution—say Estates with financial and political powers. It is another thing to explain why at a given point their role within a given society changed qualitatively. 'To unearth the seed is not the same as revealing the causes for its germination.'[94] Maitland's argument (to risk repetition), that 'legal ideas never reach very far beyond practical needs' implies something similar: whose needs did these various inquisitions serve?[95] There are various elements of Roman law bound up in canonical inquisitions, but to say that Roman law influenced the canon law on inquisitions does not explain why canonical inquisitions existed, or were developed in the later twelfth century.[96] That, accordingly, is what the final part of this chapter does, focusing on canonical inquisitions, using English secular

---

[92] Bartlett, *Trial by Fire and Water*, 154.
[93] On the danger of 'confusing ancestry with explanation', Marc Bloch, *The Historian's Craft*, trans. Peter Putnam (Manchester, 1954), 32 and 29–35.
[94] Bloch, 'Pour une histoire comparée des sociétés européennes', in his *Mélanges historiques*, 2 vols. (Paris, 1963), i. 16–40 at 25.
[95] Maitland, *Township and Borough*, 27. Bruno Lemesle makes the same point in relation to witness inquiries in twelfth-century Anjou, arguing that explanations based on societal need are more instructive than simply citing 'Anglo-Norman influence'. Lemesle, 'L'Enquête contre les épreuves: Les Enquêtes dans la région Angevine (XIIe–début XIIIe siècle)', in Claude Gauvard (ed.), *L'Enquête au Moyen Âge*, Collection École française de Rome 399 (Rome, 2008), 41–74 at 50. Cf. William C. Jordan's similar point that Carolingian *missi dominici* do not explain Louis IX's *enquêteurs*, *Louis IX and the Challenge of the Crusade* (Princeton, NJ, 1979), 53.
[96] The causal relationship between Roman law and canonical inquisitorial procedure is complex. Naz argued that Innocent III, not Roman law, was the efficient cause of inquisitorial procedure —see *Dictionnaire de droit canonique*, ed. R. Naz, 7 vols. (Paris, 1935–65), v. 'Inquisition', R. Naz, cols. 1418–26 at 1418. G. R. Evans, *Law and Theology in the Middle Ages* (London, 2002), 123–9 discusses Roman *infamia* in this context, noting divergences. Trusen notes *inquisitio* was used generically in Roman law without specific legal meaning ('Inquisitionsprozeß', 170). His caution about overinterpreting 'prefigurements' of inquisitorial procedure is juridically sensible, but not so useful when asking why law was socially useful and therefore what such prefigurements mean. *Ex officio* action existed in Roman law too. See J. Dahyot-Dolivet, 'La Procédure pénale d'office en droit romain', *Apollinaris* 41 (1968), 89–105, and also his 'La Procédure judiciaire d'office dans l'église jusqu'à l'avènement du Pape Innocent III', *Apollinaris* 41 (1968), 443–55. Being *infamatus* in Roman law entailed serious loss of legal and public status. See W. W. Buckland, rev. Peter Stein, *A Textbook of Roman Law from Augustus to Justinian*, 3rd edn. (Cambridge, 1963), 91–2. More generally *publica fama* had legal powers well outside ecclesiastical contexts in the twelfth century as shown by Wickham, *Courts and Conflict*, see s.v. '*publica fama*' and 'Fama and the Law in Twelfth-Century Tuscany', in Thelma Fenster and Daniel Lord Smail (eds.), *Fama: The Politics of Talk and Reputation in Medieval Europe* (Ithaca, NY, 2003),

analogues as a counterpoint, and closing with a shorter consideration of some later thirteenth century inquisitions.

The Politics of Inquisitorial Accountability

It is to ask, again, 'Who, whom?'. Who is it that exacts what from whom? What is exacted and how; how stable is the relation between the giver and receiver of the account; how is it achieved? There are two ways in which the inquisitorial procedure described here is coercive with respect to a bishop's office. One aspect is that forms of accountability (always) play an important role in constructing and reinforcing norms of office. Norms frame the terms of disputes about the proper discharge of a role—because the transgression of the norms implicit or explicit in that role is what the dispute hangs on. Even if York Minster ultimately felt it could press its case no further at the Curia in 1196, it had been successful in securing an inquisition into Geoffrey's conduct by appealing to recognizable episcopal norms which it said he had traduced. A second aspect of coercion is more basic still and has already been implied: successfully requiring that one person account to another is itself an act of coercion, and itself a political achievement.[97] Procedure was needed to uphold right norms, but also needed to be politically practicable: laws, ethics, politics. Innocent III in fact articulated a three-part test of this sort to gauge when the papacy's dispensing power could be used. Such decisions, he said, needed to follow 'what is allowed (*liceat*) according to equity, what is appropriate (*deceat*) according to morality, and what is expedient (*expediat*) according to utility'.[98] Canonical inquisitions offered answers of considerable sophistication and interest to each of these aspects.

Norms of Office: deceat

The Gregorian reforms were, in large part, about competing ideas of what Christendom's shepherds needed to look like. One crude way of characterizing the

---

15–26; and generally in Wickham's 'Gossip and Resistance among the Medieval Peasantry', *P&P* 160 (1998), 3–24.

[97] Cf. Bisson, *Crisis of the Twelfth Century*, arguing that real politics is made possible from the late twelfth century only because of secular officials' growing institutionalized accounting to lord-kings, but arguably conceding too little to the idea that once they have established forms of accountability they may be just as coercive as their less subtle predecessors (perhaps more so). There are relevant comments and discussion of this important interpretation at 5, 19, 91, 452, 488, 490, 491–4, 497, 524, 529, 536–9.

[98] *Magnae devotionis inditium*, 15 March 1198 (*Reg. Inn. III*, i. #100 at 101; X. 3.34.7; 3 Comp. 3.26.3; Potthast #48). The context was the dispensing of a crusading vow. The trio is taken from Bernard, *De Consideratione*, §III.iv.15 with 1 Cor. 6: 12, 10: 22–3. For other uses by Innocent see on the imperial election in 1200/1 in *Regestum Innocentii III papae super negotio Romani imperii*, ed. Friedrich Kempf, Miscellanea Historiae Pontificiae 12 (Rome, 1947), #29 at 77 and regarding Ingeborg of Denmark and Philip Augustus, *Reg. Inn. III*, xi. #178 (183) at 292. Comment in Cheney, 'Letters of Pope Innocent III' in his *Medieval Texts and Studies*, 16–38 at 35, and on Hostiensis's gloss Kenneth Pennington, *Prince and the Law: Sovereignty and Rights in the Western Legal Tradition* (Berkeley, Calif., 1993), 61–4.

later eleventh and earlier twelfth century ecclesiastically was that during this period the papacy was principally preoccupied with establishing some specific norms for the episcopacy (celibate, non-simoniacal, and a clerically distinct *ordo*).[99] Commentators stressed bishops' liturgical and moral qualities, 'rather than their duty of supervising their inferiors in the hierarchy and managing the affairs of their dioceses'.[100] A distinct approach is apparent from the later twelfth and early thirteenth century which can be exemplified by a 1205 letter of Innocent III to Peter des Roches. Addressing the new Bishop of Winchester as a *rector*, Innocent stressed that 'it is incumbent on a ruler to ensure that he should skilfully guard against being negligent—God forbid— in those matters which relate to his administration, since cursed is the man who does the work of God negligently'.[101]

The later period was more preoccupied with working out the implications of that *ordo* and institutionalizing it. Part one of 'Gratian's' *Decretum*, at D. 21–101, has been called a 'mirror for bishops', but it is not structurally concerned with the organizational relations of bishops and others.[102] By contrast Huguccio of Pisa (d. 1210) was concerned with this when he clarified that only by papal delegation could a bishop be judged.[103] The wider question of how to ground norms of episcopal conduct is well illustrated by the contemporary comment of those who felt distinctly ambivalent about the relationship between the spirit and the letter that institutionalized it.[104] That medieval ambivalence now has its place in the modern historiography with the thesis arguing for a transition from a twelfth-century episcopacy concerned

---

[99] e.g. Gregory VII (*Register*, 2.64, 25 March 1075) calling the Abbot of St Denis to account for his alleged simony; generally see I. S. Robinson, 'The Institutions of the Church, 1073–1216', in David Luscombe and Jonathan Riley-Smith (eds.), *The New Cambridge Medieval History*, iv. c.*1024*–c.*1198 Part 1* (Cambridge, 2004), 368–460 at 432–45.

[100] Robinson, 'Institutions of the Church', 442–3.

[101] *Reg. Inn. III*, viii. #145 (144); *Innocent III English Letters*, #23 at 79; Potthast #2594, alluding to Jer. 48: 10.

[102] Jean Gaudemet, 'Patristique et pastorale: La Contribution de Grégoire le Grand au « Miroir de l'Évêque » dans le Décret de Gratien', in *Études d'histoire du droit canonique dédiées à Gabriel Le Bras*, 2 vols. (Paris, 1965), i. 129–39.

[103] Pennington, *Pope and Bishops*, 75–6, 79–80, on Huguccio, 81–5.

[104] e.g. *The Arundel Lyrics* and *The Poems of Hugh Primas*, ed. and trans. Christopher J. McDonough, Dunbarton Oaks Medieval Library 2 (Cambridge, Mass., 2010), Arundel lyrics ##24 (against episcopal degeneration), 25 (against Bishop Manasses of Orléans, 1146–85), 26 (against the corruption of the Curia, esp. Franco, *camerarius* of Alexander III, 1174–9), 27 (in praise of an unknown English bishop); Peter of Blois, *Tractatus de institutione episcopi* in *PL*, 207, cols. 1097–12 and Ep. 14, 150 (*PL* 207, cols. 42–51, 439–42), for discussion Lachaud, *Éthique du pouvoir*, 158–9, 260–2; Bernard of Clairvaux, *De moribus et officio episcoporum* (letter 42) in *S. Bernardi opera*, vii.100–31, and on this Damien Boquet, 'Le Gouvernement de soi et des autres et selon Bernard de Clairvaux. Lecture de la lettre 42, *De moribus et officio episcoporum*', in Claude Carozzi and Huguette Taviani-Carozzi (eds.), *Le Pouvoir au Moyen Âge* (Aix-en-Provence, 2005), 279–96. See also *Petri Cantoris Parisiensis Verbum adbreviatum*, ed. Monique Boutry, Corpus Christianorum Continuatio Mediaevalis 196 (Turnhout, 2004), 361–81, 'De officio praelatorum et quid eis ex officio incumbat', and 'Contra negligenciam prelatorum' (§1.54–5). Cf. the 1283–4 *Liber de prelato* of Salimbene de Adam (on Elia da Cortona) in his *Cronica*, ed. Giuseppe Scalia, 2 vols. Scrittori d'Italia 232–3 (Bari, 1966), i. 136–239. A short, fourteenth-century approach is Bishop Simon Ghent of Salisbury, *Meditatio de statu prelatu*, in BL Royal MS 5 C III, fo. 301 (*Solus aliquociens sedens*). See Kathleen Edwards, 'Bishops and Learning in the Reign of Edward II', *Church Quarterly Review* 138 (1944), 57–86; William A. Pantin, *The English Church in the Fourteenth Century* (Cambridge, 1955), 111–12.

with spiritual and moral integrity to a thirteenth-century one more preoccupied by merely 'administrative' capabilities.[105] The thesis has its roots in twelfth-century sources, with Bernard of Clairvaux's *De consideratione* the classic expression of considered regret for the propensity of ecclesiastical administration to reproduce itself gratuitously.[106] But Bernard's view can be readily contrasted with other prelates' documented pride in their administrative capabilities.[107] Certainly the definitions of good bishops varied, both within and across communities. Philip II and Peter the Chanter disputed about whether the quality of French prelates had declined since the early Middle Ages.[108] The Paris schools were bothered more generally about the right contours of episcopal character—notably the question of how to distinguish between ideal prelates and princes.[109] For themselves, the English could not decide about Hubert Walter. Was he a good archbishop, or illegally transgressing cap. 12 of the Third Lateran Council by holding secular office?[110] This chapter opened with Gerald of Wales finding fault that Hubert Walter's profile did not conform to Gerald's idealized outline. The point of Gerald's outline was that a correlation with it should produce good prelates. Gerald's test was fallible though. Stephen Langton fitted the profile—but Langton was sufficiently inattentive to pastoral care to be reproached for

---

[105] Marion Gibbs and Jane Lang, *Bishops and Reform 1215–1272: With Special Reference to the Lateran Council of 1215* (Oxford, 1934), may represent analysts who find the thirteenth-century episcopate too bureaucratic (see 174–9). A far subtler version is Brentano's *Two Churches*. Cheney, by contrast, argued for substantive improvements from *c*.1150, and held the 'bureaucratic' Hubert Walter in high regard (*From Becket to Langton*, 32–41, 154, and *Hubert Walter*, 181–6). See also Pantin, *English Church in the Fourteenth Century*, 9–26. For negative judgements conscious of their own preferences, see Brentano's reflections in *Two Churches*, 353–80, esp at 362, 371, 377 on Gregory IX, Celestine V, and the conventual Franciscans. Aaron Hope, 'Hireling Shepherds: English Bishops and their Deputies *c*.1186 to *c*.1323' (Ph.D. thesis, UCL, 2013) is a major re-evaluation of diocesan administration.

[106] A recent analysis following this theme is Elaine Graham-Leigh, 'Hirelings and Shepherds: Archbishop Berenguer of Narbonne (1191–1211) and the Ideal Bishop', *EHR* 116 (2001), 1083–1102, counterpointing a twelfth-century diocesan, administrative ideal against a later twelfth/thirteenth-century papal, spiritual ideal. Cf. Constance Brittain Bouchard, *Spirituality and Administration: The Role of the Bishop in Twelfth-Century Auxerre* (Cambridge, Mass., 1979), 139–44.

[107] Suger, *Œuvres*, i. 54–154; *Chronicle of Jocelin*, *passim*. For other examples see François Louis Ganshof and Adriaan Verhulst, 'France, the Low Countries and Western Germany', in M. M. Postan (ed.), *The Cambridge Economic History of Europe*, i. *The Agrarian Life of the Middle Ages*, 2nd edn. (Cambridge, 1966), 291–339 at 320–1, 323 (Meinhard of Marmoutier, 1132–46; Henry and Baudouin of Sint-Bavo, Ghent in the early thirteenth century; Hugues-Varin at Liessies (Hainault); Willem van Rijckel at Sint-Truiden 1249–72 (Liège)).

[108] Delisle, 'Etienne de Gallardon', 23–4. Comment in John W. Baldwin, *Masters, Princes and Merchants: The Social Views of Peter the Chanter and His Circle*, 2 vols. (Princeton, NJ, 1970), i. 170–1. Compare the, possibly confected, 1194 view of Jean Bellesmains, Archbishop of Lyons, who retorted to English episcopal complaints about Richard I's exactions that, compared to Philip Augustus, Richard was a 'hermit': William of Newburgh, *Historia rerum Anglicarum* in *Chronicles of the Reigns of Stephen, Henry II and Richard I*, ed. Richard Howlett, RS, 4 vols. (London 1884–9), ii. 421–2 (§5.3). Comment in Jörg Peltzer, 'Les Évêques de l'empire Plantagenêt et les rois angevine: un tour d'horizon', in Martin Aurell and Nöel-Yves Tonnerre (eds.), *Plantagenêts et Capétiens: confrontations et heritages*, Histoire de Famille. La parenté au Moyen Âge 4 (Turnhout, 2006), 461–84 at 461–42.

[109] See e.g. Nigellus de Longchamp, *Tractatus contra curiales et officiales clericos*, i. 176, 199 (*c*.1193 to William Longchamp, Bishop of Ely and chief justiciar, who had served Geoffrey of York). Comment and further references: Baldwin, *Masters, Princes*, i. 161–6, 170–2, 186–97.

[110] See William of Newburgh's positive and Roger of Howden's negative judgement, analysed in Gillingham, 'Historian as Judge', esp. 1277–81.

it by Honorius III.[111] Any absolute prescription of sanctity and learning as the necessary and sufficient predicates of episcopal excellence is demonstrably false. Likewise the presumption that administrative ability connotes pastoral death: it would be a mistake to see any absolute transition from unregulated charisma to bureaucratized pastoral oversight. The *acta* and biography of St Hugh of Avalon, Bishop of Lincoln, demonstrate that there was no necessary contradiction between a more spiritual charisma and administrative, even fiscal ability—it is Hugh who leaves the earliest extant set of synodal statutes.[112] Robert Grosseteste or Eudes Rigaud would likewise disprove any presumption that charismatic pastoral care fitted a single holy shape, in which 'mere' administration was a source of indifference. Louis IX may make the point for charisma and institutionalized secular accountability.[113]

De bonis uel malis episcopis multum disputandum est.[114] Manifestations and perversions of good episcopal conduct varied with the beholder. Timothy Reuter's maxim on kings is also applicable to bishops: so to be a bishop was 'not simply a matter of status or of action, but also of style', and consequently a 'social construct'.[115] Robert Brentano's incisively analysed the 'total styles' of the English and Italian churches in this periods, arguing that 'thirteenth century English saints

---

[111] Reg. vat., xi. fo. 222, 'Miramur plurimum', 26 March 1222 (*Reg. Hon. III*, ii. #3891). David Carpenter has argued that Langton's own conduct reflected no high ideals, at least in relation to the 'Mandeville debt': 'Archbishop Langton and Magna Carta: His Contribution, His Doubts and His Hypocrisy', *EHR* 126 (2011), 1041–65.

[112] 'Decreta domini Hugonis Lincoliniensis pontificis', in Howden, *Gesta regis Henrici secundi*, i. 357. See also Mayr-Harting (ed.), *St Hugh of Lincoln*, v–vi, and in the same volume, David M. Smith, 'Hugh's Administration of the Diocese of Lincoln', 19–47, esp. 40–5. For Brentano, Hugh exemplified 'with misleading precision the change from one sort of prevailing religious sentiment to another, from the hair shirt to the shepherd's crook, from the twelfth to the thirteenth century' (*Two Churches*, 176).

[113] See Grosseteste's mandates, visitations, and statutes in *C&S*, ii.1. 201–5, 261–78, and his conception of such activity in letter #127, in *Roberti Grosseteste, episcopi quondam Lincolniensis, epistolae*, ed. H. R. Luard, RS (London, 1861), and a further defence of his position ('propositum') at Lyons (1250) in Servus Gieben (ed.), 'Robert Grosseteste at the Papal Curia, Lyons 1250. Edition of the documents', *Collectanea Franciscana* 41 (1971), 375–7; James Herbert Strawley, 'Grossteste's Administration of the Diocese of Lincoln', in D. A. Callus (ed.), *Robert Grosseteste, Scholar and Bishop: Essays in Commemoration of the Seventh Centenary of his Death* (Oxford, 1955), 146–77 and Adam J. Davis, *The Holy Bureaucrat: Eudes Rigaud and Religious Reform in Thirteenth-Century Normandy* (Ithaca, NY, 2006), esp. 176–9. Administration as a means of pastoral care, then, did not necessitate spiritual emasculation, but note Brentano's comment that 'Grosseteste's sanctity *could* be built into institutions, made to do an orderly job' (*Two Churches*, 222, my stress, and in contrast to St Francis). What is interesting about all these individuals is the way they used institutional means as vehicles for pastoral care, and the way in which their charisma was understood through such activity. For Louis IX, see Joinville, *Histoire de saint Louis*, ed. M. Natalis de Wailly, 9th edn. (Paris, 1921), chs. 140–7 and here pp. 126–7, 256–7.

[114] For the diversity of various groups of bishops see e.g. Morris, *Papal Monarchy*, 219–26, 527–35; Gibbs and Lang, *Bishops and Reform*, part 1 and App. C. A more recent *tour d'horizon* of the Angevin episcopate 1150–1204/6 is Peltzer, 'Évêques de l'empire Plantagenêt'; also Paul B. Pixton, *The German Episcopacy and the Implementation of the Decrees of the Fourth Lateran Council, 1216–1245: Watchmen on the Tower*, Studies in the History of Christian Thought 64 (Leiden, 1995), table C, 195–202.

[115] '*Regemque, quem in Francia pene perdidit, in patria magnifice recepit*: Ottonian Ruler Representation in Synchronic and Diachronic Comparison', in Timothy Reuter, *Medieval Polities and Modern Mentalities*, ed. Janet L. Nelson (Cambridge, 2006), 127–46 at 128–9, with comments on bishops at 129 n. 6, 138.

were in fact bishops. In Italy [. . .] the bishop and the saint were different things. The [Italian] saint was a saint [. . .] because he was not what a bishop seemed to be in Italy. England was Martha and Italy was Mary.'[116] Episcopal preaching was a central definition of a good bishop in Italy, pastoral care was in England; registering documents was an English practice, but not generally an Italian one; the English had 'manor bishops', the Italians 'local' city-bishops; the English scholar-bishops, the Italians largely not; the English, episcopal registers, the Italians, largely not.[117]

Any idea of a bishop was the result of hammering a relatively malleable set of moulded parts into a character of one's preference. The idea of pastoral responsibility was a longstanding focus however. Isidore of Seville's definition expressed a well-established ideal:

> The term episcopacy [*episcopatus*] is so called because he who is placed over it has oversight [*superintendere*], exercising pastoral care, that is, over his subjects, for the term σκοπειν in Latin means 'watch over' [*intendere*]. Bishop then, in Greek, means 'overseer' [*speculator*] in Latin, for he is set over the Church as an overseer. He is so called because he keeps watch [*speculari*], and oversees [*praespicere*] the behaviour and lives of the people placed under him.[118]

Norms would be an important way of internalizing the conscience of such responsibility—as Hugh of Avalon said on his deathbed to Hubert Walter. But such internalized self-coercion would be erratic. Hugh also granted as much about his own conduct. How much more erratic then across all Christendom's prelates? In this context it is an interesting feature of Bernard of Clairvaux's *De consideratione* that his exhortation to the Bishop of Rome to right conduct avoids the presumption that the content of episcopal/papal duties (*officia*) is a sufficient guide to such right conduct.[119] Bernard wished to see worldly, administrative activities—including all tallying and totting—distanced from episcopal duties.[120] 'How', not just 'what', mattered.[121] If one was concerned with some sort of consistency, this created a regulatory problem, at least practically. Conscience alone was inadequate; yet bare functional description was insufficient. Could a single procedure help to regulate the same officers through their accountability when those offices might exist quite distinctively in different parts of Christendom?

---

[116] Brentano, *Two Churches*, 222, using Grosseteste and St Francis as exemplars of the ideal types. On criteria for choosing prelates and their qualities, see Salimbene de Adam, *Cronica*, i. 173–90, 200–4, 207–11.

[117] Brentano, *Two Churches*, ch. 3, esp. 183–4, 206–7, 211–13, 217, 221; on records, ch. 5, e.g. 291–4.

[118] *Etymologies of Isidore*, 171 (§VII.xii.9–12). This idea is picked up by Bernard in *De consideratione*, §II.vi.10 where he discusses episcopal eminence as a function of the need to oversee.

[119] This is partly because Bernard wishes to criticize many of those damaging activities that have become associated with ecclesiastical/papal office. This is reflected in his use of terms such as *occupatio*, *negotio*, *opus* (*De consideratione*, §§II.xiv.23; IV.iv.9; IV.iv.12). *Officium* is used (e.g. *De consideratione*, §§II.vi.10; III.v.19) but it does not seem a favoured term.

[120] Bernard, *De consideratione*, §IV.vi.19.

[121] Cf. Bernard Williams, 'Professional Morality and its Dispositions', in his *Making Sense of Humanity and Other Philosophical Papers 1982–1993* (Cambridge, 1995) at 200.

Canonical inquisitions were a clever, sophisticated, and seemingly simple solution. (Though Bernard can scarcely be expected to have approved of the consequences, given his criticism of ecclesiastical litigiousness.[122]) But if norms and functions of episcopal office provided for what bishops should do (*deceat*), there was no necessary reason why episcopal accountability to the papacy should be taken as a given. Establishing the norm that bishops were thus accountable (*liceat*) was an act of political coercion itself, by the papacy, on bishops.

Securing Accountability: liceat *and* expediat

The need for episcopal responsibility was a theme of longstanding importance in the Western Church beyond Isidore.[123] The generally disastrous social effects attributed to the 'negligent bishop' were identified as the tenth of the 'twelve abuses of the age', in an early eighth-century Irish text attributed to Cyprian.[124] Abbatial responsibility had figured prominently in Gregory the Great's *Pastoral Care*,[125] and Bernard of Clairvaux would transpose it to the Bishop of Rome himself.[126] 'Gratian's' *Decretum* left the precise question of the accountable relationship between pope and bishops open to interpretation.

Even if episcopal responsibility was a longstanding *desideratum*, episcopal accountability to the papacy was a contested value that needed to be established. Lateran IV cap. 8 used Luke 16 as a proof text on the obligations of clerics and bishops to account for their offices, like the unjust steward in the parable. The ruling drew a comparison between bishops and mere estate managers, *villici*. In so doing, at the largest council of bishops and other prelates then ever held, *Qualiter et quando* definitively established as an axiom of episcopal accountability what was once a controversial equation of prelates and bailiffs. One hundred and fifty years earlier Luke 16 would have looked less like a *proof* of bishops' liability to account and more like a disproof of such liability, for all bar the most committed to ideas of terrestrial accountability.[127] Then Gregory VII came under sustained criticism for seeking to 'remove the anointed of the Lord like bailiffs by common lot as often

---

[122] Bernard, *De consideratione*, §III.ii.
[123] Jean Gaudemet, 'Charisme et droit: le domaine de l'évêque', *ZRG Kan. Abt.* 74 (1988), 44–70; Steffen Patzold, *Episcopus: Wissen über Bischöfe im Frankenreich des späten 8. bis frühen 10. Jahrhunderts*, Mittelalter-Forschungen 25 (Ostfildern, 2008); Donald Edward Heintschel, *The Mediaeval Concept of an Ecclesiastical Office: An Analytical Study of the Concept of an Ecclesiastical Office in the Major Sources and Printed Commentaries from 1140–1300* (Washington, 1956). For representations of bishops see Eric Palazzo, *L'Évêque et son image: L'Illustration du pontifical au Moyen Âge* (Turnhout, 1999).
[124] Ed. in Siegmund Hellmann, 'Pseudo-Cyprianus, *De xii abusivis saeculi*', *Texte und Untersuchungen zur Geschichte der altchristlichen Literatur* 34 (Leipzig, 1910), 1–60 at 53–6. For *episcopi negligentes* in ninth-century Francia see de Jong, *Penitential State*, 114–15, 183.
[125] For discussion of some relevant Benedictine aspects see pp. 203, 217. For a twelfth-century application 'de incuria praelatorum', see Bernard of Clairvaux, *Apologia ad Guillelmum Abbatem*, in *S. Bernardi opera*, iii. 103 (§XI.27). Jean Gaudemet in 'Patristique et pastorale' argued that Gregory was particularly important to Gratian in producing *Decretum*, D. 21–101 on episcopal conduct.
[126] Bernard, *De consideratione*. See esp. the emphasis on stewardship versus lordship at §III.i.2.
[127] It is interesting to find in Wulfstan of York's *Institutes of Polity* a reference to bishops as beadles (*bydelas*) which the *Toronto Old English Dictionary* translates here as 'preacher, minister of the Gospel',

as pleased'.[128] There might be precedents that could be pointed to, but episcopal accountability to the papacy was not established as a unarguable norm.[129] It looked distinctly unnatural to Wenrich of Trier. For Liemar of Bremen, accountability was something a *potens* expected of a *pauper* (see pp. 42–3). It was certainly *infra dignitatem* for a bishop; even a bailiff, Robert of Chilton might argue (pp. 26–9).[130] Even worse, *Qualiter et quando* enabled inquisitions into prelates to be triggered by a *clamor* from anyone, regardless of their official status, even if mindful of their social standing.[131] Yet, the proof texts that the Curia eventually settled on as scriptural models for *inquisitio veritatis*—Sodom and Gomorrah, Christ's words himself in Luke, even Adam and Eve in Eden—*were* powerful totems for papal authority.[132] This 'theory in practice' can be seen at the end of the twelfth century, set out by Celestine III in his preambles to the letters in Geoffrey of York's case.[133]

The citation of Luke 16 specifically in this context is more apposite still. The parable of the unjust steward concerned menial administration. In *Qualiter et quando* Innocent both reminded prelates that they were mere *villici* and at the same time specified as a remedy only the loss of their administrative/temporal powers—at least initially.[134] This was not a new moral. As Bernard of Clairvaux stressed to the Pope himself in the mid-twelfth century, the *villa* is to the *villico*, but he is not the *dominus*. So the Pope should go out into the field of the Lord, 'not as a lord, but as a steward, to see and provide that you call to account where you should'.[135] The corrective medicine prescribed under Innocent III was a treatment, not a purgative (perhaps he had learnt the

---

but which in other Old English contexts can mean 'overseer, officer', as it does in *Rectitudines singularum personarum*. Cf. *Die «Institutes of polity, civil and ecclesiastical»: ein Werk Erzbischof Wulfstans von York*, ed. and trans. (into German) Karl Jost, Schweizer Anglistische Arbeiten 47 (Berne, 1959), 62 (cap. 5) with the *Rectitudines* in F. Liebermann (ed.), *Die Gesetze der Angelsachsen*, 3 vols. in 4 (Halle, 1903–16), i. 451 (§18).

[128] Wenrich of Trier, *Epistola*, in MGH, *LdL*, i. 289, ll. 34–5.

[129] See Gelasius I, 'Quid ergo isti', on Rome's power to punish bishops (496), *Acta Romanorum Pontificum a S. Clemente I (An. c. 90) ad Coelestinum III († 1198)* (Rome, 1943), #188. Cf. Nicholas I, 'Proposueramus quidem' (865), #322.

[130] Cf. the stress placed by Gregory the Great on obedience in (especially but not only) monastic contexts: Carole Straw, *Gregory the Great: Perfection in Imperfection* (Berkeley, Calif., 1988), 84–9. Good and bad flow up the chain, but the liability to account is extracted from inferiors by superiors, not vice versa. The stress caused in tensions between lay attempts to discipline criminous clerics was of course significant. For an earlier twelfth century dispute about lay versus clerical accountability, see the interesting dispute at Winchester about Roger of Salisbury's arrest and the seizure of his castles by Stephen in 1139: William of Malmesbury, *Historia novella*, ed. Edmund King, trans. K. R. Potter, OMT (Oxford, 1998), 48–59, including Roger's contemptuous rejection of the idea that he was a salaried *serviens* or *minister* of Stephen and hence accountable as such (56).

[131] On 'Gratian's and later assaults against the idea that only those of the same hierarchical level could accuse bishops, see Ronald Knox, 'Accusing Higher Up', *ZRG Kan. Abt.* 77 (1991), 1–31.

[132] *Constitutiones Concilii quarti Lateranensis*, 54–7. See further *Summa 'omnis qui iuste iudicat' sive Lipsiensis*, ed. Rudolf Weigand, Peter Landau, Waltraud Kozur, et al., Monumenta iuris canonici, Ser. A: Corpus glossatorum 7 (Rome, 2007), i. 1 (preface). Further references (into the seventeenth century) in Pennington, *Prince and the Law*, 142–5, 162, 200, 228, 252, 264, 274.

[133] Thinking especially of 'Mediator Dei et' and 'Cum sacrosancta Romana', Howden, *Chronica*, iii. 279, 312.

[134] *Constitutiones Concilii quarti Lateranensis*, 56, 'quatenus si fuerit grauis excessus, etsi non degredetur ab ordine, ab amministratione tamen amoueatur omnino'.

[135] Bernard, *De consideratione*, §§III.i.2 and II.vi.12, 'non tamquam dominus, sed tamquam villicus, videre et procurare unde exigendus es rationem'.

lesson Gregory VII would not).[136] An example is provided by the 1232 inquisition into Heinrich I von Müllenark, Archbishop of Cologne. During that investigation Gregory IX had it proclaimed that the Archbishop was not to alienate any church property—jerking back his administrative leash.[137] *Qualiter et quando*'s sanctions were produced by a calculus of risk and damage that had clear political preferences built into it.

How did the papacy get to the point where Luke 16 seemed to be a normal rather than abnormal rule with which to secure episcopal accountability? The case of prelates and bishops seems a particular, ecclesiastical instance of a wider twelfth-century phenomenon. That phenomenon was twelfth-century institutions' general attempts to aggrandize their power and assert it as 'public', which produced a need for their officers' conduct to be consonant with their aspirations or pretensions. For the Church, episcopal accountability emerged as a corollary of its pastoral interest in others. Hugh of Lincoln's synodal statutes of 1186 (by *c*.1192 in Roger of Howden's account), described how Hugh, 'while in his episcopal office, built up the people entrusted to him by his conduct and through the word of fatherly exhortation, and by the power of obedience ordered in his synods, both the whole clergy and the people subject to him, to observe these decretals inviolably'.[138] The Bishop of Lincoln's synodal canons were the statutory expression of concern for those he was responsible for as a reflection of his concern for his own self and duties. Self-images and ideas of responsibility paved the way for practices of accountability.

The conditional algebra linking prelates' spiritual accountability and the conduct they themselves required of others was a commonplace of the period.[139] Innocent III seems to have felt it particularly strongly.[140] A 1213 letter illustrates the point to an English addressee in an important idiom. Writing to Stephen Langton and other English bishops, the Pope warned

> Brother bishops and archbishop, you should so strive to guard both yourselves and the flocks which have been entrusted to you, by ripping out vice and planting down virtues, so that on the very last day of the exacting examination, before the awful judge, 'who will render to each according to his works', you may render a worthy account.[141]

---

[136] Cf. Tillmann, *Innocent III*, 'willingly practiced mildness where he hoped to attain his end without severity', 'Innocent's reforms do not aim at subverting existing conditions, but they do try to obviate the dangers resulting from them and to diminish their bad consequences', (respectively 208, 211).

[137] 'Cum olim in', clearly indicates the canonical inquisitorial process following Lateran IV, *Epistolae saeculi xiii e regestis pontificum Romanorum*, ed. C. Rodenberg, MGH Epistolae, 3 vols. (Berlin, 1883–94), i. #529 (28 May 1233). See also i. ##459, 472, 520, 523, 530, 532, 540, 579, 637, ii. #50; *Reg. Greg. IX*, i. ##748, 828, 1214, 1233, 1347, 1355, 1362, 1366, 1371, 1378, 1380, 1381, 1384, 1419, 1847; *Chronica regia Coloniensis (Annales maximi Colonienses), cum continuationibus in monasterio s. Pantaleonis scriptis*, ed. G. Waitz, MGH, SRG 18 (Hannover, 1880), 263, 264, 272. Comment: Michael Matscha, *Heinrich I. von Müllenark, Erzbischof von Köln (1225–1238)*, Studien zur Kölner Kirchengeschichte 25 (Siegburg, 1992), 153–73; Pixton, *German Episcopacy*, 390–1.

[138] Howden, *Gesta regis Henrici secundi*, i. 357.

[139] e.g. numerous biblical episodes in the later thirteenth-century *bible moralisée* BL Additional MS 18719 are interpreted as lessons for prelates and stress this theme. Thus on fo. 296ʳ Paul's account of a man taken up into the third heaven (2 Cor. 12: 2) signifies that prelates who rule and teach others should surpass them in their conduct so as to be easier models for imitation.

[140] Expressed powerfully in Innocent III's 'salt' sermon on the consecration of pontiffs, *PL* 217, *Sermones de diversis*, #4, cols. 666–72; more routinely, 'Querelam Thome militis', *Innocent III English Calendar*, #954 at 266 (3 March 1214).

[141] 'Ei qui non' (6 July 1213), *Innocent III English Letters*, #54 at 153 (Potthast #4777), alluding to Romans 2: 6. Cf. *Innocent III English Letters*, #56 at 156 (15 July 1213), 'Quartodecimo die Iulii'

Even Gerald of Wales's 'unlearned' Hubert Walter had absorbed this idiom, an internalized sense of temporal responsibility achieved by envisaging an ultimate spiritual accountability. In a 1203/4 ordinance for Christ Church Canterbury, Walter, as Archbishop, set out rules and regulations for reducing priory staff and for appointing and dismissing them. His *exordium* describes how all should be attentive to the 'day of the Lord which will come like a thief' and which

> should be especially attended to by those whom God has set and established over others, either with a share of responsibility or in fullness of power, so that they should strive to make provision for the sheep entrusted to them in such a way that on the day of their stewardship [*in die villicationis sue*] the strict judge need not repay them for their negligence or sloth but with a celestial reward for their earthly care and work.[142]

Accidentally or deliberately, here the key office (*villicatio*) from Luke 16's scriptural proof has become the sign of accountability itself. In setting out which Canterbury offices are to be abolished, Walter repeatedly refers to requirements which the 'common utility' exacts of him and of all those at Canterbury. It is with reference to such *utilitas* that Walter holds Canterbury to account, a duty his own accountability (here, to God) pragmatically necessitates.

Such thinking reflects the establishment of a reciprocal connection between prelates' assertion of power and their meriting of authority. This not quite per se to establish episcopal *accountability* as a norm. It was a small step to go on to do so though, and to apply some sanction on bishops if it was thought they were not behaving in a meritorious way. Ecclesiastical order, as Hubert Walter said, needed to be public and useful.[143] Indeed these two aspects might well be synonymous, the useful being definably what was more in the public rather than private interest.[144] (Celestine asked if Geoffrey of York was *utilis*, though Gerald of Wales thought prelates attended too much to the wrong sort of 'useful'.) It was entirely fitting in this context that episcopal conduct that was both scandalous and public should be deemed intolerable. The idea of *excessus* as the transgression of official powers has been noted already. Its crucial role here as a premise for papal intervention has been demonstrated by Bruno Lemesle.[145] Part of its resonance came from the expansiveness of its meaning (as perhaps with the modern totem of 'accountability'). The

---

to Stephen Langton; 'In corrigendis excessibus' alluding to Ezekiel 3: 18–20, 33: 6–8, to Peter des Roches *c.*27 October 1205 (*Reg. Inn. III*, viii. #147 (146); *Innocent III English Calendar*, #647); or indeed the opening of cap. 7 on the correction of *excessus* at Lateran IV (*Constitutiones Concilii quarti Lateranensis*, 53–4).

[142] *Canterbury, 1193–1205* ed. C. R. Cheney and Eric John, EEA 3 (Oxford, 1986), #389 at 58–9 (March 1203–March 1204). See 1 Thess. 5: 2, 2 Peter 3: 10. The final clause enjoining obedience also invokes the accountability of Judgement Day.

[143] Cf. e.g. Alexander III, 'Inter caetera sollicitudinis', *PL* 200, col. 930 (Jaffé #12254, part included in X 1.17.3). Cf. also X 3.24.2, where Alexander III in 'Fraternitatem tuam credimus' warns the Bishop of Paris of the need to be a *procurator* not a *dominus*.

[144] For the malleable idea of *utilitas* in later medieval theology and political thought see M. S. Kempshall, *The Common Good in Late Medieval Political Thought* (Oxford, 1999) *s.v.*; in medieval rhetoric see Kempshall, *Rhetoric and the Writing of History, 400–1500* (Manchester, 2011), *s.v.*; in the *ius commune* see Ennio Cortese, *La norma giuridica: spunti teorici nel diritto comune classico*, 2 vols. (Milan, 1962–4) i. 105, 128, 185–7, 264–9 and *s.v.* For Hostiensis see Pennington, *Pope and Bishops*, 108, and 'A *Quaestio* of Henricus de Segusio and the Textual Tradition of his *Summa super decretalibus*', *Bulletin of Medieval Canon Law* 16 (1986), 91–6.

[145] Lemesle, 'Corriger les excès'.

connected idea of infamy was consequently an immensely useful way of literally publicizing such behaviour.[146] Julien Théry suggests we should speak here of *fama* societies, as distinct from honour societies.[147] The scandalizing of some 'public' became a determinant of investigation by the church into its erring agents. But the avoidance or removal of scandal was the principle thing. The inquisitorial technique formalized in Lateran IV cap. 8 enshrines this principle, saying inquisitions are to be undertaken except where great damage is done for the sake of a small gain.[148] Addressing a *scandalum* should not exacerbate that same scandal. Such logic was more generally apparent in ecclesiastical governance. Two letters of Gregory IX can make the point. In 1237 the Pope sought to shore up the impoverished see of Dunblane but only if it could be rectified without grave scandal to the episcopate.[149] The following year, Gregory likewise hazed his English legate, Cardinal Otto di Monteferrato, away from acting against pluralist clerks with powerful families, lest it disturb the kingdom and produced scandal.[150] This was a politic accountability.

This concern with scandal and active investigation of it meshed with the emerging idea that 'it is in the public interest that crimes should not go unpunished' (*rei publica interest, ne crimina remaneant impunita*).[151] This Roman law-influenced maxim was most influential through Innocent III's decretals, *Inauditum* and *Ut famae*.[152] Not coincidentally it occurs in the *Gesta* of Innocent—written by a curial

---

[146] See Bird, 'Wheat and the Tares'; Stern, 'Public Fame: A Useful Canon Law Borrowing'. Cf. on public belief, *publica fama*, Chris Wickham, '*Fama* and the Law' and *Courts and Conflict*, passim.

[147] Théry, '«Excés» et «affaires d'enquête»', i. 491.

[148] *Constitutiones Concilii quarti Lateranensis*, 57.

[149] 'Venerabilis frater noster' (11 June 1237), *Vetera monumenta hibernorum et scotorum. Historia illustrantia*, ed. Augustin Theiner (Rome, 1864), #91; calendared in *Reg. Greg. IX*, ii. #3742. The relevant phrase is '*si* absque gravi scandalo fieri poterit' (my emphasis).

[150] 'Cum, sicut intelleximus' (25 February 1238), Reg. vat., xviii. fo. 360ᵛ, calendared *Reg. Greg. IX*, ii. #4100.

[151] Richard M. Fraher's articles provide key reference points: 'Theoretical Justification'; Fraher, 'Preventing Crime in the High Middle Ages: The Medieval Lawyers' Search for Deterrence', in James Ross Sweeney and Stanley Chodorow (eds.), *Popes, Teachers, and Canon Law in the Middle Ages*, (Ithaca, NY, 1989), 212–33; Fraher, 'IV Lateran's Revolution in Criminal Procedure: The Birth of *Inquisitio*, the End of Ordeals, and Innocent III's Vision of Ecclesiastical Politics', in Rosalio Iosepho Castillo Lara (ed.), *Studia in honorem Eminentissimi Cardinalis Alphonsi M. Stickler* (Rome, 1993), 97–111. Cf. however Günter Jerouschek, '"Ne crimina remaneant impunita". Auf daß Verbrechen nicht ungestraft bleiben: Überlegungen zur Begründung öffentlicher Strafverfolgung im Mittelalter', *ZRG Kan. Abt.* 89 (2007), 323–37, arguing for the importance of Sichard of Cremona, Rufinus of Sorrento in developing this idea rather than Fraher's Anglo-Norman canonist, Innocent III, or Innocent III's legal advisers. The contributions of Rufinus and Abelard are stressed by Chiffoleau, '*Ecclesia de occultis non iudicat*?', 379 n. 49. Lotte Kéry noted Fulbert of Chartres's linking of *utilitas* and public punishment of crimes. See 'Ein neues Kapitel in der Geschichte des kirchlichen Strafrechts: Die Systematisierungsbemühungen des Bernhard von Pavia (†1213)', in Wolfgang P. Müller and Mary E. Sommar (eds.), *Medieval Church Law and the Origins of the Western Legal Tradition: A Tribute to Kenneth Pennington* (Washington DC, 2006), 229–51 at 247. Fulbert's words are 'Sed cum iuris sit ad utilitatem rei publicae cunctos punire maleficos', Frederick Behrends (ed.), *The Letters and Poems of Fulbert of Chartres*, OMT (Oxford, 1976), #29 at 54, On this case see Edward Peters, 'The Death of the Subdean: Ecclesiastical Order and Disorder in Eleventh-Century Francia', in Bernard S. Bachrach and David Nicholas (eds.), *Law, Custom, and the Social Fabric in Medieval Europe: Essays in Honor of Bryce Lyon*, Studies in Medieval Culture 28 (Kalamazoo, Mich., 1990), 51–71, esp. 52–3 and n. 5. I owe the latter reference to Bernard Gowers.

[152] *Inauditum hactenus speciem*, (*Reg. Inn. III*, i. #546 (549); Potthast #591), to Emeric of Hungary (4 February 1199); *Ut famae tuae* (X 5.39.35; 3 Comp. 5.21.8; *Reg. Inn. III*, vi. 181 (183); Potthast

insider–and specifically in the context of the numerous prelates the Pope removed from office.[153] Richard Fraher noted an Anglo-Norman canonist linking *res publica* and public prosecution in the 1190s, and other earlier parallels have been noted (Augustine provides a still earlier one).[154] Pennington doubts Fraher's canonist was any direct influence on Innocent III.[155] The question of 'originality' is one issue; more relevant here is the linking of the idea with practices. The Anglo-Norman canonist's formulation may then be especially interesting. Autonomously of papal reflection, it seemed a good idea in Anglo-Norman circles to link the prosecution of crime with some idea of public interest, and therefore of regnal activity. Pennington has stressed the importance of linking a Romanizing idea of 'public interest' with a duty of prosecution, and that particular terms connoted an especial public duty to do so (such as the use of the 'public' term *crimen*).[156] But it does not seem to have been necessary that the idea *had* to be formulated in a 'maxim [that] is the product of a skillful blend of Roman law and the common presumptions of the age'.[157] It is obviously clear that it should be the stronger for having been. But it seems simpler to assume a social-political need was groping for some pithy, compelling formulation, than that the discovery of a Romanizing formulation met a hitherto unperceived need. Well after the 1215 promulgation of *Qualiter et quando* it is possible to find instances where the principle of *ne crimina* is cited but the resonant, public, term of *crimen* has slipped away. At the August 1231 Council of St Quentin, lest *maleficia* (not *crimina*) *remaneant impunita* is cited as justification for ensuring that crimes committed in one diocese should not be evaded by an offender jumping into another.[158]

#2038) to Andreas, Archbishop of Lund (10 December, 1203). The Roman borrowing is from the Digest's reference to the *Lex aquila* at 9.2.51. See Kenneth Pennington, 'Innocent III and the Ius Commune', in Richard Helmholz, Paul Mikat, Jörg Müller, and Michael Stolleis (eds.), *Grundlagen des Rechts: Festschrift für Peter Landau zum 65. Geburtstag, Rechts- und staatswissenschaftliche Veröffentlichungen der Görres-Gesellschaft 91* (Paderborn, 2000), 349–66. I use Pennington's online version of this at http://faculty.cua.edu/pennington/Medieval%20Papacy/InnocentIuscom.htm, accessed February 2014.

[153] 'Hic, ad reformationem et correctionem excessuum vigilanter intendens, visitatores prudentes per diversas provincias delegabat, per quos faciebat diligenter inquiri de statu et conversatione, non solum Ecclesiarum, sed etiam praelatorum; et, quos inveniebat culpabiles, a suis praelationibus protinus removebat, nolens crimina relinquere impunita. Quot [corr.] enim praelatos a suis dignitatibus deposuerit, enarrare quis posset?', *PL* 214, col. clxxii.

[154] Fraher, 'Theoretical Justification', 590. This *Summa 'Induent sancti'* has been part edited by Fraher for the 'Monumenta iuris canonici, Ser. A: Corpus glossatorum'. The Stephan Kuttner Institute of Medieval Canon Law plans to complete the edition. Augustine: *De civitate dei*, §19.6, and see p. 258 for Augustine.

[155] See his 2009 online paper, 'Prosecution of Clerics in Medieval Canon Law', the relevant webpage of which is http://faculty.cua.edu/pennington/KansasFourthLateran/KansasFourthLateran.html, accessed February 2014; Jerouschek, '"Ne crimina remaneant impunita"'.

[156] Pennington, 'Innocent III and the Ius commune', at nn. 20–3 in the online version.

[157] Pennington, 'Prosecution of Clerics in Medieval Canon Law' at http://faculty.cua.edu/pennington/KansasFourthLateran/KansasFourthLateran.html.

[158] *Archives administratives de la ville de Reims, collection de pièces inédites, archives administratives*, ed. Pierre Varin, 8 vols. (Paris, 1839–53), i.2. #118 at 556 = *Les Actes de la province ecclésiastique de Reims*, ed. T. Gousset, 4 vols. (Reims 1842–4), ii. 357–63 at 361. See also *maleficia* used thus in the key 1231 text *Parens scientiarum* regulating the University of Paris, specifically regarding the Bishop's disciplinary powers over students, *CUP*, i. #79 at 138.

Formulae can be useful because they amplify the resonance of what one wanted to say anyway. On 7 July 1215, ignorant of what had been signed at Runnymede on 15 June, Innocent III berated Langton and the other English prelates for insufficient support of the papal mandate of 19 March in favour of John against the barons. Here Innocent invoked the Pseudo-Isidorian critique of passive connivance in wrongdoing whereby 'the suspicion of hidden complicity cannot be avoided by someone [i.e. the prelates] who recoils from obstructing flagrant wrongs' (*quia non caret scrupulo societatis occulte qui manifesto facinori desinit obviare*).[159]

There are, furthermore, instances where the content of *rei publica interest, ne crimina remaneant impunita* was articulated without its form. Alexander III provides an instance. In April 1177 Roger Archbishop of York wrote to Bishop Roger of Worcester. The Archbishop ordered Roger to despoil Master Hugh of Southwell of the churches of Epperton and Shelford on account of Hugh's use of forged papal letters to the Archbishop. The letter's core is the mandate from Alexander III to do so, on the basis that 'it is therefore required of us to punish such a serious misdeed most gravely, so that others should dread to attempt similar things, having the example of this punishment' (*igitur decet nos tam gravem excessum durius vindicare, ut alii exemplo pene illius similia attemptare formident*).[160]

The development of these norms provided prelates with the felt reason for imposing order on and exact accountability from their subordinates and their flocks. That at once explains not just where the demand for inquisitorial procedure came from, but also in part why the imposition of it by superiors was conceded. The right to exact such powers empowered all prelates, given both that they always had lesser clergy beneath them and the rise in the powers of pastoral care. The *quid pro quo* was that everyone had some superior who could exact accountability back. The logic of this meant in the case of the Bishop of Rome that his answerability and authority would again become a question of increasing controversy as the thirteenth century wore on. But even if the supply and demand for mechanisms of prelates' accountability can be explained like this, it risked that hierarchy itself, since how was the papacy to haul bishops and archbishops over the coals without undermining the integrity of the ecclesiastical hierarchy as a whole?

SOCIOLOGICAL ASPECTS OF CANONICAL INQUISITIONS

A sociological exploration of a canonical inquisition can help to answer this, by focusing on the social structures and institutional tensions that the procedure was

---

[159] *Decretum*, D. 83.3, 86.3, C. 2.7.55; *Innocent III English Letters*, #80 (7 July 1215) to Peter des Roches at 207; also *Constitutiones Concilii quarti Lateranensis*, cap. 71 at 115.

[160] *York, 1154–1181*, EEA 20, #110A at 125. The incipit for Alexander's letter is *Ex constanti relatione*. For a similar idea see Innocent's 'In corrigendis excessibus' to Peter des Roches *c.*27 October 1205 (*Reg. Inn. III*, viii. #147 (146); *Innocent III English Calendar*, #647); Further, Charles Duggan, 'Decretals of Alexander III to England', *Decretals and the Creation of 'New Law' in the Twelfth Century*, no. III, #404.

intended to navigate.[161] Even with the norm established that bishops were accountable (*deceat* so to speak), it remained very tricky to institutionalize it formally (*liceat*) in a way that was both practicable and did not undermine other aspects of the church hierarchy (*expediat*). An inquisition from the other end of the thirteenth century, long after the technicalities of the procedure had been developed, can provide the focus: the 1301–3 inquisition into Walter Langton, Bishop of Coventry and Lichfield.

If we return to *Qualiter et quando*, its explicit concern was clerical accountability, its rubric: 'how and in what way a prelate ought to proceed to investigate and punish the offences of his subjects'. The target then was principally a person—although, as the early commentators noted, inquisitions could also be *de statu ecclesiae*.[162] These clerics were secular ones. As an early commentary noted, there were other ways of regulating those in monastic orders.[163] The canon was framed with two distinct objectives in mind and with enormous sensitivity to their potential effects.

The first objective was the regulation of clerical *excessus*. *Excessus* was clearly linked with the insolence of office (not acting *insolenter* was important).[164] The second objective simply qualifies the first very heavily: the regulation of *excessus* should not itself hazard further the Church's stability—'Let careful precaution nevertheless be taken in all cases lest serious loss is incurred for the sake of a small gain [in reprimanding an individual].' The above analysis has shown why inquisitorial procedure should be a cause for hierarchical concern. It was a tender point.[165] The legislation therefore had to achieve a very fine balance between securing the demands of ecclesiastical, pastoral *sollicitudinem* and of ecclesiastical *utilitudinem*.

Qualiter et quando is a clever solution to this problem. It expresses a feeling for hierarchy that practically qualifies clerical status while upholding its form in principle. This may be less contradictory than it sounds. Take Mary Douglas's argument for a more flexible definition of hierarchy than historians or social scientists often use:

> Hierarchy is *not* a vertical command structure dominated by an up-down pattern of communication. It is not a system requiring unquestioning deference to arbitrary fiats issued from above... [H]ierarchy restricts position, it institutes authority. Its institutions

---

[161] I am using 'institutional' in the sense of social practices here, although it has obvious connections with the organizations and groups around bishops (their and other prelates' *familiae*, cathedral chapters, the Curia, etc.).

[162] Vincentius Hispanus, *Apparatus in concilium quartum Lateranense*, in *Constitutiones Concilii quarti Lateranensis*, 299.

[163] *Casus anonymi fuldenses* in *Constitutiones Concilii quarti Lateranensis*, 485.

[164] See Lemesle, 'Corriger les excès', 754–60. For a parallel example of official *excessus* linked to the duty of correcting superiors see Jocelin of Brakelond's (fl. 1173–*c*.1215) passage where Ranulph Glanvill berates the monks for permitting Abbot Hugh to appoint town reeves without their counsel (thus allowing the king to claim that right during the abbacy's vacancy). This licence by Hugh is described as *excessus*. Jocelin explicitly notes the tension between monastic obediency to prelates and correcting superiors since Glanvill 'non advertens quod monachorum summa religio tacere est, et excessus suorum prelatorum clausis oculis preterire', *Chronicle of Jocelin*, 73. In late twelfth-century England *excessus* can be found used in relation to public wrongs—see the *Dialogue of the Exchequer* on the wrongs Henry II determines to right at the Northampton in 1176, purprestures, or the righting of other wrongs (*DS*, II.ii, II.x, II.xiii, at 77, 94, 107).

[165] As disputes about visitation rights show, in relation to Boniface of Canterbury, Robert Grosseteste, or Eudes Rigaud. See e.g. *C&S*, ii.1. 447–8, *Annales monastici*, iii. 151, 181 (Canterbury);

work to prevent concentrations of power. It is a positional system in which everyone has a place, every place has a prescribed trajectory of roles through time, in total the pattern of positions is coherent and the roles are coordinated.[166]

This may well be over-optimistic: hierarchy *may* well be characterized by what Douglas decries. Nevertheless, her description remains valuable as an ideal type, not a transhistorical norm. Taken as such, the approach to status in *Qualiter* makes sense. The formal character of ecclesiastical hierarchy is always upheld: 'not only when a subject has committed some excess [*excedit*] but also when a prelate has done so, if the matter reaches the ears of the *superior* [my stress] through an outcry or rumour [. . .] the superior should carefully investigate the truth before senior churchmen'.[167] Inquisitions are conducted by *superiores*. But *inferiores* can instigate them. *Diffamatia* can come from anywhere. It needed to come from anywhere if the insolence of office was to be moderated, otherwise the *pauperes* would fear to speak against the *potentes*.[168] Hence the canon's anxiety to put firewalls around that licence which was *Qualiter*'s central, combustible purpose.[169]

The qualifying of *superiores*' authority in *Qualiter* should therefore be taken as a necessary intrusion to counteract official *excessus*. It transgresses the ideal order in proportion to clerics' and prelates' prior exceeding of their office. There is, therefore, a symbolic logic that the reprimand for the abuse of *status* enables *inferiores* to complain against those powers ordained by God.

A further firebreak on the risk of an inquisition damaging the wider ecclesiastical fabric was provided by the canon's guidance on penalties. Innocent knows too that prelates cannot avoid being whipping boys for diocesan complaints by virtue of their office and power. Innocent also concedes how damaging to the wider edifice of the church such proceedings may be. The Innocentine emphasis on a bishop's marriage

---

Roberti Grosseteste [. . .] *epistolae*, #127; F. A. C. Mantello, 'Bishop Robert Grosseteste and His Cathedral Chapter: An Edition of the Chapter's Objections to Episcopal Visitation', *Mediaeval Studies* 47 (1985), 367–78; *The Letters of Robert Grosseteste, Bishop of Lincoln*, ed. F. A. C. Mantello and Joseph Goering (Toronto, 2010), #127, and Apps. A–B, 432–41 and Davis, *Holy Bureaucrat*, chs. 3–4.

[166] Mary Douglas, 'A Feeling for Hierarchy', in James L. Heft (ed.), *Believing Scholars: Ten Catholic Intellectuals* (Fordham, NY, 2005), 94–120 at 95–6.

[167] *Constitutiones Concilii quarti Lateranensis*, 55 (cap. 8).

[168] The same sociology lies behind the 1164 Assize of Clarendon's regulation of accusations by credible persons and empanelled jury where people do not *dare* to accuse: *C&S*, i.2. 880; further, Helmholz, 'Early History of the Grand Jury', 618–25.

[169] The issue of correcting superiors is a broader one. See Wilfried Hartmann, 'Discipulus non est super magistrum (Matth. 10: 24), Zur Rolle der Laien und der niedern Kleriker im Investiturstreit', in Hubert Mordek (ed.), *Papsttum, Kirche und Recht im Mittelalter: Festschrift für Horst Fuhrmann zum 65. Geburtstag* (Tübingen, 1991), 187–200; I. S. Robinson, '*Periculosus homo*: Pope Gregory VII and Episcopal Authority', *Viator* 9 (1978), and *Authority and Resistance* (Manchester, 1978), 124–7, 169–170; Knox, 'Accusing Higher Up'; Philippe Buc, *L'Ambiguïté du livre: Prince, pouvoir et peuple dans les commentaires de la Bible au Moyen Âge* (Paris, 1994), ch. 6 esp. 350–408, on how scriptural encouragement for the popular correction of rulers was canalized within safe boundaries during the thirteenth century. Théry notes the rarity of procedures against prelates from very lowly clerics or laity ('«Excés» et «affaires d'enquête»', i. 450). In a different field it is worth remembering that the importance of hierarchy meant a slight mental gulp was needed to grant that even a reeve was liable on complaint to 'respond to his subjects' (*respondeat subditis suis*), *LHP*, cap. 56.4, cf. 31.7; F. M. Stenton, *The First Century of English Feudalism, 1066–1166*, 2nd edn. (Oxford, 1961), 61. Obviously cf. also above, pp. 26–9.

to his diocese would also establish a presumption against the possibility of dismissing bishops.[170]

On the count of heresy Lateran IV articulates the unequivocal rule that a negligent bishop was to be deposed from episcopal office.[171] While conceding that degradation should not immediately follow from non-heretical inquisitions, *Qualiter* readily grants suspension from all administrative responsibilities.[172] As noted (pp. 159–61), it was the lesser qualities of episcopal status that were emphatically initially at risk from inquisitorial procedure.[173]

Innocent reminded the prelates that they were mere *villici* at the same time as he suggested that the loss of administrative powers might be 'all' they would face. *Qualiter et quando*'s sanctions were produced by a calculus of risk and damage which sought to balance individual punishment and collective stability.

Perhaps, however, *Qualiter et quando* was better pastoral theology than legal procedure.[174] Despite the elegance of its legal solution, when the canon turned to address the question of prelates' accountability it did so with a considerable sense of caution.

> While this [inquiring into offences] should be observed in the case of subjects, *all the more carefully* [my emphasis] should it be observed in the case of prelates who are set as a mark for the arrow [Lam. 3: 12]. Prelates cannot please everyone since they are bound by their office not only to convince but also to rebuke and indeed sometimes even to suspend and indeed often to bind. Thus they frequently incur the hatred of many people and endure plots against them. Therefore the holy fathers have wisely decreed that accusations against prelates should not be admitted readily without careful provision being taken through which the door may be closed not only to false but also to malicious accusations, lest, with the columns being shaken, the building itself collapses [Judg. 16: 30]. They thus wished to ensure that prelates are not accused unjustly in such a way that at the same time they take care not to sin in an arrogant

---

[170] See the 21 August 1198 decretal *Quanto personam venerabilis* (3 Comp. 1.5.3; X 1.7.3; *Reg. Inn. III*, i. #335), and commentary in Pennington, *Pope and Bishops*, 16, 38, 112. The tension between immovability and modern conceptions of removable officials is noted in Udo Wolter, 'Verwaltung, Amt, Beamter, V–VI', in Otto Brunner, Werner Conze, and Reinhart Koselleck (eds.), *Geschichtliche Grundbegriffe: Historisches Lexikon zur politisch-sozialen Sprache in Deutschland*, 8 vols. in 9 (Stuttgart, 1972–97), vii. 32.

[171] *Constitutiones Concilii quarti Lateranensis*, 49 (cap. 3).

[172] *Constitutiones Concilii quarti Lateranensis*, 56 (cap. 8).

[173] *Dignitas auctoritatis* was for a bishop, *dignitas amministrandi* was for a bishop *and* for lesser officials. See *Die Summa decretorum des Magister Rufinus*, ed. Heinrich Singer (Paderborn, 1902), 151–3, ad. *Decretum*, D. 60 (*Ecce ex parte*). Discussion: Robert L. Benson, *The Bishop-Elect: A Study in Medieval Ecclesiastical Office* (Princeton, NJ, 1968), 65–6. Cf. Wolter, 'Verwaltung, Amt, Beamter, V–VI', 30, on Johannes Andreae's 1298 distinction between *dignitas* (of one who having administration has jurisdiction); *personatus* (one who has pre-eminence but not jurisdiction), and *officium* (pertaining to those having ecclesiastical administration but without jurisdiction or pre-eminence).

[174] A complementary analysis is Fraher's 'Preventing Crime in the High Middle Ages', especially his emphasis on expediency (231). The same concern with setting a balance between superiors' rights and wrongs to inferiors is visible in Lateran IV cap. 12's principle in relation to monastic visitations 'quia sic uolumus superiorum iura seruari, ut inferiorum nolimus iniurias sustinere' (*Constitutiones Concilii quarti Lateranensis*, 61). Much historiography has concentrated on the legal status of inquisitorial procedure—e.g. Kéry, '*Inquisitio—denunciatio—exceptio*', argues these actions, although not formally criminal, increasingly functioned as such (266–8).

manner, finding a suitable medicine for each disease: namely a criminal accusation that aims at loss of status, that is to say degradation [i.e. cancellation of clerical status], shall in no way be allowed unless it is preceded by a charge in a lawful form.[175]

The caution is explicable. This is an exceptionally clear expression of the papal desire to integrate the appropriate (*deceat*), the feasible (*liceat*), and the politic (*expediat*). The ethical imperative behind holding prelates to account for their excesses is uppermost. But there is the sheer problem of how an under-resourced, relatively immobile Curia could realistically aspire to hold prelates to account across Christendom. Realizing this jurisdiction practically requires that the policing of delicts be delegated, just as with papal judges-delegate more generally.[176] Indeed when canonical inquisitions are triggered by action *at* the Curia, papally appointed inquisitors are simply a species of papal judge-delegate (as in the case of Geoffrey of York). Even the nature of the knowledge that could provide a satisfactory criterion for triggering an inquisition would remain to be specified. The solution, adopting *infamia* and *scandalum* as the touch-paper for sparking inquisitions, was as inspired as it was problematic.

It was inspired because it was a solution which made a virtue of necessity. Surveillance was 'outsourced' and secured by using the sheep to watch the shepherd. It was inspired because it was a flexible, *local*, and, strikingly, subjective measure.[177] It was also problematic: to initiate an inquisition into a prelate on the basis of *publica fama* was to institutionalize a subjective measure as the criterion for legal proceedings. *Deceat* and *expediat* are knotted at the heart of the formula that renders inquisitions of this sort possible (*liceat*). 'Communities' or, more neutrally, groups, determined whether its clergy's faults and failings were intolerable enough to produce a *scandalum*. There is no objective metric for that.[178]

---

[175] *Constitutiones Concilii quarti Lateranensis*, 55–6 (cap. 8).
[176] See in general, Jane E. Sayers, *Papal Judges Delegate in the Province of Canterbury 1198–1254* (Oxford, 1971).
[177] I stress 'local' because this partly qualifies R. I. Moore's sharp contrast between the justice of the 'little community' and the justice of the lord. For Moore, justice belonged 'either to the little community of custom, tradition and face-to-face authority, or to the large one of written law, literacy and the clerks'. Moore implicitly sees the change from the former to the latter as a largely bad thing for communities. His analysis is not dissimilar from Bisson's in *Crisis of the Twelfth Century*, but he draws the opposite inference. For Bisson such changes are implicitly a good thing. Inquisitions (qua Lateran IV cap. 8), however, offer, at least in principle, a mediate case between those two mutual exclusives of 'community' and 'public authority'. They are mediate because they both rely on 'central' papal or episcopal authority for their resolution, and on 'local' demonstrable *scandalum* for their trigger. This is notable since Moore sees Lateran IV specifically as marking the closing phase of his *First European Revolution* in which the little community distinctly loses out to a hardening world of bureaucrats and inquisitors. See *First European Revolution*, 170, 174. Moore's contrast anyway risks sentimentalism about that little community. See Edward Peters, 'Moore's Eleventh and Twelfth Centuries: Travels in the Agro-literate Polity', in Michael Frassato (ed.), *Heresy and the Persecuting Society in the Middle Ages: Essays on the Work of R. I. Moore* (Leiden, 2006), 11–29, at 27. For the opposite risk of idealizing government see below pp. 248–53.
[178] In several important articles Julien Théry has stressed the subjectivity of canonical inquisitions from the opposite direction: that they provide enormous discretion, not so much to the communities

The early commentaries on Lateran IV presumed two important things in this context. The first was a presumption, already noted, in favour of inquisitions being sparked by some person(s) *actively* initiating the case (*cum aliquo instigante*), despite the ostensible point of inquisitions being to investigate crimes without any such activity. The general presumption of the legal commentaries made shortly after Lateran IV was that, despite *clamor*'s provision of an inquisition's formal motive power, that there would be someone instigating it.[179] Inquisition became a relatively risk-free way of accusing someone to all intents and purposes. As Lotte Kéry has pointed out, the membrane separating the related legal proceedings of accusation, inquisition, and exception was in fact highly permeable.[180] The second presumption of early Lateran IV commentators and which qualified the first, was that any complainant would be from the affected community.[181]

The problematic aspects of this canny solution are brought out further by reflecting on the rationality of what was permitted to spark *Qualiter et quando*-type inquisitions. The canon said,

> But when because of their excesses someone will be notorious such that now an outcry rises up which cannot be ignored any further without scandal or tolerated without danger, then without the slightest hesitation, let action be taken to inquire into and punish his excesses, not out of hate but rather out of charity.[182]

There is a functional logic here. (It is clear why an inquisition should be conducted if communities/solidarities are this upset.) Yet, despite the canon's earlier warning about unfounded allegations, these criteria offer no guidance on whether a group's upset is rational, proportionate, or real. From this perspective an inquisition is carried out whenever enough (of the right sort of) people think it ought to be. That is justification enough. It makes political sense. The collapse of relations between groups (indicated by *clamor* and *scandalum*) proves an investigation should be held. The logic is not quite 'no smoke without fire', but rather 'if you have smoke you have a problem'. Thereafter an inquisition proceeds on formally rational grounds. (There

---

instigating the inquisitions, but to the judge evaluating whether the *infamia* was *infamia* or the offence offensive. This is true, but it also seems to me that communities similarly obtained some subjective latitude to judge or assert whether a cleric was scandalous, a latitude that was as open to abuse as the judge's discretion, and on which I comment shortly. See Julien Théry, '*Atrocitas/enormitas*. Esquisse pour une histoire de la catégorie d'«énormité» ou «crime énorme» du Moyen Âge à l'époque moderne', *Clio@Themis: Revue électronique d'histoire du droit* 4 (2011), 1–48, at 30–6; Théry, '*Fama*: L'Opinion publique comme preuve judiciare: Aperçu sur la révolution médiévale de l'inquisitoire (XIIe–XIVe siècle)', in Bruno Lemesle (ed.), *La Preuve en justice de l'Antiquité à nos jours* (Rennes, 2003), 119–47, esp. 119–20, 132–5, 141; Théry, '«Excés» et «affaires d'enquête»', i. 470–1, 475, 487–93. Vallerani stresses both, *Medieval Public Justice*, 38–9, 106–13; see also Stern, 'Public Fame: A Useful Canon Law Borrowing', esp. 671–2. On the importance of the community as judge, 'the hidden foundation of all legal systems in practice', see Alexander Murray, *Suicide in the Middle Ages*, ii. *The Curse on Self-Murder* (Oxford, 2000), 452–82 (quote 468).

[179] See Johannes Teutonicus, *Apparatus in concilium quartum Lateranense*, and Vincentius Hispanus, *Apparatus in concilium quartum Lateranense* on an *impetrator* (in *Constitutiones Concilii quarti Lateranensis*, respectively 197–201, 298–303, both *passim*).

[180] Kéry, '*Inquisitio—denunciatio—exceptio*', 267.

[181] *Apparatus in concilium quartum Lateranense* in *Constitutiones Concilii quarti Lateranensis*, 201 (Johannes Teutonicus); 300 (Vincentius Hispanus).

[182] *Constitutiones Concilii quarti Lateranensis*, 56 (cap. 8).

are headings of complaint: they are investigated by competent judges; the proceedings are formal, with certain summary qualifications.) They can, though, be initiated on non-rational or incoherent grounds. The fact that the inquisition must be then conducted on rational grounds (technically at least) is intended to ensure the rationality of the overall process. Practices of accountability vary in where they are at their most subjective. Judgements on sheriffs were at their most unpredictable (political or 'irrational' if you will) in the final assessment of how much a sheriff might be actually expected to pay straight away: 'where financial matters were concerned, judgement in a court simply meant a judicial reinforcement of the King's will'.[183] Canonical procedure arguably risked being most subjective or unpredicable at the point where the inquisition was triggered. Parallel observations of politicized inquisitorial techniques have been made about non-ecclesiastical examples.[184]

A pragmatic cost–benefit analysis accompanied the 'no serious loss for the sake of a small gain' rule. This produced an in-principle inconsistency between a mere cleric's *excessus* and a prelate's. The former might merit investigation, although a prelate's might not—because the relative 'loss' might be more serious. This law was a respecter of persons. The practical value of this for communities was that it both laid the burden of policing the system on them and required them to determine transgressions by unavoidable reference to locally dominant, and acceptable, styles of being a bishop. If there was no offence taken, there was no offence. It also, however, reserved judgement on discerning a prelate's excessiveness to papal judges, or the pope himself.

That is to offer a reading of the ideal dynamics allowed by the law. But an important, actual qualification is that the offended solidarities might 'only' be competing clerical factions, not an oppressed 'little community', to use Moore's phrase. To the extent that those instigating inquisitions into prelates and clerics are themselves members of often clerical élites, the more likely they are to frame their complaints in terms that they imagined other clerical élites would take seriously. Such complaints are proportionately less 'vernacular'. Such was the case with many complaints of episcopal *excessus*, as, again, with the case of Geoffrey of York above. It was the same with Walter Langton, Bishop of Coventry and Lichfield (see pp. 173–83).

A connected problem was the fact that many inquisitorial charges were so manifold that one has the strong suspicion they are the result of such disaffected élites massing sufficient charges to make an inquisition irresistible, because clearly scandalous. Indeed the premium placed on *scandalum* as the relevant criterion for initiating an inquisition quite probably meant that contentious figures magnetically attracted multiple counts of scandalous conduct by legally informed *instigantes*. On balance this seems likely for instance regarding the multiple charges relayed by the

---

[183] J. C. Holt, *Northerners: A Study in the Reign of King John*, rev. edn. (Oxford, 1992), 182, speaking specifically about King John. Cf. Wendy Davies, 'Judges and Judging: Truth and Justice in Northern Iberia on the Eve of the Millennium', *Journal of Medieval History* 36 (2010), esp. 201–3 on the rhetorical stage management of juridical decisions, but where that may not detract from their content.

[184] Serena Morelli, '«*Ad extirpenda vitia*»: normativa regia e sistemi di controllo sul funzionariato nella prima età angioina', *Mélanges de l'École française de Rome: Moyen-Âge, temps modernes* 109.2 (1997)', esp. 472–3, 474–5.

Chapter of Laon against Bishop Anselm de Mauny 1233–7.[185] That legal procedures were used for non-legal ends is a necessary consequence of humans' use of them. The non-juridical aims of litigation is well-acknowledged in the literature. Cases might be abandoned part-way through, once some other purpose had been served.[186] Church courts, like others, could serve as a place of dispute-resolution, rather than of law-enforcement.[187] In the same way, inquisitorial procedure could be irrational yet functional, lending support to the idea that part of its usefulness to communities was the space it provided aggrieved and influential members of a diocese to express grievances about a prelate or cleric.[188] The risk of licensing this was central to what Maitland saw as the key difference between canonical inquisitions and English inquests and presentment (accusatory) juries.[189] He argued that the key thing was the way in which sworn declarations were validated by either procedure. In the common law it was taken as accusatory, and subject to scepticism accordingly. Post-1215 and the banning of ordeals a judge terminated a case with a (non-presentment) jury's verdict (a finding of fact).[190] In the romano-canonical *ius commune* it was taken as testimony with a judge using it to determine truth and give judgement.[191] Given the play made with the law in practice one may wonder how nice these distinctions are. But the model of rumours is functionally very similar between presentment jury and communal rumours ascending towards an prelate inquiring *ex officio*. Further, the scope for preliminary canonical inquiries into the standing of the *infamia* indicates too that reliance upon it was not unqualified.

The structure of inquisitions, then, both enabled subjective complaints—since it is the outraged community that effectively triggers an inquisition—while simultaneously encouraging complaints to be framed in recognizable terms—since the complaints would demonstrably need to lead to *scandalum* or *infamia* to produce

---

[185] Sabapathy, 'Accountable *rectores* in comparative perspective: the theory and practice of holding *podestà* and bishops to account (late twelfth to thirteenth centuries)', in Agnès Bérenger and Frédérique Lachaud (eds.), *Hiérarchie des pouvoirs, délégation de pouvoir et responsabilité des administrateurs dans l'Antiquité et au Moyen Âge*, Centre de Recherche Universitaire Lorrain d'Histoire, Université de Lorraine—Site de Metz 46 (Metz, 2012), 215–20.

[186] Brundage, *Medieval Origins of the Legal Profession*, 445–6.

[187] Charles Donahue, Jr., 'Roman Canon Law in the Medieval English Church: Stubbs vs. Maitland Re-Examined after 75 Years in the Light of Some Records from the Church Courts', *Michigan Law Review* 72 (1974), 647–716 at 706; Vallerani, *Medieval Public Justice, passim*; late thirteenth-century Bolognese patterns in Sarah Rubin Blanshei, *Politics and Justice in Late Medieval Bologna* (Leiden, 2010), 273–4, 343–4.

[188] By 'irrational yet functional' I mean that there was an incoherence between the means and ends of inquisitorial procedure (as I have demonstrated) but that the functions that it served, while inconsistent with some of those ends, are apparent and demonstrable. See further D. L. d'Avray, *Rationalities in History: A Weberian Essay in Comparison* (Cambridge, 2010).

[189] Frederick Pollock and Frederic William Maitland, *The History of English Law before the Time of Edward I*, reissued edn. by S. F. C. Milsom, 2 vols. (Cambridge, 1968), i. 151–3, ii. 656–9; *Britton*, i. 22.

[190] Pollock and Maitland, *History of English Law*, i. 139–40; Robert Bartlett, *Trial by Fire and Water: The Medieval Judicial Ordeal* (Oxford, 1986), 137–9; Paul Brand, 'The English Medieval Common Law (to c.1307) as a System of National Institutions and Legal Rules: Creation and Functioning', in Paul Dresch and Hannah Skoda (eds.), *Legalism: Anthropology and History* (Oxford, 2012), 173–96 at 177–8.

[191] Vallerani, *Medieval Public Justice, passim*.

an inquisition. Even if an inquisition was granted, however, there was still considerable latitude open to papal judgement.[192] Prior, recognized norms of being a bishop were needed in order to demonstrate their breach. The development of inquisitorial legislation then can be seen as one marker in the much longer dialectical process of articulating those norms.[193]

The sociological interpretation then is that inquisitorial procedure was a practical, inspired answer to the question of 'who will guard the guards?'. It was, though, a compromise, in that not only was there little understandable ecclesiastical appetite for radically circumscribing episcopal status, but the practical problems in enabling those inferior to bishops to complain about them were significant. It also made a virtue out of a papal weakness. Beyond prelates themselves the papacy lacked any group through whom it could supervise prelates (papal legates are a partial exception, but could not be expected to cover the ground). The reliance therefore on—in principle—local standards to determine problematic prelates (determined by judges-delegate through *scandalum* and *publica fama*, etc.) was a very intelligent one. Were the aims of the legislation met by application of the procedure in practice? Is scandal avoided and infamy controlled? Were malicious prosecutions avoided or not by the development of this sort of formidable procedure? One final example may provide an illustration of the problems.

The Inquisition into Walter Langton, Bishop of Coventry and Lichfield

The inquisition into Walter Langton stands at the opposite end of the thirteenth century to Geoffrey of York's, long after inquisitorial procedures had been fully elaborated. It is well known at one level, but its interest in relation to canonical inquisitions has been little explored.[194] Like Geoffrey of York's, the inquisition into Walter Langton involved a cleric at the heart of royal government; was based on grave allegations; was ultimately summarily dismissed; and can again be twinned with a later, separate, and better-known investigation into Langton's wrongdoings in the secular sphere.[195] Unlike Geoffrey's—and many other canonical inquisitions—Langton's case was pushed not by an unhappy ecclesiastical group, but by a knight,

---

[192] See Théry, '*Fama*: L'Opinion publique comme preuve judiciare', 131–5, 145–7.
[193] Two classic treatments are Benson, *Bishop-elect* and Pennington, *Pope and Bishops*.
[194] Julien Théry offers a complementary analysis in his invaluable *habilitation* '«Excés» et «affaires d'enquête»', which I read having substantively completed this study. I thank him again for his kindness in sending me a copy. See i. 304, 381, 403–4, 409, 411, 451, 453–4, 494, 506–7, 518, 524–5.
[195] For the chronology of the canonical inquisition see *The Register of Walter Langton Bishop of Coventry and Lichfield, 1296–1321*, ed. J. B. Hughes, C&Y 91, 97, 2 vols. (2001–7), esp. i. at xxx–xxxii, xxxv–xxxvi; Roy Martin Haines, 'Langton, Walter (d. 1321)', *ODNB*; Jeffrey H. Denton, *Robert Winchelsey and the Crown, 1294–1313: A Study in the Defence of Ecclesiastical Liberty* (Cambridge, 1980), *passim*, esp. 53–4; Alice Beardwood, 'The Trial of Walter Langton, Bishop of Lichfield, 1307–1312', *Transactions of the American Philosophical Society* NS 54.3 (1964), 1–45 at 6–8. For the secular 1307–12 trial, Beardwood, 'The Trial of Walter Langton' and *Records of the Trial of Walter Langton*, ed. Beardwood.

John de Lovetot.[196] Langton, in fact, received strong support from his chapter during the inquisition.[197]

These were the allegations against Langton:

That the said bishop was and is publicly defamed [*diffamatus*] in the Kingdom of England and elsewhere because he did homage to the Devil [*diabolo fecit homagium*] and kissed him on the back [*in tergo*], and spoke to him frequently. Item, that concerning this, here [and] among the English at the Roman Curia there was and is that public knowledge and rumour [*publica vox et fama*]. Item, that the said bishop for over two years before obtaining the said episcopate, and after obtaining it, was and is publicly and seriously defamed [*diffamatus*] throughout the Kingdom of England amongst the clergy and people, and especially in parts of London for having committed adultery with Lady Joan de Brianzon, the stepmother of the said knight [John de Lovetot] wife of the late Sir John Lovetot, justiciar of the illustrious King of England [. . . and after his death] had the said Lady Joan as his concubine publicly, and both were attached to each other publicly and she followed the said Bishop through various parts of England up to the time of her death. Item, that concerning this there was at that time and is now public knowledge and rumour [*publica vox et fama*] in the Kingdom of England and especially in [London] and even among the English at the Roman Curia. Item, he [i.e. John de Lovetot, Jr.] intends to prove that the said Bishop before he acceded to the said episcopate and after was and still is publicly and seriously defamed in the Kingdom of England and especially in parts of London that, in order to more freely contract the bond of fornication with the said Lady Joanna, at an opportune time, together with the said Lady Joanna, slew, strangled, and killed the said Sir John her husband, sleeping, at night, at home, and in his own bed. Item, that concerning this it was and is the public knowledge and rumour [*publica vox et fama*] in the said places and among the English at the Roman Curia. Item, he [i.e. John de Lovetot, Jr.] intends to prove that the said lord Bishop before obtaining the said episcopate, and after obtaining it, was and is publicly and seriously diffamed in the Kingdom of England for simoniacal depravity, and that he has committed many wrongs [*mala*] by himself and through others against clerics and ecclesiastical persons and places of those parts, against ecclesiastical liberty and even by going against constitutions of the holiest father Pope Boniface VIII. Item, that concerning this there was and is the public knowledge and rumour in those parts and among the English at the Roman Curia. Item, that he intends to prove that the said Bishop before his promotion to the said episcopate held very many benefices, having care of souls, and he held these dignities without the dispensation of the Apostolic See. Item, that concerning this the same Bishop is publicly defamed in the said parts.[198]

This admixture of 'official' and personal crimes comprised the inquisitorial articles relating the allegations against Langton. It barely needs stressing

---

[196] On Lovetot's namesake father, Paul Brand, 'Lovetot, Sir John de (b. in or before 1236, d. 1294)', rev. *ODNB*.

[197] *Register of Walter Langton*, i. at xxxvi n. 122.

[198] Reg. vat., l. fos. 279ᵛ–280ʳ, *articuli* appended to 'Ad audientiam nostram' (1 March 1302). The text of *Reg. Bon. VIII*, #5012 (Potthast #25129) has several omissions, including the most lurid aspects; Winchelsey also omitted the articles from his recapitulation in his 16 February 1303 'Sanctissimo patri in' (*Registrum Roberti Winchelsey*, ii. 648–52). The letter indicates Joan was dead by March 1302 although Brand, 'Lovetot, Sir John de (b. in or before 1236, d. 1294)' states she died around August.

that the articles are at almost 'maniacal' pains to specify the public *fama* about Langton, its persistency, its occurrence both before and after his election, and the nature of crimes pertaining to clerical office (simony, pluralism) while also bringing his holding of it into disrepute more personally (concubinage, fornication, murder, perverse diabolism).[199] Boniface VIII sent the articles on 1 March 1302 to the inquisitors Robert Winchelsey, Archbishop of Canterbury, Thomas Jorz, Dominican Prior in England, and Hugh of Hartlepool, Minister of the English province of the Franciscans.[200]

Analysis of Langton's inquisition requires resketching the chronology of events. By 6 February 1301 repeated rumours and allegations against Langton were circulating at the Curia, provoking Boniface to summon Langton personally.[201] At this stage the rumours were not linked to anyone; Lovetot went unmentioned. On 6 February Boniface ordered Langton to appear at the Curia within three months. On 1 May Winchelsey issued this citation directly to Langton.[202] On 10 May Langton received it; on 26 May Winchelsey issued his *certificatio* recounting the events to date and his compliance with Boniface's orders.[203] Meanwhile Boniface appears to have written to Winchelsey demanding why he had not acted on the allegations against Langton. At least, on 5 June Winchelsey wrote defending himself.[204] By August the deadline for appearing at the Curia had expired; but at the end of August Langton was in York. By the end of 1301 he was in France.[205] A supportive letter of Queen Margaret may date from this period.[206] She appealed for Langton's excusal from personally justifying himself at the Curia 'not least because it would threaten manifold danger and intolerable loss not only for the Lord King, but also for the whole kingdom'. Langton manages her estates which 'had he abandoned, he would have left us all at sea, without direction, since no one knows these estates like him'. Langton 'is deemed the very king's right eye', and 'royal affairs are ruled through him before all others'.[207] Between January and May Langton was at the Curia. Certainly royal letters supporting Langton reached Boniface before March since he mentioned them on 1 March 1302 in 'Ad audientiam

---

[199] 'Maniacal' is Jacques Chiffoleau on such contexts, 'Dire l'indicible. Remarques sur la catégorie du *nefandum* du XIIe au XVe siècle', *Annales: Économies, Sociétés, Civilisations* 45, (1990), 289–324 at 305.

[200] Hugh of Hartlepool died before the investigation was complete: *Registrum Roberti Winchelsey*, ii. 648; *Reg. Bon. VIII*, #5239. On Hugh see Jeremy Catto, 'Hartlepool, Hugh of (*c*.1245–1302)', *ODNB*.

[201] 'Grave nimis non', *Chronicon de Lanercost M.CC.I.–M.CCC.XLVI.: e codice Cottoniano nunc primum typis mandatum*, ed. Joseph Stevenson, Bannatyne Club 65 (Edinburgh, 1839), 200–1, also reproduced within Winchelsey's 26 May 1301 letter to Boniface certifying that he has acted in accordance with the Pope's instructions (*Registrum Roberti Winchelsey*, ii. 600–1). The two editions have multiple variants between them and a composite reading is necessary.

[202] *Registrum Roberti Winchelsey*, ii. 601, 'Litteras apostolicas nuper'.

[203] *Registrum Roberti Winchelsey*, ii. 600–1, 'Litteras apostolice celsitudinis' is the incipit of the overall *certificacio* containing the other letters.

[204] *Registrum Roberti Winchelsey*, ii. 602, 'Sinistra quorundam suggestio'.

[205] Counting from his receipt of the citation in early May. His itinerary is given in *Register of Walter Langton*, ed. Hughes, ii. App. D. For this period see 210–11.

[206] *The Liber epistolaris of Richard de Bury*, ed. N. Denholm-Young, Roxburghe Club (Oxford, 1950), #447 at 316–17, 'Altis ad sancte'.

[207] *Liber epistolaris of Richard de Bury*, #447 at 317.

nostram'.²⁰⁸ By then one inquisition into Langton's *infamia* had already been carried out. The *articuli* quoted on p. 174 were its product, the result of a preliminary test of the *infamia*, compiled by the Franciscan Gentile da Montefiore, Cardinal of Saint Martin in the Mountains, interviewing the English *curiales* at the Curia.²⁰⁹ They signal that inquisitorial matters had taken a clear turn *cum promovente* since Boniface says the articles are at Lovetot's *petitionem et instantiam*. With Lovetot acting as an active and supporting *promotor*, 'Ad audientiam nostram' suspended Langton and, on the basis of Gentile's inquisitorial findings, appointed Winchelsey, Jorz, and Hartlepool as Langton's inquisitors in England. A striking feature of the letter is Boniface's unease in openly describing the detailed charges against Langton, arguably a sign of their seriousness. One aspect, the kissing of the Devil's 'back', would reappear as a key feature in the inquisitorial trial of the Templars.²¹⁰ (And Boniface would have problems of his own with allegations of diabolism.) On 30 March Boniface appointed three Lichfield canons as procurators during Langton's suspension. Possibly their competence and closeness to Langton implies he had some influence over the Pope's selection.²¹¹ On 6 April 1302 Boniface ordered the inquisitors to examine the witnesses Lovetot would provide.²¹² The same day he wrote to the King asking him 'not to have ill-will or rancour against [Lovetot], lest he, for fear of you, cease from pursuing this business and the truth be hidden'.²¹³ In May Langton was in France, but was back in London for the July–August parliament. In August, in an unlikely coincidence, Lovetot was (briefly) arrested by the King.²¹⁴ The Lichfield chapter and John Dalderby, Bishop of Lincoln, wrote in support of Langton.²¹⁵ Through August and September 1302 so too did the King, making brutal attacks on Lovetot's character in passing, Boniface's earlier plea for good-will having failed.²¹⁶ In early December Boniface, himself now frustrated with Lovetot's foot-dragging, ordered the inquisitors to compel him to produce evidence he had promised but was allegedly withholding.²¹⁷ Around then Lovetot was attacked and left for dead in St Paul's cemetery.²¹⁸ On 16 February 1303 Winchelsey, completing his inquisitorial responsibility, summarized the chain of events to date,

---

[208] Reg. vat., l. fo. 279, 'Ad audientiam nostram'. As noted, this is printed with numerous omissions and an incomplete version of Gentile's charge sheet, in *Reg. Bon. VIII*, #5012. The main letter also appears within Winchelsey's 16 February 1303 letter, 'Litteras vestre sanctitatis', but lacking the *articuli* (*Registrum Roberti Winchelsey*, ii. 648–52).

[209] Gentile was Cardinal from 2 March 1300 and became a faithful adherent of Boniface: Laura Gaffuri, 'Gentile da Montefiore (Gentilis de Monteflore)', *DBI*, liii. 167–70 at 167.

[210] *Le Dossier de l'affaire des Templiers*, ed. Georges Lizerand, 2nd edn. (Paris, 1964), 18, from the original arrest order of 14 September 1307. Philip IV alleged that initiates 'in posteriori parte spini dorsi primo, secundo in umbilico, et demum in ore [. . .] deosculantur ab ipso' [i.e. the Templar receiving the initiate].

[211] Hughes's suggestion, *Register of Walter Langton*, i. xxx.

[212] *Reg. Bon. VIII*, #4627, 'Nuper nobis per' = 'Nuper vobis [*sic*] per' as transcribed in Winchelsey's 'Litteras vestre sanctitatis' to Boniface (*Registrum Roberti Winchelsey*, ii. 651, as 'secunda bulla').

[213] *Foedera*, i.2. 939, 'Eam gerimus de'.   [214] *CR 1296–1302*, 604.

[215] *Register of Walter Langton*, i. xxxvi n. 122.

[216] *Foedera*, i.2. 943 ('Dum gemitus frequentiam', 'Non sine cordis amaritudine', both 24 August 1302); calendared with others in *Liber epistolaris of Richard de Bury*, ##78–81 at 43–4.

[217] Reg. vat., l. fos. 237ʳ⁻ᵛ; *Reg. Bon. VIII*, #4849, 'Dudum vobis per'.

[218] *Registrum Roberti Winchelsey*, i. 448–9, 'Apostolice sedis auctoritas', 20 December 1302, excommunicating the attackers.

and noted he was sending on the inquisitors' report separately.[219] It does not appear to survive. A few days later Winchelsey wrote to Edward asking for letters of safe conduct for the understandably nervous Lovetot since 'he fears danger from his opponents threatening him between here and the sea'.[220] The implication is clear that it was the journey from London (where Winchelsey wrote) to the Channel that worried Lovetot. Lovetot did not go to the Curia at Anagni.[221] In 1303, presumably before this point, Edward wrote again to Boniface in support of Langton.[222] On 8 June at Anagni Boniface, reviewing Winchelsey's inquisition, found that 'the inquisitorial witnesses have deposed nothing which has damaged you. And it seems that many of these witnessed against you with respect to the public rumour, however they added to their words that [the rumour] originated with your opponents.'[223] Boniface 'therefore, who delights especially in the fragrance of prelates' good reputation' found that Langton's, combined with the proof that Lovetot senior 'ended his days with a natural not a violent death', combined with the infamy's origination with Langton's enemies, justified ending his suspension, his office's delegation to the Lichfield canons, and the Bishop's absolution of infamy.[224] The only qualification was that Langton had to purge himself with thirty-seven other senior clerics.[225] Boniface afterwards explained his reasoning as follows: 'You would not have had to undergo purgation, but, not so much out of legal necessity as for your protection, lest you should be slandered further regarding what has been said, and subjected to the biting of thieves, we declared you had to undergo canonical purgation regarding what had been objected in the said Curia.'[226]

Langton returned home. He maintained a high position for the rest of Edward I's reign: royal ambassador to the Curia in 1305; keeper of the realm in 1306; royal executor in 1307. Between August 1307 and January 1312 Langton was caught up in Edward II's energetic prosecution of him at the Exchequer for damages to royal and other property, and for his conduct at the Exchequer as Treasurer. Eventually exonerated, Langton returned to the treasurership in early 1312, but his subsequent career was one of oscillating inclusion and exclusion from royal and ecclesiastical favour.[227] He died in 1321.

---

[219] 'Litteras vestre sanctitatis', *Registrum Roberti Winchelsey*, ii. 652.
[220] 'In negotio inquisicionis', 20 February 1303, *Registrum Roberti Winchelsey*, ii. 773.
[221] He is held contumacious for his absence in Reg. vat., l. fos. 332ᵛ–333, 'Dudum ad audientiam', 8 June 1303. *Reg. Bon. VIII*, #5239 has been cut and gives the incipit as 'Propter quod nos', but this is to start some way into the letter.
[222] 'Anxietatis nimiae torquemur', *Foedera*, i.2. 956, trans. *CR 1302–1307*, 81–2.
[223] Reg. vat., l, fo. 333 (*Reg. Bon. VIII*, #5239).
[224] Reg. vat., l. fo. 333 (*Reg. Bon. VIII*, #5239).
[225] Reg. vat., l. fo. 333 (*Reg. Bon. VIII*, #5239). Cf. 'Inter sollicitudines nostras' (X 5.34.10) requiring the Dean of Nevers to have fourteen compurgators. See Théry, '*Atrocitas/enormitas*', 35; Hirte, *Papst Innocenz III*, 142–4; R. H. Helmholz, 'Crime, Compurgation and the Courts of the Medieval Church', *Law and History Review* 1 (1983), 1–26 at 17 cites Antonius de Butrio *Commentaria* (Venice, 1578), at 102ʳ (#24); Cynthia J. Neville, 'Homicide in the Ecclesiastical Court of Fourteenth-Century Durham', in *Fourteenth Century England* 1 (2000), 103–14; Kéry, '*Inquisitio—denunciatio—exceptio*', 261–6.
[226] Reg. vat., 50, fo. 333 (*Reg. Bon. VIII*, #5239).
[227] See Haines, 'Langton, Walter (d. 1321)', *ODNB*; Beardwood, 'The Trial of Walter Langton, Bishop of Lichfield, 1307–1312', *passim*.

178 *Bishops*

Langton's 1301–3 inquisition can serve as a way of reviewing the dynamics of episcopal accountability by the end of the thirteenth century, as institutionalized through canonical inquisitions.

First, inquisitorial procedure was exceptionally flexible, as others have recently argued.[228] Its procedural boundaries readily blurred with others. It was a properly mixed action, so to speak. The case begins in 1301 as a citation of Langton to the Curia ('Grave nimis non immerito'). Boniface does not at this stage make any clear allusion to inquisitorial procedure; he simply orders Winchelsey to cite Langton to the Curia.[229] It seems possible in principle that at this stage the proceedings could develop *per notorium* or *per inquisitionem*.[230] Nevertheless a number of the keynotes of inquisitorial procedure are present—*excessus* by prelates, the threat of *scandalum*, the need for superiors to act on persistent rumours, a *clamor* validated by repetition.[231] It seems that Boniface's initial citation was *not* an inquisition with someone instigating it (*cum aliquo promovente*)—that is, the initial *fama* seems not to have been 'helped' by Lovetot or anyone else, as was permitted procedurally. This had happened by the time that Cardinal Gentile carried out his preliminary inquisition, as detailed in 'Ad audientiam nostram', where Lovetot is acting as *promotor*. The importance that *inquisitionis promotor* could assume is a further illustration of a functional smudging specifically between inquisitorial and accusatorial procedure.[232] But an inquisition *cum aliquo promovente* was a wholly orthodox way of running an inquisition even though the basic inquisitorial logic was that (in the words of Lateran IV cap. 8) *fama* and *clamor* acted as *actor* and *iudex*.[233] Determining whether an inquisition was *cum aliquo promovente* was one of the first things Johannes Teutonicus said was necessary in an inquisition in his commentary on Lateran IV cap. 8.[234] Functionally Lovetot was an accuser, with the important proviso that since he was not one formally, he avoided the risk of the *poena talionis* associated with making such serious charges. Lovetot's role as *promotor* furthermore was essential to the case's

---

[228] Théry, '*Atrocitas/enormitas*'; '*Fama*: L'Opinion publique comme preuve judiciaire'; and '«Excés» et «affaires d'enquête»', i. *passim*, esp. 60–1, 477–8, 530–3; Kéry, 'Inquisitio—denunciatio—exceptio'; Vallerani, *Medieval Public Justice*, 35–44, stresses differences within a set of similar practices.

[229] Contrast e.g. the case against Anselm de Mauny, Bishop of Laon, where Gregory IX's 4 January 1233 letter of inquisition, 'Quia potestatem ligandi', very clearly quotes from *Qualiter et quando: Reg. Greg. IX*, i. #1017, and cf. Lateran IV, cap. 8, *Qualiter et quando, Constitutiones Concilii quarti Lateranensis*, 54–7.

[230] On *per notorium*, see Fournier, *Officialités au Moyen Âge*, 281–3; Brundage, *Medieval Canon Law*, 144–7; cf. Pennington, *Prince and the Law*, 256–7.

[231] 'Grave nimis non', *Chronicon de Lanercost*, 200–1; *Registrum Roberti Winchelsey*, ii. 600–1.

[232] Lovetot is described as such in e.g. *Reg. Bon. VIII*, #4627; Reg. vat., l. fo. 237ʳ (calendared, *Reg. Bon. VIII*, #4849).

[233] *Constitutiones Concilii quarti Lateranensis*, 55. The procedural separation of elements was important. In 1088 Bishop William of St Calais of Durham had objected to the judicial process coordinated against him by William Rufus involving his co-bishops where he said they were simultaneously 'accusers and judges'. See further Boureau, *Loi du royaume*, 96. Cf. Vallerani, *Medieval Public Justice*, 250–2 for communal inquisitorial equivalents and for Bologna, Blanshei, *Politics and Justice in Late Medieval Bologna*, 313–20, 337–66, esp. 343–9, 364.

[234] Johannes Teutonicus, *Apparatus in concilium quartum Lateranense*, 197: 'Item. It should be distinguished whether a judge inquires *ex officio*, namely to the outcry of the rumour, or whether the judge knows the inquisition is with someone instigating it [*cum aliquo promovente*], because if

development and collapse. Such involvement illustrates the permitted potential for inquisitions to develop following a very accusatorial dynamic.

Secondly, this fact had consequence in the proliferation of allegations. Accusatory procedure had inbuilt curbs against extravagant insinuations and allegations. In the event of a failed accusation, an accuser was liable for the penalties associated with their accusations to rebound on them.[235] One effect was to prevent allegations from escalating (or getting anywhere at all). This firewall was lowered significantly for inquisitorial procedure. It is not always easy to tell how justified any litany of complaints against a prelate may be, but at the very least inquisitions permitted, arguably encouraged, the circulation of speculative allegations. It is, for instance, hard to determine whether Anselm de Mauny, Bishop of Laon in 1233 was really guilty of alienation of church property, involvement in a homicide, corruption, disciplinary failures, failure to offer the last rites, fraud, misuse of bequests, nepotism, pastoral neglect, simony, theft, and tolerance of clerics' sexual assaults on virgins, as his chapter alleged.[236] It seems reasonable to suppose that these allegations were so framed deliberately to trigger an inquisition. As they did.[237] The allegations against Langton are not so lengthy, but they compensate in gravity. The allegations of homicide and diabolic communication are the most spectacularly serious. Back-kissing would feature in Philip IV's charges against the Templars. Philip's charges were anatomically more precise, the Templars' kissing of the 'base of the spine' a euphemism for anus.[238] Lovetot wished something similar to be understood here. The conjunction of diabolism and homosexuality was surely not accidental either. It is 'striking the frequency with which homosexual behavior comes to be identified with heresy' in this period.[239] Some scholars have thought the charges wholly implausible.[240] But such charges were dangerous. Versions of them would lead in less than a decade to the deliberate suppression and destruction of an entire religious order, using the same scandalized logic.[241] Per se the charges against Langton were neither implausible nor hard to imagine.

Infamia then was often framed in such a way as to ensure that the relevant responsible authority felt compelled to initiate investigations. In this regard it cannot be

---

he knows the inquisition is with someone instigating it, the defendant is not to be forced to swear anything by which his opponent [*adversarius*] can be benefited [*instrui*] but he himself [i.e. the judge] will summon witnesses.'

[235] See Brundage, *Medieval Canon Law*, 142-143; Kéry, '*Inquisitio—denunciatio—exceptio*'; Trusen, 'Inquisitizionprozeß'.

[236] 'Quia potestatem ligandi', *Reg. Greg. IX*, i. #1017 (4 January 1233). Théry remarks on this problem, '«Excés» et «affaires d'enquête»', i. 416–17.

[237] Sabapathy, 'Accountable *rectores* in comparative perspective', 215–20.

[238] Anne Gilmour-Bryson, 'Sodomy and the Knights Templar', *Journal of the History of Sexuality* 7 (1996), 151–83, at 156–7 esp. n. 22, 182. On the kissing specified in the French Templar initiation rite see *Dossier de l'affaire des Templiers*, 212.

[239] James A. Brundage, *Law, Sex, and Christian Society in Medieval Europe* (Chicago, 1987), 473.

[240] Michael Prestwich, *Edward I* (London, 1988), 549, but cf. T. F. Tout and Hilda Johnston, *State Trials of Edward the First*, CS, 3rd ser. 9 (1906), xxxvii, on the period's 'remarkable ingenuity in piling upon a nucleus of truth, a strange medley of hideous crime'.

[241] *Dossier de l'affaire des Templiers*, 196–203; Malcolm Barber, *The Trial of the Templars*, 2nd edn. (Cambridge, 2006), 202–16, 259–82, with his judgement on the inquisition at 283–90.

accidental that many such allegations included both personal and 'official' delicts. The former included ones that would have led culprits to serious secular proceedings without benefit of clergy. The latter were some of the most serious clerical crimes available. (As with Langton, de Mauny's *infamia* included both personal crimes and 'official' ones such as simony.) Wider categories helped to indicate the general gravity of the matter. Generically *excessus* and *scandalum* connoted a broad, emphatic sense of official transgression, incorporating personal crimes and misdemeanours.[242] The private was parsed through the official. Given the nature of episcopal office, and the period's stress on pastoral care, it is unsurprising, if distinctive, that episcopal accountability evolved in this way. As Boniface duly said regarding the 'unpromoted' allegations against Langton,

> Wherefore, led by worthy impulses and by considered zeal we are roused to hasten to apply a remedy to correct and punish the excesses of prelates as justice demands [. . .] Thus, since we did not wish, just as we ought not, to disregard such things as offend God and scandalize men by turning a blind eye, if they can be mended by the help of truth—instead of determining to proceed with skilled attention to their due punishment, according to the law as we have seen it—lest they should grow with the passage of time [. . .][243]

Langton's case may be a good example of what one could call allegation inflation, a product of the relatively safe space that inquisitions provided for the articulation of *infamia*. This was arguably the necessary cost—in this hierarchical society—of establishing a method which actually enabled senior clerics to be investigated for *excessus*.[244] On the one hand the capacity for malicious or at least exaggerated allegations as a direct side-effect of inquisitorial procedure is notable. On the other one wonders if this was inevitable when generating a complaint serious enough to have any traction against a bishop and royal treasurer.

Thirdly, therefore, the evaluation of such charges called for a discernment proportionate to their seriousness and this inflationary tendency. Throughout the trial Boniface sought to control the allegations against Langton, and to control Langton and Lovetot. In 'Ad audientiam nostram', he says 'we do not want to publish their depositions about the said bishop' arising from the case, 'but having carefully considered the nature of the matter' suspends him 'as justice requires' (*justicia exigente*).[245] Boniface adds that he will not disclose the names of the witnesses against Langton, 'with the names of the said witnesses kept absolutely out of reach of the aforementioned bishop, lest they later be liable to some danger'.[246] This was against usual procedure, but required given the Pope's

---

[242] Lemesle, 'Corriger les excès'; Helmholz, '*Scandalum* in the Medieval Canon Law'.
[243] 'Grave nimis non', *Registrum Roberti Winchelsey*, ii. 600.
[244] On difficulties with other procedures see generally Knox, 'Accusing Higher Up'; Théry, '*Atrocitas/enormitas*' and '*Fama*: L'Opinion publique comme preuve judiciaire'.
[245] *Reg. Bon. VIII*, #5012 = *Registrum Roberti Winchelsey*, ii. 649. Depositions survive occasionally. For an instance see Marie-Claude Junod, 'L'Enquête contre Aimon de Grandson, Evêque de Gènève (1227)' in *Mémoires et documents publiés par la Société d'histoire et d'archéologie de Genève*, 48 (1979), 1–182.
[246] 'Ad audientiam nostram' (*Reg. Bon. VIII*, #5012, col. 649; *Registrum Roberti Winchelsey*, ii. 650).

obligation to protect witnesses.[247] The exception may have been made because Lovetot expressed fear for himself; equally, it may have been made because Boniface was reluctant to encourage the circulation of such rumours about Langton. The assault in St Paul's implies there was some justification for the fear. Boniface was also quite careful to send the articles under his seal separately, noting this repeatedly.[248] Winchelsey was similarly careful. His enregistered copy of Boniface's inquisitorial mandate excludes Gentile's articles of inquisition (which by definition Winchelsey had received), and Winchelsey's reference to Langton's *enormia* is often allusive.[249] Similarly, when Langton wanted to disprove the charges, and so see them, Winchelsey had a copy of the witnesses' *attestacionum* made but with the witnesses' names removed.[250] Since a large part of the legal logic driving inquisitions was to avoid or eliminate *scandalum* it was sensible to minimize the repetition of the allegations. In the context of the allegations against Langton one may be eavesdropping on the uncertainty in this period about how far one should or should not specify the 'unsayable'.[251] It is also worth saying that overinflated allegations might prove counterproductive if they led to official reluctance to cause (further) scandal by disseminating them.

Partly because of this, and especially because Winchelsey's and Jorz's final report is missing, it is hard to determine what was actually made of the diabolical allegations. They explicitly figure in Boniface's *restitutio famae* of Langton.[252] But the discretion with which they were specified implies an awareness of their potency (a sensitivity perhaps shared by the modern editors of Boniface's Register). More widely their handling suggests some prior judicial selection in determining which were the most serious and credible charges here. The Curia may have been sceptical of their credibility right from the start. Certainly it is not diabolism that seemed the stickiest charge for Langton, at least so far as 'Ad audientiam nostram' goes. That letter pays more attention to the alleged homicide of John Lovetot senior. Boniface noted that Lovetot junior had produced at the Curia letters, seemingly sealed with Langton's seal, in which Langton agreed to pay this Lovetot a 'certain amount of money' so that the 'knight would not file a complaint against him concerning this', i.e. the death of the father.[253] Langton conceded that 'it did seem to be his seal, but he added afterwards that it was a fake or stolen'.[254] The charges of homicide but not diabolism

---

[247] *Constitutiones Concilii quarti Lateranensis*, 56 (cap. 8), where the canon notes that both the articles of the inquiry (so here Gentile's *inquisitio*) and the names of the witnesses and their depositions were to be given to the defendant.
[248] See *Reg. Bon. VIII*, ##4626, 4627, 4849, 5012 (4849 only in Reg. vat., l. fo. 237^{r-v}).
[249] 'Enormia': within 'Sinistra quorundam', 5 June 1301, in *Registrum Roberti Winchelsey*, ii. 602. Enregistered copy: within 'Litteras vestre sanctitatis', *Registrum Roberti Winchelsey*, ii. 648–50. Highly allusive: e.g. *Registrum Roberti Winchelsey*, ii. 651, 'predictos articulos sub bulla vestra inclusos nobis'. On *enormia*, Théry, '«Excés» et «affaires d'enquête»', i. ch. 4, esp. 441–6, arguing it is less a juridical category than a means of galvanizing a case.
[250] 'Litteras vestre sanctitatis', *Registrum Roberti Winchelsey*, ii. 652.
[251] See Chiffoleau, 'Dire l'indicible', arguing that the early fourteenth century sees a determination to say the unsayable (303). There still seems some ambivalence about doing so in Langton's case.
[252] Reg. vat., l fo. 332^v (part edn. *Reg. Bon. VIII*, #5239).
[253] Reg. vat., l fo. 279^v (part edn. *Reg. Bon. VIII*, #5012).
[254] Reg. vat., l fo. 279^v (part edn. *Reg. Bon. VIII*, #5012).

appear as the focus of debate at the Curia. In the extant documentation then, we have a picture in which charges are handled with some apparent discernment. That may support the idea that in practice inquisitions—despite the risks of summary procedure—allowed rational adjustments to be made to canonistic inquisitorial procedure. Two final aspects offer grounds for some scepticism: the wide latitude given to judges in determining judgement and the openness of cases to outside influence.

Inquisitorial procedure gave judges (e.g. Boniface VIII) enormous latitude in dealing with suspects (e.g. Langton). Boniface could decide to conduct a further inquisition having had Gentile da Montefiore's initial report. He could determine the deadlines Langton was faced with and the delegated inquisitors. If Winchelsey was an obvious lead choice he was also a very different prelate, one who poured sand where Langton poured oil in church–state relations. Finally Boniface would ultimately determine the sanctions Langton faced. In all this there was a great deal of scope for judicial discretion which might or might not be exercised equitably.

It was suggested earlier that paradoxically, in order to enable inquisitions against powerful figures, inquisitorial procedure sought to be open to questions of reputation and repute and so ran the risk that powerful people would again exert influence there. Just this happened with the royal letters on Langton's behalf to Boniface. Arguably this necessitated some judicial freedom of manoeuvre. The procedurally 'internal' question of inappropriate judicial discretion was the problematic corollary of the 'external' issue of undue outside influence in triggering and influencing an inquisition. Judges needed discretion in evaluating the potency of allegations, and their sources.[255] In 1301 Lovetot was in debt to Langton and had mortgaged property to him.[256] Further than that it is hard to fathom additional putative motives (beyond the actual claims made in the allegations). An old idea was that Winchelsey was behind Langton's inquisitions because of his opposition to royal fiscal policy, Langton's inquisitions compromising an important ecclesiastical supporter of the King. This idea has lost support.[257] During the inquisition relations between King, Pope, and Church were better than they had been during the 1297 crisis, if not uncomplicated. In January 1301 Boniface granted Edward a crusading tenth. In March he wrote off any money taken from earlier tenths but also sought repayment of the outstanding feudal census.[258] Having headed off one parliamentary crisis in 1300, at a Lincoln parliament in January 1301 the King sought a fifteenth but had to endure a detailed bill of complaint as well as specific criticisms of Langton (as Treasurer) for unjust prises and Exchequer innovations.[259] Winchelsey's own involvement in John Ferrers's 1301 attempts to recover his inheritance led to him being accused of breaking his fealty to the King for inappropriate use of church courts.[260]

---

[255] On the issue generally, Vallerani, *Medieval Public Justice*, 52–65.
[256] Beardwood, 'Trial of Walter Langton', 7.
[257] Denton, *Robert Winchelsey*, 52–4; Théry, '«Excés» et «affaires d'enquête»', i. 453–4.
[258] *Foedera*, i.2. 931, 'Celsitudinis tuae conditiones', 'Quanto erga Romanam'; Denton, *Robert Winchelsey*, 200–4.
[259] Rishanger, *Chronica*, 453–65; *Chronicle of Pierre de Langtoft*, ii. 329–34; Matthew Paris, *Flores historiarum*, ed. H. R. Luard, RS, 3 vols. (London, 1890), iii. 108–9, 303–4; Denton, *Robert Winchelsey*, 186–200; Prestwich, *Edward I*, 525–7; Maddicott, ' "1258" and "1297" ', 7–12.
[260] Denton, *Robert Winchelsey*, 205–6.

As bishop and Edward's treasurer, Langton's inquisition was an unhelpful inconvenience at a suspiciously delicate moment—a fact obvious from royal efforts to disparage Lovetot and bolster Langton.[261]

It was a necessary evil of holding prelates to account in this way at all that the procedures should be liable to outside influence and allegations like this. Manipulation was almost entailed by reliance on *publica vox et fama*. During Langton's more famous secular trials for corruption between 1307 and 1312 it certainly seems likely that Edward II's vendetta against him found further expression in unsuccessful allegations of ecclesiastical *enormia* in 1309.[262] Once the fact of any *infamia* was established its functional role was arguably over; for even if fire was undetectable, it could prove hard to shift the smell of the smoke. *Infamia* played a clear role right up to the end of Langton's 1302–3 trial when Boniface issued the *restitutio famae* with the obligation to purge himself given the allegations. Legally this may have been gratuitous if Langton had no case to answer. Politically it was vital given canonical inquisitions' aim of eliminating ecclesiastical *scandalum*.

CONCLUSIONS

Qualiter et quando stressed the elimination of scandal, the need to ensure damage was not done to the Church, the importance of regulating *excessus*, and the need to prosecute public crimes. The unfolding of the above cases however gives reason to wonder how far these aims were met by the application of inquisitorial procedure. What the legislation said it sought and what the legal practice produced might be quite different.

Episcopal accountability, as exacted by canonical procedures, helped to shape and express expectations of episcopal conduct. The dynamic through which it expressed it—coerced liability to answer public rumours—added an important colour. That colour has been occasionally lurid here and this chapter has deliberately emphasized the dexterity in procedural gymnastics demonstrated by bishops, chapters, and others in disagreements about episcopal conduct. This leaves one far from clear that inquisitorial accountability provided a satisfactory means of evaluating and then asserting a 'positive' idea or ideal of episcopal practice. This is again to point out that it seems wrong-headed to expect institutions for securing accountability to produce compelling characterizations of official conduct. They often served as substitutes when that conduct was deemed lacking.

---

[261] *Liber epistolaris of Richard de Bury*, ##78–81, 447, at 43–4, 316–17. See also *CR 1296–1302*, 602, 603–4; *CR 1302–1307*, 81–2; Lincolnshire Record Office, Episcopal Register II (Episcopal Register of Bishop John Dalderby I), fo. 31ʳ. (I have not seen Dalderby's defence of Langton.)

[262] See esp. 'Multa mentis turbatione', 5 February 1309 (Reg. vat., lvi. fo. 11ʳ; *Reg. Clem. V*, iv. #3699), ordering Langton's citation and 'Dudum ad nostri', 7 August 1309 (Reg. vat., lvi. fo. 126ʳ; *Reg. Clem. V*, iv. #4351), providing for his absolution by the Bishop of Poitiers. See also *Registrum Roberti Winchelsey*, ii. 1049–50 ('Beatitudinis vestre mandatum', 21 May 1309) complying with 'Multa mentis turbatione' and *Reg. Clem. V*, iv. #4314–15 on Langton's loan for his expenses at the Curia (July 1309). On the secular trials, see Beardwood, 'Trial of Walter Langton' and *Records of the Trial of Walter Langeton*.

Being a bishop—like being a bailiff or sheriff—then was constructed by the interaction of positive norms and coercive regulations. As in those cases, where the stress fell varied. If the Church could not rely on positive norms as a sufficient guarantee of episcopal *sollicitudo* neither could it rely on inquisitorial procedure satisfactorily to produce that sense of episcopal conduct that a Geoffrey of York seemed so spectacularly to lack. Nor could inquisitorial procedure prevent its own manipulation in the hands of inquisitorial *impetratores*, as one suspects in Langton's case. Its openness to 'manipulation' was partly how it functioned. Langton's case is problematic not because any innocence is presumed on his part, but because there are strong reasons to suppose that the allegations made against him were exaggerated. Extreme allegations signalled both the potential seriousness of the case and the potentially spurious nature of those claims. Whatever the messy truth of his relationship with Lovetot's family, Langton's Register is demonstrable proof of some routine episcopal competence on a day-to-day basis.[263] But good administration is not incompatible with homicide, back-kissing, and devil-worship, and a large part of the difficulty arising from canonical inquisitorial accountability was that its flexibility enabled both those investigating and those triggering inquisitions to indulge in questionably unaccountable behaviour. Procedurally, there does not seem to have been a conceivable alternative to reliance on local perceptions of *scandalum* and *infamia*. It was the necessary strength and the weakness of canonical inquisitorial accountability that it risked the building to test the columns on the say-so of a potentially very broad range of people. That was the cost of guarding episcopal guards at all.

---

[263] Historians have disagreed whether Langton was negligent (Haines, 'Langton, Walter (d. 1321)') or not (Hughes in *Register of Walter Langton*, i. xxxiii). The growth of episcopal delegation in this period made bishops' own absences less problematic in practice: see Hope, 'Hireling Shepherds', 78, 140–2, 228–9. Langton's concessions during the 1307–11 trial show at least that he was a deeply unethical treasurer.

5
Wardens and Fellows

WARDENS AND COLLEGES

The head of a college, its warden, was a college's principal executive officer. (The term for both institution and the officer varies. Only sometimes is it significant.) His relationship with college scholars was key to collegial accountability. Wardens of educational colleges are somewhat different from the other officers analysed here. First, those officers were less close-fitting members of communal hierarchies. Bishops obviously had hierarchies (complicated relationships with chapters; suffragans to metropolitan; all to the pope). But the inquisitorial accountability analysed especially in Chapter 4 was less institutionalized in a community than was that of wardens. Wardens' communal hierarchies were much more determinative of their accountability. It was worked out more frequently by a collective in relation to that collective. This complicated it. Monastic heads would be more comparable (models from religious orders are discussed on pp.198–205); deans might be a better fit. Collectives certainly played a role in previous examples (the communal franchise in relation to a *podestà*; the county community and Exchequer with sheriffs). But the emphasis placed on the *universitas* containing the warden is nevertheless distinctive and the reason why wardens and fellows go together here. Secondly, wardens' institutional framework was in far greater flux than that of the other officers considered here. Wardens' rights, scholars' duties, and the relation between the two varied. The constitutional structures of the universities analysed here were the product of the thirteenth century. Colleges themselves were largely a product of the second half of that century, notwithstanding monastic and charitable antecedents. As a result of both their institutional novelty and their institutional influences—as we shall see—practical thought about accountability within them was relatively variable. The plurality of the constitutional reference points pertinent to colleges could cause problems or confusion (hospitals, monasteries, friaries). Notable too is the harnessing of the *utile* in the service of the *honestum*. Colleges' purpose was to secure their founders' charitable goals. Colleges did that through the elaboration of prescriptive statutes and by verifying their application—an *utile* technique serving a *honestum* goal. As in the previous chapter we find competing ideas of *honestum* initially rather than conflicts between the *honestum* and the *utile*. (Love's absence is mourned more here than in the previous chapter; but there is no less conflict for that, frequently in relation to statutes' 'law'.) Tensions between the expedient and the ethical sneaked in through the back door—given the importance of reputation to founders and *their* aversion to *scandalum*.

The basic complication for charitable colleges with some degree of self-government was to distinguish in their hierarchical 'positional system'[1] between the interests of the permanent but impersonal foundation and those of its members—the temporary embodiments of that charitable impulse. Certainly it was an old problem for religious institutions, though founders' motivations seem to sharpen the tension for colleges. Further, their wardens were neither fish nor flesh. They were the means of securing that charitable impulse—often not recipients of it themselves. Yet they stood at the apex of the hierarchy. Consequently, wardens both held to account and were held to account. In this they were like bishops; but they did not hold so clearly a qualitatively superior position. The need to secure colleges as reliable, permanent objects of a creditable charitable impulse, and the need to balance the interests of temporary beneficiaries, the permanent institution itself, and the needs of executive officers drove collegial accountability to develop in the interesting way it did from the mid-thirteenth century. This dynamic gave colleges their odd form and produced their particular approach to accountability. More than the others, this chapter is also therefore a study of accountability within a group.

Medieval colleges comprise an important chapter in the history of legislative skill and institutional design—specifically, endowed secular colleges with a degree of self-government.[2] Colleges were not, however, numerically dominant in universities. During the twelfth and thirteenth centuries the overall numbers of (advanced) students at such colleges was a small proportion of the total number of students at a given university.[3] Members of halls[4] and Nations[5] where greater numbers found institutional

---

[1] Mary Douglas's phrase, 'A Feeling for Hierarchy', in James L. Heft (ed.), *Believing Scholars: Ten Catholic Intellectuals* (Fordham, NY, 2005), 96.

[2] Cf. on halls and colleges Alan B. Cobban, *The Medieval English Universities: Oxford and Cambridge to c.1500* (Aldershot, 1988), 112; J. R. L. Highfield, 'The Early Colleges', in J. I. Catto (ed.), *The History of the University of Oxford*, i. *The Early Oxford Schools* (Oxford, 1984), 225–63 at 225–33. In terms of their contribution to the history of institutions, endowed colleges without any self-government belong alongside but distinct from the older 'hall'—that is, a private master's private housing arrangement for his students. A classic study is A. B. Emden, *An Oxford Hall in Medieval Times: Being the Early History of St. Edmund Hall*, rev. edn. (Oxford, 1968). Despite its name Stapeldon Hall (Oxford's future Exeter College) seems collegial from very early on given its endowment, statutes, and founder Bishop Walter Stapeldon's close supervision. See John Maddicott, *Founders and Fellowship: The Early History of Exeter College, Oxford, 1314–1592* (Oxford, 2014), ch. 1, esp. 14, 26–51.

[3] For Oxford see T. H. Aston, 'Oxford's Medieval Alumni', *P&P* 74 (1977), 3–40 at 4–5; Maddicott, *Founders and Fellowship*, 7. The Sorbonne had about thirty-two fellows. On the basis of Paris's 1329–30 *computus* William J. Courtenay estimates the University there comprised 3,000–3,500 members in the early fourteenth century: *Parisian Scholars in the Early Fourteenth Century: A Social Portrait* (Cambridge, 1999), 26, justification 19–26. For relative Parisian numbers and trends over a longer period see Alexander Murray, *Reason and Society in the Middle Ages* (Oxford, 1978), 303–6. On numbers of colleges in Paris and Oxford by 1300, Jacques Verger, 'Patterns', in Hilde de Ridder-Symoens (ed.), *A History of the University in Europe*, i. *Universities in the Middle Ages* (Cambridge, 1992), 35–74 at 60–1.

[4] Catto argues that the Oxford hall 'triumphs' through incorporation into the colleges who provide the undergraduate education it formerly did. Halls remain per se less institutionally interesting and important. Jeremy Catto, 'The Triumph of the Hall in Fifteenth-century Oxford', in Ralph Evans (ed.), *Lordship and Learning: Studies in Memory of Trevor Aston* (Woodbridge, 2004) 209–23, esp. 220–1.

[5] Pearl Kibre, *The Nations in the Medieval Universities* (Cambridge, Mass., 1948); Ian P. Wei, *Intellectual Culture in Medieval Paris: Theologians and the University, c.1100–1330* (Cambridge, 2012), 111–13. Nations were relatively unimportant at Oxford: M. B. Hackett, 'The University as a Corporate Body', in Catto (ed.), *History of the University of Oxford*, i., 37–95 at 64–9.

and actual homes appear here, however, largely in counterpoint to colleges. The significance of the colleges was not (at this time) their immediate impact on the majority of university students, but in the cunning little worlds they made. Colleges developed distinctive ways to secure their members' and officers' accountability. No single part of this was new; but the combination was oddly so. Again, England is the point of departure, but Paris is considered too. The sources used here date mostly (because of their richness), from the mid-thirteenth century to the 1330s.[6] The group providing the main focus here is the House of the Scholars of Merton, more simply Merton College, Oxford. Merton can claim to be the first secular English college with an endowment and statutes.[7] It also produced an exceptional set of records, including some produced by its 'visitor' (i.e. inspector), the Franciscan John Pecham, Oxford graduate, Regent Master of Theology at Paris, and from February 1279 Archbishop of Canterbury.[8]

THE VIEW FROM MERTON COLLEGE, OXFORD

Pecham at Merton

On 4 June 1280 in Hampton in Arden, John Pecham was irritated with the fellows of Merton College. They had appealed to Pecham as their visitor to modify certain aspects of their founding statutes, last[9] revised by Walter of Merton, Bishop of Rochester, three years before his death in 1277.[10] Walter had been a faithful but adaptable royalist during the Barons' War, and Chancellor for the second time when

---

[6] The chronological development of colleges predates this, but the sources are poorer. Pre-thirteenth-century Parisian collegiate foundations are listed in Hastings Rashdall, *The Universities of Europe in the Middle Ages*, rev. edn. F. M. Powicke and A. B. Emden, 3 vols. (Oxford, 1936), i. 536, and generally ch. 5 (all references are to this edn.). The history of non-monastic collegiate foundations in Oxford begins in the mid-thirteenth century. For an example of a far older monastic foundation see John Barron, 'Augustinian Canons and the University of Oxford: The Lost College of St George', in Caroline M. Barron and Jenny Stratford (eds.), *The Church and Learning in Later Medieval Society: Essays in Honour of R. B. Dobson. Proceeedings of the 1999 Harlaxton Symposium* (Donington, 2002), 228–54.

[7] Between Balliol, Merton, and University Colleges there is little difference in terms of age. Balliol (f. 1260–6) has statutes (a charter/letter) from 1282. John Jones, *Balliol College, A History*, 2nd edn. (Oxford, 1997), conjectures earlier, lost statutes (6). University College's original grant goes back to 1249 who some constitutional order from 1280. See Rashdall, *Universities of Europe*, iii. 175–8, 179–83; Highfield, 'Early Colleges', 243 n. 2, 244–5, 260; T. H. Aston and Rosamund Faith, 'The Endowments of the University and Colleges to c.1348', in Catto (ed.), *History of the University of Oxford*, i. 265–309 at 292–3; Robin Darwall-Smith, *A History of University College, Oxford* (Oxford, 2008), 1–14.

[8] On Pecham see Decima L. Douie, *Archbishop Pecham* (Oxford, 1952); Benjamin Thompson, 'Pecham, John (c.1230–1292)', *ODNB*.

[9] Merton made several iterations: a lost *ordinatio* (c.?1262–4), and extant revisions of 1264, 1270, and lastly 1274. For reference to the lost *ordinatio* and the text of earlier charters see *Merton Muniments*, ed. P. S. Allen, H. W. Garrod, OHS 86 (Oxford, 1929), 8–9. Later iterations: *Merton Muniments*, #2 (1264), #6 (1274); *The Early Rolls of Merton College Oxford*, ed. J. R. L. Highfield, OHS ns 18 (Oxford, 1964), App., #2 at 378–91 (1270).

[10] The scholars' letter does not appear to be extant. On Pecham at Merton: Douie *Archbishop Pecham*, 273–80; Highfield, 'Early Colleges', 260–3; G. H. Martin and J. R. L. Highfield, *A History*

his final revisions to Merton's statutes were issued. By the 1270 statutes it was clear that politically speaking Merton would be on the winning side.[11] He was more than aware that the stability following the civil war was a precondition for a secure foundation, since he said as much at the start of his last statutes.[12] Pecham thought changing them no light matter. Merton had been founded as a cure for 'study's sickening' by a man 'most prudent in scholastic discipline'. Given his prudence and the care he had taken in drafting its statutes, Pecham was reluctant to diverge from them. On the contrary, beneficiaries seeking so to improve the rules—to what purpose?—risked being thought both shameless and thankless.[13]

Instead the scholars should be quietly grateful for the statutes' existing provisions, not clamouring for improvements. They should stop bothering themselves (and Pecham).

> We encourage you in the Lord and strictly order you as you wish to take consolation in our protection, that you conform your life, behaviour and studies in all things to the sacred rulings of your aforementioned founder, and do not concern yourselves with the goods of the manors except as how he himself expressly determined, knowing for certain that if you should do otherwise, certainly setting yourself up to incur the indignation of the Most High, you will weigh down the solicitude of our humble self most heavily, we who are prepared to devote our energies to you, if you will only yearn to live in peaceful and upright study; under heaven, we do not expect anything further from you.[14]

He wanted no more partisan dissent (*dissensio partialis*), nor factional in-fighting (*patriae sectio*). Pecham sought to redirect the scholars back to their collective purpose: 'since you fight for Christ the Lord we entreat you to stand together, deployed in scholarly battle-lines, under your commander'. In these matters, Pecham placed much weight on the scholars' obligations towards this leader, the college's *custos* or warden, Peter of Abingdon. 'Furthermore you should obey your commander in all right and proper things, lest, feeling he works for ingrates, he be weighed down by depression and pursue your interests less energetically. On that basis you should give him a little support, because your most prudent founder commended you and your goods to his labours.' Pecham left the scholars with a clear threat: shut up and get back to your books lest 'with drawn sword we are forced to scourge [your] disobedience with terrible wounds'.[15]

Four years later the sword was drawn and the scholars scourged. In 1284 Pecham visited Merton, probably twice.[16] The second visit provoked his 'injunctions': an extensive, itemized gloss on the 1274 statutes that comprised mainly swingeing

---

of Merton College, Oxford (Oxford, 1997), 50–2, 69–70; G. H. Martin, 'Merton, Walter of (c.1205–1277)', *ODNB*.

[11] I am grateful to Roger Highfield for stressing this to me.
[12] *Merton Muniments*, #6 at 21 ll. 3–4; Martin, 'Merton, Walter of (c.1205–1277)'.
[13] *Reg. Peckham*, i. #106 at 123.   [14] *Reg. Peckham*, i. #106 at 123–4.
[15] *Reg. Peckham*, i. #106 at 124.
[16] The 31 August 1284 Lambeth letter to the fellows was undoubtedly the result of a personal visit. In it Pecham withdraws an earlier concession of wood and straw/chaff granted during a recent (*dudum*) visit: *Reg. Peckham*, iii. #589 at 814.

criticisms of the scholars:[17] 'So that you may more easily see your defects and reform them more clearly by rule, that rule we have broken down by chapters and send it to you separated with rubrics' (seemingly now lost).[18] Here is the *utile* serving the *honestum*. As Merton's *ex officio* protector (*patronatus*), Pecham held the college to account and did not mince his words:

> Turning our weak eyes to you, a distinguished portion of the English clergy, and provoked by the prick of fear and the spark of love, we have decided to correct certain things that we have heard about you, lest little by little the salutary design of the aforesaid man should gradually evaporate because of our negligence, and also lest it come about that you, by transgressing your rule—to the maintenance of which you know you are bound by the bond of an oath, as is clear from chapter 23 of the rule—should in the future be barred as perjured and infamous from the ecclesiastical promotion and honours to which the pious wish of your aforesaid father wanted to promote you.[19]

Using the 1274 statutes to audit the house (its common name), Pecham worked through the statutes roughly in order. There was a pattern to his order of criticism: intellectual egoism; physical self-indulgence; corruption of charitable principles; and offences against hierarchy.

As examples of intellectual egoism the Archbishop cited the admission of medical students, unmentioned in the statutes.[20] Too many scholars, furthermore, were taking canon and civil law. Although permitted, they did so not 'humbly', but rather 'presumptuously' choosing this course of study themselves.[21] Knowledge of Latin was also decaying, the relevant provisions going unheeded.[22]

These intellectual abuses merged with exhibitions of physical self-indulgence. Canonical hours were 'barely kept'; prayers for benefactors were not made;[23] mealtimes

---

[17] The edition in *Statutes of the Colleges of Oxford: With Royal Patents of Foundation, Injunctions of Visitors*, ed. E. A. Bond, 3 vols. (London, 1853), i. *Merton*, 40–5 (documents are separately paginated by college), unlike Martin's Rolls edition, edits Pecham's letter into numbered chapters. There is some palaeographical basis for this. Bond enumerated his text on the basis of the full points and upright lines punctuating Lambeth Palace Library MS Reg. Pecham, fos. 236^v–7^v, and included the marginal comments which may be only slightly later. Bond's edited version is nevertheless more 'user-friendly' than the MS—it lacks his chapter numbers. There are no such equivalents in the other version, All Souls Oxford MS 182, fos.178^r–180^r (= new foliation 181^r–3^r). Bond's edition was a product of the 1850 Royal Commission into Oxford and Cambridge. Where critical editions do not exist I have relied on him. The Cambridge equivalent is *Documents Relating to the University and Colleges of Cambridge*, 3 vols. (London, 1852).
[18] *Reg. Peckham*, iii. #589 at 812. The original copy of the 1274 statutes (Merton College Record 232) is unnumbered and offers no grounds for distinguishing particular 'chapters' (reproduced in *Merton Muniments* between 22 and 23). It is possible, up to a point, sensibly to project Pecham's numbering onto 'natural' changes in topic within the 1274 statutes. Martin offered one such reconciliation at *Reg. Peckham*, iii. #589 at 818 n. 1. Merton must have received a numbered and rubricated version of the 1274 statute from Pecham, corresponding with his letter. Pecham clearly wanted something as navigable as—in different ways—Bodley Barlow MS 49's *regule compoti* (see p. 70, n. 243) or Lambeth Palace MS 1415, Stephen Langton's Pentateuch commentary.
[19] *Reg. Peckham*, iii. #589 at 812.   [20] *Reg. Peckham*, iii. #589 at 812.
[21] *Reg. Peckham*, iii. #589 at 812–13, re *Merton Muniments*, #6 at 21 l. 9. Line numbers are those of the 1274 statutes in Merton College Record 232.
[22] *Reg. Peckham*, iii. #589 at 813, re *Merton Muniments*, #6 at 21 l. 10.
[23] *Reg. Peckham*, iii. #589 at 815, re *Merton Muniments*, #6 at 22 ll. 21–3; 23 ll. 51–2.

were not improving.[24] Scholars wandered about town at will unnecessarily.[25] The brewer and baker were paid too much.[26]

In turn these seeped into a deeper undermining of the college's purposes. Walter's golden rule was being ignored, whereby the number of scholars at Merton was a function of the total that its assets could support at 50*s*. each *per annum*.[27] Indigence did not appear to be the criterion for admission that Pecham thought it should, neither did being a relation of Walter of Merton, nor coming from the dioceses of Winchester or Canterbury—all criteria from 1274.[28] Furthermore those who gained benefices did not lose their scholarships, as the statutes envisaged.[29] What was *utile* (for the scholars) was trumping, in Pecham's view, what was *honestum* for the college. 'Who, whom?' was again a pressing question.

Underpinning all these faults Pecham perceived a general contempt for hierarchy, office, and sworn undertakings. The scholars are 'perjured and disobedient'.[30] In addition to their infringements or misinterpretations of the statutes, Pecham refers to a broken oath taken by members.[31] The scholars act 'on private arrogance, spurning their superior's judgement', they are 'presumptuous and lacking in true humility'.[32] They have 'twisted the line of the rule [here the '50*s*. ratio'] and what is worse opted out of the commandments of charity and gratitude'.[33] With respect to the warden, Peter of Abingdon, Pecham had

---

[24] *Reg. Peckham*, iii. #589 at 815–16.
[25] *Reg. Peckham*, iii. #589 at 815, re *Merton Muniments*, #6 at 21–2 ll. 12–14.
[26] *Reg. Peckham*, iii. #589 at 814.
[27] *Reg. Peckham*, iii. #589 at 813–14, re *Merton Muniments*, #6 at 21 ll. 11–12; 24 ll. 65–72. A weaker variant is in Balliol's 1340 statutes: *The Oxford Deeds of Balliol*, ed. H. E. Salter, OHS 64 (1913), #571 at 296–7. University College's *c*.1280 'statutes' offer a further version, 'Pecuniam vero collectam nulli liceat ad usus alios deputare, nisi ad illum qui fuerat de ultima voluntate testatoris; quam cito vero plures redditus empti fuerint augeatur [*corr.* angeatur] numerus et exhibitio Magistrorum', *Munimenta Academica, or, Documents Illustrative of Academical Life and Studies at Oxford*, ed. Henry Anstey, RS, 2 vols. (London, 1868), ii. 780–3 at 782. Also, *The Register of Walter de Stapeldon, Bishop of Exeter* (A.D. *1307–1326)*, ed. F. C. Hingeston-Randolph (London, 1892), 307 (Stapeldon Hall/Exeter College, 1316).
[28] *Reg. Peckham*, iii. #589 at 816–17 re *Merton Muniments*, #6 at 22 ll. 25–8.
[29] *Reg. Peckham*, iii. #589 at 817 re *Merton Muniments*, #6 at 22 ll. 29–30. On collegial fellowship as a benefice that a real benefice should displace see Nathalie Gorochov, 'La Notion de pauvreté dans les statuts de collèges fondés à Paris de Louis IX à Philippe le Bel', in Jean Dufour and Henri Platelle (eds.), *Fondations et œuvres charitables au Moyen Âge* (Paris, 1999), 119–28.
[30] *Reg. Peckham*, iii. #589 at 814.
[31] Scholars had to swear to the statutes (*Merton Muniments*, #6 at 23 ll. 50–1). Pecham refers to a separate oath (he again cites/gives numbers). He says there were nine headings to this ('contra proprium juramentum, sicut patet ex quarto articulo illorum ix, quos servaturos se jurant singuli ingressuri'), *Reg. Peckham*, iii. #589 at 817. See also 812 ('juramenti vos novistis astrictos'); 814 ('contra proprium juramentum, sicut patet ex articulorum septimo quos jurastis'). Pecham distinguishes this smaller *juramentum* from the set of statutes to which scholars have also sworn e.g. 815 ('sextodecimo capitulo regulae quam jurastis'). A fifteenth-century oath is known: George C. Brodrick, *Memorials of Merton College*, OHS 4 (Oxford, 1885), 29. The Sorbonne had an oath distinct from its statutes: Palémon Glorieux, *Aux origines de la Sorbonne*, i. *Robert de Sorbon*, ii. *Le Cartulaire*, 2 vols. (Paris, 1965–6), i. #4 at 203 (1280–90). For a Nation's oath see e.g. *Statuta Nationis Germanicae Universitatis Bononiae (1292–1750)*, ed. Paolo Colliva, Acta Germania 1 (Bologna, 1975), #16 at 107 (1345–8).
[32] *Reg. Peckham*, iii. #589 at 813. [33] *Reg. Peckham*, iii. #589 at 813.

understood with no little astonishment that furthermore you [the scholars] will not admit the master [Peter] to hear the customary weekly accounts,[34] nor anyone in his place who is able to be present at the accounting, although it is through him that whatever may be surplus or deductible from absentees ought to be converted to the good of the house, and in spite of his being in charge of all things and persons. For such an exclusion of a president can have no other reason other than that light is hateful to evildoers.[35]

Pecham had likewise heard that with the fellows' connivance, the brewer, butler, and 'other servants of your community' would not obey the Warden, nor would the scholars 'help the Master to correct wrongdoers'. Given these offences to the Warden's standing, Pecham was even obliged to state what should have been obvious, that 'everyone whether within and without, greater or lesser is obliged to obey the master following the rule'.[36]

The ultimate outcomes of all this are only partly clear. We can tell the provisions against studying medicine were never effective.[37] The desire to increase the fellowship would, however, be met, although it remained a longstanding issue.[38] Furthermore, Peter of Abingdon did indeed resign the wardenship, as we shall see.[39] What can be learnt from this history with respect to collegial accountability?

Lessons from Merton

Instrumental Constitutions

Most obviously, the constitutional documents played an instrumental role in securing collegial accountability. Merton's earliest constitutional documents are not statutes by name. That word is written on early founding documents in later hands.[40] In 1264 the constitution is *ordinatio et prouisio*.[41] In 1270 it is a *donacionem* which is *sub forma et condicionibus subscriptis* with the overall group termed an *institucionem* and *collegium*.[42] In 1274 the constitution was called *obseruancias uel statuta* and the dispositive verb is *statuere* when it comes to the rules.[43] But notwithstanding

---

[34] *Weekly* accountings are not specified by the 1274 statutes. Merton's previous visitor, Archbishop Kilwardby, had visited in 1276 giving a set of *ordinationes* which refer to weekly doles. *Merton College: Injunctions of Archbishop Kilwardby, 1276*, ed. H. W. Garrod (Oxford, 1929), 11.
[35] *Reg. Peckham*, iii. #589 at 814.
[36] *Reg. Peckham*, iii. #589 at 818, similar sentiments to the latter also at 815.
[37] Aston, 'Oxford's Medieval Alumni', 16; Highfield. 'Early Colleges', 245.
[38] Martin and Highfield, *History of Merton*, 43 n. 7: 57 cumulative members before 1281, 136 by 1299.
[39] *Early Rolls of Merton*, 70–1; Brodrick, *Memorials of Merton College*, 153–4.
[40] See Highfield's description of the 1264 statutes (*Early Rolls of Merton*, App., #1 at 377–8).
[41] *Merton Muniments*, #2 at 17 l. 45. 'Statuo' is used (15 l. 5) with 'fundo et stabilio', also 'inuingo' (17 l. 40). For conveyancing: 'do, assigno, et concedo' (15 ll. 2–3). For discussion of such language at the Sorbonne, see John Sabapathy, 'Regulating Community and Society at the Sorbonne in the Late Thirteenth Century', in Fernanda Pirie and Judith Scheele (eds.), *Legalism: Community and Justice* (Oxford, forthcoming 2014).
[42] *Early Rolls of Merton*, App., #2, caps. 1, 2, 45. *Societas* is also used (e.g. cap. 5), *congregatio* (e.g. cap. 34).
[43] *Merton Muniments*, #6 at 21 l. 7; 26 l. 97, where *lex* is used alongside *statutum*. Other verbs: 21 ll. 3–6.

terminology, these constitutions were inherently instrumental. They establish the terms of the trust Walter founded.

They were treated as such by both insiders and outsiders—both when observed and when transgressed. A late but vivid parallel occurs in the German dialogue collection the *Manuale scholarium* where student Camillus complains about the fines he has run up from breaking various collegial or hall statutes. Bartoldus, his companion asks him if the prohibition 'was specified' (*fuitne publicatum*)? When Camillus says that it had been, Bartoldus retorts, 'It's your own fault, you've no excuse' (*Culpabilis es; nullam habes excusationem*).[44] That Merton's scholars took theirs as binding is clear because they wanted to change them. Pecham's pre-31 August 1284 allowances of wood and straw were modifications to the constitution made presumably at the fellows' request.[45] Both Pecham's and Kilwardby's (1276) visitation ordinances likewise show its statutes being used to hold the college to account. Perhaps significantly both these friars, one Dominican, one Franciscan, call Merton's statutes a 'rule' (*regula*)—seeing a religious order behind the college's gates.[46] This chapter will suggest that how one perceived such a community had important consequences for accountability within it.

Even if Pecham's own numbered and rubricated version of the Merton statutes is lost, his letter to the college clearly implies he had made a list of the statutes, turning them into a veritable, verifiable checklist. The format of Merton College Record 232 itself is hard to use like this (it has 30+ words a line, is 20 in. wide, has 111 lines and no paragraphs). Evaluating how the statutes' norms were, or were not, applied is the method used for bringing Merton into line—just as the action of account was for bailiffs or *sindacatio* for *podestà*. Statutes are, of course, not new nor a form particular to colleges. Walter of Merton was making use of a technique (normative statutes, lists) especially characteristic of bishops and monasteries, and widespread in this period.[47] Pecham had too his own rule as a Franciscan and had found just such a practice of numbered division helpful when commenting on it (in good scholastic style).[48] His numbering of the statutes was his attempt to make Merton's statutes more usable *as statutes* for holding the college's members to account.

One needs to ask, though, how drafters imagined the statutes would work. Roger Highfield argues that 'once the statutes of colleges were established their government should have proceeded smoothly in accordance with their

---

[44] *Die deutschen Universitäten im Mittelalter: Beiträgezur Geschichte und Charakteristik derselben*, ed. Friedrich Zarncke (Leipzig, 1857), 1–48, at 28–9 (cap. 11), trans. as *The Manuale scholarium: An Original Account of Life in the Mediaeval University*, trans. R. F. Seybolt (Cambridge, Mass., 1921). The text is *c.*1481 with strong impressions of life at Heidelberg.

[45] *Reg. Peckham*, iii. #589 at 814.

[46] *Injunctions of Archbishop Kilwardby, passim*; *Reg. Peckham*, e.g. iii. #589 at 812. *Statuta* could sometimes be used in a mendicant context to mean *regula*, though I think the argument stands here. See Rosalind B. Brooke, *Early Franciscan Government: Elias to Bonaventure* (Cambridge, 1959), 224.

[47] Cf. on diocesan statutes C. R. Cheney, 'Statute-making in the Thirteenth Century', *Texts and Studies* (Oxford, 1973), 138–57, esp. 138–9, 142–3; Highfield, 'Early Colleges', 244.

[48] *Doctoris seraphici S. Bonaventurae* [...] *Opera omnia*, ed. R. P. Bernardini and Portu Romatino, 10 vols. (Ad Claras Aquas, 1882–1902), viii. 391–437, Pecham's commentary (formerly attributed to Bonaventure) on the Franciscan *regula bullata* with frequent enumerated and subdivided references to the headings of the rule and also to the structure of the papal bull framing it. On lists and formulae see e.g. Jack Goody, *The Domestication of the Savage Mind* (Cambridge, 1977), esp. chapters on 'What's in a List?' and 'Following a Formula'.

implementation'.[49] It is not necessarily clear that such a smooth unscrolling of corporate life was conceived by founders as the axiomatic effect of their constitutions. The point of the constitutions was rather to establish a framework that could resolve unforeseen problems, given a group's charitable purpose. College constitutions may make better sense if we see them as creating a rational space for regulating foreseeable and unforeseeable conflicts between founders' intentions, members, and collegial rules—as Exchequer rules did for sheriffs.[50] Some college statutes are simply too brief to be all-encompassingly final. One early collegial 'constitution'— that of University College, Oxford—is in fact a university ruling on how to rectify a neglected bequest.[51] The written text was to be supplemented by a constitutional blend of internal procuratorial responsibility and external oversight by the University Chancellor and the Masters of Theology. The history of religious orders is relevant again here. Members' identification with colleges, and their founders' charisma, though, seem seldom highly charged enough to lead to the anxious originalism and glossing that the Franciscans themselves produced in agonizing over their own rules. Pecham had entered the order at the watermark of its constitutional elaboration. He would have known all too well that formal documents seldom had the last word. He came to the question of Merton's statutes with some 'previous' that it is worth noting.

By the 1280s the Franciscans had an institutional complex about the relationship between founder, Order, and rule. Having withdrawn in *c*.1217–18 from any formal determinative role in the Order, Francis had nevertheless set out his views on important aspects of the Order's life in his *Testament*, shortly before dying in 1226.[52] It should not be taken, he said, as a *regula* but rather his 'recordatio, admonitio, exhortatio, et meum testamentum'. Still it must, he said, be taken with (*semper iuxta*) the official rule of 1223, the *regula bullata*, which had itself succeeded an earlier rule.[53] This short, extraordinary, contradictory *Testament* was of deeply problematic standing. It was simultaneously Francis's elegiac lament, authoritative history of origins, tacit critique, confession of obedience, plea to

---

[49] Highfield, 'Early Colleges', 259.

[50] Cf. Stuart Hampshire's argument that we should not deceive ourselves into thinking that justice relates to the elimination of conflict rather than to the ongoing regulation of rational spaces for articulating and regulating conflict: 'Conflict is perpetual: why then should we be deceived [it could be otherwise]?' (*Justice is Conflict* (Princeton, NJ, 2000), 48). The issue of being able to disentangle the ultimate point of the rules from the rule itself would have been a familiar one from Pecham's time through Aristotle's discussion in *Nicomachean Ethics*, V.10 (1137a35–1138a1). See e.g. the discussion in Aquinas, *Summa Theologiae*, Ia–IIae q. 96 a. 6 and q. 97. Cf., on statutory over-proliferation, Brooke, *Early Franciscan Government*, 281–2.

[51] For the story of William of Durham's mishandled 1249 bequest, Darwall-Smith, *History of University College*, 1–14 and 18–21 on the 1292 statutes; the 1280/1 commission's findings edited in *Munimenta Academica*, ii. 780–3, the 1292 statutes in i. 56–61. Further statutes were issued in 1311, *Mediaeval Archives of the University of Oxford*, ed. H. E. Salter, OHS 73, 77, 2 vols. (Oxford, 1920–1), i. 84–6.

[52] Brooke, *Early Franciscan Government*, 76–83 for 1217–18 (not 1220), and generally on the struggles over governance.

[53] François d'Assisi, *Écrits*, ed. K. Esser, Sources chrétiennes 285 (Paris, 1981), 204–10 at 210. The *regula bullata* ratified within Honorius III's 29 November 1223 bull *Solet annuere sedes* (*Reg. Hon. III*, ii. #4582; Potthast #7108 = Reg. vat. xii, fos. 155–6ᵛ). For the earlier (by 1221) *regula non bullata*, see *Écrits*, 122–78.

be constrained to obedience, and founder's heartfelt last word. Reaction to it was complex enough to lead to Gregory IX's arbitration of 1230 (*Quo elongati a*), ruling that the *Testament* had no legal standing for the Order.[54] Partly in response to this, partly because of the Order's expansion, much more statutory regulation followed.[55] A related consequence was a steady stream, increasingly problematic, of Franciscan and papal comment on the 1223 rule.[56] Pecham himself contributed with an *Expositio super Regulam Fratrum Minorum*, c.1276–9, almost certainly written while Prior of the English Franciscan province and just before he visited Merton.[57] In his *Expositio* Pecham glossed his own rulebook, explicitly differentiating between requirements that he argued were of different standing.[58] Pecham came to review Merton's statutes with some particular institutional baggage when it came to interpreting founders' statutes. He had done something similar before.

Collegial statutes could be of as long gestation as those of religious orders. Where constitutional texts were more expansive it was often because they had been stewing for a long time. Robert de Sorbon took an extremely close interest—acting as the Sorbonne's first *provisor* during his lifetime. He will have reflected on the 'customs' and 'statutes' of his graduate theologians' college for more than seventeen years.[59] Walter of Merton drafted and redrafted Merton's constitutions over at least a twelve-year period.[60] There was a hidden preparatory period if, as Sethina Watson reckons, his Hospital of St John's Basingstoke (f. c.1240) was the regulatory model for Merton.[61] Certainly in that analogous field of hospital foundations founders' constitutions were similarly developed over decades (and functioned very similarly).[62] Founders appreciated the length of time needed to get constitutions right. They may have thought that their final

---

[54] *Reg. Greg. IX*, i. #504; Potthast ##8620, 8627 = Reg. vat., xv, fos. 36ʳ–38r reiterated by Innocent IV's 1245 *Ordinem vestrum*; Rosalind B. Brooke, *The Image of St Francis: Responses to Sainthood in the Thirteenth Century* (Cambridge, 2006), 26; David Burr, *The Spiritual Franciscans: From Protest to Persecution in the Century after St Francis* (University Park, Pa., 2001), 3–4, 15, 49–50.

[55] 'Statuta generalia ordinis edita in capitulis generalibus celebratis. Narbonae an. 1260, Assisii an. 1279 atque Parisiis an. 1292', ed. Michael Bihl, *Archivum Franciscanum Historicum* 34 (1941), 13–94, 284–358, incorporating pre-1260 traces.

[56] André Vauchez, *François d'Assise, entre histoire et mémoire* (Paris, 2009), 168–71, 240–7, 269–76; Brooke, *Image of St Francis*, 77–101; cf. Bert Roest, *A History of Franciscan Education (c.1210–1517)* (Leiden, 2000), 253 n. 63.

[57] *Bonaventurae* [...] *Opera omnia*, viii. 391–437. Conrad Harkins offered an exhaustive case for Pecham's authorship of this *Expositio* in 'The Authorship of a Commentary on the Franciscan Rule Published Among the Works of St Bonaventure', *Franciscan Studies* 29 (1969), 157–248, offering (244) a case for narrowing composition to 1276–9.

[58] *Bonaventurae* [...] *Opera omnia*, viii. 393–4, 436–7.

[59] From Louis IX's 1257 donation and the customary foundation of the college until his death (1274). The start could be moved a few years earlier (Glorieux, *Origines de la Sorbonne*, i. 35–6).

[60] Counting from the 7 May 1262 charter of Richard of Clare (*Merton Muniments*, 8).

[61] I am grateful to Sethina Watson for discussion. The hospital's influence on the college will be considered in her forthcoming study of medieval hospitals. There are no statutes extant for St John's. At present see Watson, *Fundatio, Ordinatio and Statuta*, 135-9. Alexander Murray suggests William of Durham (University College's founder) was a possible hidden influence through the foundations of both Balliol, Merton, and the 'Norman' Collège du Trésorier. See Murray, '1249', *University College Record* 12/4 (2000), 52–73 at 62–4, 66–7. For William see also A. D. M. Cox, 'Who was William of Durham?', *University College Record* 8 (1981), 115–23.

[62] Watson, *Fundatio, Ordinatio and Statuta*, 26, 144; Jacques Verger, 'Fonder un collège au XIIIᵉ siècle', in Andreas Sohn and Jacques Verger (eds.), *Die Universitären Kollegien im Europa des Mittelalters*

iterations were 'right' enough to create long-lasting groups. It need not follow that they thought these texts wound up an institutional clockwork that would enable a college to whirr off happily ever after. Walter of Merton knew that 'known unknowns' must persist (how many fellows would the golden rule permit; will Oxford remain a centre of learning?). Colleges' constitutional texts provided the basis for resolving these future imponderables, through a mixture of guidance and stipulation.[63]

It is better therefore to treat such constitutions as a necessary minimum for any collegial life, rather than as sufficient for peaceful collegial life. Some statutes stressed the need to restrict their interpretative licence. 'The rule for living ought to be fixed, defined and limited,' said the Spanish College statutes at Bologna.[64] R. N. Swanson's assessment seems right: 'These are generally utilitarian codes, concerned with the actual workings of the institution, not its validation. Yet an idealism is there [. . .] The statutes often appear not primarily as prescriptive towards an end, but as erecting safeguards against its distortion.'[65] (One is reminded of discussions about the prescriptiveness of estate management texts.) As—sometimes still—at modern universities, constitutions were predicated on the basis of the 'interminable discussion and interminable participation' to which they must give rise.[66]

Interminable discussion and participation are vividly recorded in the 1338–9 Merton *scrutinia* records.[67] Although edited some time ago the minutes merit greater consideration. Their value is precisely the remedy they offer (over a very short period) for an equally well-known problem in early university history: seeing beyond formal statutes to their interaction with the people they were supposed to guide.[68]

---

und der Renaissance (Bochum 2011), 29–38 at 31. More widely Gisela Drossbach (ed.), *Hospitaler in Mittelalter und Früher Neuheit. Frankreich, Deutschland und Italien. Eine vergleichende Geschichte; Hôpitaux au Moyen Âge et aux temps modernes: France, Allemagne et Italie: une histoire comparée*, Pariser Historische Studien 75 (Munich, 2007).

[63] In the language of contemporary moral philosophy, they provided for 'guidance control' (i.e. allowing some interpretative licence) as well as 'regulative control' (i.e. stipulative): see John Martin Fischer, *My Way: Essays on Moral Responsibility* (Oxford, 2006); John Martin Fischer and Mark Ravizza, *Responsibility and Control: A Theory of Moral Responsibility* (Cambridge, 1998).

[64] Berthe M. Marti (ed.), *The Spanish College at Bologna in the Fourteenth Century* (Philadelphia, 1966), 214. For Corpus Christi Oxford's later emphasis on the need for clear (and lengthy) statutes so as 'to breed the fewest possible questions' (ut paucissimas pariant quaestiones), *Statutes of the Colleges of Oxford*, ii. *Corpus*, 112 (1517).

[65] Swanson, 'Godliness and Good Learning: Ideals and Imagination in Medieval University and College Foundations', in Rosemary Horrox and Sarah Rees Jones (eds.), *Pragmatic Utopias: Ideals and Communities 1200–1630* (Cambridge, 2001), 43–59 at 47.

[66] The phrase is from K. C. Wheare's memoir of the medievalist G. D. G. Hall and a twentieth-century sub-rector of Exeter and president of Corpus Christi College Oxford. As an ideal of a self-governing, collegiate university Wheare's description can be applied to thirteenth-century Oxford: 'The price of liberty and efficiency at a university such as Oxford, which professes to be self-governing, is interminable discussion and interminable participation. ' "Academic politics," [Hall] thought, "were not interesting or worthwhile in themselves. Their only proper purpose was the service of the University as a place of learning. [Hall] had no sympathy with those who were too busy to contribute but not too busy to grouse, and he had too no sympathy for those whose taste for the corridors of power he had adjudged unworthy." ' 'George Derek Gordon Hall, 1924–1975', *PBA* 62 (1976), 427–33 at 429. Wheare quotes from Hall's memorial service address.

[67] *Merton Muniments*, ##13–15.

[68] I try a different approach in 'Regulating Community and Society at the Sorbonne in the Late Thirteenth Century', in Fernanda Pirie and Judith Scheele (eds.), *Legalism: Community and Justice* (Oxford, forthcoming 2014).

The 1274 statutes required that, 'with the warden and seniors of the House and all the fellows then present, three times a year [. . .] a chapter or *scrutinium* should be celebrated at the House itself, in which careful inquiry will be undertaken into individuals' lives, conduct, intellectual progress and all matters which will be rightly worthy of correction or re-shaping'.[69] The run of extant minutes appear to show each fellow speaking in turn.[70] In April 1338 the principal complaint was that there were too few students and fellows. Students were racing about inns and eating-houses too. They would bring wine and drink it standing just on Merton's threshold—provocatively, presumably.[71]

In between these constants, bubbles from bigger problems were surfacing.[72] The summer scrutiny records a full-blown row revolving around Warden Robert of Tring (former fellow and bursar) and fellows William of Wantyng and John of Wyly.[73] It related to the latters' failure to audit the bailiffs' accounts. The minutes allow competing interpretations of the discord (and factions) to be faintly traced. Bursar and philosopher William of Heytesbury's version shows the constitution in action—as well as the interminable discussion it gave rise to.[74]

> There is rancour between the Warden and Wyly and Wantyng because the latter two have been assigned to hear the bailiffs' accounts and he [Heytesbury] believes that there may be a problem with their conduct and with respect to the Warden's, given they fail to hear the accounts. Having been delegated to hear the accounts they are bound to attend, unless they have reasonable cause and in his [Heytesbury's] judgement, they have none. Regarding the hearing of accounts, five should be present for the accounting, but only three of those named do.[75] So if there is a problem, it would be better to substitute others and to trust to their counsel, so that they can conduct the common business and so there may be the peace between the fellows that there should.
>
> Wantyng behaves much like a stranger to the Warden, and Wyly and Wantyng are bound to be present to hear the accounts lest they can offer some other excuse which he [Heytesbury] has not heard.
>
> Wyly and Wantyng ought to have been compelled to hear the accounts, or they should have offered some other excuse, after all no clear reason was given, and thus the

---

[69] *Merton Muniments*, #6 at 23 ll. 47–8.

[70] Minuting was contentious. In 1339 Richard of Aynho, for one, complained, 'it is not appropriate that there are so many listening at the *scrutinium*'. The text is partly corrupt, but he seems to allege the previous recording of a dispute has created problems with the sub-warden. *Merton Muniments*, #15 at 35 (fo. 3ᵛ ll. 236–7).

[71] *Merton Muniments*, #13 at 33 (fo.1 ll. 18–23, Finmere's complaint). Seemingly verbatim records are tricky. Cf. Alexander Murray (on inquisitorial transcripts) in 'Time and Money', in Miri Rubin (ed.), *The Work of Jacques Le Goff and the Challenges of Medieval History* (Woodbridge, 1997), 3–25 at 7 with John Arnold, *Inquisition and Power: Catharism and the Confessing Subject in Medieval Languedoc* (Philadelphia, 2001), 5.

[72] Brief mention of the episode in Highfield, 'Early Colleges', 262 ('the impression is strongly given of a quarrelsome community').

[73] *BRUO*, iii. 1908 (Tring), 1979 (Wantyng), 2118 (Wyly).

[74] For Heytesbury, *BRUO*, ii. 927–8, and E. J. Ashworth, 'Heytesbury, William (d. 1372/3)', *ODNB*.

[75] A reference to the 1274 rule requiring three bursars to be selected from the fellowship who will hear with the separately selected five the bailiffs' accounts annually. They were also all involved in hearing the warden's accounts. *Merton Muniments*, #6 at 24 ll. 55–8.

rule in this respect has not been observed according to the form of the statutes [*iuxta formam statuti*].

That while there should be accountability [*respondendum*] towards all the fellows in the approved and proper manner as they are bound in handling the business of the house amongst the fellows, [yet] Elindon[76] and Wantyng mockingly bandy honest words about.

There are too few fellows. The number is insufficient to hear accounts, as noted already, and about the college gate.[77]

A second bursar, William of Humberston, seemingly allied with Heytesbury, put it more concisely: 'two of the fellows [presumably Wyly and Wantyng] are deficient in this respect: that they will not shoulder the responsibilities of the House as they are bound to'.[78] The third bursar Robert Finmere thought Wyly and Elindon 'too rebellious', and criticized Wantyng and Elindon who 'in handling communal business refuse to give counsel as other fellows'.[79] There seems to have been a distinct hostility between Finmere and Wyly, since numerous fellows commented on it.

Of the three problematic fellows Wyly himself was not present (or did not speak). Elindon defended the Warden's discretion in some matters ('he may correct himself'), but also complained about Tring's numerous absences. On the whole, Elindon appeared more bothered by his feud with Finmere. Finmere, he said, made 'mortal threats' against Wyly. Elindon said he also 'treats him [Elindon] badly and that nothing is noted in this quarrel lest it comes from his accomplices, and that the Warden acts hostilely towards him, and does not treat him as he ought because [Warden Tring] supports Finmere against him'. Wantyng's retort rests on formal grounds (and implies either that Warden Tring was not present or that his presence inhibited Wantyng's tongue not at all).

If there is a disagreement between the fellows, about whether someone should be thrown from office, they should make it known so that they have the warden with them and have his clear view [*propositum*]. Also if there is discord between the fellows, the Warden's good intentions and desire to please regarding the fellows is an obstacle for the deans and bursars lest they can all agree as in a case such as Finmere and Wyly.[80]

Having made this self-interested, 'principled' defence of himself and Wyly, Wantyng put the boot into Warden Tring. He prevented the increase of fellows, made them hostile towards the learned, sustained his relatives at the college (and so was held in contempt), and would not correct himself in those matters which had earlier been put before him (Wantyng then lists these).[81]

The alliances can be conjectured thus: Bursar Finmere stood with Warden Tring against Wyly, Wantyng, and Elindon. The other bursars Heytesbury and Humberston saved their fire mostly for Wantyng and Wyly whom they particularly blamed for

---

[76] *BRUO*, i. 634; it is not clear if Richard Elindon had a particular dereliction.
[77] *Merton Muniments*, #13 at 33 (fo. 1^{r-v} ll. 45–69).
[78] *Merton Muniments*, #13 at 33 (fo. 1 ll. 30–1). *BRUO*, ii. 982 (Humberston). Emden lists Heytesbury and Finmere both as first and Humberston as second bursar (each bursar was responsible for one of the three four-monthly periods during the course of the year).
[79] *Merton Muniments*, #13 at 33 (fo. 1 ll. 33–5). *BRUO*, ii. 685 (Finmere).
[80] *Merton Muniments*, #14 at 34 (fo. 2 ll. 95–101).
[81] *Merton Muniments*, #14 at 34 (fo. 2 ll. 101–7 then on to 129).

failing to hear the bailiffs' accounts. Of those under fire, Elindon seemed more preoccupied by his quarrel with Wyly than with any failings of Warden Tring. Wantyng sought protection behind constitutional proprieties and a blistering attack on Tring. Wyly and Tring's feelings are not recorded. The final fellow to speak, Robert of Hardley,[82] summed up this tangle of mutual hostility. He noted only that 'peace must be rebuilt between Wyly and Finmere, and between Elindon and Finmere, and between Wantyng and [John de] Wylot,[83] and between the Warden and Elindon, Wantyng and Wyly'.[84]

Like other methods of securing accountability discussed here, that which proceeded from the constitutions of Merton College was laborious, partial, and inconclusive. Its laboriousness is hopefully tangible, given the detail already cited. It was partial in two senses, first in that Elindon alleged Finmere and his allies conspired against him. Whether the *scrutinium* really was biased would depend presumably on one's view about Elindon's actual dereliction of duty. Second, Warden Tring was the apparently absent centre of the whole affair (in none of the four extant scrutinies of 1338–9 is he recorded). It is hard to see how the problems could be resolved without his participation in *scrutinia*.[85] The statutes required his presence. It is unsurprising that accountability was inconclusive. At the least, this is another proof that notwithstanding how articulate the provision for accountability, the justice or equity its mechanisms could immediately produce was quite fragmentary.

Hierarchy

Merton also has interesting lessons to teach about the relationship between collegial hierarchy and accountability. The question simmers through Merton's *scrutinia* records. Before returning to them it is worth going back to John Pecham. As the 'visitor' (external inspector) Pecham stood at the apex of Merton's hierarchical chain of accountability. He held Merton College to account. But Pecham reframed the nature of collegial hierarchy most revealingly, especially in the 1280 letter previously quoted. His ideal of community conflicted interestingly with other ideals one could institutionalize at a community like Merton.

In the 1280 letter there is a general current away from granting autonomy of judgement to the fellows and towards enforcing hierarchical obedience (to the warden).[86]

---

[82] *BRUO*, ii. 871.
[83] *BRUO*, iii. 2119, a future University chancellor. He established the poor scholars ('postmasters') fund at Merton.
[84] *Merton Muniments*, #14 at 34 (fo. 2 ll. 144–6).
[85] The point stands, even assuming Tring was present but silent. I assume we have, more or less, all the minutes that were made at this *scrutinium*.
[86] Pecham would share an affinity with Mary Douglas. See again her 'A Feeling for Hierarchy', esp. her 'ten principles' of hierarchy (98, 104), and n.b. 95–6, 109. Her points about the function of hierarchy being to limit competition and institute authority are at the centre of the Merton case (96). The claim that *as a rule* hierarchical 'institutions work to prevent concentrations of power' (96) works here. As with inquisitions and clerical hierarchies, there remains a question about justified dismissal from office, and whether collegial hierarchies place the barriers too high, or whether that height is a good price to pay for institutional stability.

Arguably, Kilwardby and Pecham's perception of Merton's *statuta* as a religious *regula* compounded this, implying, as it seems, the 'classic' monastic stress on the absolute authority of an abbot. It was as *regula* that Pecham had commented by definition on his own rule.[87] It was not unusual for monastic hierarchical thought to influence college foundations, as with the Benedictine rule at Peterhouse.[88] Pecham's description of Merton's *custos* as their *dux* also implies a lesson. Ostensibly Pecham was simply sustaining the military metaphor that entreated the scholars 'to stand together, at your commander's side, deployed in the battles of the schools'.[89] But the underlying reason the metaphor was chosen in the first place is clear: soldiers obey; they neither judge their commanders, nor quibble with the battle-plan. Due obedience is a strong theme in Pecham's approach to collegial accountability in 1280—to such a degree that Pecham seems subtly to bend the emphases of Merton's 1274 rule. In this it may again reflect the stresses of Pecham's commentary on his own rule. 'Without a single head, no *respublica* can flourish', he had written of the Franciscan minister general's sway.[90] The reluctance to allow the fellows much autonomy might also be seen within a Franciscan educational context since their *studia* had no formal corporate autonomy.[91] Franciscan *studia* existed to serve the Order and its provinces' needs. Many questions pertaining to its individual *studia* were therefore reserved to the provincial or general chapter, or even the minister general. No matter where they studied Franciscans were always constitutionally 'internal' to the Order, their community (*universitas*) always the Order's, not the university's.[92] This basic question of which community students and masters belonged to was at the root of Parisian university conflict and competition between 'seculars' and 'regulars' (those in orders).[93]

A *custos* was also a specifically Franciscan office, but it is hard to prove how that idea leaked into Merton's *custos*. Franciscan office was in principle a burden not an honour. A Franciscan *custos* was nevertheless a significant officer, the warden of provincial

---

[87] *Bonaventurae* [...] *Opera omnia*, viii. 391, 393–4, reflection on his act of commenting at 391, 436–7.

[88] Henry Mayr-Harting, 'The Foundation of Peterhouse, Cambridge (1284), and the Rule of Saint Benedict', *EHR* 103 (1988), 318–38. On Peterhouse see further Roger Lovatt, 'The Triumph of the Colleges in Late Medieval Oxford and Cambridge: The Case of Peterhouse', *History of Universities* 14 (1998), 95–142. Gregory IX's 1235–7 reform of the Benedictine rule (and Innocent IV's 1253 reissue of it) is an important qualifier of that 'classic' position. On the rule and the reform see p. 217 n. 227.

[89] *Reg. Peckham*, i. 124 (#106).

[90] '*Bonaventurae* [...] *Opera omnia*, viii. 427, also 393, 396 and (on correction) 431–5.

[91] For the friars' Oxford *studia* see M. W. Sheehan, 'The Religious Orders 1220–1370', in Catto (ed.), *History of the University of Oxford*, i. 193–223 at 198–201. Pure and simple *scholae* lacked life, legally speaking (Pierre Michaud-Quantin, *Universitas: expressions du mouvement communautaire dans le Moyen-Âge latin* (Paris, 1970), 54). The law could really matter. Lincoln College, Oxford narrowly escaped collapse after it's rector's death in 1474 because its statutes made no provision for a successor: see Virginia Davis, 'The Making of English Collegiate Statutes in the Later Middle Ages', *History of Universities* 12 (1993), 1–23 at 13. Balliol needed to seek a papally approved 'reconciliation' of divergences between its 1282 and 1340 statutes, *Oxford Deeds of Balliol*, #573 (1363/4).

[92] Roest, *History of Franciscan Education*, 102, 92 ('internal'); John R. H. Moorman, *A History of the Franciscan Order, From its Origins to the Year 1517* (Oxford, 1968), 123–6.

[93] Jacques Le Goff, 'How Did the Medieval University Conceive of Itself?', *Time, Work, and Culture in the Middle Ages*, trans. A. Goldhammer (Chicago, 1980), 122–34 at 127–8.

subdivision. Their accountability oscillated with Franciscan politics. After Elias's generalship important changes made *custodes* more accountable to their provinces, but alterations in 1242 amended this to stress their answerability to chapters and other offices.[94] Our ignorance of the specific nature of the fellows' discontent prevents a proper contextualization of Pecham's response. But the lack of latitude Pecham was willing to extend in 1280 is partly explicable in terms of his own institutional background.

Pecham's 1284 visitation letter of course makes clear that by then he certainly was attending to the letter of Merton's statutes; he enumerates his points following the statutes' order. So it is notable, given the fellows' unhappiness with the Warden, that Pecham is less interested in statutes relating to the warden's accountability. Pecham is not generally interested in the scholars' role in regulating the college, although the statutes held that the warden himself was to account annually to the vice-warden and five other fellows for 'his administration and for those things from the goods of the said house which have come into his hands'. His more general conduct was also inquired into along with the lesser servants by the fellow vice-warden and scholars.[95] The fellows also selected the three-person shortlist from which the *patronus* appointed the warden.[96] And, in straight contradiction to Pecham's 1280 criticisms, the 1274 statutes awarded a group of senior scholars, with the warden, the power to add to the existing statutes.[97] Members were even given the very large discretion of being able to relocate the whole scholarly body elsewhere than Oxford if they saw fit.[98] Their judgement therefore on what was expedient for the college served its wider charitable purpose following Walter of Merton's original vision. Having said that, Walter of Merton might well have agreed with Pecham that in admitting medical students the scholars had gone too far in permitting 'custom [*consuetudo*] to be the interpretor of the law [*juris*]'.[99] Pecham's injunctions actually offer very little evaluation of how the scholars were executing their powers of governance and administration, in contrast to their failings as vehicles for Walter of Merton's charity.[100] This focus was a choice—Pecham focused not necessarily on what Walter of Merton had, but on what he thought important, just as he had in his *Expositio* of the Franciscan rule. His ideas about community affected his ideas about the accountability within it.

The story can be taken one turn further. Two months after his injunctions to the scholars, Pecham wrote to *magistri* William of Montfort, precentor of Hereford, and Simon Ghent, Archdeacon of Oxford.[101] He instructed them to

---

[94] On custodies, François d'Assise, *Écrits*, 192–4 (*Regula bullata*, cap. 8); Brooke, *Early Franciscan Government*, 130–1, 233–4, 237–43, 266–7, and 106–7, 186 on the burden of office.
[95] *Merton Muniments*, #6 at 24 l. 57; ll. 61–2.
[96] *Merton Muniments*, #6 at 25 ll. 82–4.   [97] *Merton Muniments*, #6 at 26 ll. 97–8.
[98] *Merton Muniments*, #6 at 26 ll. 98–101. This was also the case elsewhere, e.g. Balliol: *Oxford Deeds of Balliol*, #571 at 296 (1340 statutes).
[99] *Reg. Peckham*, iii. #389 at 812. On custom and law in these contexts see further Sabapathy, 'Regulating Community and Society at the Sorbonne'.
[100] Pecham had clearly worked through all the 1274 statutes. He numbers the founder's kin rule 43, which occurs towards the end of the 1274 statutes. His numbering concentrates mostly on early 'chapters'.
[101] See Roy Martin Haines, 'Ghent, Simon (c.1250–1315)', *ODNB*; John Le Neve, rev. J. S. Barrow, *Fasti Ecclesiae Anglicanae 1066–1300 VIII Hereford* (London, 2002), 16; John Le Neve, rev. Diana E. Greenway, *Fasti Ecclesiae Anglicanae 1066–1300 I* (London, 1968), 8; *Registrum Thome de Cantilupo, Episcopi Herefordensis, A.D. 1275–1282*, ed. R. G. Griffiths and W. W. Capes, C&Y 2

faithfully inquire into, on our authority, the whole question of the discord or dispute between the scholars [of Merton] and master Peter of Abingdon warden (*custos*) of them and their goods; how it arose; and the resulting accusations and justifications. In order to do this the warden is indeed to be compelled, to give an account of his administration, before you or other credible persons, suspect to neither party and whom you may appoint as deputies.[102]

The inquiry clearly betrays a problem with Peter of Abingdon's accountability, notwithstanding the absence of any significant discussion in Pecham's injunctions. The inquiry itself is perfectly regular, but it implies that Pecham preferred to use a private and discreet process to deal with the Warden, not the injunctions to the fellowship as a whole.[103] The inquisitorial set-up is reminiscent of the considerations from the previous chapter about ensuring that the investigation of rumours did not produce a greater scandal than the original offence. The situation had seemingly gone beyond any collegial, fraternal correction. The August 1284 injunctions' failure to acknowledge any shortcomings on Abingdon's part also perhaps implies that Pecham was uncomfortable with the hierarchy of accountability that Walter of Merton had provided for in 1274. Pecham was happy enough for the fellows to be accountable, to him and to the Warden. But he seems not to have wanted them to be responsible for anything beyond their own behaviour. His implicit view was that the fellows could not direct themselves as a self-governing community, perhaps in principle as well as in practice.

The sequel is quickly told. Peter of Abingdon resigned a year or so later in 1286 and retired to his rectory at Nuneham Courtenay.[104] It seems unlikely that his withdrawal had nothing to do with the preceding disputes.[105] His house in Merton he granted in 1291–2 to three fellows of the college, not to Merton itself, though he did leave it three glossed biblical books.[106] Abingdon was replaced by Richard of Werplesdon, a fellow and also a former bursar.[107]

Richard of Werplesdon was a scholar and Peter of Abingdon a career administrator. Before Abingdon became warden he had been warden of St John's Basingstoke. Before

---

(London,1907), lxix, 111, 119, 122, 221–2, 248–9, 253. Montfort was ostensibly an odd choice for Pecham since he was Cantilupe's vicar-general for the latter's Normandy and Orvieto trips during his jurisdictional disputes with Pecham. Montfort was also one of Cantilupe's executors. See William W. Capes (ed.), *Registrum Ricardi de Swinfield, Episcopi Herefordensis, A.D. 1283–1317*, C&Y 6 (London, 1909), 70–2 (9 July 1285 bull of Honorius IV citing Swinfield, Montfort, and others). A letter of Alexander IV (*Registrum Ricardi de Swinfield*, 101, 19 December 1258) says that our William was the son of 'our devoted Peter de Montfort of the diocese of Worcester'. This was the Peter de Montfort who died at Evesham and was the lifelong friend of Walter Cantilupe, Bishop of Worcester (1237–66). There is a Merton connection since William's brother—another Peter—gave the advowson of Ponteland (Northumb.) to Walter of Merton in 1268. See *Burke's Peerage*, ix. 127. Martin and Highfield, *History of Merton*, 64–5 state that the grant came direct from Peter. More generally, D. A. Carpenter, 'Montfort, Peter de (*c.*1205–1265)', *ODNB*, and 'St Thomas Cantilupe: His Political Career', *Reign of Henry III*, 293–307 at 298 n. 27.

[102] *Reg. Peckham*, iii. #605.
[103] He entrusts the process to Montfort and Ghent's 'discretion', *Reg. Peckham*, iii. #605 at 836.
[104] *BRUO*, i. 4; *Early Rolls of Merton*, 70–1.
[105] Martin and Highfield, *History of Merton*, 70, suggest the 'agreed transfer' was better-natured than the preceding events imply.
[106] *Early Rolls of Merton*, App., #67; F. M. Powicke, *The Medieval Books of Merton College* (Oxford, 1931), 95.
[107] *BRUO*, iii. 2017.

Werplesdon became warden, he was a fellow of Merton. When Werplesdon became warden he ceased to be a fellow.[108] Fellows were the objects of Walter of Merton's charitable foundation. Merton's wardens, like its bailiffs, were merely officers. This helps to explain their ambivalent standing. They were the instrumental means for the values a charitable institution sought to sustain. Even when wardens are formal members of a college, they need not embody its purposes in the same way as the poor scholars do. Viewed from this angle they were servants not managers (to *prodesse* not *preesse*). That formality may be easily forgotten given a warden's institutional status. Viewed from that angle they may readily become managers. Likewise, the scholars embody the point of the foundation; they are its members. In this they are superior to administrative officials. Yet constitutionally the scholars will be at least partially subject to those officers, even at a relatively 'democratic' foundation like Merton. There was ambiguity about who really served whom. There is some truth in Michael Prestwich's contrast between medieval universities where administrators served rather than managed and modern ones where they manage and do not serve.[109] But it is not an uncomplicated truth. Had Merton been a literally corporate body in this period it might well have looked like a man punching himself in the face.

Comparison draws out this ambiguity further. College wardens were distinct from abbots, a clearly analogous 'head of house'. Two things particularly generally distinguish the relations of abbots-to-monks and wardens-to-scholars. First, scholars were not always the *ordo* out of which wardens were drawn, as monks constituted the *ordo* from which abbots were drawn. At Stapeldon Hall where the rector *was* a fellow there was a tight one-year tenure.[110] At Merton the fellows could not quite have repeated for their warden the claim of Bury St Edmunds's monks of their abbot: 'Out of us he came, for us he was and always is, and as he was so he is.'[111] That was a strong statement articulated in reaction to a head perceived as overmighty and unaccountable to his franchise.[112] An abbot was of a piece with his monks, not set apart. Pecham said the same of the minister general. His custody pertained not to a difference of status (*gradum*), but to one of function (*actum*).[113] The qualifications for Merton's warden were only that he be a man of probity and honesty, chosen from those 'reliable and

---

[108] The same would be true today; the warden is not a fellow. The 1274 statutes provide for the warden being 'siue de dicta Domo siue aliunde' (*Merton Muniments*, #6 at 25 l. 82).

[109] *Plantagenet England, 1225–1360* (Oxford, 2005), 131 n. 33, quoting Alan Cobban *English University Life in the Middle Ages* (London, 1999), 235. Prestwich cites as a regrettable portent the proliferation of administrative staff over and against the number of 'mere academics' following Kilwardby's 1276 injunctions. Given though that Kilwardby's new offices were given to *scholarly* fellows, not to 'external' or 'administrative' officials, the issue would be how far they remained 'scholarly' or how became 'administrative'. The issue has not gone away.

[110] *Register of Stapeldon*, 304–5.

[111] *The Customary of the Benedictine Abbey of Bury St Edmunds in Suffolk*, ed. Antonia Gransden, Henry Bradshaw Society 99 (Chichester, 1973), 36 ll. 18–19 (*c*.1234).

[112] See *Customary of the Benedictine Abbey of Bury*, introduction; Gransden, 'A Democratic Movement in the Abbey of Bury St Edmunds in the Late Twelfth and Early Thirteenth Centuries', *JEH* 26 (1975), 25–39; Gransden, *A History of the Abbey of Bury St Edmunds 1182–1256: Samson of Tottingham to Edmund of Walpole*, Studies in the History of Medieval Religion 31 (Woodbridge, 2007), ch. 5.

[113] *Bonaventurae* [. . .] *Opera omnia*, viii. 427; Francis's view: Brooke, *Early Franciscan Government*, 106–7, 112.

experienced in spiritual and temporal matters'.[114] Highfield argues that 'The Warden was as much an estates bursar as he was the head of an academy.'[115] It is not clear from Peter of Abingdon's story however, nor from the 1338–9 *scrutinia*, how far Merton's fellows conceded the Warden was their *academic* head.[116] They would have been far happier seeing him as a *mere* estates bursar. The statutes give them some justification for doing so. His title of warden (*custos*) after all probably derived from that for estates bailiff.[117]

Secondly because of, not despite, monastic solidarity Benedictine monks needed to obey their abbot irrespective of his actions (though this was modified in the 1230s). He acted as Christ's deputy.[118] The monks of Bury might well assert the abbot's obligation to consult with his monks, but in terms of 'Who, whom?' they were struggling with the Benedictine Rule's general stress on obedience. Unlike Merton it established a simpler internal hierarchy.[119] The abbot was like God, and should be obeyed without delay; so quickly indeed that order and obedience would simultaneously converge 'all in a whirl from the fear of God'.[120] Self-abnegation, 'following another's judgement and mandate' without 'murmur or reluctance' was the order of the day.[121] The monks were accountable to the abbot; the abbot was accountable to God. Accountability flowed up, not down (as with kings: p. 99). 'The abbot should not frighten the flock entrusted to him, nor should he act unjustly, like one yielding arbitrary power, but he should reflect constantly that all his judgements and actions are to be accounted for to God.'[122] From a Franciscan perspective (Pecham's) the upwards drift would have been similar, even with respect to temporal governance. 'The servant is not greater than the lord', said Pecham in relation to the servants' disobedience to Peter of Abingdon.[123] While Franciscan visitation allowed for the strictly regulated private accusation of brother by brother (peer-to-peer), *excessus* involving provincial ministers should gravitate up to the provincial chapter, and

---

[114] *Merton Muniments*, #6 at 25 ll. 82, 83.   [115] *Early Rolls of Merton*, 3.

[116] Compare Abelard's fine gradations between the powers of 'provost' and 'deaconess' in his proposed double-monastery (Clanchy, *Abelard*, 257).

[117] Highfield, 'Early Colleges', 231; *Early Rolls of Merton*, 68–9.

[118] *La Règle de Saint Benoît*, ed. Adalbert de Vogüé, and Jean Neufville, Sources chrétiennes 181–6, 7 vols. (Paris, 1971–7), i. cap. 4.61, 'praeceptis abbatis in omnibus oboedire, etiam si ipse aliter—quod absit!—agat, memores illud dominicum praeceptum: "Quae dicunt facite, quae autem faciunt facere nolite"' (cf. Matt. 23: 3).

[119] *Règle de Benoît*, ii. cap. 63, 'De ordine congregationis', and caps. 63. 5–10; 63. 15–17.

[120] *Règle de Benoît*, i. caps. 5.4; 5.9. Cf. also ii. cap. 63.12.

[121] *Règle de Benoît*, i. caps. 5.12; 5.14.

[122] *Règle de Benoît*, ii. cap. 63.2–3. Cf. 1 Kings 3 and Daniel 13: 44–62. Cf. also *Règle de Benoît*, ii. cap. 64.7, citing also Augustine's 'Rule', 15.200–1, and Luke 16: 2 on the unjust steward. Cap. 64.8, cites the Augustinian distinction between *prodesse* and *preesse* discussed at p. 135 n. 3. The theme of abbatial accountability to God is the touchstone for his accountability in Benedict's rule: i. caps. 2.37–8; 3.11; ii. 65.22. The cellarer is also directed to it, ii. cap. 31.9. The theme occurs also in the *Regula Magistri*, probably an earlier text drawing on a common model. Compare *La Règle du Maître*, ed. Adalbert de Vogüé et al., Sources chrétiennes 105–7, 3 vols. (Paris, 1964–5), i. caps 2.32–3; 7.55–6; ii. 93.18–23 (the accountable shepherd); Also *Règle du Maître* i. prologue 6 (general accountability after death); i. caps. 10.21–2 and ii. 11.51 (monks accountable for every foolish word); ii. caps. 11.20–6 (appointment of prior enables the abbot to worry less about his accountability).

[123] *Reg. Peckham*, iii. #589 at 818; cf. Matthew 10: 24 (I thank Sylvie Jaffrey for reminding me of this). A 'regular' example: *Reg. Peckham*, ii. #504 at 650–1.

thoroughly intractable problems could go higher still. Legislation against conspiracy further canalized challenges to superiors.[124]

Such hierarchical thinking existed generally in a university or collegial context. It was a function of learning and teaching. Students should be humble.[125] In the mid-twelfth century, William of Conches refused to concede to Parisian students the right to judge their masters.[126] A central purpose of Elias of Trikinghorn's *De disciplina scholarium* (1230–40) was to show 'how the exuberance of the adolescent should be subjected to his master and bound to discipline'.[127] Criticism of one's superiors had a place in satire, not serious thought; students had their own dreadful manners to worry about first.[128] Pecham would have given the head (*lector*) of Franciscan *studia* the same standing, since he (unlike Merton's *custos*) taught his members. This sensitivity can be discerned with respect to academic and university pastoral thought. Peter of Auvergne, commenting between 1272 and 1296 on Aristotle's *Politics*, offered a nuanced account of a multitude's superiority in judgement compared to an individual superior, and his permissions for its right to judge its leader were carefully qualified.[129] In the early thirteenth century, Thomas of Chobham talked of masters' accountability at the Last Judgement for their teaching of students.[130] In his university allegory of the Last Judgement, Robert de Sorbon

---

[124] 'Statuta generalia [. . .] Narbonae an. 1260, Assisii an. 1279 atque Parisiis an. 1292', cap. 8 on visitation, cap. 7 on correction, respectively 284–92 esp. 8.18, 8.20, 8.22 (287 for 'Narbonne', 290 for Assisi and Paris revisions). The regulations are strongly influenced by the sorts of inquisitorial concerns and approaches discussed in Ch. 4 (*excessus, infamia*, etc). Brooke has shown that cap. 8 is probably a 1239 introduction reacting to Elias's generality; cap. 7 both 1260 and perhaps 1244–7 (*Early Franciscan Government*, 232, 251, 277–8 and App. 4).

[125] See Hannah Skoda, *Medieval Violence: Physical Brutality in Northern France, 1270–1330* (Oxford, 2013), ch. 4 on student stereotyping.

[126] Wilhelm von Conches, *Philosophia*, ed. Gregor Maurach with Heidemarie Telle (Pretoria, 1980), 88 (book 4, preface).

[127] *PL* 64, cols. 1223–48 at 1225. Cf. the (ideally) subservient matriculating student's dialogue with his master in the late-fifteenth-century *Manuale Scholarium*, in *Die deutschen Universitäten im Mittelalter*, 3–4 (cap. 1).

[128] e.g. the 1241 *Morale Scolarium of John of Garland (Johannes de Garlandia) a Professor in the Universities of Paris and Toulouse in the Thirteenth Century*, ed. Louis John Paetow (Berkeley, Calif., 1927), 225–6, cap. 15, 'De prelatis voluptatis. . .': 'Ut Moysen Ietro, maiores instruo metro' etc. (l. 381). The following chapter deals with table manners.

[129] Peter's continuation of Aquinas's commentary on the *Politics* (for III.11, III.15) in *S. Thomae Aquinatis opera omnia: ut sunt in indice Thomistico: additis 61 scriptis ex aliis medii aevi auctoribus*, ed. Roberto Busa, 7 vols. (Stuttgart-Bad Cannstatt, 1980), vii. 414–15 (Peter's III cap. 9), 419–20 (Peter's III cap. 14); his later *quaestio* treatment is edited in Christoph Flüeler, *Rezeption und Interpretation der aristotelischen Politica im späten Mittelalter*, Bochumer Studien zur Philosophie 19, 2 vols. (Amsterdam, 1992), i. 214–16. Both are trans. in Arthur Stephen McGrade, John Kilcullen, and Matthew Kempshall (eds.), *The Cambridge Translations of Medieval Philosophical Texts*, ii. *Ethics and Political Philosophy* (Cambridge, 2001), at 230–8, 240–9 (literal commentary); 249–51 (Book 3, *quaestio* 17). See also Jean Dunbabin, 'The Reception and Interpretation of Aristotle's *Politics*', in Norman Kretzmann, Anthony Kenny, and Jan Pinborg with Eleanore Stump (eds.), *The Cambridge History of Later Medieval Philosophy: From the Rediscovery of Aristotle to the Disintegration of Scholasticism, 1100–1600* (Cambridge, 1982), 723–37 at 733–4. On the scholastic tendency to avoid explicating political problems by analogy with university institutions see Sabapathy, 'Regulating Community and Society at the Sorbonne'.

[130] Thomas de Chobham, *Summa confessorum*, ed. F. Broomfield, Analecta mediaevalia Namurcensia 25 (Louvain, 1968), 298. The *Summa* is dated 1215–17 (Joseph Goering, 'Chobham, Thomas of (d. 1233 x 6)', *ODNB*).

discussed how the Chancellor of Paris (i.e. God) will beat both bad students and their teachers if the latter are responsible for the former's failings at their examination (i.e. at the Last Judgement).[131] That is, in this context a restricted or no emphasis is placed on allowing scholars to hold their betters to account here and now. Their accountability is rather deferred or internalized.

In so far as he was held accountable annually, Merton's warden lacked such relief. In so far as he is accountable at all the constitution of Merton seemed to subvert a 'classic' Benedictine hierarchy. Accountability flows down and up. Pecham was unhappy with the flow; perhaps partly because he approached the question from a Franciscan perspective; partly because colleges were at this point still unknown quantities in regulating the current of accountability. Different ideals of community entailed different arrangements of accountability within them. As this study has shown, however, the flat impunity of office was increasingly untenable in a wide variety of fora. Within collegiate institutions themselves Merton should be seen as one of a number of related experiments exploring how best to arrange the accountability between wardens and fellows.[132]

Charitable college foundations institutionalized a friction between conflicting values. On the one hand students should be humble; on the other colleges often involved them in positions of responsibility, which risked conceitedness.[133] On the one hand was the norm that answerability should follow hierarchy and flow up not down; on the other was the problem that sometimes non-scholarly 'superiors' oversaw the institution but scholarly 'inferiors' embodied it.[134] Who in this was above, who below?[135] Pecham's problem could not have been absolutely the principle that the warden was accountable downwards. His minister general could be removed by the general chapter if he was inadequate. Accusations against Elias had indeed led to his deposition by Gregory IX in 1239; Innocent IV deposed Crescentius of Jesi in 1247.[136] The issue seems rather to have been that alongside norms about student humility fellows were the objects of charity. Poor scholars ought to behave as such.[137] That scholars should arrogate authority from the receipt of charity was, as he makes clear, a hard thought for Pecham to think. At the same time Merton's fellows treated the warden as little more than an obedientiary. This was not so much a struggle between Weberian 'experts' and 'dilettantes' as one between different experts from different cadres (administrative, scholarly)

---

[131] Robert de Sorbon, *De Consciencia et de tribus dietis*, ed. Félix Chambon (Paris, 1902), 30, §24.
[132] On fluidity, Highfield, 'Early Colleges', 230.
[133] Skoda, *Medieval Violence*, 125, citing norms of humility expected by a number of Parisian colleges of their students.
[134] Contrast the long-term academic master and annual 'administrative' warden of the Augustinian St George's Oxford: Barron, 'Augustinian Canons', 252–3.
[135] In this spirit, contemporary fellows of St John's College, Oxford (f. 1555 on the Cistercian foundation of St Bernard's College) are advised regarding hierarchy in the Senior Common Room following dinner that 'the senior Fellow presides (not the President of College even if present) [. . .] The President is simply a member of Common Room and has no authority there', Malcolm Vale, *Notes on the Senior Common Room for Fellows and Lecturers at St John's College* (privately printed, 2009), 3.
[136] François d'Assise, *Écrits*, 192 (*regula bullata*, cap. 8); Brooke, *Early Franciscan Government*, 161–7, 255.
[137] Cf. Gorochov, 'Notion de pauvreté'.

whose position simultaneously boosted their status in one direction as it undercut it in another.[138] Pure official administrators had an overarching stewardship but merely administered. Fellows embodied the institution but as the recipients of charity. Were Merton a hospital it would be one thing for the brothers running it to have some control over their head. But was the correct comparator for Merton's fellows a hospital's administering brothers, or the inmates who were the beneficiaries of its charity?

That there was some conceptual division at Merton between the two ideal types is clear from its constitutional material. The 1274 statutes handle warden's and scholars' respective accountabilities apart. The warden is accountable along with the bailiffs and his duties pertain to his administrative competence (in this more estates bursar than academic head).[139] The fellows meanwhile are accountable at the *scrutinia*, as described above, where their moral and intellectual conduct are the *interroganda*. The warden should attend the *scrutinium*, though his 'life, conduct, and integrity' were evaluated separately below stairs with the other servants after their accounts had been audited.[140] Pecham may have thought that Merton was a case of the inmates running the asylum. But that was, up to point, what Walter of Merton had designed.

Different views about how most productively to handle the friction at the heart of colleges are reflected in the plurality of constitutional models into the fourteenth century.[141] Definitions inflected accountabilities. In 1341 the Parisian college of Autun specified a one-member, one-vote plebiscite when choosing a head. The whole college was to gather in the chapel and swear an oath to choose the best master, while the senior scholar held the gospels, taking singly and secretly the votes whose result would be announced before them. Only if there was no majority choice did the appointment bounce upwards to the Chancellor of Notre Dame and three Masters of Theology, and failing that, the Bishop of Paris.[142]

Balliol's 1282 charter describes an Oxford principal who sounds functionally more like a twelfth-century master than either an abbot or a warden. Elected out of the fellowship he clearly belonged to their *ordo*[143] and retained a scholarly function. He

---

[138] Weber, *Wirtschaft und Gesellschaft*, 572, 'Einerlei [. . .] der Herr [. . .] stets befindet er sich den im Betrieb der Verwaltung stehenden geschulten Beamten gegenüber in der Lage des "Dilettanten" gegenüber dem "Fachmann" '.

[139] On e.g. the warden's visitation of Merton's estates see P. D. A. Harvey, *A Medieval Oxfordshire Village: Cuxham, 1240–1400* (Oxford, 1965), 87–90.

[140] Their accountings are textually distinct. *Merton Muniments*, #6 at 23 ll. 47–9, for the accountability of the scholars at scrutiny; at 24 ll. 56–65 for the stewards' (*yconomi*) and warden's annual accounts.

[141] See Maddicott, *Founders and Fellowship*, 30, 43.

[142] *The Mediaeval Statutes of the College of Autun at the University of Paris*, ed. David Sanderlin, Texts and Studies in the History of Mediaeval Education 13 (Notre Dame, 1971), ch. 5 at 40, 'prestito vero hujusmodi sacramento, dictus antiquior scolaris in Theologia sigillatim, secreto [. . .] vota singulorum de dicto collegio exquirat, sacerdote dicte domus et uno notario publico et testibus sufficientibus sibi assistentibus [. . .] Ea omnibus ibidem presentibus publicet in communi et ille in quem omnes vel major pars numero de facto consenserint eligatur.' The other provisions at 41. Cf. Queen's Oxford c.1340, *Statutes of the Colleges of Oxford*, i. *Queen's*, 9–10 (repeated voting to break deadlocks for *prepositus*) and 13 (election of fellows).

[143] 'Item uolumus quod scolares nostri ex semetipsis eligant unum principalem cui ceteri omnes humiliter obediant in hiis que officium principalis contingunt secundum statuta & consuetudines

regulated the in-house disputations of the most able before they proceeded to public ones in the schools.[144] He had no clear disciplinary remit initially (apart from ensuring Latin was spoken).[145] Two external procurators instead provided Balliol's explicit disciplinary mettle. They validated the scholars' choice of principal; penalized overspending from the weekly dole according to means; prevented the baiting of poorer members; expelled those refusing to speak Latin; and appointed the poor scholar who received in-house charity.[146] Sixty years later the system was deemed inadequate and the 1340 statutes (diverging from the 1280 charter) displaced the principal with a master, an administrator-scholar of a recognizable sort.[147]

The Sorbonne provides a further contrast.[148] It did not appoint its *provisor*. He was appointed by a broad representative committee of Paris's archdeacon, the University's Chancellor and Rector, its Regent Masters in Theology, the deans of Medicine and Canon Law, and the procurators of the Four Nations. It is hard to imagine which other university officials might have been involved. He was likewise accountable to them annually and could be removed by them as they saw fit.[149] The impression (post-Robert de Sorbon) of a well-tethered *provisor* is negatively and tentatively supported by the relative lack of evidence for problems relating to him. This group was more hobbled than the one at Merton. The *provisor* and members could in no way alienate property.[150] As to problems, the Sorbonne's cartulary contains one document addressing the *provisor*'s rights and powers—perhaps implying difficulties—but the two provisorates in the thirty-odd years following Robert de Sorbon's own do not imply overall the constitutional stress (liveliness?) of a Merton.[151] Sorbon had emphasized that 'we are all as equal fellows'.[152] It is hard to tell how far this was an achieved reality. It would be the

---

inter ipsos uisitatas & approbatas' (Devorguilla of Balliol's letter/charter of 22 August 1282), in *Oxford Deeds of Balliol*, #564 at 277.

[144] 'Si uero aliquis sophista ita prouectus fuerit quod merito possit in breui in scolis determinare, tunc ei dicatur a principali quod prius determinet domi inter socios suos [...] prefigat principalis diem disputacionis sequentis et disputacionem regat & garrulos cohibeat & assignat sophisma proximo disputandum,' etc., *Oxford Deeds of Balliol*, #564 at 279.

[145] The principal seems quickly to have filled the vacuum arising from no clear administrative head. Jones, *Balliol College*, 7.

[146] *Oxford Deeds of Balliol*, #564.

[147] See the 1340 statutes of Philip of Somerville in *Oxford Deeds of Balliol*, #571 esp. at 290–1 (his annual accounting to the whole fellowship or a delegated part of it), 292 (procedures for removing him for mismanagement/delicts). Somerville also established a complicated visitatorial board (abolished in 1364). See Jones, *Balliol College*, 17–20; Highfield, 'Early Colleges', 243.

[148] See further, Sabapathy, 'Regulating Community and Society at the Sorbonne'. There is a helpful map of Parisian colleges in André Tuilier, *Histoire de l'Université de Paris et de la Sorbonne*, 2 vols. (Paris, 1994), i. between 96–7.

[149] *CUP*, i. #421 (letter of Clement IV, 23 March 1268). Rashdall argued that nevertheless they interfered little (*Universities of Europe*, i. 508 n. 6). But if its appointees were partly placemen, interference might be less necessary.

[150] *CUP*, i. #421; and ##458–9 (letters of Gregory IX, 5 January 1275). See also L. J. Paetow's note on the university's jurisdiction over colleges in Rashdall, *Universities of Europe*, i. 533–6.

[151] Though one can infer some problems from Glorieux, *Origines de la Sorbonne*, i. ##7 (1297), 17, 20 (1318–19). The *provisores* Guillaume de Montmorency (1274–86), Pierre de Villepreux, (1286–1304), and Jean de Vallibus (1304–15) spent a good deal of time obtaining or securing property for the college: Glorieux, *Origines de la Sorbonne*, i. 118–29.

[152] Glorieux, *Origines de la Sorbonne*, i. 40.

more remarkable given Paris's intellectual and institutional ferment: the ongoing violent struggle between seculars and mendicants of the 1250s and beyond; the 1272 crisis about the university rector's election; the theological disputes of the 1270s; the 1290s controversy over the University's chancellor, Berthaud of St Denis; the Arnaud de Villeneuve affair of 1300–1; the university's involvement in the Templars' destruction.[153] Perhaps having a 'live-in' founder for seventeen years riveted the institutional fault-line that might have been produced by combining poor students of unequal means, the self-regard of an intellectual élite, a semi-administrative warden, some expectation of collegial parity, and traditional hierarchical norms.

Any resulting stability was not wholly at the expense of self-government. Indeed the Sorbonne placed a particular emphasis on temporary, rotating internal offices. This was accountability 'going across' peers—parallel to accountabilities going 'up' or 'down'. Thus with its *provisor* the Sorbonne had two annual procurators and a disciplinary prior (or *lator rotuli*), four-monthly lesser procurators, elected from fellows, and weekly officials chosen from members.[154] In these respects it was similar to the Parisian Nations, whose proctors were democratically elected but held office for only four to six weeks (similar to the rector of the Faculty of Arts that the Nations went on to elect).[155] Merton had four-monthly bursars too. Stapeldon Hall (a college in all but name) had an annually elected fellow-rector, preventing the highest official from becoming too entrenched. John Maddicott has interestingly suggested that the idea driving that may well have been reforming ideas about fixed-term shrieval tenures, exemplifying again how transferable ideas of official accountability could be.[156] Part of the point must have been to ease the tensions between scholars and administrators by blurring the divisions between them. Likewise, rotating officers presumably reduced, or equalized, the extent to which authority and status attached to persons rather than offices.[157] (Pecham's point in his *Expositio* about the minister general being a *custos* because of function not status was similar.) A related logic clearly lies behind the automatic dismissal and audit of administrative servants at Merton before any reappointment could take place.[158] Reappointment was consequent on satisfactory tenure of office. The academic

---

[153] Luca Bianchi, 'Gli articoli censurati nel 1241/1244 e la loro influenza da Bonaventura a Gerson', in F. Morenzoni. J.-Y. Tilliette (ed.), *Autour de Guillaume d'Auvergne (†1249)* (Turnhout, 2005), 155–71; Glorieux, *Origines de la Sorbonne*, i. 106–7, 115–23, 128–9; Wei, *Intellectual Culture in Medieval Paris*, 161–9; *CUP*, ii. ##569, 571–2, 577, and 592 on Berthaud; Joseph Ziegler, *Medicine and Religion, c.1300: The Case of Arnau de Vilanova* (Oxford, 1998), 24–8.

[154] Glorieux, *Origines de la Sorbonne*, i. ##1 at 194 (by 1274); 2 (late 1260s–early 1270s?); 8–9 (1300–4); 26 (1327); discussion at 97–9 with uncertainty about the dating of #2 at 114, 124; Rashdall, *Universities of Europe*, i. 508–9.

[155] Wei, *Intellectual Culture in Medieval Paris*, 111.

[156] *Register of Stapeldon*, 304–5; Maddicott, *Founders and Fellowship*, 41–2; Highfield 'Early Colleges', 231–2. For the fourteenth-century annual *computi rectoris* that preceded the (re-)election, see *Register of the Rectors, Fellows and Other Members on the Foundation of Exeter College, Oxford*, ed. Charles William Boase, OHS 27 (Oxford, 1894), 339–48.

[157] Marti, *Spanish College*, 188 notes the dangers of office: 'officium periculosum est et ualde suspectum'.

[158] *Merton Muniments*, #6 at 24 ll. 61–5.

equivalent was Merton's *scrutinium* of intellectual and moral progress itself. Other institutions had such 'security clauses'.[159] Some attempt to remind office-holders, even so, of their strictly limited authority seems behind the Sorbonne's complicated system of official key-holders, including a non-office-holding fellow who may have acted like a 'surety' (having no office to lose).[160] As a final net, criss-crossing the formal checks and counter-checks and indifferent to office, went mutual supervision—bluntly, spying.[161] As the Spanish College at Bologna said regarding its *rector*'s co-counsellors: 'where there is much counsel there is much benefit'.[162]

'COLLEGE PECULIARS'

The above argument has suggested that colleges embodied frictions that were a function of their intermixing a particular charitable purpose and their constitutional affiliations with religious institutions of one sort or another. Like all the officers and institutions for accountability analysed here, the intelligent construction of institutions for regulating conflict was at the centre of colleges' own approaches.

The fault-lines, this section suggests (pp. 214–20), are mostly a consequence of colleges' need to embody various accountabilities (the plural is important). But colleges' oddness has also been stressed, partly in order to see them as novelties (and distinct from halls or older private masters' schools). Many college histories have been written for *almas matres* with some level of filial piety, and some consequent idealization.[163] This can take some of the rough edges off them

---

[159] 1228, Bishop of Paris to scholars of St Thomas du Louvre: *CUP*, i. #60 (students to leave after a year, can be readmitted on basis of previous conduct). Compare the Sorbonne: Glorieux, *Origines de la Sorbonne*, i. #1 at 195 (removal if no progress in seven years). The accountable distraint envisaged by cap. 61, the security clause, of Magna Carta of course was exacted by inferior of superior. See comment in Robert Bartlett, *England under the Norman and Angevin Kings, 1075–1225* (Oxford, 2000), 65–6.

[160] Glorieux, *Origines de la Sorbonne*, i. #20 at 213 (1319), the text partly corrupt. The general problem in religious communities was longstanding. Cf. e.g. Alexander III's confirmation of the ruling of Archbishop Guillaume aux-Blanches-Mains of Sens, c.1171, at Chartres granting administrative responsibility for the chapter's lands to small groups of two to four canons, removing the wide-ranging responsibilities of the four great canon-*prepositi* whose abuses had not been halted over the previous decades by obligations to swear various oaths: *Cartulaire de Notre-Dame de Chartres*, E. de Lépinois and Lucien Merlet, 3 vols. (Chartres, 1862–5), i. ##33–4 at 119–22 (1114); #57–8 at 155–9 (1149–55); #86 at 188–90 (8 April 1171/2), comment, lxxxv, xcvii–c.

[161] *Lupi* who spy and report on students who do not speak in Latin: *Manuale scholarium*, ed. Zarncke, 25–6, 28 (caps. 9, 11), also Seybolt's trans., 66 n. 4, 72 n. 2; whispering campaigns, *Merton Muniments*, #13 at 33 (fo. 1ᵛ ll. 88–9). On denouncing *lecturers* in Italy see Alan B. Cobban, 'Medieval Student Power', *P&P* 53 (1971), 28–66 at 41, 43.

[162] Marti, *Spanish College*, 130 quoting Prov. 11: 14 on the four elected counsellors from different disciplines assisting the internally elected, fixed-term rector. Annually they 'racionem et compotum uniuersalem reddere teneantur' (250). Luke 16: 2 is again referenced.

[163] e.g. Glorieux, *Origines de la Sorbonne*, i. 39–42, 94–102. On the historiography of 'Oxbridge' see Mordechai Feingold, 'Oxford and Cambridge College Histories: An Outdated Genre?', *History of Universities* 1 (1981), 207–13 revisited by Robin Darwall-Smith, 'Oxford and Cambridge College Histories: An Endangered Genre?', *History of Universities* 22.1 (2007), 241–9. The contours of university historiographies unsurprisingly vary with place. See e.g. Peter Denley, 'Recent Studies on Italian Universities of the Middle Ages and Renaissance', *History of Universities* 1 (1981), 193–205.

institutionally.[164] There is also a risk that self-administering, endowed, communal colleges, for the education of poor students, are seen as both a significant innovation and a teleological inevitability, a position with some potential for paradox.[165] This is made the easier by the durability and hence familiarity of the institution. Medieval descriptions of college administrators can be transposed to their modern equivalents (and vice versa). The parallel tendency to view especially Oxford and Cambridge—and consequently their colleges—as ever-present centres of scholarship should likewise be resisted. In the mid-thirteenth century Lincoln or Northampton might look equally likely English scholarly centres—as collegial statutes providing for the relocation of colleges remind us.[166]

So it is hard to recapture the oddness and insecurity of colleges. It has been argued that William of Durham's bequest for supporting ten to twelve Theology Masters (the future University College) was mishandled because 'people were not sure what to do with it'—his 'Parisian [collegial] concepts were too advanced for the Oxford of 1249'.[167] Similarly, whether Pecham would not or could not recognize what he saw at Merton, his misapprehensions about its organization seem a conservative Franciscan's misreading of one institutional form (a college) for a more traditional hierarchy that he could, or would, recognize (a monastery or perhaps a Franciscan *studium*). Merton certainly looked wrong to him, probably in principle, certainly in practice. This begs a simple question though: if colleges were that odd and insecure, why did they exist at all, and why did they persist?

Intellectuals, Poverty, Self-administration

There were a number of elements in tension within secular, self-administering, endowed colleges, as we have seen. Pecham wanted Merton's scholars to be accountable. He showed every sign of disbelieving they could be responsible for much at all. But colleges' claim to institutional significance hangs on this premise: the Bishop of Rochester made his scholars accountable because they were responsible for the college. (The ways in which currents flow between officers' accountability and responsibility is of course a wider concern of this study.) In many ways Merton's (or the Sorbonne's)

---

[164] Darwall-Smith, *History of University College* begins refreshingly with the perversion of its founder William of Durham's original bequest (1–17).

[165] Tuilier, *Histoire de l'Université de Paris*, i. 119–21 stresses the ambiguous purpose of the Sorbonne at its origins.

[166] See Frans van Liere, 'The Study of Canon Law and the Eclipse of the Lincoln Schools, 1175–1225', *History of Universities* 18.1 (2003), 1–13; H. G. Richardson, 'The Schools of Northampton in the Twelfth Century', *EHR* 56 (1941), 595–605; C. H. Lawrence, 'The University in State and Church', in *History of the University of Oxford*, i. 97–150 at 127–32. Irrespective of the precise timing of the decline of these schools, founders' provisions for relocation indicates their uncertainty about the stability of study where they were establishing colleges.

[167] Darwall-Smith, *History of University College*, 13, 12. It is not evident how clear William of Durham's 'original' 'collegiate endowment' was (12). The 1280/1 inquiry into its mishandling does not offer strong proof for its coherence. It could be argued that the presence of a founder or close family member was a key (see Merton, Balliol, the Sorbonne). Maddicott stresses the personal involvement of Walter Stapeldon and his family in Stapeldon Hall (Exeter College): *Founders and Fellowship*, 31, 45–6, 48–9.

solution was wholly unoriginal. It was an institutionalization of the need for bright young scholars to be trained for the sorts of responsibility they would assume on leaving those colleges. As Archbishop of Canterbury Pecham after all had to arrange for the management of things as un-Franciscan as its extensive estates.[168] The trope of learned monks' and priests' scorn for, evasion of, or resignation to the responsibilities of office was as old as the established Church.[169] Yet equally scholarship as a means to beneficed bursarial responsibilities was a marriage as openly disavowed as it was privately anticipated.[170] There was not a little *ressentiment* in the scorn we saw Gerald of Wales express for Hubert Walter (pp. 93, 135–6). In some ways, though, the intermixture of learning and administering was more problematic for colleges.

There was the question of scholars' administrative competence to begin with. The Sorbonne's greater and lesser procurators were appointed from its membership and the college was responsible as a whole for setting its own monthly budget.[171] But the Sorbonne also needed provisions for recovering bad debts from its own procurators.[172] By 1318 the greater procurators were required to account weekly, implying that less frequent accounting was a bad idea.[173] Two paid fellows kept University College's financial and disciplinary matters in order, a *procurator* with the former day-to-day responsibilities and a senior fellow with responsibility for the latter and overall oversight.[174] Merton itself used some of the most up-to-date accounting methods on its estates, which, again, fellows were involved in regulating.[175]

Effective self-administration was predicated on collaboration. This need cut across the contrasting impulse towards intellectual rivalry. At least since Abelard, the 'battle of the schools' had encouraged ill-tempered competition.[176] That study led to community *dissensionem* was an argument Aquinas felt obliged to rebut when justifying peaceable religious orders' involvement in it.[177] The violence of medieval university towns was a logical corollary (other factors contributed too). Many of the texts in Denifle and Châtelain's *Chartularium Universitatis Parisiensis* are concerned with student violence and behaviour.[178] Constraining scholars to collaborate collegially might be putting cats in a sack. The same was true of the more straightforwardly self-interested Nations.[179] The Nations were there to advance the collective interests of their members. The colleges were there to advance the charitable aims of their founders. Both faced challenges ordering individual egos towards institutional interests.

---

[168] *Survey of Archbishop Pecham's Kentish Manors 1283–85*, ed. Kenneth Witney, Kent Records 28 (Maidstone, 2000); Douie, *Archbishop Pecham*, 85–94.
[169] R. A. Markus, *Gregory the Great and His World* (Cambridge, 1997), 12–14, 17–26; Carole Straw, *Gregory the Great: Perfection in Imperfection* (Berkeley, Calif., 1988), 188–93.
[170] Murray, *Reason and Society*, ch. 9.
[171] Glorieux, *Origines de la Sorbonne*, i. #2 at 199.
[172] Glorieux, *Origines de la Sorbonne*, i. #2 at 199–200.
[173] Glorieux, *Origines de la Sorbonne*, i. #17.
[174] *Munimenta Academica*, i. 57 (1292); ii 782 (1280/1281).
[175] *Manorial Records of Cuxham*, 32, 30.   [176] Murray, *Reason and Society*, 234–7.
[177] *Summa Theologiae*, IIa–IIae q. 188 a. 5 obj. 2.
[178] See further, Skoda, *Medieval Violence*, 119–58.
[179] For a 1345–8 Bolognese example, *Statuta Nationis Germanicae Bononiae*, 101–23 esp. caps. 24 on discord, 25 on exclusion, 29 on infamy, reputation, and purgation. The earlier 1292 statutes are far briefer (95–7).

Tensions between members of colleges were further exacerbated by disparities in wealth, a third problem.[180] A charitable *raison d'être* for colleges was supporting poor scholars.[181] Students at the Collège des Bons-Enfants (f. *c.*1209) were instructed to add to their incomes by begging.[182] Neither Robert de Sorbon nor Walter of Merton were from wealthy backgrounds and both had raised themselves through literacy, though Walter's learning was more modest than Robert's.[183] A recurrent worry was the scandalous potential of dress.[184] Robert de Sorbon had himself got into a row about his *vilain* parentage with Jean de Joinville, when he ticked off the seneschal at court for wearing better clothes than the King.[185] The sumptuary legislation *universitates* issued simultaneously shows that there could be considerable gaps in wealth and that these caused tensions.[186] Food was another concern, particularly private dining. Hostility to private dining arose partly from the value placed on communal life.[187] But loud, lavish private dining was also a potential source of external scandal or internal resentment.[188] Other status symbols caused problems. Merton's 1338 *scrutinium* minutes find one fellow complaining about the number of horses the college was burdened by (presumably belonging to fellows).[189]

The attitudes of college members towards poverty itself in all this are hard to sift. That scholars should be needy was a given for founders, and so poverty is a *desideratum* in their statutes. Sumptuary legislation implies scholars might not feel the same way. One suggestion of how scholars themselves felt can be obtained from John of Garland's 1241 poem *Morale scolarium*.[190] Garland, an English grammarian who had studied at Oxford, Paris, and Toulouse provides in the poem a cynical-cum-realist portrait of a scholar's difficulties. His attitude to poverty may

---

[180] Oxford Colleges' policies on poverty summarized by Highfield, 'Early Colleges', 252–4. General remarks on poverty in universities, Miri Rubin, *Charity and Community in Medieval Cambridge* (Cambridge, 1987), 269–71, 275–8.

[181] Though Tuilier, *Histoire de l'Université de Paris*, i. 119 wonders whether Sorbon's original intention was charitable. See Gorochov, 'Notion de pauvreté' for her reservations about whether 'poor scholars' was meant literally.

[182] Murray, '1249', 60–1, citing J. M. Reitzel, 'The Founding of the Earliest Secular Colleges within the Universities of Paris and Oxford' (Ph.D. thesis, Brown University, 1971), 130. I have been unable to consult this.

[183] Robert's background is stressed in William Chester Jordan, *Men at the Center: Redemptive Governance under Louis IX* (Budapest, 2012), 1–22.

[184] Glorieux, *Origines de la Sorbonne*, i. #1 at 194. The need for personal marks sewn into clothing was a corollary of having an identical 'uniform' (195).

[185] Joinville, *Histoire de Saint Louis*, ed. M. Natalis de Wailly, 9th edn. (Paris, 1921), ch. 6.

[186] *Oxford Deeds of Balliol*, #564 at 278 (1282), 'Et ut melius prouideatur sustentacioni pauperum ad quorum utilitatem intendimus laborare, uolumus quod diciores in societate scolarium nostrorum ita temperate studeant uiuere ut pauperiores nullo modo grauentur propter expensas onerosas.' For Bolognese rules on livery, Marti, *Spanish College*, 216–18. The requirement to have one's name sewn into (identical) clothing in colleges was obviously a corollary of such parity.

[187] Glorieux, *Origines de la Sorbonne*, i. #1 at 193.

[188] Glorieux, *Origines de la Sorbonne*, i. #1 at 194; *Statutes of Autun* (1345 statutes), cap. 15 at 86–7, passage beginning, 'Rursus ad evitandum turpia et indecentia, murmurationes, contentiones'. The Merton 1339 minuted complaint 'de tumultu sociorum in cameris' of Simon of Westcombe was presumably of a similar nature (*Merton Muniments*, #15 at 35 (fo. 3ᵛ l. 204)). On scandal see here pp. 214–20.

[189] *Merton Muniments*, #14 at 34 (fo. 3 l. 154), William of Humberston's complaint.

[190] Traugott Lawler, 'Garland, John of (b. *c.*1195, d. in or after 1258)', *ODNB*.

be contradictory rather than nuanced, but that may also point towards contradictions in wider university life.[191] On the one hand poverty is a virtuous challenge to be overcome. 'The victor over poverty is a recruit to probity, a soldier of honesty, a prince of peace, a man of piety.'[192] But poverty is also a hazard: 'Poverty will root up many and fling them from their home.'[193] It is not bad to be poor, but the poor are treated badly.[194] Garland knows, resentfully, that only lucrative scholarship is its own reward.[195] Poverty seems to run in tandem with Garland's theme of *rusticitas* which is treated as both the virtuous accent of the inverse snob[196] and the shibboleth that the successful scholar must quash.[197] So Garland lists the 'seven signs of a peasant according to Thales', justifying their removal, 'Even were you Socrates, you'll just be a ditch-digger if you can't curb your crudity.'[198]

The question of rusticity returns us to the relationship between social standing, collegial administration, and self-government. A fourth and final question is suggested. Was there anything *infra dignitatem* of a scholar who undertook an administrative job? The obligation of such office-holders to give an account of their tenure has been well-stressed. Yet the phrase's Gospel derivation and connotations (see e.g. pp. 26–9, 42–3, 160, 203) are subservient and/or rural: hardly an edifying comparator for an upwardly mobile scholar.[199] It is a interesting question whether self-governing colleges had to struggle to persuade their members to undertake such offices.[200] This may well have been the case at the Sorbonne, finding expression in financial penalties imposed for evading office-holding.[201] On the other hand ecclesiastical office provided a constant link between administration, financial security, status, and some intellectual competence. This was the self-made route of Walter of Merton; he would hardly despise it. It was the Church in some shape or form that would provide livings for many scholars. Scholars can't be choosers. With all his contradictions, John of Garland can be cited to make that point too. He rounds on an imagined nepotistic prelate he knew at the schools: 'O prelate, you've given not a thing to your naked old friend. But why should you

---

[191] Murray, *Reason and Society*, 231, 237–44, is again suggestive on this theme and *rusticitas*.
[192] *Morale scolarium*, cap. 10 p. 207 ll. 209–10.
[193] *Morale scolarium*, cap. 26 p. 238 l. 515.
[194] 'Pauper deprimitur, teritur, pauper quia scitur; | Nudus despicitur baculo ferroque feritur', *Morale scolarium*, cap. 6 p. 197 ll. 109–10.
[195] '. . .Sapiens, procul eicieris. | Si nichil attuleris, demens eris, indignus eris. | Que lucrative sunt artes sunt modo vive, | Ut causative, specierum compositive, | Et celeres misse que posssunt es habuisse, | Resque foro misse que possunt lucra dedisse', *Morale scolarium*, cap. 1 p. 189 ll. 20–4.
[196] 'Natum rure chorum presignit mente decorum', *Morale scolarium*, cap. 10 p. 208 l. 220.
[197] 'Hanc modo defendo [i.e. curialitas], sunt rustica que reprehendo' (on table manners), *Morale scolarium*, cap. 9 p. 202 l. 164.
[198] *Morale scolarium*, cap. 21 p. 232 l. 453.
[199] Niermeyer, *Mediae Latinitatis Lexicon Minus*, ii. 1439–40. On upwardly mobile scholars see Murray, *Reason and Society*, esp. chs. 9–12. See further Olga Weijers, *Terminologie des Universités au XIIIe Siècle*, Lessico Intellettuale Europeo 39 (Rome 1987), 73–9.
[200] Murray's *Reason and Society* does not frame precisely this question, but 237–9 provide food for thought. I address aspects in 'Regulating Community and Society at the Sorbonne in the Late Thirteenth Century'.
[201] Glorieux, *Origines de la Sorbonne*, i. #2 at 197–8.

care unless you have proved him worthy through witnesses; if you did so you could loosen your right hand and give out a gift.'[202]

There was no insurmountable contradiction between being a scholar and desiring a post; nor of being a scholar of distinction and a serious administrator—as the careers of Pecham or Kilwardby show. Yet questions of status, the standing of collegial administrative offices, poverty, and intellectuals' self-regard must show, again, that historians should not take collegial self-governance as a self-evident given: the ingredients were a potentially volatile combination. Pecham at Merton exemplifies it.

Sources and Reasons

Constitutionally, those ingredients are a pick-and-mix from pre-existing institutional forms.[203] And to reiterate, it is only their combination that risks incoherence and is novel. How did the whole differ from the sum of its parts?

There were parallels with the Nations in colleges' self-government. But student guilds' most pronounced (democratic) forms cannot be completely reconciled with more hierarchical colleges, even where 'superiors' were accountable to 'inferiors' as at Merton.[204] Ultimately, Nations' principle interests were their own. That might have encouraged violence, but it did not make them institutional sociopaths. Nations still worried, as colleges did, about members' *scandalum* and how to control it.[205]

In Nations the identity between members and institution was very close. Colleges had a rather more subtle dynamic given their endowed status and founders' intentions. College members' interests bisected temporarily and only to a degree with the enduring charitable impulse which gave the whole endeavour life and was intended to outlast any individual's membership. That charitable impulse to endow a trust is most closely paralleled in hospital foundations. As noted, many college foundations have their roots in or alongside hospitals. Walter of Merton's first charitable impulse produced St John's Hospital, Basingstoke (where Peter of Abingdon had also been warden).[206] That hospital went on to offer elderly fellows a rest home until the early

---

[202] *Morale scolarium*, cap. 8 p. 202 ll. 160–2. Compare the description of the student from Chaucer, *The Canterbury Tales*, Prologue, ll. 285–308.

[203] Contiguously, the fact that Merton as a foundation bears parallels with Islamic *awqaf* seems more a testament to humans' ability independently to produce similar objects that meet similar needs—rather than an argument for Islamic influence. For the Islamic influence argument see Monica M. Gaudiosi, 'The Influence of the Islamic Law of Waqf on the Development of the Trust in England: The Case of Merton College', *University of Pennsylvania Law Review* 136 (1988), 1231–61. See further pp. 241–6.

[204] Kibre, *Nations in the Medieval Universities*, 43 (Germans at Bologna), 70–5 (Nations at Paris). For Bolognese students' control over teachers see Cobban, 'Medieval Student Power', 35–43 esp. 39–43. Parisian Nations were different again, only feeding into the Arts faculty and governed by its Masters. 'The nation was a masters' institution run by and for those who taught. As such it reflected the concerns of magisterial life': Gordon Leff, *Paris and Oxford Universities in the Thirteenth and Fourteenth Centuries: An Institutional and Intellectual History* (New York, 1968), 51–60 at 60. Cobban's hypothesis that collegial universities defused 'student power' would require separate consideration; 'Medieval Student Power', 64.

[205] See e.g. *Statuta Nationis Germanicae Bononiae*, 114 (cap. 23), 120–1 (cap. 29).

[206] Martin and Highfield, *History of Merton*, 4; *Early Rolls of Merton*, 21–2; *CCR 1257–1300*, 44; Merton College Record, #1731, trans. in Francis Joseph Baigent and James Elwin Millard, *A History*

fifteenth century at least.[207] A 1272 document calls the college itself a *hospitalis*.[208] Alongside Canterbury and Winchester, Oxford had the most hospitals in England.[209] The town's association of chantries for the sick and chantries for the clever was not limited to Merton. Pairings of Oxford college and hospital included: Oriel and St Bartholomew's, Cowley; Queen's and St Julian's (God's House), Southampton; and later Magdalen with St John the Baptist.[210] The connection was also early at Cambridge: Peterhouse budded off from a hospital, St John's.[211] The earliest collegiate foundation in Paris, the Collège des Dix-Huit was a room in the Hôtel-Dieu next to Notre Dame.[212] Their 1330 statutes still characterized them as the 'Scholars of the House of God'.[213] Paris in turn had about sixty hospitals for a population of over 200,000 by the mid-fourteenth century.[214] Further comparison would be needed to test how far colleges and hospitals were fellow-travellers. Certainly the association was not only Northern European. Siena's Casa della Sapienza arose out of early discussions to convert the hospital Casa della Misericordia (1388).[215]

Those hospital roots flowed out of monastic ones and into colleges: shared worship and prayers for a founder; communal eating accompanied by edifying reading; common dress. Writing about Cambridge's charitable foundations, Miri Rubin has argued that given their communal, regular lives and commemorative functions, Cambridge's colleges and hospitals shared striking similarities.[216] Merton College had monastic and hospital roots—it was originally a trust for students held by the Augustinian Priory at Merton.[217] Walter's own priory education had quickly led to practical office there (as attorney and land agent).[218] His foundation encouraged

---

of the Ancient Town and Manor of Basingstoke (London, 1889), 44–5; Watson, '*Fundatio, Ordinatio and Statuta*', 135–9.

[207] Martin and Highfield, *History of Merton*, 324 n. 257.

[208] *Early Rolls of Merton*, 69 n. 9.

[209] Michel Mollat, *The Poor in the Middle Ages: An Essay in Social History*, trans. A. Goldhammer (New Haven, Conn., 1986), 147.

[210] *Early Rolls of Merton*, 50–1. See also Nicholas Orme, *Medieval Schools: From Roman Britain to Renaissance England* (New Haven, Conn., 2006), 208–9.

[211] Mayr-Harting, 'Foundation of Peterhouse', 319, 326 n. 1, 334; *Documents Relating to Cambridge*, ii. 2–3; Rubin, *Charity and Community*, 271–6.

[212] *CUP*, i. *Pars introductoria* #50 (1180 acceptance by the Dean and Chapter of Paris of Josse of London's endowment).

[213] E. Coyecque, 'Notice sur l'ancien collège des Dix-Huit', *Bulletin de la Société de l'Histoire de Paris et de l'Île de France* 14 (Paris, 1887), 176–86, statutes edn. 181–4 at 184.

[214] Mollat, *Poor in the Middle Ages*, 147; difficulties of estimation at 146, 173–7, 265–71. *Histoire des hôpitaux en France* ed. Jean Imbert (Toulouse, 1982), 101, has a map of the nineteen main hospitals in central Paris.

[215] Peter Denley, *Commune and Studio in Late Medieval and Renaissance Siena* (Bologna, 2006), 299–305; the earliest examples are French-influenced Bolognese ones (Collegio Avignonese, 1256; Collegio Bresciano, 1326), 301.

[216] Rubin, *Charity and Community*, 182, 191. On Western medieval hospitals' greater emphasis on spiritual and palliative care as contrasted with Islamic and Byzantine foundations' medical emphasis, John Henderson, Peregrine Horden, and Alessandro Pastore (eds.), *The Impact of Hospitals, 300–2000* (Berne, 2007), 21.

[217] Martin and Highfield, *History of Merton*, 5, 11–13. See 15 arguing the Surrey properties' prayers were 'the chief and essential function of the house, and their performance a guarantee that its contingent business would be duly and effectively performed'. Also Highfield, 'Early Colleges', 251.

[218] *Early Rolls of Merton*, 8–9.

subtle and useful fellows in principle and practice. Nor were his links with the religious limited to monks. Although Kilwardby's Register is lost, we can tell from his correspondence that the Dominican had cordial relations with Merton's college.[219] Likewise, for Robert of Sorbon a key influence seems to have been the Franciscans, an unsurprising empathy for Louis IX's chaplain.[220] Franciscans' preoccupation with poverty and its value converged with—or surpassed—the colleges' emphasis on poor scholars (however relative or partial).[221] Aside from being young and able to benefit from learning, indigence was the key quality that Pecham reminded Merton's scholars to select members on. He did not stress (as he might) that they should be honest, chaste, peaceful, humble, fit for study.[222] (Given his views on the fellowship perhaps this was too much to ask.) Such influences are consistent with the twelfth- and thirteenth-century tendency for university institutions to monasticize themselves partially, if only to neutralize their monastic critics.[223]

There were differences though.[224] An important one has been touched on already. Fellows were not quite so coterminous with monks and/or hospital brethren as they might look to outsiders. College fellows were the recipients of charity. Were college fellows then really stewards or rather inmates and beneficiaries; and if the latter, what were they doing regulating the actual stewards, such as the bailiffs and warden of Merton? This seems at root to be Pecham's problem. Nor were the values of collegiate founders and monks or friars completely consonant here. Douie suggested that, as a good Franciscan, one of the things irritating Pecham at Merton was its building programme.[225] Similarly a monastic disavowal of 'acceptance of persons' can hardly have been more flagrantly in conflict with collegial rules favouring founder's kin.[226] So the affinities between religious orders and colleges are partial and partially contradictory. There was space for consensus about whether officers' accountability to inferiors or peers was acceptable (as warden to fellows). It is a central argument of this chapter that whether such accountability was acceptable depended on what sort of community one saw a college as: *natio, studium, hospitalis, ordo*. Such accountability of officers to members was most customary for Nations; most problematic if the correct

---

[219] TNA SC 1/18/173 (1277–8) to Edward I; SC 1/10/72 (1277–8) to John of Kirkby.

[220] Nicole Bériou, 'Robert de Sorbon, maître en théologie, 1201–1274', in Marcel Viller et al. (eds.), *Dictionnaire de spiritualité ascétique et mystique: doctrine et histoire*, 17 vols. (Paris, 1937–95) xiii. cols. 816–24 at 817, 823; but cf. Gorochov, 'Notion de pauvreté', 126–8.

[221] Cobban, *Medieval English Universities*, 304–5 analyses some of the earliest available data from New College Oxford *c*.1380–*c*.1500. Of poor scholars, 61.4% were children of rural smallholders, 0.1% children of urban labourers or serfs.

[222] Cf. *Reg. Peckham*, iii. #589 at 816, 'quia solos debetis recipere indigentes', and the 1274 rule in *Merton Muniments*, #6 at 22 l. 26.

[223] See e.g. Highfield, 'Early Colleges', 251–2; Wei, *Intellectual Culture in Medieval Paris*, 72–8, 85–6, 99–100, 122; Stephen C. Ferruolo, *The Origins of the University: The Schools of Paris and Their Critics, 1100–1215* (Stanford, Calif., 1985); Ferruolo, 'The Paris Statutes of 1215 Reconsidered', *History of Universities* 5 (1985), 1–14.

[224] See Verger, 'Fonder un collège au XIIIᵉ siècle', 31–2; Tuilier, *Histoire de l'Université de Paris*, i. 121.

[225] Douie, *Archbishop Pecham*, 275. For relevant remarks within a Dominican context see Joanna Cannon, *Religious Poverty, Visual Riches: Art in the Dominican Churches of Central Italy in the Thirteenth and Fourteenth Centuries* (New Haven, Conn., 2013), 18–21, 339–40.

[226] Well stressed by Mayr-Harting, 'Foundation of Peterhouse', 326, 330.

comparanda for Merton's fellows were a hospital's inmates. As we have seen with the Franciscans, for religious orders the accountability of heads to brothers was acceptable, even if God was in the detail. By the mid-thirteenth century Benedictines too would be less able to criticize a quasi-monastic common life whose head was accountable to its members. Gregory IX had sought to provide precisely for more accountable abbots in his 1235–7 revisions to the Benedictine Rule.[227] As a result the abbot was far more accountable internally and (in principle) his scope for unilateral action significantly limited—particularly regarding asset management, even if the tension between an accountable abbot and obedient monks beneath him remained.[228]

College founders were magpies, picking up bright fragments from a range of institutions to feather their own nests. In their new settings, some of those borrowings diverged from the purpose of their original setting. The above argument suggested that the new pattern risked incoherence. Yet it lasted. So something about it worked. What?

The argument has been that colleges were a striking institutional intermixture drawn from other contexts that also had various fault-lines or tensions running through them. So the reasons justifying these institutional cross-breeds must have been stronger than the strains on their joints. The last part of this chapter argues this. In particular it argues that the strain on colleges' joints are mostly a consequence of their need to embody certain mutually reinforcing accountabilities.

The reasons that drive these specific accountabilities are a mixture of the simple and the relatively sophisticated. The principal driver relates fundamentally to founders' needs. The others fall out of this: the control of violence and *scandalum*; the requirement for housing; and the complexity of charitable objectives.

Volo is the first word of the Sorbonne's statutes.[229] *Ego* is Merton's after its divine invocation: 'ego [. . .] do, assigno et concedo'.[230] This was self-government at the founder's command. Endowed colleges were designed to be vehicles of charity fulfilling their founder's express purposes; the same is true of hospitals.[231] Otherwise charitable energy would be misspent.[232] So reliability must come first. That entailed writing down what

---

[227] *Registrum Gregorii IX*, ii. #3045. There are two recensions in the Register, from 1235 ('a') and 1237 ('b'), the latter confirmed in 1253 by Innocent IV, with a mixed text in Matthew Paris's *Additamenta* (*Chronica majora*, vi. 235–47). See e.g. *Registrum Gregorii IX*, ii. #3045, caps. 26–9, 31, 34, 47, 51; also *Documents Illustrating the Activities of the General and Provincial Chapters of the English Black Monks, 1215–1540*, ed. W. A. Pantin, CS 3rd ser. 45, 47, 54, 3 vols. (1931–7), i. #13 at 45 (14 October 1249, General Chapter, Canterbury Province), #34 at 110–11 (1279 'scheme' for interpreting the Rule).
[228] David Knowles, *The Religious Orders in England*, 3 vols. (Cambridge, 1948–59), i. 270–1.
[229] Glorieux, *Origines de la Sorbonne*, i. #1 at 193.
[230] *Merton Muniments*, #2 at 15 ll. 1–3 (1264); in 1274, a confirmation and extension, it is 'ego [. . .] approbo, stabilio et confirmo', #6 at 21 ll. 1–4.
[231] Stressed by Watson, *Fundatio, Ordinatio and Statuta*, ch. 2, 77, 98–110, and suggesting (299) that constitutional *hospitales* provided a model for later medieval monastic patrons eager to hold *their* foundations 'accountable'. See also Astrik L. Gabriel, 'Motivation of the Founders of Medieval Colleges', *Garlandia: Studies in the History of the Medieval University* (Notre Dame, Ind., 1969), 211–23 at 212; Rashdall, *Universities of Europe*, i. 498–500, esp. 500 n. 1.
[232] See e.g. a thirteenth-century French *Summa pastoralis* including instructions for archdeacons evaluating the administration of almshouses in relation to their charitable purpose and edited by Félix Ravaisson, *Catalogue général des manuscrits des bibliothèques publiques des départements*, 7 vols. (Paris,

was wanted. By definition, for founders of colleges and hospitals, reliability means upholding charitable ambitions beyond masses and prayers for them and their families. 'Caritas non querit quae sua sunt', Paul told the Corinthians: so a philanthropist who pays only for his or her own salvation might only be an egotist.[233] Whether those more altruistic intentions were broadly medicinal or broadly educational, the easiest way to ensure that a charitable bequest remained expressly devoted to these purposes was to stipulate it carefully. (Those foundations that served both hospital and educational functions and eventually split illustrates this).[234] Reliability also meant endurance, so foundations needed to be as near to permanent as a founder could afford (hence the enormous volume of early conveyancing records for both the Sorbonne and Merton). From that, two things could be deduced. A permanent foundation implies a populated foundation. And a reliable, populated, permanent foundation implies a foundation enclosed in a specific place. The affinities between colleges, hospitals, and monasteries are at root a function of the need for founders to fix their charity on something they could count on. It is a reflection of how reliable colleges seemed to Louis IX in 1270 that they could compete with the friars in his will as objects of charity.[235]

For them to be *worth* relying on implied some control over the virtues of their members—a donor's reputation would otherwise be ill reflected. The Nations' concern with their reputation is mostly political. 'Exceedingly dear to us is the good reputation of the scholars of our Nation, which ought to be put before all financial benefit', said the German Nation at Bologna.[236] Colleges' attention to reputation was a consequence of the desire to well reflect founders' charitable piety. (Hospital founders felt the same.[237]) Robert de Sorbon justified his various statutory provisions in relation to the scandal they prevented.[238] Sir Philip Somerville's statutes for Balliol specified homicide, adultery, theft, rape, perjury, sacrilege, and simony as the sort of 'serious fault' or 'serious carnal failing or sign of depravity' through which 'a grave scandal in the said house could be sparked'.[239] Walter of Merton made the public aspect of criminous clerks a clear reason for their expulsion.[240] Pecham glossed it inimitably. If after warnings a fellow still transgressed a third time (a frequent collegial qualification), 'he should be completely cut off from your

---

1849–85), i. [Autun, Laon, Montpellier, Albi], 132, Laon MS 183 ed. 592–649 at 634–41. Comment in A. J. Davis, 'Preaching in Thirteenth-Century Hospitals', *Journal of Medieval History* 36 (2010), 72–89 at 74, 84–7.

[233] 1 Cor. 13: 5.   [234] e.g. Peterhouse, Cambridge, or the Collège des Dix-huit, Paris.

[235] *CUP*, i. #430ª (February 1270).

[236] *Statuta Nationis Germanicae Bononiae*, cap. 29, 120.

[237] Watson, *Fundatio, Ordinatio and Statuta*, 25, 28, 274–5.

[238] e.g. Glorieux, *Origines de la Sorbonne*, i. #1 at 194 (students to be quiet while eating in rooms lest those passing by in the street be scandalized), 195 (no student to have extravagant shoes or clothes by which any scandal could be generated; students not to lecture prematurely with scandalous effects). Cf. the similar concerns about resolving problems discreetly and internally at the Collège des Dix-Huit, Coyecque, 'Notice sur l'ancien collège des Dix-Huit', 1330 statutes, caps. 11–14 at 182.

[239] *Oxford Deeds of Balliol*, #571 at 292–3 (*scandalum* caused by fellows), 294 (public turpitude of chaplain).

[240] Merton *Muniments*, #6 at 22 ll. 30–1 (1274). The same concern in #2 at 15 ll. 12–13 (1264). One of the reasons to think that Kilwardby was less critical than Pecham of Merton during his visitation is that he does not use the language of scandal or infamy; his modifications are instead often *utile*—often as a pairing with *honestas*: *Injunctions of Archbishop Kilwardby*, 11, 13, 14.

company, like a putrid limb'.[241] In such matters it was better to be safe than fair. At Queen's Oxford, unless a scholar was able to purge himself of 'the rumour (*fama*) or rather infamy (*infamia*)' levelled against him he would be taken as guilty whether the crime was great or small.[242] Concern for external reputation naturally informed colleges' overwhelming desire to resolve disputes internally.[243] When we can test this, as at Merton in 1338–9, the scholars look less concerned with others' perceptions and more upset or irritated themselves. They are bothered about *discordia* or *dissentio* rather than *scandalum*. At several 1338 scrutinies a recurrent sorrow around the table was that 'there is not the love between fellows that there ought to be'.[244] At Merton in so far as they appear concerned about public appearances it is more a matter of the proper relations between fellows *internally*: 'Wylie went far too far against Finmere in front of all the fellows publicly.'[245] By contrast Pecham, the external visitor, seems galvanized to protect the college's wider reputation.

There is no explicit sign that Walter of Merton envisaged his foundation would improve the violent tenor of life at Oxford. But sensitivity to corporate reputation meant colleges were more likely to overcome that professional hazard of medieval university life. Walter's correspondence does in fact show a concern and an awareness of order and disorder in Oxford.[246]

That colleges made some (minor) contribution to the control of extreme student behaviour (overall) may be deduced from the substitutes university authorities made in the absence of colleges. Nations could be one mediate form of control on students.[247] But often, in Paris, the university was forced to issue general regulations with the mass of individual masters as their target, the legislative equivalent of shooting a swarm of mosquitos.[248] As lords for servants, so masters were individually liable for their students and students were invidually accountable to him, notably for fees.[249] It is possible to see the role that housing could play in the regulation of behaviour through a source such as the 1329/30 Paris *computus*

---

[241] *Reg. Peckham*, iii. #589 at 817–18 on *Merton Muniments*, #6 at 22–3 ll. 33–5 (1274).

[242] *Statutes of the Colleges of Oxford*, i. Queen's, 20 (1340); *Munimenta Academica*, i. 59, 60 (University College 1292 and need for discreet co-disciplining and decorous conduct). Similar concerns in *Statutes of the Colleges of Oxford*, i. Oriel, 9 (May 1326). *Oriel College Records*, #4 has the January 1326 statutes. For concern about reputation and scandal see e.g. also *Historia universitatis Parisiensis*, ed. C. Egasse du Boulay, 6 vols. (Paris 1665–73), iv. 158 cap. 48 (Harcourt); Marti, *Spanish College*, 324–6; *Statuta Nationis Germanicae Bononiae*, caps. 23, 29, 114–15, 120–1.

[243] E.g. *Statutes of the Colleges of Oxford*, i. Oriel, 14 (1329); *Origines de la Sorbonne*, i. #41 at 230 (1357); see above for Merton.

[244] *Merton Muniments*, #13, all at 33: Bernard (fo. 1 ll. 37–8); Hotham (fo. 1 ll. 43–4); Heriard (fo. 1ᵛ l. 70); Doyly (fo. 1ᵛ l. 77). At Exeter/Stapeldon Hall, *dissensiones* are ideally resolved internally: Charles William Boase, *Register of the Rectors and Fellows, Scholars, Exhibitioners and Bible Clerks of Exeter College, Oxford with Illustrative Documents and a History of the College*, 2 vols. (Oxford, 1879), i. xl (Stapeldon's 1322 answer to a question about this).

[245] *Merton Muniments*, #15 at 35 ll. 243–4.

[246] TNA SC 1/22/56 (*c*.25 January 1274) Thomas de Cantilupe to Robert Burnel, Merton and others; SC 1/28/139 (*c*.February 1274) the mayor, bailiffs, and commonalty of Oxford to Walter of Merton.

[247] e.g. Honorius III's suspension of the seals to forestall violence according to Nations, *CUP*, i. #45 (May 1222).

[248] e.g. *CUP*, ii. #561 (October 1289 obligations of masters to have records of students). Comment on Oxford, Highfield, 'Early Colleges', 225.

[249] Baldwin, *Masters, Princes*, i. 128–9, 175.

roll.[250] In Paris, housing was regulated by the university and run through the masters, hiring accommodation out for their students.[251] In 1328 the university needed to pay for the costs of legal appeal to the Pope concerning a student, Jean le Fourbeur, fined for the rape of a woman, Symonette.[252] An indirect product of this legal appeal was a summarized list of all the students liable to pay their contribution to its costs. What is interesting here is that the collectors travelled around area by area, house by house, listing the masters or institutions and the numbers of liable students: a pattern that can be read off the sequence and descriptions the collectors made.[253] Provision of housing was the most basic element in regulating the behaviour of students.[254] By extension, putting their students in one place was a collegial founder's first step in creating an accountable college.

The final reason for the construction of collegial corporate bodies as described was founders' needs to separate the charitable wood from the trees. This has been alluded to several times, so a brief summary can conclude this chapter.

CONCLUSIONS: *OMNIBUS ET SINGULIS*

Midway up Mount Purgatory, in the middle of Dante's *Commedia*, Virgil gives an extended theological discussion of the heavenly good.

> Perchè s'appuntano i vostri disiri
> dove per compagnia parte si scema,
> invidia move il mantaco a' sospiri.
> Ma se l'amor de la spera suprema
> torcesse in suso il disiderio vostro,
> non vi sarebbe al petto quella tema;
> ché, per quanti si dice più lì 'nostro',
> tanto possiede più di ben ciascuno,
> e più di caritate arde in quel chiostro.[255]

Dante is a 'high' medieval source to cite. But the ideal of individuals subsuming themselves within a wider collective without sacrificing their individuality was one that founders such as Sorbon or Merton were attempting to institutionalize practically. Their institutions were not (quite) as grand then as their names sound today, and these founders had a very mundane question in view: how to secure a balance

---

[250] Comment and edn. in Courtenay, *Parisian Scholars*.
[251] Baldwin, *Masters, Princes*, i. 130.
[252] Following Courtenay's account, *Parisian Scholars*, ch. 3.
[253] Courtenay, *Parisian Scholars*, Apps. 1–2. A similar approach was used in 1284–5 (30–8).
[254] A side-effect of university requirements to allocate students to masters was to stamp out wandering scholars. See Cobban, 'Medieval Student Power', 31 n. 12.
[255] 'Because your human longings point to where | portions grow smaller in shared fellowship, | meanness of mind must make the bellows sigh. | If love, though, reaching for the utmost sphere, | should ever wrench your longings to the skies, | such fears would have no place within your breast. | For, there, the more that we speak of 'ours', | the more each one possesses of the good | and, in that cloister, love burns brighter.' Dante, *Purgatorio*, 15 ll. 49–57, trans. Robin Fitzpatrick, slightly modified (London, 2007).

between *omnes et singulos* within their foundations.[256] Dante's envisaged balance was heavenly and frictionless. Merton's and Sorbon's was not—although 'love' and solidarity played dominant roles which their 'law' sought to regulate.[257] Once founders were dead there were three prisms through which to focus on the charitable purposes they had outlined. One was through the merely temporary, living embodiments of a foundation's charitable purpose: the perspectives of a John of Wyly, a Robert Finmere, or a William of Heytesbury at Merton. Another was through the necessary officers who regulated them: the Warden Trings. Yet another was through that of the permanent, impersonal interests of the foundation itself: its bricks and mortar. It was to be hoped that a Tring or a Heytesbury could articulate those permanent, impersonal interests. In case they could not, a visitor, a Pecham, was provided for. Each perspective alone was inadequate or unreliable—too partial in the first two cases, too detached perhaps in the third. Combining them offered the best chance to see the wood for the trees and the trees for the wood. Hence the odd combination above was required, and hence the calculated eclecticism of collegiate constitutions in seeking to create wholes greater than the sum of their parts. Merton was one solution, the Sorbonne's another. The optimal configuration was arguable, not least because of the ambiguous status of fellows as both beneficiaries and regulators of the institutions that housed them. And because it was arguable, it was argued about. Just as Pecham did in 1280.

Founders attempted to construct accountable, collegial statutes through interlocking mechanisms that both asserted group solidarity and reconciled variant interests within that group. The strength of the approach adopted by drafters was the prescriptive licence they offered to temporary members, officers, and visitors in resolving this. Intentions and aims were specified, but significant levels of discretion variously reserved for members in disciplining, accounting, or determining what was useful for serving the institution's purposes. This was a challenge. Far bigger institutions—such as the Franciscans—can be seen ungainfully wrestling with the question. The *utile* apparatus of statutes and rules was intended to articulate the *honestum* purpose. It was critical that accountability went up, down, and across if this was to work, involving both warden and fellows. In observing that, we observe an interlocking mechanism where weight braces counterweight. Collegial statutes provided for both the resolution of disputes and the avoidance of them. If accountability is ultimately a way of regulating conflict, the threat of that conflict may well also have been a disincentive— forestalling other conflicts of which we lack all trace. It is anyway the longevity of the foundations rather than some imperfect avoidance of *dissentio* or *discordia* which is the better measure of how far founders' ideals of collegiate accountability were achieved. The institutions for holding the temporary members of colleges to account—wardens and fellows both—were after all only a means to that enduring end.

---

[256] A common form of address in statutes: e.g. *Statutes of the Colleges of Oxford*, i. Oriel, 10, 12 (May 1326); Glorieux, *Origines de la Sorbonne*, i. #41 at 230; *A Cartulary of the Hospital of St John the Baptist*, ed. H. E. Salter, 3 vols., OHS 66, 68–9 (Oxford, 1914–17), iii. #1 at 6; *Statutes of Autun*, 1341 statutes, caps. 15, 19 at 46, 47. See Maddicott's complementary discussion of 'collegiality' at Stapeldon Hall, *Founders and Fellowship*, 49–50.

[257] I use the terms, again, à la Clanchy, 'Law and Love'.

6

Conclusions

> Medieval government was concerned before all else with managing men. The question—what is being administered? was closely related to other equally important questions. Who is conducting the administration? Who is profiting from office? Who is enjoying the King's favour, and with what justification?[1]

If 'government' is extended beyond royal forms to seigneurial, ecclesiastical, and collegial government then Sir James Holt's comments on the northern barons and knights whose rebellion led to Magna Carta may be extended to the officers analysed here, *mutatis mutandis*. During the later twelfth and thirteenth centuries a way of thinking took hold that trusted to procedures of accountability as a means of regulating officers' conduct. Some specific administrative, legal, and institutional expressions of these accountable approaches have been this study's focus. The stance was not inherently new, but it became qualitatively more complex and quantitatively more widespread in this period, across European countries, and across different sorts of officer—including in England. The officers exposed to these methods were not only 'state' ones, but included seigneurial, ecclesiastical, and university-college officers, as well as urban-communal ones.

The relationship between formal accountability and the cultivation of responsible conduct varied. In given cases the amount of English attention given to *both* the cultivation of officials' responsible character *and* the elaboration of needful bits and curbs for restraining them could differ markedly. Seigneurial bailiffs experienced both (unusually perhaps in England). Wardens experienced both. Bishops both likewise, but the cultivation of responsible character more than the others. Sheriffs experienced mostly the bits and curbs (again perhaps unusually). Stress on one therefore did not by definition preclude stress on the other. Elaboration of character did not displace elaboration of procedure. Bishops' liability to canonical inquisitions did not negate the considerable thought given to the character of the bishop. It is not clear to me that it had a particular English complexion. Likewise with *podestà*, reflection on the character of office did not preclude the machinery of accountability. Nor should it be inferred that the more 'hard' accountability and the less 'soft' responsibility, the more robust the office. In the case of sheriffs, the relatively reduced amount of interest in the 'softer' side of shrieval responsibility did not seem to strengthen the office per se. Some contrasts are marked in this chapter with a range of contemporary Continental practices.

---

[1] J. C. Holt, *The Northerners: A Study in the Reign of King John*, rev. edn. (Oxford, 1992), 217.

Conclusions 223

The generic problems that drove the holding of officers to account were of a deep-seated nature. Those with power in the Middle Ages often sought to bridge the distance between them and their subject communities through their officials. Delegated officials of some sort were any *rector*'s way of making himself manifest on the ground.[2] Even 'self-government at the king's command' required some local oversight.[3] How delegating authorities, delegated officials, and entangled communities regulated their relationships was therefore a permanent question for all three groups. Answers varied.

One response of communities to those problems was a fantasy of access. An *exemplum* about Philip Augustus's justice on a corrupt royal *prévôt* from Ralph of Coggeshall's *Chronicon* (fl.1207–26) illustrates this while conveniently summarizing that insolence of office which accountability should be a solution to.[4] A *prévôt*, long envious of a neighbour's vineyard, formulates a cunning plan to steal it following the neighbour's death. With two accomplices he goes to the tomb, puts 100*l*. in the dead man's hands, and says, 'This money I give to you for your vineyard'. Taking his money back the *prévôt* tells his accomplices, 'Now you can confidently say, swear, and offer your testimony that I, in your presence, exchanged that vineyard for so much money with that man' (all technically true). He seizes the land and ejects the dead man's widow. She gets nowhere with the local courts because of the *prévôt*'s standing and witnesses. It is only when she goes directly to the King that she gets justice. Philip separates the three culprits. He tells one accomplice to quietly recite the Lord's Prayer to one side. He tells the other that the first has confessed the truth, 'as it is in the Lord's Prayer' (again, technically true). In a nice medieval instance of the 'prisoner's dilemma', this second accomplice promptly confesses. The *prévôt* is hanged, the widow restored. The *exemplum*'s lessons are these. That *mediocres* officials are corrupted by their power and lusts. That such men can play the rules of the game to endorse the frauds they commit, or at least to prevent detection. That rules and legal language can be twisted technically both for good (Philip's narrowly truthful statement to the second accomplice), and ill (the *prévôt*'s graveside chicanery). That routine legal procedures may be worse than useless. That status counts at law. That the powerless (the proverbial widows and orphans) have only the fount of justice, the king, to appeal to when intermediate sources of justice predictably fail. That the king is Solomonic: available, attentive, canny, just. That through him fraud is found out and punished, and the downtrodden—despite their status but only if they heroically persist—get their just deserts.

---

[2] *Die Konstitutionen Friedrichs II. für das Königreich sizilien*, ed. Wolfgang Stürner, MGH Leges, Const. Suppl. 2 (Hannover, 1996), cap. 1.17, 'et sic nos etiam, qui prohibente individuitate persone ubique personaliter esse non possumus, ubique potentialiter esse credamur'. See also 1.31 at 186. See also the ideal legal hierarchy of the *Sachsenspiegel*, 3.53 (book and chapter numbers from the Wolftenbüttel MS), trans. Maria Dobozy as *The Saxon Mirror: A Sachsenspiegel of the Fourteenth Century* (Philadelphia, 1999).

[3] Albert Beebe White, *Self-Government at the King's Command: A Study in the Beginnings of English Democracy* (Minneapolis, 1933), and invoked e.g. by Jean Dunbabin, *Charles I of Anjou: Power, Kingship and State-Making in Thirteenth-Century Europe* (London, 1998), 66; J. R. Maddicott, *Origins of the English Parliament, 924–1327* (Oxford, 2010), 452.

[4] *Radulphi de Coggeshall Chronicon Anglicanum*, ed. Joseph Stevenson, RS (London 1875), 197–9.

Pessimistic about intermediary justice, the *exemplum* is optimistic about the quality of the king's, as well as of his accessibility.[5]

That fantasy of access is a longstanding one of communities faced with intermediary officers mediating between them and their lord. Another response—its opposite—is the despair of distance, perhaps a more likely response. At the end of the sixth century, John the Almsgiver, Patriarch of Alexandria, dreamt that his planned voyage to Constantinople to petition the Emperor for help from Arab raiders would be futile. 'God is always close at hand; but the emperor is far, far away', he was told.[6] He abandoned the attempt. In the nineteenth century, Russian peasants at the terminus of the state's reach likewise recognized the limits of the thread tying emperor and village through local officials. 'God is in his heaven, and the tsar is far away,' they disconsolately reflected.[7]

Between fantasy and despair have stood other, more pragmatic expressions of optimism and pessimism. Innocent III remarked that since he could not fly across Christendom in the blink of an eye he would just have to make do with papal legates. Innocent saw his agents here as limbs (*membra*) of a wider corporate whole, a formulation not restricted to writers such as John of Salisbury.[8] Before *Britton* (*c.*1291) made Edward I spool out England's judicial hierarchy, he has the King begin by admitting that 'since we cannot provide in our own person to hear and adjudge all the complaints of our people we have split our responsibility [*charge*] into many parts'.[9] Charlemagne said much the same in 802, though his solution was oath-taking.[10] The shapes of some other pragmatic solutions in England during the later twelfth and thirteenth centuries have been studied above. They should be understood within their wider political economy. This too had been done before, and the body politic metaphor is just one way of thinking about officials' reliability within a self-contained system. The Arabic *Kitāb Sirr al-asrār*, Aristotle's supposed advice to Alexander, explained its self-reinforcing system like this:[11]

---

[5] A longer version is in Richer of Senones, *Gesta Senonensis Ecclesiae*, ed. G. Waitz in MGH, SS 25 (Hannover, 1880), 249–345 at 288–90 (§3.5). This slightly longer version offers the same Solomonic model but the *prévôt* is the higher *bailli*, the widow goes straight to the King without seeking any intermediary justice, the *bailli*'s corruption is explicitly contrasted by Philip with the benefits the *bailli* has gained from office, and he is banished and disinherited, not executed.

[6] Quoted in Peter Brown, *The World of Late Antiquity: From Marcus Aurelius to Muhammad* (London, 1971), 187.

[7] Quoted in Geoffrey Hosking, *Rulers and Victims: The Russians in the Soviet Union* (Cambridge, Mass., 2006), 12.

[8] 'Licet commissa nobis', August 1198, *Reg. Inn. III*, i. #345 at 515. For Castilian texts of Alfonso X with interesting senses of the parts forming a unitary whole see Jular Pérez-Alfaro, 'King's Face on the Territory: Royal Officers, Discourse and Legitimating Practices in Thirteenth and Fourteenth Century Castile', in Isabel Alfonso, Hugh Kennedy, and Julia Escalona (eds.), *Building Legitimacy: Political Discourses and Forms of Legitimacy in Medieval Societies*, The Medieval Mediterranean 53 (Leiden, 2004), 114–17.

[9] *Britton*, ed. Francis Morgan Nichols, 2 vols. (Oxford, 1865), i. 2.

[10] Oath of the General Capitulary. The oath to the Emperor enjoins a personal liability to God, 'quia ipse domnus imperator non omnibus singulariter necessariam potest exhibere curam et disciplinam', MGH Leges, *Capitularia regum francorum*, i. #33 cap. 3 p. 92.

[11] Linda T. Darling's study *A History of Social Justice and Political Power in the Middle East: The Circle of Justice from Mesopotamia to Globalization* (Abingdon, 2013) is now the key reference point, esp. 39–82 for the idea's early history. See also Yassine Essid, *A Critique of the Origins of Islamic Economic Thought* (Leiden, 1995), 56–61. On the Arabic version see Mahmoud Manzalaoui, 'The

There can be no justice and government without the subject. There can be no subject without a king. There can be no king without an army. There can be no army without a state. There can be no state without men (soldiers). There can be no soldiers without money. There can be no money without population (and peace). There can be no population and peace without justice and government.[12]

Vernacular and Latin versions of this c.950–80 Arabic 'circle of justice' circulated widely from 1140. The idea, though, was not novel. An earlier ancestor, stressing the supervision of officials, was attributed to Khusro I Anushirwan, Shah of Persia (AD 531–79) and used seven not eight terms: 'The monarchy depends on the army, the army on money, money comes from the land-tax, the land-tax comes from agriculture. Agriculture depends on justice; justice on the integrity of officials, and integrity and reliability on the ever-watchfulness of the king.'[13]

These analogues raise broader questions of parallels and influence. That the formula could be passed on did not mean that it would be. A useful illustration of the need for some further complementarity is the Bûyid administrator/historian Abū ʿAlī Aḥmad ibn Muḥammad Miskawayh (c.932–?1030), active when the Sirr al-Asrār was compiled.[14] Miskawayh drew on sixth-century sources and recorded texts attributed to Khusro I. He was also the author of the al-Ḥikmah al-khālidah (Perennial

Pseudo-Aristotelian "Kitāb Sirr al-asrār." Facts and Problems', Oriens 23–4 (1970–1), 147–257. On the Latin version: Manzalaoui, 'The Secretum secretorum: The Mediaeval European Version of "Kitāb Sirr-ul-Asrār"', Bulletin of the Faculty of Art, Alexandria University 15 (1961), 83–107; Alexander Murray, Reason and Society in the Middle Ages (Oxford, 1978), 83–4, 119–22, 445 nn. 37–8 and plate II; Pseudo-Aristotle, The Secret of Secrets: Sources and Influences, ed. W. F. Ryan and Charles B. Schmitt, Warburg Institute Surveys 9 (London, 1982); Steven J. Williams, The Secret of Secrets: The Scholarly Career of a Pseudo-Aristotelian Text in the Latin Middle Ages (Ann Arbor, Mich., 2003).

[12] Opera hactenus inedita Rogeri Baconi, v. 227. This is the translation from the Arabic text and this portion is not included in the Latin MSS of the Secretum secretorum. The Latin does include a version of related material that precedes this list: 'The world is a garden or orchard, its timber or hedge is judgement. Judgement is the master [dominator] walled in by law. Law is the kingdom that the king rules. The king is the shepherd protected [defenditur] by his lords. The lords are mercenaries [stipendarii] sustained by money. Money is fortune [fortuna] gathered by subjects. Subjects are servants [servi] subject to justice. Justice is that which stretches itself out and is itself the health [salus] of subjects.' Cited from BL Royal MS 12 C. VI, fol. 34ᵛ where this is given the title 'De lege regis et pecunia et quod uniusquisque fuerit'. For Bacon's edition see Opera hactenus inedita Rogeri Baconi, v. 126. This idea, sometimes also called the circle of the sphere or the octagon of justice, as well as the circle of justice (Arabic but not Latin MSS include a diagram) bears comparison with the body politic metaphor used by John of Salisbury and others.

[13] Quoted, Brown, World of Late Antiquity, 166. See Masʿūdī, Les prairies d'or, trans. Charles-Adrien-Casimir Barbier de Meynard and Abel Pavet de Courteille, rev. Charles Pellat, 3 vols. (Paris, 1962–71), i. 236 (§631 = II.210) and cf. 223 (§597 = II.172); Janine Sourdel-Thomine, 'Les Conseils du Šayḫ al-Harawī à un prince ayyūbide', Bulletin d'études orientales 17 (1961–2), 205–68 at 219. Cf. The History of al-Ṭabarī, ed. E. Yar-Shater, 40 vols. (Albany, 1985–2007), v. (trans. C. E. Bosworth), 155. More generally on Khusro, Zeʾev Rubin, 'The Reforms of Khusro Anushirwan', in Averil Cameron (ed.), The Byzantine and Early Islamic Near East, iii. States, Resources and Armies, Studies in Late Antiquity and Early Islam 1 (Princeton, 1995), 227–97, and 'The Sasanid Monarchy', in Averil Cameron, Bryan Ward-Perkins, and Michael Whitby (eds.), The Cambridge Ancient History, xiv. Late Antiquity: Empire and Successors, A.D. 425–600 (Cambridge, 2000), 638–61 at 652–9. On all this now see Darling, A History of Social Justice, esp. 39–46, 60–5, 74–82.

[14] Tajārib al-umam (Experiences of the Nations) and Tahdhīb al-akhlāq (Health of the Soul). Parts of the Tajārib al-umam are translated in The Eclipse of the ʿAbbasid Caliphate: Original Chronicles of the Fourth Islamic Century, ed. H. F. Amedroz and D. S. Margoliouth, 7 vols. (Oxford, 1920–1). See also on the Tajārib al-umam, Michael Richard Jackson Bonner, Three Neglected Sources of Sasanian History in the Reign of Khusraw Anushirvan, Studia Iranica 46 (Paris, 2011). The Tahdhīb al-akhlāq is translated as The Refinement of Character: A Translation from the Arabic of Aḥmad ibn-Muḥammad

Philosophy) a text suggested as bearing a 'distinct family resemblance' to the *Kitāb Sirr al-asrār*, although he does not quote the latter.[15] However, even if a strong textual thread could be strung from Khusro I to Miskawayh to the Pseudo-Aristotle it would be mistaken to take it as a sufficient explanation of such sentiments' recurrence in these texts and societies. Intellectual antecedents and sources can help to explain such recurrences, but attention needs also to be given to the environment in which such ideas per se resonated. Such debates can otherwise risk missing the wood for the trees. So, for instance, historians have argued whether Roman legal ideas provided an essential conceptual vocabulary for justifying mid-/late thirteenth-century English royal taxation.[16] English arguments for royal taxes may well have made appeal to Roman legal precedent in order to assert the 'necessity' required to legitimize the taxes, but this alone does not give a sufficient account of either royal demands or parliamentary retorts. One should also ask why there are trees here in the first place. What were the immediate phenomena that made it a useful thing at all to reach for political-legal concepts validated by their pedigree? Bartlett may be quoted a final time: 'The important thing is not the putative descent of some practice or institution, but its function and significance in the living society in which it has a place.'[17] This need not entail a reductionist functional explanation (it does not in Bartlett's analysis). It is, however, to stress explanations that, though they may address practices' ultimate origins, also focus on their redeployed meanings and functions within the societies in question. On this basis one can consider the patterns formed by the various official accountabilities discussed in earlier chapters. This chapter, then, first examines some parallels, differences, and similarities between the forms of accountability already described; secondly, tries to establish the causes and 'elective affinities' underlying them; and thirdly and finally, considers some of their effects and consequences. It also widens its perspective to note a number of further non-English examples, intended to contextualize this material.

PARALLELS, DIFFERENCES, SIMILARITIES

'Who, Whom?'

'Who, whom?' lies at the root of Holt's questions in this chapter's epigraph. In all the classes of officers treated here there was a tricky balance to be found between

Miskawayh's Tahdhīb al-Akhlāq, trans. Constantine K. Zurayk (Beirut, 1968). See M. Arkoun's entry on Miskawayh in *The Encyclopaedia of Islam*, ed. H. A. R. Gibb et al., 12 vols. (Leiden, 1960–2009), accessed online.

[15] Manzalaoui, 'The Pseudo-Aristotelian "Kitāb Sirr al-asrār"', 164–5. The text is edited as *al-Ḥikmah al-khālidah: Jāvīdān khirad*, ed. 'Abd al-Raḥmān Badawī (al-Qāhirah, 1952) and excerpted in *An Anthology of Philosophy in Persia*, i. *From Zoroaster to 'Umar Khayyām*, ed. Seyyed Hossein Nasr and Mehdi Aminrazavi (Oxford, 1999), 326–55.

[16] Michael Prestwich, *Documents Illustrating the Crisis of 1297–1298 in England*, CS 4th ser. 24 (1980), 28–30 (sceptical of Roman law's relevance *tout court*); G. L. Harriss, *King, Parliament and Public Finance in Medieval England to 1369* (Oxford, 1975), 61–3 (arguing for learned law's relevance); Maddicott, *Origins of the English Parliament*, 176–7 (a middle way but where the legal ideas are not indispensable). Cf., *mutatis mutandis*, Andrew Lewis, 'On Not Expecting the Spanish Inquisition: The Uses of Comparative Legal History', *Current Legal Problems* 57 (2004).

[17] Robert Bartlett, *Trial by Fire and Water: The Medieval Judicial Ordeal* (Oxford, 1986), 154.

autonomy and authority on the one side, and obedience and effectiveness on the other. A powerful, authoritative figure risked being too autonomous of the power that had appointed him. A more junior, more obedient, less prepossessing figure risked being simply ineffective, captured by local interests.[18] 'Who, whom?' was a see-saw. Holt's focus was on officers particularly close to or appointed by the king. One argument of this study is that over the course of the later twelfth and thirteenth centuries, across a wide spectrum, his questions were focused and augmented by very practical answers specifically preoccupied with lesser (*mediocres*) officials' accountability ('Who, how, for what?').

More widely 'Who, whom?' has been a basic guiding question throughout this analysis. '*Kto kogo?*' when applied to those in power and authority is a question of how and whether holding to account goes down or 'simply' up. Are those above liable to justify themselves to those below, and how, and for what? It might be put in particular historiographical frames. Walter Ullmann's theories of government is one that has not been discussed so far. For Ullmann, medieval political thought was 'to a very large extent a history of the conflicts between these two theories of government', where the ascending ('populist') model derived its legitimacy and origin from the people, while the descending ('hierocratic') model derived it from the highest powers. There is some similarity of concern between 'down/up' accountability and Ullmann's conception of ascending or descending political legitimacy. The particular shape of Ullmann's interpretation is sufficiently problematic, however, for it to be unclear whether reassembling it would serve a useful purpose.[19] It is simpler and more useful to say that the later twelfth and thirteenth centuries saw a period of acute interest in the question of who it was that was liable to justify their official actions to others. Since this interest was also practical it found legal and administrative expression.

Beyond this, the general, unsurprising, drift of many of the mechanisms for holding officers to account has been that superiors hoisted their officers up to account to them: sheriffs at the Exchequer, bailiffs to their employers or through the action of account; bishops to the pope; wardens to their governing bodies; one can add *podestà* to their communes too. These superiors define officers' accountability, and in so doing define offices too. Yet there is some place also for inferiors or 'subject' communities to yank officers down to account to them. This would be a further qualification of

---

[18] See Daniel Power's comments in 'Guérin de Glapion, Seneschal of Normandy (1200–1201): Service and Ambition under the Plantagenet and Capetian Kings', in Nicholas Vincent (ed.), *Records, Administration and Aristocractic Society in the Anglo-Norman Realm. Papers Commemorating the 800th Anniversary of King John's Loss of Normandy* (Woodbridge, 2009), 153–92 esp. 153, also 167–9, 178–82. Guérin's career is particularly recoverable because of Louis's 1247 Norman *enquêtes*. See *RHF*, xxiv.1. 1–73; Charles Petit-Dutaillis, '*Querimoniae Normannorum*', in A. G. Little and F. M. Powicke (eds.), *Essays in Medieval History Presented to Thomas Frederick Tout* (Manchester, 1925), 99–118.

[19] Walter Ullmann, *A History of Political Thought: The Middle Ages*, rev. edn. (London, 1970), 12–13. For criticism see Francis Oakley, 'Celestial Hierarchies Revisited: Walter Ullmann's Vision of Medieval Politics', *P&P* 60 (1973), 3–48 esp. 6–10, 22–44. Oakley's critique hinges on the anachronistic, mutually exclusive, and tendentious development of this pairing in Ullmann's writings. For reference to Ullmann's approach in relation to the types of sources dealt with here, see e.g. Leonard E. Scales, 'The Cambridgeshire Ragman Rolls', *EHR* 113 (1998), 553–79 at 553.

the utility of Ullmann's ascending/descending model. Even where complaints 'ascend' they are assimilated into a complaints structure that 'descends' from on high—at the discretion of those on high. This often occurred within the formal framework of an (inferior) official accounting to his superior official and is therefore somewhat masked. The best example of this is episcopal accountability, especially given the early and high medieval concern and effort expended on establishing the clergy—and bishops pre-eminently—as a caste apart.[20] The issue in the late twelfth/thirteenth century is not so much episcopal accountability directly *to* inferiors (communities, chapters) as the exposure of bishops to judicially potent rumours or scandals emerging from *anywhere*—and the licence of 'promoters' or *ex officio* judges to take such *scandala* forward into juridical arenas. Inquisitorial legislation was well aware of the institutional risks. The control retained by clerical élites in determining the reality of scandal was crucial, but the fact remained that clerics and priests were effectively open to complaints from below them within their hierarchies, and from those outside them. Here practice might be more assertive than theory.[21] The practical recommendation for this openness was the administrative reason that it would be hard to police ecclesiastical behaviour without some means for local complaints to move up church hierarchies, even bypassing senior knots in them. As Innocent III noted, papal legates might be of some use, but it is hard to envisage them as a significant bulwark force. Diocesan or provincial discipline might be of little help, especially given these units variable sizes across Christendom, and especially given that the scandalous problems might *be* at those levels. *Infamia* was therefore an enormously flexible and seemingly simple way to resolve this, while retaining ecclesiastical control of the detailed determination of inquisitorial cases. Episcopal liability to inferiors was a necessary consequence of a workable episcopal accountability to superiors.

Aside from episcopal accountability there was an equitable stress on the *right* of anyone from a commune to complain about *podestà* at the end of their term of office as communal executives at *sindacatio*. For sheriffs, general eyres provided a similar space, as increasingly from the later thirteenth century did *querelae*. But as with canonical inquisitions, such secular communal enquiries were quite as likely to result in dubiously politicized allegations, as in the 1274 Hundred Roll inquiries.[22] One of Robert le Vavasur's 1255 inquiries was initiated by the King against him through 'various rumours'. Like romano-canonical inquiries it proceeded with *ex officio* judges plus jury to investigate the rumour; the judges empowered to remit it to the King.[23] Inquests of sheriffs such as that of 1258–9 were specifically designed to elicit anyone's complaints about sheriffs, and the same was equally true in the case of

---

[20] Peter Brown, *Through the Eye of a Needle: Wealth, the Fall of Rome, and the Making of Christianity in the West, 350–550 AD* (Princeton, NJ, 2012), pt. V, *passim*, esp. 517–22, 530; R. I. Moore, *First European Revolution, c.970–1215* (Oxford, 2000), *passim*, esp. *s.v.* 'clergy'.

[21] Philippe Buc, *L'Ambiguïté du livre: Prince, pouvoir et peuple dans les commentaires de la Bible au Moyen Âge* (Paris, 1994), 312–408, shows that while this fact might be tolerated in the field of *praxis*, when it came to *theoria* theologians generally sought to qualify it to death.

[22] Caroline Burt, *Edward I and the Governance of England, 1272–1307* (Cambridge, 2013), 91, 102–3.

[23] *CPR 1247–1258*, 432.

French *enquêtes*.[24] In the case of sheriffs there was, arguably until Edward I, a somewhat schizophrenic spasming from an established 'Exchequer' accountability that stressed fiscal returns, to another more equitable concern with accountability, and emphasizing broader measures of conduct beyond the fiscal (though the Exchequer of Pleas played a role here). Sheriffs' contributions to England's political divisions in the later twelfth and thirteenth centuries seem largely a function both of governmental failures to provide a satisfactory synthesis of fiscality and equity. Overall, the growing sophistication of interest in officers' accountability necessitated a softening of officers' hierarchical imperviousness to criticism from below. The question of whether officers were dismissible in relation to such criticisms may also be seen in this context.[25] In some cases the issue seems to have been principally practical (e.g. bailiffs' reliability). In others, questions of principle complicated matters (e.g. bishops' 'marriage' to their dioceses).

Delegation and Access

This is already to raise the question of how direct were lines of accountability between officers and their ultimate lords. If anyone could complain about a *podestà*, it was also true that, at *sindacatio*, *podestà* were accountable directly to the franchise that had elected them. In this they are somewhat at variance with other forms of accountability analysed here. In many cases the line between *mediocrem* officer and ultimate lord is indirect and somewhat attenuated. Sometimes a delegated judge (lay or ecclesiastical) may have been granted summary powers of judgement. But that does not reduce the levels between the accountable officer and his ultimate superior. The fantasy of access regarding Philip Augustus's finagling *prévôt* from Ralph of Coggeshall is partly a fantasy because in it all intermediaries between abusing officer and his final judging superior are triumphantly elided. Indeed, the insinuation of that *exemplum* was that middling points of appeal between abused, abuser, and ultimate judge are simply spaces where the abuser can stretch the insolence of office a little further. Such hierarchical simplicity is heavily qualified in many of the cases here, wherein the person exacting accountability from *mediocres* officers is not the person to whom they are ultimately liable. It is seigneurial auditor, Exchequer official, itinerant judge, papally delegated investigator, internal collegial auditors. It is often not lord, king, pope, or visitor. Sometimes the latters' involvement is a sign that the officers' lack of accountability has got out of hand (e.g. Geoffrey of York, at least as his chapter saw it; Pecham at Merton). In others it is because an accountable official has a form of appeal against a holding to account he himself thinks abusive (John de Valle at the Exchequer of Pleas). In others it is because the ultimate superior of the official wishes to reserve final judgement to himself (Walter Langton). One might

---

[24] *1258–1259 Special Eyre of Surrey and Kent; RHF*, xxiv.
[25] Cf. Udo Wolter, 'Verwaltung, Amt, Beamter, V–VI', in Otto Brunner, Werner Conze, and Reinhart Koselleck (eds.), *Geschichtliche Grundbegriffe: Historisches Lexikonzur politisch-sozialen Sprache in Deutschland*, 8 vols. in 9 (Stuttgart, 1972–97), vii. 32.

think about this feature of these methods in terms of 'mesne'—intermediary—judgement in English common law.[26] The mesne nature of these accountable judgements is sometimes strictly a judgement provisional on a later, final one. For bailiffs, *monstravit de compoto* allows for mesne judgement once *ex parte* is in operation since it is a way of appealing seigneurial auditors' judgements out into a royal court. It would also be the case for canonical inquisitions where final judgements may be reserved to the pope but a preliminary inquisition is delegated out. In the case of sheriffs the idea of mesne judgement may be applied more loosely. Exchequer accountability could be seen as a curious rolling form of mesne judgement, since debts may roll over from year to year. Any ultimate reckoning is only reached when 'and he is quit' appears in the pipe roll's ledger. It is true too that the king could forgive debts as he pleased, a further sign of the potential of the process to be personally politicized, and of the ongoing potential for Exchequer's judgement to be shown as merely mesne.[27] (Henry III's problems with wardrobe financing operating outside the Exchequer's purview could be seen in this context.)

The reason for such intermediary accountability is a function of the increasing complexity of the institutions that were trying to regulate themselves. Battle Abbey had at least temporarily lost track of what was going on at Wye. John de Valle had been delegated significant responsibilities, dealing with long-distance merchants and moving around a great deal. Sheriffs operated at a distance across the whole kingdom through the writ system, and bishops not dissimilarly across the whole of Christendom where papal letters provided for delegated direction. Tiny Merton College had pockets of land from Elham in Kent to Embleton in Northumberland.[28] The attenuated nature of accountable control was a consequence of institutional complexity across distant spaces. It is unsurprising that alongside them arose parallel attempts to achieve in fact the fantasy of access. With respect to royal officers and injustice, plaints and *querelae* seeking justice on complaint to the king were an attempt to shortcut the bureaucracy of accountability, as *Britton*'s Edward I knew.[29] Sometimes the delegated means of holding to account may have been sufficiently flexible to allow for this within its own terms—if one had the money and time. It is arguable that canonical inquisitions could in effect be initiated directly like this, 'on plaint' to the pope. This is in part how John de Lovetot seems to act at the Curia in relation to Walter Langton. If there was variation in how lords exacted accountability from those beneath them there was also variation in how those subject to their officials could seek to access those ultimate superiors from whom they hoped for redress.

---

[26] See John Hudson, *The Oxford History of the Laws of England*, ii. *871–1216* (Oxford, 2012), 78–9, 317–18.

[27] Cf. Olivier Mattéoni, 'Vérifier, corriger, juger: Les Chambres des comptes et le contrôle des officiers en France à la fin du Moyen Âge', *Revue historique* 641 (2007), 64–5.

[28] See the map of 1274 holdings in P. D. A. Harvey, *A Medieval Oxfordshire Village: Cuxham, 1240–1400* (Oxford, 1965), 88.

[29] Alan Harding, *Medieval Law and the Foundations of the State* (Oxford, 2002), 160–70, 178–86, and 'Plaints and Bills in the History of English Law, Mainly in the Period 1250–1350', in Dafydd Jenkins (ed.), *Legal History Studies 1972* (Cardiff, 1975).

Control of Officers: Insiders and Outsiders

'Who, whom?' and the question of delegated accountability is connected to the question of whether 'insiders' or 'outsiders' were the preferred choice for particular offices. Subject communities generally preferred insiders; *rectores* generally outsiders. This is readily comprehensible. Local élites and communities hope one of their own will sympathize with their needs. A *rector* at some remove from the relevant community will hope that an agent more beholden to him rather than them will be a more reliable projection of his 'face on the territory'. Canonical inquisitions kept papal options open: the pope could decide which delegated judges to appoint, those nearer or further politically to either himself or the defamed prelate. In an English context the classic example is the counties' demand for sheriffs who knew local laws and customs. The polarity exists, though, in other cases. Castilian nobles prefer *adelandados* of their status to lesser *merinos* more amenable to the king;[30] local men seek local bishops.[31] Likewise counts of Provence may naturally prefer non-Provençal justiciars and kings of the Regno non-Sicilians.[32] It is equally clear why those in charge of officials at a distance would want men who were *not* local, since they would hope such men would be more loyal to their superiors' needs.[33] Without discounting specific resentments against Poitevins or Savoyards, the English controversy about the influence of 'aliens' can be seen as part of a wider European story in which rulers sought to counterbalance longstanding regional power bases through the use of officials lacking local loyalties.

---

[30] The lesser *merino* has less discretionary judicial and military autonomy, the *adelantado* more. There were five regional *adelantados mayores* 1258–67 before Alfonso X's gradual sidelining of them. The 1271–3 aristocratic rebellion was partly tied up in a dispute about the relative functions and status of the more noble *adelantados* who had been displaced by lesser but more amenable (from the King's perspective) *merinos*. The *Leyes de los Adelantados Mayores* describing that office is possibly a projected revision of the roles or a revision of the earlier 1258 arrangement. For all this see *Leyes de los Adelantados Mayores: Regulations, Attributed to Alfonso X of Castile, Concerning the King's Vicar in the Judiciary and in Territorial Administration*, ed. Robert A. MacDonald, Hispanic Seminary of Medieval Studies 25 (New York, 2000), 16–29; Jular Pérez-Alfaro, 'King's Face on the Territory', 112–20, 121–4. For the Burgos 1272 complaints and Cortés see *Crónica de Alfonso X, Según el Ms. II/2777 de la Biblioteca del Palacio Real (Madrid)*, ed. Manuel González Jiménez (Murcia, 1998), caps. 23–5, but see also 87 n. 142 (cf. MacDonald's comments in *Leyes* at 25). The Burgos complaints about oppressive officers, ignorance or disregard of local customs, and onerous military services bear some comparison with the baronial and knightly complaints against John and Henry III in England. Passing comparison, Peter Linehan, *Spain, 1157–1300: A Partible Inheritance* (Oxford, 2008), 114–15, 187.

[31] e.g. *The Arundel Lyrics and The Poems of Hugh Primas*, ed. and trans. Christopher J. McDonough, Dunbarton Oaks Medieval Library 2 (Cambridge, Mass., 2010), Hugh Primas #16 at 192 ll. 71–2 (the laudable episcopal choice of Sens, in contrast to Beauvais's).

[32] See in Provence Raymond Berenger V's (1209–45) use of Guillaume de Cotignac and Romée de Villeneuve as comital lieutenants, both of Catalan extraction: Thierry Pécout, '*L'Invention de Provence: Raymond Bérenger V (1209–1245)* (Paris, 2004), 241, 247–50. For Charles I of Anjou's use of non-Provençals in Provence, see Dunbabin, *Charles I of Anjou*, 51–2. For Charles' majority use of French and Provençal justiciars in the Regno (but local fiscal specialists centrally under heavy supervision) see Dunbabin, *Charles I of Anjou*, 734, and *The French in the Kingdom of Sicily, 1266–1305* (Cambridge, 2011), 177–80.

[33] e.g. cap. 21 of the 1194 eyre wanting non-local sheriffs, *Select Charters and Other Illustrations of English Constitutional History from the Earliest Times to the Reign of Edward I*, ed. W. Stubbs, rev. H. W. C. Davis, 9th edn. (Oxford, 1913), 254.

Podestà are an interesting exception proving this rule. In their 'classic' form they are accountable to the local communities that select them. Were the rule true about local élites preferring local officers one would suppose that *podestà* should be local as a matter of course. Famously, though, *podestà* are legislated to be outsiders for the specific reason that insiders proved too partial to one or other factional grouping. The rule, however, is simply seeking to control an excess of communities' 'natural' tendency to want pliable insiders; the problem of *podestà* becoming assimilated into local political groupings similarly confirms the rule. In this case too the issue of dismissible officers was a practical one rather than an in-principle issue.

Mention of *podestà* in this context raises the related question of finite tenure. In Italy the rule might be more honoured in the breach, but again the logic of finite tenure was to minimize official entitlement. Opposite views could be justified, however. To Louis IX, Guibert of Tournai argued for the principle of infrequent changes in local (royal) officials, just as a wounded man beset by flies might not thank a passer-by for brushing them off since 'the flies which you have shooed away were full of blood, and hardly troubling me. But those which cover me and take their place will bite all the more sharply'. Prolonged attachment to the same body means that the thirst for blood levels off, whereas frequent changes in personnel will simply mean a faster turnover of ravenous bloodsuckers.[34] The English baronial arguments to Louis in 1264 argued precisely the opposite. The reformers had made shrieval appointments annually, with neither prejudice to nor presumption against re-election, precisely so that sheriffs should not become 'overproud in office'.[35] In practice it was more problematic, as Roger of Howden's disparaging remarks about the counterproductive 1170 Inquest of Sheriffs showed.[36] Both perspectives are comprehensible. But the problems identified by both Guibert and the reformist barons would apply to each other's solutions when it came to officers' finite tenures. In practice anyway most middling officers were subject to review and removal. Bishops are something of an exception here. But even their immunity weakened over the period. Innocent III's practice of removing heretical or otherwise unacceptable bishops signalled that principled hurdles to removing prelates were not insurmountable.[37]

Local Political Structures, Values, and Officers' Accountability

An officer's accountability was very significantly a function of the 'local' political structures around an office. This itself is unsurprising; more interesting is how

---

[34] *Le Traité Eruditio regum et principum de Guibert de Tournai, O.F.M.*, ed. A. de Poorter, Les Philosophes belges, 9 (Louvain, 1914), 78 (§2.2.9).
[35] *DBM* #37b cap. 11 at 263.
[36] *Gesta regis Henrici secundi Benedicti abbatis* [Roger of Howden], ed. William Stubbs, RS, 2 vols. (London, 1867), i. 4–5. See p. 114.
[37] The *Gesta* of Innocent specifies twenty removals before its cut-off of 1209: see *PL* 214, cols. clxxii–clxxv (cap. 130).

different institutional-jurisdictional contexts gave rise to different practices of accountability.[38]

Bailiffs and *podestà* are a case in point. The offices differ in many ways—but Andrew Horn's interest in both again serves as an encouragement to comparison. Both were executive officers with financial and legal responsibilities. *Podestà* were certainly greater men, with greater legal powers and with military responsibilities. Still, it is interesting to compare the method of accountability in either case. Both bailiff and *podestà* underwent an end-of-term audit of their actions. Around both officers grew a similar-shaped worry about their accountability. *Monstravit de compoto* addressed the possibility of a landless bailiff absconding after finishing a term of office and having embezzled (fraud) or mismanaged (incompetence) his land-lord's assets. *Sindacatio* sought to prevent a professional *podestà* leaving the commune before he had given an adequate account of his and his officers' actions. Beyond this though the socio-political structure entailed by the action of account differs from that of *sindacatio*. The action of account presumed that a nationwide county network would provide a sticky net in which to catch a bailiff who had run out of the jurisdiction in which he—allegedly—committed the offences.[39] It was predicated on royal government of a particular degree and depth. One cannot imagine a pan-Italian institution whereby allegedly criminal *podestà* would be sent by one helpful city-state back to their previous employer (take Siena and Florence's thirteenth-century antagonism). But, in contrast perhaps to *podestà*, we can wonder whether bailiffs were enough of a 'profession' for previous poor performance to pose an obstacle to future work. The role of professionalism may here have varied in relation to these jurisdictional nets, as well as in relation to the relative power of the positions. One can more easily imagine how a *podestà* would seek to avoid a truly disastrous *sindacatio* for reputational as well as financial reasons. Reputation was thought to matter more explicitly for *podestà*, and indeed as bigger figures they were the more visible. Much of the literature addressed to *podestà* discusses how they should seek to smooth the path of *sindacatio* for this reason. English bailiffs also had experience and skills and hawked around for work—as Adam Marsh's correspondence showed. They could also be quite 'senior' in the sense of having heavy responsibilities—as John de Valle's case showed. Aside from relevant differences between the two offices, issues of professionalism, reputation, and the political structure of either England or Italy show why *sindacatio* and actions of account could develop as they did where they did.

In the same way, the argument about the specific emphases of shrieval accountability stemmed from an argument about the mainly fiscal interests of

---

[38] See more widely Michael Borgolte, *Europa entdeckt seine Vielfalt, 1050–1250*, Handbuch der Geschichte Europas 3 (Stuttgart, 2002), esp. pt. 4.

[39] English government was well used to jurisdictional boundaries being manipulated. See the ruse whereby debtors to the king would hide their goods outside their county of residence to prevent that county's sheriff from extracting the debt. *DS*, II.i at 71–2. For problems produced in Germany of discrete judicial districts (*Gericht*) and their imperial judicial hierarchies in relation to the pursuit of crime see *Saxon Mirror*, §§2.71 (breaking the peace), 3.24 (outlawry), 2.35 (stolen goods found in another district).

the major institution responsible for routinely holding them to account—the Exchequer—and can be counterpointed with the different emphases of French *enquêtes* into *baillis*, where the chronological development of its relevant fiscal institution—the *Chambre des comptes*—did indeed differ. College wardens are a further contrasting case, where accountability was a consequence of local institutional (organizational) structure, but where institutional (social) forms had more, not less in common across Europe; perhaps again unsurprising given the monastic humus on which they were based, as across Merton and the Sorbonne. Episcopal accountability fits in midway here, as both generic (the procedure of canonical *inquisitio* is applicable throughout Christendom) and local (subjective local groups/élites may play a determinative role in assessing what constitutes a *scandalum* in the first place).

This is to offer a portrait of English official accountability in which any 'Englishness' in these features is a recognizable variant of a wider European continuum. Although the values underpinning these different European experiments in official accountability were very similar, their different political and administrative backgrounds led to them being instrumentalized and institutionalized in quite distinct ways. Holt's brilliant analysis of the English crisis of '1215' rightly set it in its wider European context.[40] His near contemporary Jacques Le Goff, however, never had 'such a profound feeling of exoticism as in England'—'l'Angleterre est un pays bien étrange'.[41] But, in the area of officers' accountability at least, Le Goff's comment seems more not less *outré*. When one asks Susan Reynolds's question, 'How different was England?' in terms of the complexity of the accountability exacted from its officials, the answer must be, 'Distinctive, but of a piece with the rest of Europe.'[42] Reynolds—Holt and Le Goff's younger contemporary—has stressed in her major works the common ground of European social institutions and legal practices, at least to the thirteenth century.[43] The English forms may be variable, the underlying impulses are not, and no more exotic than those of France or the Regno. With respect to officials' accountability, there was commonality of values and variety of institutional expressions as a function of underlying economic and political structures—but also as a consequence of the encouragement given by authoritative individuals, be they Walter of Merton, Louis IX, Innocent III, Richard of Ilchester, Henry III, or Frederick II.

This bears in turn on David d'Avray's Weberian thesis about the relationship between values and their instrumental expression. Here that would mean the value placed on being accountable in relation to a given instrumental practice of

---

[40] J. C. Holt, *Magna Carta*, 2nd edn. (Cambridge, 1992), 23–49, puts the charter in this wider context.

[41] The first quote is Le Goff's, the second Boureau's, both in Alain Boureau, *La Loi du royaume: Les Moines, le droit et la construction de la nation anglaise (XI*e*–XIII*e* siècles)* (Paris, 2001), 11.

[42] Susan Reynolds, 'How Different was England?', *TCE* 7 (1999).

[43] Susan Reynolds, *Kingdoms and Communities in Western Europe, 900–1300*, 2nd edn. (Oxford, 1997), and *Fiefs and Vassals: The Medieval Evidence Reinterpreted* (Oxford, 1994).

securing that accountability (say a bailiff's duty to give account and the action of account).

> Since values mould instrumental rationality, the degree to which instrumental rationality in different cultures coincides depends on the degree of overlap between their value rationalities [. . .] The key is the causal dependence of instrumental technique on values. Similar values generate similar instrumental techniques [. . .] differences in underlying values can cause the whole character of the instrumental rationalities they generate to look entirely different, as vodka changes its taste with different mixers.[44]

The forms of instrumental techniques are a function of their underlying values. So the norms asserting that officials be accountable would determine the institutional form that instrumentalizes this claim. The material evaluated here certainly illustrates a more complex dialectic between values and institutional expression. The value of accountability as expressed in the parable of the unjust steward and invoked in relation to both *podestà* and bishops is insufficient to explain the differing shapes of *sindacatio* and canonical inquisition. One gets closer by adding the value of episcopal status (and the consequent *caveat* about ensuring an investigation produces 'no serious loss for the sake of a small gain'), since this goes some way to explaining the prominence of *infamia* procedurally. But the structure of inquisitions seems as much a practical consequence of the limits of papal oversight. This itself may have little to do with values. The Exchequer's definition of what constituted shrieval accountability defined what sheriffs were accountable for. But that focus also imposed real limits on (e.g.) Henry III's faltering attempts to assert the importance of non-fiscal aspects of sheriffs' conduct.[45] Institutional form (that is, instrumental rationality) could constrain or enable ideals (that is, value rationality) in practice. The explanation for the difference between Henry III and Louis IX's handling of their 'shrieval' officers is not only that Louis's values were arguably more coherent than Henry's; it is that the instrumental rationalities institutionalized in their administrative traditions conditioned either king's freedom of manoeuvre differently.

This draws attention to the difficulty of isolating the specific roles that values play in determining given institutional practices. (It is not at all to deny that role.) If it is right that ideals or values of official accountability were relatively common throughout Christendom, then would one expect to see them given the same institutional form? Institutional forms may be more regionalized (e.g. southern European *sindacationes*)[46] or less (non-canonical *inquisitiones* generally). If, as it seems, ideals of accountability were relatively common then political/institutional context and purpose may play determinative roles. Values may shape instrumental practices, but they are not the only thing that matters.

---

[44] d'Avray, *Rationalities in History*, 112–13.
[45] On Henry III's motivations and speeches, Maddicott, *Origins of the English Parliament*, 170, 174–5.
[46] See further Moritz Isenmann, *Legalität und Herrschaftskontrolle (1200–1600): Eine vergleichende Studie zum Syndikatsprozess: Florenz, Kastilien und Valencia* (Frankfurt, 2010).

This is to suggest something about the importance of institutional need and rectores' own thinking, raising the question of causation.

CAUSES, CONDITIONS, CORRELATIONS

Institutional Development, Intellectual Capability, and the *rector*'s Conscience

This 'accountable' way of thinking, some of whose influence and forms are analysed here, seems principally the product of three factors. Its dominance was required by one much broader phenomenon, enabled by a second, and shaped by a third: respectively, institutional growth, scholastic rationalization, and public power's self-consciousness. The massive elaboration of institutions *tout court*, going hand in hand with the development of these practices made the practices necessary and strongly influenced their shape. It explains the relationship between delegation and access treated already. It could not, however, give the practices their intellectual method, or their faith in that method. This was manifested in that wider 'scholastic' faith in humans' power to establish the truth about things through systematic inquiry.[47] Peter Abelard, in the 1120s, writing about theological inquiry and the reconciliation of different authorities, used Augustine as a springboard to articulate the germ of this approach's axiomatic method: 'it is by doubting that we come to inquiry [*inquisitionem*] and by inquiring that we perceive the truth'.[48] There was a pessimistic flipside to this optimistic upside (see this chapter pp. 253–60), but epistemologically this is the basis for the forms of accountability considered here. Twelfth- and thirteenth-century belief in inquiry and accountability was no less potent than that modern confidence that regularly produces routine inquests and audits as well as massive quasi-judicial inquiries into a variety of phenomena: the 'culture, practices and ethics of the press'; alleged state complicity in the death of a United Nations arms inspector; governmental intelligence on weapons of mass destruction in the context of the 2003 Iraqi war; and an inquiry 'to identify lessons that can be learned from the Iraq conflict'—to take only the most prominent British inquiries conducted during the writing of this

---

[47] R. W. Southern, *Scholastic Humanism and the Unification of Europe*, 2 vols. (Oxford, 1997–2001) is an exploration of the intellectual phenomena in relation to the institutional need. For a different perspective see Moore, *First European Revolution*, 112–59, 188–98.

[48] 'Dubitando quippe ad inquisitionem venimus; inquirendo veritatem percipimus', the prologue to Peter Abailard, *Sic et non: A Critical Edition*, ed. Blanche B. Boyer and Richard McKeon (Chicago, 1976), 103 ll. 338–9. On Augustine—and Abelard's addition of *inquisitionem* and *inquirendo*—see Beryl Smalley, '*Prima clavis sapientiae:* Augustine and Abelard', in Smalley, *Studies in Medieval Thought and Learning from Abelard to Wyclif* (London, 1981), 1–10. Relevant notes of Abelard's usage include Alain Boureau, 'Introduction', in Claude Gauvard (ed.), *L'Enquête au Moyen Âge*, Collection École française de Rome 399 (Rome, 2008), 1–10 at 8, and Paul Hyams, 'Due Process versus the Maintenance of Order: The Contribution of the *ius commune*', in Peter Coss (ed.), *The Moral World of the Law* (Cambridge, 2000), 85. For a minimal interpretation of the maxim, M. T. Clanchy, *Abelard: A Medieval Life* (Oxford, 1997), 107–8, and for broader comment 6, 34, 36–7, 121, 216, 273–4, 331.

study.[49] If demand came from institutional growth and wherewithal from scholastic confidence, the underlying impetus came—thirdly—from the reflections of those in 'public power'.[50]

There were two general sides to these reflections. The first was pragmatically self-interested. The second was a more complicated matter of self-consciousness and conscience. As argued earlier, there is no especial reason the two may not be expressed at the same time.[51] The pragmatic side can be seen in the quote from *The Mirror of Justices*, where a land-lord is blamed for losses incurred by his servants, since he 'can put this rightly down to his own stupid contract, in so far as he did not take sufficient surety for complete loyalty and discretion'.[52] Some of the pseudo-Aristotelian *Secretum secretorum*'s stress on selecting bailiffs comes from the same impetus. But *rectores*' self-consciousness about themselves as holders of power, and the responsibility that entailed, must not be discounted as a real motor of official accountability. The great stress on rulers' (and officials') character as the guarantee of justice was noted at the outset and has recurred throughout.[53] 'The powerful shall be powerfully tormented' (Wisdom 6: 7) is a scriptural precept frequently quoted in relation to the need for those in authority to rule justly and to see those beneath them did so.[54] These ideas passed back and forth from secular to ecclesiastical positions of responsibility, just as Gregory the Great had thought of *rectores* as being of either quality.[55] Ideas of right rule (what John of Salisbury called 'public power') were connected to reformed practices of accountability. Frederick II explained the existence of princes in terms of the need for people to be corrected after the Fall of man; so did Charles I of Anjou.[56] Walter Map wrote of the

---

[49] Respectively the 'Leveson Inquiry', 'Hutton Inquiry', 'Butler Inquiry', and 'Chilcot Inquiry' (formally the Iraq Inquiry). Part 1 of The Leveson Inquiry (2011–12) has concluded (http://www.levesoninquiry.org.uk/). The Hutton Inquiry (2003–4) is archived at The National Archives's website (http://www.nationalarchives.gov.uk/webarchive/). The 'Butler Review' (2004) is available at http://www.archive2.official-documents.co.uk/document/deps/hc/hc898/898.pdf, all accessed February 2014. The 'Chilcot Inquiry' is open at time of writing (2009–) http://www.iraqinquiry.org.uk/, accessed February 2014. A review of both the Hutton and Butler inquiries is *Hutton and Butler: Lifting the Lid on the Workings of Power*, ed. W. G. Runciman (Oxford, 2004). It touches on many issues relevant to medieval inquiries including: judicial discretion in interpreting the terms of enquiry (13); the 'problem' of oral reports vs. written records in government (73); the tension between the fact of an inquiry and public expectations of it (40, 50); the difficulty of separating 'pure' fact-finding and (public) expectations of blame-apportioning (34–8, 121). While this volume was in proof, the British Home Secretary announced, on 7 July 2014, a further panel inquiry, into public bodies' handling of sex abuse allegations, permitting its conversion into an inquiry (like Leveson) under the 2005 Inquiries Act. See also p. 260 n. 176.

[50] For the term in late-twelfth-century royal government, Beryl Smalley, *The Becket Conflict and the Schools: A Study of Intellectuals in Politics* (Oxford, 1973), 228–9, 231, 239–40.

[51] See pp.127–34.

[52] *Mirror of Justices*, ed. William Joseph Whittaker, intr. Frederic William Maitland, SS 7 (London, 1895), 76.

[53] Ch. 1 *passim*, esp. pp. 23–4.

[54] e.g. Gerald of Wales, *Liber de principis instructione* in *Giraldi Cambrensis Opera*, RS, 8 vols. (London, 1861–91), viii. ed. George F. Warner, 327 (Dist. 3, cap. 31).

[55] R. A. Markus, 'Gregory the Great's *rector* and his Genesis', in Jacques Fontaine, Robert Gillet, and Stan Pellistrandi (eds.), *Grégoire le Grand* (Paris, 1986), 137–46 esp. 142–3.

[56] *Konstitutionen Friedrichs II. für das Königreich sizilien*, Prooemium, 147; cf Charles I of Anjou's preamble to 'Post corruptionis amara discrimina' (10 June 1282), *RCA*, xxv. Documenti tratti da altre fonti, #5 at 194–5. On Frederick and Louis IX in this context see Jacques Chiffoleau, 'Saint Louis, Frédéric II et les constructions institutionelles du XIIIᵉ siècle', *Médiévales* 34 (1998)', 16.

rector as *corrector*, associating ruling with the control of those beneath the ruler.[57] Innocent III chastised Peter des Roches by the same token.[58] It was an essential part of Innocent III's reforms that in 1213, two years before the Church's planned general council, he should require prelates across Christendom to 'to inquire carefully into everything which seems to need thorough correction or reform, and faithfully recording this, you will send on the report for examination by the Sacred Council'.[59] Louis IX's reparative actions before leaving on crusade were a parallel move. The most recent study of Edward I argues that the reason for his distinctive approach to governance was a function of his (self-)regard for regal office.[60] Rulers' conscience of their accountability to God above was a genuinely influential justification for their impositions of accountability down below. Ideas of right rule contributed to reformulated practices of official accountability.[61]

One need not be naïve about these motives. Neither Edward's nor Louis's reforms need be taken at the face value of the 'reformist' sensibility they ostensibly reveal. Louis's regulation of and 'distinction between public and private violence was a rhetorical weapon of the monarchy as it entered, one contestant among many, an arena of conflicting powers and authorities'.[62] Such concern may also be seen as much an expression of rulers' vanity as of their conscience. Thus attacks on a prince's officials are taken as an attack on the prince himself.[63] The prince was transparent through his official, and what struck the official passed straight through to the prince. 'For the *bailli* while he is a *bailli* represents his lord's person, and so who wrongs a *bailli*, wrongs the lord', said Philippe de Beaumanoir.[64] This could have an effect, as in the Regno, on the attitude taken towards officials' delicts.[65] As Frederick II specified in his oath for bailiffs 'the purity which we ourselves pursue, we demand especially from our officials in administering justice'.[66] Delegated responsibility could find expression

---

[57] Walter Map, *De nugis curialium*, ed. M. R. James, rev. C. N. L. Brooke and R. A. B. Mynors, OMT (Oxford, 1983), 510 (§5.7).

[58] 'In corrigendis excessibus', *c.*27 October 1205 (*Reg. Inn. III*, viii. #147 (146); *Innocent III English Calendar*, #647)

[59] 'universa subtiliter inquiratis que correctionis, aut reformationis studio indigere videntur, et ea fideliter conscribentes, ad sacri concilii perferatis examen', in 'Vineam Domini Sabaoth', 19 April 1213, *Innocent III English Letters*, #51 at 147.

[60] Burt, *Edward I and the Governance of England*, 88–9, 113, 116, 176, 191–2, 237.

[61] Cf. Adam J. Davis, *The Holy Bureaucrat: Eudes Rigaud and Religious Reform in Thirteenth-Century Normandy* (Ithaca, NY, 2006), 10–11.

[62] Robert Bartlett, 'The Impact of Royal Government in the French Ardennes: The Evidence of the 1247 Enquête', *Journal of Medieval History* 7 (1981), 95–6.

[63] *Konstitutionen Friedrichs II. für das Königreich sizilien*, caps 1.30, 3.40; see also Romain Telliez, «*Per potentiam officii*»: *Les Officiers devant la justice dans le royaume de France au XIVe siècle* (Paris, 2005), 62–70, 413–14, 681–3.

[64] Philippe de Beaumanoir, *Coutumes du Beauvaisis*, ed. André Salmon, 2 vols. (Paris, repr. 1970), i. cap. 1 §15.

[65] *Konstitutionen Friedrichs II. für das Königreich sizilien*, caps 1.36.1–2 (negligent/corrupt officials), 3.41 (punishments of officials who use their office as the cover for the pursuit of their personal vendettas). These provisions and those on attacks against officials (1.30, 3.40) follow on associatively from each other in the minds of their drafters.

[66] 'Puritatem, quam nos ipsi sectamur, ab officialibus nostris, in iudiciis maxime postulamus', *Konstitutionen Friedrichs II. für das Königreich sizilien*, cap. 1.62.1 at 227, also 1.31. This view is explored in a thirteenth-century Castilian context in Jular Pérez-Alfaro, 'King's Face on the Territory', esp. 110–20. Cf. for Louix IX, Guibert of Tournai, *Eruditio regum et principum*, e.g. 44, 67–8, 84–5, 87–8 (§§2.1.1, 2.2.2, 3.2, 3.5).

in the vanity of self-regard—'By acting badly you impugn *me*', so to speak. The idea that subordinates' actions needed to be a right reflection of their superiors' integrity is also articulated in Lateran IV's important proportionate papal algebra expressing the reason for canonical inquiries: 'A prelate should act the more diligently in correcting the offences of his subjects in proportion as he would be worthy of condemnation were he to leave them uncorrected.'[67] Holding *mediocres* officials to account was a further means of burnishing the self-image of their superiors. As a political ideal, officials' accountability was closely tied to rulers' self-regard.

Étatisation and Official Accountability?

One might be therefore tempted to infer the centrality of 'state' or regnal institutions to such practices of accountability. No accountability, no state; no state, no accountability. Many important interpretations of practices of accountability— especially in relation to inquisitions *ex officio* and/or action following public *infamia* develop a version of this line of thought, rooted as they are in explanations of the state.[68] 'The slow movement from accusation by the injured party to inquest of witnesses by a royal official was perhaps the most obvious sign of the emergence of the state in France'.[69] In León and Castile, 'proof by inquisition was an essential part of a procedure in which criminal proceedings were initiated by the king or a royal judge *de su oficio*, instead of by the victim of the crime or his kin [. . .] it was a procedure aimed at bringing about royal control of criminal justice'.[70]

---

[67] *Constitutiones Concilii quarti Lateranensis una cum Commentariis glossatorum*, ed. Antonio García y García, Monumenta iuris canonici, Ser. A: Corpus glossatorum 2 (Vatican City, 1981), 56 (cap. 8).
[68] Thomas N. Bisson, *The Crisis of the Twelfth Century: Power, Lordship, and the Origins of European Government* (Princeton, NJ, 2009), *passim*; Élisabeth Lalou, 'L'Enquête au Moyen Âge', *Revue historique* 313 (2011), 151–3 (on *enquêtes* and the state); R. C. van Caenegem, 'Public Prosecution of Crime in Twelfth Century England' and 'Criminal Law in England and Flanders under King Henry II and Count Philip of Alsace' in R. C. van Caenegem, *Legal History: A European Perspective* (London, 1991), respectively 1–36 and 37–60; Théry, '*Fama*: L'Opinion publique comme preuve judiciaire: Aperçu sur la révolution médiévale de l'inquisitoire (XIIe–XIVe siècle)', in Bruno Lemesle (ed.), *La Preuve en justice de l'Antiquité à nos jours* (Rennes, 2003), 147 (on *fama* and the state); Claude Gauvard, '*De grace especial*': *Crime, état et société en France à la fin du Moyen Âge* (Paris, 2010 edn.), 946–52, *s.v.* 'renommée'; Patrick Wormald, *Lawyers and the State: The Varieties of Legal History*, SS Lecture (London, 2006). See also Sarah Rubin Blanshei, *Politics and Justice in Late Medieval Bologna* (Leiden, 2010), *passim*, and 'Crime and Law Enforcement in Medieval Bologna', *Journal of Social History* 16 (1982), 121–38, esp. 124–5, 127 on Bologna's dysfunctional dual state/private criminal system; Harding, 'Plaints and Bills', esp. 82–3, and *Medieval Law and the Foundations of the State*, esp. 33–7, 118–23, 134–5, 147–60; J. H. Mundy, *Liberty and Political Power in Toulouse 1050–1230* (New York, 1954), 163, 320 n. 41. Important dissent in Massimo Vallerani, *Medieval Public Justice*, trans. Sarah Rubin Blanshei (Washington, 2012), *passim*, and e.g. 1–2. A stimulating account for the early modern and modern period is Jakob Soll, *The Reckoning: Financial Accountability and the Making and Breaking of Nations* (New York, 2014), focusing on the erratic relationship between fiscal accounting, political stability, and governmental and financial accountability from the fourteenth century on. Soll stresses the influence of accounting, its quantitative increase, and its qualitatively questionable and volatile modern effects (esp. ch. 13 and 205–8). He discusses medieval accounting innovations in their religious cultural context at 6–28.
[69] Dunbabin, *French in the Kingdom of Sicily*, 240, 245, relevantly citing Philippe de Beaumanoir, *Coutumes du Beauvaisis*, i. cap. 1 §14.
[70] Evelyn S. Procter, *The Judicial Use of 'Pesquisa' (Inquisition) in León and Castille, 1157–1369*, English Historical Review Suppl. 2 (London, 1966), 34.

'[French] officers' abuses and subjects' resistance to them must [. . .] be understood as a mode of operationalizing political power and as a reaction faced with this. Their history is therefore fully bound up in a history of the State, conceived not simply as the history of political institutions but also as a history of the relationships which sustain these institutions and particularly of the men who give life to them and those on whom their power is exercised'.[71]

There seems then a wider prima facie link between what is called *étatisation* in French, 'public' office-holding, and any sort of fiscal or criminal accountability. The ecclesiastical sphere has good grounds for claiming a central role in the articulation of the idea of 'office' itself.[72] The ideological space pontiffs had cleared for summary inquisitions into their episcopal 'bailiffs' was probably borrowed by kings more than has been realized.[73] Within German lands, a historian might even argue that proximity to the prince is the likeliest preventative of accountability in governmental institutions.[74] In 1347 Cologne a list of officials feels no need to qualitatively distinguish between town, princely, and burgher officials.[75] As to officials' accountability, the deliberate consideration here of seigneurial, collegial, and of ecclesiastical forms is intended to question systematically the presumption of a necessarily state-based point of origin and impetus. It would—true—be possible to argue that English treatises on seigneurial officials were imitative of public pretensions of royal power (more 'learned moralizing' perhaps)[76], and can therefore be parsed in that light.[77] It would be possible to argue that collegial concern with its members' and officers' accountability is a consequence of these foundations' 'public interest' purposes and therefore explicable, again, in relation to 'The' Public Power's image of itself, and consequently also an extended product of *étatisation*. It would be possible to argue that papal concern with ecclesiastical government is simply an aspirant version of 'stately' *étatisation* in a religious register. (Especially if one thinks the Church is the state *manqué*.) Eventually, though, enough non-state sources for officials' accountability would appear so uncomfortably subordinated to a privileged statist version that one must

---

[71] Telliez, «*Per potentiam officii*», 679–80.
[72] Wolter, 'Verwaltung, Amt, Beamter, V–VI', 30–1, 40. See also Wolter, 'The *Officium* in Medieval Ecclesiastical Law as a Prototype of Modern Administration', in Padoa-Schioppa (ed.), *Legislation and Justice*, 17–36 (a partial English version of the German article). Notwithstanding these quotes of Wolter's, in the context of regional German administration, he also sees the (fiscal) accountability of the *Amtmann* as, again, a consequence of growing state appetites (Wolter, 'Verwaltung, Amt, Beamter, V–VI', 43–4).
[73] Julien Théry, '«Excès» et «affaires d'enquête»: Les Procès criminels de la papauté contre les prélats, XIIIe–mi–XIVe siècle', 2 vols. (Université Paul-Valéry—Montpellier III, Dossier pour l'habilitation à diriger des recherches en histoire médiévale, 2010), i. 539–41 on Philip IV and Jean d'Aunay, sénéschal of Carcassonne in 1309.
[74] Wolter, 'Verwaltung, Amt, Beamter, V–VI', 46. In this latter section Wolter is generally talking about Bavaria. Louis XIV's abandonment of Colbert's miniature account books produced for him by his minister when the latter died in 1683 provides an ambivalent miniature of the wider relationship in Soll's *Reckoning*, ix–x.
[75] Wolter, 'Verwaltung, Amt, Beamter, V–VI', 41.
[76] The term is Bisson's, *Crisis of the Twelfth Century*, 445–56.
[77] On the context of the practical *Rectitudines singularum personarum*, see further P. D. A. Harvey, '*Rectitudines singularum personarum* and *Gerefa*', *EHR* 426 (1993), 20–1, for a non-royal, possibly monastic context.

ask whether a statist part has been mistaken for the bigger whole. 'Each good lord should be a good magistrate and judge,' said John of Ibelin of a lord's duty to investigate claims of murder on his doorstep.[78] 'At the beginning of *every* administrative system was the estate manager', not the king.[79] Kings used the same point of departure themselves. 'If mere lords appoint and judge their bailiffs and stewards, cannot then kings their officers?' demanded Henry III, and Edward I, bristling against attempts to restrict their control of (royal) officers.[80] The concerns of lords in controlling their officials, popes in regulating their prelates, colleges in disciplining their wardens, do indeed bear comparison with kings in controlling their agents, but these practices and institutions seem sufficiently autonomous to justify treating them as species of a common concern, rather than variations of a *ur*-regal/*étatiste* tendency. Some degree of predictable—not peaceful—order is needed for the development of these practices, and to this degree some basically stable division of power is needed (as Western Europe's ninth or late twelfth to thirteenth centuries show).[81] Given that, it seems more useful to stress the similarities, even the mutual influence between kings' and others' experiments in holding their officers accountable.[82] But if forms of accountability flourish in the shadow of kings, kings keep no monopoly in casting shadows. It is better to say that it is predictable that powers seeking power should appropriate to themselves 'rights' of inquiry and judgement which depend on their own volition, not on that of a plaintiff. The grounds of those powers may be various. From the appropriation by kings of such powers, *étatisation* may follow, be that Carolingian or Angevin. There are others—lords, colleges—appropriating accountability likewise and there seems no necessary reason to associate practices of accountability per se with *étatisation* per se. Such appropriations were a further turn of these powers' civilizing process. Formalizing officers' accountability helped to legitimize all forms of power in this period, seigneurial to imperial.

Elective Affinities

If *étatisation* does not provide an infallible skeleton key for explaining the diverse coherence that characterizes officials' accountability in the later twelfth and thirteenth centuries, how may it be explained? Implicit in the analysis just given is that the underlying conditions of institutional development, intellectual capability, and public powers' self-consciousness interacted and mutually strengthened one another when combined with various practices of holding officers to account. That is to say that between these phenomena there was an elective affinity that provides

---

[78] John of Ibelin, *Le Livre des assises*, ed. Peter W. Edbury (Leiden, 2003), 192.
[79] Joseph R. Strayer, 'The Development of Bureaucracies', *Comparative Studies in Society and History* 17 (1975), 504–9 at 505, my stress.
[80] Paris, *Chronica majora*, v. 20–1; *The Song of Lewes*, ed. C. L. Kingsford (Oxford, 1890), ll. 485–526; *DBM* #37a, caps. 1–6; *Chronicle of Pierre de Langtoft*, ii. 330.
[81] Not peaceful because regnal power seeks to arrogate rights of violence, not to restrict violence: Norbert Elias, *The Civilizing Process: Sociogenetic and Psychogenetic Investigations*, trans. Edmund Jephcott, rev. edn. (Oxford, 2000), esp. 187–362.
[82] Vallerani, *Medieval Public Justice* has much of relevance; Moore, *First European Revolution*, 171–3 stresses the parallel ambitions of both secular and ecclesiastical practices.

the basis for explaining parallel, 'vernacular' developments in multiple fields and regions. The idea of an elective affinity (*Wahlverwandtschaft*) between phenomena is easy to describe. It suggests (following Weber's development of the older German tradition), that distinct social, religious, or economic phenomena may have complementary features that, if brought together, can strengthen the parts and reinforce a whole.[83] Although one cannot tell from the standard English translation, an elective affinity between particular patterns of religious belief and practical ethics is Max Weber's explanation for the relationship between 'the Protestant ethic' and the 'spirit of capitalism'.[84] It is best to avoid the general idea that an elective affinity is simply a kind a 'operating system' that two phenomena share.[85] Weber instead stressed the active complementarity between different phenomena as the characteristic link for hypothesizing any such affinity.[86] The whole was greater than the sum of its disparate parts. In Weber's Protestant case, there is no reason why the affinity he identified could not be produced elsewhere by a work ethic that was *not* definitively Protestant *nor* linked to a singularly specific form of capitalism. The more general point concerned the relationship between a (Protestant) sort of belief and an (early modern) form of capitalism. To describe one variation is therefore not to exhaust the potential repertoire of related affinities.[87] There is nothing to preclude similar conjunctures in other places at other times. So for accountability. One finds similar concerns to those articulated in this book expressed distinctively in the Carolingian Empire with its *missi*, *inquisitiones*, and stress on responsibility;[88]

---

[83] Michael Löwy, 'Le Concept d'affinité élective chez Max Weber', *Archives de sciences sociales des religions* 49 (2004), 93–103 esp. 94–5, 99–102. References to Weber's usages can be found in Richard Herbert Howe, 'Max Weber's Elective Affinities: Sociology Within the Bounds of Pure Reason', *American Journal of Sociology* 84 (1978), 366–85 at 366; also Hubert Treiber, '"Elective Affinities" between Weber's Sociology of Religion and Sociology of Law', *Theory and Society* 14 (1985), 809–61 at 810–12.

[84] See 'Die protestantische Ethik und der Geist des Kapitalismus', in *Gesammelte Aufsätze zur Religionssoziologie* 1 (Tübingen, 1988, repr. of 1920 edn.), 83, 145. Cf. *The Protestant Ethic and the Spirit of Capitalism*, trans. Talcott Parsons (London, 2001), 49, 88. The few uses of the term in the original do not fully reflect its centrality to Weber's explanation.

[85] So Pierre Bourdieu (e.g.) seems to assimilate *Wahlverwandtschaft* to the idea of a *habitus*, which is for him a style of thinking, following Erwin Panofsky, that could explain the aesthetic parallels between gothic architecture and scholastic thought: 'Postface' to Erwin Panofsky, *Architecture gothique et pensée scolastique*, trans. Pierre Bourdieu (Paris, 1967), 135–67 at 135, and on *habitus*, 151–2, 157–67.

[86] See Max Weber, *Wirtschaft und Gesellschaft: Grundriss der Verstehenden Soziologie*, ed. Johannes Winckelmann, 5th edn. (Tübingen, 1972), 201: 'Wohl aber läßt sich Allgemeines über den Grad der Wahlverwandtschaft konkreter Strukturformen des Gemeinschaftshandelns mit konkreten Wirtschaftsformen aussagen, d. h. darüber: ob und wie stark sie sich gegenseitig in ihrem Bestande begüngstigen oder umgekehrt einander hemmen oder ausschließen: einander "adäquat" oder "inadäquat" sind'.

[87] There is an interesting parallelism here with Aby Warburg's fascination with the meaning and reception of the same artistic motif erupting in different contexts (such as the 'maenad's' flowing dress in Ghirlandaio's fresco in S. Croce, Florence).

[88] Stefan Esders, 'Die römischen Wurzeln der fiskalischen *inquisitio* der Karolingerzeit', in Gauvard (ed.), *L'Enquête au Moyen Âge*, 13–28; Mayke de Jong, *The Penitential State: Authority and Atonement in the Age of Louis the Pious, 814–840* (Cambridge, 2009), ch. 3; Abigail Firey, *A Contrite Heart: Prosecution and Redemption in the Carolingian Empire* (Leiden, 2009), *passim*; Paul Fouracre, 'Carolingian Justice: The Rhetoric of Improvement and Contexts of Abuse', in *La giustizia nell'alto medioevo (secoli v–viii)*, Settimane di studio del Centro italiano di studi sull'alto medioevo 42 (Spoleto,

through the oaths, frankpledges, and tithings of later Anglo-Saxon England;[89] in the inquiries of and relatable to the Domesday Book;[90] or in Mamluk Egypt (1250–1517). The latter is worth pausing at because of its distance from the tradition that links the European parallelisms and because of its specific legal provision for 'trials of suspicion' (*daʿāwīal-tuham*).[91] Trials of suspicion could be initiated following the investigative initiative of military authorities, governors, or important market inspectors (*muḥtasib*); did not require a plaintiff/accuser; and were undertaken for the purposes of forbidding wrong (*ḥisba*), a judgement made by the authorities.[92] Here is another 'vernacular' version, strikingly comparable with canonical inquisitions specifically. Through these trials torture was also licensed in order to provide for the convictions that could not be secured through regular testimonial procedure (*fiqh*). Stressing this aspect, Baber Johansen comments that the

> introduction of judicial torture accompanies the rationalization of the system of proof and procedure in the Near East as well as thirteenth-century Europe [. . .] I find it hard to believe that jurists living in Europe and the Near East in the thirteenth century simultaneously introduced a process of rationalization of the law accompanied by the legitimation of judicial torture without there having been any mutual influence and exchange.[93]

It is not clear whether Johansen is talking generally about European legal torture and the systematization of the *ius commune* in this period, or if he has canonical inquisitions specifically in mind. Certainly the inquisitorial procedure led *ex officio* by a judge on the basis or rumour or suspicion and justified with reference to some public good is a striking parallel with *daʿāwī al-tuham*. So one should stress that in *daʿāwī al-tuham* 'What needed to be proved was not the specific crime as much as the fact that the defendant was suspicious with a history of criminality. "Suspicion", therefore, became a formal legal category that had to be established in court before

---

1995); Rosamund McKitterick, *Charlemagne: The Formation of a European Identity* (Cambridge, 2008), 142–55, and chs. 4–5; Janet L. Nelson, 'Kingship and Royal Government', in Rosamund McKitterick (ed.), *The New Cambridge Medieval History*, ii. c.700–c.900 (Cambridge, 1995), 410–27.

[89] For ninth- to eleventh-century England see esp. Patrick Wormald, *The Making of English Law: King Alfred to the Twelfth Century*, i. *Legislation and its Limits* (Oxford, 1999), *passim*; David Pratt, *The Political Thought of King Alfred the Great* (Cambridge, 2007), *passim*; Stephen Baxter, 'Archbishop Wulfstan and the Administration of God's Property' in *Wulfstan, Archbishop of York: The Proceedings of the Second Alcuin Conference*, ed. Matthew Townend, Studies in the Early Middle Ages 10 (Turnhout, 2004), and the texts previously discussed: *Rectitudines singularum personarum*, *Gerefa*, and the 'Institutes of Polity, Civil and Ecclesiastical'. I am grateful to Stephen Baxter for access to a copy of Patrick Wormald's unpublished draft chapter (c.1990) on 'The Pursuit of Crime' from the unfinished second volume of *The Making of English Law*, which discusses many relevant issues.

[90] Sally Harvey, 'Domesday Book and its Predecessors', *EHR* 86 (1971), and 'Domesday Book and Anglo-Norman Goverance', *TRHS* 5th ser. 25 (1975); R. H. C. Davis, 'Domesday Book: Continental Parallels', in *Domesday Studies: Papers Read at the Novocentenary Conference of the Royal Historical Society and the Institute of British Geographers, Winchester 1986*, ed. J. C. Holt (Woodbridge, 1987).

[91] I first came across this legal procedure through Yossi Rapoport's ongoing work on the legal history of the Mamluk Sultanate and am grateful to him for references to Baber Johansen's work.

[92] Baber Johansen, 'Signs as Evidence: The Doctrine of Ibn Taymiyya (1263–1328) and Ibn Qayyim al-Jawziyya (d. 1351) on Proof', *Islamic Law and Society* 9.2, *Evidence in Islamic Law* (2002), 168–93 at 190–1.

[93] Johansen, 'Signs as Evidence', 193. Cf. Lewis, 'On Not Expecting the Spanish Inquisition'.

the fact-finder could use these procedures [i.e. summary means, including imprisonment and beating].'[94]

Michael Cook in his study of individual Muslims' private responsibility to 'command right and forbid wrong' has noticed other relevant medieval European/Islamic parallelisms.[95] Focusing on Aquinas, *Summa Theologiae*, IIa-IIae q. 33 a. 1–8, Cook notes: 'the duty of fraternal correction modified by material considerations (time, place); the counter-obligation to avoid investigating others' lives; the general nature of the charitable obligation to correct irrespective of relative status; the burden to do so privately unless there is a public interest reason for its publicity; and further, if private reproof is ultimately unsuccessful, that public reproof should be undertaken'. Amongst differences, Cook notes that Aquinas is dogmatic about the obligation to correct irrespective of the consequences (where Islam is more accommodating), but lacks a general responsibility of physical reproof (as distinct from verbal reproof)—which Islamic thought has (correction 'with the hand').[96] Broader examination of the Western material beyond 'high grade' thinkers such as Aquinas would certainly reveal a wider medieval story. Ibn Taymiyya is certainly helpful in extracting it. As well as his discussions of 'trials of suspicion', Ibn Taymiyya's writings stress the importance of cost–benefit judgements when forbidding wrong and commanding evil for communal ends.[97] That mode of thinking bears strong comparison with the same cost–benefit decision-making which characterized both the legislation and the practice of canonical inquisitions.

Cook and Johansen come to different conclusions, though, about the meaning of such similarities. Johansen believes that the legal similarities must be explicable through direct European-Egyptian influence. Cook allows that 'monogenetic' explanations may indeed be the answer (however unprovable), but concedes too that there may be 'an elective affinity between forbidding wrong and monotheism'. The two complement and strengthen each other. Cook also acknowledges, however, that the doctrinal drivers one might propose for such an affinity (God's righteousness, his involvement with the world, and a belief in communal, fraternal correction) do not fit quasi-monotheistic Zoroastrianism, which despite its highly moralistic worldview had a strong disposition against correcting others.[98] Perhaps though this is to hope for too tight a set of infallible parallelisms.

---

[94] Mohammad Fadel, 'Adjudication in the Mālikī Madhhab: A Study of Legal Process in Medieval Islamic Law', 2 vols. (Ph.D. thesis, University of Chicago, 1995), 192, but also 184–99 esp. 190–9. See also Fadel, 'Proof and Procedure in Islamic Law', in Stanley N. Katz (gen. ed.), *The Oxford International Encyclopedia of Legal History*, 6 vols. (Oxford, 2009), iv. 427–31.

[95] Michael Cook, *Commanding Right and Forbidding Wrong in Islamic Thought* (Cambridge, 2010). Cook excludes rulers' and censors' functions in commanding right and forbidding wrong (xii).

[96] Cook, *Commanding Right and Forbidding Wrong*, 573–9, for 'correction with the hand' see index *s.v.* 'hand' and on the division of labour of the 'three modes' of correction (hand, mouth, heart), esp. 474, 583.

[97] Baber Johansen, 'A Perfect Law in an Imperfect Society: Ibn Taymiyya's Concept of "Governance in the Name of the Sacred Law"', *The Law Applied: Contextualizing the Islamic Shari'a*, ed. P. Bearman, W. Heinrichs, and B. G. Weiss (London, 2008), 259–94 at 282–4.

[98] Cook, *Commanding Right and Forbidding Wrong*, 578–82.

It is more fruitful to follow Cook's Weberian line of thought. Similar practices may originate independently given similarities of local need and similarities of religious-socio-political structure.[99] This is surely the deeper logic in explaining the parallelisms between, for instance, *daʿāwī al-tuham* and canonical inquisitions and *infamia*. The advantage of this approach historiographically is that one cuts knotty (and sometimes chauvinistic) debates about priority and invention in relation to given practices. It may also help to avoid the 'wood for the trees' problem discussed on p. 226: i.e. a text that showed the definitive transmission of European inquisitorial practice to Mamluk Egypt would still need to explain why it was attractive and feasible to Mamluk rulers, adminstrators, and jurists. One is missing the wood for the trees if one stops at a precedent/source to 'explain' a given transmission.

Similarities *within* Europe may be understood on a similar basis. There were no European patents pending on the use, deployment, or fact of *inquisitiones*, accounts, audits, *infamia*, *scrutinia*, end-of-tenure justifications, fixed-term appointments, or regional rotation of officers.[100] In China the regulation of local magistrates by fixing tenures of one to two years, and their geographical rotation, dated at least to the Qin and Han (respectively 221–206 BC, 206 BC–AD 220). Debate about such measures was of comparable duration. In China it was still being debated in the second half of the thirteenth century, much as it was in late medieval Italy.[101] Late Roman tax registers bear similarities to the record of Domesday Book, but a direct causal connection is not per se therefore apparent.[102] Anthropologists in contemporary northern Nepal have detailed the end-of-term accountability or trial of village elders in Mustang province, a procedure rather

---

[99] Cf. Chris Wickham on inventing desmesnes, *Framing the Early Middle Ages: Europe and the Mediterranean 400–800* (Oxford, 2005), 273: 'To use a Darwinian image: I see the desmesne as a little like the development of the wing: separately pterodactyls, birds, and bats evolved wings from different sets of body parts to meet the same sort of environmental needs and opportunities. We see their wings as analogous, and all three can/could certainly fly, but the three developments are actually entirely unrelated, and could in principle recur in different ways again.'

[100] For the creativity of 'un-Romanized' Italian law (including the use of *publica fama*) Chris Wickham, *Courts and Conflict in Twelfth-Century Tuscany* (Oxford, 2003), *passim*. For parallel arguments about the development in the later twelfth and thirteenth centuries about a general capacity for judicial abstraction see Alain Boureau, 'Droit naturel et abstraction judiciaire. Hypothèses sur la nature du droit médiéval', *Annales. Histoire, Sciences Sociales* 57 (2002), 1463–88, his exploration of this in England in *Loi du royaume*; also John Hudson on the common law in the 1170s and the emergence of a novel royal 'form of legal expertise [. . .] displaying abstraction, generalisation, sustained legal reasoning', in 'From the *Leges* to *Glanvill*: Legal Expertise and Legal Reasoning', in Stefan Jurasinski, Andrew Rabin, and Lisi Oliver (eds.), *English Law before Magna Carta: Felix Liebermann and Die Gesetze der Angelsachsen* (Leiden, 2010), 221–49 at 245.

[101] See Ma Duanlin's (1254–?), negative judgement in his *Comprehensive Study of Literary Remains*, excerpted in William Theodore de Bary and Irene Bloom (eds.), *Sources of Chinese Tradition*, i. *From the Earliest Times to 1600*, 2nd edn. (New York, 1999), 665. For Italy see Aurelio Lippo Brandolini's c.1490 *Republics and Kingdoms Compared*, ed. James Hankins, I Tatti Renaissance Library 40 (Cambridge, 2009), 76–86.

[102] See Davis, 'Domesday Book: Continental Parallels', 16–17; Harvey, 'Domesday Book and Anglo-Norman Governance', 186–8 explains the variable ploughland figures in Domesday by citing both Roman (*jugum*) and pre-/post-1086 (*bovate, carucate, iugum, sulung*) examples of fiscal units of fixed value, but not fixed area.

reminiscent of the *sindacatio* of *podestà*, to which it is surely unrelated.[103] This is not to be flippant about particular connections. Investigating concrete links between one usage and another clarifies some of the ways in which ideas were disseminated, but other explanations may still be needed when analysing the context in which such connections flourished, the interests that they served, and the dispositions that made them possible.

EFFECTS

How can the effects of these practices and dispositions be characterized? Did they have unintended consequences? What was the effectiveness of these practices, their costs, and their perceived value; likewise the relationship between these practices and broader ideals about particular offices? If the requirements of accountability provided some practical definition of the contours of office, manorial manuals, *podestà* literature, and the ideal prelates of ecclesiastical treatises (for example) still had a non-trivial influence. Finally, since accountability is so frequently, if arguably, associated with the creation of justice, the book closes by reflecting on their relation in the light of the material analysed here.

Unintended Consequences

Forms of accountability can have unexpected sources, their causes unintended consequences. Take a different arena to that of this study, parliamentary accountability. The growing dynamism of the English parliament between 1189 and 1225 was, it has been convincingly argued, the consequence of an absentee or weak crown's need to implicate a credible political community in securing taxation.[104] In the more modest fora discussed here, inquiries established for royal purposes could be turned to communal ends.[105] Writ large, this could be seen as a general effect of the increased accountability in the period considered here. Before, there were fewer spheres providing a secure space in which the weaker could complain of the stronger; afterwards there were more. This seems circular in part since, as it was argued above, the growing complexity of methods for securing accountability was a function of the growth and growing complexity of institutional life more generally in this period. The point remains though.

Were there consequences for formal or self-conscious thought about accountability because of altered practices of it? An increased focus on officers' accountability

---

[103] Charles Ramble, *The Navel of the Demoness: Tibetan Buddhism and Civil Religion in Highland Nepal* (Oxford, 2008), ch. 10. I am grateful to him for discussion.
[104] Maddicott, *Origins of the English Parliament*, 141, 147, 154, ch. 7 *passim*; note also his stress (e.g. 152, 157) on the contingent effects of the specific reigns and personalities of Richard, John, and Henry III within the wider European pattern.
[105] See also Scales, 'Cambridgeshire Ragman Rolls', 578; Helen M. Cam, *Studies in the Hundred Rolls: Some Aspects of Thirteenth-Century Administration*, Oxford Studies in Social and Legal History 6 (Oxford, 1921),190; T. N. Bisson, *Tormented Voices: Power, Crisis and Humanity in Rural Catalonia, 1140–1200* (Cambridge Mass., 1998), *passim*.

did sometimes enable a more developed conversation about institutional equity. Jean Dunbabin has drawn attention to the greater interest in institutions amongst thinkers such as Ptolemy of Lucca (Tolomeo Fiadoni) in and around 1282 following the Sicilian Vespers. She has suggested that 'the traumatic events of [Charles of Anjou's] reign overcame the powerful intellectual blockage that had restricted political discussion largely to the motivation of princes, and as a consequence the floodgates opened, investigation began into the control of royal administrators, into just limits of taxation, and into appropriate definitions of treason'.[106] Political crisis, prompting practical measures or reforms, did not however invariably lead to self-conscious reflection on underlying problems. In the Regno it might. In England, as noted, there seems a curious dearth of thirteenth-century political thought on sheriffs. A text as interesting as the *Mirror of Justices* comes late in the century.[107] Lesser English seigneurial officials are rich in both practice and theory. (Specific reasons for this difference were offered earlier.[108]) By contrast in France, lacking crises such as '1215' or '1258', one can nevertheless point to rich discussions of officials' capacity for *excessus* as in Guibert of Tournai's *Eruditio regum et principum*, or extended considerations such as those of Philippe de Beaumanoir.[109] (Reasons for this difference between France and England were offered above.[110]) As for ecclesiastical accountability, because the method of canonical legal regulation went alongside a tradition of commenting on those texts, one does find thought engaging with practice in that field. As was argued in Chapter 1, the *practices* analysed previously should anyway be seen as applied political thinking on their own terms. But on the subject of *mediocres* officials' accountability, sophisticated political thinking only sometimes produced sophisticated political thought. The latter is only a partial index of the former. When it did, however, the cause and effect seem largely to be this way round: ideas followed from practical needs.

One unintended consequence arguably flowed from lesser *mediocres* to some greater *rectores*. The period discussed here was also one in which the highest rulers came under increased scrutiny or criticism in some cases leading to deposition or removal. It is tempting to interrelate that grander political narrative to the intensification of *mediocres* officials' accountability as discussed here. Sancho II, Frederick II, Henry III, Alfonso X, Adolf of Nassau, Boniface VIII, John XXII, Edward II: all may be cited as rulers held to account somehow and found wanting in one forum or another. One can find, though, a sufficient number of earlier rulers being deposed, assaulted, or otherwise 'held to account'—e.g. Leo III (d. 816), Henry IV of Germany (1050–1106), Gregory VII (*c*.1025–85), even Stephen of England (*c*.1096–1154) or Alexander III (1100–81)—to disprove any argument that such

---

[106] Dunbabin, 'Charles I of Anjou and the Development of Medieval Political Ideas', 111.
[107] See the discussion in Frédérique Lachaud, *Éthique du pouvoir au Moyen Âge: L'Office dans la culture politique (Angleterre, vers 1150–vers 1330)*, Bibliothèque d'histoire médiévale 3 (Paris, 2010), 635–62.
[108] See pp. 60–82.
[109] Guibert de Tournai, *Eruditio regum et principum*, esp. the second letter and Jacques Le Goff, *Saint Louis* (Paris, 1996), 407–17; *Coutumes de Beauvaisis*, i. cap. 1 §16–42.
[110] See pp. 121–34.

forms of accountability as discussed here were a prerequisite for *rectores* being held 'accountable' in some way. What is true is that the language of office's growing sophistication was used within debates on the relative standing of the highest offices. Dante did so in discussing a vicar's standing (and by extension of the pope's); the relative standing of pope and emperor; and the distinct derivations of each office's power.[111] Thomas of Lancaster, in setting himself up against Edward II in 1321, likewise drew on official ideas of stewardship in promoting the Steward of England's office. (Whether others were convinced is another matter.[112]) So too did the wardens or guardians (*custodes*) of Scotland during the interregnum following Alexander III's death in 1286.[113] The development of a strictly regal accountability in England seems mainly a parliamentary story, not one of transposing the devices developed here to the 'office' of kings.[114] A better case can be made for popes as prelates. The liability of Boniface VIII or John XXII to allegations of heresy (or more) may be more reasonably seen as a consequence of the technique described here in relation to other prelates. More generally still, the language of office, and the accountability it enabled and could entail, became, through the mechanisms discussed above, a potent means of contesting political control.

Effects and Their Problems

What did these forms of accountability achieve? One end has already been touched on: that *rectores* holding their officials to account should demonstrate their own probity to those watching. Historians' judgements differ regarding the effectiveness of these methods for securing officials' accountability. Some have worried that historiographical specialization in the field of high politics and governmental records may itself compromise historical judgement—historians could become unwitting apologists and the state's or the 'king's friends'.[115] In terms of wider efficacy some have tended to side with the Dunstable Annalist's well-known judgement on England's 1274–5 Hundred Roll enquiries: 'Nothing useful came of it.'[116] Extensive bureaucratic accountability could certainly perpetuate itself with little substantive impact on what it was supposed to

---

[111] Dante, *Monarchia*, ed. Prue Shaw (Cambridge, 1995), §§3.6–7, 3.8–9, 3.12. More widely Edward Peters, *The Shadow King: Rex Inutilis in Medieval Law and Literature, 751–1327* (New Haven, Conn., 1970).

[112] 'Hic annotatur quis sit senescallus Anglie et quid ejus officium', BL Cotton MS Vespasian B. VII, fos. 104^v–105^v; Cotton MS Nero C. I, fos. 4^v–5^v; L. W. Vernon Harcourt, *His Grace the Steward and Trial of Peers* (London, 1907), 164–7. See J. R. Maddicott, *Thomas of Lancaster, 1307–1322: A Study in the Reign of Edward II* (Oxford, 1970), 241–3; 289–92 (on the place of the Steward of England in the *Modus tenendi parliamentum*); Michael Prestwich, *Plantagenet England*, 224–6; Lachaud, *Éthique du pouvoir*, 574–7.

[113] See G. W. S. Barrow, *Robert Bruce and the Community of the Realm of Scotland*, 4th edn. (Edinburgh, 2005), 20–4 and ch. 6.

[114] See Maddicott, *Origins of the English Parliament*.

[115] K. B. McFarlane, *The Nobility of Later Medieval England: The Ford Lectures for 1953 and Related Studies* (Oxford, 1973), 2; see also Rees Davies, 'The State: The Tyranny of a Concept?', *Journal of Historical Sociology* 16 (2003), 280–300 at 288–9.

[116] *Annales Monastici*, iii. 263. Cf. the more neutral Hagnaby Chronicle's notice on Edward's country-wide sworn inquiries into the basis of tenures (BL Cotton MS Vespasian B XI, fo. 27); Sandra Raban, *A Second Domesday? The Hundred Rolls of 1279–80* (Oxford, 2004), 24 and to 36. On (e.g.) the *use* made of John's 1212 feudal tenure inquiries see Holt, *Magna Carta*, 212.

improve or inform. In the Hundred Rolls case it is possible that the crown's intention was *not* to do anything with the retrospective indictments, but to restrict *henceforth* sheriffs' jurisdictions and licence for abusive behaviour, as happened.[117] That possibility is instructive since it begs the question of what one might expect the function of such practices to be at all. In fact the existence of extracts from the 1274–5 rolls, made 1280–94, and including the *De ministris* roll that comprised officers' abuses alone, does imply that something more was intended than occurred.[118] Other historians have made more positive arguments for the sorts of administrative practices analysed here. 'Familiarity with the innumerable records produced by the government during this period may lead to the conclusion that this was an unnecessarily bureaucratic age, and that there could have been easier and quicker ways of doing things. The overriding impression, however, is of men who were doing their best and working very hard.'[119]

There are inherent difficulties however in correlating administrative sophistication with standards of official conduct, procedural effectiveness, and equity in medieval government.[120] One is the question of what officials' hard work is taken to indicate governmentally speaking. In the Regno Charles I integrated a highly routinized and literate administration with high expectations of probity on the part of his officials (or at least a tendency to blame them when things went wrong). That these men were working very hard may have been of little comfort to the taxable population of the Regno—if we follow Saba Malaspina's account of Charles's oppression through officials and their *excessus*.[121] Unjust exactions were justified by invoking the *utilitas fisco*.[122] (One might be reminded of Richard of Ely.) Notwithstanding Malaspina's antipathy to Charles, it is hard to dismiss the inference he drew between the Capetian's compulsion to extract and his compulsion for accountability. Effectiveness of administration here goes hand in hand with extractive rule. Many histories of English local government in the later twelfth and thirteenth centuries entail at least a partially similar narrative.[123] 'The king's eye is ever fresh there', Walter Map wrote of the twelfth-century English Exchequer. Ostensibly this therefore indicated equity's consequent presence, just as Khusro I had also assumed. Thomas Bisson has argued recently that, by the early thirteenth century, partly as a function of officers' accountability, there are signs that lordly European government was becoming less 'intrusive'

---

[117] Robert C. Palmer, *The County Courts of Medieval England 1150–1350* (Princeton, NJ, 1982), 228–9.

[118] TNA SC 5/8/4, Northumbrian part published in H. H. E. Craster, 'An Unpublished Northumbrian Hundred Roll', *Archaeologia Aeliana*, 3rd ser. 3 (1907), 187–90; Tunstead hundred (Norfolk) published in *A Formula Book of English Official Historical Documents*, ed. Hubert Hall, 2 vols. (Cambridge, 1908–9), ii. 146; comment in Raban, *A Second Domesday?*, 24–5. I hope to discuss the *De ministris* roll properly elsewhere.

[119] Prestwich, *Plantagenet England*, 77. Similar perspectives, M. L. Holford, 'Under-sheriffs the State, and Local Society, c.1300–1340: A Preliminary Survey', in Chris Given-Wilson, Ann Kettle, and Len Scales (eds.), *War, Government, and Aristocracy in the British Isles, c.1150–1500: Essays in Honour of Michael Prestwich* (Woodbridge, 2008), 68; Palmer, *County Courts*, 38. A quite positive assessment of French royal officers' held to account *c.*1254–*c.*1380 is Telliez, «*Per potentiam officii*», 684–5.

[120] Cf. Reynolds, 'How Different was England?', 4–7, 14–16.

[121] *Die Chronik des Saba Malaspina*, ed. Walter Koller and August Nitschke, MGH, SS 35 (Hannover, 1999), 179–80 (§4.2), 241 (§6.1), 282–3 (§7.13), 331 (§9.22).

[122] *Chronik des Saba Malaspina*, 251 (§6.7).

[123] The works cited by Barratt, Carpenter, Holt, Maddicott, and Waugh are relevant.

(meaning sporadic and unsystematic).[124] There is much in this. The practices analysed here certainly point to a greater systematization of government (not only royal government). But it is not clear that government became less intrusive in the more usual sense, as an important strand of British historiography suggests.[125] High historiographical expectations of government may be better established in relation to French than English government (or at least in relation to some French kings, notably Louis IX). In France, judgements on Louis IX's 'moralisation de l'administration', his 'equitable justice' in holding his bailiffs to account, have tended to the positive.[126] More recent judgements have also tempered older views by additionally stressing the public propaganda value of Louis' *enquêtes* as well as finding room for an admixture of both self-interest and altruism in later Capetian *enquêtes*.[127] Something of the same can be said for Edward I and his supposed masterfulness.[128] For Italy there is a sense that the pursuit of the accountable letter of the law could well strip it of its spirit.[129]

The problem of judging the effects of accountability is related to the problem of the documentary base. Better documented government does not mean better government.[130] Here, since the holding of officials to account often produces evidence of problems, there is an irony that a greater interest in holding officials to account may produce an optical illusion of increased official wrongdoing. The lens sharpens and the clouds gather. Cadoc of Pont-Audemer may well be a bad *bailli*

---

[124] Bisson, *Crisis of the Twelfth Century*, 572. See also 417 and his sect. V, 'Resolution: Intrusions of Government (1150–1215)'.

[125] John Gillingham, *The Angevin Empire*, 2nd edn. (London, 2001), 56–7; M. T. Clanchy, 'Law, Government and Society in Medieval England', *History* 59 (1974); Bartlett, 'Impact of Royal Government', esp. 89–92, 95–6, and 'Lords of Pride and Plunder', *New York Review of Books* 57/11 (24 June 2010), 48, 'bureaucratic government does not necessarily mean less violent, or even less arbitrary, government' (reviewing Bisson's *Crisis of the Twelfth Century*); Dunbabin on historians' tendency to elide advanced government with more bureaucratic government, *French in the Kingdom of Sicily*, 250; and Paul A. Brand, 'Edward I and the Judges: The "State Trials" of 1289–93', *TCE* 1 (1986) at 34, suggesting the purpose of the 1289 'state trials' was raising money, not justice. A recent general *sed contra* is Burt, *Edward I*, e.g. 15–16, 141–7, 236–41.

[126] Le Goff, *Saint Louis*, 218 (and more generally 658–62, 701–4). See W. C. Jordan, *Louis IX and the Challenge of the Crusade: A Study in Rulership* (Princeton, NJ, 1979), e.g. 47 for the situation before Louis takes charge, and for his success, 61–3, 158, 167–8, 170–1, 181. Use of Le Goff's phrase in e.g. Laure Verdon, 'Le Roi, la loi, l'enquête et l'officier: procédure et enquêteurs en Provence sous le règne de Charles II (1285–1309)', in C. Gauvard (ed.), *L'Enquête au Moyen Âge*, École française de Rome (Rome, 2008), 328–9, and cf. Lachaud, *Éthique du pouvoir*, 412–13.

[127] Respectively, Marie Dejoux, 'Mener une enquête générale, pratiques et méthodes: L'Exemple de la tournée ordonnée par Louis IX en Languedoc à l'hiver 1247–48', in Thierry Pécout (ed.), *Quand gouverner c'est enquêter: Les Pratiques politiques de l'enquête princière (Occident, XIIIe–XIVe siècles)* (Paris, 2010), and Canteaut, 'Le Juge et le financier: Les Enquêteurs-réformateurs des derniers Capétiens (1314–1328)', in Gauvard (ed.) *L'Enquête au Moyen Âge*, 269–318.

[128] Marc Morris, *A Great and Terrible King: Edward I and the Forging of Britain* (London, 2008), 119–22; Maddicott, *Origins of the English Parliament*, 448; Raban, *A Second Domesday?*, 25.

[129] Philip Jones, *The Italian City-State: From Commune to Signoria* (Oxford, 1997), 637–8, 621–4.

[130] The issue was a bone of contention between Timothy Reuter and Thomas Bisson in the *Past & Present* 'Feudal Revolution' debate in relation to levels of violence (full references, p. 18 n. 92). See further Reuter's comments in 'Modern Mentalities and Medieval Polities', *Medieval Polities and Modern Mentalities*, ed. Janet L. Nelson (Cambridge, 2006), 13–14. See also Susan Reynolds's overarching argument in *Fiefs and Vassals* that 'feudalism' is a product less of actual historical change but more of late twelfth- and thirteenth-century lawyers reifying and standardizing older, far more varied practices.

of Normandy under Philip Augustus, revealed through Louis IX's *enquêtes*, but it is hard to quantify how the *enquêtes* consequently improved local government. Still, in themselves Louis IX's 1247 *enquêtes* in Maine and Anjou 'do not make reassuring reading about the quality of thirteenth century administration'.[131]

Medieval advocates of administration and accountability expressed their own reservations. Richard of Ely admits that Richard of Ilchester, his great predecessor, had overreached himself in his craze for recording writs in duplicate.[132] The system could become self-defeating. Charles of Anjou said that 'On account of the multitude of officials the performance of duties to the crown and the movements of the crown's servants are often delayed'.[133] Effort was needed to investigate whether officials had done as instructed.[134] In matters where accountability was a function of collecting and collating information there was the overwhelming effort of processing and acting on it.[135]

But as institutions became more extensive and extended, those in charge of them were faced with the need to elaborate institutional procedures further, irrespective of the measurable costs and limitations of so doing. Just as oaths were unreliable but indispensible devices for securing officials' conduct, so too had accounts, inquests, and audits become.[136] Medieval perceptions that these practices had limits is clear from the adoption then abandonment of some sophisticated devices for accountability. Accounting had always been and would continue to be an expensive way of controlling servants and officials.[137] In England, 'for-profit' experiments with royal 'in-land' demesne management, custodian sheriffs, and 'phase two' accounting were all temporary measures of some complexity taken up and then abandoned.[138] Some of these games turned out not to be worth the candle.

---

[131] Dunbabin, *Charles I of Anjou*, 29. Robert Bartlett commented that the 1247 Ardennes *enquêtes* demonstrate that 'royal government often made its impact in these upland villages in the form of the seizure of property and the imprisonment of the inhabitants', Bartlett, 'Impact of Royal Government', 89–90.

[132] *DS*, II.ii at 74–5.

[133] Dunbabin's trans. (with comment, *Charles I of Anjou*, 76) on *RCA*, xxi. Reg. lxxxvii #108, quote at 29.

[134] In England e.g. 1279 distraint of knighthood, *CPR 1272–1281*, 342–3. In the Regno e.g. the inquiry into whether Urso Rufolo, *secretus* of the Regno, had followed provisioning orders in 1270, *RCA*, vi. Reg. xxii #965; comment Dunbabin, *Charles I of Anjou*, 75; see also Serena Morelli, *Per conservare la pace: I giustizieri del regno di Sicilia da Carlo I a Carlo II d'Angiò* (Naples, 2012), 253, 273.

[135] Prestwich, *Edward I*, 96–8; Raban, *A Second Domesday?*, 36, 181, both on the 1274–5 Hundred Roll inquiries. On the arguable use of information collected on knights not performing their duties, Scott L. Waugh, 'Reluctant Knights and Jurors: Respites, Exemptions, and Public Obligations in the Reign of Henry III', *Speculum* 58 (1983), 937–86 at 953.

[136] The twelfth-century attempts by various bishops and supervising archbishops and popes to regulate the behaviour of the canon-*prévôts* of Chartres through oaths variously exacted and arranged is a case in point: E. de Lépinois and Lucien Merlet (eds.), *Cartulaire de Notre-Dame de Chartres*, 3 vols. (Chartres, 1862–5), i. ##33–4 at 119–22 (1114); ##57–8 at 155–9 (1149–55); #86 at 188–90 (8 April 1171/2).

[137] For comments up to 1200 see Wickham, *Framing the Early Middle Ages*, 245–9, 265–72 esp. 270. For the later period, e.g. McFarlane, 'Continuity of Great Estates', *Nobility of Later Medieval England*, 139.

[138] See pp. 79, 117–9, and 72–6.

Profit however might be only one purpose of such mechanisms.[139] Strict supervision, as embodied in intrusive accountability might also be undertaken *pour encourager les autres*. Even from the later fourteenth century it was unclear whether the point of supervising seigneurial officials was to improve productivity or discourage peculation.[140] It is not clear in many cases whether the 'cost' of such encouragement was 'worth' the initial outlay. For seigneurial lords it was principally an issue of fiscal accountability. Where the accountability of office or the conduct of officers was a value in and of itself it is easier to say that the effort embodied in these mechanisms was 'worth it'. This would be the case with prelates. A more pragmatic reason for this affirmative answer though is that the costs of holding prelates to account lay principally on the communities and *promotores* who wished to see such prelates brought to book through canonical inquisition. The costs to the Curia were in terms of its time and stationery.

This leads on to the broader effects of these technical practices on an ethics of office.[141] The period saw the officialization of power, but with limits.[142] Furthermore, while accountability may be a sign that some office is held, the argument regarding sheriffs sought to show that this might imply relatively little with respect to any especially equitable concept of that office. Conversely, liability did not only arise from formal office. The 'action of account' created legal bailiffs where no actual 'bailiffship' was held. In 1289 the trials of the king's ministers included a debate whether the lesser fish at several removes from the king were actually his ministers. With bailiffs and *monstravit de compoto* one could be a 'bailiff' less because of specific tasks one discharged and more because of the pattern of one's relationship to a superior. Similarly in 1289 responsibilities could arise from actions taken that implied some involvement in some task, and therefore some wider responsibility *to the king* because of it.[143] Accountability here was not so much a sign of office as a means of constructing it.

This bears on arguments related to the supposed increased rationality of formalized procedures, compared with more personal methods of dispute resolution. These forms however could continue to act as very personal ways of resolving disputes—as the Walter Langton case showed.[144] The assumption that an increase in formal regulation reflected the inherent progress and superiority of those forms over older ones is related to the presumption that more administration is better government. But

---

[139] See Wickham's helpful comments on variety of accounting/supervisory purposes in an early medieval estate management context, *Framing the Early Middle Ages*, 264–71.
[140] Stressing the latter, McFarlane, 'Landlord versus Minister and Tenant', *Nobility of Later Medieval England*, 213–14 (on *valores*).
[141] See also here Lachaud, *Éthique du pouvoir*; Bisson, *Crisis of the Twelfth Century*, both *passim*.
[142] See e.g. Karn, 'Secular Power and its Rewards in Dorset in the Late Eleventh and Early Twelfth Centuries', *Historical Research* 82 (2009) on informal/formal officials.
[143] See the debates about whether William of Alevent is liable as bailiff of the hundred of Lothingland (TNA JUST 1/541A m. 22d), Richard le Draper as mayor of Bristol (m. 38), John of Louthis as mayor of Wallingford (m. 22d), John of Olivestede as a royal bailiff of Essex (m. 22d), Robert le Blaunchas clerk of the hundred of Pershore (m. 31), edited in T. F. Tout and Hilda Johnston (eds.), *State Trials of Edward the First, 1289–1293*, CS, 3rd ser. 9 (1906), xxvii–xxviii.
[144] It seems feasible that the complex of inquisitorial-type procedures were used in resolving ecclesiastical disputes in a way that accusatorial process functioned in lay contexts such as communal Bologna. On the latter, see Blanshei, 'Crime and Law Enforcement', 124–5.

a kind of capillary attraction invariably drew petitioners and plaintiffs towards the highest point of legal, administrative, and political appeal—be it papal or regal—thus tending towards institutional convergence in those fields.[145] This shift towards more routinized inquisitions, audits, scrutinies, and accounting is a sign of changed attitudes towards due process, rather than any clearer sign of 'progress'.[146] Inquisitions, after all, determined not only officials' wrongdoing, but also sanctity and heresy.

Such practices were more rational, in the limited but important sense that they were more regularized and the basis and conditions for disputes about officers' conduct more explicit. Whether they were proportionately more just is less clear. In ecclesiastical inquisitions or *monstravit de compoto*—where law was more, not less, involved—the procedural regulation did not lead to more predictable outcomes, as noted. Legal reasoning could take on a life of its own. An increase in legalized formality often meant an increase in expensive claim and counter-claim, rather than the swift delivery of personal justice by a king at ease in an apple orchard.[147] It might seem that having procedures for regulating the conduct of officials was more important than the effects of those procedures. The threshold for triggering an inquisition into a prelate was, for instance, cynical or pragmatic depending on your perspective. Devices for accountability may most sensibly be seen as pertaining to procedural aspects of justice—they created a space for more substantive disagreements about conduct.[148] In their modest and limited character many of the above procedures attempted to provide the terms for that disagreement. How, and by whom the question was asked, however, made an obvious difference. Nevertheless, the ability of provisions such as *Qualiter et quando* to establish measures for the evaluation of conduct should not be underestimated. Rules like this, or like college statutes, by establishing the definition of official misbehaviour, created one important measure of the contents of office. Even if the quality of outcomes varied, a space for debate—and for conflict—regarding determined measures of official conduct stood established.

Accountability and Justice?

Practices of accountability then did not promote justice in an uncomplicated way. The most obvious reason is that those practices could themselves be corrupted, subverted, or discarded.

The image that illustrates this book's cover is from a manuscript produced in London or Westminster in the late 1280s–early 1290s, perhaps at the request of

---

[145] See e.g. Frederic L. Cheyette on the thirteenth-century emergence of French legal practices in '"Suum cuique tribuere"', *French Historical Studies* 6 (1970), 289–90, 297–8; Jean Dunbabin on Charles I of Anjou's Great Court at Naples, *Charles I of Anjou*, 123. Cf. Raoul van Caenegem, 'L'Histoire du droit et la chronologie. Réflexions sur la formation du "Common Law" et la procédure romano-canonique', *Études d'histoire du droit canonique dédiées à Gabriel Le Bras*, 2 vols. (Paris, 1965).

[146] I would see a direct parallelism between this shift and the shift of belief in terms of the shape of proof in relation to medieval ordeals. For the latter shift see Bartlett, *Trial by Fire and Water*.

[147] Cf. M. T. Clanchy, 'Law and Love in the Middle Ages', in John Bossy (ed.), *Disputes and Settlements: Law and Human Relations in the West* (Cambridge 1983), 53.

[148] See John Sabapathy, 'A Medieval Officer and a Modern Mentality: *Podestà* and the Quality of Accountability', *Mediaeval Journal* 1.2 (2011) 68–76.

the French royal court. It is a *bible moralisée*, a compendium of biblical images and quotes in which each biblical image has a connected moralized pendent interpreting it.[149] This image is a moralized pendent, an unhappy bishop having his mitre removed by other prelates while the pope looks on. Its caption describes how 'when some bad prelate through his bad examples corrupts the souls of his subjects some accuse him before the pope and he is convicted and deprived of his dignity'. It is an obvious reassuring allusion to the effectiveness of the sorts of inquisitions, denunciations, and accusations analysed in Chapter 4. The image to which the de-mitred bishop refers telescopes the events of 2 Maccabees 4: 39–44. A prelude to the full Maccabean revolt (*c*.166–57 BC) against the Seleucids of Judah, this episode concerns the simoniac, murderous, treacherous, embezzling, sacrilegious, hellenizing high priest Menelaus. Menelaus's deputy and brother has died bloodily suppressing a riot in Jerusalem protesting against his and his brother's practices (170 BC). A trio delegated by the Jewish council (*gerousia*) accuses Menelaus to King Antiochus IV Epiphanes (175–164 BC) in Tyre (control at a distance in action). This is the freeze-framed moment that the *bible moralisée* illustrates, the delegation's accusation of Menelaus to Antiochus paralleling that of the bishop before the pope below it.[150] The biblical episode offers rich connections to episcopal accountability: an abusive officer, public outcry and *fama*, denunciation before a higher authority, due process, the appeal to the public good. The actual end of the scriptural story is less edifying (vv. 45–50). Menelaus bribes Antiochus to sentence to death the men who have brought the case against him. Menelaus gets off. 'He stayed in power, growing in malice and in betrayal of the citizens.' The whole episode of 2 Maccabees 4: 39–50 illustrates the subversion of that accountability that the interpreted abbreviation purports to deduce. The *bible* indeed considers the subsequent events of vv. 45–50 in terms of curial corruption and bad counsellors leading fallible popes astray.[151] In the parable of the unjust steward of Luke 16 one is left wondering just where the accountability is located that one is supposed to admire. Taking 2 Maccabees 4: 39–50 as a *whole* a reader might think that the story illustrates the fallibility, not the strength, of practices of accountability when faced with brute politics. (To which a response might be 'What else is there?'. At least Menelaus's due deserts come eventually when his Seleucid allies ritually execute him by throwing him from

---

[149] BL Additional MS 18719, fo. 239ʳ. On *biblés moralisées* see John Lowden, *The Making of the biblés moralisées*, 2 vols. (Philadelphia, 2000), on Additional 18719 at i. 2, 5, 8–9, 147, 149, 151, 155–9, 180, 185, 187, ch. 6, and figs. 85–96, plates xxii–xxiii, and ch. 7 on Paris, BNF MS fr. 167, based on Additional 18719. Vol. ii is a comparative study of the Book of Ruth in the *biblés moralisées*, including many notes on 18719. Far less colourful than its relations, 18719 has some beautiful work in it, notably Artist E's and F's. Fo. 239ʳ may be by Artist A or D (Lowden argues i. 206 that 'D' may be 'A' when he is not rushing his work). See further: Babette Hellemans, *La Bible moralisée: Une œuvre à part entière, création, sémiotique et temporalité au XIIIᵉ siècle* (Turnhout, 2010); Christopher de Hamel, *The Book: A History of the Bible* (London, 2001), 146–53.

[150] Both compositions are adapted from the manuscript's exemplar, the so-called Oxford-Paris-London manuscript; its equivalent image is in BL Harley MS 1526, fo. 28ᵛ. The image is viewable on the BL's Catalogue of Illuminated Manuscripts at http://www.bl.uk/catalogues/illuminatedmanuscripts/ILLUMIN.ASP?Size=mid&IllID=34402.

[151] BL Additional MS 18719, fo. 239ᵛ. Further work still seems to be needed on interpretations offered in the *bibles*. For instructive commentary, Lowden, *Making of the bibles moralisées*, ii. 3–5.

the top of a tower fifty cubits high into a great pit of ash—'by such a law did death come to the transgressor of the law', 2 Maccabees 13: 7.)

Ways of securing accountability can try to forestall their own subversion but, if others connive in this, ultimately subjects have few alternatives beyond the revolt which eventually toppled Menelaus. This problem is longstanding and intractable. It is present in one of the first extended discussions of official accountability and its limits, Aristotle's account of the tyrant's subversion of *euthyna*.[152] A tyrant who can subvert accounting 'will not appear as a tyrant but a responsible steward [*dispensans yconomus*]' because, in Peter of Auvergne's gloss, 'he will appear to work for the common good [*bonum commune*] and will not appear to be a tyrant'.[153] The human problem too lies behind one of the modern period's most famous 'answers', Bentham's panopticon, which sought to do away with the problem by reducing officers to a bare, monitoring minimum.

That officers and rulers can subvert the practices designed to restrain them is a straightforward qualification to the justice of accountability. A still more basic point may be made. There is nothing about practices of accountability that themselves imply more equitable official conduct, for the simple reason that such practices need imply little about the ends to which they are put.

Gregory the Great described how, just as God held his court of justice, so the Devil called his demons to account for their wrongdoings.[154] It is the ends not the means of government which give it normative content. 'Without justice what are kingdoms but great gangs?' asked Augustine, modifying the pirate's taunt to Alexander the Great that the only thing determining their different titles was the scale of their operations, not the difference of their conduct.[155] Devices for establishing accountability *sensu strictu* too are devoid of value to create anything but a rather thin official ethic.[156] For that some ideology of responsible office is also required.[157] Often some mix of the two was present, but not always. Sheriffs, it was argued, were rather unusual in lacking a more positively developed ideology

---

[152] Aristotle, *Politics*, 1314b1–10 (V.11), discussed in Sabapathy, 'A Medieval Officer and a Modern Mentality', 72–4, see also 68–9.

[153] In William of Moerbeke's translation and Peter's literal commentary on *Politics* 1314b6–14 (V.11, VIII.11 in William): *Aristotelis Politicorum libri octo. Cum vetusta translatione Guilelmi de Moerbeka*, ed. Franciscus Susemihl (Leipzig, 1872), 581; *Aquinatis opera omnia: ut sunt in indice Thomistico: additis 61 scriptis ex aliis medii aevi auctoribus*, ed. Roberto Busa, 7 vols. (Stuttgart-Bad Cannstatt, 1980), vii. 446 (Peter's 5.12).

[154] 'Cumque singuli spiritus ad inquisitionem eius exponerent, quid operati contra bonos fuissent'. The *inquisitio* is that of the 'humani generis antiquus inimicus'. Grégoire le Grand, *Dialogues*, ed. Adalbert de Vogüé, Sources chrétiennes, 3 vols. (Paris, 1978–80), ii. 280 (§3.7.4–5).

[155] *De civitate dei*, 4. 4, relevantly recalled to Louis IX by Guibert of Tournai in his *Eruditio regum et principum*, 49 (§2.1.6). For relevant Carolingian reflections, Janet L. Nelson, 'Kings with Justice, Kings without Justice: An Early Medieval Paradox', in *La giustizia nell'alto medioevo (secoli ix–xi)*, Settimane di studio del Centro italiano di studi sull'alto medioevo 44 (Spoleto, 1997), 797–823, and Fouracre, 'Carolingian Justice'.

[156] I set out the theoretical basis informing this section in Sabapathy, 'A Medieval Officer and a Modern Mentality', 68–79.

[157] Cf. Nelson's stress on the personal responsibility Charlemagne sought in his 802 oath: Janet L. Nelson, 'Charlemagne and Empire', in Jennifer R. Davis and Michael McCormick (eds.), *The Long Morning of Medieval Europe* (Aldershot, 2008), 219–34 at 230–2. It can be seen as the counterpart to the Carolingian practice of giving officials overlapping duties to diffuse power and encourage co-supervision, as Davis argues in the same volume ('Pattern for Power').

of responsibility from the crown's side. It was in such a context that much of the period's ideals about shrieval office were expressed negatively as complaints or in the form of alternate schemas such as the 1258 ordinance of sheriffs. A further reason for caution about how practices of accountability contribute towards some ideal of office is that a purely accountable office strips an agent of latitude and institutionalizes distrust. For this reason, such purely accountable officers seldom exist, if 'purely accountable' means officers are controlled only by the formal mechanisms of accountability, and not by 'softer' social expectations and internalized norms. Accountability, often associated with trust, is, strictly speaking, a compensation for trust's absence.[158] Given the reliance of delegated power at a distance throughout most forms of medieval government, a *purely* accountable office would be hard to sustain practically. It is the relationship between practices of accountability and related ideals of office that is an important proxy for any equitable effects from the officialization of power. Louis IX's 1254 *Grande ordonnance* is consequently an interesting example of regulating officials' conduct by appealing to responsibility and imposing accountability from a sequence of different, specified angles. Like Charlemagne, Louis relied on both internalized norms and externalized rules. So *baillis* and *prévôts* swear an oath at the assizes before others 'so they will dread to incur the vice of perjury, not only from fear of God and us, but for worldly shame' (personal obligation operating through religious conscience, dread of the king, and social opprobrium).[159] They should also have a sufficient sense of their office's ethics that 'if they know of any official, sergeant, *prévôt*, who is disloyal, a thief, usurer, or full of other vices for which he should lose our service [. . .] they will punish and judge him in good faith' (responsible self-policing).[160] Finally *baillis*, *viscontes*, *prévôts*, and mayors are to remain forty days in their bailiwick after ending their office in order to be judged 'so that they may answer the incoming *baillis* should there be any alleged wrongdoing

---

[158] The paradox is encapsulated by this rule of McFarlane's: a lord's 'ministers could only be trusted if they were efficiently watched and made to watch each other', *Nobility of Later Medieval England*, 52–3. See also 139–40. Bisson's comment is relevant: 'Accounting was the remedy for malfeasance. It rather looks as if [. . .] lords who trusted their servants were unlikely to insist on auditing them with regularity' (*Crisis of the Twelfth Century*, 328). Cf. delegated manorial control at a distance: 'the local lord was distancing himself [through the twelfth to thirteenth centuries] from the vill and its inhabitants; his relations with his tenants were being redefined through the interventions of cash payments and the formalised procedures of the manorial court', P. D. A. Harvey, 'Non-agrarian Activities in Twelfth Century English Estate Surveys', in Daniel Williams (ed.), *England in the Twelfth Century: Proceedings of the 1988 Harlaxton Symposium* (Woodbridge, 1990), 101–11 at 111, and 'Initiative and Authority in Settlement Change', in Michael Aston, David Austin, and Christopher Dyer (eds.), *The Rural Settlements of Medieval England: Studies Dedicated to Maurice Beresford and John Hurst* (Oxford, 1989), 31–43 at 38–43.

[159] Jean de Joinville, *Histoire de Saint Louis*, ed. M. Natalis de Wailly, 9th edn. (Paris, 1921), 295 (ch. 140, §701), 'que il doutent à encorre le vice de parjurer, non pas tant seulement pour la paour de Dieu et de nous, mais pour la honte dou monde'.

[160] Joinville, *Histoire de Saint Louis*, 294 (ch. 140, §699), 'Et jureront et promettront que se il saivent souz aus nul official, sergant ou prevost qui soient desloial, rapineur, usurier ou plein d'autres vices, par quoy il doivent perdre nostre service [. . .] ainçois les puniront et jugeront en bone foy.' This implies a particular onus on *baillis*, and does *not* envisage that lesser officials can judge *baillis*, but it does imply that officials other than *baillis* can judge officials other than *baillis*.

which some may wish to complain of' (formal accountability).[161] It stands useful comparison with the 1258 reforming English ordinance of sheriffs, prescribing conduct towards the county, and Edward I's 1274 oath stressing a more developed ethic of responsibility to the king. The ordinance similarly made explicit that the point of fixed annual tenure was to help communities 'fear [royal officers] less and more confidently describe their wrongs'.[162]

Different historians have framed these distinctions in various ways though the phenomena they are differentiating seem basically similar. Michael Clanchy's attractive distinction between law and love fits well again here.[163] (Though loyalty might need stressing here within love.) The applicability to Louis's *ordinance* is obvious. If love relies on public undertakings it also depends on some internalized inner conscience. By and large love polices itself. The devices for accountability discussed here largely lean on law not love. A similar contrast is Cristina Jular Pérez-Alfaro's between 'positive' norms and 'negative' corrective complaints procedures (though perhaps such normative language is better avoided).[164] Thomas Bisson's contrast between older, more feudal bonds of fidelitarian accountability and a later twelfth- and thirteenth-century accountability of competent office draws a similar contrast.[165] It is the relationship between these two dynamic tendencies that is needed to supplement the question of 'Who, whom?'. There is no general answer about how these tendencies came to be balanced in this period. There were officers in whose case an excess of 'law' over 'love' created difficulties (Plantagenet sheriffs, arguably). Bishops, however, provide a case of an office that had both some of the richest literature about love-cum-fidelity, and an increasingly formalized method of accountability that could lead to interminably complex legal cases of indeterminate outcome. It could also be abused and abusive—as with Philip IV's use of inquisitorial techniques to destroy the Templars.[166] As for bailiffs and stewards, there was both a rich English literature on manorial 'love', and also a highly legalistic procedure for dealing with bailiffs' lack of love through the action of account. (The same is true of *podestà*, an exceptionally interesting case given that their literature of responsibility and 'love' was sometimes explicitly articulated to neutralize the application of *sindacatio*'s law to them.)[167] Wardens stand a little apart since their regulation was informed by a longstanding monastic literature of responsibility and by the greater ability to regulate that given their collegial institutionalization. There the paradox seemed to be rather one of status, an uncertainty about how to correlate the relative standing of fellows and wardens.

[161] Joinville, *Histoire de Saint Louis*, 297–8 (ch. 140, §714), 'affin qu'il puissent respondre aus nouviaus bailliz, pour ce que il auroient mesfait contre ceus qui se vourroient pleindre d'aus'. They may be present by proxy.
[162] *DBM*, #8 at 122; see also TNA E159/32 m. 2. On the 1274 oath (E 159/49, m. 1d), see Prestwich, *Edward I*, 93; Maddicott, 'Edward I and the Lessons of Baronial Reform', 20.
[163] Clanchy, 'Law and Love', 47, 50. Clanchy discusses Louis IX at 52–4, 56.
[164] Jular Pérez-Alfaro, 'King's Face on the Territory', 111, 119, 120.
[165] Bisson, *Crisis of the Twelfth Century*, passim.
[166] For the Templars' attack on the irregularities in applying summary procedures against them see Malcolm Barber, *The Trial of the Templars*, 2nd edn. (Cambridge, 2006), 157, 161.
[167] See Sabapathy, 'A Medieval Officer and a Modern Mentality'. A much needed review of this literature is being conducted by David Napolitano of Cambridge.

The great qualification to this critique of accountability's justice, as noted, is that nevertheless these procedures did create various objective, 'official', rules for conflict and various sorts of more or less level playing fields.[168] These procedures might be costly, partial, or distant—but they were there. The material explored here is clearly an expression of a renewed belief in the desirability and possibility of officials' accountability. Definitions of what constituted that accountability varied and were contested, but it is very striking that, even if practices left a deal to be desired, even in cases of strong hierarchies predisposed against *inferiores*' involvement in holding their *superiores* to account, that there was both a pragmatic and principled acknowledgement that officials' accountability was possible. Office might well be insolent, but in the later twelfth and thirteenth centuries across important groups of *mediocres* officers, the right to insolence was increasingly open to question.

This equivalent judgement recognizes that much medieval accountability was connected to some wider idea of a common good, but that this perspective was inevitably partial in practice and principle. Versions of this view lie behind some thoughts, again, of Augustine and Peter Abelard that may terminate this study. Both articulated the principle, discussed in earlier chapters, that the investigation of crimes was needed in order to serve the public good. One version (*ne crimina remaneant impunita*) was earlier discussed regarding the justification of prelates' accountability.[169] Abelard and Augustine articulated the principle in distinctly ambivalent ways. Augustine's view is clear, bleak, scornful:

> Will the wise man sit as judge amidst the darkness of our social life, or not dare to? Of course he will sit. For human society binds and drags him to this office, which he thinks it a crime to abandon. He does not think it a crime that innocent witnesses are tortured because of someone else's case; that those accused are often overcome by the force of torture, make false confessions and are punished although innocent; that, even if not liable to the death penalty, many die under or after torture; that sometimes those who accuse others, perhaps wishing to benefit human society by ensuring that crimes do not go unpunished [*ne crimina inpunita sint*], are instead condemned by an ignorant judge because witnesses lie and the fiercely obdurate defendant does not confess under torture, so that they cannot prove what they allege, although they spoke the truth. The wise judge does not reckon so many and such great evils to be sins. For he does not act out of the desire to harm but under the necessity of ignorance, just as human society compels the necessity of judgement.[170]

Society's compulsion to judge is as unavoidable as a judge's ignorance in judging.

---

[168] See esp. pp. 58, 107–8, 170–1, 193, 253. For a theory of this, which he calls '*officialisation*', see Pierre Bourdieu, *Le Sens pratique* (Paris, 1980), 183–8. For a relevant example of seigneurial (abbatial) inquisitions whose effects provide both some security of peasant conditions and the inquiring Lord Benard I Ayglier with his rights, see Laurent Feller, 'Les Enquêtes seigneuriales de Bernard Ier Ayglier, abbé du Mont-Cassin (1267–1270)', in Julie Claustre, Olivier Mattéoni, and Nicolas Offenstadt (eds.), *Un Moyen Âge pour aujourd'hui: Mélanges offerts à Claude Gauvard* (Paris, 2010), 326–38.

[169] See pp. 163–5. See e.g. also a version in a Sicilian communal context in *Konstitutionen Friedrichs II. für das Königreich sizilien*, cap. 2.7 at 299.

[170] Augustine, *De civitate dei*, §19.6.

Abelard's view is perhaps not so bleak. Abelard's confidence about inquiry [*inquisitionem*] as a means to truth has already been quoted (p. 236). Elsewhere, however, he suggested more cautionary inferences were needed regarding the capacity of human institutions to establish the truth. Speaking specifically about the public punishment of moral crimes, Abelard contrasted men's limited perspicacity with God's—'inspector of intent and consent', 'tester of the heart and guts'.[171] Human justice's necessarily limited perspective meant that it can only be scandalized by what it can see; 'so that we seek to forestall public rather than correct individual wrongs'.[172] For Abelard 'public' becomes a hazardous criterion, both an unavoidable proxy for demonstrable wrongs, and a limited proof of offences committed: 'For whatever can redound to the common ruin or public detriment should be punished with greater correction, and what causes greater wrong deserves among us a heavier penalty, and the greater the scandal [*scandalum*] with men the greater the punishment which it incurs among men, even though a lighter fault has preceded it.'[173] Abelard thinks these judgements necessarily limited by our dependence for judgement on outward acts (*opera*) not inner faults (*culpas*). Adulterers receive milder punishments than fire-starters. A man having sex in a church scandalizes less for his corruption of a woman and the spiritual temple, and more for his social offence. Abelard judges that

> These things take place following the exigencies of stewardship [*dispensationis temperamento*] more than the dues of justice so that [. . .] we attend to collective utility by preventing public wrongs. [. . .] Thus, reserving mental wrongs to divine judgement, we prosecute with our own judgement the [outward] effects of those faults which we have to judge, attending, as we said, to what is stewardly in such things, that is, the logic of foresight rather than pure equity.[174]

Human accountability is constituted by the politics of the visible and the possible. Public judgement follows public exigency. Judgements need to look 'right'.[175]

---

[171] *Peter Abelard's Ethics*, ed. D. E. Luscombe, OMT (Oxford, 1971), 42.

[172] 'Magis publica preueniamus dampna quam singularia corrigamus', *Peter Abelard's Ethics*, 42. See also Augustine, *De civitate dei*, 19. 6 and 19. 8. The problem had a long future: see Jacques Chiffoleau, '«*Ecclesia de occultis non iudicat*»? L'Église, le secret, l'occulte du XIIe au XIVe siècle', *Il Segreto, The Secret*, Micrologus 14 (Florence, 2006), esp. 419–20; Alain Boureau, 'Une parole destructrice: la diffamation. Richard de Mediavilla et le droit individuel au péché', in Julie Claustre, Olivier Mattéoni, and Nicolas Offenstadt (eds.), *Un Moyen Âge pour aujourd'hui: Mélanges offerts à Claude Gauvard* (Paris, 2010), 306–14.

[173] 'Omne namque quod in communem perniciem uel in publicum redundare potest incommodum castigatione maiori est puniendum, et quod contrahit maiorem offensam, grauiorem inter nos promeretur penam et maius hominum scandalum maius inter homines incurrit supplicium, et si leuior precessit culpa,' *Peter Abelard's Ethics*, 42, Luscombe's trans.

[174] 'Et haec quidem non tam iusticiae debito quam dispensationis aguntur temperamento, ut, [. . .] publica preueniendo dampna communi consulamus utilitati. [. . .] Culpas itaque animi diuino reseruantes iudicio, effecta earum de quibus iudicare habemus prosequimur nostro, dispensationem in talibus, hoc est, prouidentiae quam diximus rationem magis quam aequitatis adtendentes puritatem', *Peter Abelard's Ethics*, 44. His tone seems to oscillate between approval, resignation, and criticism in these pages.

[175] Mary Douglas's thinking about institutions is relevant here: 'when an [classificatory/scientific] analogy matches a structure of authority or precedence, then the social pattern reinforces the logical patterns and gives it prominence', Douglas, *How Institutions Think* (Syracuse, 1986), 65 and 90, on the 'coherence principle': an idea has to fit with others to take off (a necessary but not sufficient

260   *Conclusions*

Some 712 years separate Abelard's and Augustine's deaths. Some 872 years separate Abelard from the present and such judgements remain intractable. The British Government's 2005 Inquiries Act legislating for public inquiries empowers a minister to 'cause an inquiry to be held under this Act in relation to a case where it appears to him that—(a) particular events have caused, or are capable of causing, public concern, or (b) there is public concern that particular events may have occurred'.[176] By their lights, the medieval solutions considered above were no less elegant, no less simplistic. The hazardousness of medieval institutional judgements when it came to holding officers to account has certainly been seen: in the initial arrangement of who was accountable to whom for what; in the matter of who judged what constituted 'a reasonable account'; in the question of whose utility was served by accounted judgement; by the arguable nature of determining infamy and scandal; or by conflicting judgements regarding the competing claims of individual dues as distinct from those of the institution 'itself'.[177]

The later twelfth and thirteenth centuries saw a great intensification and extension of practices of holding officers to account, mostly for the benefit of the institutions responsible for such officers, but with some, sometimes unintended, knock-on gains for the communities amongst which the officer lived. The elaboration of devices for holding these officials to account generated a dynamic of its own, one that did not preclude 'love', even if, by nature, it preferred 'law'. Any justice from accountability was perhaps a consequence of some complementarity between these two ways of resolving conflicts.[178] These devices for institutionalizing accountability, in whatever sphere, reflected an extraordinarily creative response in England—and beyond—to the problem of complex government and control at a distance: accountings, *inquisitiones*, *sindacationes*, *scrutinia*. Many of these institutions and methods for securing accountability persist in modified forms today. Many of the problems and limitations consonant with the solutions they offer persist likewise. There is nothing, however, to imply that medieval conceptions of the possibilities and limitations of earthly accountability were less pragmatic or more deluded than contemporary ones. Indeed it is possible, in so far as medieval expectations of divine accountability tempered expectations of worldly accountability, that medieval realism about the limits of worldly accountability was of a comparable, sometimes superior, quality to our own.

---

condition). See also her remarks that 'scientific formulae [. . .] always carry the marks of their social origins', *How Institutions Think*, 56. For 'scientific formula' here read 'socially legitimate means of holding to account'.

[176] *The Inquiries Act 2005* (London, 2005), 1 (available at http://www.legislation.gov.uk/ukpga/2005/12/contents, accessed February 2014). For (e.g.) the Leveson Inquiry see p. 237 n. 49. Select Committee on the Inquiries Act [House of Lords], *The Inquiries Act 2005: Post-legislative Scrutiny*, Report of Session 2013–14 (London, 2014) raises issues and limitations relevant to the preceding analysis; see esp. summary and §§44–52, 63–5, 95–7, 106, 110, 119, 147–50, 162–4, 202, 208–10, 211–15, 226, 281, 291–3, 298–9.

[177] Cf. for the present, Anthony King and Ivor Crewe, *The Blunders of our Governments* (Oxford, 2013), 347–59.

[178] Cf. Soll's stress in the later period that a beneficial relationship between fiscal accounting, political stability, and wider accountability seems to belong to 'those societies that managed to harness accounting as part of their general cultures' (*Reckoning*, 207).

Bibliography

LIST OF MANUSCRIPTS AND ROLLS CONSULTED

London, British Library (BL)
Additional 15668 (Newent Priory Cartulary, s.xiii–s.xiv).
Additional 18719 (*Bible moralisée*, late 1280s–early 1290s).
Additional 30024 (Brunetto Latini, *Tresor*, s.xiii[ex]).
Cotton Claudius D. II (part of Andrew Horn's *Magnum librum c.*1322).
Cotton Julius B. VIII (*Fleta*, 1290–1300).
Cotton Julius D. II (Irish register of writs, *c.*1227).
Cotton Nero C. I (Tract on the steward, *Modus tendendi parlamentum*, statutes, s.xv[ex]–s. xvi[2]).
Cotton Vespasian B. VII (Tract on the steward, *Modus tendendi parlamentum*, list of kings).
Cotton Vespasian B. XI (Hagnaby Chronicle).
Cotton Vespasian E. III (Burton Annals).
Egerton 3724 (Mohun Register, 1350).
Harley 645 (Mid-thirteenth-century obedientiary accounts).
Harley 3601 (*Liber memorandum* of Barnwell Priory).
Royal 5 C. III (theological miscellany, s.xv).
Royal 6 E. VI and VII, each in two parts (James le Palmer, Omne bonum, s.xiv[med]).
Royal 9 A. VII (*Vade mecum* of statutes, ready reckoners and manuals, English, s.xiii[ex] with later additions).
Royal 12 C. VI (s.xiii[ex]–s.xiv tracts, including the *Secretum secretorum*).

London, Lambeth Palace Library
Reg. Pecham (s.xiii[ex], John Pecham's Register).

London, The National Archives (TNA)
C 150/1 (Cartulary, St Peter's Abbey, Gloucester, presented to the abbey by abbot John de Gamages).
E 13/1a (Exchequer of Pleas, Plea Rolls, 1236–7).
E 13/1e (Exchequer of Pleas, Plea Rolls, 1269–70).
E 13/9 (Exchequer of Pleas, Plea Rolls, 1281–2).
E 13/12 (Exchequer of Pleas, Plea Rolls, 1285–6).
E 13/17 (Exchequer of Pleas, Plea Rolls, 1291–2).
E 101/505/34 (Accounts and Tallies of John of Tarrant for Ufford (Northampton), 1296–9).
E 159/32 (King's Remembrancer Memoranda Rolls, 1258–9).
E 159/43 (King's Remembrancer Memoranda Rolls, 1268–9).
E 159/49 (King's Remembrancer Memoranda Rolls, 1274–5).
JUST 1/82 (Cambs. eyre, 1260–1).
JUST 1/541a (General oyer and terminer, various counties, proceedings against the King's judges and ministers 1290–1).
SC 1/6 (Special Collections: Ancient Correspondence of the Chancery and the Exchequer, 1195–1214; 1280–1).
SC 1/10 (As above, *c.*1269–72; 1296–1321).
SC 1/12 (As above, 1262–1329).

SC 1/18 (As above, 1267–1327).
SC 1/22 (As above, 1272 x 1274–1282 x 1292).
SC 1/28 (As above, 1274–1342).
SC 5/8/4 (1274–5 Hundred roll extracts).

Oxford, All Souls College
All Souls College 182 (Letter compilation of s.xiii–s.xiv, including a version of John Pecham's Register).

Oxford, Bodleian Library (Bodley MSS)
Ashmole 1524 (includes a *Husbandry*, a (?Kentish) copy, *c*.1300).
Barlow 49 (Faringdon accounts of Beaulieu Abbey, 1269–70).
Bodley 784 (Copy of the notabilia used by James le Palmer used for Omne bonum (BL MS Royal 6 E. VI and VII)).

Rome, Archivio Segreto Vaticano
Registra vaticana, 523 vols. [accessed from the *Registra vaticana* database].

EDITIONS OF SOURCES[1]

The 1235 Surrey Eyre, ed. C. A. F. Meekings, completed by David Crook, 3 vols., Surrey Record Society 31, 32, 37 (Guildford, 1979–2002).
The 1258–9 Special Eyre of Surrey and Kent, ed. Andrew H. Hershey, Surrey Record Society 38 (Woking, 2004).
The 1263 Surrey Eyre, ed. Susan Stewart, Surrey Record Society 40 (Woking, 2006).
Acta Romanorum Pontificum a S. Clemente I (An. c. 90) ad Coelestinum III († 1198) (Rome, 1943).
Actes du Parlement de Paris. 1. série, de l'an 1254 a l'an 1328, ed. E. Boutaric, 2 vols. (Paris, 1863–7).
ADAM MARSH, *The Letters of Adam Marsh*, ed. C. H. Lawrence, OMT, 2 vols. (Oxford, 2006–10).
ADAM OF EYNSHAM, *Magna Vita Sancti Hugonis*, ed. Decima L. Douie and Hugh Farmer, OMT, 2 vols. corr. edn. (London, 1985).
ALESSANDRO DI TELESE, *Alexandri Telesini abbatis Ystoria Rogerii regis Sicilie Calabrie atque Apulie*, ed. Ludovica De Nava and Dione Clementi, FSI 112 (Rome, 1991).
The Anglo-Saxon Chronicles, trans. Michael Swanton, rev. edn. (London, 2000).
Anglo-Saxon Prose, trans. Michael Swanton, rev. edn. (London, 1993).
Annales monastici, ed. H. R. Luard, RS, 5 vols. (London, 1864–9).
An Anthology of Philosophy in Persia, i. *From Zoroaster to 'Umar Khayyām*, ed. Seyyed Hossein Nasr and Mehdi Aminrazavi (Oxford, 1999).
ANONYMOUS OF ST DENIS, *Gesta sancti Ludovici noni*, in *RHF* xx.
Archives historiques du département de la Gironde, 58 vols. (Paris/Bordeaux, 1859–1932).
ARISTOTLE, *Aristotelis Politicorum libri octo. Cum vetusta translatione Guilelmi de Moerbeka*, ed. Franciscus Susemihl (Leipzig, 1872).

---

[1] Medieval texts are alphabetized by author's first name (e.g. Thomas Aquinas) or by institution if appropriate (e.g. Merton College); other editions are alphabetized by title.

The Arundel Lyrics and The Poems of Hugh Primas, ed. Christopher J. McDonough, Dunbarton Oaks Medieval Library 2 (Cambridge, Mass., 2010).

AUGUSTINE, *Sancti Aurelii Augustini episcopi De civitate Dei, libri XXII*, ed. Bernard Dombart and Alfons Kalb, Bibliotheca scriptorum Graecorum et Romanorum Teubneriana, 5th edn., 2 vols. (Stuttgart, 1981).

AURELIO LIPPO BRANDOLINI, *Republics and Kingdoms Compared*, ed. James Hankins, I Tatti Renaissance Library 40 (Cambridge, 2009).

BALLIOL COLLEGE, OXFORD, *The Oxford Deeds of Balliol*, ed. H. E. Salter, OHS 64 (1913).

'BARNWELL CHRONICLER', *Memoriale fratris Walteri de Coventria*, ed. William Stubbs, RS, 2 vols. (London, 1872–3).

BATH AND WELLS, *Charters of Bath and Wells*, ed. S. E. Kelly, Anglo-Saxon Charters 13 (Oxford, 2007).

BATTLE ABBEY, *The Chronicle of Battle Abbey*, ed. Eleanor Searle, OMT (Oxford, 1980).

BEC ABBEY, *Select Documents of the English Lands of the Abbey of Bec*, ed. Marjorie Chibnall, CS, 3rd ser. 73 (1951).

BERNARD OF CLAIRVAUX, *De consideratione*, in *Sancti Bernardi opera*, ed. J. Leclercq, C. H. Talbot, and H. M. Rochais, 8 vols. in 9 (Rome, 1957–77), iii. 381–493.

BERNARD OF CLAIRVAUX, *Sancti Bernardi opera*, ed. J. Leclercq, C. H. Talbot, and H. M. Rochais, 8 vols. in 9 (Rome, 1957–77).

Biblioteca Arabo-Sicula, ed. Michele Amari, 2 vols. (Turin, 1880).

BONAVENTURE, *Doctoris seraphici S. Bonaventurae* [...] *Opera omnia*, ed. R. P. Bernardini and Portu Romatino, 10 vols. (Ad Claras Aquas, 1882–1902).

BONIFACE VIII, *Les Registres de Boniface VIII: Recueil des bulles de ce pape publiées ou analysées d'après les manuscrits originaux des archives du Vatican*, ed. Georges Digard, Maurice Faucon, Antoine Thomas, and Robert Fawtier, 4 vols. (Paris, 1882).

Borough Customs, ed. Mary Bateson, 2 vols., SS 18, 21 (1904–6).

'BRACTON', *Bracton on the Laws and Customs of England*, ed. George E. Woodbine, rev. S. E. Thorne, 4 vols. (Cambridge, Mass., 1977).

Briefsammlungen der Zeit Heinrichs IV, ed. Carl Erdmann Norbert Fickermann, MGH, Die Briefe der Deutschen Kaiserzeit, 500–1500, 5 (Weimar, 1950).

Britton, ed. Francis Morgan Nichols, 2 vols. (Oxford, 1865).

Brevia Placitata, ed. G. J. Turner and T. F. T. Plucknett, SS 66 (1951).

BRUNETTO LATINI, *Li Livres dou Tresor*, ed. P. Chabaille (Paris, 1863).

BRUNETTO LATINI, *Li Livres dou Tresor*, ed. Francis J. Carmody (Berkeley, Calif., 1948).

BRUNETTO LATINI, *Li Livres dou Tresor*, ed. Spurgeon Baldwin and Paul Barrette (Tempe, 2003).

BRUNETTO LATINI, *Tresor*, ed. Pietro G. Beltrami, Paolo Squillacioti, Plinio Torri, and Sergio Vatteroni (Turin, 2007).

The Buckinghamshire Eyre of 1286, ed. Lesley Boatwright, Buckinghamshire Record Society 34 (Aylesbury, 2006).

BURY ST EDMUNDS ABBEY, *The Customary of the Benedictine Abbey of Bury St Edmunds in Suffolk*, ed. Antonia Gransden, Henry Bradshaw Society 99 (Chichester, 1973) (*see also* JOCELIN OF BRAKELOND).

CALENDAR OF CHARTER ROLLS, HENRY III–EDWARD I, *Calendar of the Charter Rolls Preserved in the Public Record Office*, ii. *Henry III–Edward I: 1257–1300* (London, 1906).

Calendar of Documents relating to Ireland, ed. H. S. Sweetman (vol. v with G. F. Hancock), 5 vols. (London, 1875–86).

Calendar of the Justiciary Rolls, or, Proceedings in the Court of the Justiciar of Ireland, Preserved in the Public Record Office of Ireland, ed. James Mills [vols. 1–2], Herbert Wood, Albert E. Langman, and rev. Margaret C. Griffith, 3 vols. (Dublin, 1905–56).

Calendar of Ormond Deeds, ed. Edmund Curtis, 6 vols. (Dublin, 1932–43).

CALENDAR OF INQUISITIONS MISCELLANEOUS, HENRY III–EDWARD I, *Calendar of Inquisitions Miscellaneous Preserved in the Public Record Office*, i. 1219–1307 (London, 1916).

CALENDAR OF PATENT ROLLS, EDWARD I, *Calendar of the Patent Rolls Preserved in the Public Record Office, Edward I*, 4 vols. (1873–1971).

CALENDAR OF PATENT ROLLS, HENRY III, *Calendar of the Patent Rolls Preserved in the Public Record Office, Henry III*, 6 vols. (London, 1901–13).

The Cambridge Translations of Medieval Philosophical Texts. ii, *Ethics and Political Philosophy*, ed. and trans. A. S. McGrade, John Kilcullen, and Matthew Kempshall (Cambridge, 2000).

CAMBRIDGE, UNIVERSITY AND COLLEGES, *Documents Relating to the University and Colleges of Cambridge*, 3 vols. (London, 1852).

Capitularia regum Francorum, MGH Leges, ed. Alfred Boretius and Victor Krause, 2 vols. (Hannover, 1883–7).

Cartulaire Normand, de Philippe-Auguste, Louis VIII, Saint Louis, et Philippe-le-Hardi, ed. Léopold Delisle (Caen, 1882, repr. Geneva, 1978).

Catalogue des actes de Philippe-Auguste: avec une introduction sur les sources, les caractères et l'importance historique de ces documents, Léopold Delisle (Paris, 1856).

'La Chambre des comptes du roi de France', Élisabeth Lalou, in *Les Chambres des comptes en France aux XIVe et XVe siècles. Textes et documents*, ed. Philippe Contamine and Olivier Mattéoni (Paris, 1998), 1–18.

CHARTRES, *Cartulaire de Notre-Dame de Chartres*, E. de Lépinois and Lucien Merlet, 3 vols. (Chartres, 1862–5).

Chronica regia Coloniensis (Annales maximi Colonienses), cum continuationibus in monasterio s. Pantaleonis scriptis, ed. G. Waitz, MGH, SRG 18 (Hannover, 1880).

Chronicon de Lanercost M.CC.I.–M.CCC.XLVI.: e codice Cottoniano nunc primum typis mandatum, ed. Joseph Stevenson, Bannatyne Club 65 (Edinburgh, 1839).

The Civil Pleas of the Suffolk Eyre of 1240, ed. Eric James Gallagher, Suffolk Record Society 52 (Woodbridge, 2009).

CLEMENT V, *Regestum Clementis papae V*, 10 vols. in 8 (Rome, 1885–92).

CLOSE ROLLS, EDWARD I, *Calendar of the Close Rolls Preserved in the Public Record Office. Edward I*, 5 vols. (London, 1900–08).

CLOSE ROLLS, HENRY III, *Close Rolls of the Reign of Henry III*, 14 vols. (London, 1902–38).

COLLÈGE D'AUTUN, *The Mediaeval Statutes of the College of Autun at the University of Paris*, ed. David Sanderlin, Texts & Studies in the History of Mediaeval Education 13 (Notre Dame, 1971).

COLLÈGE DES DIX-HUIT, E. Coyecque, 'Notice sur l'ancien collège des Dix-Huit', *Bulletin de la Société de l'Histoire de Paris et de l'Ile de France* 14 (Paris, 1887), 176–86.

Le Compte Général de 1187, connu sous le nom de «Gros Brief», et les institutions financières du comté de Flandre au XIIe siècle, ed. A. Verhulst and M. Gysseling (Brussels, 1962).

Constitutiones Concilii quarti Lateranensis una cum Commentariis glossatorum, ed. Antonio García y García, Monumenta iuris canonici, Ser. A: Corpus Glossatorum 2 (Vatican City, 1981).

Corpus iuris canonici, ed. E. Richter, rev. E. Friedberg, 2 vols. (Leipzig, 1879; repr. Graz, 1959).

Councils and Synods with Other Documents Relating to the English Church i. *A.D.871–1204*, ed. Dorothy Whitelock, Martin Brett, and C. N. L. Brooke, 2 vols. (Oxford, 1981); ii. *1205–1313*, ed. F. M. Powicke and C. R. Cheney, 2 vols. (Oxford, 1964).

The Court Baron, ed. Frederic William Maitland and William Paley Baildon, SS 4 (London, 1891).

Crónica de Alfonso X, Según el Ms. II/2777 de la Biblioteca del Palacio Real (Madrid), ed. Manuel González Jiménez (Murcia, 1998).
Crown Pleas of the Devon Eyre of 1238, ed. Henry Summerson, Devon and Cornwall Record Society (Torquay, 1985).
Crown Pleas of the Wiltshire Eyre, 1249, ed. C. A. F. Meekings, Wiltshire Archaeological and Natural History Society 16 (Devizes, 1961).
Curia Regis Rolls Preserved in the Public Record Office, 1196–1243, 17 vols. (London, 1922–91).
CUXHAM, *Manorial Records of Cuxham, Oxfordshire, circa 1200–1359*, ed. P. D. A. Harvey, Oxfordshire Record Society 50/Historical Manuscripts Commission Joint Publications 23 (London, 1976).
DANTE ALIGHIERI, *Monarchia*, ed. Prue Shaw (Cambridge, 1995).
DANTE ALIGHIERI, *Purgatorio*, trans. and ed. Robin Fitzpatrick (London, 2007).
Decretales ineditae saeculi XII, ed. Walther Holtzmann, rev. Stanley Chodorow and Charles Duggan, Monumenta iuris canonici. Ser. B: Corpus collectionum 4 (Vatican City, 1982).
Die deutschen Universitäten im Mittelalter: Beiträge zur Geschichte und Charakteristik derselben, ed. Friedrich Zarncke (Leipzig, 1857).
Dispute between the Priest and the Knight, ed. Norma N. Erickson, *Proceedings of the American Philosophical Society* 111 (1967), 288–309.
Documents Illustrating the Activities of the General and Provincial Chapters of the English Black Monks, 1215–1540, ed. W. A. Pantin, CS 3rd ser. 45, 47, 54, 3 vols. (1931–7).
Documents Illustrating the Crisis of 1297–1298 in England, ed. Michael Prestwich, CS 4th ser. 24 (1980).
Documents of the Baronial Movement of Reform and Rebellion, 1258–1267, ed. R. E. Treharne and I. J. Sanders, OMT (Oxford, 1973).
Documents on the Affairs of Ireland Before the King's Council, ed. G. O. Sayles (Dublin, 1979).
Domesday Book, trans. Ann Williams and G. H. Martin, repr. (London, 2002).
Le Dossier de l'affaire des Templiers, ed. Georges Lizerand, 2nd edn. (Paris, 1964).
The Earliest English Law Reports, vols. iii–iv, ed. Paul A. Brand, SS 122–3 (London, 2005–7).
Early Registers of Writs, ed. Elsa de Haas and G. D. G. Hall, SS 87 (London, 1970).
The Eclipse of the 'Abbasid Caliphate: Original Chronicles of the Fourth Islamic Century, ed. H. F. Amedroz and D. S. Margoliouth, 7 vols. (Oxford, 1920–1).
English Episcopal Acta, ii. *Canterbury, 1162–1190*, ed. C. R. Cheney and Bridgitt E. A. Jones (Oxford, 1986).
English Episcopal Acta, iii. *Canterbury, 1193–1205*, ed. C. R. Cheney and Eric John (Oxford, 1986).
English Episcopal Acta, iv. *Lincoln, 1186–1206*, ed. David M. Smith (Oxford, 1986).
English Episcopal Acta, xvi. *Coventry and Lichfield, 1160–1182*, ed. M. J. Franklin (Oxford, 1998).
English Episcopal Acta, xx. *York, 1154–1181*, ed. Marie Lovatt (Oxford, 2000).
English Episcopal Acta, xxvii. *York, 1189–1212*, ed. Marie Lovatt (Oxford, 2004).
English Historical Documents, i. c.*500–1042*, ed. D. Whitelock, rev. edn. (London, 1979); ii. *1042–1189*, ed. D. C. Douglas and G. W. Greenaway (London, 1953); iii. *1189–1327*, ed. H. Rothwell (London, 1975).
English Lawsuits from William I to Richard I, ed. R. C. van Caenegem, SS 106–7, 2 vols. (London, 1990–1).
Enquêtes menées sous les derniers Capétiens, ed. Xavier Hélary and Élisabeth Lalou, Ædilis, Publications scientifiques 4 (Orléans, 2006–9), online only at <http://www.cn-telma.fr/enquetes/>, accessed February 2014.
Epistolae saeculi xiii e regestis pontificum Romanorum, ed. C. Rodenberg, MGH Epistolae, 3 vols. (Berlin, 1883–94).

ETIENNE DE GALLARDON, Léopold Delisle, 'Etienne de Gallardon, clerc de la chancellerie de Philippe Auguste, chanoine de Bruges', *Bibliothèque de l'École des chartes* 60 (1899), 5–44.

EUSTACHE LE MOINE, *Le Roman d'Eustache le moine*, ed. A. J. Holden and J. Monfrin (Louvain, 2005).

The Eyre of London, 14 Edward II, AD 1321, ed. H. M. Cam, 2 vols., SS 85–6 (1968–9).

The Eyre of Northamptonshire: 3–4 Edward III, A.D. 1329–1330, ed. Donald W. Sutherland, SS 97–8 (1983).

EXETER COLLEGE, OXFORD, Charles William Boase, *Register of the Rectors and Fellows, Scholars, Exhibitioners and Bible Clerks of Exeter College, Oxford with Illustrative Documents and a History of the College*, 2 vols. (Oxford, 1879).

EXETER COLLEGE, OXFORD, *Register of the Rectors, Fellows and Other Members on the Foundation of Exeter College, Oxford*, ed. Charles William Boase, OHS 27 (Oxford, 1894).

FALCONE DI BENEVENTO, *Chronicon Beneventanum: città e feudi nell'Italia dei Normanni*, ed. Edoardo D'Angelo (Florence, 1998).

Fiscal Accounts of Catalonia under the Early Count-Kings (1151–1213), ed. T. N. Bisson, 2 vols. (Berkeley, Calif., 1984).

Fleta, ed. H. G. Richardson and G. O. Sayles, SS 72, 89, 99, 3 vols. (1955–84).

Flores historiarum, ed. H. R. Luard, RS (London, 1890).

Foedera, conventiones, litteræ et cujuscunque generis acta publica inter reges Angliæ, et alios quosvis imperatores, reges, pontifices, principes vel communitates: ab ingressu Gulielmi I. in Angliam, A.D. 1066, ad nostra usque tempora habita aut tractata, ed. Thomas Rymer and Robert Sanderson, rev. Adam Clarke, Frederic Holbrooke, and John Caley, 4 vols. in 7 (London, 1816–69).

A Formula Book of English Official Historical Documents, ed. Hubert Hall, 2 vols. (Cambridge, 1908–9).

FRANCIS OF ASSISI, François d'Assisi, *Écrits*, ed. K. Esser, Sources chrétiennes 285 (Paris, 1981).

FULBERT OF CHARTRES, *The Letters and Poems of Fulbert of Chartres*, ed. Frederick Behrends, OMT (Oxford, 1976).

GERALD OF WALES, *Giraldi Cambrensis Opera*, var. eds., RS, 8 vols. (London, 1861–91).

GERALD OF WALES, *'De Invectionibus'*, ed. W. S. Davies, *Y Cymmrodor* 30 (1920).

GERMAN NATION, BOLOGNA UNIVERSITY, *Statuta Nationis Germanicae Universitatis Bononiae (1292–1750)*, ed. Paolo Colliva, Acta Germania 1 (Bologna, 1975).

GERVASE OF CANTERBURY, *The Historical Works of Gervase of Canterbury*, ed. W. Stubbs, RS, 2 vols. (1879–80).

Die Gesetze der Angelsachsen, ed. F. Liebermann, 3 vols. in 4 (Halle, 1903–16).

GILBERT FOLIOT, *The Letters and Charters of Gilbert Foliot: Abbot of Gloucester (1139–48), Bishop of Hereford (1148–63), and London (1163–87)*, ed. Z. N. Brooke, Adrian Morey, and C. N. L. Brooke (Cambridge, 1967).

'GLANVILL', *The Treatise on the Laws and Customs of the Realm of England Commonly Called Glanvill*, ed. G. D. G. Hall, NMT (London, 1965); reissued with 'Guide to Further Reading' by Michael Clanchy, OMT (Oxford, 1993).

The Great Roll of the Pipe for the Thirty First Year of the Reign of Henry I, Michaelmas 1130 (Pipe Roll 1), ed. Judith A. Green, Pipe Roll Society NS 57 (95) (Loughborough, 2012).

GREGORY IX, *Les Régistres de Grégoire IX*, ed. Lucien Auvray, Bibliothèque des Écoles françaises d'Athènes et de Rome. 2nd ser., Registres des papes du 13. Siècle 9, 4 vols. (Paris, 1896–1955).

GUIBERT DE TOURNAI, *Le Traité Eruditio regum et principum de Guibert de Tournai, O.F.M.*, ed. A. de Poorter, Les Philosophes belges 9 (Louvain, 1914).

GUILLAUME LE BRETON, *Œuvres de Rigord et de Guillaume le Breton: historiens de Philippe-Auguste*, ed. H.-François Delaborde, Société de l'histoire de France, 2 vols. (Paris, 1882–5).

GUISBOROUGH PRIORY, *Cartularium prioratus de Gyseburne, Ebor. dioceseos, ordinis Sancti Augustini, fundati A.D. MCXIX*, ed. William Brown, Surtees Society 86, 89, 2 vols. (1889–94).

HINCMAR OF REIMS, *De ordine palatii*, ed. Thomas Gross and Rudolf Schieffer, MGH, Fontes iuris germanici antiqui 3 (Hannover, 1980).

The Historians of the Church of York and its Archbishops, ed. James Raine, RS, 3 vols. (London, 1879–94).

The Historical Charters and Constitutional Documents of the City of London, ed. W. de Gray Birch, rev. edn. (London, 1887).

The History of al-Ṭabarī, ed. E. Yar-Shater, 40 vols. (Albany, 1985–2007).

HONORIUS III, *Regesta Honorii Papae III*, ed. Petrus Pressutti, 2 vols. (Rome, 1888–95; repr. Hildesheim, 1978).

Imperial Lives and Letters of the Eleventh Century, ed. and trans. T. E. Mommsen and K. F. Morrison, rev. edn. (New York, 2000).

INNOCENT III, *Regestum Innocentii III papae super negotio Romani imperii*, ed. Friedrich Kempf, Miscellanea Historiae Pontificiae 12 (Rome, 1947).

INNOCENT III, *Selected Letters of Pope Innocent III Concerning England (1198–1216)*, ed. C. R. Cheney and W. H. Semple, NMT (Edinburgh, 1953).

INNOCENT III, *Die Register Innocenz' III*, ed. Othmar Hageneder et al., Historischen Instituts beim Österreichischen Kulturinstitut in Rom. II. Abt.: Quellen. 1, 10 vols. in 13 (Graz, 1964–).

INNOCENT III, *The Letters of Pope Innocent III (1198–1216) Concerning England and Wales: A Calendar with an Appendix of Texts*, ed. C. R. Cheney and Mary G. Cheney (Oxford, 1967).

ISIDORE OF SEVILLE, *The Etymologies of Isidore of Seville*, trans. Stephen A. Barney, W. J. Lewis, J. A. Beach, and Oliver Berghof (Cambridge, 2006).

JEAN DE JOINVILLE, *Histoire de Saint Louis*, ed. M. Natalis de Wailly, 9th edn. (Paris, 1921).

JOCELIN OF BRAKELOND, *The Chronicle of Jocelin of Brakelond Concerning the Acts of Samson, Abbot of the Monastery of St Edmund*, ed. H. E. Butler, NMT (London, 1949).

JOHN OF GARLAND, *Morale Scolarium of John of Garland (Johannes de Garlandia) a Professor in the Universities of Paris and Toulouse in the Thirteenth Century*, ed. Louis John Paetow (Berkeley, Calif., 1927).

JOHN OF IBELIN, *Le Livre des assises*, ed. Peter W. Edbury (Leiden, 2003).

JOHN OF SALISBURY, *The Letters of John of Salisbury*, i. *The Early Letters*, ed. W. J. Millor and H. E. Butler, rev. C. N. L. Brooke, NMT (London, 1955).

JOHN PECHAM, *Registrum epistolarum fratris Johannis Peckham Archiepiscopi Cantuariensis*, ed. C. T. Martin. RS, 3 vols. (London, 1882–6).

JOINVILLE, *see* JEAN DE JOINVILLE.

JORDAN FANTOSME, *Jordan Fantosme's Chronicle*, ed. R. C. Johnston (Oxford, 1981).

Die Konstitutionen Friedrichs II. für das Königreich sizilien, ed. Wolfgang Stürner, MGH Leges, Const., Suppl. 2 (Hannover, 1996).

LATERAN COUNCIL, FOURTH, *see Constitutiones Concilii quarti Lateranensis*; 'Die Teilnehmerliste des Laterankonzils vom Jahre 1215'.

Layettes de trésor des chartes, ed. A. Teulet, J. de Laborde, E. Berger, and H.-F. Delaborde, Inventaires et documents, 5 vols. (Paris, 1863–1909; repr. Nendeln, 1977).

Legal and Manorial Formularies, Edited from Originals at the British Museum and the Public Record Office in Memory of Julius Parnell Gilson (Oxford, 1933).

Leges Henrici Primi, ed. L. J. Downer (Oxford, 1972).

La Legislazione angioina, Romualdo Trifone, Documenti per la storia dell'Italia meridionale 1 (Naples, 1921).

Leyes de los Adelantados Mayores: Regulations, Attributed to Alfonso X of Castile, Concerning the King's Vicar in the Judiciary and in Territorial Administration, ed. Robert A. MacDonald, Hispanic Seminary of Medieval Studies 25 (New York, 2000).

Libelli de lite imperatorum et pontificum saeculis xi. et xii., MGH, 3 vols. (Hannover, 1891–7).

The Liber epistolaris of Richard de Bury, ed. N. Denholm-Young, Roxburghe Club (Oxford, 1950).

LINCOLN CATHEDRAL (*see also under* ROBERT GROSSETESTE), 'Bishop Robert Grosseteste and His Cathedral Chapter: An Edition of the Chapter's Objections to Episcopal Visitation', ed. F. A. C. Mantello, *Mediaeval Studies* 47 (1985), 367–78.

The Manuale scholarium: An Original Account of Life in the Mediaeval University, trans. R. F. Seybolt (Cambridge, Mass., 1921).

MASʿŪDĪ, *Les Prairies d'or*, trans. Charles-Adrien-Casimir Barbier de Meynard and Abel Pavet de Courteille, rev. Charles Pellat, 3 vols. (Paris, 1962–71).

MATTHEW PARIS, *Matthæi Parisiensis, monachi Sancti Albani, Chronica majora*, ed. H. R. Luard, RS, 7 vols. (London, 1872–83).

MATTHEW PARIS, *Flores historiarum*, ed. H. R. Luard, RS, 3 vols. (London, 1890).

MERTON COLLEGE, OXFORD, *Memorials of Merton College*, George C. Brodrick, OHS 4 (Oxford, 1885).

MERTON COLLEGE, OXFORD, *Merton Muniments*, ed. P. S. Allen and H. W. Garrod, OHS 86 (Oxford, 1929).

MERTON COLLEGE, OXFORD, *The Early Rolls of Merton College Oxford*, ed. J. R. L. Highfield, OHS NS 18 (Oxford, 1964).

Mirror of Justices, ed. William Joseph Whittaker, intr. Frederic William Maitland, SS 7 (London, 1895).

MISKAWAYH, *The Refinement of Character: A Translation from the Arabic of Aḥmad ibn-Muḥammad Miskawayh's Tahdhīb al-Akhlāq*, trans. Constantine K. Zurayk (Beirut, 1968).

Munimenta Gildhallæ Londoniensis: Liber albus, Liber custumarum, et Liber Horn, ed. Henry Thomas Riley, RS, 3 vols. in 4 (London, 1859–62).

NIGEL OF CANTERBURY, *Nigellus de Longchamp dit Wireker, i. Introduction, Tractatus contra curiales et officiales clericos*, ed. A. Boutemy (Paris, 1959).

The Northumberland Eyre Roll for 1293, ed. Constance M. Fraser, Surtees Society 211 (Woodbridge, 2009).

ORDERIC VITALIS, *The Ecclesiastical History of Orderic Vitalis*, ed. Marjorie Chibnall, OMT, 6 vols. (Oxford, 1969–80).

Ordonnances des roys de France de la troisième race: recueillies par ordre chronologique, 21 vols. (Paris, 1723–1849).

The Oxfordshire Eyre, 1241, ed. Janet Cooper, Oxfordshire Record Society 56 (Oxford, 1989).

OXFORD, UNIVERSITY AND COLLEGES (*see also under individual colleges*), *Statutes of the Colleges of Oxford: With Royal Patents of Foundation, Injunctions of Visitors*, ed. E. A. Bond, 3 vols. (London and Oxford, 1853).

OXFORD, UNIVERSITY AND COLLEGES, *Munimenta Academica, or, Documents Illustrative of Academical Life and Studies at Oxford*, ed. Henry Anstey, RS, 2 vols. (London, 1868).
OXFORD, UNIVERSITY AND COLLEGES, *Mediaeval Archives of the University of Oxford*, ed. H. E. Salter, OHS 70–3, 2 vols. (Oxford, 1920–1).
PARIS, UNIVERSITY AND COLLEGES (*see also under individual colleges*), *Historia universitatis Parisiensis*, C. EGASSE DU BOULAY, 6 vols. (Paris 1665–73).
PARIS, UNIVERSITY AND COLLEGES, *Chartularium Universitatis Parisiensis*, ed. H. Denifle and E. Chatelain, 4 vols. (Paris, 1889–97).
Parliament Rolls of Medieval England 1275–1504, gen. ed. Chris Given-Wilson, 16 vols. (Woodbridge and London, 2005).
PATROLOGIA LATINA, Jacques-Paul Migne (ed.), *Patrologiae cursus completus [. . .] omnium SS. patrum: doctorum scriptorumque ecclesiasticorum . . . ad aetatem Innocentii III [. . .] series latina*, 221 vols. (Paris, 1844–55, 1862–5).
PETER ABELARD, *Peter Abelard's Ethics*, ed. D. E. Luscombe, OMT (Oxford, 1971).
PETER ABELARD, Peter Abailard, *Sic et non: A Critical Edition*, ed. Blanche B. Boyer and Richard McKeon (Chicago, 1976).
PETER OF AUVERGNE, see *Rezeption und Interpretation der aristotelischen Politica*, ed. Flüeler; in THOMAS AQUINAS, *Thomae Aquinatis opera omnia* ed. Busa 1980, vii; *Cambridge Translations of Medieval Philosophical Texts*, ed. McGrade et al.
PETER THE CHANTER, *Petri Cantoris Parisiensis Verbum adbreviatum*, ed. Monique Boutry, Corpus Christianorum Continuatio Mediaevalis 196 (Turnhout, 2004).
PHILIPPE DE BEAUMANOIR, *Coutumes de Beauvaisis*, ed. André Salmon, 2 vols. (Paris, repr. 1970).
PHILIP II AUGUSTUS, *Recueil des Actes de Philippe Auguste, roi de France*, gen. ed. Élie Berger, Chartes et diplômes relatifs à l'histoire de France, 6 vols. (Paris, 1916–)(see also *Catalogue des actes*, Delisle).
PHILIP II AUGUSTUS, *Les Registres de Philippe Auguste*, ed. John W. Baldwin with Françoise Gasparri, Michel Nortier, and Élisabeth Lalou, Recueil des historiens de la France, Documents financiers et administratifs 7 (Paris, 1992).
PIERRE DE LANGTOFT, *The Chronicle of Pierre de Langtoft*, ed. Thomas Wright, RS, 2 vols. (1866–8).
The Pipe Roll of the Bishopric of Winchester for the Fourth Year of the Pontificate of Peter des Roches, 1208–1209, ed. Hubert Hall (London, 1903).
The Pipe Roll of the Bishopric of Winchester 1210–1211, ed. N. R. Holt (Manchester, 1964).
PIPE ROLLS (*see also The Great Role of the Pipe*), *Pipe Rolls, 1184–5, 1186–7, 1191–2, 1200, 1207, 1208, 1221*, 7 vols. (London, 1913–90).
Pleas of the Crown for the County of Gloucester, A.D. 1221, ed. F. W. Maitland (London, 1884).
Le Premier Budget de la monarchie française: Le Compte général de 1202–1203, ed. Ferdinand Lot and Robert Fawtier, Bibliothèque de l'École des Hautes Études, Sciences, historiques et philologiques 259 (Paris, 1932).
PSEUDO-CYPRIAN, 'Pseudo-Cyprianus, *De xii abusivis saeculi*', *Texte und Untersuchungen zur Geschichte der altechristlichen Literatur* 34 (Leipzig, 1910), 1–60.
Quinque Compilationes Antiquae, nec non collectio canonum Lipsiensis, ed. E. Friedberg (Leipzig, 1882, repr. Graz, 1882).
RALPH DICETO, *Radulfi de Diceto Decani Londoniensis, Opera historica*, ed. William Stubbs, RS, 2 vols. (London, 1876).
RALPH OF COGGESHALL, *Radulphi de Coggeshall Chronicon Anglicanum*, ed. Joseph Stevenson, RS (London 1875).
RAMSEY ABBEY, *Cartularium monasterii de Rameseia*, ed. William Henry Hart and Ponsonby A. Lyons, RS, 3 vols. (London, 1884–93).

Recueil de jugements de L'échiquier de Normandie au XIIIe siècle (1207–1270) suivi d'un mémoire sur les anciennes collections de ces jugements, ed. Léopold Delisle (Paris, 1864).
Recueil des historiens des Gaules et de la France, gen. ed. L. Delisle, 24 vols. in 25 (Paris, 1869–1904, repub. Farnborough, 1967).
The Red Book of the Exchequer, ed. Hubert Hall, RS, 3 vols. (London, 1896).
Regesta pontificum romanorum: ab condita ecclesia ad annum post Christum natum MCXCVIII. ed. P. Jaffé, rev. S. Loewenfeld, F. Kaltenbrunner, and P. Ewald, 2 vols. (Leipzig, 1885–8).
Regesta pontificum romanorum inde ab a. post Christum natum MCXCVIII ad a. MCCCIV, ed. Augustus Potthast, 2 vols. (Berlin, 1874–5, repr. Graz, 1957).
Regesta Regum Anglo-Normannorum 1066–1154, ed. C. Johnson, H. A. Cronne, and H. W. C. Davis, 4 vols. (Oxford, 1913–69).
I registri della Cancelleria angioina, ed. Riccardo Filangieri et al., Testi e documenti di storia napoletana, 49 vols. (Naples, 1950–).
Registrum omnium brevium, tam originalium quam judicialium (London, 1634).
La Règle du Maître, ed. Adalbert de Vogüé et al., Sources chrétiennes 105–7, 3 vols. (Paris, 1964–5).
La Règle de Saint Benoît, ed. Adalbert de Vogüé and Jean Neufville, Sources chrétiennes 181–6, 7 vols. (Paris, 1971–7).
REIMS, *Archives administratives de la ville de Reims, collection de pièces inédites, archives administratives*, ed. Pierre Varin, 8 vols. in 5 (Paris, 1839–53).
REIMS, *Les Actes de la province ecclésiastique de Reims*, ed. T. Gousset, 4 vols. (Reims 1842–4).
Rerum Britannicarum Medii Aevi Scriptores ('Rolls Series'), 99 vols. in multiple parts (London, 1858–96).
Rerum Italicarum Scriptores, new edn., 34 vols. in multiple parts (various publishers, 1900–).
Rezeption und Interpretation der aristotelischen Politica im späten Mittelalter, Christoph, Flüeler, Bochumer Studien zur Philosophie 19, 2 vols. (Amsterdam, 1992).
RICHARD OF ELY, *Dialogus de scaccario: The Course of the Exchequer by Richard, Fitz Nigel and Constitutio domus regis: The Establishment of the Royal Household*, ed. Charles Johnson, rev. F. E. L. Carter, and D. E. Greenway, OMT (Oxford, 1983).
RICHARD OF ELY, *Dialogus de Scaccario and Constitutio Domus Regis*, ed. (respectively) Emilie Amt and S. D. Church, OMT (Oxford, 2007).
RICHARD DE MEDIAVILLA, *Questions disputées*, ed. Alain Boureau, 6 vols. (Paris, 2012–14).
RICHARD SWINFIELD, *Registrum Ricardi de Swinfield, Episcopi Herefordensis, A.D. 1283–1317*, C&Y 6 (London, 1909).
RICHER DE SENONES, *Gesta Senonensis Ecclesiae*, ed. G. Waitz, in MGH, SS 25 (Hannover, 1880), 249–345.
RIGORD, *Histoire de Philippe Auguste*, ed. and trans. Élisabeth Carpentier, Georges Pon, and Yves Chauvin (Paris, 2006).
ROBERT DE SORBON (*see also* SORBONNE), *De Consciencia et de tribus dietis*, ed. Félix Chambon (Paris, 1902).
ROBERT GROSSETESTE, *Roberti Grosseteste, episcopi quondam Lincolniensis, epistolae*, ed. H. R. Luard, RS (London, 1861).
ROBERT GROSSETESTE, 'Robert Grosseteste at the Papal Curia, Lyons 1250. Edition of the documents', ed. Servus Gieben, *Collectanea Franciscana* 41 (1971), 340–93.
ROBERT GROSSETESTE, *Templum Dei, edited from MS 27 of Emmanuel College, Cambridge*, ed. Joseph Goering and F. A. C. Mantello (Toronto, 1984).
ROBERT GROSSETESTE, *The Letters of Robert Grosseteste, Bishop of Lincoln*, trans. F. A. C. Mantello and Joseph Goering (Toronto, 2010).
ROBERT KILWARDBY, *Merton College: Injunctions of Archbishop Kilwardby, 1276*, ed. H. W. Garrod (Oxford, 1929).

ROBERT WINCHELSEY, *Registrum Roberti Winchelsey, Cantuariensis Archiepiscopi, A.D. 1294–1313*, ed. Rose Graham, C&Y 51–2, 2 vols. (1952–6).
ROGER BACON, *Opera hactenus inedita Rogeri Baconi*, ed. Robert Steele, 16 vols. (Oxford 1905–40).
Roger II and the Creation of the Kingdom of Sicily, trans. Graham A. Loud, Manchester Medieval Sources (Manchester, 2012).
ROGER OF HOWDEN, *Gesta regis Henrici secundi Benedicti abbatis*, ed. William Stubbs, RS, 2 vols. (London, 1867).
ROGER OF HOWDEN, *Chronica magistri Rogeri de Houedene*, ed. William Stubbs, RS, 4 vols. (London, 1868–71).
The Roll of the Shropshire Eyre of 1256, ed. Alan Harding, SS 96 (1981).
The Rolls of the 1281 Derbyshire Eyre, ed. Aileen M. Hopkinson, intr. David Crook, Derbyshire Record Society 27 (Chesterfield, 2000).
Rolls of the Justices in Eyre: Being the Rolls of Pleas and Assizes for Gloucestershire, Warwickshire and Staffordshire, 1221, 1222, ed. Doris Mary Stenton, SS 59 (London, 1940).
Rotuli chartarum in Turri londinensi asservati, i.1, ed. T. D. Hardy (London, 1837).
Royal and Other Historical Letters Illustrative of the Reign of Henry III, ed. W. W. Shirley, RS, 2 vols. (London, 1862–6).
Royal Writs in England from the Conquest to Glanvill, ed. R. C. van Caenegem, SS 77 (London, 1959).
RUFINUS OF BOLOGNA/ASSISI/SORRENTO, *Summa decretorum*, ed. Heinrich Singer (Paderborn, 1902, repr. 1963).
RYMER, THOMAS, *see Foedera*.
SABA MALASPINA, *Die Chronik des Saba Malaspina*, ed. Walter Koller and August Nitschke, MGH, SS 35 (Hannover, 1999),.
ST AUGUSTINE'S CANTERBURY, Thomas of Elmham, *Historia monasterii S. Augustini Cantuariensis*, ed. Charles Hardwick, RS (London, 1858).
ST GILES AND ST ANDREW PRIORY, BARNWELL, *The Observances in Use at the Augustinian Priory of S. Giles and S. Andrew at Barnwell, Cambridgeshire*, ed. John Willis Clark (Cambridge, 1897).
ST GILES AND ST ANDREW PRIORY, BARNWELL, *Liber memorandum ecclesie de Bernewelle*, ed. John Willis Clark, intr. F. W. Maitland, (Cambridge, 1907).
ST JOHN THE BAPTIST HOSPITAL, DUBLIN, *Register of the Hospital of S. John the Baptist*, ed. Eric St. John Brooks (Dublin, 1936).
ST JOHN THE BAPTIST HOSPITAL, OXFORD, *A Cartulary of the Hospital of St John the Baptist*, ed. H. E. Salter, OHS, 66, 68–9, 3 vols. (Oxford, 1914–17).
ST PETER'S GLOUCESTER, *Historia et cartularium monasterii Sancti Petri Gloucestriae*, ed. William Henry Hart, RS, 3 vols. (London, 1863–7).
SALIMBENE DE ADAM, *Cronica*, ed. Giuseppe Scalia, Scrittori d'Italia 232–3, 2 vols. (Bari, 1966).
The Saxon Mirror: A Sachsenspiegel of the Fourteenth Century, trans. Maria Dobozy (Philadelphia, 1999).
Siegmund Hellmann, ed., 'Pseudo-Cyprianus, *De xii abusivis saeculi*', *Texte und Untersuchungen zur Geschichte der altchristlichen Literatur* 34 (Leipzig, 1910), 1–60 at 53–6.
Select Cases before the King's Council, 1243–1482, ed. I. S. Leadam and J. F. Baldwin, SS 35 (Cambridge, Mass., 1918).
Select Cases concerning the Law Merchant, 1239–1633, ii. *Central Courts*, ed. Hubert Hall, SS 46 (London, 1930).
Select Cases in the Exchequer of Pleas, ed. Hilary Jenkinson and Beryl E. R. Formoy, SS 48 (London, 1932).

Select Charters and Other Illustrations of English Constitutional History from the Earliest Times to the Reign of Edward I, ed. W. Stubbs, rev. H. W. C. Davis, 9th edn. (Oxford, 1913).
Select Pleas in Manorial Courts and Other Seignorial Courts, ed. F. W. Maitland, SS 1 (London, 1889).
The Song of Lewes, ed. C. L. Kingsford (Oxford, 1890).
SORBONNE, COLLEGE (*see also* ROBERT DE SORBON), *Aux origines de la Sorbonne*, i. *Robert de Sorbon*, ii. *Le Cartulaire*, Palémon Glorieux, 2 vols. (Paris, 1965–6).
Sources of Chinese Tradition, i. *From the Earliest Times to 1600*, ed. William Theodore de Bary and Irene Bloom, 2nd edn. (New York, 1999).
SPANISH COLLEGE AT BOLOGNA, *The Spanish College at Bologna in the Fourteenth Century*, ed. Berthe M. Marti (Philadelphia, 1966).
State Trials of Edward the First, 1289–1293, ed. T. F. Tout and Hilda Johnston, Camden Society, 3rd ser. 9 (1906).
Lo stato normanno svevo, lineamenti e ricerche, Gennaro M. Monti (Trani, 1945).
'Statuta generalia ordinis edita in capitulis generalibus celebratis. Narbonae an. 1260, Assisii an. 1279 atque Parisiis an. 1292', ed. Michael Bihl, *Archivum Franciscanum Historicum* 34 (1941), 13–94, 284–358.
*The Statutes of the Realm: From Original Records, etc. (*1101–1713), ed. A. Luders, T. Edlyn Tomlins, J. France, W. E. Tauton, and J. Raithby, 11 vols. (London, 1810–28).
SUGER, *Œuvres*, ed. Françoise Gasparri, Classiques de l'histoire de France au Moyen Âge 37, 41, 2 vols. (Paris, 1996–2008).
Summa 'omnis qui iuste iudicat' sive Lipsiensis, ed. Rudolf Weigand, Peter Landau, Waltraud Kozur, et al., Monumenta iuris canonici, Ser. A: Corpus glossatorum 7 (Rome, 2007).
Survey of Archbishop Pecham's Kentish Manors 1283–85, trans. Kenneth Witney, Kent Records 28 (Maidstone, 2000).
THOMAS AQUINAS, *S. Thomæ Aquinatis doctoris angelici summa theologica*, 6 vols. (Turin, 1932).
THOMAS AQUINAS, *Selected Political Writings*, ed. A. P. d'Entrèves, trans. J. G. Dawson (Oxford, 1974).
THOMAS AQUINAS, *S. Thomae Aquinatis opera omnia: ut sunt in indice Thomistico: additis 61 scriptis ex aliis medii aevi auctoribus* ed. Roberto Busa, 7 vols. (Stuttgart-Bad Cannstatt, 1980).
THOMAS AQUINAS, *Politial Writings*, trans. R.W. Dyson (Cambridge, 2002).
THOMAS CANTILUPE, *Registrum Thome de Cantilupo, Episcopi Herefordensis, A.D. 1275–1282*, ed. R. G. Griffiths and W. W. Capes, C&Y 2 (London, 1907).
THOMAS OF CHOBHAM, *Summa confessorum*, ed. F. Broomfield, Analecta mediaevalia Namurcensia 25 (Louvain, 1968).
THOMAS OF MARLBOROUGH, *History of the Abbey of Evesham*, ed. Jane Sayers and Leslie Watkiss, OMT (Oxford, 2003).
UGO FALCANDO, *La historia o liber de regno Sicilie e la epistola ad Petrum Panormitane urbis thesaurium di Ugo Falcando*, ed. G. B. Siragusa, FSI 22 (Rome, 1897).
'An Unpublished Northumbrian Hundred Roll', H. H. E. Craster, *Archaeologia Aeliana*, 3rd ser. 3 (1907), 187–90.
Vetera monumenta hibernorum et scotorum. Historia illustrantia, ed. Augustin Theiner (Rome, 1864).
WACE, *The History of the Norman People: Wace's Roman de Rou*, trans. Glyn S. Burgess, notes with Elisabeth van Houts (Woodbridge, 2004).

WALTER LANGTON, *Records of the Trial of Walter Langeton, Bishop of Coventry and Lichfield, 1307–1312*, ed. Alice Beardwood, CS 4th ser. 6 (1969).
WALTER LANGTON, *The Register of Walter Langton Bishop of Coventry and Lichfield, 1296–1321*, ed. J. B. Hughes, C&Y 91, 97, 2 vols. (2001–7).
WALTER MAP, *De nugis curialium*, ed. M. R. James, rev. C. N. L. Brooke and R. A. B. Mynors, OMT (Oxford, 1983).
WALTER OF GUISBOROUGH, *The Chronicle of Walter of Guisborough*, ed. Harry Rothwell, CS 3rd ser. 89 (1957).
Walter of Henley and Other Treatises on Estate Management and Accounting, ed. Dorothea Oschinsky (Oxford, 1971).
Walter of Henley's Husbandry together with an anonymous Husbandry, Seneschaucie and Robert Grosseteste's Rules, ed. Elizabeth Lamond (London, 1890).
WALTER STAPELDON, *The Register of Walter de Stapeldon, Bishop of Exeter (A.D. 1307–1326)*, ed. F. C. Hingeston-Randolph (London, 1892).
WILLIAM LONGCHAMP, Exupère Caillemer, 'Le Droit civil dans les provinces anglo-normandes au XIIe siècle', *Mémoires de l'Académie nationale des Sciences, Arts et Belles-Lettres de Caen* (Caen, 1883) [edition of *Practica legum*].
WILLIAM OF CONCHES, *Wilhelm von Conches, Philosophia*, ed. Gregor Maurach with Heidemarie Telle (Pretoria, 1980).
WILLIAM OF MALMESBURY, *Historia novella*, ed. Edmund King, trans. K. R. Potter, OMT (Oxford, 1998).
WILLIAM OF NEWBURGH, *Historia rerum Anglicarum*, in *Chronicles of the Reigns of Stephen, Henry II and Richard I*, ed. Richard Howlett, RS, 4 vols. (London 1884–9), 1–2.
WILLIAM RISHANGER, *Willelmi Rishanger, Chronica et annales*, ed. Henry Thomas Riley, RS (1865).
Wimbledon's Sermon: Redde Racionem Villicationis Tue, a Middle English Sermon of the Fourteenth Century, ed. Ione Kemp Knight (Pittsburgh, 1967).
The Worcester Eyre of 1275, ed. Jens Röhrkasten, Worcestershire Historical Society NS 22 (Trowbridge, 2008).
WULFSTAN OF YORK, *Die «Institutes of polity, civil and ecclesiastical»: ein Werk Erzbischof Wulfstans von York*, ed. and trans. (into German) Karl Jost, Schweizer Anglistische Arbeiten, 47 (Berne, 1959).
Yorkshire Hundred and Quo Warranto Rolls, ed. Barbara English, Yorkshire Archaeological Society, Record Series 151 (Leeds, 1996).

SECONDARY SOURCES

ABULAFIA, DAVID, *The Western Mediterranean Kingdoms, 1200–1500: The Struggle for Dominion* (Harlow, 1997).
ADAMS, JENNY, *Power Play: The Literature and Politics of Chess in the Later Middle Ages* (Philadelphia, 2006).
AIRLIE, STUART, 'Bonds of Power and Bonds of Association in the Court Circle of Louis the Pious', in Peter Godman and Roger Collins (eds.), *Charlemagne's Heir: New Perspectives on the Reign of Louis the Pious (814–840)* (Oxford, 1990), 191–204.
ALTHOFF, GERD, *Family, Friends and Followers: Political and Social Bonds in Early Medieval Europe*, trans. C. Carroll (Cambridge, 2004).
AMBLER, SOPHIE, 'On Kingship and Tyranny: Grosseteste's Memorandum and its Place in the Baronial Reform Movement', *TCE* 14 (2013), 115–28.

AMT, EMILIE, 'The Reputation of the Sheriff, 1100–1216', *Haskins Society Journal* 8 (1996), 91–8.
ANDERSON, PERRY, *Passages from Antiquity to Feudalism* (London, 1974).
ANGELOV, DIMITER, *Imperial Ideology and Political Thought in Byzantium, 1204–1330* (Cambridge, 2007).
ARKOUN, M., 'Miskawayh', in H. A. R. Gibb, et al. (eds.), *The Encyclopaedia of Islam*, 12 vols. (Leiden, 1960–2009) [consulted online].
ARNOLD, BENJAMIN, *German Knighthood, 1050–1300* (Oxford, 1985).
ARNOLD, BENJAMIN, 'Instruments of Power: The Profile and Profession of *Ministeriales* within German Aristocratic Society (1050-1225)', in T. N. Bisson (ed.), *Cultures of Power* (Philadelphia, 1995), 36–55.
ARNOLD, JOHN, *Inquisition and Power: Catharism and the Confessing Subject in Medieval Languedoc* (Philadelphia, 2001).
ARTIFONI, ENRICO, 'I podestà professionali e la fondazione retorica della politica comunale', *Quaderni storici* 63 (1986), 687–719.
ARTIFONI, ENRICO, 'Sull'eloquenza politica nel Duecento italiano', *Quaderni medievali storici* 35 (1993), 57–78.
ARTIFONI, ENRICO, 'Retorica e organizzazione del linguaggio politico nel Duecento italiano', in Paolo Cammarasono (ed.), *Le forme della propaganda politica nel Due e nel Trecento*, Collection de l'École française de Rome 201 (Rome, 1994), 157–82.
ASHWORTH, E. J., 'Heytesbury, William (d. 1372/3)', *ODNB*.
ASTON, T. H., 'Oxford's Medieval Alumni', *P&P* 74 (1977), 3–40.
ASTON, T. H., and Faith, Rosamund, 'The Endowments of the University and Colleges to c.1348', in J. I. Catto (ed.), *History of the University of Oxford* (Oxford, 1984), i. 265–309.
AUBENAS, R., *Étude sur le notariat provençal au Moyen Âge et sous l'Ancien Régime* (Aix-en-Provence, 1931).
BAGGE, SVERRE, GELTING, MICHAEL H., and LINDKVIST, THOMAS (eds.), *Feudalism: New Landscapes of Debate*, The Medieval Countryside 5 (Turnhout, 2011).
BAIGENT, FRANCIS JOSEPH, and MILLARD, JAMES ELWIN, *A History of the Ancient Town and Manor of Basingstoke* (London, 1889).
BAKER, J. H., *An Introduction to English Legal History*, 3rd edn. (London, 1990).
BAKER, J. H., *Why the History of English Law has not been Finished* [Inaugural Lecture] (Cambridge, 1999).
BALDWIN, JOHN W., *Masters, Princes and Merchants: The Social Views of Peter the Chanter and His Circle*, 2 vols. (Princeton, NJ, 1970).
BALDWIN, JOHN W., *The Government of Philip Augustus: Foundations of French Royal Power in the Middle Ages* (Berkeley, Calif., 1986).
BALDWIN, JOHN W., 'Paris et Rome en 1215: Les Réformes du IVe Concile de Latran', *Journal des Savants* 1 (1997), 99–124.
BALTEAU, J., et al. (eds.), *Dictionnaire de biographie française*, 19 vols. (Paris, 1933–).
BARBER, MALCOLM, *The Trial of the Templars*, 2nd edn. (Cambridge, 2006).
BARLOW, FRANK, 'Apulia, Simon of (d. 1223)', *ODNB*.
BARLOW, FRANK, *Thomas Becket* (London, 1986).
BARRATT, NICK, 'The Revenue of King John', *EHR* 111 (1996), 835–55.
BARRATT, NICK, 'English Revenue of Richard I', in S. D. Church (ed.), *King John: New Interpretations* (Woodbridge, 1999), 651–2, 656.
BARRATT, NICK, 'The Revenues of John and Philip Augustus Revisited', in S. D. Church (ed.), *King John: New Interpretations* (Woodbridge, 1999), 75–99.
BARRATT, NICK, 'The English Revenues of Richard I', *EHR* 116 (2001), 635–56.
BARRON, CAROLINE M., *London in the Later Middle Ages: Government and People 1200–1500* (Oxford, 2004).

BARRON, JOHN, 'Augustinian Canons and the University of Oxford: The Lost College of St George', in Caroline M. Barron and Jenny Stratford (eds.), *The Church and Learning in Later Medieval Society: Essays in Honour of R. B. Dobson* (Donington, 2002), 228–54.

BARROW, G. W. S., *Robert Bruce and the Community of the Realm in Scotland*, 4th edn. (Edinburgh, 2005).

BARTHÉLEMY, DOMINIQUE, 'The "Feudal Revolution"', *P&P* 152 (1996), 196–205.

BARTLETT, ROBERT, 'The Impact of Royal Government in the Ardennes: The Evidence of the 1247 *Enquête*', *Journal of Medieval History* 7 (1981), 83–96.

BARTLETT, ROBERT, *Trial by Fire and Water: The Medieval Judicial Ordeal* (Oxford, 1986).

BARTLETT, ROBERT, *Gerald of Wales: A Voice of the Middle Ages*, repr. edn. (Stroud, 2006).

BARTLETT, ROBERT, *England under the Norman and Angevin Kings, 1075–1225* (Oxford, 2000).

BARTLETT, ROBERT, 'Lords of "Pride and Plunder"', *New York Review of Books* 57/11 (24 June 2010), 47–50.

BAXTER, STEPHEN, 'Archbishop Wulfstan and the Administration of God's Property', in Matthew Townend (ed.), *Wulfstan, Archbishop of York. The Proceedings of the Second Alcuin Conference*, Studies in the Early Middle Ages 10 (Turnhout, 2004), 161–205.

BEARDWOOD, ALICE, 'The Trial of Walter Langton, Bishop of Lichfield, 1307–1312', *Transactions of the American Philosophical Society* NS 54/3 (1964), 1–45.

BEJCZY, ISTVÁN P., *The Cardinal Virtues in the Middle Ages: A Study in Moral Thought from the Fourth to the Fourteenth Century* (Leiden, 2011).

BENSON, ROBERT L., *The Bishop-elect: A Study in Medieval Ecclesiastical Office* (Princeton, NJ, 1968).

BENTHAM, JEREMY, *Panopticon; Or The Inspection House*, 2 vols. (Dublin and London, 1791).

BÉRENGER, AGNÈS, and LACHAUD, FRÉDÉRIQUE (eds.), *Hiérarchie des pouvoirs, délégation de pouvoir et responsabilité des administrateurs dans l'Antiquité et au Moyen Âge*, Centre de Recherche Universitaire Lorrain d'Histoire, Université de Lorraine—Site de Metz 46 (Metz, 2012).

BÉRIOU, NICOLE, 'Robert de Sorbon, maître en théologie, 1201–1274', in Marcel Viller et al. (eds.), *Dictionnaire de spiritualité ascétique et mystique: doctrine et histoire*, 17 vols. (Paris, 1937–95), xiii. cols. 816–24.

BERKHOFER III, ROBERT F., *Day of Reckoning: Power and Accountability in Medieval France* (Philadelphia, 2004).

BERKHOFER III, ROBERT F., COOPER, ALAN, and KOSTO, ADAM J. (eds.), *The Experience of Power in Medieval Europe, 950–1350* (Aldershot, 2005).

BESNIER, R., '«*Inquisitiones*» et «*Recognitiones*». Le Nouveau Système des preuves à l'époque des Coutumiers normands', *Revue historique de droit français et étranger* 28 (1950), 183–212.

BIANCHI, LUCA, 'Gli articoli censurati nel 1241/1244 e la loro influenza da Bonaventura a Gerson', in F. Morenzoni and J.-Y. Tilliette (eds.), *Autour de Guillaume d'Auvergne (†1249)* (Turnhout, 2005), 155–71.

BINSKI, PAUL, *Becket's Crown: Art and Imagination in Gothic England, 1170–1300* (New Haven, Conn., 2004).

BIRD, JESSALYNN, 'The Wheat and the Tares: Peter the Chanter's Circle and the *Fama*-based Inquest Against Heresy and Criminal Sins, *c*.1198–*c*.1235', in Uta-Renate Blumenthal, Kenneth Pennington, and Atria A. Larson (eds.), *Proceedings of the Twelfth International Congress of Medieval Canon Law: Washington, D.C. 1–7 August 2004*, Monumenta iuris canonici, Ser. C: Subsidia 13 (Vatican City, 2008), 763–856.

BISSON, T. N., *The Medieval Crown of Aragon: A Short History* (Oxford, 1986).

BISSON, T. N., 'Les Comptes des domaines au temps du Philippe Auguste: essai comparatif', in his *Medieval France and her Pyrenean Neighbours: Studies in Early Institutional History* (London, 1989), 265–83.

BISSON, T. N., 'The "Feudal Revolution"', *P&P* 142 (1994), 6–42.
BISSON, T. N. (ed.), *Cultures of Power: Lordship, Status and Process in Twelfth-century Europe* (Philadelphia, 1995).
BISSON, T. N., 'Medieval Lordship', *Speculum* 70 (1995), 743–59.
BISSON, T. N., 'The "Feudal Revolution": Reply', *P&P* 155 (1997), 208–25.
BISSON, T. N., *Tormented Voices: Power, Crisis and Humanity in Rural Catalonia, 1140–1200* (Cambridge, Mass., 1998).
BISSON, T. N., Review of R.I. Moore, *The First European Revolution*, *Speculum* 77 (2002), 1366–8.
BISSON, T. N., *The Crisis of the Twelfth Century: Power, Lordship, and the Origins of European Government* (Princeton, NJ, 2009).
BISSON, T. N., 'Author's response' to Theo Riches's review of *Crisis of the Twelfth Century*, in *Reviews in History* (2009) (<http://www.history.ac.uk/reviews/review/754, accessed February 2014>).
BLANSHEI, SARAH RUBIN, 'Crime and Law Enforcement in Medieval Bologna', *Journal of Social History* 16 (1982), 121–38.
BLANSHEI, SARAH RUBIN, *Politics and Justice in Late Medieval Bologna* (Leiden, 2010).
BLOCH, MARC, *The Historian's Craft*, trans. Peter Putnam (Manchester, 1954).
BLOCH, MARC, 'Pour une histoire comparée des sociétés européennes', in his *Mélanges historiques*, 2 vols. (Paris, 1963), i. 16–40.
BLOCH, MARC, *La Société féodale* (Paris, 1994 edn.).
BLOCH, MARC, and FEBVRE, LUCIEN, 'A nos lecteurs', *Annales d'histoire économique et sociale* 1 (1929), 1–2.
BOLTANSKI, LUC, *De la critique: Précis de sociologie de l'émancipation* (Paris, 2009).
BOORMAN, JULIA, 'The Sheriffs of Henry II and the Significance of 1170', in George Garnett and John Hudson (eds.), *Law and Government in Medieval England and Normandy: Essays in Honour of Sir James Holt* (Cambridge, 1994), 255–75.
BOQUET, DAMIEN, 'Le Gouvernement de soi et des autres et selon Bernard de Clairvaux. Lecture de la lettre 42, *De moribus et officio episcoporum*', in Claude Carozzi and Huguette Taviani-Carozzi (eds.), *Le Pouvoir au Moyen Âge* (Aix-en-Provence, 2005), 279–96.
BORGOLTE, MICHAEL, *Europa entdeckt seine Vielfalt, 1050–1250*, Handbuch der Geschichte Europas 3 (Stuttgart, 2002).
BOUCHARD, CONSTANCE BRITTAIN, *Spirituality and Administration: The Role of the Bishop in Twelfth-Century Auxerre* (Cambridge, Mass., 1979).
BOULET-SAUTEL, MARGUERITE, 'Le *Princeps* de Guillaume Durand', *Études d'histoire du droit canonique, dédiées à Gabriel Le Bras*, 2 vols. (Paris, 1965), ii. 803–13.
BOUREAU, ALAIN, 'How Law Came to the Monks: The Use of Law in English Society at the Beginning of the Thirteenth Century', *P&P* 167 (2000), 29–74.
BOUREAU, ALAIN, *La Loi du royaume: Les Moines, le droit et la construction de la nation anglaise (XIe–XIIIe siècles)* (Paris 2001).
BOUREAU, ALAIN, 'Droit naturel et abstraction judiciaire. Hypothèses sur la nature du droit médiéval', *Annales. Histoire, Sciences Sociales* 57 (2002), 1463–88.
BOUREAU, ALAIN, 'Introduction', in Claude Gauvard (ed.), *L'Enquête au Moyen Âge*, Collection École française de Rome 399 (Rome, 2008), 1–10.
BOUREAU, ALAIN, 'Une parole destructrice: La Diffamation. Richard de Mediavilla et le droit individuel au péché', in Julie Claustre, Olivier Mattéoni, and Nicolas Offenstadt (eds.), *Un Moyen Age pour aujourd'hui: Mélanges offerts à Claude Gauvard* (Paris, 2010), 306–14.
BOURDIEU, PIERRE, *Le Sens pratique* (Paris, 1980).
BOURGAIN, PASCALE, and HUBERT, MARIE-CLOTILDE, *Le Latin médiéval*, L'Atelier du médiéviste 10 (Turnhout, 2005).

BOUTOULLE, FRÉDÉRIC, 'L'Enquête de 1236–1237 en Bordelais', in Thierry Pécout (ed.), *Quand gouverner c'est enquêter* (Paris, 2010), 117–31.
BRADLEY, HENRY, rev. JOHN HUDSON, 'Buckland, Hugh of (d. 1116 x 19)', *ODNB*.
BRAND, PAUL A., 'Edward I and the Judges: The "State Trials" of 1289–93', *TCE* 1 (1986), 31–40.
BRAND, PAUL, *The Origins of the English Legal Profession* (Oxford, 1992).
BRAND, PAUL, 'Ethical Standards for Royal Justices in England, c.1175–1307', *University of Chicago Law School Roundtable* 8 (2001), 239–79.
BRAND, PAUL, *Kings, Barons and Justices: The Making and Enforcement of Legislation in Thirteenth-Century England* (Cambridge, 2003).
BRAND, PAUL, 'Stewards, Bailiffs and the Emerging Legal Profession' in Ralph Evans (ed.), *Lordship and Learning: Studies in Memory of Trevor Aston* (Woodbridge, 2004), 139–53.
BRAND, PAUL, 'The English Medieval Common Law (to c.1307) as a System of National Institutions and Legal Rules: Creation and Functioning', in Paul Dresch and Hannah Skoda (eds.), *Legalism: Anthropology and History* (Oxford, 2012), 173–96.
BRAND, PAUL, 'Carleton, William (c.1250–1311)', *ODNB*.
BRAND, PAUL, 'Lovetot, Sir John de (b. in or before 1236, d. 1294)', rev. *ODNB*.
BREMOND, CLAUDE, LE GOFF, JACQUES, and SCHMITT, JEAN-CLAUDE, *L'Exemplum*', *TSMAO* 40 (1982).
BRENTANO, ROBERT, *Two Churches: England and Italy in the Thirteenth Century*, new edn. (Berkeley, Calif., 1988).
BRITNELL, RICHARD (ed.), *The Winchester Pipe Rolls and Medieval English Society* (Woodbridge, 2003).
BROOKE, ROSALIND B., *Early Franciscan Government: Elias to Bonaventure* (Cambridge, 1959).
BROOKE, ROSALIND B., *The Image of St Francis: Responses to Sainthood in the Thirteenth Century* (Cambridge, 2006).
BROWN, PETER, *The World of Late Antiquity: From Marcus Aurelius to Muhammad* (London, 1971).
BROWN, PETER, *Through the Eye of a Needle: Wealth, the Fall of Rome, and the Making of Christianity in the West, 350–550 AD* (Princeton, NJ, 2012).
BRUNDAGE, JAMES A., *Law, Sex, and Christian Society in Medieval Europe* (Chicago, 1987).
BRUNDAGE, JAMES A., *Medieval Canon Law* (Harlow, 1995).
BRUNDAGE, JAMES A., *The Medieval Origins of the Legal Profession: Canonists, Civilians, and Courts* (Chicago, 2008).
BUC, PHILIPPE, *L'Ambiguïté du livre: Prince, pouvoir et peuple dans les commentaires de la Bible au Moyen Âge* (Paris, 1994).
BUCKLAND, W. W., rev. PETER STEIN, *A Textbook of Roman Law from Augustus to Justinian*, 3rd edn. (Cambridge, 1963).
BÜHLER-REIMANN, THEODOR, '*Enquête—Inquesta—Inquisitio*', *ZRG Kan. Abt.* 61 (1975), 53–62.
BURGER, MICHAEL, 'The Date and Authorship of Robert Grosseteste's Rules', *Historical Research* 74 (2001), 106–16.
BURR, DAVID, *The Spiritual Franciscans: From Protest to Persecution in the Century after St Francis* (University Park, Pa., 2001).
BURT, CAROLINE, 'The Demise of the General Eyre in the Reign of Edward I', *EHR* 120 (2005), 1–14.
BURT, CAROLINE, *Edward I and the Governance of England, 1272–1307* (Cambridge, 2013).

CAENEGEM, R. C. VAN, 'L'Histoire du droit et la chronologie. Réflexions sur la formation du «Common Law» et la procédure romano-canonique', in *Études d'histoire du droit canonique dédiées à Gabriel Le Bras*, 2 vols. (Paris, 1965), ii. 1459–65.

CAENEGEM, R. C. VAN, 'History of European Civil Procedure', *International Encyclopedia of International Law*, XVI.2 (Tübingen, 1973).

CAENEGEM, R. C. VAN, *The Birth of the English Common Law*, 2nd edn. (Cambridge, 1988).

CAENEGEM, R. C. VAN, 'Public Prosecution of Crime in Twelfth-Century England', in his *Legal History: A European Perspective* (London, 1991), 1–36.

CAENEGEM, R. C. VAN, 'Criminal Law in England and Flanders under King Henry II and Count Philip of Alsace', in his *Legal History: A European Perspective* (London, 1991), 37–60.

CAM, HELEN M., *Studies in the Hundred Rolls: Some Aspects of Thirteenth-century Administration*, Oxford Studies in Social and Legal History 6 (Oxford, 1921).

CAM, HELEN, M., *The Hundred and the Hundred Rolls: An Outline of Local Government in Medieval England* (London, 1930).

CAMMAROSANO, PAOLO, 'L'Éloquence laïque dans l'Italie communale (fin du XIIe–XIVe siècle)', *Bibliothèque de l'École des Chartes* 158 (2000), 431–42.

CAMPBELL, B. M. S., *English Seignorial Agriculture, 1250–1450*, Cambridge Studies in Historical Geography 31 (Cambridge, 2000).

CANNON, JOANNA, *Religious Poverty, Visual Riches: Art in the Dominican Churches of Central Italy in the Thirteenth and Fourteenth Centuries* (New Haven, Conn., 2013).

CANTEAUT, OLIVIER, 'Le Juge et le financier: Les Enquêteurs-réformateurs des derniers Capétiens (1314–1328)', in Claude Gauvard (ed.), *L'Enquête au Moyen Âge* (Rome, 2008), 269–318.

CARAWAN, EDWIN M., '"Eisangelia" and "Euthyna": The Trials of Miltiades, Themistocles and Cimon', *Greek, Roman and Byzantine Studies* 28 (1987), 167–208.

CAROLUS-BARRÉ, LOUIS, 'La Grande Ordonnance de 1254 sur la réforme de l'administration et la police du royaume', in *Septième centenaire de la mort de Saint Louis: actes des colloques de Royaumont et de Paris, 21–27 mai 1970* (Paris, 1976), 85–96.

CARPENTER, D. A., 'The Decline of the Curial Sheriff in England 1194–1258', *EHR* 91 (1976), 1–32.

CARPENTER, D. A., *The Minority of Henry III* (London, 1990).

CARPENTER, D. A., *The Reign of Henry III* (London, 1996).

CARPENTER, D. A., 'Matthew Paris and Henry III's Speech at the Exchequer in October 1256', in his *The Reign of Henry III* (London, 1996), 137–50.

CARPENTER, D. A., 'St Thomas Cantilupe: His Political Career', in his *The Reign of Henry III* (London, 1996), 293–307.

CARPENTER, D. A., 'Abbot Ralph of Coggeshall's Account of the Last Years of King Richard and the First Years of King John', *EHR* 113 (1998), 1210–30.

CARPENTER, D. A., 'The Second Century of English Feudalism', *P&P* 168 (2000), 30–71.

CARPENTER, D. A., *The Struggle for Mastery: Britain 1066–1284* (London, 2003).

CARPENTER, D. A., 'Archbishop Langton and Magna Carta: His Contribution, His Doubts and His Hypocrisy', *EHR* 126 (2011), 1042–65.

CARPENTER, D. A., 'Montfort, Peter de (c.1205–1265),' *ODNB*.

CASSIDY, RICHARD, '*Adventus Vicecomitum* and the Financial Crisis of Henry III's Reign, 1250–1272', *EHR* 126 (2011), 614–27.

CASSIDY, RICHARD, 'The 1259 Pipe Roll', 2 vols. (Ph.D. thesis, University of London, 2012).

CASSIDY, RICHARD, '*Recorda splendidissima*: The Use of Pipe Rolls in the Thirteenth Century', *Historical Research* 85 (2012), 1–12.

CASSIDY, RICHARD, 'William Heron, "Hammer of the Poor, Persecutor of the Religious", Sheriff of Northumberland, 1246–1258', *Northern History* 50 (2013), 9–19.

CASSIDY, RICHARD, 'Bad Sheriffs, Custodial Sheriffs, and Control of the Counties', *TCE* 15 (forthcoming 2015).

Catalogue général des manuscrits des bibliothèques publiques des départements, 7 vols. (Paris, 1849–85).

CATTO, J. I., 'Andrew Horn: Law and History in Fourteenth Century England', in R. H. C. Davis, J. M. Wallace-Hadrill with R. J. A. I. Catto, and M. H. Keen (eds.), *The Writing of History in the Middle Ages: Essays Presented to Richard William Southern* (Oxford, 1981), 367–91.

CATTO, J. I. (ed.), *The History of the University of Oxford*, i. *The Early Oxford Schools* (Oxford, 1984).

CATTO, J. I., 'The Triumph of the Hall in Fifteenth Century Oxford', in Ralph Evans (ed.), *Lordship and Learning: Studies in Memory of Trevor Aston* (Woodbridge, 2004), 209–23.

CATTO, J. I., 'Hartlepool, Hugh of (*c*.1245–1302)', *ODNB*.

CATTO, J. I., 'Horn, Andrew (*c*.1275–1328)', *ODNB*.

CHENEY, C. R., *From Becket to Langton: English Church Government 1170–1213* (Manchester, 1956).

CHENEY, C. R., *Hubert Walter* (London, 1967).

CHENEY, C. R., *Notaries Public in England in the Thirteenth and Fourteenth Centuries* (Oxford, 1972).

CHENEY, C. R., 'Statute-making in the Thirteenth Century', in his *Medieval Texts and Studies* (Oxford, 1973), 138–57.

CHENEY, C. R., 'Letters of Pope Innocent III', in his *Medieval Texts and Studies* (Oxford, 1973), 16–38.

CHENEY, C. R. (ed.), rev. MICHAEL JONES, *A Handbook of Dates for Students of British History*, Royal Historical Society Guides and Handbooks 4 (Cambridge, 2000).

CHEYETTE, FREDRIC L., '"Suum cuique tribuere"', *French Historical Studies* 6 (1970), 287–99.

CHIFFOLEAU, JACQUES, 'Saint Louis, Frédéric II et les constructions institutionelles du XIIIe siècle', *Médiévales* 34 (1998), 13–23.

CHIFFOLEAU, JACQUES, 'Dire l'indicible. Remarques sur la catégorie du *nefandum* du XIIe au XVe siècle', *Annales. Économies, Sociétés, Civilisations* 45 (1990), 289–324.

CHIFFOLEAU, JACQUES, '«*Ecclesia de occultis non iudicat*»? L'Église, le secret, l'occulte du XIIe au XIVe siècle', in *Il Segreto, The Secret*, Micrologus 14 (Florence, 2006), 359–481.

CLANCHY, M. T., 'Did Henry III Have a Policy?', *History* 53 (1968), 203–16.

CLANCHY, M. T., 'Remembering the Past and the Good Old Law', *History* 55 (1970), 165–76.

CLANCHY, M. T., 'Law, Government, and Society in Medieval England', *History* 59 (1974), 73–8.

CLANCHY, M. T., '*Moderni* in Education and Government in England', *Speculum* 50 (1975), 671–88.

CLANCHY, M. T., 'A Medieval Realist: Interpreting the Rules at Barnwell Priory, Cambridge', in Elspeth Attwooll (ed.), *Perspectives in Jurisprudence* (Glasgow, 1977), 176–94.

CLANCHY, M. T., Review of S. F. C. Milsom, *Historical Foundations of the Common Law*, *Modern Law Review* 44 (1981), 597–600.

CLANCHY, M. T., 'Law and Love in the Middle Ages', in John Bossy (ed.), *Disputes and Settlements: Law and Human Relations in the West* (Cambridge 1983), 47–67.

CLANCHY, M. T., *Abelard: A Medieval Life* (Oxford, 1997).

CLANCHY, M. T., *England and its Rulers, 1066–1307*, 3rd edn. (Oxford, 2006).

CLANCHY, M. T., *From Memory to Written Record: England 1066–1307*, 3rd edn. (Chichester, 2013).
COBBAN, ALAN, 'Medieval Student Power', *P&P* 53 (1971), 28–66.
COBBAN, ALAN B., *The Medieval English Universities: Oxford and Cambridge to c.1500* (Aldershot, 1988).
COBBAN, ALAN, *English University Life in the Middle Ages* (London, 1999).
COKAYNE, G. E. C. et al. (eds.), *The Complete Peerage of England, Scotland, Ireland, Great Britain and the United Kingdom, Extant, Extinct or Dormant*, new edn., 14 vols. (London, 1910–59).
CONDREN, CONAL, *Argument and Authority in Early Modern England: The Presupposition of Oaths and Offices* (Cambridge, 2006).
CONSTABLE, GILES, 'The Structure of Medieval Society According to the *Dictatores* of the Twelfth Century', in Kenneth Pennington and Robert Somerville (eds.), *Law, Church and Society: Essays in Honour of Stephan Kuttner* (Philadelphia, 1977), 253–67.
CONSTABLE, GILES, *Three Studies in Medieval Religious and Social Thought* (Cambridge, 1995).
COOK, MICHAEL, *Commanding Right and Forbidding Wrong in Islamic Thought* (Cambridge, 2010).
CORTESE, ENNIO, *La norma giuridica: spunti teorici nel diritto comune classico*, 2 vols. (Milan, 1962–4).
COURTENAY, WILLIAM J., *Parisian Scholars in the Early Fourteenth Century: A Social Portrait* (Cambridge, 1999).
COVILLE, ALEXANDRE, *Recherches sur l'histoire de Lyon du Vme siècle au IXme siècle, 450–800* (Paris, 1928).
COX, A. D. M., 'Who was William of Durham?', *University College Record* 8 (1981), 115–23.
COX, GARY W., 'War, Moral Hazard, and Ministerial Responsibility: England after the Glorious Revolution', *Journal of Economic History* 71 (2011),133–61.
CROOK, DAVID, *Records of the General Eyre*, Public Record Office Handbooks 20 (London, 1982).
CROOK, DAVID, 'Freedom, Villeinage and Legal Process: The Dispute between the Abbot of Burton and his Tenants of Mickleover, 1280', *Nottingham Medieval Studies* 44 (2000), 123–40.
DAGRON, GILBERT, *Emperor and Priest: The Imperial Office in Byzantium*, trans. Jean Birrell (Cambridge, 2003).
DAHYOT-DOLIVET, J., 'La Procédure pénale d'office en droit romain', *Apollinaris* 41 (1968), 89–105.
DAHYOT-DOLIVET, J., 'La Procédure judiciaire d'office dans l'église jusqu'à l'avènement du Pape Innocent III', *Apollinaris* 41 (1968), 443–55.
DARLING, LINDA T., *A History of Social Justice and Political Power in the Middle East: the Circle of Justice from Mesopotamia to Globalization* (Abingdon, 2013).
DARWALL-SMITH, ROBIN, 'Oxford and Cambridge College Histories: An Endangered Genre?', *History of Universities* 22.1 (2007), 241–49.
DARWALL-SMITH, ROBIN, *A History of University College, Oxford* (Oxford, 2008).
DAVIES, JOHN, 'Accounts and Accountability in Classical Athens', in Robin Osborne and Simon Hornblower (eds.), *Ritual, Finance, Politics: Athenian Democratic Accounts Presented to David Lewis* (Oxford, 1994), 201–12.
DAVIES, R. R., 'The State: The Tyranny of a Concept?', *Journal of Historical Sociology* 16 (2003), 280–300.
DAVIES, WENDY, 'Judges and Judging: Truth and Justice in Northern Iberia on the Eve of the Millennium', *Journal of Medieval History* 36 (2010), 193–203.
DAVIES, WENDY, and FOURACRE, PAUL (eds.), *The Settlement of Disputes in Early Medieval Europe* (Cambridge, 1986).

DAVIES, WENDY, and FOURACRE, PAUL (eds.), *Property and Power in the Early Middle Ages* (Cambridge, 1995).

DAVIES, WENDY, and FOURACRE, PAUL (eds.), *The Languages of Gift in the Early Middle Ages* (Cambridge, 2010).

DAVIS, A. J., *The Holy Bureaucrat: Eudes Rigaud and Religious Reform in Thirteenth-century Normandy* (Ithaca, NY, 2006).

DAVIS, A. J., 'Preaching in Thirteenth-Century Hospitals', *Journal of Medieval History* 36 (2010), 72–89.

DAVIS, JENNIFER R., 'A Pattern for Power: Charlemagne's Delegation of Judicial Responsibilities', in Jennifer Davis and Michael M. McCormick (eds.), *The Long Morning of Medieval Europe: New Directions in Medieval Studies* (Aldershot, 2008), 235–46.

DAVIS, R. H. C., 'Domesday Book: Continental Parallels', in J. C. Holt (ed.), *Domesday Studies: Papers Read at the Novocentenary Conference of the Royal Historical Society and the Institute of British Geographers, Winchester 1986* (Woodbridge, 1987), 15–39.

DAVIS, VIRGINIA, 'The Making of English Collegiate Statutes in the Later Middle Ages', *History of Universities* 12 (1993), 1–23.

D'AVRAY, D. L., *The Preaching of the Friars: Sermons Diffused from Paris Before 1300* (Oxford, 1985).

D'AVRAY, D. L., *Rationalities in History: A Weberian Essay in Comparison* (Cambridge, 2010).

DEAN, TREVOR, and LOWE, KATE, 'Writing the History of Crime in the Italian Renaissance', in their (eds.), *Crime, Society and the Law in Renaissance Italy* (Cambridge, 1994), 1–15.

DEJOUX, MARIE, 'Mener une enquête générale, pratiques et méthodes: L'Exemple de la tournée ordonnée par Louis IX en Languedoc à l'hiver 1247-48', in Thierry Pécout (ed.), *Quand gouverner c'est enquêter* (Paris, 2010), 133–55.

DELISLE, LÉOPOLD, 'Etienne de Gallardon, clerc de la chancellerie de Philippe Auguste, chanoine de Bruges', *Bibliothèque de l'École des chartes* 60 (1899), 5–44.

DELISLE, LÉOPOLD, and PASSY, LOUIS (eds.), *Mémoires et notes de M. Auguste Le Prévost pour servir à l'histoire du département de l'Eure*, 3 vols. (Evreux, 1862–9).

DENHOLM-YOUNG, N., *Seignorial Administration in England* (London, 1937).

DENHOLM-YOUNG, N., 'The "Paper Constitution" Attributed to 1244', *EHR* 232 (1943), 401–23.

DENLEY, PETER, 'Recent Studies on Italian Universities of the Middle Ages and Renaissance', *History of Universities* 1 (1981), 193–205.

DENLEY, PETER, *Commune and Studio in Late Medieval and Renaissance Siena* (Bologna, 2006).

DENTON, JEFFREY H., *Robert Winchelsey and the Crown, 1294–1313: A Study in the Defence of Ecclesiastical Liberty* (Cambridge, 1980).

Dictionnaire de biographie française, ed. J. Balteau et al., 19 vols. (Paris, 1933–).

DIONYSIA VON DORNUM, DEIRDRE, 'The Straight and the Crooked: Legal Accountability in Ancient Greece', *Columbia Law Review* 97 (1997), 1483–518.

Dizionario biografico degli italiani, 71 vols. (Rome, 1960–).

DOHERTY, HUGH, 'Robert de Vaux and Roger de Stuteville, Sheriffs of Cumberland and Northumberland 1170-1185', *Anglo-Norman Studies* 28 (2006), 65–102.

DONAHUE JR., CHARLES, 'Roman Canon Law in the Medieval English Church: Stubbs vs. Maitland Re-Examined after 75 Years in the Light of Some Records from the Church Courts', *Michigan Law Review* 72 (1974), 647–716.

DONAHUE JR., CHARLES, *Why the History of Canon Law is not Written*, SS Lecture (London, 1986).
DOSSAT, YVES, 'Inquisiteurs ou enquêteurs? À propos d'un texte', *Bulletin philologique et historique* (1957), 105–13.
DOUGLAS, MARY, *How Institutions Think* (Syracuse, 1986).
DOUGLAS, MARY, *Thought Styles* (London, 1996).
DOUGLAS, MARY, *Natural Symbols: Explorations in Cosmology*, 2nd edn. (London, 2003).
DOUGLAS, MARY 'A Feeling for Hierarchy', in James L. Heft (ed.), *Believing Scholars: Ten Catholic Intellectuals* (Fordham, NY, 2005), 94–120.
DOUIE, DECIMA L., *Archbishop Pecham* (Oxford, 1952).
DOUIE, DECIMA L., *Archbishop Geoffrey Plantagenet and the Chapter of York*, Borthwick Institute of Historical Research 18 (York, 1960).
DRESCH, PAUL, 'Legalism, Anthropology and History: A View from Part of Anthropology', in Paul Dresch and Hannah Skoda (eds.), *Legalism: Anthropology and History* (Oxford, 2012), 1–37.
DRESCH, PAUL, and SKODA, HANNAH (eds.), *Legalism: Anthropology and History* (Oxford, 2012).
DROSSBACH, GISELA (ed.), *Hospitaler in Mittelalter und Früher Neuheit. Frankreich, Deutschland und Italien. Eine vergleichende Geschichte; Hôpitaux au Moyen Âge et aux temps modernes: France, Allemagne et Italie: une histoire comparée*, Pariser Historische Studien 75 (Munich, 2007).
DUBY, GEORGE, *Les Trois Ordres ou l'imaginaire du féodalisme* (Paris, 1978).
DUGGAN, CHARLES, 'The Reception of Canon Law in England in the Later-Twelfth Century', in Stephan Kuttner and J. Joseph Ryan (eds.), *Proceedings of the Second International Congress of Medieval Canon Law: Boston College, 12–16 August 1963* (Vatican City, 1965), 359–90, repr. in Duggan, *Canon Law in Medieval England: The Becket Dispute and Decretal Collections* (London, 1982), #XI.
DUGGAN, CHARLES, *Decretals and the Creation of 'New Law' in the Twelfth Century: Judges, Judgements, Equity and Law* (Aldershot, 1998).
DUGGAN, CHARLES, 'Honorius (d. c.1213)', *ODNB*.
DUNBABIN, JEAN, 'Aristotle in the Schools', in Beryl Smalley (ed.), *Trends in Medieval Political Thought* (Oxford, 1965), 65–85.
DUNBABIN, JEAN, 'Robert Grosseteste as Translator, Transmitter, and Commentator: The "Nicomachean Ethics"', *Traditio* 28 (1972), 460–72.
DUNBABIN, JEAN, 'The Reception and Interpretation of Aristotle's Politics', in Norman Kretzmann, Anthony Kenny, and Jan Pinborg with Eleanore Stump (eds.), *The Cambridge History of Later Medieval Philosophy: From the Rediscovery of Aristotle to the Disintegration of Scholasticism* (Cambridge, 1982), 723–37.
DUNBABIN, JEAN, 'Government', in J. H. Burns (ed.), *The Cambridge History of Medieval Political Thought, c.350–c.1450* (Cambridge, 1988), 477–519.
DUNBABIN, JEAN, 'Guido Vernani of Rimini's Commentary on Aristotle's Politics', *Traditio* 44 (1988), 373–88.
DUNBABIN, JEAN, *Charles I of Anjou: Power, Kingship and State-Making in Thirteenth-Century Europe* (London, 1998).
DUNBABIN, JEAN, *France in the Making, 843–1180*, 2nd rev. edn. (Oxford, 2000).
DUNBABIN, JEAN, 'Charles I of Anjou and the Development of Medieval Political Ideas', *Nottingham Medieval Studies* 45 (2001), 110–26.
DUNBABIN, JEAN, *The French in the Kingdom of Sicily, 1266–1305* (Cambridge, 2011).
DURLIAT, JEAN, 'De conlaboratu': faux rendements et vraie comptabilité à l'époque carolingienne', *Revue historique de droit français et étranger*, 4th ser. 56 (1978), 445–7.

DYER, CHRISTOPHER, *Making a Living in the Middle Ages: The People of Britain 850–1520* (London, 2003).
EDWARDS, KATHLEEN, 'Bishops and Learning in the Reign of Edward II', *Church Quarterly Review* 138 (1944), 57–86.
ELIAS, NORBERT, *The Civilizing Process: Sociogenetic and Psychogenetic Investigations*, trans. Edmund Jephcott, rev. edn. (Oxford, 2000).
EMDEN, A. B., *A Biographical Register of the University of Oxford to A.D. 1500*, 3 vols. (Oxford, 1957–9).
EMDEN, A. B., *An Oxford Hall in Medieval Times: Being the Early History of St. Edmund Hall*, rev. edn. (Oxford, 1968).
ESDERS, STEFAN, 'Die römischen Wurzeln der fiskalischen *inquisitio* der Karolingerzeit', in Claude Gauvard (ed.), *L'Enquête au Moyen Âge* (Rome, 2008), 13–28.
ESMEIN, A., *A History of Continental Criminal Procedure, with Special Reference to France*, trans. J. Simpson (London, 1914).
ESSID, YASSINE, *A Critique of the Origins of Islamic Economic Thought* (Leiden, 1995).
EVANS, G. R., *Law and Theology in the Middle Ages* (London, 2002).
FADEL, MOHAMMAD, 'Adjudication in the Mālikī Madhhab: A Study of Legal Process in Medieval Islamic Law', 2 vols. (Ph.D. thesis, University of Chicago, 1995).
FADEL, MOHAMMAD, 'Proof and Procedure in Islamic Law', in Stanley N. Katz (gen. ed.), *The Oxford International Encyclopedia of Legal History*, 6 vols. (Oxford, 2009), iv. 427–31.
FARMER, DAVID H., 'The Cult and Canonization of St Hugh', in Henry Mayr-Harting (ed.), *St Hugh of Lincoln: Lectures Delivered at Oxford and Lincoln to Celebrate the Eighth Centenary of St Hugh's Consecration as Bishop of Lincoln* (Oxford, 1987), 75–87.
FEINGOLD, MORDECHAI, 'Oxford and Cambridge College Histories: An Outdated Genre?', *History of Universities* 1 (1981), 207–13.
FELLER, LAURENT (ed.), *Contrôler les agents du pouvoir. Actes du colloque organisé par l'Équipe d'acceuil «Histoire Comparée des Pouvoirs» (EA 3350) à l'Université de Marne-la-Vallée, 30, 31 mai et 1ᵉʳ juin 2002* (Limoges, 2004).
FERM, OLLE, and HONEMANN, VOLKER (eds.), *Chess and Allegory in the Middle Ages* (Stockholm, 2005).
FERRUOLO, STEPHEN C., *The Origins of the University: The Schools of Paris and Their Critics, 1100–1215* (Stanford, Calif., 1985).
FERRUOLO, STEPHEN C., 'The Paris Statutes of 1215 Reconsidered', *History of Universities* 5 (1985), 1–14.
FICHTENAU, HEINRICH, *Living in the Tenth Century: Mentalities and Social Orders*, trans. P. J. Geary (Chicago, 1991).
FIREY, ABIGAIL, *A Contrite Heart: Prosecution and Redemption in the Carolingian Empire* (Leiden, 2009).
FISCHER, JOHN MARTIN, *My Way: Essays on Moral Responsibility* (Oxford, 2006).
FISCHER, JOHN MARTIN, and RAVIZZA, MARK, *Responsibility and Control: A Theory of Moral Responsibility* (Cambridge, 1998).
FLASCH, KURT, *Introduction à la philosophie médiévale*, trans. Janine de Bourgknecht (Paris, 1998).
FLETCHER, CHRISTOPHER, 'Morality and Office in Late Medieval England and France', *Fourteenth Century England* 5 (2008), 178–90.
FLICHE, AUGUSTIN, THOUZELLIER, CHRISTINE, and AZAIS, YVONNE, *Histoire de l'Église depuis les origines jusqu'à nos jours*, x. *La Chrétienté romaine (1198–1274)* (Paris, 1950).
FLOWER, C. T., *Introduction to the Curia Regis Rolls, 1199–1230*, SS 62 (London, 1944).

FLÜELER, CHRISTOPH, *Rezeption und Interpretation der aristotelischen Politica im späten Mittelalter*, Bochumer Studien zur Philosophie 19, 2 vols. (Amsterdam, 1992).

FOURACRE, PAUL, 'Carolingian Justice: The Rhetoric of Improvement and Contexts of Abuse', in *La giustizia nell'alto medioevo (secoli v–viii)*, Settimane di studio del Centro italiano di studi sull'alto medioevo 42.

FOURNIER, PAUL, *Les Officialités au Moyen Âge: Étude sur l'organisation, la compétence et la procédure des tribunaux ecclésiastiques ordinaires en France, de 1180 à 1328* (Paris, 1880).

FOWLER-MAGERL, LINDA, *Ordines iudiciarii and Libelli de ordine iudiciorum (from the Middle of the Twelfth to the End of the Fifteenth Century)*, TSMAO 63 (Turnhout, 1994).

FRAHER, RICHARD M., 'The Theoretical Justification for the New Criminal Law of the High Middle Ages: "rei publicae interest, ne crimina remaneant impunita"', *University of Illinois Law Review* 577 (1984), 577–95.

FRAHER, RICHARD M., 'Preventing Crime in the High Middle Ages: The Medieval Lawyers' Search for Deterrence', in James Ross Sweeney and Stanley Chodorow (eds.), *Popes, Teachers, and Canon Law in the Middle Ages* (Ithaca, NY, 1989), 212–33.

FRAHER, RICHARD M., 'IV Lateran's Revolution in Criminal Procedure: The Birth of *Inquisitio*, the End of Ordeals, and Innocent III's Vision of Ecclesiastical Politics', in Rosalio Iosepho Castillo Lara (ed.), *Studia in honorem Eminentissimi Cardinalis Alphonsi M. Stickler* (Rome, 1993), 97–111.

FRAME, ROBIN, 'Fitzgerald, Maurice [called Muiris Ruadh] (d. 1268)', *ODNB*.

FRANSEN, GÉRARD, and LEGENDRE, PIERRE, 'Rectifications et additions', *Revue historique de droit français et étranger* 44 (1966), 115–18 (*see also* WILLIAM LONGCHAMP).

FRIDENSON, PATRICK, 'Les Organisations, un nouvel objet', *Annales. Histoire, Sciences Sociales* 44 (1989), 1461–77.

FRÖHLICH, PIERRE, *Les Cités grecques et le contrôle des magistrats (IVe–Ier siècle avant J.-C.)* (Geneva, 2004).

GABRIEL, ASTRIK L., 'Motivation of the Founders of Medieval Colleges', in his *Garlandia: Studies in the History of the Medieval University* (Notre Dame, 1969), 211–23.

GANSHOF, FRANÇOIS LOUIS, and VERHULST, ADRIAAN, 'France, the Low Countries and Western Germany', in M. M. Postan (ed.), *The Cambridge Economic History of Europe*, i. *The Agrarian Life of the Middle Ages*, 2nd edn. (Cambridge, 1966), 291–339.

GARCÍA Y GARCÍA, ANTONIO, 'The Fourth Lateran Council and the Canonists', in Wilfried Hartmann and Kenneth Pennington (eds.), *The History of Medieval Canon Law in the Classical Period, 1140–1234: From Gratian to the Decretals of Pope Gregory IX* (Washington DC, 2008), 367–78.

GAUDEMET, JEAN, 'Patristique et Pastorale: La Contribution de Grégoire le Grand au «Miroir de l'Évêque» dans le Décret de Gratien', in *Études d'histoire du droit canonique dédiées à Gabriel Le Bras*, 2 vols. (Paris, 1965), i. 129–39.

GAUDEMET, JEAN, 'Charisme et droit: le domaine de l'évêque', *ZRG Kan. Abt.* 74 (1988), 44–70.

GAUDIOSI, MONICA M., 'The Influence of the Islamic Law of *Waqf* on the Development of the Trust in England: The Case of Merton College', *University of Pennsylvania Law Review* 136 (1988), 1231–61.

GAUVARD, CLAUDE (ed.), *L'Enquête au Moyen Âge*, Collection de l'École française de Rome 399 (Rome, 2008).

GAUVARD, CLAUDE, *'De grace especial': Crime, état et société en France à la fin du Moyen Âge* (Paris, 2010 edn.).

GENET, JEAN-PHILIPPE, 'Chambres des comptes des principautés et genèse de l'état moderne', in Philippe Contamine and Olivier Mattéoni (eds.), *La France des principautés: Les*

Chambres des comptes XIVe et XVe siècles. Colloque tenu aux Archives départementales de l'Allier, à Moulins-Yzeure, 6, 7, 8 avril 1995 (Paris, 1996), 267–79.
GEUSS, RAYMOND, *Philosophy and Real Politics* (Princeton, NJ, 2008).
GEUSS, RAYMOND, 'Moralism and Realpolitik', in his *Politics and the Imagination* (Princeton, NJ, 2010), 31–42.
GIBB, H. A. R., et al. (eds.), *Encyclopaedia of Islam*, 12 vols. (Leiden, 1960–2009).
GIBBS, MARION, and LANG, JANE, *Bishops and Reform 1215–1272: With Special Reference to the Lateran Council of 1215* (Oxford, 1934).
GILLINGHAM, JOHN, *Richard I* (New Haven, Conn., 1999).
GILLINGHAM, JOHN, *The Angevin Empire*, 2nd edn. (London, 2001).
GILLINGHAM, JOHN, 'The Historian as Judge: William of Newburgh and Hubert Walter', *EHR* 119 (2004), 1275–87.
GILMOUR-BRYSON, ANNE, 'Sodomy and the Knights Templar', *Journal of the History of Sexuality* 7 (1996), 151–83.
GIUSEPPI, M. S., 'The Wardrobe and Household Accounts of Bogo de Clare, A.D. 1284-6', *Archaeologia* 70 (1920), 1–56.
GLAUTIER, M. W. E., 'A Study in the Development of Accounting in Roman Times', *Revue internationale des droits de l'antiquité*, 3rd ser. 19 (1972), 311–43.
GLÉNISSON, JEAN, 'Les Enquêteurs-réformateurs de 1270 à 1328', in *Positions des thèses soutenues par les élèves de la promotion de 1946 pour obtenir le diplôme d'archiviste paléographe, École nationale des chartes* 98 (1946), 81–8.
GLÉNISSON, JEAN, 'Les Enquêtes administratives en Europe occidentale aux XIIIe et XIVe siècles', in Werner Paravicini and Karl Ferdinand Werner (eds.), *Histoire comparée de l'administration (IVe–XVIIIe siècles): Actes du XIVe Colloque historique franco-allemand, Tours, 27 mars–1er avril 1977*, Beihefte der Francia 9 (Munich, 1980), 17–25.
GLORIEUX, PALÉMON, *Aux origines de la Sorbonne*, i. *Robert de Sorbon*, ii. *Le Cartulaire*, 2 vols. (Paris, 1965–6).
GOERING, JOSEPH, 'Chobham, Thomas of (d. 1233 x 6)', *ODNB*.
GOLDIE, MARK, 'The Unacknowledged Republic: Officeholding in Early Modern England', in Tim Harris (ed.), *The Politics of the Excluded, c.1500–1800* (Basingstoke, 2001), 153–94.
GOODY, JACK, *The Domestication of the Savage Mind* (Cambridge, 1977).
GOROCHOV, NATHALIE, 'La Notion de pauvreté dans les statuts de collèges fondés à Paris de Louis IX à Philippe le Bel', in Jean Dufour and Henri Platelle (eds.), *Fondations et œuvres charitables au Moyen Âge* (Paris, 1999), 119–28.
GORSKI, RICHARD, *The Fourteenth-Century Sheriff: English Local Administration in the Late Middle Ages* (Woodbridge, 2003).
GOURON, ANDRÉ, 'Royal *Ordonnances* in Medieval France', in Antonio Padoa-Schioppa (ed.), *Legislation and Justice*, The Origins of the Modern State in Europe, 13th to 18th Centuries (Oxford, 1997), 57–71.
GRAHAM-LEIGH, ELAINE, 'Hirelings and Shepherds: Archbishop Berenguer of Narbonne (1191–1211) and the Ideal Bishop', *EHR* 116 (2001), 1083–102.
GRANSDEN, ANTONIA, 'A Democratic Movement in the Abbey of Bury St Edmunds in the Late Twelfth and Early Thirteenth Centuries', *JEH* 26 (1975), 25–39.
GRANSDEN, ANTONIA, *A History of the Abbey of Bury St Edmunds 1182–1256: Samson of Tottingham to Edmund of Walpole*, Studies in the History of Medieval Religion 31 (Woodbridge, 2007).
GREEN, JUDITH A., 'Praeclarum et Magnificum Antiquitatis Monumentum: The Earliest Surviving Pipe Roll', [*Bulletin of the Institute of*] *Historical Research* 55 (1982), 1–17.
GREEN, JUDITH A., *The Government of England under Henry I* (Cambridge, 1986).

GREEN, JUDITH A., *English Sheriffs to 1154*, Public Record Office Handbooks 24 (London, 1990).
GUREVICH, AARON, *The Origins of European Individualism*, trans. Katharine Judelson (Oxford, 1995).
HAGGER, MARK, 'A Pipe Roll for 25 Henry I', *EHR* 122 (2007), 133–140.
HAINES, ROY MARTIN, 'Ghent, Simon (*c.*1250–1315)', *ODNB*.
HAINES, ROY MARTIN, 'Langton, Walter (d. 1321)', *ODNB*.
HAINSWORTH, D. R., *Stewards, Lords and People: The Estate Steward and his World in Later Stuart England* (Cambridge, 1992).
HAMEL, CHRISTOPHER DE, *The Book: A History of the Bible* (London, 2001).
HAMPSHIRE, STUART, *Justice is Conflict* (Princeton, NJ, 2000).
HARDING, ALAN, 'Plaints and Bills in the History of English Law, Mainly in the Period 1250–1350', in Dafydd Jenkins (ed.), *Legal History Studies 1972*, (Cardiff, 1975), 65–86.
HARDING, ALAN, *Medieval Law and the Foundations of the State* (Oxford, 2002).
HARKINS, CONRAD, 'The Authorship of a Commentary on the Franciscan Rule Published Among the Works of St Bonaventure', *Franciscan Studies* 29 (1969), 157–248.
HARRIS, BRIAN E., 'King John and the Sheriffs' Farms', *EHR* 79 (1964), 532–42.
HARRISS, G. L., *King, Parliament and Public Finance in Medieval England to 1369* (Oxford, 1975).
HART, H. L. A., *The Concept of Law*, 2nd edn. (Oxford, 1994).
HARTLAND, BETH, '"To serve Well and Faithfully": The Agents of Aristocratic English Lordship in Leinster *c.*1272–*c.*1315', *Medieval Prosopography* 24 (2003), 195-246.
HARTLAND, BETH, 'English Lords in Late Thirteenth and Early Fourteenth Century Ireland: Roger Bigod and the de Clare lords of Thomond', *EHR* 122 (2007), 318–48.
HARTLAND, BETH, 'The Liberties of Ireland in the Reign of Edward I', in Michael Prestwich (ed.), *Liberties and Identities in the Medieval British Isles* (Woodbridge, 2008), 200–16.
HARTMANN, WILFRIED 'Discipulus non est super magistrum (Matth. 10, 24), Zur Rolle der Laien und der niedern Kleriker im Investiturstreit', in Hubert Mordek (ed.), *Papsttum, Kirche und Recht im Mittelalter: Festschrift für Horst Fuhrmann zum 65. Geburtstag*, (Tübingen, 1991), 187–200.
HARVEY, P. D. A., *A Medieval Oxfordshire Village: Cuxham, 1240–1400* (Oxford, 1965).
HARVEY, P. D. A., 'Agricultural Treatises and Manorial Accounting in Medieval England', *Agricultural History Review* 20 (1972), 170–82.
HARVEY, P. D. A., 'The Pipe Rolls and the Adoption of Desmesne Farming in England', *Economic History Review* NS 27 (1974), 345–59.
HARVEY, P. D. A., 'Initiative and Authority in Settlement Change', in Michael Aston, David Austin, and Christopher Dyer (eds.), *The Rural Settlements of Medieval England: Studies Dedicated to Maurice Beresford and John Hurst* (Oxford, 1989), 38–43.
HARVEY, P. D. A., 'Non-agrarian Activities in Twelfth Century English Estate Surveys', in Daniel Williams (ed.), *England in the Twelfth Century: Proceedings of the 1988 Harlaxton Symposium* (Woodbridge, 1990), 101–11.
HARVEY, P. D. A., '*Rectitudines Singularum Personarum* and *Gerefa*', *EHR* 426 (1993), 1–22.
HARVEY, P. D. A., 'Mid-Thirteenth Century Accounts from Bury St Edmunds Abbey', in Antonia Gransden (ed.), *Bury St. Edmunds: Medieval Art, Architecture, Archaeology, and Economy* (Leeds, 1998), 128–38.
HARVEY, P. D. A., *Manorial Records*, Archives and the User 5, rev. edn. (London, 1999).
HARVEY, P. D. A., 'The Manorial Reeve in Twelfth-century England', in Ralph Evans (ed.), *Lordship and Learning: Studies in Memory of Trevor Aston* (Woodbridge, 2004), 125–38.
HARVEY, SALLY, 'Domesday Book and its Predecessors', *EHR* 86 (1971), 753–73.

HARVEY, SALLY, 'Domesday Book and Anglo-Norman Governance', *TRHS* 5th ser. 25 (1975), 175–93.
HARVEY, SALLY, *Domesday: Book of Judgement* (Oxford, forthcoming 2014).
HASKINS, C. H., 'Henry II as a Patron of Literature', in A. G. Little and F. M. Powicke (eds.), *Essays in Medieval History Presented to Thomas Frederick Tout* (Manchester, 1925), 71–7.
HEINTSCHEL, DONALD EDWARD, *The Mediaeval Concept of an Ecclesiastical Office: An Analytical Study of the Concept of an Ecclesiastical Office in the Major Sources and Printed Commentaries from 1140–1300* (Washington, 1956).
HEISER, RICHARD, 'The Sheriffs of Richard I: Trends of Management as Seen in the Shrieval Appointments from 1189 to 1194', *Haskins Society Journal* 4 (1993), 109–22.
HEISER, RICHARD, 'Richard I and His Appointments to English Shrievalties', *EHR* 112 (1997), 1–19.
HELLEMANS, BABETTE, *La Bible moralisée: Une Œuvre à part entière, création, sémiotique et temporalité au XIII*ᵉ *siècle* (Turnhout, 2010).
HELMHOLZ, R. H., 'The Early History of the Grand Jury and the Canon Law', *University of Chicago Law Review* 50 (1983), 613–27.
HELMHOLZ, R. H., 'Crime, Compurgation and the Courts of the Medieval Church', *Law and History Review* 1 (1983), 1–26.
HELMHOLZ, R. H., *The Ius Commune in England: Four Studies* (Oxford, 2001).
HELMHOLZ, R. H., *The Oxford History of the Laws of England*, i. *The Canon Law and Ecclesiastical Jurisdiction from 597 to the 1640s* (Oxford, 2004).
HELMHOLZ, R. H., '*Scandalum* in the Medieval Canon Law and in the English Ecclesiastical Courts', *ZRG Kan. Abt.* 127 (2010), 258–74.
HERSHEY, ANDREW H., 'An Introduction to and Edition of the Hugh Bigod Eyre Rolls June 1258–February 1259: P.R.O. Just 1/1187 & Just 1/873', 2 vols. (Ph.D. thesis, University of London, 1991).
HERSHEY, ANDREW H., 'Success or Failure? Hugh Bigod and Judicial Reform during the Baronial Movement, June 1258–February 1259', *TCE* 5 (1995), 65–87.
HERSHEY, ANDREW H., 'Justice and Bureaucracy: The English Royal Writ and "1258"', *EHR* 113 (1998), 829–51.
HERSHEY, ANDREW H., 'The Rise and Fall of William de Bussey: A Mid-Thirteenth Century Steward', *Nottingham Medieval Studies* 44 (2000), 104–21.
HIGHFIELD, J. R. L., 'The Early Colleges', in J. I. Catto (ed.), *The History of the University of Oxford*, i. *The Early Oxford Schools* (Oxford, 1984), 225–63.
HIRTE, MARKUS, *Papst Innozenz III., das IV. Lateranum und die Strafverfahren gegen Kleriker: Eine registergestützte Untersuchung zur Entwicklung der Verfahrensarten zwischen 1198 und 1216*, Rothenburger Gespräche zur Strafrechtsgeschichte 5 (Tübingen, 2005).
HOLFORD, M. L., 'Under-sheriffs, the State, and Local Society, *c.*1300–1340: A Preliminary Survey', in Chris Given-Wilson, Ann Kettle, and Len Scales (eds.), *War, Government, and Aristocracy in the British Isles, c.1150-1500: Essays in Honour of Michael Prestwich* (Woodbridge, 2008), 55–68.
HOLLISTER, C. WARREN, and BALDWIN, JOHN W., 'The Rise of Administrative Kingship: Henry I and Philip Augustus', *AHR* 83 (1978), 867–905.
HOLT, J. C., 'Philip Mark and the Shrievalty of Nottinghamshire and Derbyshire in the Early Thirteenth Century', *Transactions of the Thoroton Society of Nottinghamshire* 56 (1952), 8–24.
HOLT, J. C., *The Northerners: A Study in the Reign of King John*, rev. edn. (Oxford, 1992).
HOLT, J. C., *Magna Carta*, 2nd edn. (Cambridge, 1992).

HOLTZMANN, WALTHER, *Studies in the Collections of Twelfth-Century Decretals*, ed. C. R. Cheney and Mary G. Cheney, Monumenta iuris canonici, Ser. B: Corpus collectionum 3 (Vatican City, 1979).

HOPE, AARON, 'Hireling Shepherds: English Bishops and their Deputies c. 1186 to c. 1323' (UCL Ph.D. thesis, University College London, 2013).

HORNBLOWER, SIMON, and SPAWFORTH, ANTHONY (eds.), *The Oxford Classical Dictionary*, 3rd edn. (Oxford, 1996).

HOSKING, GEOFFREY, *Rulers and Victims: The Russians in the Soviet Union* (Cambridge, Mass., 2006).

HOWE, RICHARD HERBERT, 'Max Weber's Elective Affinities: Sociology Within the Bounds of Pure Reason', *American Journal of Sociology* 84 (1978), 366–85.

HOUBEN, HUBERT, *Roger II of Sicily: A Ruler between East and West*, trans. Graham A. Loud and Diane Milburn (Cambridge, 2002).

HUDSON, JOHN, 'Administration, Family and Perceptions of the Past in Late Twelfth-Century England: Richard FitzNigel and the Dialogue of the Exchequer', in Paul Magdalino (ed.), *The Perception of the Past in Twelfth Century Europe* (London, 1992), 75–98.

HUDSON, JOHN, *The Formation of the English Common Law: Law and Society in England from the Norman Conquest to Magna Carta* (London, 1996).

HUDSON, JOHN, 'Court Cases and Legal Arguments in England, c.1066-1166', *TRHS* 6th ser. 10 (2000), 91–115.

HUDSON, JOHN, 'Magna Carta, the *Ius Commune*, and English Common Law', in J. S. Loengard (ed.), *Magna Carta and the England of King John* (Woodbridge, 2010), 99–119.

HUDSON, JOHN, 'From the *Leges* to *Glanvill*: Legal Expertise and Legal Reasoning', in Stefan Jurasinski, Andrew Rabin, and Lisi Oliver (eds.), *English Law before Magna Carta: Felix Liebermann and Die Gesetze der Angelsachsen* (Leiden, 2010), 221–49.

HUDSON, JOHN, *The Oxford History of the Laws of England*, ii. *871–1216* (Oxford, 2012).

HUDSON, JOHN, rev. HENRY BRADLEY, 'Buckland, Hugh of (d. 1116 x 19)', *ODNB*.

HUNNISETT, R. F., *The Medieval Coroner* (Cambridge, 1961).

HUSCROFT, RICHARD, 'Robert Burnell and the Government of England, 1270–1274', *TCE* 8 (2001), 59–70.

HYAMS, PAUL, 'Due Process versus the Maintenance of Order in European Law: The Contribution of the *ius commune*', in Peter Coss (ed.), *The Moral World of the Law* (Cambridge, 2000), 62–90.

IMBACH, RUEDI, *Dante, la philosophie et les laïcs: initiations à la philosophie médiévale*, Vestigia 21 (Fribourg, 1996).

INGLESE, G. 'Latini, Brunetto', *DBI*.

THE INQUIRIES ACT 2005 (London, 2005).

ISENMANN, MORITZ, *Legalität und Herrschaftskontrolle (1200–1600): Eine vergleichende Studie zum Syndikatsprozess: Florenz, Kastilien und Valencia* (Frankfurt, 2010).

JACOB, E. F., *Studies in the Period of Baronial Reform and Rebellion, 1258–1267*, Oxford Studies in Social and Legal History 8 (Oxford, 1925).

JAMME, ARMAND, and PONCET, OLIVIER (eds.), *Offices et papauté (XIVe–XVIIe siècle): charges, hommes, destins*, Collection de l'École française de Rome 334 (Rome, 2005).

JAMME, ARMAND, and PONCET, OLIVIER (eds.), *Offices, écrit et papauté (XIIIe–XVIIe siècle)*, Collection École française de Rome 386 (Rome, 2007).

JEROUSCHEK, GÜNTER, '*Ne crimina remaneant impunita*. Auf daß Verbrechen nicht ungestraft bleiben: Überlegungen zur Begründung öffentlicher Strafverfolgung im Mittelalter', *ZRG Kan. Abt.* 89 (2007), 323–37.

JOBSON, ADRIAN, 'The Oxfordshire Eyre Roll of 1261', 3 vols. (Ph.D. thesis, University of London, 2006).

JOBSON, ADRIAN, 'John of Crakehall: The "Forgotten" Baronial Treasurer, 1258–1260', *TCE* 13 (2011).

JOHANSEN, BABER, 'Signs as Evidence: The Doctrine of Ibn Taymiyya (1263–1328) and Ibn Qayyim al-Jawziyya (d. 1351) on Proof', *Islamic Law and Society* 9.2, Evidence in Islamic Law (2002), 168–93.

JOHANSEN, BABER, 'A Perfect Law in an Imperfect Society: Ibn Taymiyya's Concept of "Governance in the Name of the Sacred Law"', in P. Bearman, W. Heinrichs, and B. G. Weiss (eds.), *The Law Applied: Contextualizing the Islamic Shari'a* (London, 2008), 259–94.

JOLLIFFE, J. E. A., *Angevin Kingship*, 2nd edn. (London, 1963).

JONES, JOHN, *Balliol College, A History*, 2nd edn. (Oxford, 1997).

JONES, PHILIP, *The Italian City-State: From Commune to Signoria* (Oxford, 1997).

JONG, MAYKE DE, *The Penitential State: Authority and Atonement in the Age of Louis the Pious, 814–840* (Cambridge, 2009).

JORDAN, WILLIAM CHESTER, *Louis IX and the Challenge of the Crusade: A Study in Rulership* (Princeton, NJ, 1979).

JORDAN, WILLIAM CHESTER, 'Communal Administration in France, 1257–1270: Problems Discovered and Solutions Imposed', in his *Ideology and Royal Power in Medieval France: Kingship, Crusades and the Jews* (Aldershot, 2001), III, 292–313.

JORDAN, WILLIAM CHESTER, 'Anti-corruption Campaigns in Thirteenth-century Europe', *Journal of Medieval History* 35 (2009), 204–19.

JORDAN, WILLIAM CHESTER, *Men at the Center: Redemptive Governance under Louis IX* (Budapest, 2012).

JULAR PÉREZ-ALFARO, CRISTINA, *Los Adelantados y Merinos Mayores de León (siglos XIII–XV)* (León, 1990).

JULAR PÉREZ-ALFARO, CRISTINA, 'The King's Face on the Territory: Royal Officers, Discourse and Legitimating Practices in Thirteenth and Fourteenth Century Castile', in Isabel Alfonso, Hugh Kennedy, and Julia Escalona (eds.), *Building Legitimacy: Political Discourses and Forms of Legitimacy in Medieval Societies*, The Medieval Mediterranean 53 (Leiden, 2004), 107–37.

JUNOD, MARIE-CLAUDE, 'L'Enquête contre Aimon de Grandson, Evêque de Gènève (1227)', *Mémoires et documents publiés par la Société d'histoire et d'archéologie de Genève* 48 (1979), 1–182.

KANTOROWICZ, ERNST, H., *Kaiser Friedrich der Zweite* (Berlin, 1927).

KANTOROWICZ, ERNST, H., *The King's Two Bodies: A Study in Mediaeval Political Theology* (Princeton, NJ, 1957).

KARN, NICHOLAS, 'Secular Power and its Rewards in Dorset in the Late Eleventh and Early Twelfth Centuries', *Historical Research* 82 (2009), 2–16.

KARN, NICHOLAS, 'Rethinking the *Leges Henrici Primi*', in Stefan Jurasinski, Andrew Rabin, and Lisi Oliver (eds.), *English Law before Magna Carta: Felix Liebermann and Die Gesetze der Angelsachsen* (Leiden, 2010), 199–220.

KEATS-ROHAN, K. S. B., *Domesday Descendants: A Prosopography of Persons Occurring in English Documents 1066–1166*, ii. *Pipe Rolls to Cartae Baronum* (Woodbridge, 2002).

KELLY, HENRY ANSGAR, 'Inquisitorial Due process and the Status of Secret Crimes', in Stanley Chodorow (ed.), *Proceedings of the Eighth International Congress of Medieval Canon Law*, Monumenta iuris canonici, Ser. C: Subsidia 9 (Vatican City, 1992), 407–27, repr. in Kelly, *Inquisitions and Other Trial Procedures in the Medieval West* (Aldershot, 2001), no. II.

KEMPSHALL, M. S., *The Common Good in Late Medieval Political Thought* (Oxford, 1999).

KEMPSHALL, MATTHEW, *Rhetoric and the Writing of History, 400–1500* (Manchester, 2011).

KER, N. R., 'Liber Custumarum, and Other Manuscripts Formerly at the Guildhall', *The Guildhall Miscellany* 3 (1954), 37–45.

KER, N. R., *Medieval Manuscripts in British Libraries*, i. London, 4 vols. (Oxford, 1969).

KÉRY, LOTTE, 'Inquisitio—denunciatio—exceptio: Möglichkeiten der Verfahrenseinleitung im Dekretalenrecht', *ZRG Kan. Abt.* 87 (2001), 226–68.

KÉRY, LOTTE, 'Ein neues Kapitel in der Geschichte des kirchlichen Strafrechts: Die Systematisierungsbemühungen des Bernhard von Pavia (†1213)', in Wolfgang P. Müller and Mary E. Sommar (eds.), *Medieval Church Law and the Origins of the Western Legal Tradition: A Tribute to Kenneth Pennington* (Washington DC, 2006), 229–51.

KIBRE, PEARL, *The Nations in the Medieval Universities* (Cambridge, Mass., 1948).

KIECKHEFER, RICHARD, 'The Office of Inquisition and Medieval Heresy: The Transition from Personal to Institutional Jurisdiction', *Journal of Ecclesiastical History* 46 (1995), 36–61.

KING, ANTHONY, and CREWE, IVOR, *The Blunders of our Governments* (London, 2013).

KING, EDMUND, 'Estate Management and the Reform Movement', in W. M. Ormrod (ed.), *England in the Thirteenth Century: Proceedings of the 1989 Harlaxton Symposium*, Harlaxton Medieval Studies 1 (Stamford, 1991).

KING, EDMUND, *King Stephen* (New Haven, Conn., 2010).

KITTELL, ELLEN E., *From Ad Hoc to Routine: A Case Study in Medieval Bureaucracy* (Philadelphia, 1991).

KNOWLES, DAVID, *The Religious Orders in England*, 3 vols. (Cambridge, 1948–59).

KNOX, RONALD, 'Accusing Higher Up', *ZRG Kan. Abt.* 77 (1991), 1–31.

KOELBLE, THOMAS A., 'The New Institutionalism in Political Science and Sociology', *Comparative Politics* 27 (1995), 231–43.

KOSTO, ADAM J., 'What about Spain? Iberia in the Historiography of Medieval European Feudalism', in Sverre Bagge, Michael H. Gelting, and Thomas Lindkvist (eds.), *Feudalism: New Landscapes of Debate*, The Medieval Countryside 5 (Turnhout, 2011), 135–58.

KUTTNER, STEPHEN, and GARCÍA Y GARCÍA, ANTONIO, 'A New Eyewitness Account of the Fourth Lateran Council', *Traditio* 20 (1964), 115–78.

KUTTNER S., and RATHBONE, E., 'Anglo-Norman Canonists of the Twelfth Century', *Traditio* 7 (1949–51), 279–358 at 305–8; repr. with corrections in Kuttner, *Gratian and the Schools of Law 1140–1234* (London, 1983), #VIII.

LACEY, NICOLA, *A Life of H. L. A. Hart: The Nightmare and the Noble Dream* (Oxford, 2004).

LACHAUD, FRÉDÉRIQUE, 'La Notion d'office dans la littérature politique en France et en Angleterre, XIIe–XIIIe siècles', *Comptes rendus de l'Académie des Inscriptions et Belles-Lettres* (November–December 2009), 1543–70.

LACHAUD, FRÉDÉRIQUE, *L'Éthique du pouvoir au Moyen Âge: L'Office dans la culture politique (Angleterre, vers 1150–vers 1330)*, Bibliothèque d'histoire médiévale 3 (Paris, 2010).

LALOU, ÉLISABETH, 'La Chambre des comptes de Paris: sa mise en place et son fonctionnement (fin XIIIe–XIVe siècle)', in Olivier Contamine and Philippe Mattéoni (eds.), *La France des principautés* (Paris, 1996), 3–15.

LALOU, ÉLISABETH, 'L'Enquête au Moyen Âge', *Revue historique* 313 (2011), 145–53.

LANGLOIS, Ch.-V., 'Doléances recueillis par les enquêteurs de Saint Louis et des derniers Capètiens directs', *Revue historique* 92 (1906), 1–41.

LAWRENCE, C. H., 'The University in State and Church', in J. I. Catto (ed.), *History of the University of Oxford*, i. *The Early Oxford Schools* (Oxford, 1984), i. 97–150.

LAWLER, TRAUGOTT, 'Garland, John of (b. *c*.1195, d. in or after 1258)', *ODNB*.

LEA, H. C., *A History of the Inquisition of the Middle Ages*, 3 vols. (London, 1888).

LEFF, GORDON, *Paris and Oxford Universities in the Thirteenth and Fourteenth Centuries: An Institutional and Intellectual History* (New York, 1968).
LE GOFF, JACQUES, 'How Did the Medieval University Conceive of Itself?', in his *Time, Work, and Culture in the Middle Ages*, trans. A. Goldhammer (Chicago, 1980), 122–34.
LE GOFF JACQUES (ed.), *The Medieval World*, trans. Lydia G. Cochrane (London, 1990).
LE GOFF, JACQUES, *Saint Louis* (Paris, 1996).
LE GOFF, JACQUES, *Héros du Moyen Âge, le saint et le roi* (Paris, 2004).
LEMESLE, BRUNO, 'L'Enquête contre les épreuves: Les Enquêtes dans la région Angevine (XIIe–début XIIIe siècle)', in Claude Gauvard (ed.), *L'Enquête au Moyen Âge* (Paris, 2010), 41–74.
LEMESLE, BRUNO, 'Corriger les excès. L'Extension des infractions, des délits et des crimes, et les transformations de la procédure inquisitoire dans les lettres pontificales (milieu du XIIe siècle-fin du pontificat d'Innocent III)', *Revue historique* 313 (2011), 747–79.
LE NEVE, JOHN, rev. DIANA E. GREENWAY, *Fasti Ecclesiae Anglicanae 1066–1300*, i. *St Paul's London* (London, 1968).
LE NEVE, JOHN, rev. J. S. BARROW, *Fasti Ecclesiae Anglicanae 1066–1300*. viii. *Hereford* (London, 2002).
LEWIS, ANDREW, 'On Not Expecting the Spanish Inquisition: The Uses of Comparative Legal History', *Current Legal Problems* 57 (2004), 53–84.
LIERE, FRANS VAN, 'The Study of Canon Law and the Eclipse of the Lincoln Schools, 1175–1225', *History of Universities* 18.1 (2003), 1–13.
LEYSER, KARL, 'The German Aristocracy from the Ninth to the Early Twelfth Century: A Historical and Cultural Sketch', *P&P* 41 (1968), 25–53.
LIEBERMANN, F., *Einleitung in den Dialogus de Scaccario* (Göttingen, 1875).
LIH, LARS T., 'The Soviet Union and the Road to Communism', in Ronald Grigor Suny (ed.), *The Cambridge History of Russia*, iii. *The Twentieth Century* (Cambridge, 2006), 706–31.
LINEHAN, PETER, *Spain, 1157–1300: A Partible Inheritance* (Oxford, 2008).
List of Sheriffs for England and Wales: From the Earliest Times to A.D. 1831, Public Record Office, Lists and Indexes 9, repr. (New York, 1963).
LOVATT, MARIE, 'Geoffrey (1151?–1212), Archbishop of York', *ODNB*.
LOVATT, ROGER, 'The Triumph of the Colleges in Late Medieval Oxford and Cambridge: The Case of Peterhouse', *History of Universities* 14 (1998), 95–142.
LOWDEN, JOHN, *The Making of the Bibles moralisées*, 2 vols. (Philadelphia, 2000).
LÖWY, MICHAEL, 'Le Concept d'affinité élective chez Max Weber', *Archives de sciences sociales des religions* 49 (2004), 93–103.
LUCHITSKAYA, S. I., 'Chess as a Metaphor for Medieval Society', in Yelena Mazour-Matusevich and Alexandra S. Korros (eds.), *Saluting Aron Gurevich: Essays in History, Literature and Other Related Subject* (Leiden, 2010), 277–99.
LYDON, JAMES, 'The Years of Crisis, 1254–1315', and 'A Land of War', in Art Cosgrove (ed.), *A New History of Ireland*, ii. *Medieval Ireland 1169–1534* (Oxford, 1987), 179–204, 240–74.
LYON, BRYCE, and VERHULST, ADRIAAN, *Medieval Finance: A Comparison of Financial Institutions in Northwestern Europe* (Bruges, 1967).
MCCORMICK, MICHAEL, *Charlemagne's Survey of the Holy Land: Wealth, Personnel, and Buildings of a Mediterranean Church between Antiquity and the Middle Ages* (Washington DC, 2011).
MCFARLANE, K. B., *The Nobility of Later Medieval England: The Ford Lectures for 1953 and Related Studies* (Oxford, 1973).
MACINTYRE, ALASDAIR, *After Virtue: A Study in Moral Theory*, 2nd edn. (London, 1985).
MACINTYRE, ALASDAIR, *Whose Justice? Which Rationality?* (London, 1988).

MACINTYRE, ALASDAIR, *Three Rival Versions of Moral Enquiry: Encyclopaedia, Genealogy, and Tradition* (London, 1990).
MCKITTERICK, ROSAMUND, *Charlemagne: The Formation of a European Identity* (Cambridge, 2008).
MADDICOTT, J. R., *Thomas of Lancaster, 1307–1322: A Study in the Reign of Edward II* (Oxford, 1970).
MADDICOTT, J. R., 'Magna Carta and the Local Community', *P&P* 102 (1984), 25–65.
MADDICOTT, J. R., 'Edward I and the Lessons of Baronial Reform: Local Government, 1258–1280', *TCE* 1 (1986), 1–30.
MADDICOTT, J. R., *Simon de Montfort* (Cambridge, 1994).
MADDICOTT, J. R., '"1258" and "1297": Some Comparisons and Contrasts', *TCE* 9 (2003), 1–14.
MADDICOTT, J. R., *The Origins of the English Parliament, 924–1327* (Oxford, 2010).
MADDICOTT, JOHN, *Founders and Fellowship: The Early History of Exeter College, Oxford, 1314–1592* (Oxford, 2014).
MAILLOUX, ANNE, 'Pratiques administratives, définition des droits et fixation territoriale d'après l'enquête ordonnée par Robert sur les droits de l'évêque de Gap entre 1305 et 1309', in Jean-Paul Boyer, Anne Mailloux and Laure Verdon (eds.), *La Justice temporelle dans les territoires angevins aux XIIIe et XIVe siècles: théories et pratiques*, Collection de l'École française de Rome 354 (Rome, 2005), 249–62.
MAITLAND, FREDERIC WILLIAM, *Township and Borough* (Cambridge, 1898).
MAITLAND, FREDERIC WILLIAM, *Roman Canon Law in the Church of England: Six Essays* (London, 1898).
MAITLAND, FREDERIC WILLIAM, 'The History of the Register of Original Writs', in *The Collected Papers of Frederic William Maitland*, ed. H. A. L. Fisher, 3 vols. (Cambridge, 1911), ii. 110–73.
MAITLAND, FREDERIC WILLIAM, *The Forms of Action at Common Law* (Cambridge, 1954).
MANZALAOUI, MAHMOUD, 'The Pseudo-Aristotelian "Kitāb Sirr al-asrār". Facts and Problems', *Oriens* 23/4 (1970–1), 147–257.
MANZALAOUI, MAHMOUD, 'The *Secretum secretorum*: The Mediaeval European Version of "Kitāb Sirr al-Asrār"', *Bulletin of the Faculty of Art, Alexandria University* 15 (1961), 83–107.
MARENBON, JOHN, 'Ce que les historiens de la philosophie anglophones pourraient apprendre en lisant Kurt Flasch' (2005) (<http://www.trin.cam.ac.uk/show.php?dowid=200, accessed February 2014>).
MARKUS, R. A., 'Gregory the Great's *rector* and his Genesis', in Jacques Fontaine, Robert Gillet, and Stan Pellistrandi (eds.), *Grégoire le Grand* (Paris, 1986), 136–46.
MARKUS, R. A., *Saeculum: History and Society in the Theology of St Augustine*, rev. edn. (Cambridge, 1988).
MARKUS, R. A., *Gregory the Great and His World* (Cambridge, 1997).
MARTIN, G. H., 'Merton, Walter of (c.1205–1277)', *ODNB*.
MARTIN, G. H., and HIGHFIELD, J. R. L., *A History of Merton College, Oxford* (Oxford, 1997).
MARTINES, LAURO, *Power and Imagination: City-States in Renaissance Italy* (Harmondsworth, 1980).
MARX, WILLIAM, 'The *Conflictus inter Deum et Diabolum* and the Emergence of the Literature of Law in Thirteenth Century England', *TCE* 13 (2011), 57–66.
MATSCHA, MICHAEL, *Heinrich I. von Müllenark, Erzbischof von Köln (1225–1238)*, Studien zur Kölner Kirchengeschichte 25 (Siegburg, 1992).
MATTÉONI, OLIVIER, 'Vérifier, corriger, juger: Les Chambres des comptes et le contrôle des officiers en France à la fin du Moyen Âge', *Revue historique* 641 (2007), 31–69.

MAYR-HARTING, HENRY (ed.), *St Hugh of Lincoln: Lectures Delivered at Oxford and Lincoln to Celebrate the Eighth Centenary of St Hugh's Consecration as Bishop of Lincoln* (Oxford, 1987).

MAYR-HARTING, HENRY, 'The Foundation of Peterhouse, Cambridge (1284), and the Rule of Saint Benedict', *EHR* 103 (1988), 318–38.

MEEKINGS, C. A. F., and CROOK, DAVID, *King's Bench and Common Bench in the Reign of Henry III*, SS Supplementary Series 17 (London, 2010).

MICHAUD-QUANTIN, PIERRE, *Universitas: expressions du mouvement communautaire dans le Moyen-Âge latin* (Paris, 1970).

MILLER, EDWARD, *The Abbey and Bishopric of Ely: The Social History of an Ecclesiastical Estate from the Tenth to the Early Fourteenth Century* (Cambridge, 1951).

MILLS, MABEL H., 'Experiments in Exchequer Procedure, 1200–1232', *TRHS* 4th ser. 8 (1925), 151–70.

MILLS, MABEL H., 'Reforms at the Exchequer, 1232–1242', *TRHS* 4th ser. 10 (1927), 111–33.

MILSOM, S. F. C., *The Legal Framework of English Feudalism* (Cambridge, 1976).

MILSOM, S. F. C., *Historical Foundations of the Common Law*, 2nd edn. (London, 1981).

MITTEIS, HEINRICH, *The State in the Middle Ages: A Comparative Constitutional History of Feudal Europe*, trans. H. F. Orton (Amsterdam, 1975).

MOLLAT, MICHEL, *The Poor in the Middle Ages: An Essay in Social History*, trans. A. Goldhammer (New Haven, Conn., 1986).

MOORE, R. I., *The First European Revolution, c.970–1215* (Oxford, 2000).

MOORE, R. I., *The War on Heresy: Faith and Power in Medieval Europe* (London, 2012).

MOORMAN, JOHN R. H., *Church Life in England in the Thirteenth Century* (Cambridge, 1945).

MOORMAN, JOHN R. H., *A History of the Franciscan Order, From its Origins to the Year 1517* (Oxford, 1968).

MORELLI, SERENA, '«Ad extirpenda vitia»: normativa regia e sistemi di controllo sul funzionariato nella prima età angioina', *Mélanges de l'École française de Rome. Moyen-Âge, temps modernes* 109.2 (1997), 463–75.

MORELLI, SERENA, *Per conservare la pace: I giustizieri del regno di Sicilia da Carlo I a Carlo II d'Angiò* (Naples, 2012).

MORRIS, COLIN, *The Papal Monarchy: The Western Church from 1050 to 1250* (Oxford, 1989).

MORRIS, MARC, *A Great and Terrible King: Edward I and the Forging of Britain* (London, 2008).

MORRIS, W. A., *The Frankpledge System* (Cambridge, Mass., 1910).

MORRIS, W. A., *The Medieval English Sheriff to 1300* (Manchester, 1927).

MORRIS, W. A., and STRAYER, JOSEPH R. (eds.), *The English Government at Work, 1327–1336*, ii. *Fiscal Administration* (Cambridge, Mass., 1947, 1950).

MUNDY, J. H., *Liberty and Political Power in Toulouse 1050–1230* (New York, 1954).

MURRAY, ALEXANDER, *Reason and Society in the Middle Ages* (Oxford, 1978).

MURRAY, ALEXANDER, 'Time and Money', in Miri Rubin (ed.), *The Work of Jacques Le Goff and the Challenges of Medieval History* (Woodbridge, 1997), 3–25.

MURRAY, ALEXANDER, '1249', *University College Record* 12/4 (2000), 52–73.

MURRAY, ALEXANDER, *Suicide in the Middle Ages*, ii. *The Curse on Self-Murder* (Oxford, 2000).

NAGEL, THOMAS, 'Ruthlessness in Public Life', in his *Mortal Questions* (Cambridge, 1979), 74–90.

NAZ, R. (ed.), *Dictionnaire de droit canonique: contenant tous les termes du droit canonique, avec un sommaire de l'histoire et des institutions et de l'etat actuel de la discipline*, 7 vols. (Paris, 1935–65).

NELSON, JANET L., 'Gelasius I's Doctrine of Responsibility, a Note', *Journal of Theological Studies* 18 (1967), 154–62.
NELSON, JANET L., '"Not Bishops' Bailiffs but Lords of the Earth": Charles the Bald and the Problem of Sovereignty', in Diana Wood (ed.), *The Church and Sovereignty, c.*590–1918, SCH Subsidia 9 (Oxford, 1991).
NELSON, JANET L., *Charles the Bald* (London, 1992).
NELSON, JANET L., 'Kingship and Royal Government', in Rosamund McKitterick (ed.), *The New Cambridge Medieval History*, ii. c.*700*–c.*900* (Cambridge, 1995), 383–430.
NELSON, JANET L., Review of Joseph Canning, *A History of Medieval Political Thought*, 300–1450, 1st ed. (London, 1995), *Reviews in History* 33 (1997), (<http://www.history.ac.uk/reviews/review/33, accessed February 2014.>)
NELSON, JANET L., 'Kings with Justice, Kings without Justice: An Early Medieval Paradox', in *La giustizia nell'alto medioevo (secoli ix–xi)*, Settimane di studio del Centro italiano di studi sull'alto medioevo 44 (Spoleto, 1997), 797–823.
NELSON, JANET L., 'Charlemagne and Empire', in Jennifer R. Davis and Michael M. McCormick (eds.), *The Long Morning of Medieval Europe: New Directions in Medieval Studies* (Aldershot, 2008), 219–34.
NELSON, JANET L., 'Organic Intellectuals in the Dark Ages?', *History Workshop Journal* 66 (2008), 1–17.
NEVILLE, CYNTHIA J., 'Homicide in the Ecclesiastical Court of Fourteenth-Century Durham', *Fourteenth Century England* (2000), i. 103–14.
NEVILLE, LEONARA. *Authority in Provincial Byzantine Society, 950–1100* (Cambridge, 2004).
NIERMEYER, J. R. and VAN DE KIEFT, C., rev. J. W. J. BURGERS, *Mediae Latinitatis Lexicon Minus*, 2 vols. (Leiden, 2002).
NOKE, C., 'Agency and the *Excessus* balance in Manorial Accounts', in R. H. Parke and B. S. Yamey (eds.), *Accounting History: Some British Contributions* (Oxford, 1994), 139–59.
Ó CLÉIRIGH, CORMAC, 'The Absentee Landlady and the Sturdy Robbers: Agnes de Valence', in Christine Meek and Katharine Simms (eds.), *'The Fragility of her Sex'? Medieval Irishwomen in their European Context* (Blackrock, 1996), 101–18.
Ó CLÉIRIGH, CORMAC, 'Fitzgerald, John fitz Thomas, First Earl of Kildare (d. 1316)', *ODNB*.
OAKLEY, FRANCIS, 'Celestial Hierarchies Revisited: Walter Ullmann's Vision of Medieval Politics', *P&P* 60 (1973), 3–48.
OGILVIE, SHEILA, 'Whatever Is, Is Right? Economic Institiutions in Pre-Industrial Europe', *Economic History Review* NS 60 (2007), 649–84.
OIKONOMIDES, NICOLAS, 'The Role of the Byzantine State in the Economy', in Angeliki E. Laiou (gen. ed.), *The Economic History of Byzantium from the Seventh through the Fifteenth Century*, 3 vols. (Washington DC, 2002), iii. 973–1058.
ORME, NICHOLAS, *Medieval Schools: From Roman Britain to Renaissance England* (New Haven, Conn., 2006).
OSCHINSKY, DOROTHEA, 'Notes on the Editing and Interpretation of Estate Accounts', pts. 1 and 2 in *Archives* 9 (1969–70), 84–9, 142–52.
OTWAY-RUTHVEN, A. J., *A History of Medieval Ireland* (London, 1968).
OWEN, DOROTHY M., 'Eustace (d. 1215)', *ODNB*.
Oxford Dictionary of National Biography: From the Earliest Times to the Year 2000, ed. H. C. G. Matthew and Brian Harrison, 61 vols. (Oxford, 2004); regularly updated online, current editor Lawrence Goldman (all citations from online edn.).
PAGE, WILLIAM (ed.), *The Victoria History of the County of Gloucester*, ii. (London, 1907).
PANOFSKY, ERWIN, *Architecture gothique et pensée scolastique*, trans. Pierre Bourdieu (Paris, 1967).
PANTIN, W. A., *The English Church in the Fourteenth Century* (Cambridge, 1955).

PALAZZO, ERIC, *L'Évêque et son image: L'Illustration du pontifical au Moyen Âge* (Turnhout, 1999).
PALMER, ROBERT C., *The County Courts of Medieval England 1150–1350* (Princeton, NJ, 1982).
PARAVICINI, WERNER, and WERNER, KARL FERDINAND (eds.), *Histoire comparée de l'administration (IVe–XVIIIe siècles): Actes du XIVe Colloque historique franco-allemand, Tours, 27 mars–1er avril 1977*, Beihefte der Francia 9 (Munich, 1980).
PASTOUREAU, MICHEL, *L'Échiquier de Charlemagne: Un jeu pour ne pas jouer* (Paris, 1990).
PASTOUREAU, MICHEL, *Une histoire symbolique du Moyen Âge occidental* (Paris, 2004).
PATZOLD, STEFFEN, *Episcopus: Wissen über Bischöfe im Frankenreich des späten 8. bis frühen 10. Jahrhunderts*, Mittelalter-Forschungen 25 (Ostfildern, 2008).
PEACEY, JASON, *Print and Public Politics in the English Revolution* (Cambridge, 2013).
PÉCOUT, THIERRY, *L'Invention de Provence: Raymond Bérenger V (1209/1245)* (Paris, 2004).
PÉCOUT, THIERRY (ed.), *Quand gouverner c'est enquêter: Les Pratiques politiques de l'enquête princière (Occident, XIIIe–XIVe siècles): Actes du colloque international d'Aix-en-Provence et Marseille 19–21 mars 2009* (Paris, 2010).
PELTZER, JÖRG, 'Les Évêques de l'empire Plantagenêt et les rois angevine: un tour d'horizon', in Martin Aurell and Nöel-Yves Tonnerre (eds.), *Plantagenêts et Capétiens: confrontations et heritages*, Histoire de Famille. La parenté au Moyen Âge 4 (Turnhout, 2006), 461–84.
PENNINGTON, KENNETH, *Pope and Bishops: The Papal Monarchy in the Twelfth and Thirteenth Centuries* (Philadelphia, 1984).
PENNINGTON, KENNETH, 'A Quaestio of Henricus de Segusio and the Textual Tradition of his Summa super decretalibus', *Bulletin of Medieval Canon Law* 16 (1986), 91–6.
PENNINGTON, KENNETH, *The Prince and the Law, 1200–1600: Sovereignty and Rights in the Western Legal Tradition* (Berkeley, Calif., 1993).
PENNINGTON, KENNETH, 'Innocent III and the Ius commune', in Richard Helmholz, Paul Mikat, Jörg Müller, and Michael Stolleis (eds.), *Grundlagen des Rechts: Festschrift für Peter Landau zum 65. Geburtstag*, Rechts- und staatswissenschaftliche Veröffentlichungen der Görres-Gesellschaft 91 (Paderborn, 2000), 349–66.
PENNINGTON, KENNETH, 'Law, Criminal Procedure', in *Dictionary of the Middle Ages: Supplement 1* (New York, 2004), 309–20.
PENNINGTON, KENNETH, 'Prosecution of Clerics in Medieval Canon Law' [online paper at http://faculty.cua.edu/pennington/kansasfourthlateran/LexAquilia-2.htm, accessed February 2014.
PETERS, EDWARD, *The Shadow King: Rex Inutilis in Medieval Law and Literature, 751–1327* (New Haven, Conn., 1970).
PETERS, EDWARD, *Inquisition* (New York, 1988).
PETERS, EDWARD, 'The Death of the Subdean: Ecclesiastical Order and Disorder in Eleventh-century Francia', in Bernard S. Bachrach and David Nicholas (eds.), *Law, Custom, and the Social Fabric in Medieval Europe: Essays in Honor of Bryce Lyon*, Studies in Medieval Culture 28 (Kalamazoo, 1990), 51–71.
PETERS, EDWARD, 'Moore's Eleventh and Twelfth Centuries: Travels in the Agro-literate Polity', in Michael Frassato (ed.), *Heresy and the Persecuting Society in the Middle Ages: Essays on the Work of R. I. Moore* (Leiden, 2006), 11–29.
PETIT-DUTAILLIS, CHARLES, '*Querimoniae Normannorum*', in A. G. Little and F. M. Powicke (eds.), *Essays in Medieval History Presented to Thomas Frederick Tout* (Manchester, 1925), 99–118.
PETIT-DUTAILLIS, CHARLES, *La Monarchie féodale en France et Angleterre* (Paris, 1933).
PIÉRART, MARCEL, 'Les Euthenoi athéniens', *L'Antiquité classique* 40 (1971), 526–73.

PIRIE, FERNANDA, and SCHEELE, JUDITH (eds.), *Legalism: Community and Justice* (Oxford, forthcoming 2014).
PIXTON, PAUL B., *The German Episcopacy and the Implementation of the Decrees of the Fourth Lateran Council, 1216–1245: Watchmen on the Tower*, Studies in the History of Christian Thought 64 (Leiden, 1995).
PLUCKNETT, T. F. T., *Legislation of Edward I* (Oxford, 1949).
PLUCKNETT, T. F. T., *The Mediaeval Bailiff* (London, 1954) (repr. with same pagination in his *Studies in English Legal History* (London, 1983), essay V).
PLUCKNETT, T. F. T., *A Concise History of the Common Law*, 5th edn. (London, 1956).
POLLOCK, FREDERICK, and MAITLAND, FREDERIC WILLIAM, *The History of English Law before the Time of Edward I*, reissued, ed. S. F. C. Milsom, 2 vols. (Cambridge, 1968).
POOLE, REGINALD L., *The Exchequer in the Twelfth Century* (Oxford, 1912).
POST, GAINES, *Studies in Medieval Legal Thought: Public Law and the State, 1100–1322* (Princeton, NJ, 1964).
POWER, DANIEL, 'Guérin de Glapion, Seneschal of Normandy (1200–01): Service and Ambition under the Plantagenet and Capetian Kings', in Nicholas Vincent (ed.), *Records, Administration and Aristocractic Society in the Anglo-Norman Realm: Papers Commemorating the 800th Anniversary of King John's Loss of Normandy* (Woodbridge, 2009), 153–92.
POWER, MICHAEL, *The Audit Society: Rituals of Verification* (Oxford, 1997).
POWICKE, F. M., *The Medieval Books of Merton College* (Oxford, 1931).
POWICKE, F. M., *The Loss of Normandy, 1189–1204: Studies in the History of the Angevin Empire*, 2nd edn. (Manchester, 1961).
POWICKE, F. M., *The Thirteenth Century, 1216–1307*, 2nd edn. (Oxford, 1962).
PRATT, DAVID, *The Political Thought of King Alfred the Great* (Cambridge, 2007).
PRESTWICH, MICHAEL, *Edward I* (London, 1988).
PRESTWICH, MICHAEL, *Plantagenet England, 1225–1360* (Oxford, 2005).
PREVOST, M., 'Cadoc', *DBF*.
PROCTER, EVELYN S., *The Judicial Use of 'Pesquisa', (Inquisition) in León and Castille, 1157–1369*, English Historical Review Suppl. 2 (London, 1966).
QUELLER, DONALD E., *The Office of the Ambassador in the Middle Ages* (Princeton, NJ, 1967).
RABAN, SANDRA, 'Edward I's Other Inquiries', *TCE* 9 (2003), 43–57.
RABAN, SANDRA, *A Second Domesday? The Hundred Rolls of 1279–80* (Oxford, 2004).
RADDING, CHARLES M., 'Fortune and her Wheel: The Meaning of a Medieval Symbol', *Mediaevistik: Internationale Zeitschrift für interdisziplinäre Mittelalterforschung* 5 (1992), 129–40.
RAFTIS, J. AMBROSE, *The Estates of Ramsey Abbey: A Study in Economic Growth and Organziation*, Studies and Texts 3 (Toronto, 1957).
RAMBLE, CHARLES, *The Navel of the Demoness: Tibetan Buddhism and Civil Religion in Highland Nepal* (Oxford, 2008).
RASHDALL, HASTINGS, *The Universities of Europe in the Middle Ages*, rev. edn. F. M. Powicke and A. B. Emden, 3 vols. (Oxford, 1936).
REUTER, TIMOTHY, 'The "Feudal Revolution"', *P&P* 155 (1997), 177–95, repr. in his *Medieval Polities and Modern Mentalities* (Cambridge, 2006), 72–88.
REUTER, TIMOTHY, *Medieval Polities and Modern Mentalities*, ed. Janet L. Nelson (Cambridge, 2006).
REUTER, TIMOTHY, 'Modern Mentalities and Medieval Polities', in his *Medieval Polities and Modern Mentalities* (Cambridge, 2006), 3–18.
REUTER, TIMOTHY, '*Regemque, quem in Francia pene perdidit, in patria magnifice recepit*: Ottonian Ruler Representation in Synchronic and Diachronic Comparison', in his *Medieval Polities and Modern Mentalities* (Cambridge, 2006), 127–46.

REVEL, JACQUES, 'L'Institution et le social', *Un parcours critique: Douze exercices d'histoire sociale* (Paris, 2006), 85–110.
REYNOLDS, SUSAN, *Fiefs and Vassals: The Medieval Evidence Reinterpreted* (Oxford, 1994).
REYNOLDS, SUSAN, *Kingdoms and Communities in Western Europe, 900–1300*, 2nd edn. (Oxford, 1997).
REYNOLDS, SUSAN, 'How Different was England?', *TCE* 7 (1999), 1–16.
RHODES, P. J. *Euthynai (Accounting): A Valedictory Lecture Delivered before the University of Durham* (Durham, 2005).
RICHARD, JEAN, *Saint Louis: Roi d'une France féodale, soutien de la Terre sainte* (Paris, 1983).
RICHARDSON, H. G., 'Richard fitz Neal and the *Dialogus de Scaccario*', *EHR* 43 (1928), 161–71, 321–40.
RICHARDSON, H. G., 'The Schools of Northampton in the Twelfth Century', *EHR* 56 (1941), 595–605.
RICHARDSON, H. G., and SAYLES, G. O., *Governance of Medieval England from the Conquest to Magna Carta* (Edinburgh, 1963).
RICHES, THEO, Review of Thomas N. Bisson, *The Crisis of the Twelfth Century: Power, Lordship, and the Origins of European Government* (Princeton, NJ, 2009), *Reviews in History* 754 (2009) (<http://www.history.ac.uk/reviews/review/754, accessed March 2014>).
RICHTER, MICHAEL, *Giraldus Cambrensis: The Growth of the Welsh Nation*, rev. edn. (Aberystwyth, 1976).
RIDGEWAY, H. W., 'Mid Thirteenth-Century Reformers and the Localities: The Sheriffs of the Baronial Regime, 1258–1261', in P. F. Fleming, A. Gross, and J. R. Lander (eds.), *Regionalism and Revision: The Crown and its Provinces in England, 1200–1650* (London, 1998), 59–86.
RIDGWAY, H. W., 'Valence, [Lusignan], William de, earl of Pembroke (d. 1296)', *ODNB*.
ROBERTS, JENNIFER TOLBERT, *Accountability in Athenian Government* (Madison, Wis., 1982).
ROBINSON, I. S., '*Periculosus homo*: Pope Gregory VII and Episcopal Authority', *Viator* 9 (1978), 103–31.
ROBINSON, I. S., *Authority and Resistance in the Investiture Contest* (Manchester, 1978).
ROBINSON, I. S., 'The Institutions of the Church, 1073–1216', in D. Luscombe and J. Riley-Smith (eds.), *New Cambridge Medieval History*, iv. c.*1024*–c.*1198* (Cambridge, 2004), pt. 2, 368–460.
ROBINSON, JAMES, *The Lewis Chessmen* (London, 2004).
ROEST, BERT, *A History of Franciscan Education (c.*1210–1517*)* (Leiden, 2000).
ROFFE, DAVID, *Domesday: The Inquest and the Book* (Oxford, 2000).
RUBIN, MIRI, *Charity and Community in Medieval Cambridge* (Cambridge, 1987).
RUBIN, ZE'EV, 'The Reforms of Khusro Anushirwan', in Averil Cameron (ed.), *The Byzantine and Early Islamic Near East*, iii. *States, Resources and Armies*, Studies in Late Antiquity and Early Islam 1 (Princeton, NJ, 1995), 227–97.
RUBIN, ZE'EV, 'The Sasanid Monarchy', in Averil Cameron, Bryan Ward-Perkins, and Michael Whitby (eds.), *The Cambridge Ancient History*, xiv. *Late Antiquity: Empire and Successors, A.D. 425–600* (Cambridge, 2000), 638–61.
RUNCIMAN, W. G. (ed.), *Hutton and Butler: Lifting the Lid on the Workings of Power* (Oxford, 2004).
RYAN, W. F., and SCHMITT, CHARLES B. (eds.), *Pseudo-Aristotle, The Secret of Secrets: Sources and Influences*, Warburg Institute Surveys 9 (London, 1982).
SABAPATHY, JOHN, 'A Medieval Officer and a Modern Mentality? *Podestà* and the Quality of Accountability', *The Mediæval Journal* 1.2 (2011), 43–79.
SABAPATHY, JOHN, 'Accountable *rectores* in comparative perspective: the theory and practice of holding *podestà* and bishops to account (late twelfth to thirteenth centuries)', in Agnès

Bérenger and Frédérique Lachaud (eds.), *Hiérarchie des pouvoirs, délégation de pouvoir et responsabilité des administrateurs dans l'Antiquité et au Moyen Âge*, Centre de Recherche Universitaire Lorrain d'Histoire, Université de Lorraine—Site de Metz 46 (Metz, 2012), 201–30.

SABAPATHY, JOHN, 'Regulating Community and Society at the Sorbonne in the Late Thirteenth Century', in Fernanda Pirie and Judith Scheele (eds.), *Legalism: Community and Justice* (Oxford, forthcoming 2014).

ST. JOHN BROOKS, ERIC, *Knights' Fees in Counties Wexford, Carlow, and Kilkenny (13th–15th Century)* (Dublin, 1950).

SANDLER FREEMAN, LUCY, *Omne Bonum: A Fourteenth Century Encyclopedia of Universal Knowledge, BL MSS Royal 6 E. VI—6 E. VII*, 2 vols. (London, 1996).

SAYERS, JANE E., *Papal Judges Delegate in the Province of Canterbury 1198–1254* (Oxford, 1971).

SCALES, LEONARD E., 'The Cambridgeshire Ragman Rolls', *EHR* 113 (1998), 553–79.

SEARLE, ELEANOR, *Lordship and Community: Battle Abbey and its Banlieu, 1066–1538*, Pontifical Institute of Mediaeval Studies, Studies and Texts 26 (Toronto, 1974).

SEARLE, JOHN R., *The Construction of Social Reality* (London, 1995).

SEARLE, JOHN R., 'What is an Institution?', *Journal of Institutional Economics* 1 (2005), 1–22.

SEARLE, JOHN R., *Making the Social World: The Structure of Human Civilization* (Oxford, 2010).

SEIPP, DAVID J., 'Fleta (fl. 1290–1300)', *ODNB*.

SELECT COMMITTEE ON THE INQUIRIES ACT 2005 [HOUSE OF LORDS], *The Inquiries Act 2005: Post-legislative Scrutiny*, Report of Session 2013–14 (London, 2014).

SHEEHAN, M. W., 'The Religious Orders', in J. I. Catto (ed.), *History of the University of Oxford* (Oxford, 1984), 193–223.

SHOEMAKER, KARL BLAINE, 'Criminal Procedure in Medieval European Law', *ZRG Kan. Abt.* 85 (1999), 174–202.

SIVÉRY, GÉRARD, *Saint Louis et son siècle* (Paris, 1983).

SIVÉRY, GÉRARD, 'Le Mécontentement dans le royaume de France et les enquêtes de saint Louis', *Revue historique* 269 (1983), 3–24.

SKINNER, QUENTIN, 'The Principles and Practice of Opposition: The Case of Bolingbroke versus Walpole', in Neil McKendrick (ed.), *Historical Perspectives: Studies in English Thought and Society in Honour of J. H. Plumb* (London, 1974), 93–128.

SKODA, HANNAH, 'A Historian's Perspective on the Present Volume', in Paul Dresch and Hannah Skoda (eds.), *Legalism: Anthropology and History* (Oxford, 2012), 39–54.

SKODA, HANNAH, *Medieval Violence: Physical Brutality in Northern France, 1270–1330* (Oxford, 2013).

SMALLEY, BERYL, *The Becket Conflict and the Schools: A Study of Intellectuals in Politics* (Oxford, 1973).

SMALLEY, BERYL, '*Prima clavis sapientiae*: Augustine and Abelard', in her *Studies in Medieval Thought and Learning from Abelard to Wyclif* (London, 1981), 1–8.

SMITH, DAVID M., 'Hugh's Administration of the Diocese of Lincoln', in Henry Mayr-Harting (ed.), *St Hugh of Lincoln* (Oxford, 1987), 19–47.

SOLL, JACOB, 'Accounting for Government: Holland and the Rise of Political Economy in Seventeenth-Century Europe', *The Journal of Interdisciplinary History* 40 (2009), 215–38.

SOLL, JACOB, *The Reckoning: Financial Accountability and the Making and Breaking of Nations* (New York, 2014).

SOURDEL-THOMINE, JANINE, 'Les Conseils du Šayḫ al-Harawī à un prince ayyūbide', *Bulletin d'études orientales* 17 (1961–2), 205–68.

SOUTHERN, R. W., *The Making of the Middle Ages* (London, 1953).

SOUTHERN, R. W., *Medieval Humanism and Other Studies* (Oxford, 1970).

SOUTHERN, R. W., 'The Place of England in the Twelfth Century Renaissance', in his *Medieval Humanism and Other Studies* (Oxford, 1970), 158–80.
SOUTHERN, R. W., 'England's First Entry into Europe', in his *Medieval Humanism and Other Studies* (Oxford, 1970), 135–57.
SOUTHERN, R. W., 'Ranulf Flambard', in his *Medieval Humanism and Other Studies* (Oxford, 1970), 183–205.
SOUTHERN, R. W., *Robert Grosseteste: The Growth of an English Mind in Medieval Europe*, rev. edn. (Oxford, 1992).
SOUTHERN, R. W., *Scholastic Humanism and the Unification of Europe*, ii. *The Heroic Age* (Oxford, 2001).
STACEY, ROBERT, C., 'Agricultural Investment and the Management of the Royal Desmesne Manors, 1236–1240', *Journal of Economic History* 46 (1986), 919–34.
STACEY, ROBERT C., *Politics, Policy, and Finance under Henry III 1216–1245* (Oxford, 1987).
STACEY, ROBERT C., 'Crusades, Crusaders, and the Baronial *Gravamina* of 1263–1264', *TCE* 3 (1991), 137–50.
STE. CROIX, GEOFFREY DE, 'Greek and Roman Accounting', in A. C. Littleton and B. S. Yamey (eds.), *Studies in the History of Accounting* (London, 1956), 14–74.
STENTON, F. M., *The First Century of English Feudalism, 1066–1166*, 2nd edn. (Oxford, 1961).
STERN, LAURA IKINS, 'Public Fame: A Useful Canon Law Borrowing', in Manlio Bellomo and Orazio Condorelli (eds.), *Proceedings of the Eleventh International Congress of Medieval Canon Law: Catania, 30 July–6 August, 2000*, Monumenta iuris canonici, Ser. C: Subsidia 12 (Vatican City, 2006), 661–72.
STOLJAR, S. J., 'The Transformations of Account', *Law Quarterly Review* 80 (1964), 203–24.
STONES, JEANNE, and STONES, LIONEL, 'Bishop Ralph Neville, Chancellor to King Henry III, and His Correspondence: A Reappraisal', *Archives* 16 (1984), 227–57.
STRAW, CAROLE, *Gregory the Great: Perfection in Imperfection* (Berkeley, Calif., 1988).
STRAWLEY, JAMES HERBERT, 'Grossteste's Administration of the Diocese of Lincoln', in D. A. Callus (ed.), *Robert Grosseteste, Scholar and Bishop: Essays in Commemoration of the Seventh Centenary of his Death* (Oxford, 1955), 146–77.
STRAYER, J. R., *The Administration of Normandy under Saint Louis* (Cambridge, Mass., 1932).
STRAYER, J. R., 'La conscience du roi: les enquêtes de 1258–1262 dans la sénéchaussée de Carcassonne-Béziers', in *Mélanges Roger Aubenas*, Recueil de memoires et travaux publie par la Societe d'histoire du droit et des institutions des anciens pays de droit ecrit 9 (Montpellier, 1974), 725–36.
STRAYER, J. R., 'The Development of Bureaucracies', *Comparative Studies in Society and History* 17 (1975), 504–9.
STUBBS, WILLIAM, *The Constitutional History of England in Its Origin and Development*, 3rd edn., 3 vols. (Oxford, 1880).
SWANSON, R. N., 'Godliness and Good Learning: Ideals and Imagination in Medieval University and College Foundations', in Rosemary Horrox and Sarah Rees Jones (eds.), *Pragmatic Utopias: Ideals and Communities 1200–1630* (Cambridge, 2001), 43–59.
TELLIEZ, ROMAIN, *«Per potentiam officii»: Les Officiers devant la justice dans le royaume de France au XIVe siècle* (Paris, 2005).
THÉRY, JULIEN, '*Fama*: L'Opinion publique comme preuve judiciare: Aperçu sur la révolution médiévale de l'inquisitoire (XIIe–XIVe siècle)', in Bruno Lemesle (ed.), *La Preuve en justice de l'Antiquité à nos jours* (Rennes, 2003), 119–47.

THÉRY, JULIEN, 'Justice et gouvernement dans la Chrétienté latine: recherches autour du modèle ecclésial (v. 1150–v. 1330). «Excès» et «affaires d'enquête»: Les Procès criminels de la papauté contre les prélats, XIIIe–mi-XIVe siècle', 2 vols. (Université Paul-Valéry—Montpellier III, Dossier pour l'habilitation à diriger des recherches en histoire médiévale, 2010).

THÉRY, JULIEN, '*Atrocitas/enormitas*. Esquisse pour une histoire de la catégorie d' «énormité» ou «crime énorme» du Moyen Âge à l'époque moderne', *Clio@Themis. Revue électronique d'histoire du droit* 4 (2011), 1–48.

THOMPSON, BENJAMIN, 'Pecham, John (*c*.1230-1292)', *ODNB*.

TILLMANN, HELENE, *Innocent III*, trans. Walter Sax (Amsterdam, 1980).

TOUBERT, PIERRE, 'Byzantium and the Mediterranean Agrarian Civilization', in Angeliki E. Laiou (gen. ed.), *The Economic History of Byzantium from the Seventh through the Fifteenth Century*, 3 vols. (Washington DC, 2002), i. 377–91.

TREHARNE, R. F., *The Baronial Plan of Reform, 1258–1263*, rev. edn. (Manchester, 1971).

TREIBER, HUBERT, '"Elective Affinities" between Weber's Sociology of Religion and Sociology of Law', *Theory and Society* 14 (1985), 809–61.

TRONZO, WILLIAM L., 'Moral Hieroglyphs: Chess and Dice at San Savino in Piacenza', *Gesta* 16/2 (1977), 15–26.

TRUSEN, WINFRIED, 'Der Inquisitionsprozeß, seine historischen Grundlagen und frühen Formen', *ZRG Kan. Abt.* 74 (1988), 168–230.

TUILIER, ANDRÉ, *Histoire de l'Université de Paris et de la Sorbonne*, 2 vols. (Paris, 1994).

TYERMAN, C. J., 'Trubleville, Sir Henry de (d. 1239)', *ODNB*.

ULLMANN, WALTER, *A History of Political Thought: The Middle Ages*, rev. edn. (London, 1970).

VALE, MALCOLM, *Notes on the Senior Common Room for Fellows and Lecturers at St John's College* (Privately printed, 2009).

VALLERANI, MASSIMO, *Medieval Public Justice*, trans. Sarah Rubin Blanshei, Studies in Medieval and Early Modern Canon Law 9 (Washington, 2012).

VAUCHEZ, ANDRÉ, *François d'Assise, entre histoire et mémoire* (Paris, 2009).

VEALE, ELSPETH, 'Chigwell, Hamo (d. 1332)', *ODNB*.

VERDON, LAURE, 'Le Roi, la loi, l'enquête et l'officier: Procédure et enquêteurs en Provence sous le règne de Charles II (1285–1309)', in Claude Gauvard (ed.), *L'Enquête au Moyen Age* (Paris, 2010), 319–29.

VERGER, JACQUES, 'Patterns', in Hilde Ridder-Symoens (ed.), *A History of the University in Europe*, i. *Universities in the Middle Ages* (Cambridge, 1992), 35–74.

VERGER, JACQUES, 'Fonder un collège au XIIIe siècle', in Andreas Sohn and Jacques Verger (eds.), *Die Universitären Kollegien im Europa des Mittelalters und der Renaissance* (Bochum, 2011), 29–38.

VERNON HARCOURT, L. W., *His Grace the Steward and Trial of Peers* (London, 1907).

VICENS VIVES, JAIME, *Approaches to the History of Spain*, trans. Joan Connelly Ullman, 2nd edn. (Berkeley, Calif., 1970).

VINCENT, NICHOLAS, 'Why 1199? Bureaucracy and Enrolment under John and his Contemporaries', in Adrian Jobson (ed.), *English Government in the Thirteenth Century* (Woodbridge, 2004), 17–48.

WARREN, W. L., *Henry II*, new edn. (London, 1973).

WATSON, SETHINA C., '*Fundatio, Ordinatio* and *Statuta*: The Statutes and Constitutional Documents of English Hospitals to 1300' (D.Phil. thesis, Oxford University, 2004).

WATSON, SETHINA C., 'The Origins of the English Hospital', *TRHS* 6th ser. 16 (2006), 75–94.

WATT, J. A., 'The Theory of Papal Monarchy in the Thirteenth Century: The Contribution of the Canonists', *Traditio* 20 (1964), 179–317.

WATT, J. A., 'The Papacy', in David Abulafia (ed.), *New Cambridge Medieval History,* v. c.*1198–c.1300* (Cambridge, 1999), 107–63.

WAUGH, SCOTT L., 'Reluctant Knights and Jurors: Respites, Exemptions, and Public Obligations in the Reign of Henry III', *Speculum* 58 (1983), 937–86.

WAUGH, SCOTT L., 'Tenure to Contract: Lordship and Clientage in Thirteenth Century England', *EHR* 101 (1986), 811–39.

WEBER, MAX, *Wirtschaft und Gesellschaft: Grundriss der verstehenden Soziologie*, ed. Johannes Winckelmann, 5th edn. (Tübingen, 1972).

WEBER, MAX, *Gesammelte Aufsätze zur Religionssoziologie*, i. (Tübingen, 1988 edn.).

WEBER, MAX, 'Die »Objectivität« sozialwissenschaftlicher und sozialpolitischer Erkenntnis', in his *Schriften zur Wissenschaftslehre*, ed. Michael Sukale (Stuttgart, 1991), 21–101.

WEBER, MAX, *The Protestant Ethic and the Spirit of Capitalism*, trans. Talcott Parsons (London, 2001).

WEI, IAN P., *Intellectual Culture in Medieval Paris: Theologians and the University, c.1100–1330* (Cambridge, 2012).

WEIJERS, OLGA, *Terminologie des universités au XIIIe siècle*, Lessico Intellettuale Europeo 39 (Rome 1987).

WEILER, BJÖRN K., 'Royal Justice and Royal Virtue in William of Malmesbury's *Historia Novella* and Walter Map's *De Nugis Curialium*', in István P. Bejcy and Richard G. Newhauser (eds.), *Virtue and Ethics in the Twelfth Century* (Leiden, 2005), 317–39.

WEILER, BJÖRN K., 'The King as Judge: Henry II and Frederick Barbarossa as Seen by Their Contemporaries', in Patricia Skinner (ed.), *Challenging the Boundaries of Medieval History: The Legacy of Timothy Reuter* (Turnhout, 2009), 115–40.

WERNER, JAKOB, 'Die Teilnehmerliste des Laterankonzils vom Jahre 1215', *Neues Archiv der Gesellschaft für ältere deutsche Geschichtskunde* 31 (1906), 575–93.

WHEARE, K. C., 'George Derek Gordon Hall, 1924–1975', *Proceedings of the British Academy* 62 (1976), 427–33.

WHITE, ALBERT BEEBE, *Self-Government at the King's Command: A Study in the Beginnings of English Democracy* (Minneapolis, 1933).

WHITE, STEPHEN D., 'The "Feudal Revolution"', *P&P* 152 (1996), 205–23.

WICKHAM, CHRIS, 'The "Feudal Revolution"', *P&P* 155 (1997), 196–208.

WICKHAM, CHRIS, 'Gossip and Resistance among the Medieval Peasantry', *P&P* 160 (1998), 3–24.

WICKHAM, CHRIS, *Courts and Conflict in Twelfth-Century Tuscany* (Oxford, 2003).

WICKHAM, CHRIS, 'Fama and the Law in Twelfth-Century Tuscany', in Thelma Fenster and Daniel Lord Smail (eds.), *Fama: The Politics of Talk and Reputation in Medieval Europe* (Ithaca, NY, 2003), 15–26.

WICKHAM, CHRIS, *Framing the Early Middle Ages: Europe and the Mediterranean 400–800* (Oxford, 2005).

WILKINSON, LOUISE J., 'Pawn and Political Player: Observations on the Life of a Thirteenth Century Countess', *Historical Research* 73 (2000), 105–23.

WILKINSON, LOUISE J., 'The *Rules* of Robert Grosseteste Reconsidered: The Lady as Estate and Household Manager in Thirteenth Century England', in Cordelia Beattie et al. (eds.), *The Medieval Household in Christian Europe, c.850–c.1550* (Turnhout, 2003), 294–306.

WILKINSON, LOUISE, J., 'Women as Sheriffs in Early Thirteenth Century England', in Adrian Jobson (ed.), *English Government in the Thirteenth Century* (Woodbridge, 2004), 111–24.

WILKINSON, LOUISE J., *Women in Thirteenth-Century Lincolnshire* (Woodbridge, 2007).

WILLARD, JAMES F, and MORRIS, WILLIAM A (eds.), *The English Government at Work, 1327–1336*, i. *Central and Prerogative Administration* (Cambridge, Mass., 1940).
WILLARD, JAMES F., MORRIS, WILLIAM A., and DUNHAM, WILLIAM H. (eds.), *The English Government at Work, 1327–1336*, iii. *Local Administration and Justice* (Cambridge, Mass., 1950).
WILLIAMS, BERNARD, 'Professional Morality and its Dispositions', in his *Making Sense of Humanity and Other Philosophical Papers 1982–1993* (Cambridge, 1995), 192–202.
WILLIAMS, STEVEN J., *The Secret of Secrets: The Scholarly Career of a Pseudo-Aristotelian Text in the Latin Middle Ages* (Ann Arbor, Mich., 2003).
WINTERS, JANE FRANCES, 'The Forest Eyre, 1154–1368' (Ph.D. thesis, University of London, 1999).
WOLFF, JONATHAN, *An Introduction to Political Philosophy*, rev. edn. (Oxford, 2006).
WOLTER, UDO, 'Verwaltung, Amt, Beamter, V–VI', in Otto Brunner, Werner Conze, and Reinhart Koselleck (eds.), *Geschichtliche Grundbegriffe: Historisches Lexikon zur politisch-sozialen Sprache in Deutschland*, 8 vols. in 9 (Stuttgart, 1972–97), vii. 26–47.
WOLTER, UDO, 'The *Officium* in Medieval Ecclesiastical Law as a Prototype of Modern Administration', in Antonio Padoa-Schioppa (ed.), *Legislation and Justice*, The Origins of the Modern State in Europe, 13th to 18th Centuries (Oxford, 1997), 17–36.
WORBY, SAM, *Law and Kinship in Thirteenth Century England* (Woodbridge, 2010).
WORMALD, PATRICK, 'The Pursuit of Crime' (unpublished, c.1990).
WORMALD, PATRICK, *The Making of English Law: King Alfred to the Twelfth Century*, i. *Legislation and its Limits* (Oxford, 1999).
WORMALD, PATRICK, 'Archbishop Wulfstan and the Holiness of Society', in his *Legal Culture in the Early Medieval West: Law as Text, Image and Experience* (London, 1999), 225–51.
WORMALD, PATRICK, *Lawyers and the State: The Varieties of Legal History*, SS Lecture (London, 2006).
ZIEGLER, JOSEPH, *Medicine and Religion, c.1300: The Case of Arnau de Vilanova* (Oxford, 1998).

ONLINE RESOURCES (ALL WEBSITES ACCESSED MARCH 2014)

Comptabilité(S): <http://comptabilites.revues.org/>.
The Butler Review (2004): <http://webarchive.nationalarchives.gov.uk/*/http://www.butlerreview.org.uk/>.
Early English Laws project: <http://www.earlyenglishlaws.ac.uk/>.
Enquêtes historiques sur les comptabilités, XIVe–XIXe siècles: <http://irhis.recherche.univ-lille3.fr/00-Comptabilites/Index.html>.
ENQUÊTES MENÉES SOUS LES DERNIERS CAPÉTIENS, ed. Xavier Hélary, Élisabeth Lalou, Ædilis, Publications scientifiques 4 (Orleans, 2006–9): <http://www.cn-telma.fr/enquetes/>.
The Hutton Inquiry (2003–2004): archived at <http://www.nationalarchives.gov.uk/webarchive/>.
The Iraq Inquiry ('Chilcot Inquiry', 2009–): <http://www.iraqinquiry.org.uk>.
The Leveson Inquiry (2011–): <http://www.levesoninquiry.org.uk/>.
Revista Española de Historia de la Contabilidad: <http://www.decomputis.org/>.

Indices

INDEX OF CITATIONS

I. *The Bible*
Genesis 18: 20–1	141, 160
Numbers 27: 17–19	93n.
Judges 16: 30	168
1 Samuel 7: 3	42n.
1 Kings 3	203n.
2 Chronicles 10: 11	116n.
Proverbs 21: 1	99n.
Proverbs 11: 14	209n.
Wisdom of Solomon 6: 7	99n.
Ecclesiasticus 15: 5	138n.
Jeremiah 48: 10	155n.
Lamentations 3: 12	168
Ezekiel 3: 18–20	162n.
Ezekiel 33: 6–8	162n.
Daniel 13: 44–62	203n.
2 Maccabees 4: 39–50	254
2 Maccabees 13: 7	254–5
Matthew 6: 21	102n., 107
Matthew 6: 24	102n.
Matthew 6: 33	42n.
Matthew 23: 3	203n.
Matthew 10: 24	203n.
Matthew 18: 15–17	137–8
Luke 16: 1–14	26-29, 39, 41–3, 102n., 159–62, 203n., 209n., 254
Romans 2: 6	161n.
Romans 13: 1	96, 99
Romans 14: 4	99n.
1 Corinthians 6: 12	154n.
1 Corinthians 10: 22–3	154n.
1 Corinthians 13: 5	218
2 Corinthians 12: 2	161n.
1 Thessalonians 5: 2	162n.
2 Timothy 2: 4	136n.
Hebrews 13: 17	41n., 99
1 Peter 2: 8	144n.
2 Peter 3: 10	162n.

II. *Roman law*
Institutes 1.2.6	99
Institutes 1.1.3	102n.
Code 1.49	10
Digest 1.1.10	102n.
Digest 1.4.1	99
Digest 9.2.51	163n.

III. *Canon law*
Decretum
D. 21–101	155
D. 83.3	165
D. 86.3	165
C. 2.7.55	165

Quinque compilationes antiquae
1 Comp. 5.29.7	141n.
1 Comp. 5.32.3	149n.
1 Comp. 5.32.4	149n.
2 Comp. 5.2.10	144n., 149
3 Comp. 1.5.3	168n.
3 Comp. 3.26.3	154n.
3 Comp. 5.1.3	141n., 146n.
3 Comp. 5.1.4	141n.
3 Comp. 5.2.3	141n., 145n.
3 Comp 5.2.4	141n.
3 Comp. 5.17.1	141n., 177n.
3 Comp. 5.21.8	141n., 149n., 163
4 Comp. 5.1.4	*see* Lateran Council, Fourth – cap. 8

Liber extra
X. 1.7.3	168n.
X 1.23.6	149n.
X 3.2.8	145n.
X 3.7.6	149n.
X 3.8.7	149n.
X 3.34.7	154n.
X 5.1.16	141n., 146n.
X 5.1.17	141n.
X 5.1.21	146n.
X 5.1.24	*see* Lateran Council, Fourth – cap. 8
X 5.3.28	144n., 149
X 5.3.30	149, 152
X 5.3.31	141n., 145n.
X 5.3.32	141n.
X 5.34.6	141n.
X 5.34.10	141n., 177n.
X 5.37.3	149n.
X 5.39.35	141n., 149n, 163

GENERAL INDEX[1]

accountability (*see also particular officers*)
- abbots' 202–4
- aspects of 20–2
- communities and officers'
  accountability 50, 76n., 82, 113, 122,
  128, 165–73, 184, Ch. 5 *passim* (*esp.*
  185, 191, 192, 198–201, 205, 209n.,
  216), 223–5, 227–8, 231–2, 257, 260
- comparative 20–3, 121–34, 151–5, 171,
  184, 192, 199–200, 208, 214, 216–17,
  Ch. 6 *passim*
- conflict and 21, 58, 72, 103–10, 151,
  170–1, 193, 209, 221, 253, 258, 260
- delegated 223–4, 227–30
- fiscal 17–19, 21n., 89–90, 100–1, 116–20,
  121–8, 132–4, 233–4
- forms across different types of officer 8–10,
  42–3, 77–80
- hierarchy and (*see also* 'Who, whom?')
  20–1, 41–3, 137, 166–7, 180, 198–209
- justice and 22, 35–6, 37, 93–4, 107, 109,
  132–4, 253–60
- modern 162, 236–7, 260
- office and – *passim*
- politics and 5–6, 132–4, 154n.
- responsibility and 2–5, 23, 59–60, 72–5,
  79–82, 121–34, 183–4, 193, 195n.,
  201, 204–5, 210–11, 222, 224, 237–8,
  242, 252, 255–7
- royal/imperial 23, 98–100, 236–9, 247–8
- state and (*see also* government, and
  accountability) 19–20, 22, 24, 239–41
- trust and 63, 77, 78n., 79, 80, 89, 99,
  107, 131, 138, 144, 161–2, 203, 256
accounts (*see also* Exchequer; *Chambres des
comptes*; accountability, fiscal) 100–101,
104, 124, 127, 191, 196–7, 198, 201,
205, 206, 245, 251
- manorial – *see* manorial accounts
- 'reasonable' 29–30, 35, 45–7, 75–6, 260
accusatio, accusation 143–6, 150–1, 168–70,
172, 179, 201, 203, 205, 239, 254
action of account – *see* writs
Adam of Eynsham OSB, Abbot,
hagiographer 136–40
Adam Marsh OFM, scholar 69, 77n.
adelantados 231
administration (*see also* accountability; accounts;
audits; *Chambres des comptes*; county
administration; desmesne farming;
enquêtes; estate management; Exchequer;
government; inquiries and inquisitions,
secular; inquisitions, canonical; statutes;
Vivier-en-Brie; writs) 10–19, 100–1, 157

– *moralisation de l'administration* 55–60, 76,
  96–101
administrative history 14–19
Agnes de Valence, landowner, aristocrat 29–37,
  51, 63
Alexander III, Pope 141, 149, 151n., 162n.,
  165, 209n., 247
Alexander Nequam, Abbot, scholar 106
Alexander of Telese, historian 101
Alfonso X King of Castile and León ('the
  Wise') 2, 224n., 231n., 247
Alphonse II King of Aragon, Count of
  Barcelona (Alfonso II, Alfons I) 94
Anagni 177
Andrew Horn, chamberlain, writer 1–5,
  49, 233
– Liber Horn 25
– Magnum librum 1, 45
Annales 'school' 6, 14, 17
Anselm de Mauny, Bishop 150n., 171–2,
  178n., 179–80
Aragon 92, 94
arbitrium 98–9, 105
Aristotle (*see also Secretum secretorum*)
– *Nicomachean Ethics* 80–1, 193n.
– *Politics* 8, 204, 255
Articuli super cartas (1300) 128
audits (*see also euthyna*; Exchequer; *scrutinium*;
  sindacatio) 22, 61–2, 64, 100, 189,
  196, 206, 208, 233, 236, 245, 251,
  253, 256n.
auditors 29, 33, 35, 36, 44, 49–50, 54, 58, 60,
  61, 63, 72, 73, 75, 229–30
Augustine of Hippo, Saint, bishop and
  scholar 42, 135n., 164, 203n., 236,
  255, 258–60
Aurelius Augustinus – *see* Augustine of Hippo

bailiffs 9, 22, Ch. 2 *passim* (*esp.* 63–70), 85, 89,
  100, 114, 120, 132, 159–60, 184, 192,
  196, 197–8, 202, 203, 206, 216, 222,
  227, 229, 230, 233, 234–5, 237, 238,
  240, 241, 252, 257
– oath 69
baillis 78n., 81, 85, 87, 121–5, 128–9, 131–2,
  224n., 234, 238, 250–1, 256
Barnwell chronicler 13, 37n.
Barratt, Nick 117
Bartlett, Robert 10, 153, 226
Battle Abbey (Sussex) 26–9, 66, 67, 230
– *Chronicle of Battle* 26–9, 39, 41
Benedictine Order and rule 12, 199, 203,
  205, 217
Bentham, Jeremy 74, 108n., 255

---

[1] Medieval names are indexed by first name (Thomas Aquinas); modern names are selectively indexed by surname (Bisson, Thomas N.), except in some family groups (e.g. Bigods).

Indices 305

Bernard of Bologna, *dictator* 7
Bernard of Clairvaux OC, Abbot, scholar 159
  – *De consideratione* 135n., 137n., 154n., 156, 158, 159, 160
bibles moralisées 107, 161n., 254–5
Bigods
  – Hugh Bigod, justice, Chief Justiciar, baron 111
  – Roger Bigod II, Earl, Exchequer baron, justice 143
  – Roger Bigod IV, Earl, marshal 32
bishops 9, 22, Ch. 4 *passim* (*esp.* 134–7, 143, 154–65, 167–8, 183–4), 185, 186, 192, 222, 227, 228, 229, 230, 231, 232, 235, 254, 257
  – accountability of – see Ch. 4 *passim, and* inquisitions, canonical; Anselm de Mauny; Geoffrey of York; Walter Langton
Bisson, Thomas N. 5–6, 58n., 82n., 121, 154n., 169n., 250n.
  – on accountability 17–18, 67n., 68, 87, 89–90, 125–7, 132, 249–50, 256n., 257
Bloch, Marc 14, 115n., 153
Bogo de Clare, figure of scandal 34, 68n., 76
Bologna, University of 190n., 214n., 218
  – Spanish College 195, 209
Boniface VIII, Pope 13, 174–83, 247, 248
Bourdieu, Pierre 104n., 108n., 242n., 258n.
Boureau, Alain 12–13, 234, 245n.
Bracton 51, 60
Brand, Paul 51
Brentano, Robert 22, 156n., 157–8
Briouze family 105
Britton 1, 62n., 128, 152n., 224, 230
Brunetto Latini 2–5
  – *Livres dou Tresor* 2–5, 9, 13, 25
'Bucknell Group' 14
Burt, Caroline 122
Bury St Edmunds, Abbey 27, 75n., 202

Cadoc of Pont-Audemer, *bailli, routier* 124–5, 250–1
Caenegem, R. C. van 38
canon law (*see also index of citations*; Lateran Council, Fourth) 12, Ch. 4 *passim* (*esp.* 138–9, 148–54, 165–73), 189, 207, 247
Canterbury, Christ Church 162
Canterbury, St Augustine's 38–9
capitularies, Carolingian 56, 88n.
Castile 2, 82n., 224n., 231n., 239
Catalonia 5n., 18, 59n., 85
Celestine III, Pope 142–6, 160
chamberlain of London 1
Chambres des comptes (*see also* Vivier-en-Brie) 19, 106, 107n., 125–6, 234
character – *see under* officers
Charlemagne, King of the Franks, Emperor 224, 255n., 256
Charles the Bald, King of West Francia, Emperor 42–3
Charles I ('of Anjou'), Count of Anjou, Maine, Provence, King of Sicily, Jerusalem 128n., 129, 130, 132, 133, 134, 231n., 237, 247, 249, 251
Charles II ('of Salerno'), King of Sicily 122
chess 7, 103–7
Chiffoleau, Jacques 15
clamor 48, 131, 141, 160, 170, 178
Clanchy, Michael (*see also under* law) 13, 59, 68, 96, 102, 257
colleges, in general Chapter 5 *passim esp.* 185–7
  – and hospitals 185, 194, 206, 214–8, 221n.
  – and religious orders 192, 193–4, 199–200, 202–4, 205, 208, 216–17, 218, 221
colleges, of Cambridge
  – Peterhouse 199, 215, 218n.
colleges, of Oxford 22
  – Balliol 187n., 190n., 194n., 199n., 200n., 206–7, 210n., 212n., 218
  – Corpus Christi 195n.
  – Exeter (Stapeldon Hall) 134n., 186n., 190n., 195n., 202, 208, 210n., 219n., 221n.
  – Merton (*see also* Walter of Merton) 16, 187–209, 210–13, 215–21, 229, 230, 234
    – accounting at 191, 196–7, 198, 201, 205, 206
    – scholars' oath 189–190
    – founding documents of 187–98, 199, 200, 205, 206, 215, 216, 217
    – minuting at 195–8, 212
    – *scrutinium* of 195–8, 203, 206, 209, 212, 219, 245, 253, 260
  – Oriel 215, 219n., 221n.
  – St John's 205n.
  – University 187n., 190n., 193, 194n., 210, 211, 242n.
colleges, of Paris
  – Autun 206, 212n., 221n.
  – Bons-Enfants 212
  – Dix-Huit 215, 218n.
  – St Thomas du Louvre 209n.
  – Sorbonne (*see also* Robert de Sorbon) 186n., 190n., 191n., 194, 207, 208–9, 210–11, 213, 217–18, 221, 234
  – Treasurer (Trésorier) 194n.
colleges, of Siena, Casa della Sapienzia 215
common law (English) (*see also* writs) Ch. 2 *passim* (*esp.* 38–52), 128, 172, 230, 245n.
Cook, Michael 244–5
county administration, English (*see also* sheriffs) 26–9, 83–5, 91–2
  – and manorial jurisdictions 26–9, 29–37, 61–3, 67–8
  – compared with other European polities 92, 233
Court baron 66, 69n.

Coventry and Lichfield, diocese of (*see* Walter Langton)
Crescentius of Jesi OFM, Minister General 205
crimina, ne crimina remaneant impunita ('lest crimes go unpunished') 163–5, 258, cf. 49, 99, 112
Crusades 87, 120, 123, 128, 129, 140
– officers' accountability during 131–2, 238
custodes 188, 199–200, 201, 203, 204, 208, 248

daʿāwī al-tuham ('trials of suspicion') (*see also* inquiries and inquisitions, secular; inquisitions, canonical) 243–5
Dante Alighieri 7
– *Monarchia* 12
– *Purgatorio* 220–1
d'Avray, David 11n., 234–5
denunciation, *per denunciationem* 137, 145n., 147, 150–2, 254
desmesne farming (*see also* Exchequer, reforms at) 52–5, 60–64, 251
devil, kissing his back 174, 176, 184
Dialogue of the Exchequer (*see also* Richard of Ely) 22, 93–110, 125–6, 132
dice 106–7
Domesday Book 88n., 89n., 100
Douglas, Mary 41n., 69n., 166–7, 198n., 259n.
Dunbabin, Jean 128, 133n., 247
Dunblane, diocese 163

ealdorman 56
Edward I, King of England 1, 29–31, 38, 44, 49, 78n., 177, 224, 238, 241, 250
– and shrieval accountability 85, 111, 119, 120, 122, 126, 128, 133–4, 229, 257
Edward II, King of England 177, 183, 247, 248
elective affinity (*Wahlverwandtschaft*) (*see also* Weber) 152n., 226, 241–6
Elias of Cortona OFM, Minister General 200, 204n., 205
Elias of Trikinghorn, *De disciplina scholarium* 204
Ely (*see also* Eustace of Ely; Nigel of Ely; Richard of Ely; William Longchamp) 96
enquêtes, French (*see also* inquiries and inquisitions, secular; Louis IX; Philip II) 23, 88–91, 125–9, 132n., 228–9, 234, 250–1
estate management (*see also* Fleta; *Gerefa*; *Husbandry*; Manuscripts and rolls (BL Royal MS 9 A VII, Durham, Dean and Chapter Library MS Loc. 2. 15, TNA C 150/1); *Rectitudines singularum personarum*; Robert Grosseteste (*Rules, Statuta*); *Seneschauncy*; Tidenham; *and Walter of Henley*) Ch. 2 *passim* (*esp.*

52–63, 76–82), 101, 241
estate officers – *see* bailiffs; *prepositi*; reeves; stewards
étatisation – *see under* accountability, state and
Eudes Rigaud OFM, Archbishop, scholar 157
Eustace of Ely, Bishop 149–50
Eustache le moine, *roman* of 123–4
euthyna ('straightening'; *see also* audits) 18, 93n., 255
ex parte – *see* writs
excessus 65, 112, 138, 139, 144–5, 147, 160n., 162, 166–7, 171, 178, 180, 183, 203–4, 247, 249
Exchequer (*see also* audits) 16, Ch. 2 *passim*, 185, 230, 249
– account and audit 78, 86, 91–2, 103–10, 112–3, 127, 227, 229, 233–4
– account as *conflictus* and chess game 72, 103–10
– barons of 91n., 93–4, 104–6, 107–10, 112, 134
– compared with other European parallels 92, 106, 107n., 121–34
– court 29–37, 68, 91, 93, 110, 112, 173, 229
– equity at 30, 94, 102, 108, 109–10, 235
– law, rules, and customs of 92–110, 130, 134, 135–6, 193
– officers of 102–4, 108, 135, 229
– reforms at 79, 116–20
– repayment at 93, 104–10, 112–13, 171
– science of (*scientia*) 103–6
– *voluntas* at 104–6
eyres (*see also* 'Hundred Rolls') 4, 40–6, 50, 86–91, 110–13, 121, 228
– 1194 114, 120, 144, 231n.
– *c*.1245–6, articles of 110–11
– 1254, articles of 111
– 1258–9, Surrey and Kent 111, 228–9
Ezra, prophet 95, 101–2

fama ('rumour', 'report') (*see also infamia*; *publica fama*) 76, 112, 138–40, 141n., 145–7, 150, 151n., 153n., 163, 169, 174–5, 178, 181, 183, 219, 239, 254
fellows – *see under* colleges
Fitzgeralds, family 30–7
Flanders 85, 92
Flasch, Kurt 11
Fleta 60–1
fortune 105–7, 225n.
Fraher, Richard M., 164
France (*see also baillis*; *Chambres des comptes*; *prévôts*; Louis VII; Philip II; Louis IX; Philip IV; Philip V) 22, 85, 87, 92, 109, 121–34
Francis, Saint 157n., 158n.
– *Testament* of 193–4
Franciscan rules and statutes 140, 192–4, 199–200, 203–4, 216–17, 221

Franciscan *studia* 199, 204, 210, 243
frankpledge 41n., 54n., 85
Frederick II, Emperor 13, 132, 234, 247
– *Constitutions* ('Constitutions of Melfi', *Liber Augustalis*) 88, 106–7, 119n., 223n., 237, 238, 258n.

Ganshof, François-Louis 16
Gentile da Montefiore OFM, Cardinal 176, 182
Geoffrey Chaucer, poet 7
Geoffrey de Geneville, Justiciar 33
Geoffrey de Lusignan, half-brother of Henry III 67, 75
Geoffrey of St Calais, *procurator* of Battle Abbey 26–9, 39, 66
Geoffrey of York, Archbishop, illegitimate son of King Henry II 142
– canonical inquiry into 142–51, 154, 160, 162, 169, 171, 173, 184, 229
Gerald of Wales, scholar 96, 101, 135–7, 142, 148, 156–7, 162, 211
– *De invectionibus* 92–4, 135–6
– *Gemma ecclesiastica* 136
– *Liber de principis instructione* 23n., 135n., 237n.
Gerefa 56–7, 59–60
Gervase of Canterbury OSB, scholar 114, 142
Geschichtliche Grundbegriffe 20–1
Gilbert de Clare 66, 75
Gilbert of Sempringham, monastic reformer 8
Gillingham, John 15
Glanvill 40–1, 61, 65, 95n., 97, 152n.
Glénisson, Jean – *see under* inquiries
government, and accountability (*see also* accountability, state and; Bisson) 5–6, 13, 90, 121–34, 248–51
government, as business 94, 98, 101, 133
'Gratian' 155, 159
Gregory I ('the Great'), Pope 3n., 160n., 237
– *Pastoral Care* 159
– *Dialogues* 255
Gregory VII, Pope 13, 42–3, 154–5, 159, 161, 163, 247
Gregory IX, Pope (*see also* index of citations, *Liber extra*) 149, 161, 178n., 194, 199n., 205, 217
Guibert of Tournai, *Eruditio regum et principum* 23, 135n., 232, 238n., 247, 255n.
Guildhall, London 1

Hadrian II, Pope 42–3
Hamo Chigwell, Mayor of London 4
Harvey, P. D. A. 53–5, 72
Heinrich von Müllenark, Archbishop 161
Henry I, King of England 115
Henry II, King of England 94, 95–7, 100, 107, 114–16, 128, 142

Henry III, King of England 1, 13, 30, 50, 112, 118–20, 128, 130, 132, 134, 230, 234, 247
– Bordelais inquiry of 127
– on bailiffs 66, 241
– on sheriffs 118, 235
Henry of Battle Abbey OSB, Abbot 26, 28, 39, 67
Henry of Huntingdon, historian 1
Highfield, J. R. L. 192–3
Hincmar of Laon, Bishop 42
Holt, J. C. 222, 226, 234
honestas, etc. (*see also utilitas*) 69, 80, 88, 110, 113, 115, 120, 123, 185, 189, 190, 218n., 221
Honorius III, Pope 156–7
Honorius, canonist 148–9
hospitals – *see under* colleges
Howden – *see* Roger of Howden
Hubert Walter, Archbishop of Canterbury, Justiciar, Chancellor 8, 92–3, 114, 115n., 135–7, 142–4, 146, 149, 151–2, 156, 158, 162, 211
– and Hugh of Avalon 136–7
Hudson, John 152n., 245n.
Hugh of Avalon, Saint, bishop 136–40
– and Hubert Walter 136–7
Hugh of Hartlepool OFM, Provincial Minister, scholar 175–6
Hugo Falcandus, historian 100, 101n.
Huguccio of Pisa, Bishop, canonist 155
'Hundred rolls' enquiries (1274–5) (*see also* eyres) 228
– *capitula* of 111
Husbandry 54–5, 60, 63, 72

Ibn Miskawayh, administrator, scholar 95n., 225–6
Ibn Taymiyya, jurist 244
ideal types (*see also* Weber) 6–8, 90n.
al-Idrīsī, scholar 101
infamia, infamatus (*see also fama; publica fama; scandalum*) 106–7, 131, 138–141, 145, 152n., 153n., 162–3, 169, 172–3, 176–83, 184, 189, 204n., 211n., 218n., 219, 228, 235, 239, 243–6, 260
Innocent III, Pope (*see also* Lateran Council, Fourth) 7n., 41, 135n., 136, 140–2, 146–8, 149–52, 154–5, 160–1, 163–5, 167–9, 224, 228, 232, 234, 238
– *Gesta* (*Deeds*) 163–4, 232n.
Innocent IV, Pope 199n., 205, 217n.
'inquest of sheriffs' (1170) 86, 89, 109, 113–18, 120, 128, 130, 232
inquiries and inquisitions, secular (*see also* Bisson; *daʿāwī al-tuham; enquêtes*; 'inquest of sheriffs'; *pesquisa*) 8, 86–9, 114–15, 173, 177, 183, 200–1

inquiries and inquisitions, secular (*Cont.*)
- *ex officio* 88, 143–4, 151–4, 189, 228–9, 239–41, 241–6
- modern 236–7, 260
- 'reformist' vs. 'fiscal' (Jean Glénisson) 87–9, 111, 121, 127, 132
- relation with canonical inquisitions 8, 38n., 128, 139, 151–4, 171–2, 200–1, 228–9, 241–6

inquisitions, canonical (*see also accusatio*; *da'āwī al-tuham*; *excessus*; *fama*; *infamia*; Lateran Council, Fourth; *scandalum*) 8, 22, 41, Ch. 4 *passim esp.* 140–2, 150–1, 159–61, 166–73
- canonization 8, 253
- *ex officio* 138–40, 141, 145, 149–54, 172, 178n., 228, 239, 243
- promotion of (*promotor, cum promovente*) 150, 176, 178, 252
- rationality of 165–73, 234–5
- relation with secular inquisitions – see above

institutions (*see also specific institutions and administration*) 5, 14–19, 93–4, 109–10, 121–34, 165–73, Ch. 5 *passim* (*esp.* 185–6, 193–5, 205–11, 214, 217, 220–1), 235–41, 247, 251–3, 259–60
- definitions of/senses of 16

Ireland, courts and administration of 29–37
Isabella of Angoulême, Countess, Queen of England 30
Isabella de Fortibus, Countess 66
Isidore of Seville, encyclopaedist, bishop 42, 158, 159
ius commune 12, 98n., 139n., 243

James le Palmer, Exchequer clerk – see Manuscripts and rolls, BL Royal MSS 6 E. VI-VII
Jean d'Avesnes, baron 30
Jean de Joinville, knight, biographer 212
Johannes Teutonicus, canonist 12, 150, 170, 178
Johansen, Baber 243–5
John, King of England 13, 92, 105, 117, 120, 126, 130, 132, 134, 165
John the Almsgiver, Patriarch 224
John of Crakehall, steward, Exchequer Treasurer 8, 69, 78
John Dalderby, Bishop of Lincoln 176
John Francis, bailiff 35
John of Garland, *Morale scolarium* of 204n., 212–4
John of Hotham, tenant, bailiff 32, 35–6
John of Ibelin, Count of Jaffa and Ascalon, jurist 241
John de Lacy, Earl of Lincoln (*see also* Margaret de Quincy) 79
John de Lovetot, knight 174–83, 184, 230
John Pecham OFM, Archbishop, Prior Provincial, scholar 214
- and Merton College 187–94, 198–206, 210–11, 214, 216, 218–9, 221, 229
- *Expositio super Regulam Fratrum Minorum* 194, 200, 202, 208

John of Salisbury, Bishop, scholar 224, 237
- *Policraticus* 95n., 109, 225n.
John de Valle, bailiff 25, 29–37, 50, 63, 66, 69, 75, 76, 82, 110, 229, 230, 233
John Wogan, Justiciar 32
John of Wyly, scholar 196–8, 221
Jordan Fantosme, *Chronicle* of 97
Jular Pérez-Alfaro, Cristina 82n., 257
justices in eyre (*see* eyres)

Karn, Nicholas 41, 61
Kéry, Lotte 151n., 163n., 168n., 170
Khusro I Anushirwan, Shah of Persia 225–6, 249
King, Edmund 76
kingship (*see also* accountability, royal/imperial; *arbitrium*) 96–101, 130–4, 203, 236–9
'*Kto kogo?*' – see 'Who, whom?'

Lachaud, Frédérique 17
Laon, bishopric of (*see also* Anselm de Mauny) 42
Lateran Council, Fourth 140–2
- cap. 8, *Qualiter et quando* (*see also* inquisitions, canonical) 138, 140–1, 145, 150, 152, 159–61, 163–4, 166–73, 178, 181n., 183–4, 239, 253
- commentaries on 150, 166, 170, 178
Lateran Council, Third 156
law (*see also* canon law; common law; *ius commune*; Roman law) 9, 10, 11–13, 23, 138–9, 148–54
- 'law and love' (Michael Clanchy) 57, 59, 62, 68–70, 81–2, 99, 185, 219–21, 257, 260
- rationality of 139, 165–73
Le Goff, Jacques 6n., 15, 234
Leges Henrici Primi 41, 61–3, 70
Lemesle, Bruno 153n., 162
Lenin, Vladimir – see 'Who, whom?'
León 239
Leyes de los Adelantados Mayores 231n.
Liemar of Bremen, Archbishop 42–3
London 1–5
- Charter of 1319 4
lords, liability for officers' actions 62, 65–6, 219, 237–9
Louis VII, King of France 106
Louis IX, King of France 6n., 15, 59, 76, 119–20, 126–9, 132, 133, 157, 194n., 216, 218, 232, 234, 235, 238, 250
- crusade of 1248–54 129
- *enquêtes* of 1247 x 1269 23, 87–8, 122–3, 124, 250–1
- *ordonnances* of (1254) 58, 122, 125, 128–9, 256–7

– ordonnances of, for mayors (1262) 127
'Luffield Book' of John of Oxford 69

Maddicott, J. R. 17, 123, 130, 208
Magna Carta 98, 120, 121, 132, 133, 165, 234, 247
Maitland, F. W. 10, 51, 139, 150, 153, 172
Manegold of Lautenbach, polemicist 11
manorial accounts Ch. 2 (*passim esp.* 26–9, 29–37, 70–6, 78, 79–81), 106, 211
Manuale scholarium 192, 204n., 209n.
Manuscripts and rolls, discussion of
 – Bod. Barlow MS 49 70n.
 – BL Additional MS 18719 107, 161n., 253–5
 – BL Additional MS 30024 2–4, 9
 – BL Royal MSS 6 E VI-VII (Omne bonum) 73n., 77
 – BL Royal MS 9 A VII 70–1
 – BL Royal MS 12 C. VI 78n., 225n.
 – Durham, Dean and Chapter Library MS Loc. 2. 15 64, 73–4
 – Lambeth Palace Library MS Reg. Pecham 189n.
 – TNA E 13/17 29–37
 – TNA C 150/1 54, 74–5
Margaret, Queen of England 175
Margaret de Quincy, Countess 53n., 79–80
Marshal family 30
 – Henry Marshal, Bishop 142
 – William Marshal II, Earl 65
Mattéoni, Olivier 19, 106
Matthew Paris OSB, historian 51
mayors 2–5, 9, 127, 252n., 256–7
mediocres (middling status groups) 7–10, 13, 23, 82, 223, 227, 229, 239, 247, 249, 258
Menelaus, high priest 254–5
merinos 231
Merton College (*see under* colleges, of Oxford)
Milsom, S. F. C. 68
ministeriales 132
Mirror of Justices 1, 49–50, 62, 237, 247
missi, Carolingian 85, 153n., 242
monstravit de compoto – see writs
Montaperti, battle of 2
Moore, R. I. 139n., 169n., 171

Nations, at universities 186, 190n., 207, 208, 211, 214, 216, 218, 219
Nelson, Janet. L. 11
Newburgh, *see* William of Newburgh
Nigel of Ely, Bishop, Exchequer treasurer 96
Northampton, Schools of 148, 210
notorium, proceedings *per notorium* 145, 178

oaths 16, 69, 73–4, 79, 93n., 108, 119, 125, 129, 189, 190, 206, 209n., 224, 238, 243, 251, 256–7
Odo, Bishop of Bayeux, Earl of Kent 28, 39

office *passim but esp.* 89–90, 96n., 107–8
 – norms of 5–10, 23, 55–60, 69, 76–82, 132–3, 135–7, 154–65, 173, 183–4, 235, 256–7
 – professionalization and specialization *passim, esp.* 5, 7, 9, 57, 82, 102, 108–9, 120–2, 125, 139, 233
 – status and (*see also* accountability, hierarchy and; *mediocres*) 7–8, 23, 37, 43, 160n.
officers (*see also under specific types*) *passim but esp.* 20–3, 89–90
 – conduct and character *passim but esp.* 1–10, 59, 69–71, 77–78, 81–2, 94, 108–9, 132–4, 137, 154–8, 183–4, 222–223, 237
 – comparisons (across officers/ institutions) 8–10, 20–3, 77, 135–6, 184, 199–200, 202–4, 214–19, Chapter 6 *passim*
 – comparisons (geographical) 22–3, 121–34, 157–8, 206–9, 210–12, 220–1, Chapter 6 *passim*
 – dismissible (*see also* writs, *monstravit de compoto*) 21, 42, 64, 86, 113, 114, 119, 128n., 136, 162, 167–9, 198n., 208, 229, 232
ordeal 10, 153, 172, 253n.
Orderic Vitalis, *Ecclesiastical History* 100
'Ordinance of the Magnates' (1259) 50
Oschinsky, Dorothea 52–3, 60, 72
Otto di Monteferrato, Cardinal, Papal legate *a latere* 163
Oxford, University of
 – colleges (*see also under* colleges) 192–3, 194–5, 202–7, 210–21, 222, 234, 240, 241, 253, 257
 – halls at 186–7, 208, 209

Paris, University of (*see also* colleges, of Paris) 156, 164n., 186n., 199, 204–5, 206, 207–8, 210, 211, 214n., 219–20
Parliament 19–20, 35, 48, 79, 111, 112, 123, 128, 176, 182, 226, 246, 248
Pennington, Kenneth 164
Pershore, Abbot of 112
pesquisa ('inquisition') (*see also* inquiries and inquisitions, secular) 239
Peter II, King of Aragon, Count of Barcelona (Pedro II, Pere I) 94n.
Peter Abelard, scholar 203n., 211, 236, 258–60
Peter of Abingdon, Warden of Merton College 188–91, 201, 203–4, 214
Peter of Auvergne, Bishop, scholar 204, 255
Peter of Blois, cleric, courtier, scholar 7, 101n., 147n.
Peter Damian, reformer 106
Peter the Chanter, scholar 66n., 135n., 156
Peter des Roches, Bishop, Justiciar, Exchequer baron 152, 155, 161n., 165n., 238
'Petition of the Barons' (1258) 48

Philip II ('Augustus'), King of France 122, 123–5, 135n., 156, 223–4, 229, 251
– *inquisitiones* of 127
– *Ordonnance* of (1190) 128, 131–2, 133
Philip IV ('the Fair'), King of France 176n., 179, 257
Philip V, King of France 125
Philippe de Beaumanoir, *Coutumes de Beauvaisis* 81, 132, 238, 247
Philip Mark, sheriff 126
pledges 31–7, 62, 63, 85, 143, 243
Plumstead (Kent) 39
podestà 2–5, 8, 9, 46, 70, 122, 132, 185, 192, 222, 227–8, 229, 232–3, 235, 245–6, 257
'political thought'/'political thinking' 5, 8, 9, 10–19, 52, 96, 100, 101, 113, 122, 142, 247
precedents, and historical explanation 10, 153–4, 224–6, 241–6
preesse/prodesse ('strutting'/'serving') 135–6, 202, 203n.
prepositi ('those placed above') 7, 26–9, 37, 41–2, 55n., 61, 62, 70, 74n., 85, 144n., 206n., 209n.
Prestwich, Michael 202, 249
prévôts 85, 87, 128–9, 131–2, 223–4, 229, 251n., 256–7
procuratores 26–9, 45, 162n., 176, 193, 207, 208, 211
Provence, county of 133n., 231
Provisions of Oxford (1258) 78n.
Provisions of Westminster (1259) 12, 63, 48–52, 68, 78n.
Pseudo-Aristotle – *see Secretum secretorum*
Ptolemy of Lucca OP (Tolomeo Fiadoni), Prior, historian 247
publica fama (*see also fama*, *infamia*) 141n., 145, 153n., 163, 169, 173, 245n.
purgation 145, 177

querelae 34n., 50n., 112, 228, 230

Ralph of Coggeshall OC, Abbot, historian 116, 223–4
Ralph de Neville, Bishop, Chancellor 66
Ranulf Flambard, *exactor*, bishop 100
Rectitudines singularum personarum 56–60
rector, rectores 8, 155, 202, 207, 208, 209, 223, 231, 247–8
– conscience of 137–8, 236–9
reeves 28, 41, 55–64, 69n., 70–4, 132, 167n.
'Reform movement' of 1258–67 71, 78, 122, 132, 133, 247
Regno (*see also* Roger II; Frederick II; Charles I; Charles II) 121, 128, 130–131, 133, 134, 231, 234, 238, 247, 249, 251
reputation – *see fama*; *infamia*; *scandalum*

res publica etc. (*see also status regni*) 98n., 130–1, 132n., 136–7, 163–5, 199, 259–60
responsibility, relation with accountability – *see under* accountability
Reuter, Timothy 157
Reynolds, Susan 139, 234, 250n.
Richard I, King of England 112, 114–15, 116–17, 120, 123, 143, 156n.
Richard II, Duke of Normandy 94n., 100
Richard Elindon, scholar 197–8
Richard of Dover, Archbishop 149
Richard of Ely, Bishop of London, Exchequer Treasurer (*see also Dialogue of the Exchequer*) 90–1, 93, 94–110, 115, 125, 126, 130, 132, 249, 251
Richard of Ilchester, Bishop, Exchequer baron 38, 92, n., 234, 251
Richard fitz Nigel – *see* Richard of Ely
Richard of Werplesdon, scholar, warden 201–2
Robert Bagot, Exchequer baron 36
Robert of Chilton, steward 25, 26–9, 30, 39, 43, 62, 66–7, 69, 82, 160
Robert Finmere, scholar 196–8, 198, 219, 221
Robert Grosseteste, Bishop of Lincoln, scholar 8, 69, 157, 166n.
– *Rules* 53–4, 57, 66, 78–81
– *Statuta* 54, 80
Robert Kilwardby OP, Archbishop, scholar 191n., 192, 199, 202n., 214, 216, 218n.
Robert de Sorbon, royal chaplain, scholar, college founder, *provisor* (*for the Sorbonne see under* colleges) 194, 204–5, 207, 212, 216, 218, 220–1
Robert of Tring, warden 196–8, 221
Robert le Vavasur, sheriff 112–13, 228
Robert Winchelsey, Archbishop 54, 175–82
Roger II, King of Sicily 100–1
– *Assizes* of (1140s) 130–1
Roger of Howden, clerk, historian 112, 114, 136n., 144–6, 156n., 161, 232
Roger de Lovetot, sheriff 112
Roger of Salisbury, Bishop, minister, *procurator* 103, 160n.
Roger of York, Archbishop 165
Roman law (*see also index of citations*) 3n., 10, 12, 99, 102n., 138–9, 140, 141, 153, 163–4, 226
Romuald of Salerno, historian 100
rules 16, 20, 38–44
– H. L. A. Hart's definition of 23n.
rumour – *see fama*; *infamia*; *publica fama*; *scandalum*

Saba Malaspina, Bishop, historian 249
Samson of Bury St Edmunds OSB, Abbot 27, 28n.
St John's Basingstoke, hospital 194, 201, 214
St Mary's Abbey, York 143

St Paul's, London 176, 181
St Peter's Monastery, Gloucester (*see also* Manuscripts and Rolls, TNA C 150/1) 54, 74
San Martino, Parliament of (1283) 122
St Quentin, Council of 164
San Savino, Piacenza 107
Savoy 125
scandalum 139, 144–5, 151, 162–3, 169–73, 178–84, 185, 201, 212, 214, 217, 218–19, 228, 234, 259–60
scholasticism 188, 192, 236–7
scrutinium (*see also* audits) 22, 195–8, 203, 206, 209, 212, 219, 245, 253, 260
Secretum secretorum 77, 225n., 237
– *Kitāb Sirr al-asrār* 224–6
Seneschauncy 25, 60, 64, 81
sheriffs 9, 36, 39, 46, 47, Ch. 3 *passim*, 171, 185, 193, 227, 228–30, 231, 232, 235, 247, 249, 251, 252, 255–7
– accountability of at Exchequer (*see also* Exchequer) 86, 108–10, 113, 116–20
– compared with other European equivalents 85, 121–34
– conception of as responsible 108–10, 222, 255–6
– oaths of 108, 119–20
Simon of Apulia, Bishop, canonist 142–3
Simon of Ghent, Bishop, scholar 200–1
Simon Magus, sorcerer, buyer of spiritual powers 94
Simon de Montfort, Earl 78, 79
Simon of Senlis, bailiff 66, 81
Skinner, Quentin 12n.
sindacatio (*see also* accounts; audits; inquiries and inquisitions, secular; inquisitions, canonical) 2–5, 10, 13, 22, 46, 70, 122, 192, 228, 229, 233, 235, 245–6, 257, 260
sollicitudo ('responsibility') 96n., 136, 184
Sorbonne – *see* colleges of Paris; Robert de Sorbon
Southern, R. W. 121, 127, 130
speculator ('overseer') 158
state – *see* accountability, state and
status regni (*see also* accountability, state and; *res publica*) 99, 102–3
Statutes of the Exchequer (1275) 111
Statute of Marlborough (1267) 48
Statute of Rhuddlan (1284) 111
Statute of Westminster I (1275) 111
Statute of Westminster II (1285) 33, 38, 48, 49, 51, 52–3, 68
Stephen Langton, Archbishop, scholar 93–4, 101, 156–7, 161, 165, 189n.
stewards (*see also villicus*) Ch. 2 *passim*, 115, 159n., 206, 216, 241, 248, 255, 257, 259
Suger of St Denis OSB, Abbot 27

Swanson, R. N. 195

tallies 30, 34, 73–4, 91–2
Templars 106, 125, 176, 179, 208, 257
tenure 61–70
Théry, Julien 163, 167n., 169n., 173n., 181n.
Thomas Aquinas OP, theologian 11, 65, 120
Thomas Becket, Archbishop, Chancellor 66, 105, 151
Thomas Cantilupe, Bishop 64
Thomas of Chobham, scholar 204
Thomas Corbet, sheriff 46
Thomas Jorz OP, Cardinal, Prior Provincial 175–6, 181
Thomas of Lancaster, Earl, Steward of England 248
'three orders' 6–7
Tickhill (Yorkshire), honour of 112
Tidenham (Gloucestershire), survey of 58
trust, relationship with accountability – *see under* accountability

Ullmann, Walter 227–8
underworld 93
utilitas, utilis, etc. 1, 88–90, 97–8, 102–3, 108, 109–10, 113, 114–15, 120, 125, 130, 131, 145, 146n., 147, 154, 162–3, 166, 185, 189, 190, 195, 212n., 218n., 221, 249, 259–60

Valence, family (*see also* Agnes de; William de) 30–1, 34, 51
'vernacular' procedures 23–4, 47, 139, 148–54, 152, 171, 242–6
'Vespers' rebellion 122, 130, 247
Vicens Vives, Jaime 14–15
villicus, villicatio (*see also* Luke 16) 19n., 27–8, 37, 41–3, 95n., 159–62, 203n., 235, 254
virtues, cardinal 97–8
Vivier-en-Brie *ordonnance* of Philip V, King of France (1320) 125

Wace, *Roman de Rou* 100–1
Walter Castello 33
Walter l'Enfaunt, justice 32
Walter Langton, Bishop, Exchequer treasurer 66n., 110, 128, 166, 171, 173–83, 184, 229, 230, 252
Walter of Henley 25, 54, 57, 76–7
Walter Map, scholar, courtier, royal justice 96, 98, 101, 106, 249
– *De nugis curialium* 93–4, 111, 237–8
Walter of Merton, Bishop, Chancellor, college founder 187–8, 190, 192, 194, 195, 200–1, 202, 206, 210, 212, 213, 214, 218, 219, 234
Walter Stapeldon, Bishop, Exchequer treasurer, college founder (*see also* colleges, of Oxford, Exeter) 104, 134

wardens 9, 22, Ch. 5 *passim* (*esp.* 185–7, 189–209, 216–17), 222, 227, 234, 241, 248, 257
Watson, Sethina 194
Waugh, Scott L. 63
Weber, Max (*see also* elective affinity; ideal types) 20
Wenrich of Trier, scholar 159–160
'Who, whom?' 21, 37, 43, 50, 99, 101, 109, 154, 190, 203, 226–229, 231, 253, 257
Wickham, Chris 15, 22, 245n.
William de Bussey, steward 34, 51
William Cadigan, bailiff 46
William Carleton, Exchequer baron, justice 33
William of Conches, scholar 204
William Dodingseles, Justiciar 32, 36
William of Durham – *see under* colleges, of Oxford, University
William fitz Stephen, clerk 2
William of Heytesbury, scholar 196–8, 221
William of Humberston, scholar 197
William of Loges, clerk 33
William Longchamp, Bishop of Ely, Chancellor, canonist 148
William March, Bishop of Bath, Exchequer Treasurer 34
William of Molecastre, sheriff 110

William of Montfort, cleric 200–1
William of Newburgh, historian 103n., 115n., 116, 156n.
William of St Calais OSB, Abbot, bishop and royal adviser 178n.
William of Stuteville, justice, baron 143
William de Valence, Earl 30, 31, 51
William de Vescy, baron, Justiciar 35
William of Wantyng, scholar 196–8
William of Warenne IV, Earl 143
William de Wilton, justice 112
William of York, Bishop, justice 110–11
Wolter, Udo 20–1, 240
Wulfstan of York, Archbishop 59, 76
 – *Institutes of Polity* 55–6
writs 39–41, 63, 65, 91, 92, 95n., 230, 251
 – action of account (*de compoto*) 6n., 22, 38–44
 – *ex parte* 29–37, 38
 – *monstravit de compoto* (*see also* Statute of Westminster II) 29–37, 44–52, 63, 65, 71, 75–6, 230, 233, 252, 253
Wye (Kent) 26-9

York, metropolitan see of (*see* Geoffrey of York; Roger of York; Wulfstan of York)
 – Cathedral Chapter of 142–8, 150–1, 154